INTRODUCTION TO THE HISTORY OF INTERNATIONAL RELATIONS

INTRODUCTION TO THE HISTORY OF INTERNATIONAL RELATIONS

PIERRE RENOUVIN
and
JEAN-BAPTISTE DUROSELLE

Translated by
MARY ILFORD

FREDERICK A. PRAEGER, *Publishers*
New York • Washington • London

FREDERICK A. PRAEGER, PUBLISHERS
111 Fourth Avenue, New York, N.Y. 10003, U.S.A.
77–79 Charlotte Street, London W. 1, England

Published in the United States of America in 1967
by Frederick A. Praeger, Inc., Publishers

First published in France in 1964 under the aegis of the Fondation Nationale
des Sciences Politiques by Librairie Armand Colin, under the title *Introduction
à l'Histoire des Relations Internationales*

© 1964, Librairie Armand Colin
English translation © 1967, Frederick A. Praeger, Inc.

Library of Congress Catalog Card Number: 66–18918

Printed in the United States of America

INTRODUCTION

The primary purpose of the study of international relations is to analyze and explain the relations between political communities organized each within a given territorial framework—that is, relations between states. Of course, we must take into account relations established between peoples and among the individuals comprising these peoples—the exchange of goods and services, the communication of ideas, the reciprocal play of influences, whether sympathetic or hostile, among various forms of civilization. But it is an observable fact that these can seldom be dissociated from relations between states. Governments often refuse to allow unhampered contacts between peoples; they subject the movement of money or goods, or migration, or even the circulation of ideas to regulations and restrictions; they can also, with other measures, shape and direct the mood and opinions of the people. Such governmental intervention most often simply limits or modifies the relations established by personal initiative, but it can also affect their actual nature. Left to themselves, relations between individuals of different countries might make for solidarity; at worst, antagonism between individual interests would not normally entail direct political consequences. Regulated by states, however, they become the subject of official, governmental negotiation or dispute. Thus, it is the action of states that is "at the heart of international relations." This is the general position we have adopted here.[1]

Diplomatic history is that aspect of the study of international relations which is concerned with the actions or gestures of governments, their decisions, and, when possible, their intentions. Diplomatic history is an indispensable aspect of the study of international relations but it certainly does not explain everything. Fully to understand diplomacy, we have to try to discover the deeper influences that affect it so strongly. Geographical conditions, demographic movements, economic and financial interests, the collective characteristics of peoples and nations, public opinion—these are the underlying factors which make up the setting within which human groups have developed, and which largely determine the nature of the relations between them. In making decisions and plans, the statesman cannot afford to neglect them; he himself is influenced by them; and he is obliged to recognize the limits they set on his action.

Nevertheless, when a statesman possesses exceptional intellectual gifts, or particular strength of character, or a temperament that inclines him to

---

[1] It is also the position Raymond Aron adopts in *Peace and War: A Theory of International Relations* (trans. Richard Howard and Annette Baker Fox) (New York, 1966).

transcend those limitations, he can try to alter the play and effect of these deep forces and make them serve his purposes. By his economic policies, he can further develop his country's natural resources; he can attempt to influence demographic conditions; through the press or the schools, he can try to influence the national frame of mind; he is prepared, on occasion, to take action that rouses public opinion to fever pitch. To study international relations without taking sufficient account of the personal ideas, methods, and emotional reactions of the statesman, then, is to neglect an important—sometimes, indeed, an essential—factor.

These are the general lines on which we have structured this book.

To begin with, we have considered how these deep, underlying forces have in fact influenced international relations during the past century—a period that has seen tremendous economic changes, major demographic movements, and singularly vigorous assertions of various forms of national sentiment. Using data accumulated in earlier historical research, as well as material acquired in new research of our own, we have tried to demonstrate the play of these forces in international relations, to indicate the difficulties in interpreting them, and to assess their effect.

Secondly, by comparative analysis, we have examined the role which the statesman's personality and ideas have actually played in given circumstances. How did he conceive the national interest? What light is thrown on his policies by his character and temperament? In what circumstances did he come to his decisions? We have also tried to throw light on the practical processes by which the deep forces within a nation influence the statesman and, as well, how the statesman tries to modify them.

We chose to work within a historical perspective since it provided us with a documentary foundation for our work which would not have been available had we limited our study to contemporary affairs. But a few brief explanations are still called for regarding our general plan.

Should we have devoted a separate chapter to the study of public opinion and foreign affairs? It is certainly true that expressions of public opinion have often influenced the decisions of statesmen. Nevertheless, we concluded that these expressions of public opinion reflect demographic conditions, economic or financial interests, and collective psychological tendencies—subjects covered in other chapters.

Should national defense establishments be included among the influences bearing on international relations? Historically, there is no doubt that when a state possesses superiority in weapons that is likely to be eradicated in the near future, it is tempted to try to use it to advantage. But such superiority in arms is inseparable from the nation's general level of technology and from its economic, financial, and population resources; it is related to the intensity of national feeling; it is also affected by the intentions of the government and by how much authority is vested in the military establishment by constitutional texts or tradition. Technology and arms policy, we concluded, have not exerted an autonomous influence.

Thus defined, the scope of our book is certainly not original. American scholars have often dealt with these problems; in France, Raymond Aron's works have broken new ground. But, in most cases, writers have been principally interested in establishing the foundations of a "science of international relations," in examining problems of political philosophy, in discussing theories—on the relation between population increase and war, or on the sources of imperialism, or what makes national sentiment; historical examples have been adduced only as stimuli to theory. We do not underestimate the value of these investigations, but, rather than scanning history for proof of theories elaborated beforehand, we thought it wiser to look at the past with a view of forming only such conclusions as the data warranted. This method, incidentally, may enable us to provide theorists of international relations with new material or topics to reflect on, but we have tried not to be influenced by this consideration.

Our purpose, even thus circumscribed, is still overly ambitious. The study of the underlying motive forces in international relations brings us up against so many and such vast questions that it is impossible to go into them all. Some—concerning varieties of national sentiment, for instance, or the relation between nationalism and religion—have not yet been subjected to serious critical analysis. In many areas, we can do no more than outline the problems. The demographer, the economist, the social psychologist will doubtless find gaps in our documentation; they may regard our choice of certain examples as arbitrary; they may dispute certain interpretations. And our study of the role of the statesman may give rise to other criticism, since perforce we could only show individual behavior, and the exemplary value of our choices can always be disputed. We felt, however, that we should accept these risks; they were unavoidable, in any case, if we wanted to paint a general picture. Finally, we may have aggravated our problems by trying to write a relatively short work. The effort to be concise sometimes entails many disadvantages.

We hope at least to achieve two results: to provide a framework for study and suggest a mode of approach; and also to raise questions, point to the gaps in our historical knowledge, and thus suggest new fields of study.

P. R.
J.-B. D.

Paris, 1964

CONTENTS

I
THE UNDERLYING FORCES

by

PIERRE RENOUVIN

1

GEOGRAPHY

The life of human communities is influenced by climate, topography, hydrography, the quality of the soil and the nature of the sub-soil (which determine types of vegetation and availability of mineral resources), and by transportation facilities (greater by water than by land). Every human community is thus intimately affected by its physical environment, and environment thus constitutes a major factor of differentiation among human groups.[1] The historian of human societies, whether of primitive groups or of nation-states, can never afford to disregard geographical conditions; the full significance of "geo-history" has been made abundantly clear.[2]

In studying international relations also, we must make full allowance for this influence of the physical environment; it is clearly apparent in the way people behave, in their commercial and political relations, and in the relative power of various states. But we should also note that man has constantly sought to circumscribe geographical factors and to subordinate them to his will. Human groups have always tried to escape the constraints imposed on them by nature. To what extent have they succeeded? This is the central question here.

I. TERRITORIAL FACTORS

The state, as we know it, is associated with a territory over which it exercises control. According to the pioneering nineteenth-century geographer Friedrich Ratzel, the idea of the state is inseparable from that of territory.[3]

Within this territorial setting, what are the geographical factors that can increase or diminish a state's power?

---

[1] At the end of the nineteenth century, the German scholar Friedrich Ratzel pioneered in the study of these questions. See his *Politische Geographie* (Leipzig, 1897). Many works followed his; while none attained the same sweep or wealth of observation, they have resulted in important additions to our knowledge. The most recent and important is Jean Gottmann, *La Politique extérieure des états et leur géographie* (Paris, 1952).

[2] Particularly by Fernand Braudel in his great work *La Méditerranée et le monde méditerranéen à l'époque de Philippe II* (Paris, 1949).

[3] Ratzel, *op. cit.*

A. CLIMATE

Temperature affects not only human health but also human temperament
and modes of living. Excessive heat or cold hinders the development of
human activities: the arctic regions have always seemed to reject the possibility of human life; in the equatorial zone, where it is very hot and very
humid, man's aptitude for work is reduced and the formation of compact
human groups consequently becomes difficult.[4] Outside these extreme zones,
experiments in industrial plants show that optimum working activity is
achieved in regions with moderate temperatures (Great Britain, France, the
northern United States) and that it is substantially lower in places such as
the Naples area or the Nile Delta. The great modern states developed in
temperate zones.[5]

Rainfall is another essential element,[6] because it directly influences
plant life; climate, indeed, acts mainly "through the medium of the vegetable
world."[7] In arid zones, where vegetation is sparse, if present at all, human
settlement cannot be either extensive or stable, for the bases of economic life
are too fragile. In hot and very humid zones, settlement may be impeded
by excessive vegetation (equatorial forests) or by diseases (malaria, sleeping
sickness) fostered by the climatic conditions. Even in more temperate zones,
forms of vegetation influence economic activities and the way of life. The
state whose territory can supply the population with food sufficient for its needs
depends less on foreign states; it can more easily isolate itself economically
and, consequently, politically.[8] Abundant forests gave some states a great
advantage in sea power when wood was the essential material in boat construction; and dense forests along border regions formed a protective screen
which long constituted an element of security. Cotton-growing states acquired
an important role in the world economy with the development of the textile
industry. There are many other examples.

Is this influence of climatic conditions a stable, constant one? Changes
in rainfall patterns or in the position of climatic zones have certainly
occurred in the past—it is possible, for instance, that the great migrations

[4] In his study of the possibility of man adapting to extreme temperatures, Maximilien
Sorre noted that biological data on this subject were still inadequate. See *Les Fondements de la géographie humaine*, Vol. I: *Les Fondements biologiques: Essai d'une
écologie de l'homme* (Paris, 1943), and "Adaptation au milieu climatique et vie sociale:
Géographie psychologique," in H. Pieron (ed.), *Traité de psychologie appliquée* (Paris,
1954), VI, 1243–1394.
[5] Ratzel, who gave scant attention to the importance of climate, nevertheless observed that the original impetus and power of the Chinese Empire came from northern
China, where the winters are cold. *Op. cit.*, p. 235.
[6] See the comments of Pierre George, "Sur une nouvelle présentation du déterminisme en géographie humaine," *Annales de Géographie*, 1952, pp. 250–54.
[7] Lucien Febvre, *A Geographical Introduction to History* (New York, 1924; reissued,
1966), p. 115.
[8] On autarkies, see below, Chapter Three, pp. 58–59.

from central Asia in the fifth century were the result of a drought in that area —but such changes have been very gradual.[9] Relative stability in climate does not necessarily imply, however, that climate is decisive; for in one and the same climatic zone there may be different forms of social organization, and areas with both scattered and concentrated human settlement. Moreover, past experience does not provide a valid explanation of the present.[10] Prior to the eighteenth century, climate was a vital factor in the life of most human societies, since societies were then primarily agricultural and were "dominated by the ever troublesome problem of subsistence." This dependence of well-being on weather is far less close today.[11]

Forty years ago, the French historian Lucien Febvre noted that there was "nothing strict, rigid, or mechanical" about the influence of temperature and rainfall on the life of human societies, and that this influence could not be seriously studied without more adequate data concerning forms of climate.[12] His comment has lost little of its pertinence today.

B. TOPOGRAPHY

The topography of any country naturally has considerable bearing on its food resources, since altitude, the direction of slopes, and other topographical factors affect the climatic and general farming conditions. Topography also keenly affects many essential aspects of social and political life: the density of settlement; mingling of populations; national boundary lines.

1. Density of Settlement

In Europe, mountainous regions long served as "zones of refuge"; the same is true today in parts of Asia and Africa. Alluvial plains, on the other hand, remained sparsely populated until dikes were constructed. Topography, here, has played different parts at different times: mountain peoples came down into the plains searching for easier living conditions once an improved social organization had made life secure and safe in the plains and the "zones of refuge" were unnecessary, or when technical advances had reduced

[9] The effect of meteorological fluctuations on economic life is difficult to assess because there is little reliable data; climatic explanations of the great agricultural crises of human history are only hypotheses, often undemonstrated.

[10] See Pierre George, *Introduction à l'étude géographique de la population du monde* (Paris, 1951), p. 63.

[11] See E. Le Roy-Ladurie, "Histoire et climat," *Annales de Géographie*, January, 1959, pp. 3–34. Le Roy-Ladurie criticizes the views adopted by Gustaf Utterström in "Climatic Fluctuations and Population Problems in Early Modern History," *The Scandinavian Economic History Review*, XXX, No. 1, (1955), 3–47.

[12] Febvre, *op. cit.*, pp. 91–121.

the danger of flooding. In modern Europe, lands lying at the foot of mountainous regions, where the soil is fertile and communication easy, have
become heavily populated. The relative significance of mountain and plain
is thus "far more an effect of civilization than a physical fact."[13]

2. *Mingling of Populations*

The mingling of different races and the mingling of population groups
with differing histories and origins have often been impeded by natural,
geographical obstacles to the movement of men and goods. Cultural and
economic differences between varying human groups have persisted longer
in regions that are divided up by natural partitions, whereas in more open,
accessible zones, such differences have tended to vanish. But here again, we
have to guard against generalizations: the Belfort Gap—the "Burgundy
Gate"—constituted a linguistic boundary separating the French and Germans;
but, in contrast, the Gorizia-Ljubljana Gap provided a zone of contact
between Italians, Germans, and Slavs; and from medieval times on, the
Brenner Pass was frequently used by German-speaking peoples to penetrate
south across the Alps into the upper Adige valley. A "gate" can thus be an
avenue of invasion.

It would be even more rash to try to establish a connection between
topography and *types* of human society. Plateaux, which according to
some authorities have played an essential part in man's history, have done
so only in particular latitudes and particular environments.[14] In some areas
(Andorra, in the Pyrenees, or Aosta, in the Italian Alps, for instance), the
mountain terrain encouraged the development of a characteristic type of
society, but only where there was no passage across or through the mountain mass. How, then, can we infer any geographical "determinism"?

Still, it is true that a mountainous terrain has often preserved a people's
independence. Switzerland's neutrality was respected in all the great
European wars of the past 100 years; Abyssinia escaped the penetration
of Islam and, until 1935, was able to resist European colonial expansion. In
addition, the walls formed by mountain ridges undoubtedly facilitated the
establishment and long survival of separate states in the valleys of a single
mountainous zone—as in Indochina, for example. At the same time, the
effectiveness of this natural partitioning has varied greatly, depending on
the topographical features involved. Norway's rounded ridges have not had
the same effect on her history as the Carso escarpments have had in the
Trieste area of Italy and Yugoslavia. Peninsulas like Italy and Greece where
the mountains formed a barrier between them and the mainland, tended to

---

[13] George, *Introduction à l'étude géographique*, p. 67.
[14] Elisée Reclus, *La Terre* (Paris, 1876), p. 635, and Febvre, *op. cit.*, pp. 192-94.

achieve political unity,[15] although it is true that it was a long time before the inevitability of this unity was apparent.

Actually, all these various points may be summed up in a single sentence: to the extent that physical features seriously impeded communications, they exerted an influence on the character of human groups.

3. National Boundary Lines

Topography has been crucially important in the drawing of political boundaries. Actual demarcation lines depend on the will of two adjacent states and, therefore, on the pressure they exert upon each other; they express and reveal the balance of political forces far more than geographical factors. Nevertheless, military history shows us that mountains, or merely an escarpment (the banks of the Meuse River, for instance), sufficed to impede or delay armed offensives until very recent times, when the development of air power transformed the whole nature of strategic and tactical theory. And when a frontier crosses a region that is difficult of access, it is easier to guard and defend. Here, the mean altitude of a mountain range is not all-important: what counts most is the altitude of the *passes*. The Pyrenees have always been a more formidable obstacle than the Alpine frontiers because there are so few passes through them. Consequently, the state that wants to be free to conduct an offensive action against its neighbor has every interest in maintaining a bastion on the farther mountain slope beyond the pass where its "natural" frontier lies, which it could use as an operational base if the occasion arose. This consideration certainly influenced Austria to make every effort, after her defeat in 1866, to keep the southern Tyrol (Alto Adige) even though she lost Venetia. That bastion beyond the Alps in fact proved very useful in the autumn of 1917 in the Caporetto campaign, when the Italian forces suffered an enormous and demoralizing defeat at the hands of the Germans and Austrians.

We should also note a significant permanence in the use of certain topographical features as political boundary marks. The point where the Elbe River's defile cuts through the Erz Gebirge (Ore Mountains) has marked the frontier between Saxony and Bohemia, then between Germany and Austria, and now between Germany and Czechoslovakia. But even so, the idea of a natural frontier, which has so often appealed to fervent nationalists, is seldom very strictly applied.

There is also the matter of the general relation between mountain ranges and plains. Vidal de la Blache's views on the harmony of France's geographical features strongly influenced many French historians and geographers;[16] German historians, for their part, have often commented on the

[15] See Braudel, *op. cit.*, p. 131.
[16] See Vidal de la Blache, *Tableau de la géographie de la France* (Paris, 1911).

fragmentation of the habitable zones within their national territory and on the lack of a "central nucleus" capable of becoming a focus for political action. Yet the fragmentation of the littoral plains was certainly no obstacle to the existence and long duration of a united monarchy on the Japanese archipelago.

C. HYDROGRAPHY

The importance of hydrography in a nation's history is perhaps most apparent in military affairs. The difficulties encountered in crossing a marshy region or a wide river where bridges had been destroyed were important considerations for military operations in both world wars.[17] It is also important to a country's economy or social structure and, consequently, to its politics, for great rivers are avenues along which external influences enter the life of the nation. But it is chiefly the actual configuration of rivers and waterways that affect the life of states. The roughly parallel courses of the great rivers of northern Germany—the Ems, the Weser, the Elbe, the Oder—established a "compartmentalization" that probably did much to delay the development of Germany's political unity; in France, on the other hand, a number of rivers empty into the Seine River basin, and this facilitated the development of Paris as a political capital.

The existence of a great fluvial axis is conducive to the creation and expansion of a state; settlers in the river's lower valley usually seek to dominate the upper valley too, since whoever controls the upper valley can alter the water flow; the master of the upper valley, on the other hand, seeks to gain control of the lower valley since, if the river is navigable, it provides access to the outside world.

It has been said that the total occupation of a river by the strongest power possessing a part of it is "one of the principles of political geography."[18] But just how important is this principle? A river is undoubtedly of major economic importance when it is under the control of a single state, but apart from the case of Egypt, where life in the Nile Delta depends very heavily on the water flow of the Upper Nile, the examples cited in support of this theory are not too persuasive. The conflict between Bolivia and Paraguay from 1928 to 1936 certainly turned on control of the Picamayo River route, but it also was a contest over the possession of land with likely petroleum deposits. In 1919, Romania insisted on gaining control of the Danube estuary, but she was obviously not planning to control the entire

---

[17] R. Villate, *La Géographie et la Guerre* (Paris, 1927), dealing with World War I, contains an important analysis on this point.

[18] Jean Brunhes and Camille Vallaux, *La Géographie de l'histoire* (Paris, 1921), p. 277.

river. Nor did Austria-Hungary seek to establish dominion over the Danube River beyond the Iron Gates (a gorge in the Danube on the Romanian boundary with Yugoslavia). And Bismarck's German Empire, at the peak of its power, did not aspire to control the upper reaches of the Rhine. Moreover, the free use of watercourses can be safeguarded by diplomatic agreements recognizing different political sovereignties over different sections of a river. The Rhine, the Danube, and the Congo rivers have all operated as international waterways without serious dispute.

The regulation or alteration of a water flow, when technology is capable of accomplishing it, has greatly facilitated agricultural and industrial development in certain regions. Water-power has been a basic factor in the economy of mountain regions: at the close of the nineteenth century, it made possible the industrial development of northern Italy, which had long been thwarted by the inadequacy of its fuel and power resources. And thanks to irrigation works, rivers have become an essential condition for agricultural life in all semi-arid regions.

D. SOIL

The qualities of the soil and the mineral resources of the sub-soil have always exerted an important influence on the life of human communities. First, the nature of the soil largely determines a country's sufficiency in food supplies. We need only mention the most typical cases: on the one hand, the rich lands—the loess, or rich, unstratified loam of the Mississippi Basin, parts of Europe, and northern China, or, in Russia, the "black earth" of the Ukraine; on the other hand, the thin, poor soils damaged by laterite (a residual product of rock decay) in the Deccan (the south of India) or tropical Africa. Secondly, sub-soils rich in fuel products and minerals made possible the rise of the great industrial regions.

History reveals certain links between these natural conditions and the creation of states. Points of contact between regions with varying soil resources, where systems of exchange between complementary economies could be established—between wheat lands, pastures, and forests, between savannas and tropical forests—have often become the foci of organized political life.[19] The nature of the soil has also influenced the temperament and character of peoples. In regions with poor soil, where men have had to wage a harsher struggle with nature, they have acquired great physical— some even say moral—vigor, enabling them to achieve political ascendancy over their neighbors. The political triumphs of Brandenburg in German history, and of Asturias in the history of Spain, are often cited in proof of

---

[19] Febvre, *op. cit.*, Part IV.

this contention. Yet the role of "geographical liaisons" was not very marked in the development of the great modern states,[20] and the mingling of populations, as communications improved, reduced differences in temperament. Still, the role of environment in group psychology deserves serious study.[21]

To what extent have these natural conditions affected the *relative power* of states in the modern world?

Self-sufficiency in food supplies lost much of its importance when improved means of transport made it easy to make up a deficit with imports; after 1846, Great Britain's power continued to grow at the very time when it had deliberately sacrificed its agriculture to its industry; the power of the German Empire was by no means affected by an economic situation that obliged it to meet a large part of its grain requirements by imports. (In peacetime, the only disadvantage of this imports scheme was that it aggravated the trade deficit, but the balance of payments was adjusted without difficulty. In wartime, of course, it could be disturbing—witness the blockade of Germany during World War I.)

The richness of the sub-soil, on the other hand, has played an essential role in the development of political power, particularly when coal and iron-ore deposits occurred together, making the development of metallurgical industries possible and, consequently, the manufacture of arms. The advantages of possessing such deposits tended to decline as international trade expanded and as countries blessed with only meager natural resources could more easily obtain raw materials and fuels from abroad. Japan and Italy developed iron and steel industries without having any iron ore. But the need to import basic raw materials affected their trade balances adversely and constituted a threat to their economic life, in the event that their sources of supply were shut off.

Inequality in raw-material resources (including fuels) thus became a factor of primary importance in international relations. Open competition for access to raw materials constantly gave rise to conflicts or threats of conflict between the possessors of the riches and those who wanted to share in them.[22] The contests were all the more bitter when nations whose organizational abilities and technical capacities were most highly developed felt justified in asserting their rights to the riches; was it not just, they claimed, that the resources of the sub-soil should benefit those best able to put them to good use?[23]

In the struggle for power, then, the state that controls the essential raw

---

[20] Gottmann demonstrates that it is not possible to establish a link between the types of associations formed by states and the types of their economies, except in the case of association by domination, on the colonial model. *Op. cit.*, p. 200.

[21] Sorre draws attention to this point. See *Les Fondements de la géographie humaine* and "Adaptation au milieu climatique et vie sociale."

[22] See below, Chapter Three, pp. 64–69.

[23] Gottmann, *op. cit.* p. 188.

materials holds a major advantage.[24] At the same time, such wealth is not without its drawbacks, for the same kind of contrast that is found *between* states may also occur *within* states; the inhabitants of regions with reserves of raw materials enjoy a higher standard of living than their fellow citizens do, and the dissension resulting from this inequality tends to weaken national unity.

II. LOCATION

The role a state can play in the world is strongly affected by its position on the map. Thanks to their geographical location, certain states which are small in area have made a greater mark in history than larger nations endowed with far greater resources. "There are positions that possess political value," Ratzel observed in 1897. During the past half-century, the point of this observation has not been lost.

A. ACCESS TO THE SEA

Access to the sea is clearly one of these favored, valuable locations. Territory with a shore frontage has commercial advantages: the sea affords inexpensive transportation facilities, whereas the construction of land routes is a costly business. Despite the risks of navigation, sea routes ensure greater security in one's relations with the outside world, for it is easier by sea than by land to escape from an enemy who seeks to bar one's passage. These advantages were already quite apparent by the eighteenth century and became more so during the nineteenth century, as trade expanded. The nation deprived of access to the sea (Serbia before 1914; Bolivia after 1884, when Chile annexed the Pacific coastal zone of Antofagasta) was in danger of having its foreign trade brought to a halt; and it was liable to economic pressures in moments of political tension.

Consequently, sea access has been an exceptionally powerful motive and goal in foreign policy.[25] In addition to the many examples afforded by eighteenth-century history (Russia's policy of seeking access first to the Baltic Sea, then to the Black Sea; Brandenburg's conquest of Swedish Pomerania), there is more recent evidence: Bulgaria's struggle in 1912 and 1913 to gain access to the Aegean Sea (which it was to lose in 1920); Serbia's claim to a "window on the Adriatic" during World War I; the question of a Polish corridor along the Vistula River in 1919; the Chaco War

---

[24] See Pierre Birot and Jean Dresch, *Méditerranée et Proche-Orient* (Paris, 1953) (especially pp. 125 and 137), which provides a wealth of data on the influence of environment at the present time.

[25] On the significance of areas where sea and land traffic routes meet, see Gottmann, *op. cit.*, p. 78.

between Bolivia and Paraguay in 1932–35, one of whose causes (not the only one[26]) was Bolivia's desire to acquire a piece of the Atlantic coast, since it had lost its outlet on the Pacific.

Should we conclude, then, that in general the strongest powers try to occupy coastal zones, relegating the weaker to the interior? This would be going too far. It is true, of course, that the Indians in North America, the native peoples of Australia, the Hottentots of South Africa—all evacuated the coastal regions when the Europeans arrived, but it could not have been otherwise when the newcomers came by sea and had necessarily to begin their operations by occupying the coast. When conquering forces came over land—as in the case of the Muslim penetration of West Africa—they occupied the interior, driving the weaker indigenous inhabitants to the coast.[27]

Extensive development along a coast has often been a significant factor in a nation's power, provided the citizens have a "maritime vocation." But does access to the sea in itself confer this vocation? In the case of the British, the Dutch, and the Scandinavians, the answer is yes, but in other cases not. For instance, the Germans before 1880 showed no taste for maritime navigation. The people of southern India, and of Albania, remained indifferent to the sea. In the Mediterranean, where jagged coast lines and a multitude of islands provide favorable conditions for navigation, Greece and Phoenicia (modern Syria) were each a seaman's paradise, but not Corsica or Sardinia; ancient Rome possessed a maritime power that Carthage lacked.

Such differences may sometimes be ascribed to geography. In the Mediterranean, for instance, coastal shelves are rare and, where they exist, narrow;[28] fishing is therefore poor, and men are consequently less attracted to the sea in their daily lives. But the differences are also the result of a people's character: Norway, that great nation of seamen, has no more extensive coastal shelf than Corsica; on the coasts of the Baltic, the peoples of the Baltic states and the German Pomeranians have less of a maritime bent than the Swedes or Finns, although the submarine topographies of each coast are similar. There is no constant relation, therefore, between possession of a seacoast and man's temperament and mode of life.[29]

Again, a powerful state possessing a piece of coastline along a relatively small sea has often sought to extend its control to the major portion or even to the whole of the shore line. Was not this policy of *mare nostrum* Sweden's in the Baltic in 1658, when she twice invaded Denmark, and could it not explain Japan's battle with China over Korea in 1894 and then her action

---

26 For another, see above, p. 8.

27 Off the coast of East Africa, on the other hand, the island of Zanzibar is Muslim territory, but there, conquering Islam came by sea.

28 That is, where the shallow waters extend less than about 650 feet from the shore.

29 On this point, the following are most illuminating: Sorre, *op. cit.*, p. 194; Febvre, *op. cit.*, pp. 213 ff.; and Braudel, *op. cit.*, p. 165.

in the Vladivostock region in 1918–19? Tsarist Russia, when it sought to establish its influence in Bulgaria between 1870 and 1887, might have been trying to gain such control on the Black Sea. And Mussolini's Italy invoked the same principle in regard to the Mediterranean. But these inferences are far from proven, and in none of these cases was the geographical motivation obvious. Swedish policy was less to control the Baltic than to establish a bridgehead so that it might be able to intervene in German affairs. The Japanese Government wanted to prevent Korea from falling under Russian domination because it was fearful of becoming the neighbor of a great European power. Tsarist Russia, when it intervened in Bulgaria, had in view its expansion in the Balkans far more than its control of the Black Sea. Mussolini's policy, which incidentally was applied with considerable hesitation, except in the Adriatic, was merely the expression of a desire for power and prestige. To realize that a map can appeal to men's imagination is not the same as acknowledging geographical determinism.

B. CONTROL OF TRANSIT ROUTES

Another major aspect of these problems is the control that a particular geographical location enables a state to exercise over land or sea routes. Indeed, a favorite theme of political geographers is the constant significance of certain zones of land traffic.

The nation whose territory is traversed by a natural highway, especially if the government is strong enough to forbid its use to strangers, enjoys a special status. All foreigners using this highway must be in its good graces—a profitable situation, since that state can levy a transit tax on the men or goods passing through its borders. And the natural highway can become the focal point around which the state is consolidated. But this commercial traffic route can also be an invasion route. If the state is weak and has powerful neighbors, it may become the victim of its originally advantageous location; such was the case with Belgium and Iran during the two world wars. This danger disappears when the threats posed by neighboring states are, as it were, cancelled out—as in 1828, when Brazil and Argentina, after making rival claims on the River Plate delta, decided to make the best of it and leave the new state of Uruguay alone.

The role of "isthmus regions," or crossroads of land routes between two seas, is akin to that of the natural highway. The description of southwestern France as an "isthmus" connecting the Mediterranean and Atlantic is a classic one, even if its essential traits have lost some of their significance today.[30] The importance of the highways between the Persian Gulf and the Mediterranean Sea via Mesopotamia and Syria, reduced when the Suez Canal provided Europeans with a quick sea route to southern Asia, was

[30] See Vidal de la Blache, *op. cit.*

reasserted after 1919, when the exploitation of oil deposits in the Middle East made it necessary to establish pipe lines across Arabia.[31]

Again, passes through mountain ranges have often afforded privileged locations for the establishment of small states, which thereupon enjoyed an importance in international relations out of all proportion to their size. But their autonomy seldom lasted for long. In Europe, as soon as larger, neighboring states aspired to control the relevant mountain passes, the smaller states lost their independence. In Asia, the principalities of the upper Mekong disappeared at the end of the nineteenth century when the French and British colonized Indochina. Today, the small independent Himalayan states— Nepal, Bhutan, Sikkim—are the last survivors.

Here again, however, the influence of geography must not be exaggerated. A direct relation between the actual flow of traffic and the existence of natural highways is frequent but not inevitable. In Africa, Asia, and America, certain great land routes have been abandoned and neglected after being used for centuries, although the physical conditions have not changed.

From time immemorial, a nation's possession of land from which it can guard and, if necessary, seal off a major sea route has also constituted an outstanding political and economic advantage. The role of the Dardanelles and the Bosporus, the Strait of Gibraltar, the Strait of Messina between Sicily and Italy, and the Denmark Strait between Iceland and Greenland, has been clear throughout European history, especially since the large-scale development of navigation in the sixteenth century. And in Asia, the Strait of Bab al-Mandeb uniting the Red Sea and the Indian Ocean and the Straits of Malacca between Malaya and Sumatra made Aden and Singapore cities of worldwide significance.

It is hardly necessary to recall that Great Britain was long concerned to establish direct control or influence over territories commanding the great maritime routes. Possession of the "gates" to the Mediterranean and Red seas and, after 1825, of the best naval base on the sea route connecting the Indian and Pacific oceans was closely associated with the rise of British power.

Yet again, the influence of geography has varied—in this case, according to the degree of technological development. The great advances in steam-powered shipping in the second half of the nineteenth century made some cities, which had been badly situated as ports of call for sailing vessels, important as fuel supply points. And the interoceanic canals, which created new transit routes between continents, sometimes enhanced but sometimes diminished the value of positions on the natural maritime routes: the opening of the Kiel Canal across the Danish isthmus reduced—albeit on a modest scale—the maritime traffic in the Sound between Denmark and Sweden;

---

[31] The Baltic–Black seas "isthmus," cited by some authors, appears to me much more debatable.

the Suez Canal enlarged the volume of traffic in the Mediterranean and Red seas, thereby increasing the importance of Malta and Aden at the expense of African ports on the route around the Cape of Good Hope. And the mere idea for a Panama Canal, half a century before the plan was carried out, provoked diplomatic action ending with the Clayton-Bulwer Treaty of 1850 between the United States and Great Britain; conferred strategic value on the Antilles Islands, which covered the approaches to the canal; drew the world's attention to the Galapagos Islands in the Pacific; and altered traffic patterns among the archipelagos of the South Pacific.

C. Islands

As far as political power is concerned, islands have as many disadvantages as advantages. To begin with the latter, islands in the middle of an ocean are particularly valuable as bases—economically important as ports of call on sea and air routes, strategically important as potential naval and air bases. Iceland was an important naval base in the Battle of the Atlantic in 1941. The islands in the Pacific were the subject of much diplomatic rivalry from 1840 (between Great Britain and France over Tahiti) to 1919 (between the United States and Japan over Yap); in 1922, they were central to the Four-Power Pacific Treaty (one of the Washington Conference treaties); and they served as steppingstones for the American offensive against Japan launched in February, 1942.

When they lie close to the mainland, islands can be advance posts for the economic or political penetration of the state controlling the mainland coast. In 1842, the English selected Hong Kong as their base for action in China. The presence of Spaniards in Cuba was a disturbing one to the United States once her territory reached down to the Florida Keys. The Japanese occupied the large East Indian islands in 1942 not only to ensure a supply of needed raw materials but also to establish naval and air bases that would enable them, if they wished, to conduct an offensive against India.

It would also seem that an insular state enjoys greater freedom than its mainland counterpart in choosing allies.[32] But can it be argued that an insular location confers some "peculiar genius" on a people, some particular spirit of initiative that inclines it to expansionism? No such "genius" is apparent if one thinks of Iceland or Newfoundland, of Hawaii, of Formosa or Indonesia, of Corsica or Crete. It is, of course, true that Great Britain and Japan built up great empires, yet it would be rash to establish a direct link between their island life and their imperialist ambitions. From 1637 to 1854, the Japanese cut themselves off from all contact with foreign countries because their government considered this "closed door" policy a wise

---

[32] See Gottmann, *op. cit.*, pp. 75–80.

one. Nor did they show any desire to abandon this policy until external circumstances forced them to do so. As for the English, they did not feel any "vocation on the sea" before the sixteenth century;[23] economic circumstances, independent of geographical environment, altered their attitude and widened their horizons.[34]

On the other hand, islands have certain disadvantages. Except when islands are very large, they frequently lack sufficient food resources and must depend on other countries to supply them. This state of economic dependence, which is very marked in the Mediterranean islands, is not conducive to the preservation of political independence. Often, too, islands turn in on themselves too much and preserve an archaic civilization. Such is the case with the Pacific islands, particularly those that are far from frequently used maritime routes. Such was also the case, until recently, of Sardinia, although it is not far from the mainland and lies along the maritime route between Marseille and Tunis.

Insular states close to the mainland, moreover, are aware of dangers in their position: since they can serve as advance posts for a would-be conqueror of the mainland, they know it is possible that the mainland ruler will be eager to forestall this eventuality. To ensure security, the government of an island has often taken the initiative: as, for example, the doges of Venice in regard to the *terra firma;* the Danes when they invaded Schleswig in 1700 during the Northern War; the British penetration of Malaysia from Singapore; the plan to annex Korea contemplated as far back as 1873 by Japan; the conquest by the Sultan of Zanzibar of part of the East African coast in the early nineteenth century.

Hence, the consequences of being on an island differ greatly according to the size of the island and its situation—in a closed sea or in an ocean, near or far from the continental littoral, near or far from a maritime route.

Considering these various aspects,[35] then, we can reach a few tentative conclusions about the importance of location in the history of international relations. Of course, we can make certain comparisons, note certain analogies and causal relations in connection with particular cases; yet in other, ostensibly very similar, cases the same causal relationships will not obtain. Affinities between a state's geography and its foreign policy are undeniable, but they are "often unstable, nearly always different." Actually,

---

[33] Admiral Alfred T. Mahan took care to point this out. See *The Influence of Sea Power upon History: 1660–1783* (Boston, 1890).

[34] "England has changed its nature . . . owing to causes in no way dependent on race or geographical environment." Febvre, *op. cit.* pp. 178–79.

[35] I do not think it necessary to examine still another: the issue of "central location." Germany, by reason of her central geographic position, for example, could play her neighbors off against each other, yet did she not at the same time complain of the threat of encirclement?

the political value of a state's geographical position depends on what is around it; a state's history, Ratzel maintained, is always "a part of the history of the neighboring states" as well. But even this is not a factor with constant political consequences; sometimes it leads to solidarity, to the extent that contiguous states experience the same concerns in the face of the rest of the world (this is true of Scandinavia in contemporary Europe); more often, it arouses jealousies. "Cohabitation is not a very effective or strong political bond."[36]

III. SIZE

Among geographic factors, what importance should one assign to the *size* of the area a state occupies? There is certainly no permanent correlation between the extent of the area and the richness of available resources; the produce of the soil depends on climate, water flow, and the quality of land far more than on size of the territory; nor do the resources of the sub-soil have any connection with how much land there is. All one can say is that between states in the same climatic zone, the larger often possesses greater agricultural resources. Apart from this self-evident, even banal, observation, the question has been raised whether the size of a state has an intrinsic value in and of itself.

Any state, according to Ratzel, is *necessarily* in conflict with the outside world in defense of the land it possesses, and any properly organized state endeavors to enlarge its area because this will bring it either more plentiful and varied resources or greater security. The size of a nation's territory is an essential element in the idea each people forms concerning its destiny, Ratzel argued; this "space consciousness" was at the center of his theory that citizens of a large state have "broad" views because they enjoyed varied means of existence and great freedom of movement, whereas peoples occupying a "small space" generally have more timid or modest attitudes. Space was thus a "political force." In the contemporary world, he argued, the small state could no longer hope to expand, and found it hard to maintain complete independence, whereas a large state was often most "eager to expand." Still, Ratzel did not want small states to disappear: the Netherlands and Belgium, for instance, even though they occupied strategic positions at the mouths of the Rhine and Scheldt rivers, had a right to independence.[37]

Ratzel's "political geography," although it did not claim to establish a political dogma, relied on arguments that justified the territorial expansion of the German Empire. It is not surprising, therefore, that Chancellor Bethmann-Hollweg and Foreign Secretary Jagow virtually repeated Ratzel's

---

[36] Gottmann, *op. cit.*, p. 192.
[37] It would be "altogether anti-historical," Ratzel said, "to wipe them off the map." *Op. cit.*, p. 354.

definitions in 1913–14—that the state is a "living being that grows," that "small states have no future." But Ratzel's theories have now lost much of their appeal, and territorial expansion as a national ambition seems to be on the wane.

Ratzel's theories about geographical space were subjected to critical analysis by Camille Vallaux, a French geographer. The size of a territory had no intrinsic political value but was meaningful only in connection with *distance*, Vallaux thought, which varied according to the means of transportation available. As for "space consciousness," the focal point of the German geographer's argument, it was, Vallaux said, "nebulous"; the trader from Amsterdam with connections all over the world has a "space consciousness" far greater than a French peasant's. Size is not, therefore, a determinant in the formation of the national psychology. The development of no political society is "rigorously determined by the land on which it lives or the framework within which it moves."[38]

Do the preceding observations warrant a general conclusion? A political society is certainly influenced by its natural environment, but is it *determined* by that environment? Does the study of geographical data alone make it possible to define the guiding principles of a particular state's foreign policy?

Political thinkers, from Jean Bodin to Turgot, from Montesquieu to Michelet, were much concerned with these problems. Many insisted on the importance of geographical factors; Hegel and Gobineau considered them negligible. Some posited a "geographical determinism"—Victor Cousin, the early nineteenth-century French philosopher, for instance, who said:

> Give me the map of a country, its configuration, its climate, its waters, its winds, and its whole physical geography; give me its natural products, its flora, its fauna—and I will tell you *a priori* what the citizen of that country is like, and what part that country plays in history, not accidentally, but necessarily, not at a certain period, but in all.[39]

But it is only since the end of the nineteenth century that the influence of geography has been defined in anything like scientific terms.

Here again, the dominant influence was that of Friedrich Ratzel, who proposed to study the effect of geographical conditions on the character and behavior of human groups in the firm belief that his findings would help to renew the foundations of political science. The connection "between man and the land," between human activities and natural environment, was his foremost concern.

Ratzel's ideas, somewhat amended, were adopted in the early twentieth

---

[38] Camille Vallaux, *Géographie sociale* (Paris, 1911), p. 137.

[39] Victor Cousin, *Introduction à l'histoire de la philosophie* (Paris, 1828), Eighth Lesson, p. 17.

century in the United States by Ellen Churchill Semple and in Sweden by Rudolf Kjellén.[40] In England, they were simplified (and distorted) by Halford MacKinder. A balance of political forces, MacKinder contended, did not depend solely on geographical circumstances, for "virility" and "capacity for organization" also played their part; nevertheless, in his view, geographical factors exerted a coercive influence because they were more measurable and more constant. He pointed to the considerable position that Russia enjoyed in modern Europe as an example: First organized in a frontier zone, Russia expanded eastward toward the steppes that had once been the pathway for the great invasions from central Asia; she succeeded in organizing the "Eurasian space"—the pivotal region, the "heartland," of the world. A continental power, he argued, is always the strongest one, especially when it holds a central strategic position so that it can move in any direction. If Russia should expand to the "marginal" regions of Asia—to China and India—and possess a navy, she would control the world. Here as elsewhere, MacKinder made sweeping assertions but no attempt to adduce proofs.[41]

After 1919, the German school of geopolitics drew its inspiration from MacKinder as well as from Ratzel and Kjellén. The prime mover of that school, Karl Haushofer, believed that geopolitics must show how politics is "determined" by geographical factors. It must therefore examine the influence of climate, topography, forms of vegetation, demography, and location on the life of human societies. This analysis, which would establish "palpable facts" and "proven laws," would provide statesmen with the necessary principles "for elaborating practical policy." At the same time, it would show them the limits of the possible; anything a government might achieve beyond the framework drawn by "geopolitics" would be ephemeral. Haushofer's intended "science" and "guide" to political life defined the terms of his profession of faith. But his main concern was not a scientific one. He was thinking primarily of the education of public opinion, and his aim was to establish that it was Germany's vocation to regain her former power.[42]

While retaining Ratzel's ideas on "space" and the "sense of space," geopolitics gained new themes: the "malleability" of frontiers, the right of a people to possess the land around the mouth of any river intersecting its territory (whereas Ratzel had recognized the right of the Netherlands to independence), and, finally, the notion of *Lebensraum*, "room to live in," to which certain peoples were entitled.[43] After 1931, when the National Socialist movement had gained ascendancy in Germany, the geopoliticians

---

[40] Ellen Churchill Semple, *Influence of Geographic Environments* (New York, 1911), and Rudolf Kjellén, *Staten som Lifsform (The State as an Organism)* (Stockholm, 1916).

[41] Halford MacKinder, "The Geographical Pivot of History" (London, 1904).

[42] Karl Haushofer *et al.*, *Bausteine für Geopolitik* (Berlin, 1928).

[43] Ratzel had used the term *Lebensraum* in 1901, but in a bio-geographic sense. Haushofer transposed it into the economic and political arena.

were even more insistent. But they adapted their doctrine to circumstance: the "laws" they claimed to establish for the use of statesmen could not, they now said, apply to all situations, for a powerful personality could sometimes change the course of events[44]—clear evidence that they had capitulated to opportunism and propaganda.

These geopolitical theories of Ratzel, MacKinder, and the others were attacked from widely different standpoints.

The first current of opposition challenged MacKinder's and Haushofer's ideas on "natural seats of power," a challenge that drew its inspiration from the work of the American historian of sea power Alfred Mahan. While the geopoliticians emphasized land power, which they saw as the basic source of political domination, Mahan's followers attempted to show that sea power had played the preponderant role in history. According to Mahan, peoples, like individuals, however strong they may be, decline if they are deprived of the activity and external resources they need to stimulate and nourish their internal vigor. And the sea is both the surest means of communication with other peoples and the richest source for the renewal of a people's own strength. However, the development of maritime connections is risky if one does not possess naval supremacy. The state with a favorable geographical position on a coastline ought therefore to strengthen its fleet rather than to expand by land, which demands great military effort. During the seventeenth and eighteenth centuries, France had been wrong to pursue a continental policy, Mahan maintained, and Spain fell into decadence because it was unable to safeguard its communications with South America for lack of naval power. These observations would seem to imply that to be a naval power could be the result of deliberate choice. Yet Mahan did not hesitate to assert that the history of seafaring peoples had been governed by geographical conditions far more than by the perspicacity of their governments. He thus remained a stanch believer in determinism.

The other current of opposition to "geopolitics" (largely French) was directed also against this geographical determinism. The French geographers had no intention of disputing the obvious connection between natural conditions on the one hand, and inequality of resources and diversity in ways of life on the other. But they insisted, nevertheless, that human initiative reduced the influence of geographical environment, and they refused to concede that politics was *determined* by geography.

A similar attitude was adopted by those historians who believed most firmly in the relation between geography and history. Nature, one of them wrote, gives human society opportunities, but man remains master of those opportunities.[45] The geographical environment, according to another, is only

---

[44] Despite these concessions to the role of "personality," Haushofer lost virtually all his influence in official German Government circles during the 1930's.

[45] Febvre, *op. cit.*

a "partial factor of interpretation," for it does not "irrevocably constrain men." The study of geography therefore cannot produce conclusions valid for all times and all states of civilization.[46] A third, who criticized Ratzel's ideas of "space" and emphasized the role of man, nevertheless attached some importance to physical environmental conditions.[47] Finally, for Arnold Toynbee, it is always man's acts, the effect of his social organizations, and the role of religious concepts—far more than natural resources—that hold the center of the stage.[48]

IV. CONCLUSION

All the preceding remarks lead to a single conclusion: the role of geographical factors in international relations is not so clear or constant as one might at first sight believe. Man has succeeded, especially within the last century, in limiting the effect of the physical environment, thanks to technological processes he has invented.

In agriculture, natural conditions have been altered either by clearing and afforestation—which has changed not only vegetation, but also the extent and nature of eroded lands—or by irrigation and drainage systems that have increased the area of arable land. And new methods of improving the soil and new methods of cultivation have made it possible to increase agricultural production substantially even in regions where the quality of the soil is poor. But whenever man's efforts have not been continued, the earlier conditions have reappeared. Today, tropical rain forests cover the region of Central America where archaeological fragments show the Mayans once flourished; in Syria, the desert has reconquered areas where ruins attest to the existence of the once great city of Palmyra.

Advances in industrial technology, particularly since the early nineteenth century, have been closely dependent on the utilization of energy sources and thus with resources of the sub-soil. When coal was the prime fuel, the states with large coal deposits came to have overwhelming importance in global economic and political life. The era of hydro-electric power brought mountainous regions, which had previously been outside the mainstream of world economics, into the fore. Then, in the first years of the twentieth century, the discovery of oil and natural-gas deposits drew attention to the economic and political significance of regions or states that had previously

[46] Braudel, *op. cit.*, p. 3.

[47] Ancel, *op. cit.*

[48] Critical analysis has virtually demolished MacKinder's and Haushofer's theories, but not Ratzel's. Even those who most vigorously attacked Ratzel's excessive determinism took care not to identify him with the "geopoliticians" who pursued propaganda aims so alien to the scientific spirit. The French geographer Vidal de la Blache paid tribute to Ratzel's achievement and to the "wealth of observations" he had assembled, reproaching him only with having couched his ideas in a dogmatic form that was incompatible with the relativity of the phenomena.

aroused little interest. And, after 1945, the Congo's uranium deposits, exploited largely for military reasons, gave that country considerable importance, at least for a time.

Finally, technology has transformed the conditions of traffic and transport. The construction of railroads, especially the great transcontinental lines, ended the isolation of certain regions and ensured new markets for their products. The railroad made it possible to populate and develop the central plains of the United States, the Canadian prairies, the Argentine pampas, and Siberia. And airplanes, since they first became important vehicles for commercial transport between 1919 and 1939 have been largely responsible for eliminating the remaining obstacles to travel over great distances and difficult terrain. In military use, they have reduced or eliminated the importance of natural barriers—mountains, rivers, deserts—that were once regarded as impregnable, and have largely reduced the advantages of certain island states while increasing the importance of others.

The effect of government regulations, while far less marked than that of technological progress, is also far from negligible. National laws have modified the conditions under which the soil and sub-soil may be explored and exploited. And, since the eighteenth century, states have strictly delimited their frontiers and, by measures enforced at the confines of their territory through customs agents or police, impeded the circulation of men and the exchange of goods along the land routes. Alone or in agreement with other states, they have regulated traffic on sea routes, too. In some parts of the world, international treaties have imposed political divisions that disregard the characteristics of the physical environment. In all these cases, considerations of national power, security, or prestige (as well as sentiment) have taken precedence over geographical conditions. Everywhere, the restraints imposed by the physical environment have diminished markedly as a result of man's deliberate action.

2

POPULATION

During the last century, the rate of growth in the world's population has been increasing sharply and international migrations have been on a very large scale. Population changes have substantially affected the relative economic and political strength of nations and states; hence, they constitute an important aspect of international relations. Migrations, too, have had this effect; they have also been sometimes the cause, sometimes the occasion, of disagreements or conflicts between states.

I. THE POPULATION INCREASE

Despite the unreliability of any estimates made before censuses were established, it is now generally accepted that the world population in 1800 was about 900 million. According to census data, the figure in 1954 was approximately 2.46 billion, the maximum increase having occurred between 1850 and 1900.

Europe's population rose from 187 million in 1800 to 266 million in 1850, 400 million in 1900, and 555 million in 1953. (The most rapid increase took place between 1870 and 1914: from about 300 million to 452 million, or an increase of about 50 per cent in less than fifty years.) But the proportions in which the European states took part in this increase were unequal. The population of European Russia increased during this period by 60 million; of Germany, by 27 million; of Great Britain (including Ireland), by 14 million; of Italy, by 8 million; of France, by only 3.5 million.

The question then arises: what links can historical data establish between these different demographic situations and national power, whether as regards military strength, or economic prosperity, or national attitudes?

A. EFFECTS ON MILITARY STRENGTH

The size of a population could be an essential element of military power at any period when the efficacy of an army was proportionate to the number of its soldiers rather than to its fire power. This became clearly apparent at the time of the French Revolution, when a mass conscripted army was introduced; again after 1871, when all the armies on the European continent were recruited on the basis of compulsory military service; and during World War I, despite the considerable advances in the development of armaments.

Only during the past forty years has the number of soldiers lost its direct relation to the power of the army. In 1930, for instance, the report of the Preparatory Commission for the League of Nations Disarmament Conference at Geneva noted that in a "modern war," the offensive advantage belongs to the country with the greatest industrial potential rather than to the one with the largest number of reserves.[1] The development of air forces during World War II and, especially, the later development of atomic weapons have amply confirmed the validity of this observation. But even in the times when it was widely held that the military power of a state depended on the size of its population, this theory was often belied by the facts.

At a time when Italy's population was increasing most rapidly, her army was much smaller than those of other major European states: at the beginning of 1914, her peacetime mobilized force included no more than 275,000 men. Italy had simply not attempted to use her manpower resources in order to increase her military potential. Was this because the government considered it unnecessary to maintain a stronger army? It was chiefly because the parliamentary majority considered it inexpedient, or even impossible, to burden the country with the expenditures involved in any increase and was determined to hold down "unproductive" expenditures. For twenty years, from 1887 to 1907, this policy of strict economy was applied to the military establishment. Economic conditions, then, at least until the first years of the twentieth century, suffice to explain it; in a primarily agricultural country, where the peasantry in at least two-thirds of the country was bitterly poor, where would the necessary sources of revenue be found?

Russia, whose population in 1914 was double that of the German Empire, had a regular army that even had the military reforms adopted the previous year been fully implemented, would have exceeded the mobilized German forces by no more than 50 per cent. And the number of trained reserves was only a little greater than the army population. Financial considerations were involved here too, but they were less important than economic and social factors. In a country where industrial development was slow, the increase in effective forces was restricted by insufficient armaments manufacture, also by the shortage of officers, for the middle and lower middle classes, which furnished the junior officers of the reserve corps, were neither large nor particularly oriented to military affairs.

---

[1] Nevertheless, the traditional view died hard. For instance, in January, 1939, the Italian Fascist leader Count Galeazzo Ciano said, "The political significance of France as a great power must necessarily decline, for the annual deficit in its birthrate is equivalent to a lost battle." (*Les archives secrètes de la Wilhelmstrasse* [Paris, 1954], V, 412.)

The Austro-Hungarian Empire, with a population of 51 million (that is, 20 per cent more than France's), had a regular army at the beginning of 1914 of about 350,000 men (equivalent to 45 per cent of the French Army). Although it had to reckon with at least two potential enemies, Russia and Serbia, even if it could rely on its Italian ally, the heterogeneous populations possessed neither Austro-Hungarian patriotism nor even a sense of common interests; the parliaments in both Vienna and Budapest hesitated to ask any sacrifices of them.

Among the principal Continental powers (Great Britain, relying on its insular position, felt she did not need to shoulder the burden of universal military conscription), Germany and France were thus the only ones where there was a direct relation between the size of the population and the size of the armed forces. To maintain the effectives of her regular army at a level comparable to Germany's, France was obliged to impose exceptionally heavy military burdens on her people—that is, to draft into the Army a larger and larger number of men each year, lowering the physical standards for entry as she did so.

A comparison between China and Japan is even more striking. In 1894, at the time of the first Sino-Japanese War, the population of the Chinese Empire was at least eight times that of Japan's, yet Japan could field better armed, better organized, and better commanded military forces and more of them. Why could not the Chinese have had more forces, when they possessed the "human matériel" that should have enabled them to overwhelm the Japanese Army? There were financial reasons: there was not sufficient revenue to provide the imperial government with the means to maintain a large mobilized force. There were economic reasons: the armaments China required could not be manufactured at home for lack of necessary industry, and they could not be purchased abroad because the imperial government did not have the means to meet foreign payments and did not wish to contract foreign loans. There were also political reasons: the Manchu emperors did not wish to put modern weapons into the hands of the Chinese people. And there were, above all, psychological reasons: in Japan, where the bearing of arms had always been regarded as a symbol of social superiority, the spirit of sacrifice for the sake of the community was an essential feature of religious and civic ethics; but in China, the mass of the population lacked this national sentiment and despised the military profession.

Demographic strength has been a factor of military power, therefore, only where there was a convergence of the social, economic, and financial conditions needed to maintain, equip, and command the armies, and only when conditions made it possible to count on a spirit of sacrifice, or at least of resignation, among those subjected to the obligations and constraints of military service.

B. EFFECTS ON ECONOMIC POWER

Economists and sociologists in the late nineteenth and early twentieth centuries often pointed to the factor of population increase in the development of national economic power.

The examples of Belgium, Great Britain, and then Germany between 1890 and 1914 show that population increase stimulated production, and that industry would not have developed so rapidly had not the surplus rural population provided an abundant supply of industrial manpower. The pace of industrial development in the United States between 1895 and 1914 would have been much slower had it not been for the influx of immigrants, who came to constitute 60 per cent of the labor force in New England, Pennsylvania and the Chicago region.[2] Japanese industry could not have gotten off to such a good start between 1894 and 1914 without the demographic expansion that, after a long period of stagnation, had begun twenty years earlier. The large labor force made it possible for industrialists to keep salaries and costs low. Because they were cheap, Japanese products, although inferior in quality, could compete with European products in the Asian markets.

In all these cases, the working classes themselves, after some hard times, generally achieved better living conditions, for industrialization improved the over-all standard of living. But of course the demographic situation was only one factor in the rise of industry; a supply of manpower would have been useless without technology and capital.

In the agricultural sector, demographic increases made it possible to increase production not only by improving the output but by bringing once neglected land under cultivation. In areas where population pressures were strongest—Japan, central China, the Indochinese deltas, the Ganges plain—each fragment of arable land was put to use. (In 1925, in order to offset the effects of the population increase, the Japanese Government instituted a plan to extend cultivated areas to the lower slopes of the mountain ranges.) Inversely, as geographers have often pointed out, manpower shortages in underpopulated areas—most of tropical Africa, for instance, and parts of Brazil—have delayed the development of agriculture.

Nevertheless, a direct link between population and agricultural development only really obtains in countries whose populations, for lack of products in demand in the export market, are obliged to live off their own resources. It disappears when the economic life of a state is sufficiently developed to enable the nation to cover the agricultural deficit by imports financed with the revenue from exports of manufactured goods.

In many cases, rapid population growth causes an excessive fragmentation

---

[2] *Reports of the Immigration Commission*, U.S. Senate, 61st Cong., 3d Sess., Document No. 7475 (2 vols.; Washington, 1911).

of farmland, thus preventing any rational development of agricultural production. Often, small independent farmers are desperately concerned to produce *all* the food their families need, even when the soil they work does not lend itself to such varied production. The owners of these minute parcels of land are too poor to purchase the equipment or fertilizers that would enable them to improve the yield. A population increase in these conditions tends to perpetuate obsolete economic practices at the expense of developing the exchange economy that alone could improve conditions of production and increase the over-all volume. An increase in the number of men available does not necessarily lead to a corresponding increase in the products of the land;[3] in China throughout the nineteenth and early twentieth centuries, and in Ireland during the first half of the nineteenth century, it caused impoverishment and starvation; in Russia, it aggravated existing social problems.

To speak of the connection between population increase and economic development leads one inevitably to the concepts of *population pressures* and *overpopulation*. But a mere analysis of the size of an area and the number of people on it does not suffice to establish that population pressure or overpopulation exists.

What is the "optimum population" of any state—the figure to which the population may rise without incurring a decline in the living standard? This figure depends on the quality of the land and on mineral resources; on the technological level achieved and on how much capital is available to invest in new technical processes; on the internal organization of the economy; and, finally, on the amount and diversity of foreign trade by means of which national resources can be supplemented.[4] It is thus linked to a variable set of circumstances: some mineral resources may become important because of a new technical invention; some needed imports may be cut off if the balance of payments is unfavorable. But it also depends in the long run on a people's desiderata, that is, on the importance attached to prosperity[5] or, more correctly, on the position assigned to prosperity in relation to other goals—such as a large national population in the future. Any attempt to calculate the optimum population in any given case is thus quite dangerous.

Still, on the imprecise idea of an optimum population depends the notion of *over*population: to say that a country is economically overpopulated is to say that the population is greater than its economic optimum.

---

[3] See Otto Effertz, "Théorie ponophysiocratique de la population," *Revue d'économie politique*, XXVIII (1914), pp. 129-52.

[4] See Léon Buquet, *L'Optimum de population* (Paris, 1956). See also the debates of the World Population Conference, Geneva, 1927.

[5] Alfred Sauvy, *Théorie générale de la population*, chap. 5, "L'Optimum économique."

What is the significance of this definition? Although the experts pay heed to it, "moderate" overpopulation for the most part has little effect on international relations. In France, for instance, some regions had a surplus rural population in the nineteenth century, but the development of railroads reduced the demographic pressure by facilitating movement between regions. Serious overpopulation becomes apparent when the population increases too rapidly in relation to the available food resources in a country that, because it cannot practice an exchange economy, is not able to make up the deficiency; also, when the increase in the population aggravates unemployment and thereby lowers the standard of living for a portion of the inhabitants. Yet this deterioration is not *necessarily* the effect of overpopulation. Even if the material conditions of its existence remain more or less stable, a human group may become conscious of the inadequacy of its resources relative to those of neighboring groups and hence aspire more eagerly than before to improve them. This happens when contact with more sophisticated foreigners results in changes in eating habits, for instance: the society in which such a change occurs does not easily return to its previous habits, and the food resources that had once satisfied the population now appear inadequate. This collective dissatisfaction may suffice to produce reactions similar to those resulting from an actual decline in the standard of living.

Nevertheless, although overpopulation cannot be scientifically defined, it is quite important in any comparison between two states. "Relative" overpopulation can become a discordant element in international relations when the peoples concerned are conscious of it or when they associate the observed fact of overpopulation with that of unequal living conditions. Such inequality was obvious as long ago as 1919 among China, Japan, India, and the East Indies. But only Japan realized it at the time, a realization that contributed to the development of Japanese imperialism. Since 1945, this sense of inequality has become a more and more significant element in the conduct of certain non-European peoples and in their political concerns.[6] This is due to the increasing disproportion between a growing population and its available resources and also to the differences in economic progress between the "have" and "have-not" nations, differences that are increasingly considered unjust.[7] This awareness of inequality is directly related to the development of the information media—press, radio, television— which have given even the poorest peoples the chance to learn about how other people live and to make comparisons. Whether arising spontaneously

---

[6] If the "relative overpopulation" of West Germany or Italy has not brought similar consequences, it is probably because standards of living have improved in both those countries.

[7] Underdevelopment and overpopulation are not *always* connected: consider the example of tropical Africa.

or as the result of propaganda, the idea of overpopulation has become a major factor in modern life.

C. EFFECTS ON NATIONAL BELIEFS

Demographic expansion can sometimes modify the ideas and beliefs held collectively by a people. Sociologists studying this matter have come to three principal conclusions:

1. The numerical increase of a population is a sign of vitality that is considered to justify confidence in the national destiny and a sense of optimism.[8] The German Empire at the end of the nineteenth century provides an example of this development of the collective psychology: confidence and optimism were accompanied by a sense of superiority over peoples whose numbers were not increasing at the same pace. About 1890, some German newspapers remarked on the advantage this population increase gave Germany over France. Germany, they said, would have a population of 100 million by 1920, whereas France would have no more than 30 million.

2. The average age of the population is of even greater significance. In a country where the proportion of young people is large, adolescents realize that just because there are so many of them, they will find it hard to get jobs; they realize the need for effort; there is a greater spirit of initiative, enterprise, and sacrifice of personal interests.[9] On the other hand, when the average age of a population is high and the "controls" fall into the hands of older people, the mentality becomes more timorous, more wedded to routine.

3. Finally, the difficulties that young people encounter as they embark upon active life may cause them to listen to the advocates of a policy of force. In a rural population, where those who are "fated to be tillers of the soil" realize full well that few of them will be able to make a good living, rapid population growth prompts the young people to advocate expansion of the national territory. In Japan between 1919 and 1939, where 75 per cent of the junior officers were of peasant origin and thus had direct experience of rural overpopulation, the officers were the warmest supporters of armed action against China. In 1933, they constituted the principal support of General Sadao Araki's fascist movement. In an industrial population, when unemployment hits young people the moment they enter the job market, it generates in them, even more than in the adults, a sense of despair that

---

[8] The converse may also be true: confidence resulting from the prospect of economic expansion may encourage population growth.

[9] The theory was developed by A. Dumont in *Depopulation et civilisation* (Paris, 1890). During the first half of the twentieth century, demographers tried to spread the idea that there were "young" and "aging" nations.

moves them to violence; as in Germany during the economic slump of 1931–33, such young people are ready to listen to the man or the party who promises to secure new means of existence for them by the conquest of "space to live in."

These three conclusions, however, are contradicted by evidence supplied by other countries.

Whereas population growth helped to engender confidence in the future of Kaiser Wilhelm's Germany, it did not, in the same period, have the same effect in Russia. And as for China and India, where the problems of land and of feeding the population are dominant, the rapid population increase can hardly inspire optimism. Rural overpopulation was apparent in other countries besides Japan, but did not lead to the same political consequences. And the terrible (and long) unemployment crisis that plagued British labor between 1922 and 1938 in no way altered their peace-loving attitude and certainly never disposed them to subscribe to Sir Oswald Mosley's fascist program. Population pressure has offered an opportunity to supporters of violence only when the temperament of a people lent itself to this policy anyway. Moreover, the opportunities for armed action must be favorable: even if a demographic situation is "explosive," it does not lead to war unless the relative strengths of the countries concerned permit it.[10]

D. GOVERNMENT POLICY

Government policies have been able to influence the demographic situation. Legislative or administrative measures favoring population growth include development of public-health and medical services, which reduce the mortality rate, incentives offered to encourage larger families, and assistance to regions whose food supplies have been affected by adverse weather conditions.

The first type of government activity had particularly important consequences in territories colonized by Europeans, since it reduced the great epidemics and famines that had once curbed the natural population increase. The evidence shown in the demographic curve of the native population of Algeria since about 1880 is a typical example of this transformation.[11] A similar demographic pattern occurred among the native peoples of South Africa and among those of the Tonkin delta. European efforts thus increased the "population pressure," and this subsequently became a primary cause

---

[10] On this point, see Gaston Bouthoul, *La Population dans le monde* (Paris, 1935), p. 206.

[11] The observations made by Louis Chevalier in "Le problème démographique nord-africain," *Cahiers de l'Institut national études démographiques* (Paris), No. 6 (1949), were confirmed in a more recent study: André Nouschi, *Enquête sur le niveau de vie des populations constantinoises de la conquête jusqu'en 1939* (Paris, 1961).

of social and political unrest and, ultimately, of the resistance to white domination. The importance of demographic evolution to international relations is quite clear here, but it does not seem to have been anticipated in any way by the states concerned; their action was inspired by humanitarian considerations and the long-term consequences were not taken into account.

Governmental intervention to encourage population growth has been evident in three major states in the twentieth century:

Japan was the first. At first, the Japanese Government confined itself to propaganda efforts representing a higher birth rate as a national duty and a sign of prosperity, and to sponsoring the law of 1929 forbidding any form of birth control. It was only in January, 1941, ten months before entering World War II, that the Japanese Government established a system of marriage loans and subsidies to large families. Japan, it stated, must arrive at a population of 100 million by 1960. (The population of Japan proper was 72.2 million at the end of 1938.)

The German Government, as soon as Hitler came to power, adopted the same policy. Legislation was enacted in the mid-1930's to provide marriage loans to young couples (who did not have to pay the loan back if they had four children), as well as subsidies to large families.

The government of fascist Italy expressed its intentions in this area as early as 1928 by granting tax exemptions to large families, but it was not until 1937 that further legislation was passed.

In all three cases, the demographic policy had its basis in a political program; its purpose was to assert "number as force."

In the early years of the twentieth century, the German Government had invoked the demographic argument when it claimed the "place in the sun" to which Kaiser Wilhelm's empire felt entitled to aspire. Chancellor Bethmann-Hollweg revealed the line of argument in January, 1914, in the course of negotiations with the French Ambassador over certain Asian and African questions: it is not possible, he said, to refuse Germany "the share that legitimately belongs to any growing being." Then, Hitler's Germany gave this theory its most categorical expression: in *Mein Kampf*, Hitler declared that:

> The foreign policy of the racist state must secure the means of existence, on this planet, of the race which constitutes the state, by establishing a relation which is healthy, viable and in accordance with natural law between the number and growth of the population on the one hand, and the size and value of the territory on the other.

When is this relation a healthy one?—When "a people's food supply is insured from the resources of its own land." The National Socialist movement "must therefore endeavor to eliminate the discrepancy between the size of our population and the size of our territory"; it must "secure for the German people the territory to which it is entitled." And Hjalmar H. G. Schacht, Hitler's Minister of Economy and President of the Reichs-bank, went on to say, "Peace in Europe, and therefore in the rest of the world, depends on whether or not the crowded masses of central Europe can obtain an opportunity to live."[12] Minister of Propaganda Goebbels, five years later, enumerating the old problems that "war will enable us to settle," referred to Germany's demographic position: "with its growing birth rate, [Germany] found itself confined in an area which was far too small."[13] But at no time did Germany's political leaders trouble to give a more precise definition of their statements, the underlying principle of which foreign observers found most questionable.[14]

The demographic thrust was one of the arguments advanced in favor of Italian expansion from the very first. Prime Minister Francesco Crispi said, in June, 1889, that Italy must acquire a colonial territory to which it could send its "surplus rural population." And Enrico Corradini, the first theorist of this imperialism, emphasized the same point in his report to the nationalist party congress of Florence in 1911: Italy's surplus popula-tion must not be lost to countries where the emigrant was likely to be "de-nationalized"; it must be directed to Italian colonial territories, and it was therefore the state's duty to acquire them. (This argument obviously attached little value to the opportunities for Italian political action which the presence of large groups of Italian emigrants in America might have provided.) Italian Fascists simply revived these arguments. Mussolini outlined the theme in a Senate speech of December 11, 1923, and in 1926 the Italian press almost unanimously repeated it: because Italy, "of all the great nations, is the one with the greatest human resources," it was entitled to colonies to settle in.[15] A year later, in his "Ascension Speech" of May 26, 1927, Mussolini stated that France, having exercised hegemony in Europe when she possessed demographic superiority, lost that privileged position when her birth rate began to decline. To "qualify," he declared, Italy must have a population of no less than 60 million by 1950.

But it was in Japan between 1919 and 1939 that the connection between population increase and imperialism was most forcibly expressed. Advo-

---

[12] Speech at Frankfurt am Main, December 8, 1936.
[13] Article in *Das Reich,* November 9, 1941.
[14] The French Ambassador noted that Germany's birth rate (15.1 per 1,000 in 1933) was "one of the lowest in Europe. . . . The argument on population that Germany so frequently adduces to justify its desire for expansion is losing most of its cogency." (Report of June 7, 1933.) The birth rate rose to 19 per 1,000 in 1936, but it had been 27.5 per 1,000 in 1913.
[15] See *Popolo d'Italia,* April 10, 1926, for a good summary of this argument.

cates of "armed expansion," especially in military circles, pointed to over-population to justify their program of territorial expansion.[16]

The question remains, what real value these governments attached to the demographic argument. Did they consider the conquest of new "living space" necessary, or was the population issue simply a means to cover a political plan, the real motive for which was the will to power? The second inter-pretation is plausible. There is the statement Hitler made in January, 1941:

> According to the laws of nature, the soil belongs to the one who conquers it. The fact that we have children who want to live, the fact that our people is bursting out of its constricting frontiers—that is what justifies all our terri-torial claims in the east. Our population explosion will be our opportunity. Overpopulation forces a people to find a way out. We are not likely to remain frozen at our present level; necessity will force us to be always at the spear-head of progress.[17]

But although plausible, this interpretation is not watertight: one would have to have more documentary and textual proof, and this is an area that historical researchers have not yet tackled.

By encouraging population growth without regard to economic re-sources—that is, without allowing the prospect of a lower living standard to deter them—were these governments deliberately seeking to increase the "population pressures" in order to give their territorial claims a more solid foundation? It is quite possible, but here again, the evidence is lack-ing. It is not enough to point to the obvious internal contradictions in a given policy.

Historical research may eventually uncover documents or personal testimony that will answer these questions; in the meantime they remain of major significance in the study of international relations.

II. MIGRATION

The years between the 1870's and World War I were those of the great European migrations. Between 1871 and 1914, 34 million men left Europe, almost half of them during the last thirteen years of that forty-five-year period. Allowing for repatriations (the exact number of which is not known, for lack of statistical data prior to 1886), the net intercontinental

---

[16] In point of fact, other states, even in Europe, could make similar claims on similar grounds. The Poles' living standard, for instance, was appreciably lower than the Germans'. But Poland did not possess the wherewithal to back its claims by force of arms.

[17] Adolf Hitler, *Libres propos sur la guerre et la paix* (ed., Martin Bormann) (Paris, 1952), p. 254.

emigration from Europe was probably about 25 million persons, the great majority of whom were men in the prime of life.

International migrations elsewhere in the world cannot compare with these large-scale displacements of European populations. In Japan, where population pressure was not yet very marked, the average annual emigration between 1910 and 1913 did not exceed 12,000 men. Indian emigration, which brought 160,000 men to Natal and thence all over East Africa in little more than twenty years, had come to a stop by 1897. The number of Chinese peasants who left Fukien Province via the port of Amoy to go to the Dutch East Indies, Indochina, and Singapore does not seem to have exceeded 45,000 men annually between 1900 and 1910.

After World War I, which temporarily halted all international population movements, emigration from Europe was no longer on the same scale. The 820,000 departures in 1920 were only a flash in the pan; after 1921, statistics show an almost continuous decline, for the United States, which before 1914 had received 65 per cent of the emigrants, was closing its doors. (But we should also note the existence of a migratory current that bore, between 1920 and 1930, an average 100,000 Canadians annually to the United States; these were mostly persons born in Canada, particularly French Canadians.)

Asian migrations, on the other hand, somewhat increased, although they were still far from equaling the massive exodus from Europe that had taken place between 1905 and 1914. Chinese emigrants, by far the most numerous, barely exceeded an annual 70,000–80,000; the figure rose to an exceptional 220,000 only in 1926 and 1927, when central China became the arena of civil war.

How did these currents of migration affect international relations?

A. MIGRATIONS AND THE RELATIVE STRENGTH OF NATIONS

The influence of population movement on international relations can best be studied in the years between 1880 and 1914, when most governments permitted unrestricted migration.[18]

The nature of these migrations was not the same everywhere. In Great Britain (excluding Ireland), particularly after 1919, those who left were not primarily poor peasants but craftsmen or technicians who hoped to find better-paying jobs abroad, particularly in American industry.[19] The same was

---

[18] The term "migration" is used here in the most commonly accepted sense: the international displacement of individuals who freely decide to change their residence. We are not referring, therefore, to transfers of population made in consequence of treaties, or to "forcible" migrations.

[19] See Jacqueline Beaujeu-Garnier, *L'Europe de Nord et de Nord-Ouest* (Paris, 1958), I, 236.

true of Scandinavian emigrants. However, most emigrants from Continental Europe were peasants.

1. Effects in the Countries of Origin

First, one should consider the advantages and disadvantages of these massive migrations from the point of view of the European states that furnished the largest contingents of emigrants.

The domestic advantages were both social, economic, and political.

From a general social point of view, the emigrations mitigated the excessive density of population in certain agricultural regions. It therefore partially remedied the problem of peasant poverty and sometimes stilled the complaints directed against government farm policies. In industrial regions, it reduced the evils of unemployment. In Italy during the first years of the twentieth century, the government maintained that its purpose in encouraging emigration was precisely to relieve distress.

From an economic point of view, the money sent home by emigrants to their families[20] made it possible to improve homes and sometimes even agricultural techniques, whenever peasant families could afford to put the money into equipment. It also provided the state with the means to cover a deficit in its balance of payments and thus made it easier for it to import raw materials or capital goods. The money sent home by emigrants seems to have been particularly important before 1914 in Italy and Greece.[21]

From a political point of view, emigration was generally regarded as a guarantor of internal peace: not only did it provide an outlet for social malcontents (landless peasants, for instance, who otherwise might one day constitute the troops of a revolutionary movement), but it also rid the country of certain enemies of the regime or government. In the Austro-Hungarian Empire, "national minorities" tended to migrate much more than Germans or Magyars. In Tsarist Russia, where emigration was subject to the issuance of passports usually granted for only a strictly limited number of purposes (educational travel, apprenticeship) and valid for no more than five years, the administration freely granted passports of unlimited duration to Jews because it desired them to leave the country; it would appear that it adopted the same policy with regard to a number of socialists and liberals after the suppression of the revolutionary movements of 1905. The International Labor Office noted in 1922 that in the Danube region and in eastern Europe generally before 1914, large-scale emi-

---

[20] Remittances from the United States reached an annual average of $600 million between 1924 and 1929.

[21] See H. P. Fairchild, *Greek Immigration to the United States* (New Haven, Conn., 1911).

gration had often been regarded as a blessing in disguise by the governments concerned.[22]

In their foreign relations, states derived other advantages from emigration. Since the emigrants, at least for a while, retained their native customs in their new homes and continued to prefer the products of their native countries, they served as a stimulus to export. At the same time they served as instruments of commercial penetration to the extent that they popularized their national products among their new neighbors. Sometimes, especially if they had left Europe for political reasons, they also acted as channels of cultural influence. After the *coup d'état* of December 2, 1851, that paved the way for Louis Napoleon to become Emperor of France, French intellectual emigrants in Argentina, Uruguay, and Chile—men like Amédée Jacques, Alexis Peyret, Albert Larroque, Alfred Corcelle-Seneuil— helped to organize and promote secondary and higher education. And the members of religious "congregations," who left France after the Associations Law of 1910 had stringently limited the activities and freedom of French church groups, undoubtedly helped to strengthen French intellectual influence in the Ottoman Empire.

Emigrants of one country often formed groups in their new homeland, endeavoring to preserve their bonds and their individuality, and to maintain a sentimental link with their native land. The presence of such groups could give their mother country a means of political influence, or at least a lever for spreading its views.[23]

Finally, European states regarded the emigration of their nationals as a means of developing the prosperity of their colonial territories. In cases where the colonies enjoyed a climate that Europeans found suitable, they encouraged and even directly assisted such emigration. This policy was practiced by Great Britain toward New Zealand and Australia after 1830—prompted by Edward Gibbon Wakefield, a propagandist and colonial statesman who advocated cheap land and self-government as incentives to colonization,[24] and his Colonization Society. The idea was to substitute "systematic colonization" for mere emigration; to encourage emigrants by offering to pay their fares, but to select them carefully; to help settlers establish themselves on the land, but not by distributing free land to them, since free concessions might encourage newcomers to acquire more acreage than they could work. The practical results were poor, because there was no way of determining a fair price for the land sold, but the principle of

---

[22] *Methods of Compiling Emigration and Immigration Statistics* (Geneva: ILO, 1922).

[23] The presence of large groups of German-speaking Americans and German emigrants in the United States doubtless fostered Germany's hopes that the United States would not enter World War I against her.

[24] See his *A View of the Art of Colonization* (1849).

assisted emigration for colonial settlement attracted public attention and did have some application in British imperial policy.[25]

As against these advantages, what disadvantages did emigration entail? The first was "devitalization." For the state whose people emigrated, the emigration represented a loss of substance, insofar as it reduced manpower and, consequently, productive capacities. Those who left were for the most part men in the prime of life. In their youth, their families (and also the state) had shouldered the necessary expenditures for their physical or technical training;[26] then, just as they became useful to the nation's economy, they took their trained skills elsewhere. But was this disadvantage, which economists emphasize, in fact actually felt? For the most part, the emigrants were "surplus" rural workers who left precisely because they could find no opportunity to earn a living.

The second disadvantage was that it aged the population. The emigration of young men slowed demographic growth far more than the mere numbers of emigrants would indicate. The proportion of young people in the population as a whole declined, and the "age pyramid" was considerably altered. The inevitable consequence theoretically would be an early increase in the death rate, and such aging might soon affect a nation's sense of itself. But, in fact, large-scale emigration from Europe lasted hardly more than fifteen years—much too short a period for contemporaries to become aware of these changes.

The third disadvantage was that emigration reduced the available number of military effectives. Taking into account the nature of armed forces at the time, the disadvantage seemed a major one. Should reservists, some of whom, in case of general mobilization, would not want or would be unable to return, be permitted to leave the country? Even countries that placed no restraints on emigration, some that even encouraged it, took precautions in this regard. In Austria, where emigration was theoretically not subject to any administrative formalities, men of military age might not leave without prior authorization. In Hungary, where emigrants needed passports, men of military age were obliged after 1909 first to get a permit from the Ministry of National Defense. In Germany, a law of 1897 simply prohibited emigration of men between the ages of seventeen and twenty-five unless they had been released by the military authorities. In Italy, men between the ages of twenty and twenty-eight needed special authorization to emigrate, while all other reservists retained the right to emigrate at will.

But what was the practical effect of these restrictions? A comparison

---

[25] In particular in 1922, with the adoption of the Empire Settlement Act. See William Hancock, *Survey of British Commonwealth Affairs* (London, 1942), and G. Plant, *Overseas Settlement: Migration from the United Kingdom to the Dominions* (London, 1951).

[26] Evaluation of these expenses are always most uncertain.

between Austro-Hungarian statistics and American statistics on Austrian and Hungarian citizens coming to the United States, for instance, makes it clear that *clandestine* emigration of men of military age was considerable. Would such clandestine departures have been possible had there been serious administrative supervision? Actually, the matter seemed less urgent then than we now imagine it, since, in the states with most emigrants, the total annual contingent of draftees was never called to arms.

On the whole, concurring with the attitude prevalent at the time, governments were inclined to believe that emigration had more advantages than disadvantages. At an international congress on population problems held in Paris in August, 1889, which attempted, all too briefly, to study "the intervention of governmental authorities in emigration and immigration," there were no objections from the European delegates when the Argentine delegate remarked, "There is less disadvantage in allowing a useful citizen who might return to leave, than to retain one who is discouraged and might well become seditious."

After 1919, however, this passive governmental attitude to emigration vanished. Everywhere, new legislation attested to the interest of the public authorities,[27] and the spirit of these new laws was altogether different from that prevailing prior to 1914.

In the European countries that had furnished the most emigrants, governments abandoned their policies of unrestricted flow; the institution of passports, which became general, ensured the effectiveness of the new restrictions. In June, 1927, the government of fascist Italy ordered the prefects to distribute passports "sparingly"; persons desiring to emigrate had to show either a work contract assuring them of a job in the country to which they wanted to go or proof that they were leaving to join a father or brother. Czechoslovakia prohibited the emigration of men under the age of forty; Romania prohibited the emigration of men under the age of twenty-eight. In December, 1925, Poland enacted a decree that prohibited a would-be emigrant from leaving unless he obtained a special passport. Soviet Russia prohibited virtually all emigration: visas, no matter what the reason for going, would be given only as exceptions to the general rule. In Japan, emigration to China continued unrestricted but to all other destinations was subject to administrative permit. In China, by virtue of a law of 1918, emigration agencies had to obtain work contracts for the emigrants prior to their departure; they were not permitted to negotiate on behalf of married men unless the latter agreed that 20 per cent of their salaries would automatically be set aside for the use of their families.

---

[27] See *Migration Movements, 1920–1924* (Geneva: ILO, 1926), and *Migration Movements, 1925–1927* (Geneva: ILO, 1928). See also L. Varlez, "Les Migrations internationales et leurs réglementation" (The Hague: Academy of International Law, *Recueil des cours*, 1927), XX, 165–348.

It would be unwise to offer any over-all explanation for these changes in policy. Restrictive measures sometimes had no other purpose than to ensure the protection of the emigrant or his family: such was the case of the Chinese law of 1918. In Czechoslovakia, the restrictions were intended to preserve the level of army effectives in case of mobilization. But by and large, the new laws reflected a new attitude: emigration must be systematized, since otherwise it reduced the nation's vital strength (this appears to have been the reasoning in Great Britain's case, where the manifest concern was to prevent young people from leaving because those who remained were too few to ensure "demographic replacement"); the state had an obligation not to allow its citizens to leave "at random" and thereby run the risk of "losing their nationality for no purpose." It was this "loss of substance" that disturbed governments, a consideration that before 1914 had appeared unimportant to them.

Why did the attitude change? In central Europe, perhaps because the population congestion in certain agricultural regions had become less acute: during the war, the peasants had suffered the heaviest losses of any sector of the population, since they had supplied most of the infantry troops; and agrarian reforms enacted in the new states provided a partial solution to the land problem. But if this explanation is valid for Poland, Czechoslovakia, or Romania, it is not so for Italy or Russia. Soviet Russia prohibited emigration because it wished to develop the settlement of Siberia; fascist Italy restricted it because it was convinced that the strength of a people was linked to its "demographic vitality." The scale of migratory movements thus was strongly influenced by the policies of the states concerned.

Our interpretations of these pre- and post-1914 policies must necessarily remain tentative, since scholars have dealt with the demographic and economic consequences of the great emigrations only in general and not in detail, country by country. The attitude of the Austro-Hungarian government to the clandestine emigration of men of military age and that of the Tsarist government toward Jewish emigrants have been noted, but the probable explanations have never been seriously checked. The causal relation established between new economic and social factors and the restrictions introduced after 1919 in central and eastern Europe is only a hypothesis. In point of fact, a critical study of emigration policies has scarcely been begun, yet it would be the prerequisite to any valid interpretation.

2. Effects in the Countries of Settlement

Every state is free to regulate the admission of aliens to its territory; in 1919, Article 15 of the League of Nations Covenant confirmed that principle. What were the considerations likely to determine immigration policies?

In the states that received most of the migrants—by and large, the nations of the New World, where 95 per cent of the European emigrants went—the economic advantages were considerable. In agriculture, the economic awakening of the Argentine pampas proceeded *pari passu* with the arrival of new immigrants (Italians were almost exclusively responsible for the settlement of these regions); and Italian and Portuguese workers provided the manpower for the coffee plantations of southern Brazil. Similarly, a large-scale influx of immigrants from central and eastern Europe made it possible to settle and develop the central provinces of Canada.

In the United States, the direct participation of immigrants in the development of the agricultural economy was already considerable before 1895 and actually lessened between 1895 and 1914, since the newly arrived Italians and Slavs rarely went further than the eastern seaboard. But the influx of immigrants there resulted in an internal migration that took the American population of entire towns and villages westward.

The influence of the migrants on the development of industry was particularly marked in the United States, and native-born Americans were fully aware of it at the time. They emphasized the importance of immigrants in the mines; they recognized that the advances made in the processing industries would have been less rapid without the continuing stream of new labor and new consumers; they noted that the rise of certain industries (those employing less skilled workers) had been greatly assisted by special conditions in the labor market—that is, by the presence of recent immigrants who were too eager for jobs to argue over wages.

These observations, made over and over again during the first years of the twentieth century, were set out at length in reports published in 1911 by the United States Immigration Commission. To those who disputed the benefits of the migratory flow, the Federal Government replied that the constant influx of plentiful manpower was essential to the maintenance of the pace of industrial growth and, consequently, to economic prosperity.

Absorption of a mass of immigrants into a nation's economy involved expenditures on capital equipment that could be met only by new and more investments. But the nation that received immigrants readily found foreign capital, for investors anticipated that the magnitude of the immigration would encourage the economy. In any case, there is no doubt that certain governments not only were glad to admit immigrants but even organized propaganda to accelerate their arrival: such was the case of Canada, which established immigration agencies, granted facilities for sea passage, and offered free land concessions, a policy which it maintained from before 1914 and especially in the 1920's.

But if immigration benefited the *economy*, its *social* and *political* effects were not so happy. The disadvantages, like the advantages, began to be apparent in the United States just when more immigrants arrived than ever before—between 1905 and 1913.

The new immigrants, simply by their presence in the labor market, obstructed or slowed down wage increases. This was probably not so marked where skilled workers were concerned, since most of the immigrants, for the most part peasants, were unskilled. Nevertheless, the existence of an army of industrial reserves gave employers a sense of security, and they took full advantage of this.[28] By and large, the American public expressed itself on this issue—and argued it out—in terms of the extent of the injuries borne by the workers, not in terms of economic principle involved. Immigrants were also partly responsible for difficulties experienced in the American trade-union movement. The immigrants, being of peasant stock, were slow to acquire a sense of solidarity with the American working class; when they did, they were still not eager to join the American Federation of Labor, run largely by skilled workers, and tended instead toward new, more revolutionary groups. The sheer numbers of immigrants thus led to a splintering of the American working class. Observers of the Canadian and Argentine social scene noted similar developments but on a smaller scale, since industry was still young in those countries prior to 1914.

Wherever the influx of foreigners reached any considerable proportion, it could become a *political* threat to national unity and could, therefore, in some cases, weaken the state in its foreign relations. This problem actually arose almost everywhere, but under widely differing circumstances.

The problem arose in the United States in 1895, when the wave of immigrants consisted mainly of Italians or Slavs, often rougher and less educated than the earlier Germans and Scandinavians; these newcomers found it harder to learn English and, especially, to adapt themselves to America's liberal and democratic institutions. Americans who had easily assimilated European immigrants thus far, now realized that the American melting-pot was not working as well as it had. They were somewhat astonished to discover that certain groups of immigrants were trying, not to adapt themselves to their new environment, but instead to preserve their own language and customs and, as far as possible, to lead a life apart from the American people—and, moreover, that these groups sometimes displayed a "morbid" kind of nationalism.[29] These anxieties were expressed three years before the outbreak of World War I in the report of the Immigration Commission, which vainly recommended restrictive measures.

The experiences of the years 1915–20 confirmed the threat to national

---

[28] Average wages in the United States rose consistently from 1899 to 1905 but fell slightly between 1906 and 1914. Isaac, *op. cit.*, p. 205.

[29] These observations may have been deliberately exaggerated by proponents of restricted immigration.

solidarity: the partial success of German propaganda among German Americans in 1916; the protests of Italian immigrant organizations against the application of Wilson's principles of self-determination to the problems of the Adriatic at the time of the Versailles Peace Conference; anti-British demonstrations by Irish immigrants in 1920, just when the United States needed British cooperation against Japan in the Pacific; not to mention the unprecedented number of foreign-language periodicals published during the war—1,350 in thirty-six languages, among them ninety-five daily papers. Actually, none of these developments deflected the government's policy, but their repercussions did cause serious concern; it is not yet possible to determine whether the government was really alarmed.

Between 1902 and 1912, Canada received some 2.5 million immigrants, two-thirds of whom settled in the country for good, the rest soon crossing the frontier into the United States. In composition, this flood of immigrants was very different from earlier influxes: 28 per cent of the total were "non-British." And, since the newcomers settled for the most part in the west, Canada's three western prairie provinces now had a cosmopolitan population. In the 1911 Canadian census, the English (including Scots) numbered barely 3 million, the French a little over 2 million, and "other" Europeans (Germans, Scandinavians, and Slavs), 1.25 million.

The assimilation of these recent immigrants was of prime importance for Canada's political future. Would they become "Anglicized"? Would they become Canadian patriots?[30] Or would they look to the United States, whose economic magnetism had already attracted more than 700,000 of them? Was it possible, in fact, to achieve a sense of Canadian nationality at all? American immigration laws enacted in 1921 and 1924 tended to intensify these issues, for they prevented the new immigrants from crossing into the United States, but the prohibition did not apply to Canadian citizens, and there was reason to fear that Canadians would emigrate to the United States and be replaced by a new influx of Slavs or Scandinavians. This actually happened between 1920 and 1930, when 1.23 million Europeans entered Canada, and nearly 1 million Canadians crossed the border to the United States.

Why was Argentina not equally apprehensive, where in 1914 the proportion of recent immigrants to the total population reached 30 per cent in the country as a whole (twice as high as in the United States) and 75 per cent in Buenos Aires? The answer is given that the Italians, who constituted nearly one-half of the immigrant population and, by 1900, one-quarter of the country's total population, tended not to stay; they were potential re-emigrants to the United States, where opportunities for acquiring land and property were often greater than in Argentina. But does this explanation, plausible as it is, stand up to critical scrutiny?

---

[30] See below, Chapter Six, pp. 157–58.

The role of Chinese emigrants in the Dutch and British colonies of Southeast Asia and in Siam was in some respects analogous to that of European emigrants in the Americas. The Chinese emigrants, forming distinct communities in the countries where they settled, and raising and educating their children in the Chinese way, did not attempt before the early twentieth century to take any part in local political life. But the Revolution of 1911 and still more the Movement of May 4, 1919,[31] aroused their national sentiment, which was strengthened in 1928 by the victory of the Kuomintang in the Chinese civil war.

During the following years,[32] the Siamese government became concerned at the role that Chinese immigrants played in the country's economy (550,000 Chinese in a total population of 10 million); the government of the Netherlands East Indies decided to increase the tax levied on immigrants in order to check the influx of Chinese; and the British administrators in Malaya did not conceal their fears concerning the presence of 1.7 million Chinese (more than 30 per cent of the population)—legitimate fears, since, as a recent historian of the Malayan national movement has pointed out, the part played in this movement by the Chinese bourgeoisie was significant.[33]

Must we assume that fears aroused by the difficulties of assimilating immigrants were the direct cause of the restrictive measures taken after 1919 in the nations of the New World? This was the argument invoked in the United States when the 1921 and 1924 laws were enacted. But many other probably more powerful motives were operating in the same direction. The competition of immigrant workers increasingly threatened American labor, and this at a time when the United States was passing through an economic crisis; politicians feared that immigrants from central and eastern Europe might import Soviet ideas; industrialists had less use for unskilled workers than ever before since they had mechanized their factories out of the profits they had made during World War I. Economic and social considerations, therefore, were more urgent than any political desire to safeguard national unity against what were still uncertain dangers.

Economic interests also inspired Canada's immigration policy: first the policy of unrestricted European immigration followed before and after World War I despite the political drawbacks; then the policy of restrictive immigration in 1930 and the quota system established in 1934 during the depression. And economic considerations prevailed in Brazil and Argentina; restrictions were placed on immigration when, in consequence of the depression and the resulting unemployment, it was imperative to stop the flow of

---

[31] See below, Chapter Six, p. 161.

[32] See Hans Mosolff, *Die Chinesische Auswanderung* (Rostock, 1932), p. 221, and Ta Chên, *Emigrant Communities in South China* (New York, 1940).

[33] Lennox Mills, *Malaya: A Political and Economic Appraisal* (London and Minneapolis, 1958).

more European workers. (In Argentina, immigration had reached an annual 140,000 by 1929, but it was down to 30,000 in 1933, and 33,000 in 1934.)

How did all these problems affect the balance sheet of international relations? As long as they were unimpeded, the great migrations were not merely a great demographic event; they also increased the economic productivity of the Western Hemisphere at the expense of some of the European nations and thus, for the immediate future, profoundly modified the relative international importance of the European and American continents. They did not, however, create difficulties in inter-state relations and did not endanger the peace. Their influence was even beneficial in this respect, for in some areas, the migrations reduced population pressures, relieved poverty, and eliminated factors of social instability that might have touched off domestic political crises, crises that in turn might well have erupted into the international sphere by aggravating tensions or by providing imperialist designs for action with useful pretexts.

B. MIGRATIONS AND INTERNATIONAL DISPUTES

In other circumstances, however, the problems caused by these waves of migration led to conflicts, or at least to threats of conflict between states. Restrictions imposed on international migration, especially after 1919, were often the root of the trouble, but in certain cases free emigration and immigration also led to situations that endangered the peace. In such disputes, were the demographic phenomena the cause, or simply the pretext, for disagreement?

1. Unrestricted Immigration

Between 1890 and 1939, unrestricted international immigration led to diplomatic controversy or armed conflict in the Transvaal, Tunisia, Manchuria, and Palestine.

In Transvaal, where the discovery of gold in the Witwatersrand, near Johannesburg, in 1886 had attracted many Europeans, mostly Englishmen, to South Africa, the new immigrants—the *uitlanders,* or foreigners— constituted two-thirds of the adult male white population by 1895. Industry and commerce had until then existed more or less along traditional lines and social structures had been stable; now, the opening of the gold mines attracted new capital. The *uitlanders,* in addition to becoming predominant in the country's economy, wanted political rights to protect their material interests and to enable them to revamp the institutions and economic policy of the state. The Afrikaners (or Boers), who had been in Transvaal for centuries, were thus in danger of being submerged by another civilization if they enfranchised the new immigrants. The passive resistance of their government prompted the *uitlanders* to request the British Government to intervene in March, 1899.

The demographic situation thus undoubtedly contributed to the Boer crisis. But without Great Britain's political intervention, would it have led to war? In point of fact, the *uitlanders* were far from unanimous in their views on how to proceed. In late 1895, they had by and large been bystanders when Cecil Rhodes tried to settle the Transvaal question by means of the Jameson Raid, an abortive invasion of Transvaal by a private English force; in 1899, many of them (according to the British agent in Pretoria) were opposed to a conflict that might jeopardize the capital they had invested in the mines. But the British Cabinet decided to intervene, since failure to do so would have appeared as a weakness that could adversely affect Great Britain's "international position." In August, 1899, the Transvaal government finally accepted virtually all the English demands regarding the franchise, yet the Cabinet nevertheless declared, on September 8, that it was unable to accept Transvaal's claim to be an "independent and sovereign State." Protection of the *uitlanders* was thus a pretext for carrying out an imperial design inspired by political, economic, and financial interests.

When the French established a protectorate there in 1881, Tunisia had an Italian colony of 11,200 persons. (By 1895, the number of Italians had risen to 55,000, whereas the number of Frenchmen scarcely exceeded 16,000.) Since 1868, this colony had enjoyed a special status sanctified by law in an Italo-Tunisian treaty for a period of thirty years. In 1886, the Italians founded their own newspaper, *Unione,* and in 1889, they began to organize, at the prompting of the Italian Consul General. But their political aspirations found no support in Rome, where both the government and the public (according to *Unione*) displayed complete indifference to their plight. When the Italo-Tunisian treaty was about to expire, the French Government agreed to negotiate a new one on the status of the Italians, and in doing so tried to excise the old commercial clauses of the 1868 treaty and establish new regulations that would favor French trade. But the new convention retained almost in its entirety the privileges which the Italians enjoyed as regards their civil rights, their organizations, and their schools. Under this system, the Italian colony continued to grow and in 1904 numbered 83,000; in 1911, 88,000—twice as many as the French. The French-language press in Tunisia had already begun to show concern about this Italian influx when, in 1903, *Unione* demanded that Italians be represented on the Consultative Conference and in the municipal councils of Tunisia's cities.

The French and Italian governments took care to avoid intervening in this matter since they preferred to keep it local. The question of the Italians in Tunisia therefore did not become an international issue until after 1919. At that point, the French Government threatened to end the system they had perpetuated in 1896 by automatically naturalizing the Italians; otherwise, they realized, the numerical preponderance of the Italians would prevent French sovereignty being established in Tunisia "on a firm basis." But Mussolini's government not only insisted on the maintenance of the 1896 convention, but also embarked on a policy of "strengthening Italianness" in Tunisia, insinuating that it need not have done so had Italy received a colonial territory "proportionate to her needs" at the Versailles Peace Conference. In the bitter controversies that developed between France and Italy in the 1920's and early 1930's, the "colony without a flag" became an instrument of fascist policy; it had not been a cause of that policy.

Manchuria was in theory a territory of the Chinese Republic, but between 1922 and 1928, it in fact eluded the authority of the Peking government. Then, a great migratory wave from northern China inundated Manchuria (.4 million arrivals in 1923 and .5 million in 1925; 1.2 million in 1927 and 1.05 million in 1929). There might be grounds, therefore, for arguing that this immigration was responsible for the Sino-Japanese conflict of 1931. Since 1905, the Japanese had enjoyed a preponderant economic and political influence in southern Manchuria; they had reason to fear that they would now be turned out by the Chinese immigrants. In 1928, as soon as the Nationalist government of Chiang Kai-shek took over in Peking, this fear increased, for Kuomintang agents in Mukden were conducting a propaganda campaign against Japanese imperialism and the privileges accorded the Japanese. Japanese newspapers in Manchuria declared that to remove this threat, Baron Shidehara's cabinet should move to eliminate the Chinese administration in Manchuria. The Mukden Incident of September 18, 1931— when a mysterious explosion damaged the Japanese-owned South Manchuria Railway lines, and Japanese troops, without authorization from Tokyo, moved against the Chinese, whom they blamed for the damage, and occupied Mukden—afforded the opportunity.

But is this demographic interpretation of the Manchurian crisis confirmed by documented facts? Neither Japanese nor Chinese propagandists made any reference to this immigration when they set out the causes of the Japanese intervention; the League of Nations commission of inquiry, which noted the dimensions of the influx, established no direct causal relation between it and the origins of the conflict, confining itself to the remark that immigration had increased the economic interdependence of China and Manchuria and that this might have encouraged the Chinese Nationalists in Mukden to take a stand against foreign economic interests. Basically, only political interests were involved.

In these three cases, then, the migratory movement was the underlying cause of conflict, but in each case, the conflict of interests between immigrants and other sectors of the population became critical only when the governments concerned took action. The immigration created a favorable terrain for conflict, but politics gave the decisive impetus.

Palestine is the only one of the four countries discussed here where the immigration question was indubitably at the origin of the armed conflict. To that pastoral and extensively cultivated land, Jews had begun to come even before 1914; their arrival had raised no difficulties at first because they were so few. (In 1919, there were 65,000 Jews out of an estimated 700,000 inhabitants.) But the Zionists' decision in 1919 to advocate a Jewish National Home in Palestine and therefore to encourage further emigration there aroused Arab protests. The Arabs feared that the immigrants would occupy the cultivable lands and threaten their very way of life.

Lord Balfour, the British Foreign Secretary, who advocated the establishment of a Jewish National Home in Palestine under the British Mandate, recognized that this proposal had aroused the hostility of "the majority of the population" of Palestine; but he attributed this hostility to political or religious factors and relied on economic transformations to alter the Arabs' attitude, once they realized "the full advantages from the influx of Jewish money and the Jewish methods of developing the country."[34] He overlooked, however, that Jewish colonizers would take land away from the Arabs: at the end of 1936, after fourteen years of the British Mandate, there were 404,000 Jews in Palestine, 30 per cent of the population; some of these (about one-fourth) lived in 200 village settlements, having received land concessions from the government but also having purchased land from the Arabs (some 235,000 acres); they held, according to the Arabs, 20–25 per cent of the arable land in Palestine.

The connection is definite, then, between the influx of immigrants and the political disturbances which took place in 1920, 1921, 1929, 1933, and 1936. The British Government realized this when it decided to restrict immigration to Palestine in 1939, and in 1940 to prohibit the purchase of land from Arabs except on the coastal plain. But in 1945 the Arabs demanded a blanket prohibition. It is true that war did not break out until the Arab League came into existence and encouraged the Palestinian Arabs to protest. But the connection between the demographic situation and the war is in this case clear.

2. Restricted Immigration

Restrictions on international migration have given rise to many more disputes and threats of conflict than the free flow of people from one country to another. Disputes have occurred between European nations and the United States and also, on one occasion, between two European states. Threats of conflict have also arisen among Asian and Pacific states.

The "closing" of the United States following the immigration law of

---

[34] Great Britain, Foreign Office, *Documents on British Foreign Policy, 1919–1939,* First Series, Vol. IV, 1919, No. 218, note.

1921 was a serious blow to the interests of several European countries that, in 1920, had again allowed large numbers of emigrants to leave their shores. Grievances were vented immediately at the deliberations of the International Emigration Commission in 1921, but in vain, since the United States refused to participate in the Commission's work. The enactment of the 1924 law, which only accentuated the "closing," showed how indifferent the United States Congress remained to these complaints.

France, too, albeit on a very modest scale, came to adopt a policy of restricted immigration. Having opened its doors to Polish and Italian workers during the postwar reconstruction, and having encouraged the settlement of Italian peasants in southwestern France, it began to take restrictive action in February, 1927, when the first signs of an unemployment crisis appeared. Albert Thomas, Director General of the International Labour Office, noted that these measures were likely to provoke Franco-Italian tensions, but in fact, Italian complaints were muted. (The question of immigration at that time was a secondary one in the dossier of disputes between France and fascist Italy.) In 1930, the French policy of "braking" immigration became even stricter, but Italy herself in the same year adopted a similar policy and could hardly complain about the French.

The significance of the whole problem was emphasized clearly when the International Conference on Emigration and Immigration met in Rome in 1927. Mussolini, who had not yet announced or embarked on his restrictive emigration policy, remarked there that the exchange of "work forces" between nations was an economic and social necessity, and that emigration fostered "spiritual ties between peoples"; he emphasized the influence that migrations could exercise in international political relations, although he was careful not to define what kind of influence. And the resolutions of the Conference noted that "fluid and considerable migratory movements are necessary to the good organization of human society and to the appropriate settlement of the earth." In September of the same year, at the World Population Conference in Geneva, Director General Thomas recalled the dangers inherent in the migration problem: when the question was treated from a purely national point of view, he said, it involved the possibility of conflict or even war. To mitigate the international tension caused by restrictions placed on the free movement of migrants, a supranational authority was necessary to regulate the distribution of population, determine where emigration was needed, and evaluate the capacity to absorb newcomers in the countries of settlement; decide in what case an overpopulated state was entitled to send its citizens elsewhere; and direct such displacements.

The demographers also sought to define the terms of the problem.[35] If a state had "empty lands," was it entitled to close them to foreigners? And,

---

[35] See William Oualid, "Les éléments d'une solution internationale du problème des migrations humaines," a report to the International Studies Conference, 1937.

if it received immigrants, was it entitled to impose measures of assimilation on them? Was an "overpopulated" state entitled to demand lands for re-settlement of its people?

But these declarations and questions were not followed by actual diplomatic action. What, in fact, could the European nations do to induce the United States Congress to revise its immigration policy? "We cannot wait for miracles," an Italian newspaper commented. The international conferences on migration problems confined themselves to suggestions on how to improve the well-being of emigrants (supervision of emigration agencies and of the health and safety of transports); to hopes that the countries of settlement would provide equal treatment for all Europeans and would not adopt a policy of forced assimilation; and to recommendations for bilateral agreements on the protection of migrants. They were purely humanitarian and social resolutions. In the end, the terrible economic disaster that struck in 1929 deprived the whole issue of any practical interest: the United States ceased to be an irresistible magnet.

International "bad feelings" are exacerbated when racial considerations enter into the conflicts caused by migrations.

The determination to forbid Chinese immigration to the United States, for instance, provides an example. This determination was made even though the United States Government had signed an understanding with the imperial Chinese Government in 1868, expressly negotiated on a basis of equality, in which the principle of free reciprocal immigration was affirmed. But the overly rapid influx of Chinese immigrants on the American Pacific coast (100,000 between 1871 and 1878) alarmed the Californians, for the Chinese workers were satisfied with very low pay and thus were a competitive threat to American labor. In 1882, Congress passed the Chinese Exclusion Act, barring Chinese laborers from coming to the United States for a period of ten years; later, it prohibited such immigration outright, a measure clearly contrary to the understanding of 1868. Japanese immigration also became an issue: as soon as the number of Japanese immigrants increased sharply (it reached 12,000 during 1900), Californians demanded that the prohibition should apply to them too.

Was the motive for this exclusion an economic and social one? The campaign against the Chinese had been led by the labor unions, but the racial motive was equally apparent: in 1906, the city fathers of San Francisco announced their intention to establish segregated schools so that American children might be spared contact with students of the "Mongolian race." President Theodore Roosevelt thought the Californians' attitude on this issue was wrong, but he felt that they would have to be given partial satisfaction. Congress therefore inserted a clause in the Immigration Act of 1907 authorizing the President to exclude Japanese, and Roosevelt persuaded the Japanese Government not to issue any more passports to unskilled workers.

The Japanese population in the United States nevertheless continued to increase, due to the high birth rate. In 1922, therefore, difficulties reappeared. The state of California, by laws which the Supreme Court upheld as constitutional, forbade Japanese to purchase or have long-term rentals of land and denied them the right to naturalization. And in 1924, the new immigration law prohibited Japanese immigration entirely and even deprived the Japanese already settled on American soil of the right to be joined by their wives, children, or parents.

Canada immediately followed the United States' example: Chinese immigration was prohibited and Japanese immigration restricted, after 1908, to an annual quota of 150 persons. New Zealand had already adopted a similar policy. Beginning in 1871, she had freely admitted Chinese immigrants, who formed a part of the labor force needed in the gold mines, but after 1881, she tried to restrict these arrivals by imposing a special tax on vessels transporting Chinese. In 1888, she established a quota system but was unable to apply it, since the British Government requested Queen Victoria to withhold her consent from legislation expressly based on racial grounds. But New Zealanders circumvented the difficulty: in 1900, they began to apply an "education test" to all immigrants, the requirement being that candidates should be able to write fifty words in a European language. This virtually excluded persons of the yellow race. Australia, determined to keep her population white, adopted the same method by a law of 1901—the very year that Australia became a federal commonwealth.

Thus, the Chinese and Japanese were excluded from almost all territories bordering on the Pacific where they might have sought opportunities for work. South America and the Philippines, however, remained "open," and it was to those territories that the Japanese Government, in 1933, decided to direct its emigrants (between 100,000 and 150,000 annually). But Brazil, which had admitted more than 25,000 Japanese a year between 1924 and 1934, began in 1934 to apply a strict quota system. In 1936, therefore, the number of Japanese living outside the Japanese empire and Manchukuo was barely 700,000.

These policies of exclusion were clearly a source of conflict in international relations. The United States Government had been able to ignore the protests of the Chinese Government against the Chinese exclusion laws because China had been powerless. But the situation vis-à-vis Japan was not quite the same after her victory in Manchuria, still less after World War I. The protest delivered by the Japanese Ambassador in Washington on April 10, 1924, emphasized the "psychological" aspect of the matter and deliberately ignored the question of material interests: "The important thing is to determine whether Japan, as a nation, has or has not a right to the respect and consideration of other nations." And was not respect a prerequisite for friendly relations? To apply discriminatory measures against Japanese immigrants, the Japanese asserted, was seriously to affront Japan's national sensibilities.³⁶ And this bitter indignation was evident in the Japanese press as well. The American law, said Japanese commentators, reduced Japan to a position inferior to that of any European state. And the Japanese public was sure that these measures of exclusion expressed the Americans' feeling of racial superiority; Japan, they felt, had suffered an affront to her national honor.

These protests were central to a number of debates held in the summers of 1925 and 1927 at the Institute of Pacific Relations. The Japanese people, argued the Japanese delegates to the meetings, felt that they had been humiliated by being treated as inferior. Nations that closed their borders to Orientals had not exceeded their rights, but they were making wrong use of those rights—an abusive application of sovereignty which disturbed peace and international understanding. The American response did not touch on this aspect of the matter but dealt with the Japanese demand only from an economic and social point of view. Japan, ran the American argument, wanted an "export market" because of her surplus population. But why did she not try to restrain that surplus? If she did not, preferring to continue in her "demographic improvidence," could she reasonably expect other states to alter their immigration policies? The Institute thereupon "adjourned" consideration of the Japanese demands.

In Tokyo, however, ardent nationalists used this postponement as a pretext to declare that, since Japan could not rely on the good will of "underpopulated" states, she would have to endeavor to acquire territories for her people by force of arms. This assertion became a major propaganda theme when in 1931 the Tokyo government launched its policy of armed expansion in Manchuria and then in China. Were immigration restrictions at the root of this policy? Actually, there is reason to doubt it, since the expansionist doctrine had been formulated as far back as 1919, five years before the enactment of the American immigration law. But they served as an argument for those who had decided on this policy, either for economic reasons or for national prestige, and they contributed to achieving wide support for expansion among the Japanese people.

In the aftermath of World War II, the migration problem appeared in a new light. In Europe, there was urgent concern to make intercontinental migration possible as a means of assisting persons fleeing Eastern Europe who were then in Western Europe without means of support. The Intergovernmental Commission on European Migration, set up in December, 1951, was responsible for directing and assisting the migration of these "displaced

³⁶ Japan, as Duroselle remarks, would not, therefore, have protested against a quota system as applied to European immigrants, although this would have limited Japanese immigrants to the U.S. to 246 a year. See *From Wilson to Roosevelt: Foreign Policy of the United States, 1913–45* (Cambridge, Mass., 1963), p. 161.

persons."[37] Within its limited terms of reference, it did an effective job, theoretically a temporary one. But more was needed. In Asia and Australia, the prewar problems of unequal settlement took on new dimensions: the demands that Japan had been the first to voice were now echoed by many of the underdeveloped countries.

Economists and demographers have often returned to the line of thought indicated in 1927 by Albert Thomas: the need for a great international effort; the study of the capacity of absorption in "underpopulated" countries; the study of "rational estimates"; the preparation of planned migrations that might lead to a redistribution of the entire world population.[38] In 1937, Adolphe Landry had remarked that overpopulation was more dangerous than ever before because demographic imbalances were more marked, and because these imbalances led to greater disparities in living standards, even among peoples at a similar level of technical development. Landry was thinking only of Europe, but the problem now arises on a world scale.

III. CONCLUSION

Is it possible to establish any direct and constant relation between demographic conditions and international relations? The preceding observations would indicate not. The size of a population was an essential factor a century ago in establishing the respective military positions of various states; it has lost most of its importance as a result of the transformation in armaments. Migrations, at the time of their greatest magnitude, were not the cause of international difficulties so long as they were able to occur without restriction; they occasioned concern and sometimes conflict after 1919, when states restricted that freedom. The very ideas of "overpopulation" and "population pressure" were variously understood at different times, depending upon the national frame of mind in the country concerned.

At no time, therefore, can demographic factors be studied in isolation from their economic, political, and psychological contexts.

---

[37] See Jacques Vernant, *The Refugee in the Post-War World* (London, 1953).

[38] See, for instance, Maximilien Sorre, *Les migrations des peuples* (Paris, 1955), and D. R. Taft, *International Migrations: The Migrant in the Modern World* (New York, 1955).

3

ECONOMIC RIVALRY
AND CONFLICT

"The world's economy," François Perroux observed, "did not develop as a result of competition among equal partners, but through the emergence and influence of great national economies that successively became dominant." From this observation, Perroux moved on to establish a theory on the effect of "domination" in international economic relations, and to inquire into the possible effects of a "dominant economy" on the economic balance.[1]

The nation with superior resources or technology can increase or reduce the economic activities of another state by expanding or contracting the volume of its purchases; it can sometimes, by manipulating prices, alter the normal conditions of trade. Great Britain enjoyed such dominance during the second half of the nineteenth century; the United States began to assume it after 1919 and has certainly done so since World War II.

At the same time, all industrialized states enjoy considerable superiority over "developing" countries—those which in the nineteenth century were called "new" countries. Their economic penetration of these lands led to the discovery and exploitation of areas rich in mineral resources, to the improvement of agricultural methods and the introduction of new crops, and to the establishment of new processing industries. But it also led to far-reaching social changes: the end of native artisanry in areas where craftsmen lost out to the competition of machine-made goods; the emergence of a middle class whose interests were allied with those of the foreigners; and even, when the land was colonized, increased poverty, to the extent that some of the local resources were set aside for the colonizing power.

We must begin, then, with the forms of economic conflict between states: changes in trade policies; competition for export markets, raw materials, or principal maritime routes; tariff wars; and policies of embargo or boycott intended to paralyze trade relations. But the historian of international relations is less concerned to study economic mechanisms than to determine the relation between economic rivalries and conflicts of political interests. This relation may vary considerably in scope and significance.

---

[1] See François Perroux, "Esquisse d'une théorie de l'économie dominante," *Economie appliquée*, I (1948), 243–300; and "Note sur le dynamisme de la domination," *ibid.*, III (1950), 245–58.

I. CONFLICTING ECONOMIC POLICIES

Commercial competition is conducted by individuals or firms seeking to increase their sales while maintaining prices. But states, by their customs and monetary policies, determine the framework within which this international trade is conducted. The state's duty is to look beyond individual interests, motivated by the desire for immediate and personal gain, to the general interests of the nation.

Under a system of completely free trade, producers around the world would presumably be led to establish a rational division of labor among themselves. This arrangement would in theory ensure maximum returns, since the producers in each country would concentrate on those kinds of production where they were most likely to achieve the best results, leaving it to imports to satisfy other needs. The general national interest, however, favors the development within each state of *all* necessary production forces, in order to ensure a higher standard of living and greater economic independence for the people. The theory of comparative advantage, or of comparative cost, which is at the basis of free trade, would force each country to restrict itself to the types of production best suited to its natural resources, i.e., in which it has a comparative advantage, and to forego improving the organization of its economy. So the state tends to take steps that result in limiting free trade—that is, it tends to establish a system of protection.[2]

Is a danger of international conflict inherent in this tendency?

Theorists of free trade—notably Richard Cobden and Michel Chevalier—maintained that the free international movement of goods is a pledge of peace; it permits each nation, they said, to have access to the economic advantages with which the others were endowed; it thus lessens the occasions for envy and any accompanying belligerency; it could encourage solidarity among peoples in the economic sphere, and this should foster political cooperation. (A similiar theory of international trade as the generator of peace was advanced in the United States in the 1930's by Secretary of State Cordell Hull.) In point of fact, however, during the periods when free trade developed, it diminished neither the keenness of competition for new markets, nor the anxiety and frustration occasioned among peoples subject to "economic conquest" by the penetration of foreign influences.

A protectionist system, on the other hand, while it engages public authorities in matters of competitive international trade, reduces the dangers of instability in the national economy and prevents, therefore, the social disturbances that might become dangerous to the nation's domestic security. And these internal political disturbances, the possibility of which is now

---

[2] See Perroux, "Esquisse d'une théorie de l'économie dominante," p. 263.

lessened, might otherwise be a cause, or at least a pretext, for international conflicts.

For three-quarters of a century, in fact, protection held sway in continental Europe and the United States, notwithstanding the example given by Great Britain in 1846, when the Corn Laws were repealed and the Customs Law abolished many duties—a victory for free-trade advocates. For a while, there was apparently a tendency to liberalize trade; this was expressed in an Anglo-French commercial treaty of 1860 (the Cobden-Chevalier treaty). Then the German tariff law of 1879 began the trend back to protection, and Great Britain alone resisted. The causes of this triumph for protection are well known: the desire of western and central European farmers to be protected against Russian and American competition; the wish of the new industries of western Europe and the United States to defend themselves against British superiority. And this protectionism was not confined to the mother countries of Europe but extended to colonial territories as well.

In the eighteenth, and even at the beginning of the nineteenth, centuries, all the European powers followed a policy vis-à-vis their colonies that was based on a treaty forbidding the latter to establish processing industries and reserving to the mother country the monopoly over trade and shipping. The system eventually had to be abandoned because it was largely responsible for the revolt of the British, Spanish, and Portuguese colonies in the New World. But at the end of the nineteenth century, most of the colonial powers proposed to establish privileged markets in their respective colonies for products of their own industries;[3] this arrangement suited their interests and was perfectly legitimate, since they were acting within the sphere of their own sovereignty; moreover, they argued, the profits thus accrued would offset the administrative or military expenditures they had made in establishing the colonies in the first place.

In France, by a tariff law of January 11, 1892 (which by and large guided French international commerce until 1939, although the more severe measures were modified in points of detail in 1906, 1913, and 1928), Indochina, the colonies in the Western Hemisphere and Indian Ocean, French Equatorial Africa, and New Caledonia were given equal tariff treatment—that is, foreign imports were dutiable to the same degree as in France herself, while exports from the colonies, with a few exceptions, entered France duty-free. (French colonies in India, west Africa, and the central Pacific, and the territory of Obock [French Somaliland], either because of their geographical isolation or by virtue of international agreements, were excluded from this arrangement, but they shared in less than one-quarter of French colonial trade.[4]) The system was intended to substitute French

---

[3] The Netherlands' preference system in the Dutch East Indies was abandoned in 1872 under British pressure.

[4] See A. Girault, *Principes de Colonisation et de législation coloniale* (Paris, 1933), II, 379.

goods for American ones in the Caribbean market, for Japanese ones in Indochina, and for Australian ones in New Caledonia.

In Germany, a tariff law of 1902, which confirmed and strengthened the protectionist system established in 1879, did not provide for equal duties in Germany and her colonial territories. In general, unless the Bundesrat (the German Senate) decided otherwise, goods sold to Germany by her colonies were subject to German duties upon entry, but German tariffs on foreign imports were also levied in the colonies.

The United States applied a mixed system. U.S. tariffs were applied in Puerto Rico (1902), the Hawaiian islands (1900), and Alaska. After 1909, the Philippines and Guam had their own tariffs: duties on foreign goods were lower than in the United States, but American goods were duty-free. On the other hand, the Canal Zone, which in 1904 had been given customs equality with the U.S., was subsequently placed under the tariff control of the Republic of Panama out of consideration for the interests of Panamanian traders; goods originating in the United States were therefore dutiable unless they were intended for the use of employees of the Canal administration.

The economic consequences of the varied regulations were obvious: the United States controlled 98 per cent of the Alaskan market although the territory was in Canada's geographical sphere; in 1913, she supplied 50 per cent of the Philippines' import trade, whereas prior to the establishment of the preferential tariff she had supplied only 17 per cent.

These various methods, which were intended to establish special markets for the colonial powers, tended to aggravate the tensions between rival imperial systems. The right of each power to establish the tariffs was not in question, but disputes did arise when previously independent areas became colonies or protectorates and were withdrawn from the free-trade zones. Great Britain protested in vain when France established its customs system in Madagascar, although the Great Powers, at the Conference of Algeciras in 1906, forced France, as the predominant power in Morocco, to maintain "economic liberty without inequality" there. These disputes were irritating, but not really serious.

The only major industrial state that refused to use tariffs as an instrument of policy in its colonies was Great Britain.[5] In the colonies as at home, she applied the free-trade system, for her textile industry then feared no foreign competition and her merchant marine enjoyed absolute superiority. In January, 1906, the British electorate firmly rejected the views of Joseph Chamberlain, who had proposed the establishment of a system of imperial preference.

Apart from Great Britain and her Crown Colonies, then, most states considered protectionism a necessity at the turn of the century. The system was modified, however, by bilateral trade treaties establishing reciprocal

---

[5] The Dominions had autonomous customs systems.

tariff reductions between the parties. These treaties, with fairly long terms—usually ten or twelve years—ensured a relative stability in international trade, which enabled exporters to establish estimates and plan for the future; also, the treaties nearly always included a most-favored-nation clause, which provides that one or both of the signatories will enjoy whatever advantages that are or will be accorded any other state—in other words, which tends to promote uniform conditions of competition.

When these trade treaties were negotiated, the divergence of interests between manufacturers and retailers or distributors in each country often created serious difficulties, but all things considered, this contractual trade policy developed remarkably. The close of the nineteenth century and the beginning of the twentieth was the golden age of trade treaties and of the triumph of economic liberalism. And the volume of international trade increased even more rapidly than that of production.

After World War I, protectionism became more and more intense: tariff duties were increased and specialized, quotas were set on imported goods. It was the producers who encouraged this trend to economic nationalism. European governments sought to give their countries' industries the means to hold their own against foreign competition; the European and non-European states that had remained neutral in World War I and had during that time developed new industries wished to preserve the advantages they had acquired. But political interests also had their part: since the treaties signed in 1919 and 1920 did not appear to have established a durable peace in Europe, one had to develop, in order to increase preparedness for war, industries that would ensure adequate arsenals and the ability to pursue an independent defense policy, and one had to produce essential raw materials and foodstuffs. The resolutions of the World Economic Conference at London in 1927, which recommended that states lower the inordinately high tariffs that impeded international trade, remained a dead letter.

On the other hand, trade did not suffer much from the protectionist practices the Conference had censured; in 1929, the volume of international trade was nearly 30 per cent higher than in 1913. But the world-wide depression of 1929–33 sharply reduced the volume of international trade, and various national economic policies increased this paralysis. All the empirical remedies each government used in isolation to restore the trade balances and prevent a gold outflow—stringent quotas on imports, subsidies for certain exports and prohibition of others, exchange control, monetary devaluation—hindered the restoration of trade relations. Indeed, these neomercantilist practices, as the World Economic Conference of 1933 observed, aggravated the economic disorder. States hesitated to enter into long-term commitments that might prevent the requisite adaptation of their industries to their general economic needs. They preferred trade conventions, strictly limited in purpose and duration, to trade treaties. Even Great Britain had abandoned its free-trade policy and, by the agreements reached at the Ottawa Imperial Economic Conference in 1932, established a system of limited imperial preferences; as Chancellor of the Exchequer, Neville Chamberlain carried out the program advocated thirty years earlier by his father.

The result was apparent in international-trade statistics. Despite the rapid increase in world population (155 million between 1929 and 1937) and the resumption of industrial production after the depression years (higher in 1938 than in 1929), the volume of international trade in 1938 was about 17 per cent below the level it had reached ten years before.

In three European states—Russia after 1922, Italy after 1935, Germany after the adoption of the second Four-Year Plan in 1936—protectionist policy took an extreme form, which we may call autarky.

The policy of autarky is intended to ensure that national resources are, as far as possible, sufficient to satisfy the needs of the population and, thus, to give the state complete economic independence vis-à-vis other states; it is also intended to increase the state's economic power by maximum development of national productivity. To carry this out, there must be permanent and direct state intervention in the economic life of the country, combined, perhaps, with a nationalization of foreign trade.

The motive force of this autarky is usually the determination to give the state greater freedom of action in its international relations. This intention may be merely a defensive reaction in the face of the threatened or actual economic domination of another state, or against the dangers involved in maintaining a stable balance-of-trade equilibrium. It might be linked with a plan for social change: such was the case of Soviet Russia, which "withdrew" from the capitalist world and decided to fulfill her industrial requirements herself. But it is especially bound up with political considerations: the state concerned wishes to be in a position to hold out in case of war or blockade and to face armed conflict under advantageous conditions. The "preponderance of politics over economics" explains the attraction of autarky.

If an autarkic system were really possible, each state would be able to fall back on itself and give up all foreign trade. Rival efforts to gain markets or raw materials, and tariff wars, would be things of the past. Autarky would then be a warranty of peace. But, in the contemporary world, such an attitude is unrealistic. No national territory can assure its people sufficient foodstuffs and raw materials; no state can do without foreign trade. The autarky actually put into practice is thus always partial, and, far from holding out the promise of peace, it increases the danger of conflict.

In endeavoring to achieve autarky, the state subjects its people to privation, for it must increase tax burdens to cover the expenditures involved in the manufacture of substitute goods for imports. It thus lowers the standard of living for a period of "penance" (which it presents as temporary). Such sacrifices would soon become intolerable if the people did not accept them as necessary for the sake of the nation's higher interests, so, to achieve such acceptance, the government is obliged to keep the people in a ferment of excitement, which is dangerous to peace. But during this period of penance, the population of the autarkic state will observe the increasingly obvious inferiority of their standard of living as compared with other states, and this "Spartan" nation will begin to harbor sentiments of envy and bitterness toward wealthier nations. Lastly, this economic policy often leads to a desire to enlarge the national territory so as to acquire new sources for food and raw materials; autarky can best achieve its ends in a vast "economic area." But in a world where the possibility no longer exists of acquiring land at the expense of peoples lacking political organization, territorial expansion implies conquest at the expense of another organized state.

Thus, autarky, usually related in some basic way to the idea of a policy of force, leads, by its consequences, to the development of imperialism. The state that practices it tends to wish to increase its "living space"; the population that suffers it, or accepts it, begins to think that "war is not an accursed thing at all, especially if it is the one and only way to permit a nation to achieve all the hopes it cherishes."[6]

II. RIVALRIES IN ECONOMIC EXPANSION

The mechanization of industry in the last half of the nineteenth century made possible the standardized, mass production of goods. Industrial output could remain at a high level, thanks to the simultaneous expansion of trade; the discovery of new markets and sources of raw materials was facilitated by progress in transportation. To gain new export markets, to provide industry with adequate supplies of raw materials and power, and to establish some form of control over the main communication routes—these were the basic (and competing) concerns of the industrial nations. The question arises how these aims affected the political relations between states.

A. THE QUEST FOR EXPORT MARKETS

The principal instrument in the search for new markets was the trade agreement. And the application of the most-favored-nation clause, during the period when that clause was revered in theory and in practice inserted in nearly every treaty, greatly diminished rivalries. But in competing for the export markets of Asia, Africa, and the Americas, the European industrial states used other methods: by applying pressure individually or jointly, they acquired markets in the "new countries" without resorting to the usual

---

[6] Julius-Moritz Bonn, "La Paix économique: Dans quelle mesure les régimes autarciques sont-ils conciliables avec le maintien de la paix?" *Esprit International* (Paris), XII (1938), 238–55.

bilateral trade agreements; and they established, for their own profit, spheres of economic influence in other states.

1. Limited Tariff Duties

In Asia, the industrialized nations succeeded in securing, or imposing, a limitation on the tariff duties levied by the various countries.

China was the most typical example. As soon as the Opium War of 1839 had obliged the imperial Chinese Government to open the country to foreign trade, European countries and the United States began to devote particular attention to the Chinese market, on account of the enormous number of potential consumers there. In 1842, in the Treaty of Nanking ending the Opium War hostilities, Great Britain had insisted on a stipulation that the Chinese Government would apply a "fair and regular tariff" on imported goods brought to China over maritime routes. By a supplementary treaty signed in 1843, this tariff was set at 5 per cent *ad valorem*. Prior to the Opium War, foreign trade relations, confined solely to the port of Canton and rigorously controlled, had already involved the levy of import duties: some 20 per cent on cotton thread and fabric, 25 per cent on woolens— which at the time constituted Britain's principal exports to China. The 1843 convention thus reduced tariffs considerably, enabling the British textile industry, thanks to its mechanized production and despite the costs of transportation, to sell cotton goods on the Nanking market at lower prices than those demanded for domestic Chinese products.

The system established by the Treaty of Nanking was extended to France and the United States in 1844, then revamped and strengthened by the Treaties of Tientsin in 1858.[7] The preferential agreements in the latter inflicted clear and direct injury to Chinese artisans and, after 1895, hindered the development of modern industry in China, to the extent that it forbade industry to seek protection against foreign competition. The abrogation of the tariff clauses of the Treaty of Nanking was therefore one of the demands of Chinese revolutionaries as far back as 1907. This party was hostile, of course, to the Manchu Dynasty but no less opposed to the constraints the Great Powers had imposed on China. The same demand was advanced in May, 1919, by the Chinese nationalists. But it was not until 1928 that the restoration of customs autonomy began.

By *fiat* of the European states, the same conditions were applied to Morocco, Siam, and Persia. The Sultan of Morocco, when he signed a trade

---

[7] When the Chinese Government imposed a tax at internal stations on goods in transit (the likin), the rate imposed on European goods was at least 50 per cent lower than that levied on Chinese goods. In addition, the customs duties of 5 per cent *ad valorem* had been fixed for the future; as a result, because of the rise in prices, the 5 per-cent rate of 1858 amounted to only 3 per cent in 1900. Not until 1901 were duties restored to a true 5 per cent.

treaty with Great Britain in 1856, undertook to limit the import duties on British goods to 10 per cent *ad valorem*. The Siamese Government lost its customs autonomy by a treaty of April 18, 1855, under which Great Britain ensured that Siamese duties would be 3 per cent *ad valorem*. The Anglo-Persian treaty of 1857 contained similar provisions.

The Ottoman Government was placed under similar restraints within the framework of the "Capitulations." As far back as 1774, it undertook to levy customs duties no higher than 5 per cent on French goods, and in 1838 it conceded the same advantage to British goods. Between 1860 and 1862, treaties with France, Great Britain, Belgium, Switzerland, and the Netherlands raised this ceiling to 8 per cent. It was not until April 25, 1907, that the European powers agreed to raise the rate to 11 per cent, in order to provide the Ottoman Government with the funds it required to construct railroads.

Even more important than the low tariffs was the privilege European goods enjoyed after 1838 *within* Ottoman territory: internal duties, which were sometimes quite high, no longer applied to goods imported from Europe. Ottoman goods thus in effect had to pay a surtax, which only aggravated the competitive situation. Thanks to this privilege, European goods were able, after the middle of the nineteenth century, to command an increasingly large part of the domestic market of the Ottoman Empire.

The consequence was the decline of local Ottoman crafts and production, which were unable to survive the competition. Before 1850, this decline had already begun—in Syria, in the silk industry And in 1865, a commission on the reform of industry set up by the Sultan noted the impoverishment of the weavers in Istanbul and Üsküdar, and the decline of the tanneries and of the boat construction yards (foreign vessels had come to account for much of the traffic in Ottoman ports). But the ceiling set on tariff duties made it impossible for the Porte to take the steps that might have protected these industries against foreign competition. The only course open to it was to subsidize certain enterprises whose activity was essential to the nation's independence and security; such was the case with factories producing military supplies. Throughout the years before World War I, the complaints of the Ottoman Government fell on deaf ears. The situation did not change until 1923.

Japan was the only Asian nation to shake off foreign domination before World War I. By a treaty of July 29, 1858, the United States had seen to it that tariffs on imports of foreign goods would not exceed 20 per cent—a ceiling that was even lowered to 5 per cent for textiles and goods intended for naval construction, that is, for the principal items of the import trade. European nations trading in Japan succeeded almost immediately in having the same measures applied to them. But once industrialization had begun in Japan, in the 1870's, Japanese producers were quick to protest against a system that gave so many advantages to foreign competitors. In 1894, they obtained some slight satisfaction: the Japanese Government secured the right to fix customs duties freely, provided it did not exceed the maximum laid down in the 1858 treaty. But Japan did not regain customs autonomy until 1911; that she eventually did, she clearly owed to the development of her military and naval power.

These constraints imposed on the nations of Asia, Africa, the Middle East, and the New World undoubtedly contributed to the grievances in those countries against the policy of the Great Powers. They did not, however, lead to political conflict; the victims of the commercial treaties dared not risk such conflict, given the disproportion between the military powers involved. Neither did they lead to disputes between the industrial states, since virtually all of them enjoyed the same advantages.

2. Spheres of Influence

The establishment of zones of economic influence was one of the most widespread forms of expansion of the industrial states in the late nineteenth and early twentieth centuries. Germany, a latecomer, was particularly assiduous in pursuing this policy. But there was no colonial power that neglected this means of action. In the Ottoman Empire, the Chinese Empire, Persia, Ethiopia, the methods were the same: to obtain concessions for railroads, the construction of which would provide an outlet for European metallurgical products and the operation of which would enable European goods to reach the local markets; to request priority rights, or even a monopoly, on the prospecting and exploitation of mineral resources; and to make contracts with the government to supply products needed to build up the nation's capital equipment.

The division of territories into spheres of influence in which such measures could be carried out led to disputes among the expansionist states, but they were settled by compromise.[8]

Nazi Germany sought to acquire another kind of sphere of influence in southeastern Europe between 1934 and 1939. Here again, the underlying motive was political: if Germany could succeed in dominating a considerable part of the economic life of that region (whose products would be complementary to her own), she would possess an effective means of putting pressure on the foreign policies of the states concerned.[9]

The opportunity presented itself as a result of the depression of 1929–33. The Danubian states (Romania, Bulgaria, Hungary, and Yugoslavia) were all exporters of agricultural products, livestock, and wood products. In 1928,

---

[8] On the divisions into spheres of influence, see below, Chapter Four, pp. 92–97.

[9] A. Basch, *The Danube Basin and the German Economic Sphere* (London, 1944). See also, on the years 1937–38, Great Britain, Foreign Office, *Documents on German Foreign Policy, 1918–1945*, Series C, Vol. V (London, 1950).

the proportion of these exports to total exports was 73 per cent in Romania, 78.6 per cent in Bulgaria, 64.8 per cent in Hungary, and 68.2 per cent in Yugoslavia. But the depression meant that countries which normally imported these agricultural products, such as Germany and especially Czechoslovakia, had to curtail their purchases. The Danubian states thus suffered a marked decline in exports and a serious fall in prices. Their economic plight was grave, almost desperate.

It was not until 1934 that the German Government decided to take advantage of these circumstances. At the beginning of the depression, it had not considered the possibility, having struggled with Germany's own difficulties according to the usual methods. It had increased duties on foreign wheat—a measure taken in the interests of its own grain producers—but this in turn had aggravated the position of the Danubian agricultural states, and their inability to finance purchases of German goods led to a decline in German industrial exports. But in September, 1934, Germany's economic policy-makers struck out in a new direction: the Nazis' plan of action provided for increased exports with a view to buying more raw materials and foodstuffs abroad. It was in Germany's interest to make such purchases in southeastern Europe—that is, in an area that would remain accessible to it in case of war. She therefore proposed to these countries that she should buy all the raw materials they could supply, as well as a large part of their agricultural surplus, at a price considerably higher (often by 30 per cent) than the prevailing price on the world market. In return, these states would buy machinery, manufactured goods, and chemical goods from Germany at prices that would in certain cases be lower than the prevailing price. Control of the export trade would thereby enable the Nazi government to pursue a policy that took no account of cost prices. All that remained was to persuade the doubtful and to negotiate trade conventions.

Germany succeeded. Yugoslavia was glad to accept the German offers because, as a result of her vote in the League of Nations in favor of imposing sanctions on Italy in October, 1935, her export trade to Italy had collapsed, and she had not found compensatory markets in France or Great Britain. Romania was, at first, more reserved, because she feared the prospect of German economic preponderance, but in December, 1937, she signed an agreement to sell wheat and grass seed to Germany—at a higher price than the prevailing world price. By the autumn of 1938, when Czechoslovakia was in effect incorporated in the German economic sphere, the Danubian states were obliged, under pain of economic death, to accept with increasing docility the demands of the Third Reich. In an attempt to evade this coercion, Bulgaria, Romania, and Yugoslavia asked Great Britain to purchase quantities of their agricultural surpluses—but in vain. On February 14, 1939, the Romanian Government agreed to cooperate with Germany in a broad program: the "joint" development of Romanian petroleum deposits and the "adaptation of Romanian agricultural production to German needs." The conclusion of this agreement set the seal on German economic supremacy in southeastern Europe.[10]

The German negotiators were in no doubt that this association in economic affairs would pave the way for political collaboration. The rural population in the Danube area were satisfied, since they had recovered their export market; they would be grateful to Germany for the consequent restoration of their standard of living. By 1939, economic interdependence with Germany seemed to indicate that "the political development of the national States in southeastern Europe will follow the German pattern to an increasing extent." And the German Minister in Bucharest observed that the success of the trade negotiations between Germany and Romania were likely to "remove Romania increasingly from the orbit of the western powers and the Soviets." These were precisely the results the German Government had hoped to achieve in 1934: economic development had opened the way to political development. The economic plan had been conceived from the outset as a means of political action.

Did this political design affect relations among the Great Powers or increase international tension? Actually, it did not; Prime Minister Neville Chamberlain's closest associate, Sir Horace Wilson, was prepared, in the summer of 1938, to accept the division of the European markets between German and British exporters and did not refuse to concede to Germany a privileged field of action in southeastern Europe.[12]

B. The Quest for Raw Materials

A nation's consumption of raw materials varies according to its "economic maturity." The amount of raw materials needed in western Europe and the United States after the middle of the nineteenth century thus was considerable. And the disparity in resources available to them inevitably raised problems of division and allotment, which changed as new sources of raw materials were discovered and as technological advances changed the relative importance of different raw materials.

During most of the nineteenth century, however, the quest for raw materials and fuels was not urgent. Normal commerce provided, in peacetime, enough to satisfy the needs of the industrial states. (The "cotton famine" experienced in Great Britain and France in 1863–64 was due to the special circumstances of the American Civil War, which impeded

---

[10] Between 1933 and 1937, German exports to the Danube states rose in value from 154 million to 555.7 million marks, imports from 198 million to 574 million marks.

[11] Report from Wohlthat to Goering, February 27, 1939, in *Documents on German Foreign Policy 1918–1945*, Series D, Vol. V (London, 1953), note 306.

[12] As reported by Wohlthat, July 24, 1938, *ibid.*, Vol. VI (London, 1956), note 716.

acquisition of cotton from the South.) Nations therefore did not yet have any pressing need to secure food sources at each other's expense or to monopolize their exploitation. It is true, of course, that the desire to acquire land with a rich store of minerals and to acquire also the right to exploit those riches helps to explain certain cases of colonial expansion. In 1884, the most enterprising supporters of French action in Tonkin (now part of North Vietnam) were interested in the coal deposits there. (And in the French empire generally, except in New Caledonia, development concessions were reserved to French nationals. By a law of 1907, concessions were reserved to Dutch nationals in the Dutch East Indies.) In 1904, the Pan-Germanists who urged their government to claim part of Morocco had the ore deposits in Morocco's Rif Mountains in mind. British expansion in South Africa was clearly inspired by the wish to control a land that contained gold and diamond fields (in the Boer republics) and to control the systematic exploitation of resources in southern Africa. Concern to find coal and iron ore partially explains Japan's intervention in Manchuria, for she was trying to develop industry without the necessary resources on her own territory. Yet, these economic considerations usually played a subsidiary part in what were primarily political undertakings.

In the early twentieth century, some industrial nations adopted another policy with regard to raw materials: they aimed simply to gain exclusive or preferential control over the exploitation of mineral and fuel deposits in other lands. This was a more urgent problem for Japan than for any other country: she aspired to become the "England of Asia" and hoped to find the needed resources in China; she did, in fact, in 1907, achieve a privileged position in regard to certain iron-ore mines by controlling the Hanyehping deposits. German industrialists, also short on iron ore, sought to acquire shares in the working of French deposits in lower Normandy and the Ouenza, but ran into opposition from French business and government circles.

However, it was neither iron ore nor coal that gave rise to any notable international dispute during this period of industrial development, but oil. In order to acquire concessions to explore and drill, oil companies put heavy pressure on the local governments in regions that had, or appeared to have, oil deposits. The resulting activities led to controversies that went beyond financial considerations; when an activity of prime importance for the national economy was placed under foreign control, the people naturally felt a sense of outrage at what they considered to be a violation of their national independence. The oil companies, for their part, sought the support of their own governments—to get the concessions in the first place, and to protect themselves against opposition. When they obtained it, the matter could become an open conflict between the Great Powers. In 1912 and 1913, for instance, the interests of British and American oil firms clashed in

Mexico; each supported a rival candidate for the Mexican Presidency in the hope of placing into power a man favorable to their interests; the controversy was closely followed in Washington and London and at certain points directly affected relations between the United States and Great Britain.

After 1919, the question of access to raw materials became a more pressing international problem. At its first Assembly, in November, 1920, the League of Nations, at Italy's request, decided to institute an inquiry into the matter. The reluctance of producing nations to cooperate made this difficult, and the Assembly showed no real inclination to do something about it. Again, it was oil that provoked the most heated controversies; oil had become the essential fuel for land, sea, and air transport and was of major significance to the armed forces. Economic interests were thus intimately bound up with strategic interests. Among the Great Powers, only the United States and the Soviet Union had sufficient resources on their own land; the others had to rely on imports.[13] But the transport and distribution of oil were handled by only a few big concerns, whose prospecting and mining activities, and sales, were conducted on an international scale. These concerns dealt directly with national governments, to which they were often indispensable; and they sometimes possessed superior means of action. Nevertheless, they also required governmental protection or support, and they used appropriate pressures to achieve it. They were thus closely connected to the political life of their and other nations, where they enjoyed power status.

After World War I, the two major oil-company groups—Standard Oil (American) and Royal Dutch–Shell (British and Dutch)—were competing in Mexico, Venezuela, and, primarily, the Middle East. In Great Britain, foreigners were forbidden by law to acquire shares in British oil companies; in the United States, when the Geological Survey pointed out in 1920 that national oil reserves were beginning to dwindle,[14] that production would soon decline, and that the public authorities were in duty bound to lend their moral support to any American business effort to expand oil-production activities, the government showed itself disposed to respond to this appeal.

In Persia, the Anglo-Persian Oil Company (APOC) had been exploiting the large deposits in and near Abadan, on the coast of the Persian Gulf, since 1909. In July, 1914, the British Government had undertaken the responsibility of increasing the company's capital from £2 million to £4 million, and it now held a controlling 53 per cent of its shares. Russia, under an Anglo-Russian agreement of 1907,[15] was the only other country entitled to obtain oil concessions in Persia—in the five northern provinces; a Rus-

---

[13] See Jean Gottmann, *La Politique extérieure des états et leur géographie* (Paris, 1952), p. 181, and Henry Bérenger, *La politique du pétrole* (Paris, 1921).

[14] The potential of the Texas oilfields was not fully recognized until 1930.

[15] See below, Chapter Four. p. 94.

sian citizen (actually, a Georgian named Khoshtaria) had obtained a concession there in 1916. But in 1920, at a time when Georgia withdrew for a few months from the Soviet Union, Khoshtaria sold his rights to the APOC.

This British triumph drew protests from the Soviet Government, which while proclaiming its readiness to abandon the concessions Russia had acquired in Persia in Tsarist times, did not wish Great Britain to acquire a dominant economic interest in areas adjoining Soviet borders. It also disturbed the United States Government, which was interested in Middle Eastern oil because it feared the imminent depletion of American fields. The Iranian Government was also hostile, since the new arrangement would give the Anglo-Persian Oil Company a stronger hold on the country; it preferred to grant the rights to an American firm (it had refused to accept the concession purchased by the APOC as valid), since the United States at that time claimed no political role in the Middle East. But its negotiations with Standard Oil and with Sinclair had to be abandoned in the face of British and Russian protests—the Soviet Government, after attacking British interests, thus found itself supporting Great Britain to block American interests. The various pressures cancelled out, and the Iranian Government resigned itself, for the next twelve years, to letting the Anglo-Persian concession stand, despite the constant differences arising between it and the company.

When in November, 1932, the Iranian Government decided to cancel the concession, over the strong objections of the British Government, it may have been receiving encouragement from a Soviet agent. In any event, although the dispute went beyond the limits of strictly Anglo-Iranian relations and was submitted to the Council of the League of Nations, it did not lead to diplomatic action on the part of the United States or the Soviet Union. But when the new contract, signed on May 1, 1933, and amended in 1949, was voided by the nationalization law passed on March 20, 1951, by the Iranian Parliament, the matter provoked immediate action. Presidents Truman and Eisenhower sought to mediate the dispute between Iran and Great Britain over the expropriation indemnity, but their endeavors were apparently in vain—although they could not have been altogether in vain since in the new concession granted in 1954 to eight oil companies, after the repeal of the nationalization law, the American companies obtained a 40 per cent share.

On May 19, 1914, the Ottoman Government conceded the mining of the Mosul deposits to the Turkish Petroleum Company, of which British and German companies were principal shareholders. These companies had agreed that future output would be divided into three equal parts: one for the use of the British Navy, one for the use of the German Navy, and one for sale, and this agreement had been approved by all the governments concerned. But the concession was not implemented because of the outbreak of

World War I, and the German share was sequestered by the British authorities. After the war, the French Government sought to obtain this share, now "available," from Great Britain, in exchange for a new alignment of the spheres of influence in Asia Minor that the two states had worked out in the Sykes-Picot Agreement of 1916. After long discussions, slowed down by Franco-British disagreements over Syria, France succeeded in obtaining a 25 per-cent share in the capital of Turkish Petroleum, on condition that she would permit two pipelines to be constructed from Mosul to the Syrian ports in French Mandate territory. Economic and financial considerations, of course, had governed French policy in this matter. Fuel consumption in France had risen by 50 per cent since 1913, and too much of the country's available foreign exchange had to be used to pay for oil imports; a source of supply was therefore a matter of great importance.

But the Franco-British agreement drew protests from the United States Government. Repeatedly, United States diplomatic notes appealed to the principle of "equal treatment" laid down during the peace negotiations: in any territory that the peace treaties took away from a defeated state, the citizens of all nations must enjoy equal economic rights. England, declared Senator Henry Cabot Lodge, was taking possession of the oil resources of the world. As a result of this diplomatic pressure, the British Government, in December, 1922, at a time when its Ottoman policy was seriously imperiled by the defeat in Asia Minor of the Greek forces supported by the Allies, promised American oil interests a 25 per-cent share in the Turkish Petroleum Company, to be deducted from the British interests.

In this instance, had the State Department acted on its own initiative or as the instrument of American oil interests? Given the present stage of historical research on this subject, it is difficult to give a clear answer, but it is certainly true that the oil companies had a strong advocate within the government—Albert Fall, Secretary of the Interior, previously Senator from New Mexico.

So here are two cases where diplomatic action was taken in the interests of private companies.[16] Yet, in both cases, the general interests, economic or political, of the state were also involved. But can we speak, here, of an "oil war"? Nothing in the documents supports that view. The clash of material interests undoubtedly contributed to arousing diplomatic controversy, but it did not, apparently, seriously upset the political relations of the nations concerned.

Differences over raw-material supplies became more heated between 1935 and 1939—far more for political than economic reasons: policies were governed by military and strategic considerations; states wished to have

---

[16] It is worth noting, however, that, since the end of World War II, such diplomatic pressure by great powers has often been less effective, since governments are more reluctant to envisage resort to force.

access to essential raw materials, as well as to fuels required for transport, in case of war. "The raw-materials race is only a stage in the arms race."[17]

Every country was concerned about access to raw materials (except the United States and the Soviet Union, both of which were able to supply virtually all their own needs), states with few colonial territories most of all. Such was the case with Japan, Germany, and Italy, which used their lack of colonies as an argument to support policies of territorial expansion. Nations poorly endowed with raw materials, they argued, were being forced to pay an unfair "economic tribute" which drained their balance of payments; press campaigns contended that the supply of raw materials could be assured only if the producing territory were politically controlled. Freedom of access to raw materials was thus linked with a "redistribution" of colonial territories.

Is it not possible, however, to dissociate the economic from the colonial problem?

When President Franklin D. Roosevelt, in a speech of October 5, 1937, suggested that "peace-loving nations . . . make a concerted effort" to counter the violation of treaties and establish fundamental principles to be observed in international relations, he included in that program the right of free access to raw materials for all peoples; ensuring this right, he believed, would help to prevent war. His plan was abortive; the British Prime Minister preferred to attempt direct negotiations with Germany and Italy rather than appeal to a general conference.[18]

The following year, the idea was discussed again, this time less vaguely, among economists and political scientists.[19] Why not, for instance, assign the development and distribution of raw materials to international firms, thus bypassing national sovereignties? (This would be an insufficient and even dangerous remedy, perhaps; the firm might serve as a screen for territorial conquest planned by a dominant participant with political designs.) The International Studies Conference of 1938, which discussed these matters in full, did not succeed in working out a plan, but its conclusion deserves attention. The financial questions involved in the matter of arranging access to raw materials, the conference report pointed out, can be resolved easily in a peacetime economy but not in an economy geared to war preparations. The essential difficulties are not economic but political; political insecurity prevents a solution.

---

[17] Report to the twelfth International Studies Conference (1939), drafted by Etienne Dennery, *Peaceful Change*, Vol. IV: *Le Problème des matières premières* (Paris, 1939).

[18] See J.-B. Duroselle, *From Wilson to Roosevelt: Foreign Policy of the United States, 1913-45* (Cambridge, Mass., 1963), pp. 217-51.

[19] For example, among those preparing papers for the International Studies Conference. The same thought underlay certain suggestions made in 1946 for establishing international control over Middle Eastern oil activities. See George Lenczowski, *Oil and State in the Middle East* (Ithaca, N.Y., 1960), p. 173.

C. CONTROL OF COMMUNICATION ROUTES

In 1870, the rail systems of Europe and North America were already far advanced, but in the rest of the world, only 7,668 miles of track had been laid down (4,000 in India, by the British administration). By 1913, this figure had increased to 172,500 miles—a development accomplished everywhere by European capital and technicians, which transformed commercial activities in large areas of the world and opened up new opportunities for exports from the industrial states.

At the same time, maritime transport made considerable strides thanks to the increased tonnage of the merchant marines and new techniques of boat construction, and thanks also to the opening of the Suez and Panama canals, which shortened distances and altered trade patterns.

1. Railroads

In territories they controlled, Europeans could develop their railroad enterprises as they pleased, but in independent states, they needed the authorization of the government, which usually took the form of a concession.

In South America before 1914, nearly all the governments turned to European concerns to help them plan and build railroads; and the importance of these foreign companies in the economic life of the continent need hardly be stressed. All the most important lines in Argentina were built by British companies under concessions; not only did Englishmen occupy the executive posts in these companies, but the companies were entitled to fix the rates. Originally, the government had fixed a guaranteed minimum return for the foreign concerns; this became superfluous after 1895, when the latter began to make large profits. But not until 1907 was a law passed authorizing the government to reduce fares whenever the profits of a given company, for three years running, reached 25 per cent of the invested capital. In Uruguay, all the railroads were built with English capital; the government guaranteed a minimum return but retained the right to fix rates. In Brazil, almost 85 per cent of the rail network belonged to private British, French, and Belgian companies. In Peru in 1890, the government gave the railroad concession to a Peruvian company financed by British capital but, on account of difficulties in the railroad's construction, heavily subsidized the company for the next thirty years. Colombia adopted a similar policy, but instead of subsidizing the company's operations, it ceded it public lands. Chile was the only Latin American state that retained ownership of most of the railroads on its territory (although the Transandino was ceded to a British company), but construction was directed by European or American engineers.

In Asia and Africa, where European and American economic interests enjoyed great freedom of action, the participation of their technicians and capital in railroad construction was very large, extending far beyond the economic sphere. Only Japan did not give up her right to control rail rates and operation; other governments were obliged to grant wide privileges to foreign interests. The most typical examples were those of Ethiopia, China, and the Ottoman Empire.

The concession granted on March 9, 1894, by the Emperor Menelik II of Ethiopia to a Swiss engineer, Alfred Ilg, and his French associate, Leon Chefneux, may be regarded as a prototype of such contracts. In May, 1889, Menelik had signed the Treaty of Uccialli with Italy, but rejected Italy's interpretation that an Italian protectorate had thereby been established, and sought to secure for the Ethiopian plateau an access route to a port situated outside Italian control. The railroad concession therefore provided for the construction of a line from Djibouti to Harar and thence eventually to Addis Ababa. The concessionary company was to have a virtual monopoly, for Menelik undertook to have *all* goods transported by rail and no longer by caravan. The company was authorized to fix rates provided they did not exceed prevailing fares for the caravans. It was permitted to levy a 10 percent tax on goods in transit until its annual profits reached 3 million francs. Finally, it was authorized to develop mines and forests within a specified area on either side of the track. But the Ethiopian Government assumed no financial responsibility, and might even expect a profit, since the Emperor was to receive a parcel of shares in the company.

In 1864 and again two years later, the Chinese Government turned down proposals to construct a railroad, but a little later, in 1881 and 1890, it authorized two short sections (25 miles in all) for transporting coal. The building of a real rail network did not begin until 1894, when the government, weakened by defeats in the war against Japan, no longer dared refuse to give concessions to European companies.

China thereupon granted concessions on September 8, 1896, to the Russo-Chinese Bank for the Chinese Eastern Railway across northern Manchuria; on March 6, 1898, to the German Government for lines in Shantung; and on April 10, 1898, to the French Government for the Yunnan line. In all cases, China accorded the right to operate the lines with foreign personnel and to determine rates; it ceded freely (except in Shantung) the land on which to build the lines when such land belonged to the state; and it authorized mining of ore deposits in the areas adjoining the railroads. These were considerable economic advantages, but only in the first case did the Chinese Government cede its right to administer the "territory of the railroad" and agree to the presence of a foreign police force.[20] In treating with Germany and then France, it took precautions it had not been able

---

[20] The concession to the French for the Yunnan railroad provided that the line be protected by an *indigenous* militia.

to take in negotiating with Russia, whom it wanted as an ally against Japan. The precautions were inadequate, however, since the foreigners had a free hand in operating the railroads and fixing rates.

In the summer of 1898, during the Hundred Days of Reform,[21] the imperial government announced a new policy: railroads might be constructed and operated by foreign companies (their assistance was still indispensable, since they alone had the requisite technicians and capital), but they were to be controlled by Chinese authorities. Thus, the construction of the Peking-Hankow Railway was conceded to a Belgian company, which was also to operate it; construction costs were to be covered by the sale of bonds issued by the company on European financial markets on behalf of China; the railroad would thus belong to the imperial government. Similar principles were applied in ceding the Shanghai-Nanking line to a British company and the Hankow-Canton line to an American one. In a final phase of its railroads policy (1905–11), the imperial Chinese Government introduced new stipulations providing for Chinese control over the construction and operation of the lines. In 1911, on the eve of the revolution that was to sweep away the Manchu dynasty, China had some 6,160 miles of railroads, all but 230 miles of which had been constructed by foreign entrepreneurs; the foreign companies owned 2,670 miles, or about 43 per cent of the total system.

In the Ottoman Empire, interest was focused on the concession, to a German company, of a vast railroad system (more than 2,500 miles) whose principal line was to connect Anatolia (Ankara and Konya) with Mesopotamia and the Persian Gulf. The concession, approved in principle in 1899 and coming into effect in 1903, was similar, from an economic and financial point of view, to some of the Chinese railroad concessions. The Baghdad Railway Company was authorized to mine the ore deposits it might find within an area of 19 miles on either side of the line; it undertook to issue bonds, from the sale of which the Ottoman Government would be able to pay the company lump-sum compensation as the construction advanced. The Ottoman state thus owned the line and shared the profits but left the operation to the German company (for 99 years), which thus came to hold a key position in the economic life of the empire.

These railway enterprises in Africa, Asia, and the Middle East played a vital part in the diplomatic relations between the Great Powers, because they were connected with the establishment of their spheres of influence. They often gave rise to disputes, but these disputes were always settled by compromise, and partitions were worked out. On the whole, then, they were irritants rather than sources of conflict.

---

[21] That is, the period during which the young Emperor Kuang Hsu attempted to inaugurate new programs in almost every sphere of national life, at the prompting of K'ang Yu-wei, the radical Confucian scholar and advocate of reform.

2. Maritime Routes

In two important instances since the mid-nineteenth century—the Suez and Panama canals—major maritime routes occasioned international rivalries and controversies. Economic interests were clearly very largely involved; all countries wanted to be able to use these canals freely and without discrimination, and they wanted assurance that transit dues would not be excessive. But the question is whether these economic interests alone or largely sufficiently explain the bitterness of the controversies.

In the case of the Suez Canal—constructed by a private French company that had been granted the concession from Egypt's khedivial government— the question of freedom of transit did not, at first sight, seem likely to give rise to difficulties. The canal was, of course, on Egyptian territory, but the khedive could have little interest in prohibiting traffic since he owned the largest individual bloc of the company's shares and was entitled to part of the profits. The situation changed in 1875, however, when the khedive's financial difficulties forced him to sell his shares (worth 100 million francs) to the British Government, and again in 1882, when Britain's armed intervention against the Egyptian nationalist movement "temporarily" placed the canal under British control.

The question of freedom of transit now became very real. The British Government declared, however, that it would not violate this freedom and agreed that the canal's status should be established by an international convention. The Suez Canal Convention of October, 1888 (signed by Great Britain, France, Germany, Italy, Austria, Spain, the Netherlands, Russia, and Turkey), declared the canal free and open, in time of war as in time of peace, to all merchant and war vessels—therefore open even during a war involving Egypt, theoretically a vassal of the Ottoman Empire. This assurance was an important one to the economic interests of states whose merchant marines used the new waterway, and it was even more important strategically. But the application of the convention remained, *de facto* if not *de jure*, at the discretion of the British forces occupying Egypt, and the British Navy, mistress of the Mediterranean, was in a position, without violating the convention, to prohibit passage through the canal by means of long-distance blockade.

In point of fact, Great Britain did respect the canal's neutrality, both during World War I (the canal was closed only for 25 hours, in May, 1915, at the time of the Turkish offensive against Egyptian territory) and during the Ethiopian war in 1935–36. In the first case, the maintenance of neutrality corresponded to British interests, since Great Britain received a part of her raw-material supplies via Suez. But in the second case, the closure of the canal would have paralyzed the Italian expedition against Ethiopia. Why did England refuse to resort to it, in view of the policy of economic sanctions against Italy she had championed in the League of Nations? Had the Cabinet simply taken to heart the counsels of its legal advisers, who did not want to see 1888 repeated? Basically, this respect for the letter of the law coincided with British policy to impede the Italian expedition by indirect economic pressure but not to provoke Mussolini unduly; England was determined at all costs to avoid war with Italy.

The Panama Canal involved primarily the economic interests of the United States, once U.S. territory reached to the Pacific; the canal was of obvious importance for trade between California ports and those on the Atlantic seaboard, as well as for the expansion of American trade in the Pacific and the Far East. But the opening of a canal that reduced by one-half the length of the passage between Europe and Peru, Bolivia, or Chile was also of considerable interest to the British merchant marine. The canal was also of far-reaching political significance: by facilitating the movement of naval troops, it could increase the means of naval action and considerably modify the principles of naval strategy. Here, the interests of Great Britain, whose pre-eminence in this sphere remained unchallenged until 1919, were more immediately involved than those of any other state. Would Great Britain, which controlled all the great maritime routes of the world, also control this one? Assuredly not, for, as the British Cabinet well realized, the United States would never agree to having such a canal under British control, but it hoped to prevent the United States from establishing the waterway for its exclusive profit. In April, 1850, the Clayton-Bulwer Treaty provided that if the canal were constructed, it would be an Anglo-American undertaking, and that the Canal would be neutral; the two states exchanged commitments not to seek to establish exclusive control over the waterway or to erect fortifications on its banks. This was the undertaking from which the United States withdrew half a century later; the Second Hay-Pauncefote Treaty of December, 1901, between Great Britain and the United States, recognized the latter's exclusive right to construct the inter-oceanic waterway, supervise its neutrality, construct fortifications along it, and occupy it with troops. The United States Government thus wished to be in a position to prohibit transit through the canal—while declaring it free; it succeeded, by reason of the difficulties Great Britain was having at the time in South Africa. Was the United States simply concerned to protect its economic interests? No, neither the fortifications nor the military occupation of the Canal Zone were needed for the protection of those interests. The motivation was a strategic one: the United States Navy wanted to be absolutely secure in its right of transit.

III. COERCIVE MEASURES

When nations take steps to restrain each other's trade, the relation between economic and political forces is very close. Blockade is a clear example of economic coercion employed for political ends. But what of a tariff war, an embargo, or a boycott?

A. TARIFF WARS

From the point of view of the study of international relations, the most interesting tariff wars in the late nineteenth and early twentieth centuries are those involving Germany and Russia, between 1890 and 1894; Italy and France, between 1888 and 1898; and Austria-Hungary and Serbia, between 1906 and 1909. They were all quite different.

Russia had no customs treaty with Germany; she was obliged to pay the full rate of German duties, which after 1879 had been highly protectionist. Russian wheat entering Germany consequently paid much higher duties than Austrian wheat. To obtain a reduction, the Russian Government requested Germany in February, 1892, to conclude a trade treaty containing the most-favored-nation clause. The Germans refused, believing that the Russians would soon back down on their demands since they needed an outlet for their wheat. But instead, the Russian Government decided to levy higher duties on German goods—up to 20 or 30 per cent—effective August 1, 1893, and the German Government responded with similar measures.

This tariff war brought Russian wheat exports to Germany to a virtual standstill. In October, 1893, therefore, the Russian Government requested that negotiations be reopened. By a treaty of February 10, 1894, Germany undertook to apply the same tariffs to Russian as to Hungarian wheat; in return, Russia reduced its duties on most German industrial goods.

This short tariff war was apparently a simple consequence of conflicting economic interests. But how was the Russian Government, which at first dared not continue the struggle because of the excessive losses it entailed for Russian agriculture, able in the end to secure the advantages it had originally been refused?

The fact is that German economic policy changed, and it changed because of political factors. In the trade negotiations of 1892, the Germans were not disposed to show any consideration for Russian commercial interests; in preceding months, they had observed what appeared to be the first signs of a Franco-Russian "understanding," and they feared that such an entente might develop into an alliance. By February, 1894, however, the German Government felt that, if the tariff war continued, it might become a "national conflict" and encourage political dissensions. Kaiser Wilhelm II stated, at a meeting of the Crown Council, that he hoped, with the conclusion of the trade treaty, that relations between Russia and Germany would improve and the bonds between Russia and France loosen. In a word, the orientation of Germany's economic policy was subordinated to her political interests.

The long tariff war between Italy and France in the 1890's was undoubtedly due to basic economic causes. The French Chamber of Deputies had refused to ratify a navigation convention negotiated in 1886 which contained provisions on fishing and docking rights that were favorable to Italian interests. The Italian Government had riposted by denouncing the commercial treaty of 1881, which reduced duties on French industrial goods entering Italy in exchange for facilities granted to Italian goods entering France. New trade negotiations begun in 1887 were abortive, since Italy proposed to raise the duties on woolen goods, silks, and metallurgical products, and France did not want to reduce its duties on Italian livestock. On February 28, 1888, an Italian decree ruled that all French goods would be subject to the tariff adopted by the legislature a few months earlier—in other words, that very high duties would be imposed; a French decree imposed a corresponding measure. During the next two years, Italian exports to France fell by 39 per cent, and French exports to Italy by 50 per cent. But whereas France had relatively little trouble in finding alternative markets, Italy's agriculture and stock farming were seriously affected.

By 1890, the Italian Government had abandoned the retaliatory tariff and intimated that it was prepared to reopen negotiations for a commercial treaty, but the French were not amenable, even though German goods were beginning to replace French ones on the Italian market. Seven years passed before negotiations were reopened; a commercial treaty signed on November 21, 1898, restored normal trade relations, based on the most-favored-nation clause.

But can this lengthy customs conflict be explained solely by economic reasons? It is true that the north Italian industrialists were pleased at the rupture in trade relations, which spared them the competition of French industry. French business circles, for their part, were convinced in 1890 that Italy's economic crisis would soon force Italy to give in, and they believed that they could make her dance to their tune. In both countries, moreover, protectionist theories were widely mooted in parliamentary circles. Nevertheless, neither these material interests nor these theories fully account for the tariff war.

Why, in 1887, did the Italian Government refuse to maintain the tariff rates set in the 1881 treaty? Under the system established by that treaty, the balance of trade had been greatly to Italy's advantage. French negotiators[22] attributed the change in attitude to a political development: the advent to power, on July 29, 1887, of Francesco Crispi, an ardent

---

[22] Particularly Ambassador Billot, in his memoirs. See *La France et l'Italie: Histoire des années troublées 1881–99* (Paris, 1905), II, 132.

supporter of the Triple Alliance against France and a prime minister who gave to Italian diplomacy a new and inflexible intransigence. Italian farmers, who were directly affected by the tariff war, as a matter of fact accused their government of deliberately pursuing a policy of "disagreement" with France.

And why did the French Government take until 1898 to agree to negotiations that the French Ambassador in Rome had been advocating since 1892? It was paralyzed by the attitude of the parliamentary majority, which was displeased about the anticipated renewal of the treaty of the Triple Alliance, decided on in 1891, and wished to prolong the Italian economic crisis in the hope that its financial repercussions would prevent Italy from developing her armaments. It was only after the fall of Crispi's last ministry in 1896, and on account of the new direction that the Marquis di Rudini gave to Italian foreign policy, that French legislators agreed to give up the economic struggle.

In short, on either side, political considerations prolonged the commercial break.

The Austro-Serbian tariff war of 1906 is illustrative of methods of economic pressure being employed in the service of political designs. A commercial treaty concluded in 1882, renewed and amended in 1892, provided favorable conditions for imports into Austria-Hungary of Serbian livestock and grain, and for imports into Serbia of Austrian industrial goods. When the treaty expired in 1905, the Austro-Hungarian Government refused to renew it, agreeing only to a *modus vivendi* agreement; then, in November, 1906, it denounced even that, and by administrative measures prohibited the import of Serbian livestock. In effect, the territory of the Dual Monarchy was thus closed to the products of Serbian stock farming; whereas in 1905 Austria-Hungary had absorbed 90 per cent of Serbia's agricultural exports, in 1907 it accounted for only 31 per cent.

This "pig war" disturbed some Austrian industrialists, since the Serbs were cutting down on orders for their products, but it favored livestock farmers who no longer had to meet Serbian competition. Meanwhile, it threatened to ruin the livelihood of Serbian peasants. But the Belgrade government succeeded in finding new markets which, after 1909, absorbed most of the products of the nation's livestock farms. Once it was demonstrated that Serbian agriculture had escaped ruin and that the economic pressure exerted by Austria-Hungary was in vain, the government in Vienna considered negotiating a new trade treaty with Serbia in the interests of Austrian business. But it was not until 1911 that it was able to carry out this plan, for "agrarians" in Hungary, satisfied with the measures taken in November, 1906, obstructed the discussions.

What was the point of this customs war? Was it a struggle between economic interests? In point of fact, it was a political maneuver. The *coup d'état* of June, 1903, that placed Peter Karageorgević on the Serbian throne, put an end to the policy of Austro-Serbian collaboration inaugurated in 1880 by Milan Obrenović. The new Radical Party government made its foreign policy quite clear when it sold bonds on the French market in 1904, in order to buy armaments, and a year later when it attempted to conclude a customs convention with Bulgaria. It was in order to force the Serbian Government to return to its previous policy that the Austro-Hungarian Minister for Foreign Affairs, Agenor Goluchowski, decided on the Pig War; the financial and economic crisis that would sweep Serbia as a result, he thought, would show King Peter and the Radicals that they must be more docile in their general policy vis-à-vis Austria-Hungary. But this economic pressure was ineffective and only stirred up the Serbian peasants' nationalist sentiments against the Dual Monarchy. It is true at the time of the Bosnia-Herzegovina crisis of 1908–9, Goluchowski's successor, Aloys Aehrenthal, scored a political success by using force to annex the provinces, and the Serbian Government was forced to bow to the will of Austria-Hungary. But by then the Foreign Minister wanted to end the Pig War since, in his view, it had become superfluous. The opposition of Hungarian economic interests thwarted his policy for the next two years.

In this case, then, the origin of the tariff war was political, but economic interests upset political plans.

B. EMBARGOES

Embargoes on exports or imports have usually been used as means of achieving political purposes. By forbidding its citizens to sell or buy certain goods to nationals of another state, the government that decides on an embargo generally proposes either to obstruct some action undertaken by that state (in particular, to prevent armed conflict) or to induce it to modify its policy. But it may also, quite simply, wish to prevent its citizens becoming involved in international complications. In any case, economic considerations are not a determining factor.

Embargoes have most often been imposed on the export of arms and munitions. International law does not prohibit the export of arms, even in time of war. Article 7 of the Hague convention of 1907 on neutrality stipulates that a neutral state is not obliged to prohibit the export of arms to belligerents, but such merchandise may be seized as contraband of war without their owner's being able to count on his government's protection.

In point of fact, several times during the nineteenth century, European governments prohibited the exportation of arms to Africa. The declared object was to prevent wars among African tribes, but the actual result of the measure was to facilitate colonial conquest. When the International Conference in Brussels in 1890 established regulations for the export of arms to Africa, it set the seal of respectability on this policy.

The United States employed the embargo between 1905 and 1913 to back its dollar diplomacy: by prohibiting arms exports to civil-war factions in Central American nations, Washington could deprive the *de facto* governments of their means of defense against insurrection.

Nevertheless, the international regulation of arms exports was established immediately after World War I by the Treaty of Saint Germain of September 10, 1919. The object was to check the trade in weapons that might be prompted by the existence of now useless stockpiles. All arms exports were now subject to license. Supervision was established mainly in Africa, but also in the Middle East—Syria, Palestine, Iraq—that is, in regions where Great Britain and France, under cover of international mandates, were seeking to establish control and were encountering opposition. At the same time, Article 16 of the League of Nations Covenant provided for arms embargoes as a form of sanction against an aggressor state.

The United States ratified neither the Treaty of Saint-Germain nor the Covenant of the League. Instead, she enacted her own legislation, geared to her own interests: Congress authorized the President to prohibit or restrain arms exports to Latin America and China, where civil wars were in progress. A "neutrality law" of August 31, 1935, extended and amended on February 29, 1936, and again on March 1, 1937, prohibited such exports to all arenas of armed conflict—the war in Ethiopia, the Spanish Civil War, the Sino-Japanese War. There now appeared to be a general principle that American industry was not to sell war matériel to belligerents, and this principle was upheld until 1940. What motivated the United States was not concern for collective security, but solely the desire to maintain and confirm her neutrality in case of war in Europe.

Embargo on the export of raw materials was also provided for under Article 16 of the League Covenant, as another economic sanction that the League Council might apply against an aggressor state. The sanction was destined to remain ineffective, however, since the major supplier of raw materials, the United States, had not ratified the Covenant. On the one occasion when Article 16 was applied (the Resolution of October 3, 1935, providing for sanctions against Italy as the aggressor against Ethiopia), the League Council did not include oil among the goods banned for export to Italy—although oil was essential to the success of the Italian expeditionary forces, whose superiority was based on its airplanes and tanks—thus recognizing that an oil embargo could not be imposed unless the major oil suppliers participated.

The crucial factor, then, in the matter of raw-material supplies, was the attitude of the United States. The 1935 law had authorized the President to prohibit the export of goods intended for belligerents, but in January, 1936, the Senate Committee on Foreign Relations deemed it inadvisable to order an oil embargo, and its decision was enough to nullify the whole

League of Nations effort to broaden the scope of the sanctions. Why did the senators thus rule out the application of principles they had endorsed the year before? Embargoes, they felt, were an assurance against repeating the experiences of World War I, a safeguard against an involvement of commercial interests that might draw the United States into a general war. But the Ethiopian conflict, in their view, did not entail this risk, and they did not intend to use the "neutrality law" as a means to obstruct expansionist Italian policy.

A few years later, however, when American interests in the Pacific and the Far East were threatened by Japan, an embargo was used as just such a means of pressure. In October, 1940, the United States prohibited export of machinery or iron and steel goods to Japanese territories, and a similar decision was taken with regard to oil effective August 1, 1941. These measures were undoubtedly open to exceptions and special interpretations, but the political intent was clear: to check the growth of stockpiles in a state that was a probable adversary of the United States and, especially, to retaliate against Japanese policy in Indochina.

As regards embargo on imports, a significant use of this policy was made by Great Britain in 1933. Two British engineers were convicted for espionage by Soviet courts at a time when Anglo-Russian relations were already strained. This provoked a riposte: a royal proclamation of April 26, 1933, implementing a bill enacted some days earlier, prohibited the importation into Great Britain of wheat, butter, timber, or cotton originating in the U.S.S.R., whereupon the Soviet Government banned the importation of British goods. But this rupture of trade relations lasted only a few months; the British Government lifted the embargo once it received assurances that the two engineers would be released. On this occasion, then, the embargo was a retaliatory measure employed for political purposes.

C. BOYCOTTS

In international relations, the boycott[23] is intended to prohibit the sale or purchase of certain products, or the loading and unloading of vessels transporting those products. The purpose is to inflict material damage on the producers or merchants of another country. It may be employed by private groups as a retaliatory measure against competitors. Or it may be used by one state against another; in this case, it is particularly important since it can provoke public annoyance or resentment among the citizens and lead to political complications.

---

[23] This term, current since about 1880, signifies a concerted action to break off economic and social relations with an individual or group against which the authors of the boycott have grievances. In the nineteenth century, it was used in Ireland in landlord-tenant relations, and in the United States in labor disputes. Here, of course, we refer to the term as it is used in international relations only.

In Europe, the first example of a boycott seems to have occurred in 1897. Patriotic Danish professional groups decided to boycott German goods in response to the measures taken by the German administration in northern Schleswig to restrict the use of the Danish language. The purpose was thus political. So also were the decisions taken in 1908 by Turkish businessmen who, in protest against Austria-Hungary's annexation of Bosnia and Herzegovina, refused to buy or sell Austrian or Hungarian goods; and so also in 1912, when certain companies in Russian-dominated Poland proscribed German goods in order to mark their disapproval of Prussia's policy in Poznan.

Cases of boycotts which occurred between the two world wars were not appreciably different. In 1921, Hungarians boycotted Austrian goods, because Austria had annexed the territory of Burgenland; in 1923, during the French occupation of the Ruhr, French goods were boycotted in Germany; in 1934, a speech by the French Foreign Minister declaring France's support for the territorial *status quo* in Romania was countered in Hungary by the proscription of French goods. In all these instances, the decision to boycott was taken by groups, companies, or unions independent of any intervention by the state, which was content to let them act. In all cases, the effect was only partial and temporary.

The significance of the boycott in India of British goods in 1920, planned by Gandhi to support the demands of the national movement, was altogether different by reason of its scale, duration, and effectiveness. The boycott succeeded to the extent that Hindu merchants found elsewhere the manufactured goods they wanted to avoid buying from Great Britain—chiefly in Japan. (Japanese industry was not really in a position to supply machinery and metallurgical goods on any large scale, but its textile goods were available.) In 1932, a Board of Trade report noted that the British share in Indian imports, which in 1920 had amounted to 60 per cent, had fallen to 37.2 per cent—the main reason being the boycott.

Boycotts were used in China more frequently than anywhere else. In 1905, for three months, goods originating in the United States were banned because Washington refused to rescind the law prohibiting Chinese immigration. In 1925, similar action was taken against British goods, in connection with the incidents that had led to clashes between Chinese and British troops in the concessions of Nanking and Hankow. But the prime target of boycotts was Japan, China's most inconvenient neighbor and her principal supplier. The boycott was China's reply to Japanese policy and Japanese acts or threats of aggression nine times between 1908 and 1932.[24] These economic reprisals against political pressure were major policy tools in 1915, when the Japanese Government forced the Chinese Government to accept

---

[24] The Lytton report to the League of Nations lists these cases. See Earl of Lytton, *Lessons of the League of Nations Commission of Enquiry in Manchuria* (London, 1937).

the "twenty-one demands" concerning Japanese commercial interests in Shantung and elsewhere on the mainland; in 1919, when the Chinese and Japanese delegations to the Versailles Peace Conference fell out over the Shantung question; and in 1931, at the time of the Japanese intervention in Manchuria. On at least two occasions (in 1925 and 1931), the Chinese Government itself openly organized the boycott; the Kuomintang gave directions to business or student associations, and, if Japanese goods entered the country "illegally," that is, despite the boycott, the Kuomintang had officials seize them. In such a case, a boycott is akin to an extreme form of customs reprisals.

Another form of boycott was resorted to by the British Government in 1916, when it forbade its citizens to trade with American firms financed by German capital. Such firms, it said, were seeking to supply Germany, despite the blockade, through the agency of neutrals; eighty-five firms were blacklisted. The American press regarding this decision as "unpardonable interference" in United States domestic affairs, demanded reprisals, and on September 8, 1916, Congress passed a law authorizing the President to carry them out, leaving it to him to choose the means—an embargo on wheat or arms sales to Great Britain. But President Wilson, after consulting the Secretary of Commerce, declined to use these powers on the grounds that reprisals would seriously injure the interests of American producers.

The boycott has thus been an instrument that states have frequently employed in political conflicts. Such "political boycotts" have usually been the weapon of weak states unable directly to oppose actions they found reprehensible, which therefore tried to hurt the adversary materially. It has always been a difficult measure to carry out, since to be effective it should apply to consumer goods that the people most need; consumers, if they obey the boycott, must deny themselves the goods, unless they can get similar ones from another source, probably at a higher price; in most cases, only a wave of patriotism or xenophobia will induce people to make such a sacrifice.

IV. CONCLUSION

Whenever economic questions are uppermost in the rivalries among states—conflicts of economic policy, trade rivalries, trade wars—two forces appear to be at work. One is the pressure exerted by private interests for national action: groups of manufacturers or businessmen, who want only to make a profit; or agricultural producers, who demand tariffs that will protect them against the influx of foreign goods; or labor unions, which want to eliminate the competition of imported labor so as to maintain their own wage levels. The other is the nation's awareness of its people's collective interests, which move the government to satisfy, under the most favorable conditions, their material needs. Often these two forces converge; sometimes they work in contrary directions. In either case, one cannot normally study them apart from the political contexts—i.e., from the considerations of security, power, or prestige involved. The interaction is constant between economic interests and political action. It is indisputable, therefore, that in order to understand a nation's foreign policy, one must take economic interests into account—in the contemporary world more than ever before.

But when historians attempt to pin down the factors that have had a decisive influence in international affairs, they still must try to separate the respective roles of economics and politics. Does the profit motive or the mechanisms of high finance per se really explain political action? The cases we have cited would indicate that such explanations are sometimes too perfunctory: in some very important cases, economic factors motivated political action, but they also frequently served as tools or weapons of political schemes.

The decisive influence of material interests has been most evident in clashes of economic policies and in rivalries for the conquest of foreign markets; in many cases, however, a political motive was from the outset associated with expansionist plans or rapidly superimposed on it. The determination to gain access to supplies of raw materials has caused political friction and sometimes armed conflict. On the other hand, rivalries for railroad concessions were nearly always a cover for political schemes, and maneuvers to control the Suez and Panama canals were directly linked to national strategies and the exigencies of power politics. Measures of economic coercion—tariff wars, embargoes, boycotts—have generally been politically motivated. Of course, they presuppose economic power on the part of the nation that applies them, but the initiative is political, and material interests have served political ends.

Thus it is impossible to isolate economic factors. What must be determined is whether they have been dominant or subordinate. Sometimes, they have determined or guided political action; sometimes, they have served as the instrument of that action. This is not mere hair-splitting; it is an observation basic to historical interpretation, since it challenges the validity of purely economic explanations.

But it is often hard to arrive at convincing conclusions, owing to the inadequacy of the records. When interest groups attempt to induce governments to take certain political steps, they usually leave few written traces; and even if their lobbying can be established with certainty, their real influence remains unclear; it is perfectly likely that their attempt to sway the government may *not* influence the government's decision. In cases where commercial interests served as means to achieve political ends, written records are more frequent, since the government has no reason to dissimulate and the interested groups no reason not to retain proof of the services they rendered the state; for the most part, however, the records throw no light on ulterior motives.

Historians are obliged in many cases, therefore, to confine themselves to noting parallels and suggesting hypotheses. The unfortunate thing is that they too often tend to present hypotheses as certainties.

4

INTERNATIONAL ECONOMIC AGREEMENTS

In the study of international relations, does the *convergence* of economic interests deserve as much attention as economic divergencies? The diplomatic history of nineteenth-century Europe shows that indifferent economic relations did not prevent political "understandings" between states: the Franco-Russian alliance between 1892–93 and 1917 is a case in point. Still, political *rapprochement* was a fragile thing where there was a clear divergence in economic matters between states.

In 1841–46, at the time of the first Entente Cordiale between France and Great Britain, the British Government wished to encourage exports and therefore sought a reduction in French tariffs on textiles and railroad equipment. It failed to obtain such a reduction. This setback did not cause the eventual collapse of the Entente Cordiale, the immediate reason for which was a divergence of *political* interests,[1] but it prevented the accommodation between the two states from becoming fully accepted by the British public. Undoubtedly, a convergence of economic interests helps to make a favorable atmosphere for political collaboration. But does it always operate in favor of the maintenance of international peace?

I. CUSTOMS UNIONS

A close association of economic interests between two or more states, achieved within the framework of a customs union, requires the national economies to make an effort at adjustment, but the necessary conditions for this adjustment are seldom present.

In its most complete form, a customs union implies territorial unity: commercial relations among all the member states are completely free, and the single common customs border is established at the frontiers separating them from the nations outside the union; the tariffs established by negotiation among the member states are uniform. This type of association was achieved in 1834 by the German states in the Zollverein.

In a less complete form of customs union, the member states, while

---

[1] The so-called Spanish marriages affair.

presenting a common customs frontier to other states, may maintain individual customs barriers on their own borders, in order to protect their own producers in certain sectors against competition from producers in other member states. On this basis, economic "compromise" was established between the two parts of Austria-Hungary in 1867 and renewed every ten years during half a century—at the cost of often painful negotiations.

The harmony which is thus achieved in economic policy among participating states, and the resulting solidarity of commercial interests, are obviously conducive to political collaboration. In point of fact, the idea of a customs union is seldom dissociated from this basic motive.

Between 1820 and 1850, all the states of the German Confederation with the exception of Austria joined the Zollverein, following Prussia's initiatives. The purpose here from the outset was political. The memorandum that Motz, Prussian Secretary of Commerce and promoter of the enterprise, presented in 1818 to Frederick William III expressly indicated this intention: the association of commercial interests would open the way to political cooperation; the customs union would be the prelude to German unity. But luckily Prussia's economic interests worked in the same direction, especially when the industrialization of the Rhineland began between 1830 and 1835; Prussian industry there was in need of outlets and naturally hoped to find them in Germany, whose markets had thus far been dominated by British industry. Economic interests, too, prompted the German states to agree to join the Zollverein despite their political reluctance: the small states of central Germany were at Prussia's mercy, for she had the power to paralyze their economic life; the south German states, which held out longer, capitulated in 1834 when they realized that the trade routes to the North Sea would be closed to them if they did not join; Hanover was able to continue its resistance until 1850 because it possessed access to that coast.

Thus the Zollverein was a weapon of Prussian policy, but for most of the German states the motive to join was economic. The immediate practical result of the Zollverein was to reduce political divergence among the member states, but this result was not lasting: the Zollverein did not prevent the rupture between the "average" German states and Prussia in 1866. In the end, Prussia achieved German political unity by force.

Political interests, again, far more than economic ones, explain the failure of attempts to form a customs union between France and Belgium in 1842-43, between Bulgaria and Serbia in 1904, and between Austria and Germany in 1932.[2]

The plan for a customs union between France and Belgium, envisaged by the government of Louis Philippe in 1836 and again in 1842, shows how

---

[2] We could also cite the plan for a Customs League proposed in September, 1847, by Pius IX to Charles Albert; the plan failed on account of the (political) opposition of the Duchy of Modena.

economic interests and political schemes may at times coincide, at times conflict. After the collapse of the Kingdom of the Netherlands in 1830, Belgian industry lost the Dutch market; new outlets for coal and textile goods were found chiefly in France. The French Government decided to take advantage of this by proposing a customs union: goods would circulate duty-free between the two states, and the two nations would maintain a uniform and common tariff vis-à-vis other states.

At first the Belgians evaded the proposals—not for economic reasons, but for political ones: the King of the Belgians and his advisers felt that a customs union would place Belgium at the mercy of France and would be a first step toward political incorporation. In 1840, however, the Belgian Government, faced with the threat of economic crisis, declared its readiness to negotiate at least the question of common tariffs. The negotiations were difficult, for it was the other aspect—free circulation of goods between the two countries—that most attracted the French. Guizot, however, did not let objections from French business interests interfere with his plans, for what he expected to gain from the agreement with Belgium were political, not economic, advantages. The negotiations therefore progressed. When the plan was finally abandoned in January, 1843, it was because it had run into a serious *political* roadblock: Great Britain, in full agreement with Prussia and Austria, made known to the King of the Belgians her determination to oppose the customs union, if necessary by war, because she believed it would be the prelude to political union.

The 1904 plan for a customs union between Bulgaria and Serbia was also closely related to the political situation. The two small states wished to free the peoples of Macedonia—including Bulgarians (the majority), Serbs, and Greeks—from Ottoman domination; thus they had common interests against the Turks. But, at the same time they were rivals, for, in the event that their common aim should triumph, along what lines would Macedonia be partitioned? (Significantly, in the Macedonian insurrections that so greatly disturbed European diplomats in 1903, bands of Serbian and Bulgarian *komitajis* had worked together, but all the while kept a close watch on each other.) In order to ensure the implementation of the reform plan that the Great Powers imposed in Macedonia in the wake of the revolt there—the Mürzteg program of October, 1903—the Belgrade and Sofia governments were eager to demonstrate their solidarity, realizing that they would have no way to defend their interests if they kept apart. At the same time, on the economic level, they hoped to deprive Austria-Hungary of the power to exert pressure on them.

This is the context in which we must view the plan for economic collaboration between Bulgaria and Serbia. By a treaty of April 29, 1904, the two states concluded a secret five-year defensive alliance; under Article 1 of the treaty, they undertook to eliminate all customs duties on each other's goods and to apply a uniform customs policy with a view to an eventual customs union. This article remained a dead letter, however, since the Serbian Government in fact dared not risk reprisals from Austria-Hungary, to which it sold most of its livestock exports. The customs union, in the minds of its sponsors, had clearly been nothing more than the counterpart to a political agreement.

In the scheme for an Austro-German customs union in 1932, economic circumstances merely provided the occasion for a basically political move. The government of the Austrian republic had at the time of its formation in 1919 expressed the desire for reunification with Germany. The treaties of Versailles and Saint Germain prohibited this unless the League of Nations agreed to it. But could the prohibition be maintained if Austria was not economically viable as a state? In 1922, the League of Nations granted Austria financial aid and thereby gave new life to the nation's economy. But the Austrian people, or at least the parliamentary majority authorized to express its interests or sentiments, continued to demand an *Anschluss*— a plan that the French Government, in 1928, categorically refused to countenance. Then came the depression, hitting central Europe during 1931, with violent repercussions in Austria and Germany, the most serious of which was the failure, in May, 1932, of the great Austrian bank the Kreditanstalt.

At this point, the German Government offered the Austrian Government a customs union. The argument was economic: Austrian iron and steel industries and Austrian agriculture on the one hand, and the German electrical and chemical industries on the other, would find wider markets within this union. Yet, on both sides, the basic purpose was political: the customs union would engender a solidarity of material interests that would strengthen the desire for political unification. At the same time, the customs union would stabilize the central European economy, which would be to the liking of the British banks that had made considerable investments in Germany since 1926; one could therefore expect that if the customs union were a success, the British Government would accept its political implications and the French Government, isolated, would have to accept them too.

The customs union was thus expressly conceived as a stage in the march toward political union. And it was this political perspective that troubled the French. "They must take us for fools," Edouard Herriot declared, "if they think we can forget that the Zollverein led to German unification." And it was the political possibilities that finally impelled the British Government to adopt a line of conduct quite different from what was expected: it feared that if it agreed to the Austro-German customs union, this might precipitate in Paris the fall of Aristide Briand. Here again, political considerations took precedence over economic interests.

But the issue of customs unions arose not only in bilateral relations; in 1930, Briand raised it in a European context. The question is, again, with what in mind?

The preamble to a French memorandum of May 17, 1930, on the "organization of a system of European federal union," emphasized the need to ensure "cohesion in the material and moral forces" of Europe and to create "bonds of solidarity" among the European members of the League of Nations with a view to preserving the peace. The program was both political and economic: political cooperation would be achieved by a "quite flexible" federative system that would fully respect state sovereignty; the primary purpose of economic cooperation would be to facilitate the circulation of goods, capital, and persons, and its "ideal goal" would be the establishment of a "common market." But the first and most urgent concern was political organization; economic organization could be taken up later. Why this priority? Because, the memorandum said, nations would not be prepared to make economic sacrifices in the common interest unless they had confidence in the political situation. Without a stable political organization, weaker nations would fear "the risks of political domination that might result from the industrial domination of more highly organized states."

The subordination of economic to political ends was thus expressly stated. In this respect, Briand's program differed greatly from the plan favored by the Pan-European movement and promoted by Count Richard Coudenhove-Kalergi, which stressed the "consolidation of European finance and industry" in order to combat American competition. Briand's thought appears essentially to have been to confirm the territorial arrangements laid down by the peace treaties of 1919–20. And that is why the German Government headed by Chancellor Brüning, although moderate and conciliatory, hoped from the outset that the plan as outlined in the French memorandum would fail. In point of fact, when the Commission of Enquiry for European Union—a body established by the Assembly of the League of Nations—met in January, 1931, it studied only economic questions (and vainly at that), regardless of the principles set out in the French memorandum.

II. CONDOMINIUMS

Economic interests were also sometimes associated in colonial matters. During the time when colonial empires were being established all over the world, the joint economic development of colonial territories in certain cases seemed a possible remedy for the antagonisms dividing the colonial powers. In each case, the initiative came from Germany, a colonialist latecomer eager to gain her place in the overseas markets of other states.

The only area where such economic association was actually carried out was central Africa. In May, 1884, Chancellor Bismarck—in order, he said, to protect German commercial interests—suggested that, "by a general entente," principles be established which could be applied to "all parts of the globe not yet legally occupied by a recognized power"; such was the case of the Congo River basin, where the International Association of the Congo, which despite its name was really an agency controlled by King Leopold of Belgium, had set up a number of trading posts (protected by forty military garrisons) but had not yet achieved recognition of this situation by the colonial states. The principles Bismarck referred to were these: to prevent "the establishment, to the advantage of a single power, of an exclusive administration at the mouth of the Congo River"; and to ensure freedom of trade in central Africa. Bismarck was seeking to create a precedent; he was thinking not only of central Africa but of "the future colonial regime."

The General Act of the Berlin Conference on Africa, dated February 26, 1885, met Bismarck's suggestion. A free-trade zone was to include the Congo basin and extend on the west to the Atlantic and on the east to the Indian ocean coasts. Imported goods of whatever origin would enter duty free or would be charged at equal rates; vessels of all nations would have access to the ports and the river network; Europeans settling in these territories would have equal rights as regards acquisition of land or exercise of professional activities. The Congo Free State created by the International Association of the Congo—that is, by King Leopold and the European states that controlled other parts of the area in question (France in equatorial Africa; Portugal in Cabinda and Mozambique; Great Britain on the Somali coast)—therefore might not, in theory, procure economic privileges for their nationals, regardless of their sovereign rights. This system remained in effect until 1914, although the Congo in 1908 passed under Belgian sovereignty. In 1919, a revision of the arrangement authorized the colonial powers to establish customs duties, but the tariffs had to respect the principle of equality stipulated in the original act (except as relating to Germany and the other states defeated in World War I).

One may ask whether Germany, during the period when she could avail herself of the system she had induced the other powers to establish (that is, between 1885 and 1914), derived from it the economic benefits she had hoped for. The answer is that she certainly did not. The administration of the Congo Free State and, later, of the Belgian Congo retained, without violating the provisions of the general act, the means to grant priority to Belgian companies in opening mines and in public-works contracts. In 1913, Belgium accounted for 66 per cent of the Belgian Congo's imports, whereas Great Britain did not account for more than 10 per cent, and Germany only 8 per cent.

Germany pursued a similar policy on another occasion, but under very different circumstances. By the Act of Algeciras, signed on April 7, 1906, commerce in Morocco was internationalized; the Moroccan Government would grant commercial equality to all powers signatory to the act (although the "special" political position of France and Spain was also recognized). When, in 1908, the German Government realized that its tactic of pin-pricking was not affecting the continued increase of French influence in Morocco, it decided not to obstruct that influence politically *provided* that France would agree to associate Germany in the economic advantages of her enterprise.

A Franco-German agreement of February 9, 1909, recognized the "special political claims" of France in Morocco and established the principle of international economic association there: the French and German governments agreed to "seek to associate their nationals in any business they might secure." (Mining and public-works concessions were at issue.) But the association was not really an equal one; one of the codicils to the agreement noted that "French interests in Morocco are more important than German interests" and that this fact must be taken into account in any joint ventures.

This priority conceded to French interests was immediately challenged: Great Britain protested against the Franco-German entente, the effect of which, she thought, was to turn Morocco into an economic "game preserve." French diplomats were prepared to take this protest seriously; the German Government, for its part, declared that if France wanted to allow Great Britain a share in the public-works contracts, she was free to do so, but such British participation must be deducted from the French share alone. The French Government agreed to this condition. What, then, became of the planned priority for French interests? Here was a first difficulty in interpreting the agreement. Others could be anticipated.

The conflict intensified over the staking out of interests in mines and railway construction. Was it possible, it was asked, to avert a public admission of this failure and to safeguard the potential of Franco-German collaboration by trying for success in another area? A plan for the joint economic development of German and French territories in equatorial Africa by a syndicate in part of the French Congo and the Cameroons[3] was rejected in March, 1911, by the French Chamber of Deputies, partly because it was felt that the German part of the syndicate would be better equipped and would therefore gain control, and partly because it was suspected (not without justification) that the project would further the success of dubious financial schemes. German diplomats concluded from this that "Frenchmen do not want to work with Germans anywhere."

[3] This was the N'goko Sangha affair.

III. SPHERES OF INFLUENCE

On several major occasions, rivalries among the great industrial states, each of which was trying to gain the upper hand in the competition for export markets or for raw-materials sources, were settled by compromise. Rival states judged it wiser not to push competition to the point of possible armed conflict, and so they negotiated for amicable delimitations of their respective "spheres of influence" in certain "new countries"—principally in the Ottoman Empire, Ethiopia, Persia, China, and the Portuguese colonial empire.

By agreements concluded in 1899, 1902, and 1903, Germany had secured considerable economic advantages in the Ottoman Empire—the concession to build a railroad that was to connect Ismid, on the Bosporus, with Baghdad, via Ankara, Adana, and Mosul, as well as for a number of branch lines to Syria, Armenia, the borders of Persia and the Persian Gulf—a rail network of more than 2,500 miles in all. Great Britain and France attempted at first to prevent the construction of this railway system by closing their financial markets to the bond issues intended to finance it; later, they realized they had succeeded only in delaying the venture, not in preventing it. Between 1911 and 1914, therefore, they attempted to negotiate with Germany in order to limit her expansion in the Ottoman Empire. Then Italy joined in. On the eve of World War I, these nations had divided up the Ottoman Empire's railroad concessions and the corollary spheres of economic influence.

A Franco-German agreement of February 15, 1914, provided that the French financial group which had built railroads at the turn of the century from Damascus to Beirut and Aleppo, might construct more lines into the interior from Tripoli to Homs, in central Syria, and continue east as far as the Euphrates River, at Deir ez Zor. (The regions of Aleppo and Alexandretta, however, were reserved for the Germans.) A French concern was also permitted to lay down some 800 miles of track in northern Anatolia—from Samsun to Sivas and Karput—which would connect up with the Arghun copper mines on the border of Armenia.[4]

An Anglo-German agreement concluded on June 15, 1914, provided that the German railroad that was to connect Baghdad with the other end of the Persian Gulf would not extend beyond Bassorah, and that the traffic beyond that terminus should proceed by river; an English shipping company would organize transports to Shatt al Arab. In Asia Minor, the British company that for more than twenty years had operated the railroad from Izmir (Smyrna) to Aidin was authorized to extend the line to Lake Beysehir, 250 miles southeast of Izmir—that is, to establish a route for the penetration of British economic influence in a large sector of Anatolia. These were the

---

[4] In 1900, the Ottoman Government had conceded these lines to a Russian group which had not used its rights and had yielded them to a French group in 1913.

two restrictions placed on the German company's sphere of activities. Finally, the agreement provided—two weeks before the opening of the European war—for Anglo-German collaboration in developing oil deposits known to exist in the Mosul region.

Did the European negotiators have only a partitioning into spheres of *economic* influence in mind? In actual fact, the basic purposes were political.

The conduct of the British Government in the whole Baghdad Railway affair was governed by the political consideration of ensuring the security of India. If the railroad constructed by the German company extended beyond Baghdad as far as the Persian Gulf, the Ottoman Government would be able to transport troops speedily into a region close to British-controlled territories. In order to get Germany to abandon this project, England thought it necessary to sacrifice her economic interests elsewhere, and she gave up the preponderant commercial position she had held for so long in Mesopotamia.

As for the *political* importance of the Syrian railroads, in the opinion of the French Government it by far exceeded their *economic* importance. The French considered it advisable to seek a détente with Germany; for this reason, they were prepared to waive their opposition to the Baghdad Railway, but they wanted compensation for standing down in the form of an assurance that northern Syria would be clear of any German enterprise. Financiers concerned only with profits wanted the negotiations to take a different turn, whereupon the government took over and restored the negotiations to their course.

Italy had been intimately concerned with the eastern Mediterranean since the war in Tripolitania had given her the opportunity to undertake naval operations in the Aegean Sea and to occupy the islands there. In this context of political ambitions, she too sought a sphere of influence in Asia Minor. The railroad concession she wanted in the region around the ports of Mersina and Adana was intended to open the door to this influence. Geographically, the land for the rail line lay between the zone reserved for the Baghdad Railway Company, around the Gulf of Alexandretta, and the region where the British company was extending its lines southeast from Izmir (Smyrna). An Anglo-Italian agreement concluded in March, 1914, set the boundaries beyond which the Italian railroads were not to go in the interior.

What we have, then, is a compromise made among the various projects planned by financiers sponsoring railroad construction on the eve of World War I. But in the mind of the governments, this partitioning of the railway networks was a prelude to political partition. Each government concerned believed that the sphere of influence formed around the railroad was a step in the direction of the ultimate partition of Asian Turkey. The "present spheres of influence," said the French diplomat Jules Cambon, would become the "future shares." The Austro-Hungarian ambassador to Constantinople considered that the construction of the Baghdad Railway would lead to "a form of German protectorate" over the really Turkish regions of the Ottoman Empire, while the "non-Turkish" provinces might be abandoned to the other European powers.

In Ethiopia—to take another example—where Italy had endeavored to establish a protectorate in 1891 and five years later had met with disaster, French influence had grown after the Imperial Company of Ethiopian Railroads, a French concern, had obtained the concession for a railroad linking Addis Ababa with Djibouti. In the autumn of 1903, the British and Italian governments considered ways of checking this French predominance, and they made plans for a railroad connecting Italian Eritrea with the Anglo-Egyptian Sudan via Ethiopian territory. The French Foreign Minister, Théophile Delcassé, having successfully negotiated the Anglo-French accords of April, 1904, was now prepared, on the basis of these agreements, to safeguard British interests in Ethiopia, and in May he therefore suggested that they discuss the matter. The British wanted Italy to be a party to the talks, a condition to which the French agreed because they needed Italy's good will in the matter of Morocco.

Political considerations thus underlay negotiations intended to mark out spheres of economic influence. When these negotiations resulted in an agreement between France, Great Britain, and Italy on December 13, 1906, defining those spheres, political considerations were still in evidence: while the agreement provided for the maintenance of the "integrity" of Ethiopian territory, Article 4 stipulated that if incidents occurred which disturbed the *status quo*, the three powers would concert to "safeguard their interests," each in its own sphere of influence. Here again, economic considerations were secondary, serving merely as a screen for the real, political aims.

In Persia, an Anglo-Russian agreement of August 31, 1907, also established spheres of economic influence: a Russian zone in the entire northern part of the territory as far as Isphahan; a British zone in the southeast, in Seistan; and a "neutral" zone including the coast of the Persian Gulf in addition to central Persia. Russia and Great Britain reserved the right to the concessions for railroads, roads, and telegraph lines in their respective zones, as well as the authority to establish banks. In the "neutral" zone, either state might obtain concessions without hindrance from the other. Finally, if the Persian Government could not pay the interest on loans it had contracted from Russian and British banks, Russia and Great Britain might assume control of customs revenues and apply them to repayment of the loans; in such cases, however, there had to be prior agreements respecting "the principles of the present agreement."

At first sight, the plan appeared as a compromise in which the stipulated geographical distribution would prevent clashes between rival economic interests. In fact, the governing considerations were political and strategical.

The British Government felt that it must reach an accommodation with Russia in order to safeguard the Franco-British entente; but it feared that the Russians, who had taken advantage of the Boer War to extend their economic and financial enterprises on Persian territory, might achieve *de facto* domination over the whole country and arrange to be awarded control of a port on the Persian Gulf as well as a concession for a railroad connecting that port with Teheran. According to the British Viceroy in India, Lord Curzon, Russia was using these economic means to achieve a political goal: a Russian naval base in that area, which would gravely threaten Indian security. The Russians must also be prevented, the English thought, from securing a foothold in Seistan, where they would be within easy reach of Afghanistan and Baluchistan, for the same reason.

When the British public voiced criticism of the agreement, particularly on the grounds of the poverty of the economic resources of Seistan, Lord Grey replied by stressing the area's strategic importance. The wish of the British Government, the Foreign Office repeated, was to protect vital British interests by safeguarding her strategic position on the Indian frontier.[5]

The Russian Government, for its part, when it agreed to divide Persia into spheres of influence, ran into the resistance of its general staff; the military commanders did not wish to abandon Seistan to British influence and wanted rather to preserve the means to "put pressure on India." The Russian Foreign Minister had great difficulty in convincing them that Russia, after her defeat in Manchuria, needed to take account of British interests.

In China, during the years 1896–1900, when European expansion threatened the very independence of the country, international attention was focused on the railroad and mining concessions, and the financiers who sought concessions there requested and received their governments' diplomatic support. But, while financial interests were uppermost, the ulterior political motive was clearly apparent, since the railroad enterprises were nearly always associated with the cession of "leaseholds."[6]

Great Britain, which among European states had had the greatest influence on the Chinese economy, was disturbed by these schemes but did not want to oppose them by force, hoping rather to limit the ambitions of

---

[5] Memorandum of January 28, 1908, in Great Britain, Foreign Office, *British Documents on the Origins of the War*, 1898–1914, Vol. VI (London, 1931), No. 549.

[6] In Russia's expansion into Manchuria, the leaseholds she secured were the high point of her railroad policy. France succeeded in having a territory leased to her in a region where she held no railroad concessions but hoped to obtain them. Only Great Britain obtained a leasehold in an area where she had no railroads and could not have one.

her rivals and "preserve intact" for British interests the Yangtze River basin, which was the center of China's commercial life and the principal point of attraction for British companies. She succeeded not only in obtaining from the Chinese Government a "declaration of nonalienation" of territories in the provinces adjoining the Yangtze, in February, 1898, and, six months later, major rail concessions around Nanking and Hankow, but also in negotiating with Russia and Germany the delimitation of respective spheres of influence.

An Anglo-German agreement of September 2, 1898, concluded between banking groups but under direct governmental supervision, gave Germany a monopoly on rail construction in Shantung and the lower valley of the Yellow River, while the British sphere of "railroad interests" was to include all the provinces on either bank of the Yangtze River; the agreement set Shengting as the boundary of the two zones. An Anglo-Russian agreement of April 28, 1899, confirming the British monopoly in the Yangtze zone, provided that Russian railroads in Manchuria might extend into the provinces of Jehol and Shansi but were not to go beyond the Great Wall and thus not to reach Peking.

Here, then, we see the spheres of influence taking form: France in Yunnan, Kwangsi, and Kwangtung; Great Britain in central China; Germany in Shantung and part of Cheli; Russia in the three northern provinces of Manchuria and in Jehol and Shansi—a partition of China that brought protests from the United States, advocating, in the name of the rights of American trade, the doctrine of the "open door" in September, 1899.

Was this just a matter of rivalry between economic interests? The policy developing in China seemed to be leading, wrote the German Foreign Minister, to the "slow but progressive collapse of the Chinese Empire." Spheres of economic influence would become spheres of political influence.

But this was not anticipated in the near future; it only appeared probable. On March 14, 1899, von Bülow wrote in a service note that, in his view, it was not in Germany's interests to press "now" for a partition of China, for it could still improve its commercial position there and strengthen its means of naval action; in other words, Germany could not then secure the share that, a little later, she would be able to gain. "It is important for us at this moment that the process of eventual partition of China be, for the time being, postponed."[7]

By the following year, these hopes for partition had suffered a rude blow: the Boxer Rebellion, a demonstration of China's resistance to this European penetration, showed the European powers what formidable obstacles they might encounter if they pursued the policy undertaken in

---

[7] *Die grosse Politik der europaïschen Kabinette, 1871–1914* (Berlin, 1924), Vol. XIV², note 3778.

1898–99. But this was hardly a reason for abandoning the original political aims of that policy.

Political objectives, once again, underlay the negotiations initiated between Great Britain and Germany in 1898 and again in 1913 concerning Portugal's colonial empire. The agreement initialled in October, 1913, provided that the two states would offer Portugal financial assistance to "develop" her colonies, that the interest on these loans would be guaranteed by customs revenues, and that, if such payments were not made, the customs administration would pass to the control of the creditors. It defined the Portuguese African territories which, in such an event, would come under the customs control of one or other of the two states; a secret annex expressly provided that these spheres of economic influence were eventually to become ones of political influence. In other words, Great Britain and Germany counted on a partition of the Portuguese colonies. But the agreement remained a dead letter on account of the war in Europe.

IV. INTERNATIONAL CARTELS

In modern times, and especially since World War I, international organizations have repeatedly expressed the hope that economic nationalism might lessen and the harsh clash of interests between producers of different nations averted. But various international economic conferences held prior to 1939 failed to establish effective programs to achieve these ends. Moreover, between the two world wars, producers were adversely affected by the new circumstances of economic life: higher protective tariffs and monetary manipulations dislocated the mechanisms of international trade and intensified trade rivalries; the rapid transmission of news and the widening scope of the news services had violent repercussions on the production lines, which were faced now with enormous demands for goods, now with a sudden falling off of orders.

In order to protect themselves against these fluctuations, reduce the losses caused by competition, and prevent overproduction, manufacturers decided to make international agreements among themselves that would restore the supply-and-demand balance; this in turn would make it possible to rationalize industry, avoid violent fluctuations, and maintain prices. But the project was difficult due to the disparity in production costs from one country to another, and it could also be obstructed by national laws and tariff manipulations. An agreement among producers, therefore, required the encouragement or at least the toleration of the governments concerned. For the most part, they supported such agreements, either because they believed them beneficial or because they yielded to the pressure of interest groups.

Such understandings had already appeared briefly during the late nineteenth century—in the salt industry in 1867, in iron and steel in 1870, in the potash industry in 1876—but they had never been durable. And in 1904 and 1911, attempts at international agreement in the iron-smelting industry collapsed. A list drawn up in 1932 by the League of Nations included 100 or more such bilateral or multilateral agreements; they were most numerous between 1924 and 1937 and achieved effective results in many important industrial sectors.

The first major agreement was taken in agriculture—specifically, the rubber plantations. To offset a critical drop in prices (in 1921, rubber was 20 per cent less than in 1913), the Malayan rubber producers' association suggested a 25-per-cent cut in production. Then the British Parliament, on the advice of a committee headed by Sir James Stevenson, passed a law in November, 1922, establishing a ceiling on exports of rubber produced in British territories. The Stevenson plan, its sponsors believed, could have formed the basis for an international agreement among rubber producers, but planters in the Netherlands East Indies blocked any such development. After six years with the experimental law, which resulted in a considerable price recovery, if not stabilization, the British Government rescinded it, and an international agreement was not concluded until 1934.

In the iron and steel industry, results were more speedily arrived at. Agreements between Austrian and Czechoslovak producers, dealing mainly with the division of the Balkan market between them, and between French and German producers in 1924, the principal purpose of which was to restrict production, laid the groundwork for the establishment of an international cartel—founded in September, 1926, reorganized in 1933, and renewed in 1938—apportioning steel export quotas. But it did not include the United States, Great Britain, or the Soviet Union and controlled only 26 per cent of the world production.

The strongest international cartels were formed in the nonferrous-metals industry: in aluminum, where a cartel included all European producers and covered not only distribution but also the fixing of prices; in copper, where a cartel controlled 98 per cent of all production in 1935; in tin, where a cartel was established in 1928 but not fully operative until 1937.

In chemicals, a potash cartel was organized in December, 1926, among Germans, French, and Poles; for dyestuffs in 1927; for nitrates in 1930—the latter so successful that eight years later it included all producers. An international coke cartel, including Germans, British, Belgians, and Poles, was formed in 1937. And several shipping agreements were concluded to fix freight charges and apportion traffic. Considerable success was achieved even in the processing industries, especially among manufacturers of electric light bulbs, cement, and linoleum.

While they lasted, these international cartels from an economic standpoint seem to have been more advantageous than disadvantageous. Sometimes, of course, when they controlled virtually all production of a particular commodity, they took advantage of their power to raise prices; but often, by regulating production and adapting it to consumption demands, they succeeded in heading off a crisis.

Did these cartels contribute to the maintenance of peace on the international *political* level? Critics of the capitalist system have differed in their answers. Lenin regarded international industrial agreements as accidental "peaceful transactions" which could not alter the essential hostility between capitalist interests; it was "absurd," he said, to think that such compromises could become a pledge of peace. Karl Kautsky believed that cartels, to the extent that they remedied economic anarchy, would constitute "a guarantee against war." But the experiences of the inter-war years furnish no weighty argument in favor of either of these views.

During the years of economic and political optimism before the depression, the creation of the first great international cartels, especially in iron, steel, and potash, raised high hopes among the public. The "political Locarno" would be rounded off by an "economic Locarno"; cartels would reduce rivalries among industrial producers, make higher tariffs unnecessary, and have the effect of making national frontiers more flexible; this would help to relax international tension. (Cooperation between German and French companies in steel and potassium facilitated the conclusion of a Franco-German commercial treaty in 1927, the object of which was to foster a spirit of collaboration that, "sooner or later," would lead to political *rapprochement.*[8])

But prudent observers were wary of such high hopes. International cartelization, they said, was feasible in some areas (raw materials and semi-finished products), where industry was already largely organized on nation-wide bases; it was not feasible—or was only barely feasible—in processing industries, where diversity was too great. And if cartels could be achieved in only a relatively restricted area, how could they eliminate the basic causes of economic unrest? Moreover, even were they to provide a partial solution to production problems, would they be able to resolve either financial questions or the crucial difficulties of transport and distribution? Finally, their purpose was at best to achieve a compromise among "national egos"; how could a truly international spirit be founded on so narrow a base? "The problem of European organization transcends the limited and fluctuating domain of agreements," wrote Daniel Serruys, director of commercial agreements in the French Department of Commerce in 1929.

Ten years later, observers had more substantial data, for "international cartelization" had in the meantime made considerable strides. Yet there was

[8] This was the theory developed by Erwin Respondek, *Wirtschaftliche Zusammerarbeit zwischen Deutschland und Frankreich* (Berlin, 1929).

no more certainty than before. Some continued to voice confidence in the cartels,[9] on the grounds that industrial agreements might serve as economic shock-absorbers and could help to resolve problems in the distribution of raw materials, but they did not support their theory by any example drawn from recent achievements. Others were doubtful: in the area of raw materials, they noted, cartels had imposed high prices and had thus aggravated the problems of the "have not" nations. Such agreements, they even maintained (with less plausibility), might accentuate inequalities in arms manufacture to the detriment of certain states; thus, the aluminum cartel, dominated by German producers, might obstruct the progress of that industry in the United States.

Actually, neither supporters nor opponents of cartelization attempted a critical analysis of any specific case. But it suffices to consider the record of international relations between 1924 and 1939 to realize that the cartels were incapable of doing something to alter the course of history.

V. CONCLUSION

The association of economic interests effected within a customs union is a case where the primacy of political purposes is clearly apparent. Of course, such an association can be achieved only in a particular economic context, and it is greatly facilitated when the governments joining the customs union realize they are serving the interests of the majority of producers and businesses in their countries. But the political objective is paramount at the outset; in every case we have examined, the customs union was regarded as a prelude to an association of political interests, or even to territorial unification.

Plans for economic condominiums were closely linked to political considerations; indeed, they were subordinate to them. In central Africa, for instance, Bismarck's action in 1884 was intended to outline the features of a "new colonial policy"; in Morocco, in 1909, the French Government agreed to compensate Germany with an association of economic interests in order to achieve her political purpose—the establishment of a French protectorate in Mexico.

The spheres of influence negotiated among European states in China, Asia Minor, and Ethiopia were motivated by considerations of prestige and power; they were intended, certainly, to conciliate rival economic claims and eliminate a potential source of political conflict, but also to pave the way for a division of political control. The creation of international industrial cartels, on the other hand, was clearly determined by the play of economic interests. Their promoters maintained, of course, that such endeavors would

---

[9] For instance, Roger Picard, "Les ententes des producteurs," Academy of International Law (The Hague), *Recueil des Cours*, LXVII, 1939, 539–624.

serve the cause of peace; but it is hard to determine whether this peaceful purpose was really basic to the undertaking, or whether it was invoked merely to gain the cartels public acceptance. Even where economic considerations alone prevailed at the outset, they could not long retain their pre-eminence. The International Chamber of Commerce, in a report drawn up in 1927, stressed that the success of these industrial agreements depended on peace among nations; here, economic action, far from shaping politics, was reduced to awaiting an impulse from politics.

5

INTERNATIONAL FINANCE

As the international movement of capital has increased since the middle of the nineteenth century, financial matters have taken a more and more prominent place in international relations. The causes for this increase have frequently been enumerated: the growth of individual savings and, consequently, of personal fortunes in several large countries, thanks to the development of industry and the rise in the standard of living; the emergence and development of the joint stock company; the ease of commercial relations, resulting from progress in overland and sea transport; a new approach to investment in distant lands, thanks to the development of the mass news media; finally, the increasing sophistication of banking organization, through which capital is channeled and investment oriented.

Our purpose here is to attempt an over-all survey of international capital investment during the past century, to examine the part governments have played in these financial matters, and, finally, to note the effect of financial considerations on political relations.

I. THE INTERNATIONAL FLOW OF CAPITAL INVESTMENT

The first form of capital investment in foreign countries seems to have been intergovernmental loans. But the practice whereby banks with an international sphere of operations extended credits to governments had become widespread by the sixteenth century. This was a major aspect of the activities of Jacob Fugger, the great entrepreneur of Augsburg. Dutch banks in the seventeenth century and English banks in the eighteenth often engaged in this kind of business, and it was also current in the Napoleonic era. In the early nineteenth century, when Great Britain began to develop a policy of large-scale foreign capital investment, most of her operations consisted in opening lines of credit to foreign governments that would enable them to cover deficits or pay for special expenditures.

New forms of international credit emerged between 1850 and 1870 along with the general economic expansion of the time and the development of banking. In addition to direct loans from one state to another, and credit facilities granted by a bank in one country to the government of another, the practice developed of floating foreign bonds to which, through banks, private investors might subscribe. In most of the international financial operations of that period, however, the *state* initiated the transaction, and a state was nearly always one of the parties involved.

Following the economic and financial crisis of 1873, a great wave of industry and trade developed, not only in Europe, but also in the United States. As a result, the international movement of capital took on vast proportions, all currencies (most of them backed by gold) being freely negotiable. Mainly at the banks' initiative, individual investors bought shares in companies operating abroad. Such investments extended over most of the globe.

The motive for these operations was sometimes economic, sometimes purely financial. If the first, the object was to create means of production or transport—for instance, by furnishing mining equipment, building a railroad, or organizing some agricultural project. If the second (following the decline in the great railroad investments that had marked the period 1850–70), private investors and banks sought, in foreign investments, to earn larger profits than they could expect from investments at home, and they created companies that would profitably put these capital investments to work.

This kind of foreign investment was by far the most important form of international capital flow between 1870 and 1914. The search for opportunities to invest abroad was, for example, a prime concern of the great French bank Crédit Lyonnais as far back as 1878–80. "We are crushed under the weight of money," one bank director said. Contracts were continually negotiated and concluded between businessmen who were acting at some personal risk in the sole concern of making a profit. Their operations were at first conducted in the Middle East, especially in Egypt and the Ottoman Empire, and in Latin America. In the first decades, "financial" investments predominated; subsequently, during the last years of the nineteenth century, "industrial" investments—the development of mines and construction of railroads—eclipsed all others.

On the eve of World War I, British, French, and German investments outside Europe were assessed at a minimum of $25 billion, possibly as much as $32 billion. These investments were most considerable in Latin America. In Argentina, five-sixths of the railroad system had been conceded to British companies; in Uruguay and Paraguay, too, the principal lines belonged to British companies. Chile was the only state that, while calling on foreign technicians to construct the railroads, managed to keep most of the rail lines under her direct ownership and control. The exploitation of mineral resources in the mountainous countries of western Latin America was in the hands of British, German, French, and Swiss companies. And in Venezuela, in 1912, a subsidiary of Royal Dutch–Shell began to drill for oil.

In China, two-thirds of the railroad system belonged to European companies by 1911; European capital and technicians created the first major mines and most of the modern industrial plants.

In the Ottoman Empire, all the companies operating the railroads and most of those engaged in mining and what few industries there were, were European—in their capital, their management, and their workers.

The United States during this period, although her economic power had grown rapidly since the end of the Reconstruction, played a minor part in this foreign capital investment. She exported no capital to Europe, some to Canada, Mexico, and Central America, and some to China (where American participation did not exceed 12 per cent of total foreign investments) and South America (10 per cent of the total). The over-all figure for American investment abroad was much lower than that of European investment in the United States.

The outbreak of World War I produced a radical change in this pattern in the international movement of capital. The European belligerents, most of whose industry was mobilized for war, could no longer maintain their exports—and this at the very moment when they were obliged to increase imports of raw materials, foodstuffs, and matériel. To cover this balance-of-trade deficit with the United States and Latin America at least partially, and to provide some counterpart to the credits extended by American banks to finance their purchases, Great Britain and France had to give up a considerable part of their foreign holdings. Germany, through the blockade, was deprived of her trade with non-European countries, but she retained her ties with some of the European neutrals and, to pay for imports, used her holdings in Switzerland, the Netherlands, and Scandinavia. As for the United States, having granted extensive credits to Great Britain and France as long as she was neutral, she loaned the Allies close to $10 billion when she entered the war in April, 1917. Whereas in 1914 the indebtedness of Americans to nationals of other countries exceeded that of the latter to Americans by some $3.5 billion, the situation was now reversed and foreign indebtedness exceeded American by some $12.5 billion. And, of course, the war had profoundly affected the international investments made before 1914: Russian holdings were lost *in toto*; investments in Austria-Hungary and the Ottoman Empire were almost completely lost. These losses hurt British, and especially French, capital, the latter accounting for a large part of Russia's foreign debt and of the Ottoman national debt. By 1919, France's foreign portfolio was reduced to half of its 1913 total, Great Britain's by more than a third.

Between 1919 and 1929, the international movement of capital revived, operating in accordance with the now fashionable principles of economic liberalism. (Exchange controls were an exception.) But the striking new factor was the decline of Europe.

Faced with the financial burden of replenishing her stocks of raw materials, reviving her industries, and paying reparations, Germany was no longer in a position to export capital.

France was confronted with the task of restoring the devastated regions of her land, and, apart from a foreign bond issue floated on the Paris market in 1923, French foreign investment was not renewed before 1926.

Although Great Britain's industrial plant had sustained little direct damage during the war, the nation had to ₋pend considerable amounts to rebuild her merchant marine, severely hurt by the submarine war. Nevertheless, when hostilities ended, British foreign capital investment began again quite rapidly, thanks to the effort to restore parity to the pound sterling and dollar. Between 1925 and 1931, foreign bonds accounted for more than 40 per cent of all issues, but the financial crisis of 1931 and the devaluation of the pound marked the end of this recovery. Britain never regained anything like the position she had held prior to 1914.

Japan, after making considerable profits from the war, went through so widespread an economic crisis in 1919 and then, even more, in 1920–21, that she could not think of continuing foreign investments.

Among the major industrial states, only the United States emerged from the conflict economically and financially stronger. American capitalists had the necessary means to help in the reconstruction of Europe. And it was in their interest to employ them to that end, because if Europe did not recover her purchasing power, American producers would be the first to suffer. In 1914, Europe had been able to pay easily for raw materials and foodstuffs from America with the interest of her capital investments in the United States; how could she pay for them now?

American banks therefore embarked on a policy of extending credits abroad for the use either of industrial or construction companies or of public groups. Such investments were at first directed to Italy and Great Britain, but, between 1925 and 1929, the major beneficiary was Germany. Outside Europe, American investors, apart from a few in China, turned to Latin America. In the ten years between 1919 and 1929, total American investments abroad rose from almost $7 billion to more than $17 billion.

But the great economic catastrophe that began on Wall Street in October, 1929, virtually cut off this flow of investments and at the same time led many nations to establish foreign exchange controls. The standstill continued for ten years, far beyond the depression itself; American investors who had suffered heavy losses remained on their guard even after the economic situation had improved. No foreign bond issues were floated on the U.S. market, and few private credit lines were opened. In Europe, the principal movement of capital was from France to Poland.

This was the period in which modes of *private* investment became more varied and more flexible, and new financial techniques made possible the distinctions between different forms of short-term and long-term investments.[1] The first category included credits granted by individuals for one year at the most, for the settlement of commercial debts; credits granted under the same terms by banks; and deposits by individuals in bank accounts opened abroad. The second included portfolio investments—that is, stocks in commercial and industrial companies—and direct investments such as the purchase of lands, plantations, or forests; development of mines; or the establishment of commercial, industrial, or banking enterprises abroad. Sometimes, when the sole object was profit, interest rates were fixed contractually; sometimes, when the object was to organize or control specific undertakings, investors were repaid in percentages of the companies' profits.

World War II opened a new era, in which financial questions—strictly subordinated to national financial policies, since the exchange control system was in operation—came to re-occupy an important place in international relations. Here again, the United States took the initiative; the crucial factor was a decision made in Washington ten months before the United States entered the war.

The Lend Lease bill enacted into law by Congress on March 11, 1941, authorized the President to make available to all countries whose defense, in his judgment, should be assured in the interests of the United States, weapons, munitions, raw materials, foodstuffs, "or other commodity or article for defense" within the limits of the credits voted by Congress. This could be done by sale, transfer, lease, exchange, or any other means. The terms under which foreign governments received such aid were to be laid down by the President; the United States might request compensation or be content with "any other direct or indirect benefit." The terms of the Lend Lease Act were thus sufficiently vague to permit aid to be granted without assurance of reimbursement, since to win the struggle against Germany would in general be a "benefit" to the United States.

Under the Lend Lease system, $7 billion in credit was made available to countries fighting Germany in the first six months. In five years, this figure had reached $48 billion. Subtracting the facilities supplied by the European Allies to American troops, the financial participation of the United States in the common struggle amounted to some $40 billion.

As soon as hostilities ended, when the most urgent problem was economic reconstruction, nations that wished to buy raw materials and foodstuffs from the United States had to face the problem of their shortage of dollars. In 1946–47, Europe's "dollar deficit" was some $14.5 billion, only a quarter of which could be met by disposing of holdings or by shipments of bullion.

---

[1] See Cleona Lewis, *The United States and Foreign Investment Problems* (Washington, 1948).

The United States solved the problem by granting credits or by outright gifts.

In its first stage, American aid to Europe consisted of goods paid for with government funds voted by Congress and distributed through government agencies, the Import-Export Bank and the Reconstruction Finance Corporation. Great Britain, Greece, and Turkey were among the earliest beneficiaries.

In the second stage, which began on June 5, 1948, with the Marshall Plan, this aid was expanded and extended to sixteen nations. Some 70–80 per cent of this new American aid were goods offered as gifts;[2] the recipient government sold the goods and used the proceeds to stabilize their currencies, balance their budgets, and modernize their industrial or transport facilities— activities supervised by the Marshall Plan administration. In return, the recipient countries undertook to provide the United States with certain products in short supply, or with minerals of strategic value. The program provided that over a period of four years, $22.4 billion in goods would be shipped to the recipient states, of which amount the United States would underwrite, in all, $19.3 billion.

The third stage, beginning in 1949, was that of aid to underdeveloped countries. At this point, the consequences of the disparities in standards of living had begun to come to public attention. The disparities in economic development had tended to increase with the constant technological progress of more highly developed societies; capitalist nations, under a system of economic liberalism, had exploited or developed resources where and when they were most abundant, and they had therefore neglected less well endowed countries.

Archaic societies became acutely aware of these disparities as a result of the "contagion of needs" produced by the widespread dissemination of news through radio and motion pictures. Closer and more frequent contact with the outside world gave the peoples of the underdeveloped countries, two-thirds of the world's population, a greater consciousness of their poverty and moved them to demand their "right to life"—not only in order to improve the material conditions of their existence, but also to escape their dependency on more privileged nations.

In order to take the sting out of this protest, which threatened to become a source of serious conflict in international affairs, and also to improve the general conditions of economic life, it was necessary to make an intensified effort to aid these peoples—teaching them to use more up-to-date farming methods, to exploit their mineral resources, to create industries, and to carry out the necessary measures of social adaptation. This assistance, economists

---

[2] These were not only American goods, for the Marshall Plan administrators sometimes bought grain and meat from Argentina, nitrates from Chile, and oil from Venezuela for shipment to Europe.

argued, had to be not only technical but also financial: credit should be extended where it was needed for the purchase of capital goods, and there should be private foreign investment in local undertakings. The over-all plan thus presupposed an immense transfer of capital in execution of a long-term program. But, at the outset, what incentive could there be for private concerns to cooperate, given the evident risks and the prospects of delay in the return of profits? The capital had to come from public or semi-public funds.

The historical record so far shows only slight signs of how successful this new mode of international finance has been. But it is clear that it is hampered by economic and political factors.

Let us take the economic factors first. The international flow of private capital is subject to sudden variations, connected with circumstances in either the exporting state (capital is plentiful only in time of prosperity) or the recipient (investors shun a country whose economics do not permit them to reap the expected returns and where debtors are liable to default). Inter-governmental loans are less susceptible to these problems; the nation that applies for the loan often finds itself in economic difficulties it cannot solve without external aid, and if the creditor state's finances are sound, it will clearly find the necessary financial means more easily, and even if its finances are not in good shape, it will often manage to collect the necessary means if it believes that the business can offer a profitable return.

The political factors concern primarily the governmental attitudes in the nation that receives or distributes investments. Once a government has contracted a loan, does it make the necessary effort to pay interest? Does it give private investors a free hand, or does it establish a foreign exchange control that restricts the circulation of capital and prevents foreign companies established in the country from transferring their profits to their own country? Here, the governmental role, which is always considerable in the orientation of investment, becomes preponderant.

This is the role we must determine here. How does "business policy" affect diplomacy? The question is all the more important in that state intervention aggravates the consequences of competition between financial interests and can endanger world peace.

II. THE ROLE OF THE STATE

A nation's request for financial aid from abroad to meet its extraordinary expenses (national capital equipment, arms) or even its ordinary expenses may take one of three forms: loans granted by banks; bonds floated on foreign financial markets and issued through banks; and lines of credit opened to other states. In the last, the matter is of course handled in diplomatic negotiations, but in the other two as well, the state whose investors or banks are called on for a loan usually must intervene.

Let us consider how such governmental intervention has operated in the major capital-exporting states.

In the first place, the government must find out whether the foreign investments in question are in the national interest. Should investors buy foreign bonds and thereby run financial risks the magnitude of which they are not in a position to assess correctly, or should they be on their guard? Should banks that try to attract such capital so as to earn commissions be permitted to represent it in a favorable light on false premises? From an economic and financial point of view, is it advisable that available capital be exported when private business and the state itself need the resources, and when it would help to increase the productivity, and therefore the economic or military potential, of a competitor, rival, or possible enemy?

On the other hand, should not the government take into account the possible advantages of foreign investments for the general interests of the country? They make it possible to increase production in "new countries" of needed raw materials or foodstuffs, and they enable the capital-exporting state to finance imports of raw materials without creating or increasing a balance-of-payments deficit. They also create a reserve of means of payment that can be particularly useful in time of war (as France found during 1870–71). Finally, they can open the door to political influence: investment in private business abroad heightens the prestige of the creditor country and may be an opportunity for increased diplomatic pressure protecting the investors' interests;[3] extension of loans enables the creditor to lay down terms or to demand some return, and, if the borrower is weak, reimbursement may give rise to difficulties which give the creditor the chance to "slip a noose around his neck."

Governments have therefore been justified in regarding it as essential not only to intervene in the negotiation of foreign government loans on their markets—that was obvious—but also to exercise some measure of control over the foreign investments of their nationals.

The question nevertheless arises whether such decisions were motivated *only* by the desire to promote the national interest, and whether the public authorities took them *spontaneously*.

When a government authorizes a foreign loan, or encourages, albeit only tacitly, the export of capital, it cannot fail to take the condition of the financial market into account. Private interests therefore have a chance to express their views on the situation; indeed, they often do not wait to be asked. They frequently represent these views as synonymous with the general interests of the country, and, while they may well take the national interest into account, it is only natural that they should mainly be guided by the prospect of profits. Floating of the foreign bond issue will enable the banks

---

[3] The political consequences of protecting investments are discussed below, in Part III of this chapter, pp. 125-37.

to earn commissions; capital invested abroad will earn higher interest than at home.

The government is thus subject to the influence and even direct pressure of private interests. When its decision corresponds to what the financiers wanted, it may be concluded that the pressure was effective and that financial interests directed the action of the public authorities. The inference is not necessarily correct, for the government may simply have regarded this opinion as conforming to the national interests, but the coincidence establishes a strong presumption in favor of that inference.

In practice, how have the governments of creditor countries controlled foreign investments, and what results have they achieved? These questions are of great moment for the history of international relations. Detailed examination is often difficult because the public records rarely preserve written traces of the contacts between "finance" and government; banking records are usually closed to researchers; and other sources of information— press reports and personal testimonies—are of dubious value. Still, it is possible, thanks to some valuable studies,[4] to attempt an answer.

A. In Great Britain

Prior to 1914, Great Britain was the largest single exporter of capital in the world. She had been easily the first country to practice a broad policy of foreign investment, and, by 1875, such investments, according to the most reliable estimates, had reached £1.2 billion. Between 1875 and 1914, she maintained her pre-eminence in this field: in 1914, some £4 billion were invested outside the British Isles.

Great Britain owed this superiority to resources accumulated as a result of her industrial supremacy, challenged only in the last years of the nineteenth century, and merchant fleet, which had made possible the development of the warehousing business; to a monetary stability such that merchants all over the world regarded Bank of England notes as the equivalent of gold, and foreign capital was drawn to the City; and, finally, to the flexibility and soundness of a banking system of unrivaled organizational excellence and to some fifty-odd establishments specializing in foreign investments.

During this period, British capital was poured into private ventures (mines, industries, plantations, and especially railroads) far more than into foreign government or Dominion bonds. Only a very small proportion of this capital, about 6 per cent,[5] was invested in Europe. The centers of

---

[4] In particular, those of the American historian Herbert Feis. See *Europe, the World's Banker* (New York, 1930) and *The Investment of American Capital Abroad* (New York, 1925).

[5] This is the figure given by Leland Jenks, *The Migration of British Capital to 1875* (New York and London, 1927).

attraction were the United States, Latin America, Egypt, and, in the Empire, Canada, South Africa, and India.

Throughout this era of economic triumph, the British Government acted on the principles of economic liberalism that were at the foundation of all British economic life and avoided directly intervening in banking affairs so as to prevent or recommend a particular investment (except in cases involving major political interests). But it had no scruple in tendering semi-official advice, through the agency of the Bank of England or through personal contacts among Cabinet ministers and business leaders in Parliament. This advice remained secret, taking the form of "confidential communications," concerning which, as Lord Lansdowne pointed out when he was Foreign Secretary, the governmental authorities did not have to give account to Parliament.

The government dealt in the same spirit with requests from financial groups who wanted diplomatic support in their relations with foreign governments. As a rule, declared Sir Edward Grey to the House of Commons on July 10, 1914, the government preferred to rely on the "good will" of foreign governments, which must remain free to grant or refuse concessions; in practice, however, since England wished to persuade these governments that it was in their interest to approach British companies, the Foreign Office often acceded to the requests.

As we have said, the study of the connection between foreign investment and political action is particularly difficult, since there are rarely any traces of the proffered "advice," and since the requests by financial groups did not always give rise to correspondence. Yet there is no doubt that government intervention was frequent and effective.

In Egypt, between 1876 and 1881, all questions relating to the control of the Egyptian debt were primarily government business within the framework of the financial condominium of France and Britain. In South Africa, between 1890 and 1899, the British Government supported British financial groups in their constant conflict with the governments of the Boer Republics. In Turkey, too, British diplomats frequently backed British financial groups soliciting mining concessions. And it firmly "recommended" that British banks not participate in the construction of the Baghdad Railway when its German promoters wanted to push the line to the Persian Gulf—that is, to a zone where British strategic interests would be threatened.[6] And England did not hesitate to resort to a naval demonstration in the summer of 1898 to back up British requests for railway concessions in China, so that British economic and political interests there would not be challenged.[7]

In 1901, when the Japanese Government sought a substantial foreign loan, it could not obtain access to the British financial market, but as soon

---

[6] See above, Chapter Three, p. 72, and Chapter Four, p. 92.

[7] See above, Chapter Four, p. 96.

as the Anglo-Japanese alliance was concluded in January, 1902, access was open. And in Persia, after the Anglo-Russian Convention of August 31, 1907, the British Government kept a close watch on the activities of British banks so that they would not interfere with its policy of conciliating Russian interests. The Seligman bank, for instance, on the point of granting the Persian Government a loan to buy a railroad operated by Russians, was "advised" to abandon the project and did not attempt to disregard this advice.

B. In France

Large private fortunes were less common in France than in Great Britain, and France took longer to become a major international capital market. Under the Second Empire and at the beginning of the Third Republic, some credit institutions were already active in building railroads in Spain, Italy, Austria-Hungary, Switzerland, and Russia,[8] but it was not until after 1895, and thanks to the sizable number of small private investors then in the market, that there was any rapid increase in the volume of French foreign investment. Even so, annual foreign investments in the years before World War I was less than one-third the amount of British investments.

The flow of capital from France was directed mainly to other European nations—to Russia, Spain, Portugal, Austria-Hungary, the Balkans, Italy, and Turkey. Outside Europe, more was invested in Latin America than in the French colonial empire. And, in contrast to British investors, the French were drawn mostly to foreign government bond issues. It was only after 1900 that French investments in foreign industrial securities (Russian iron and steel, Spanish and South African mines, Chinese railroads) became considerable.

What position did the government take? To begin with, the French Government's means of action were far superior to the British Government's. Quotation of foreign bonds on the Paris Exchange was authorized in 1823 by royal ordinance; a letter of November 12, 1825, from the Minister of Finance laid down principles on the trading of foreign bonds and securities that were later spelled out in laws and regulations; the admission of foreign bonds to the listing of the Paris Exchange was subject to governmental authorization. This last regulation was legally applicable to transactions effected on the "official" market—operated by official stockbrokers; in practice, it also applied to transactions on the free market, although this gave rise to some dispute. The implementation of the regulation was at first somewhat loose but stricter under the Second Empire. Between 1871 and 1914, it was defined in several documents: a letter of August 12, 1873, from

---

[8] See R. E. Cameron, *France and the Economic Development of Europe, 1800–1914* (Princeton, N.J., 1961).

the Minister of Finance asserting his right to determine the financial or political reasons that might stand in the way of floating foreign securities on the French market; a decree of February 6, 1880, Article 5 of which stipulated, "The Minister of Finance may at any time prohibit the negotiation of a foreign security in France"; and laws of 1907 and 1912. Control thus became increasingly stricter especially between 1909 and 1913, when the government insisted on the need to reserve available capital for national needs.

Was public opinion prompting them to take this line? No, since the public was divided on this issue. Socialists were generally hostile to foreign investments, since they thought the export of capital would mean a higher interest rate and in turn an increase in the arrears on domestic loans, thus increasing pressure on the budget. And textile manufacturers feared that exported capital would enable other countries to set up manufacturing plants that would soon enable them to dispense with imports. But the chambers of commerce and some industrial producers, especially those in iron and steel who needed orders for machines, railroad equipment, or armaments, were generally favorable to foreign investment, provided that the Minister of Finance obtained a guarantee from the borrowers that the proceeds of the loan or of the opening of lines of credit would be used to pay for orders placed with French industry.

The considerable resources available to the Paris financial market enabled the government to exert diplomatic pressure on the foreign states concerned in these transactions.

The most significant case was that of Russia. Russia was the chief borrower on the international financial market, for she needed capital for industrial undertakings (the industrialization of the Donets basin began in 1880) and, above all, to cover the chronic deficit in her budget. (Her tax revenues were not sufficient to meet the expenditures on capital equipment and the maintenance of the armed forces.) Government bonds held by far the most important place in Russia's appeal to foreign financial markets, mainly the French market. In 1914, 80 per cent of the Russian public debt subscribed by foreigners was in French hands, and 35 per cent of the foreign investment in Russian industry originated in France.

The floating of Russian government bonds on the French market between December, 1888, and December, 1913, was prepared for by diplomatic negotiation. France favored the bond issue because she regarded it as helpful to the negotiation of an alliance she wanted to conclude with Russia. She believed, not unreasonably, that, once such negotiations had proved successful, financial aid would be a useful condition for the vitality of the alliance. In many cases, moreover—in 1900 and 1901, 1904 and 1913—the loans were intended expressly to help meet either expenditures of the army or the costs of strategic railway construction—as provided in the general staff agreements implementing the Franco-Russian military convention.

The French Government did not confine itself to admitting Russian bonds to the market; on occasion it also gave advice to the Russian Embassy in Paris on how to distribute the money for propaganda to ensure the success of the bond issues. The major French newspapers, prompted by subsidies received from the embassy's financial agent, Arthur Raffalovich, were virtually unanimous in acclaiming the Russian bonds.[9]

Nevertheless, three times—in 1897, 1901, and January, 1905—the Ministry of Finance sent a warning to the Ministry of Foreign Affairs concerning an "excessive" volume of Russian bonds, maintaining that Russia would be unable to meet its obligations. But the French Government allowed the paradoxical situation to continue, probably because it considered it necessary as a foreign-policy move. In other words, the security afforded, or apparently afforded, by the Russian military alliance appeared well worth the risks entailed, in this case, by private investment.

Throughout the history of the Franco-Russian alliance, this link between Russian financial need and French political considerations was a tenuous one, and never more so than between January and April, 1906, when France, having been asked for a large loan (1.2 billion gold francs), requested in return that Russian support her at the Conference of Algeciras.[10]

There were many other instances of such interaction between French financial and political policy. In 1902, when Delcassé, the Foreign Minister, was trying to arrange an accommodation with Italy and negotiating a secret agreement restricting the scope of the Triple Alliance, he offered the Italian Government access to the French financial market. In 1903, when the German Government had just obtained the Baghdad Railway concession and was anxious to float bonds on the Paris market to finance its construction, some French financial groups, and the French Minister of Finance, Rouvier, welcoming this prospect eagerly, considered establishing some form of collaboration between French and German capital. But Delcassé opposed it because the construction of the railroad threatened Russia's political interests, and the Cabinet supported him.

At the same time, he strongly urged the banking group formed in connection with the Banque de Paris et du Pays-Bas to grant an immediate loan of 7.5 million gold francs to the Sultan of Morocco, whose authority was threatened by an uprising in the Taza region of his Empire. A year later,

---

[9] With the exception of the Socialist and some Radical publications, which opposed the Russian bonds because they did not want French capital bolstering the finances of an autocratic regime. In the early part of 1906, this position was taken by men like Jean Jaurès, Clemenceau, and Anatole France.

[10] See Pierre Renouvin, "Finance et politique; l'emprunt russe d'avril 1906 en France," *Mélanges Werner Näf (Etudes suisses d'histoire générale*, Vol. 18/19, 1961), pp. 507–16.

he arranged for a much larger loan (62 million gold francs) for Morocco, with maritime customs receipts as security.

In 1907, two years after the Treaty of Portsmouth that registered Russia's defeat in Manchuria, France wanted to strengthen the peace in the Far East so that Russia could give greater attention to European politics. She advised the Russian Government to seek a *détente* with Japan and made a similar diplomatic approach in Tokyo, accompanied by a financial offer: if Japan would come to an agreement, or at least a *modus vivendi*, with Russia, she would be permitted to borrow at 5 per cent on the Paris exchange, which would enable her to pay off loans she had contracted at considerably higher interest rates in Britain during the Russo-Japanese war. And a year earlier, when Austria-Hungary, concerned about the development of Serbian nationalism and the tendencies voiced by Nicholas Pashitch, attempted to bring Serbia into line by means of a tariff war that seriously affected Serbia's entire economy and therefore her revenues,[11] the French market was open to Serbian bonds—financial aid that encouraged Belgrade's resistance to Vienna.

At the end of 1911, some French diplomats hoped, in fact, to disrupt the Austro-German alliance itself. The French Ambassador to Vienna, Crozier, outlined a plan of action. The crux of this plan was to offer the Austro-Hungarian Government substantial credits—1 billion gold francs, a sum equal to that which the French market had furnished Russia in 1906 to help her overcome the crisis that defeat in Manchuria and the revolutionary movements of 1905 had precipitated. These credits were to enable the Austro-Hungarian administrations to carry out a program of large-scale public works and industrial growth. The quid pro quo would be political: Austria-Hungary would undertake not to be associated with any aggressive German policy against France, and to exert her influence in favor of peace in case of a threat of conflict between France and Germany. Indeed, if a Franco-German war broke out, might she not preserve a "temporary neutrality" that would give Russia time to complete military preparations?

In truth, the only certain factor in this plan, which aroused the anxieties of the Russian Government, was Austria-Hungary's desire for a loan. But it soon became apparent that she had no intention of giving political guarantees in return. Raymond Poincaré, the French Prime Minister, therefore refused to consider the plan, in which "imagination," in his view, played too large a part.

Lastly, in 1913–14, the sale of Balkan bonds on the Paris Exchange was central to the French Government's diplomacy in Greece, where it sought to strengthen Prime Minister Venizelos against the pro-German inclinations of King Constantine; in Bulgaria, where it wished to forestall a German ban offer in the hope of subsequently influencing the policy of King Ferdinand; and

---

[11] See above, Chapter Three, p. 77.

in Turkey, where it insisted that the Ottoman Government, in return, accept the decision of the Great Powers concerning the future of the Aegean islands.

In the conduct of French foreign policy during this period, one of the rare occasions when the negotiation of a political agreement or accommodation was not backed by a bond issue on the Paris market was the Franco-British Entente Cordiale of 1904.[12] Financial questions did not arise during the negotiations except under one particular head—the worries of French subscribers to the Egyptian national debt that Great Britain might acquire undue freedom of action in the area. The French Government overruled these objections; it quite clearly regarded such financial concerns as secondary to the direction of its foreign policy as a whole.

Franco-German relations between 1871 and 1914 reveal another aspect of the use of the "financial arm" of foreign policy. The French market remained firmly closed to German bonds or issues of securities—a direct consequence of political differences between the two countries. In contrast, French capital did not scoff at the potential profits to be gained in the large-scale development of German industry after about 1893. In 1896–97, the financial attaché at the French embassy in Berlin assessed private French investments in Germany at a minimum of 500 million gold francs. (At this time, when there were no restrictions on the movement of capital, funds could be transferred at will.) But, so long as the Treaty of Frankfurt remained in effect, the French Government would not so much as consider permitting the German Government to float bonds on the Paris Bourse. Even when relations between the two countries moved toward an accommodation (1879–84; 1895–98; 1907; 1909–10), there was no question of waiving this principle. And the ban on German industrial securities[13] was similarly motivated: French resources were not to help strengthen the productive capacities of a probable adversary. (In 1903, as we have seen, the French Minister of Finance was prepared to make an exception in the case of the German Baghdad Railway Company, which had secured the participation of French investors, but the plan was frustrated by the Foreign Minister.) The only time this policy was challenged by Frenchmen was in 1907, when various financial journals asked whether it would not be possible to allow German industrial securities to be traded in Paris. Such appeals were in vain; the government was not inclined to give up its financial weapon.

After 1919, in very different circumstances, since the French market had lost most of its global importance, the connection between finance and politics was less close. Nations more or less firmly attached to the French diplomatic system—Poland, Romania, Yugoslavia, Czechoslovakia—were also those in which French investment (for the most part private) was

---

[12] See Pierre Renouvin, "Finance et politique; à propos de l'Entente Cordiale franco-anglaise," in *Hommage à Lucien Febvre* (Paris, 1954).

[13] Which does not seem to have been complete, although exceptions to it were rare.

considerable; it was natural that French investors should turn by preference toward "friendly" states. Government loans were extensive only in the case of Poland (in 1927 and 1931) and Romania. French diplomacy no longer had a financial weapon available with a range of action as effective as in the past.

C. IN GERMANY

In Germany before 1914, industry had reservations about foreign investments because they deflected resources needed for Germany's productive expansion; the banks' first duty, it was argued, was to provide for the needs of the domestic market. The government favored foreign investment, however, on the grounds that it could help to extend the economic and political influence of the Reich.

Control over the issue of foreign securities was exercised more discreetly than in France. Only after 1896 were laws enacted providing that an official bureau—consisting of bankers, brokers, and businessmen and meeting in the presence of a commissioner who conveyed the views of the government— could give or withhold the authorization to proceed to an issue. In practice, the government view was decisive: the system was simpler than the French one, but it produced similar results, and, similarly, it was most often guided by political considerations. After the conclusion of the Triple Alliance, in 1882, the government prevailed on the principal German banks to furnish Italy with funds for the development of her railroads. Then, in 1887, when the French market was closed to Italian securities (one of the consequences of the "tariff war" initiated by Crispi[14]), the German Ministry of Finance sponsored a bank syndicate to assist the Italian Government in surmounting this crisis.

In the financial relations between Germany and Russia, the action of the German Government was decisive on two occasions. In 1887, Bismarck ordered the Reichsbank to accept no more bonds as collateral for loans to German subscribers to Russian government bonds, thus encouraging the subscribers to sell the Russian bonds. This was a direct attack on the credit of the Tsarist government, which had until then sold a considerable portion of its foreign bonds in Germany. Was Bismarck's purpose to obstruct Russian economic development? No, since the German market remained open to loans contracted by Russian industrialists. Was it to delay the construction of the Russian railroads? Possibly, for the lines were of strategic as well as economic significance: they would accelerate the mobilization of armed forces in case of war with Germany, and they would also facilitate the export of Russian wheat, which seriously competed with Germany's. But

---

[14] See above, Chapter Three, pp. 76–77.

the essential motive was political: at a time when the diplomatic conflict between Austria-Hungary and Russia over the Bulgarian situation threatened to become an armed confrontation, Bismarck wanted to create financial, and as a result military, difficulties for Russia.

When, seven years later, Chancellor Leo Caprivi revoked Bismarck's decision, the governing motive was again political. Although not yet certain of the existence of the alliance just concluded between France and Russia, Germany was fully aware that Franco-Russian relations had taken a new turn. She recognized, moreover, that the step taken in 1887 to destroy Russian credit had aided in this development by forcing the Tsarist government to turn to the French market. She hoped that there was still time to restore the good will that had marked relations between Germany and Russia in the 1880's.

In 1914, as a final example, the negotiation of a Bulgarian loan floated on the German market was a corollary of political action pursued by Austria-Hungary in competition with France and Russia. At the request of the Austro-Hungarian Government, the German Government encouraged the scheme despite the opposition to it among financiers. The conclusion of this loan in early July was a major success in the policy of the Central Powers.

D. In the United States

Prior to 1914, the United States played only a minor part in international finance.[15] Her capital exports were extensive only in Canada and Central America. In Canada, American investments were associated with an economic influence that did not, apparently, serve as a cloak for political ambitions (despite President Cleveland's note of 1895). But in the Caribbean and Central America, American financial action was closely linked with political action. It was the theater of operations for "dollar diplomacy."

The conduct of dollar diplomacy varied considerably depending on whether the administration in Washington was Republican or Democratic. During the Presidency of William Howard Taft, the State Department was quite willing to take action without even waiting to be asked, and it pressed banks to develop their foreign investments. Diplomacy, said President Taft in May, 1910, must operate so as to ensure profitable investment for American capital. The purpose was economic, of course, but also political, for the protection of investments was the means of preparing for diplomatic or even military intervention in Central America.

In the Far East, in President Taft's view, the United States was called on to play a major role. Accordingly, in 1910, Secretary of State Philander Knox invited a group of American banks to make capital investments in

---

[15] See above, p. 104.

northern China. Businessmen were somewhat reluctant to embark on the plan, fearing they would run into opposition from European financial interests whose cooperation they needed elsewhere. The banking group that agreed to follow Knox's plan did so believing the State Department would, if necessary, actively protect the investments made in accordance with its advice. The principal agent of this banking group, Willard Straight, the great apostle of dollar diplomacy, had previously served as consul general in Mukden; he was still in close relations with the State Department. The policy he advocated was Knox's rather than the banks'.[16]

The Democratic administration that followed disavowed this position as a matter of principle. Woodrow Wilson believed that dollar diplomacy as President Taft conceived it served "special interests," whereas the government's role must be to serve the "national interest." When certain American banks considered making further commitments in China, they requested the government for a promise of support in case of future reverses, but Secretary of State William Jennings Bryan, after consultation with the Cabinet, refused to give it. When banks invested in "new countries," he argued, they imposed high interest rates justified on the grounds of the risks entailed; these risks would be eliminated if they received assurances of U.S. protection for their investments. The practice, he maintained, was abusive; when Americans go abroad, they must take risks, he said. And unlike "certain European governments," President Wilson made it clear, he did not wish to consider resort to force to protect contracts signed abroad by American citizens.[17] One cannot take such statements at face value, however, because the Wilson administration did not hesitate to intervene in Mexico in 1913 and Santo Domingo in 1915 to protect American financial interests; it simply refused to commit itself to such action in advance.

World War I transformed the United States' international financial position. The country was politically neutral, and the government first decided to maintain strict financial neutrality as well. By a note of August 15, 1914, the State Department let it be known that the granting of credits to belligerent states by American banks would be "incompatible with the true spirit of neutrality." Secretary of State William Jennings Bryan took the view that any violation of this principle could jeopardize political neutrality.

By October, however, when Great Britain and France, faced with the prospect of prolonged warfare, began to purchase raw materials or foodstuffs and to place orders for arms from American producers, it became clear (as the National City Bank stressed in a letter of October 23 to the State De-

---

[16] See Edward H. Zabriskie, *American-Russian Rivalry in the Far East: A Study in Diplomacy and Power Politics, 1895–1914* (Philadelphia, 1946), pp. 139 ff.; and Herbert Croly, *Willard Straight* (New York, 1924).

[17] See Zabriskie, *op. cit.*, p. 188, and the *Memoirs of William Jennings Bryan* (Philadelphia, 1925).

partment) that the European governments could not long continue to pay cash. The orders would soon stop unless American banks could open lines of credit to belligerent states or float foreign government bonds on the American market.

The argument was cogent, and, in the interests of American producers and exporters, the State Department did not take long to silence its political scruples and modify the doctrine. It authorized the opening of bank credits—unofficially in October, officially in March, 1915—and then in September, 1915, the floating of a $500-million Franco-British loan on the American market. The economic motive, in this case, was decisive.

At the end of November, 1916, however, this policy was suddenly abandoned. Just as the Morgan Bank was on the point of sponsoring a new British loan, the Federal Reserve Board issued a warning. It advised the banks not to invest in foreign government bonds for the time being—a clear reversal of the policy of "unguaranteed" loans that the President and the State Department had permitted since September, 1915. The warning, moreover, came from the highest level: the President had approved the text and had even advised that it be strengthened.[18]

Why this about-face? Economic and financial reasons certainly played their part: the Federal Reserve Board judged it advisable for the banks to preserve their liquidity; it also considered that the "excessive" outflow of American money was causing a rise in the cost of living and social unrest and should be restored to more "reasonable" proportions. But the political reasons were even more important: the governor of the Federal Reserve Bank of New York had begun to feel that the United States, by giving financial support to one of the belligerent camps, was exposing herself to "complications" with the other, and that creditors were in danger of being irrevocably bound to their debtors; and the President, who had been working for three days on a draft note to the belligerents inviting them to peace discussions, was considering exerting diplomatic pressure on England and France by threatening to block loans to them.

Wilson was really hesitating between political and economic goals that were contradictory. Three weeks later, when he realized that his peace move had failed, the Federal Reserve Board hastened to tone down the significance of its "warning," which, said the Secretary of the Treasury, might dry up the sources of United States prosperity.

After the United States entered the war in early April, 1917, the forms of financial assistance she had used to help Great Britain and France for the past two and a half years became obsolete. The United States Government itself now opened the lines of credit to governments with which it was "associated" to enable them to pay for goods purchased on the American

---

[18] According to a report of the Senate Special Committee to Investigate the Munitions Industry, popularly known as the Nye Committee.

market. The loans were thus granted from one state to another and took on considerable magnitude.

Immediately after the armistice, however, Washington indicated its intention of shortly putting an end to this financial solidarity. The allied states could no longer count on regular credit; each new request was to be judged on its own merits. The State Department thus gained a means of exerting pressure that it could use for political ends. In May, 1919, for instance, President Wilson took a very firm stand against Italian claims in the Adriatic. In so doing, he took into account the grave economic and social crisis that rocked Italy and the fact that she was incapable of ensuring a supply of raw materials unless she obtained credits abroad. Since the United States was the only country that could furnish such credits, could the Italian Government stand up to Wilson's maneuver?

On January 28, 1920, this new American financial policy in regard to the allied and associated states was clearly asserted: in a circular letter to the presidents of the Chambers of Commerce, the Secretary of the Treasury declared that there could be no question of continuing intergovernmental loans. Yet this decision threatened to paralyze European purchasing activities in the United States. It was therefore necessary, in order to maintain American exports, to give Europeans credit in the form of bank loans, or to obtain dollars for them through private investments—purchases of securities, real estate, and shares in industrial firms or railroad companies. The United States Government encouraged private citizens to acquire foreign government bonds, and it instructed its diplomatic and consular agents to assist Americans in finding good investment opportunities. It expected to derive political advantages from this policy, for by directing or slowing down the flow of investments, it could exert pressure on foreign governments.

At the same time, it exercised some control over the moves initiated by private financial interests. Under the terms of a circular of March 3, 1922, the banks, before floating a foreign bond issue on the market, were invited to inform the State Department of their intention. The State Department could not insist on such consultation, but a Treasury report later noted that from 1925 it had become routine. It was unusual, incidentally, for the State Department to advise against the proposed bonds.

But the government was not satisfied with mere surveillance. It also spelled out which parties banks should refuse loans to: foreign governments the United States did not recognize; those which requested aid in order to balance their budgets but without making fiscal effort on their part, or in order to pursue an armaments policy; and those that refused to fulfill their obligations to the United States. A link was thus clearly established between financial action and political considerations. How did this work in practice?

Between 1925 and 1929, Germany was the principal beneficiary of American investments in continental Europe. American investors believed,

after the Locarno agreements, that because German industry had not suffered heavy damage during the war, it was in a position to make a rapid
recovery. Private investments took the form of loans to credit institutions
or public services, purchase of company stocks, and acquisition of real estate
or securities. Requested for an opinion by the Morgan Bank, the State
Department in September, 1924, expressed the hope that credits would be
granted to Germany in order to avoid the dangers of "economic chaos"
there. In 1926 and 1927, it informed the banks that there was no political
objection to continuing these investments but advised caution. In general,
the policy appeared to be motivated only by economic and financial considerations and showed no ulterior political motive.

Yet the political consequences of this great flow of American capital
were obvious. On December 27, 1927, the *Münchener Neueste Nachrichten*
voiced the hope that "the billions that in the course of the past three years
have demonstrated America's interest in the prosperity of German industry
will, in a capitalist system, create a broad solidarity of aims, above and
beyond purely economic commitments." German industrialists and politicians
thought that this solidarity would enable Germany to avoid reparations
payments, for a conflict arose between the interests of American creditors
and those of the bond holders under the Dawes and Young plans, as soon
as the German Government made it clear that it could not meet both its
obligations under reparations and those it had assumed under the head of
private investments. This conflict was expressly noted in August, 1931, in a
report drawn up by an international committee of experts meeting at Basle.
It had a decisive influence on the negotiations that ended, in July, 1932,
with the cancellation of the war reparations.

In Latin America, where Brazil, Argentina, Chile, and Colombia were
the principal beneficiaries of American investments, the nature and political
consequences of the American role were very different. In addition to private
investments, which were also considerable in Mexico and Cuba, Latin American government bonds were traded on the United States market. In Brazil,
Argentina, and the other River Plate states, and in Chile, Bolivia, Peru, and
Colombia, the governments, which prior to 1914 had borrowed in Europe,
now turned to U.S. banks, as Central American states were already in the
habit of doing.

Did this give the United States an opportunity to extend her influence?
Yes, undoubtedly so in the case of Chile, where, in return for the loans
granted, the government had to agree to submit its finances to the supervision
of a "financial adviser" designated by the State Department. But in most
other states, the volume of private investment, far from promoting American
political influence, seems in the end to have impeded it. American financial
aid came to be associated with the rise of large-scale capitalism, which hurt

a number of small local businesses, and social opposition to this advancing capitalism coalesced with political opposition to Pan-Americanism.

When the great depression swept the world in 1929, the fate of American investments abroad was seriously jeopardized. In 1931, defaulting on debts began in Latin America; in 1932, this had spread to Europe. Of the foreign securities in American hands, 32 per cent were in default in 1934, 37 per cent in 1937. But at no point did the United States Government consider protecting these investments and exerting pressure on the debtors. The Good Neighbor policy followed vis-à-vis Latin America did not permit resort to measures of constraint against Latin American governments. In addition, its attitude favoring the cancellation of reparations payments did not permit a very strong advocacy of settling inter-Allied debts. The only step taken against "defaulting" states was the Johnson Act of 1934, which proclaimed an "embargo" on loans to governments that had failed to fulfill their financial obligations toward the United States, but which authorized banks to grant short-term commercial credits to finance foreign trade.[19] This sanction was supplemented by another precautionary measure: the Securities Exchange acts of 1933 and 1934 stipulated that *any* issue of foreign securities on the American market required prior authorization by a commission appointed by the government.

On the whole, then, United States laws were moving toward a solution analogous to that which had long been current in France. Nevertheless, the Johnson Act provided an exception: public agencies under the control of the Federal Government might continue to buy and sell foreign government bonds and open credit to the governments involved. The Import-Export Bank, established by Executive decree on February 2, 1934, to stimulate American exports to the Soviet Union, was assigned the task in 1936 of granting long-term credits to various other purchasers of American products. The objective was economic, of course, but the political motivation entered into the matter of *which* countries were selected. Although Japan requested the opening of credits, she did not receive them, since the United States refused to recognize the virtual Japanese protectorate of Manchukuo. But the Import-Export Bank extended credits to China, which needed industrial goods to organize her resistance to Japanese aggression; to Brazil, where the United States feared the growth of German influence; and to Haiti and Cuba, under the Good Neighbor policy. Financial credits thus remained an "arm of diplomacy" even when American foreign investment was scant.

This financial foreign policy took on considerable importance after 1940. Lend Lease was really only one of the forms of early American participation

---

[19] This law remained in effect until 1941, when the war in Europe led the United States to regard it as necessary, in her own interests, to give financial aid to Germany's enemies.

in the war.[20] Political ends clearly directed and governed financial policies.

After the war, Marshall Plan aid, granted to sixteen countries in 1948, of course had an economic purpose: with the credits voted by Congress, American goods were purchased for shipment to the beneficiary states, thereby maintaining a large flow of exports profitable to American producers; moreover, the restoration of European prosperity was essential to the restoration of international trade. But the Marshall Plan was primarily a political design—its object being to reduce the difficulties and sufferings in Central and Western Europe that would otherwise create a favorable opportunity for the spread of Communist ideas.[21] On February 25, 1947, Under Secretary of State Dean Acheson told his colleagues that such aid was necessary to prevent Soviet expansion. Two days later, he developed the same idea before Congressional leaders, making it clear that the security of the United States was considered at issue. It was the same political argument that President Truman presented on March 12, 1947, in a message to Congress: "One of the primary objectives of the foreign policy of the United States is the creation of conditions in which we and other nations will be able to work out a way of life free from coercion. . . . I believe that we must assist free peoples to work out their own destinies in their own way." And on May 8, in his address to the Delta Council, Dean Acheson repeated that these measures of assistance were only partially suggested by humanitarian considerations and were above all a matter of the national interest.

When the aid plan for Europe was extended in 1949 to underdeveloped countries, the political purpose was still paramount. It is true that in a message of February 20, 1949, President Truman stressed the desire to mitigate the sufferings of destitute and starving peoples and noted that the economic development of those countries would ultimately benefit the world economy and, therefore, U.S. trade. But the chief argument concerned the political advantages of foreign aid: to bring the countries concerned to an understanding of the advantages of democracy; to widen the circle of "free nations" which would "join" the United States. The same theme was developed by economists and finance experts.[22] Lenin, after all, had written as far back as 1918 that underdeveloped countries were the "weak sector" of the capitalist system and their citizens "potential allies" of Communism. To "strengthen the free world against Communism," and even to increase the "collective capacity of free peoples to defend themselves against aggression"—such was the essential purpose of the aid plan. Over and above

---

20 See above, p. 106.

21 See Joseph Jones, *The Fifteen Weeks: February 26–June 5, 1947* (New York, 1955), p. 40.

22 See, for example, Eugene Staley, *The Future of Underdeveloped Countries* (2d ed.; New York, 1961), p. 378.

economic problems, the global political balance was at issue; the under-developed countries were, first and foremost, a "zone in dispute between two competing systems."[23]

Investment policies thus gave creditor states a means of political pressure, a "financial weapon" that they used with more or less vigor, more or less skill. The question is whether their chosen political objectives were always the right ones. When financial expansion went unchecked and affected the domestic policies of the state that was the beneficiary, it sometimes boomeranged. The financial weapon is not easy to wield.

III. FINANCIAL IMPERIALISM AND POLITICAL CONFLICT

The question whether the international flow of capital has promoted peace or contributed to conflict is one that has concerned most theorists of imperialism.

The importance of international movements of capital to colonial expansion was perceived as far back as 1840 by an Oxford economist, Merivale. The accumulation of capital, he maintained, necessarily leads to a search for opportunities for foreign investment and, therefore, to the development of a colonial empire. This argument was more fully developed at the turn of the century by British political scientists. The geographer and "geopolitician" Halford MacKinder wrote in 1900 that it was in order to maintain their position in the world, since they were the great lenders, that the British were impelled to enlarge their empire.[24] And in 1902, the economist and sociologist J. A. Hobson, in his classic study *Imperialism*, argued that the search for new markets for not only industrial products but also capital was the very basis of imperialism. Capital could no longer, he said, find "profitable" employment at home; it must be put to work abroad. The "forces of capitalism," therefore, were pressuring the state to use its power to satisfy their particular interests.

Hobson's analysis was intended to show that the financial advantages derived from the growth of the British Empire accrued mainly to the capitalists who had made the investments and that the rest of the country had no advantage from them at all. This theme, which posited a direct connection between the growth of capital and the extension of colonial empires, was taken up in 1910 by an Austrian economist, Rudolf Hilferding, whose chief concern was to analyze the development of monopolies in the organization of credit and the growth of the banks' power.

---

[23] The terms are those of Alfred Sauvy.

[24] "The Great Trade Routes," *Journal of the Institute of Bankers* (London), March, 1900.

Finally, it was in the light of Hobson's theories, and also Hilferding's on credit monopoly, that in 1917 Lenin expounded his own theory.[25] Capitalist concentration, he said, was the essence of modern economics; it led to the establishment of "monopolies" that, by reason of the strong centralization of banks and the dependence of industrial capitalism on banking, were in the hands of a "financial oligarchy"; nevertheless, these monopolies could only delay and never completely eliminate the reduction in profits which was the inevitable consequence of capital accumulation. To check this decline, financial groups tended to seek out foreign investment possibilities, mainly in "backward" countries where higher profits could be made; and while they thus tried to satisfy their *financial* needs, they also had *political* schemes in mind. These schemes might not always involve territorial conquest, which more than anything else gave capital security, but the "sphere of influence" was a "semi-colony." Imperialism was thus a direct consequence of the "monopoly phase of capitalism," and, where the interests of the Great Powers clashed, it led to war.

Such were the major themes, strongly marked by the times in which they were formulated: Hobson had witnessed the Boer War, in which financial interests had played a great part in the conduct of British policy; Lenin wanted to demonstrate the responsibility of capitalism in the origins of World War I.

The value of these interpretations has often been challenged.[26] Prior to 1914, it has been pointed out, British capital investments flowed into foreign countries even more than into the Empire. Between financial capitalism and imperial development the link is thus neither as necessary nor as constant as Hobson and Lenin asserted. In the United States at the same period, capital investment abroad was meager since there was ample opportunity to employ capital funds at home. Yet a certain kind of American imperialism did develop which, although it rarely took a colonial form, did succeed in establishing at least indirect control over the Caribbean and some of the Pacific archipelagoes. Again, Lenin's theory that foreign investments in "new countries" eventually turned those countries into "semi-colonies" seems to have been belied by the experience of the Latin American countries, which attracted massive amounts of British capital. Finally, it may be noted, as Schumpeter pointed out, that imperialism appeared long before the Industrial Revolution and the development of capitalism.[27] These

---

[25] The later and more readily available editions of these authors' works are: J. A. Hobson, *Imperialism* (New York, 1949); Rudolf Hilferding, *Das Finanzkapital* (Berlin, 1955); and V. I. Lenin, *Imperialism: The Highest Stage of Capitalism* (New York, 1939).

[26] Among British critics, see in particular William Hancock, *Survey of British Commonwealth Affairs* (London, 1942), and John Strachey, *The End of Empire* (New York, 1960).

[27] Joseph Schumpeter, *Imperialism* (New York, 1951).

objections do not apply to all aspects of Hobson's and Lenin's theories; what they attack principally is their rigidity and determinism.[28]

To what extent does historical analysis confirm or invalidate these views?

A. INTERNATIONAL FINANCIAL EXPANSION AS A FACTOR FOR PEACE

In many cases, financial expansion seems to have contributed to peace.

By enabling backward countries to create means of production, capital investment by the industrial countries opened up new markets where they could dispose of their surplus production, and thus paved the way to economic expansion. And too, the industrial states could use the proceeds from their investments to buy raw materials and foodstuffs abroad without having to export currency; imports of this kind were essential to the maintenance of their industrial growth rate. Without this "safety valve"—this was Jules Ferry's argument in a speech of July 28, 1885—they would probably have suffered from unemployment and social unrest which, while perhaps not directly causing political strife, might have contributed to aggravating existing conflicts.

Financial expansion has sometimes made it possible to mitigate the poverty of underdeveloped or overpopulated countries (or both) by creating businesses that provide work and increase the amount of available consumer goods. In some parts of the world, this poverty might have become fuel for revolutionary movements, endangering the local social and political structure and probably international peace as well. In point of fact, however, this beneficial effect of international financial expansion has been slight, and only quite recently have we become aware of these potential consequences in the life of nations, even where the contribution of foreign capital has been considerable.

The case of China is typical. In 1913 and again in 1920, when an international bank consortium was formed to assist the government, the aim of the banks was to prevent a state of anarchy that would prejudice the economic interests of the great industrial states; the notion of alleviating the poverty of the Chinese people was never expressed.

In the cases of India and South Africa, did substantial capital investments produce more effective results in the social sphere? It is doubtful. In South Africa prior to 1899, the mines, to which much of the foreign capital flowed, provided work for some 50,000 out of a native population of 4 million. And the investments intended for agricultural development were accompanied by laws that reduced the area reserved to the native tribes. In India, where the appearance of railroads effected major changes in the

---

[28] Wolfgang Hallgarten gives an interesting analysis of these theoretical aspects in *Imperialismus vor 1914* (2 vols.; Munich, 1951), Chapter I.

country's economy, since they permitted the development of exports destined for Europe, capital investment fostered the creation of a native middle class but did little to relieve the destitution of the rural masses. It would appear, in a word, as Gunnar Myrdal has said,[29] that the play of economic forces, when they were not controlled, enriched the wealthy and improvished the poor.

Only since 1945 has the export of capital to underdeveloped countries ceased to be regarded simply as a way of making a profitable investment. Is this to say that the notion of "duty" has replaced that of "profit"? By no means. The preoccupation here is not humanitarian; the objective is to defend "Western" civilization. The disparity in standards of living can have more serious consequences today than in the past, because the masses are becoming more aware of their poverty and because they may see in Communism the hope of a remedy. The living standards in the disinherited nations must therefore be effectively raised, so as to render them less accessible to Communist influence, or at least so as to show them that "Westerners" can be generous. Investment policy is governed by the concern to preserve a balance of power between the two great global forces. Its service to the cause of peace is indirect.

It might be assumed, however, that the international movement of capital has contributed more directly to the maintenance of peace insofar as it has established a solidarity of interests among capital-owners or businessmen in different lands.

The European of the late nineteenth century who had invested some of his capital in a South American state uneasily followed the ups and downs of the domestic politics there that might jeopardize the payment of interest on his investment. And he feared even more the chance of war. To increase this kind of investment was thus likely to nurture a desire for political stability. Did the bankers and businessmen with an international outlook really have this desire? To give a valid reply, it would be necessary to have access to bank records and private correspondence; an inquiry on this scale will probably not be feasible for a long time to come; but it is possible to establish the position that business circles adopted in *specific* cases.

Nothing could be more significant in this regard than the attitude of the "City" in London of July, 1914. At this time, London was the principal center of international financial transactions. British capital investments ranged throughout the world. Foreign diplomats—first among them the French ambassador—were quick to note the concern of British financiers over the prospect of a major European war, which, they believed, was liable to become a world war. And if it did, what would happen to British capital? Until the eleventh hour—that is, right up to August 2, 1914—the City

---

[29] *An International Economy: Problems and Prospects* (New York, 1956).

remained the rallying point for opponents of British intervention in the conflict developing between the great continental powers.

Yet it is hardly possible to draw any general conclusions from this history. In 1916, faced with the prospect of United States intervention in the European war, American financial circles were divided. Some of the large banks, especially the Morgan Bank, favored intervention because they were deeply involved in a credit policy that tied them to the interests of France and England, but the directors of the Federal Reserve Board were less enthusiastic. A study of the economic and financial press of the time indicates that big business feared involvement in the war because it would give the government an opportunity to interfere in the organization of production and curtail their freedom of action. It was only in February–March, 1917, that businessmen decided to take a stand in favor of entering the war.[30]

A similar development took place between 1935 and 1941. At first, business circles were inclined to think that participation in World War I in 1917 had been a mistake from a business point of view, since it had heavily burdened the national debt and the national revenues and had given the economy an "artificial boost" that ended in the 1929 crash. In early 1939, big business was in the vanguard of the noninterventionist "peace party." Toward the end of the year, the armaments manufacturers, exporters, and financiers began to change their minds, but major industrial concerns in general continued to oppose President Roosevelt's policy. Not until June, 1940, when confronted with the prospect of a German victory in Europe, was the National Association of Manufacturers converted, and then only because it believed that Hitler's Germany might close some part of the world market to American industrial goods. The United States Chamber of Commerce remained opposed to intervention. Business thus remained divided.

It is impossible, therefore, to attribute a "pacific" influence to the international movement of capital. Such an influence *sometimes* is felt in *certain* circumstances; that is all we can safely say. Indeed, the occasions on which the international movement of capital has given rise to international difficulties and threats of conflict have been increasingly frequent. They have certainly been more newsworthy.

B. International Financial Investment as a Factor of Conflict

1. International Investment and Arms Policies

In the first place, arms policies have been directly related to international loans. Some states, of course, were able to develop their military capacity on the strength of their own resources. This was true of France, Germany, and

---

[30] See C. Styrett, "The Business Press and American Neutrality," *Mississippi Valley Historical Review*, September, 1945.

England during the land and sea arms races in the years preceding the two world wars. But most countries had to appeal for financial support from abroad.

Between 1873 and 1895, the Japanese Government was able to build its navy by means of foreign credits obtained, mainly, from British banks. In Russia between 1888 and 1914, the network of strategic railroads intended to speed the mobilization and dispersement of forces in case of war was constructed with the money made on bonds floated on the French market. Between 1906 and 1914, all the Balkan states, hostile to the Ottoman Empire but rivals among themselves, sought foreign loans, without which they could not make military preparations. (In most of these cases, the creditor state demanded in return that the order for arms be awarded to its own industry; such was the case, for instance, with the Greek and Serbian loans concluded with France in January, 1914.) And after 1919, Poland and Romania resorted to the French market for money to develop their armed forces.

Such practices did not necessarily imply a policy of aggression: in giving financial support to a Russian arms buildup before 1914 and to Polish and Romanian arms after 1919, France intended to increase the effectiveness of her alliances and to "contain" German power; she sought to establish an equilibrium of forces that would not endanger peace and might even help assure it. In the case of Japan and the Balkan states, on the other hand, the arms were directly intended for war. The governments approached for loans were not unaware of this but usually refrained from examining too closely this aspect of the matter.

2. Governmental Protection of International Investments

Protecting investments made by their citizens gave states the opportunity to exert financial pressures that did not operate in favor of peace.

When capital moved from a major industrial nation to an undeveloped one, the protection of investments operated in favor of colonial expansion and spheres of influence. The export of British capital to Japan or South America may not have had political consequences because these states were capable of defending their independence and in any case did not at the time threaten the security of the capital invested. But between 1871 and 1914, the experiences of Egypt, Tunisia, Morocco, the Ottoman Empire, and the Central American states exemplified in different degrees the methods of imperialist expansion.

In Tunisia, the Bey had contracted loans abroad, especially in France, so as to maintain his small army (which, in 1855, had taken part in the Crimean War)—solely for prestige purposes. He was unable to pay the interest on this debt and too weak to dare set aside the demands of the foreign bond holders. He was therefore obliged, in 1869, to submit his financial administration to the control of an international bond fund, on which his creditors were represented, which controlled a part of the customs and tax revenues of the Tunisian state. The French Government now realized that, since French banks were the chief creditors, it might be able to obtain the concession of a foothold "establishment" on the Tunisian coast in exchange for the financial facilities which the Bey could not fail to request. It hoped gradually to achieve a dominant influence in the regency. Twelve years later, Italian competition in Tunis caused France to force the issue and undertake a military expedition in order to impose a protectorate.

In Egypt, where the Khedive had called on British and French banks to finance major public works as well as the exotic expenditures ·of the court, the floating debt was mainly in the hands of French banks, whereas the funded debt was handled chiefly by British financial establishments.[31] Things developed at first rather as they had in Tunisia; a similar Caisse de la Dette was established in 1876. But the process went much faster, because both the British and French governments vigorously supported the creditors' claims; some months later, a Franco-British condominium was established with French and British controllers; and the next year an Englishman became Finance Minister and a Frenchman Minister of Public Works in the Egyptian Government. Foreign control over domestic Egyptian affairs thus became close; the Sultan's deposition of Khedive Ismail in June, 1879, accorded with the express will of the European creditors. It was at this point that Egyptian intellectuals, officers, and civil servants voiced protest; they had a sense of national humiliation; they were also the immediate victims of the budgetary economies imposed by the Franco-British administration. Great Britain intervened by force to put down an insurrection led by Ahmed Arabi and took advantage of it to establish British rule in Egypt.

In Morocco, the Sultan had been obliged to ask for a foreign loan in October, 1861, to pay Spain the war indemnity stipulated in the Treaty of Tetuán of 1860, and as security he had had to hand over his tax revenues. But soon realizing that he was encouraging "foreign encroachments" and the establishment of a "veiled protectorate," he refrained from renewing this appeal for foreign credits. Between 1894 and 1901, however, the authority of the Sultan collapsed, and the penetration of European economic influences, which altered commercial trends and social structures, led to unrest among the tribes. To restore order and bring in the taxes, the Sultan's government had to organize its armed forces, but this it was unable to do for lack of means and was thus obliged to apply again for a foreign loan. The French Government was waiting for this. By asking for a loan, the Sultan "put the noose around his neck."

In Central America, U.S. investment usually began as a matter of private

---

[31] See Jean Bouvier, "L'installation des groupes financiers au Moyen-Orient, 1862–1882," *Bulletin de la Société d'Histoire moderne*, Series 12, May 3, 1959.

initiative. Either individual Americans asked the governments to grant them concessions for public works, mining, or agricultural development, or banks offered the governments financial aid to help them organize their administration or stabilize the currency.

The United States Government confined itself to lending diplomatic support to such requests or offers. Its role became more active in cases where these capital investments required protection against discriminatory measures or defaults. By negotiation or by armed pressure, it demanded the repeal of any such measures and insisted that specific revenues—usually customs revenues—be applied to the payment of interest on the foreign debt. The United States thus established partial control over the legislation and budgetary resources of the countries concerned. Washington sometimes went so far as to state that in countries where American capital was invested the maintenance of order was essential to the security of those investments. And on December 2, 1904, President Theodore Roosevelt declared that the United States was justified in exercising powers for "purposes of international police." The supply or withholding of arms and credits to a government threatened by revolution and, in some cases, armed intervention were the chosen instruments of this policy, which sometimes led to the establishment of a "veiled protectorate." There is little doubt that dollar diplomacy in practice produced political advantages, whether or not this was premeditated.

In the case of the Ottoman Empire, the Russo-Turkish war of 1853 (in which the Porte was allied with Great Britain and France) was the starting point for the application for foreign credits. The war made this both necessary and easy, since the Sultan was assured of a favorable reception on the part of his allies. But the Ottoman Government acquired a taste for this ease in finances. After the end of the war, it continued to ask for a loan almost every year to cover the regular budget deficit. The Banque Imperiale Ottomane, a private institution established on England's initiative, in which French capital was preponderant, was the principal agent of these transactions. The British and French banks apparently had no "imperialist" designs; they simply sought investments for "unemployed" capital with a view to making a profit. By 1871, however, the British Government had realized that in a few years' time, the Porte would be unable to pay the interest on these loans. In 1875, the debt reached almost 5.3 billion francs, and the interest (including amortization) 300 million francs, while the actual budget receipts of the Ottoman Government did not exceed 380 million francs. Consequently, in the autumn of that year, after the Christian nationalities movement had erupted, threatening the Empire with grave crisis, the Porte government found itself on the verge of bankruptcy.

The major European powers did not take a direct part in the negotiations between the Ottoman Government and the bond holders, but they followed them closely. The bond holders' representatives were retired diplomats, well placed to know the position of their governments. The Muharrem decree of December, 1881, wiped out the bankruptcy, established a Caisse de la Dette directed by delegates of the bond holders, and placed about a third of the state revenue under the control of a Ottoman Public Debt Administration. The Ottoman Government thus found itself in the same position as the Egyptian Government had in 1875. How did it succeed in stopping the European intervention at that point, and how did it avoid more direct diplomatic pressures? The answer is that it did not obstruct the action of the Public Debt Administration, which "improved the receipts from the conceded revenues"—that is, which tightened up the internal-revenue system and the salt and tobacco monopolies. Even more important, it took advantage of the rivalries among the great powers.

In a word, a debtor state, when it found itself politically weak or unstable, was led to grant exceptional guarantees to foreign investors, guarantees that were liable to curtail its independence. The sovereignty of such a state, as Lord Curzon remarked, could become a "constitutional fiction" in which only a jurist could continue to believe and which a statesman scorned.[32] At the same time, such a state did not find itself politically dependent upon the creditor except when the latter was prepared to resort to arms to ensure the implementation of contractual obligations. Such resort to military force was practiced at times prior to 1914 but ceased between the two world wars.

3. Rivalries Between Creditor States

Capital investments in underdeveloped countries very easily led to rivalries between creditor states, which sought to secure economic advantages or political *quid pro quos* by forestalling competitors. When such rivalries became acute, however, efforts were made to secure international cooperation in the area concerned.

This situation arose in China in 1913, but it was resolved, at least on paper. After the 1911 revolution and the collapse of the Manchu dynasty in February, 1912, the President of the Chinese Republic, General Yüan Shih-k'ai, who had demanded the emperor's resignation but had never subscribed to the program of the revolutionaries, came into conflict with the "father of the revolution," Sun Yat-sen, and with the legislative majority. With the exception of Russia, which was only too willing for the internal unrest to continue, the European powers, in the interests of their trade, hoped that the Chinese Government would be able to maintain order and thought that Yüan was capable of achieving it.[33]

---

[32] Great Britain, Foreign Office, *British Documents on the Origins of the War, 1898–1914*, Vol. IV (London, 1927), No. 319.

[33] J. G. Reid, in *The Manchu Abdication and the Powers, 1908–1912* (Berkeley, Calif., 1935), studies the hesitations of the powers in this matter and their eventual decisions.

In order to reorganize the army and administration and carry through
a policy of major public works, however, Yüan could not avoid applying for
a large foreign loan. European businessmen had predicted for some years
that China would be obliged to resort to that solution, but they wanted to
acquire some control over Chinese finances in order to protect the bond
holders. At the start of the revolutionary movement, the foreign governments had not wished to give financial aid to the dynasty because this would
have prolonged the civil war. They had no objection to granting loans to
Yüan's government, however, since he seemed able to ensure stability.

The Chinese Government could try to obtain these funds by approaching
a number of banking groups, which would doubtless compete with one
another and request support from their respective governments. The negotiations, in such a case, would increase and aggravate the competition in
which the Great Powers were engaged in China, and it would offer the two
most enterprising states, Russia and Japan, an opportunity to secure
"dominant advantages" from the Chinese Government. It was to prevent
this eventuality that the French Government, in January, 1912, proposed
creating an international banking consortium that would organize this
financial assistance and obtain the desired guarantees from China.[34]

France had no difficulty in getting support for this project from Great
Britain and also from the United States, which had never favored the division
of China into spheres of influence; Germany eventually took the same position. Russia was reluctant at first, for she feared losing the "special position"
she had acquired in northern China, but she resigned herself to it on condition that the "reorganization loan" not be used to build up a strong Chinese
army, whose existence would conflict with Russian interests.

The consortium would (despite the later withdrawal of the American
banks, which had not obtained from Wilson's Democratic administration
the guarantee promised them by the previous Republican administration[35]),
its promoters believed, facilitate Western economic penetration and make it
possible to impose financial advisers on the Chinese Government who would
direct the expenditure of the loan. Yüan held out against this for a long
time, believing, not unreasonably, that such control would violate China's
sovereignty. In the end he yielded, since he needed the money to make himself
independent of the legislature.

The contract signed on April 27, 1913, provided for a loan of £25 million
from the consortium to be applied to certain categories of expenditures
(excluding the army) and supervised by foreign officials; the Chinese Government, as security for the payment of interest, would turn over salt-tax

[34] See the instructions given on January 9 to the French ambassador in Russia, and
the conversation between Poincaré and Isvolsky on March 9. *Documents diplomatiques
français, 1871–1914,* Third Series, I, No. 448, and III, No. 78.
[35] See above, p. 119.

revenues. Thus the policy of the European powers seemed to be moving in the direction of joint economic exploitation of the Chinese market, but the new system did not have time to prove itself, since the outbreak of war in Europe put an end to it fifteen months later. It is nonetheless interesting as the expression of an attitude that took the edge off political rivalry.

The same tendency, on a much larger scale, has characterized the aid projects for underdeveloped countries since 1949. To prevent such assistance becoming a subject for bargaining between the United States and the Soviet Union in particular and arousing political suspicions, it seemed advisable for the United Nations to assume responsibility. U.N. action, stated the Secretary General in his report of May, 1949, was all the more necessary since the underdeveloped countries had not forgotten the abuses to which "development" had given rise in the past, and they would be more likely to have confidence in a program "elaborated under international auspices."

The principle adopted by the United Nations General Assembly in November, 1949, on this matter[36] was approved by the United States and the Soviet Union, but it remains in the realm of theory. Is this simply because even in the international framework, bargaining continues over each nation's share in expenditures and, consequently, in the influence it will have over the funds? Or because the appointment of experts to carry out the technical-assistance programs is likely to engender rivalries among nations? Above all, it is because foreign aid, as Raymond Aron has said,[37] is by reason of its potential effect an act of politics.

It would seem, therefore, that genuine international cooperation in foreign investments and aid still lies in the future.

4. Major Powers as Debtors

Indebtedness among major states has occurred in altogether special circumstances, when the creditor state was not, for moral or political or even more imperative reasons, in a position to constrain the defaulting debtor.[38]

The considerable foreign debt contracted by Russia between 1888 and 1917 was almost exclusively in the hands of French bond holders. (British capital was largely tied up in private investments.) The money from French loans was intended partly for economic and administrative purposes and partly for new strategic railroads, which were needed, of course, for purposes of purely national defense but also for the proper functioning of the Franco-Russian military alliance.

---

[36] United Nations, *Official Records of the Fourth Session of the General Assembly, Resolutions*, Resolution 304 (IV).

[37] In *Le Figaro* (Paris), April 30, 1960.

[38] We are not dealing here with indemnities or reparations stipulated in a peace treaty, which are of a quite different order.

The Soviet state voided both the commercial and the public debt. The nationalization of Russian industry in 1920 was not accompanied by any provision for the indemnification of foreign capital; obligations contracted by the Tsarist government were repudiated by the new regime, which was not recognized by the other states. Creditors had no way of asserting their claims except by appealing to their own governments, but the only way open to the latter to force the Soviet Government to recognize its debts was military action, which was abandoned after brief attempts made in 1919.

In 1921, the Soviet Union felt the need to resume economic relations with the major industrial powers and therefore agreed to negotiate the question of the debts. But neither the Genoa Conference of 1922, called to consider the Russian problem, nor the talks held in 1924 with Great Britain and France led to any bases for agreement. The Soviet Government envisaged partial payment of the interest on its debts, but only to the extent that it received fresh foreign credits.

This defaulting hit France particularly hard, since Russian bonds were held by a considerable number of French small private investors—some 1.6 million of them. It was therefore strongly condemned by a large sector of the French public. But in the history of Franco-Soviet relations, marked by profound differences in social principles and political goals, this condemnation was minor; it was no longer apparent when, a decade later, in 1935, the French Government concluded a mutual-assistance pact with the Soviet Union in which the debt question was not even mentioned.

The debts contracted by the Allies with the United States in 1917–18 in their common war against Germany and Austria-Hungary are an altogether different matter. Considerable sums had been placed at the disposal of the associated states to pay for the arms, raw materials, and food shipped to them by American producers; they were expended in full on the spot and helped to increase the number of salaries paid as well as the profits reaped by the producers or shippers. But the credits the United States extended were covered by domestic bonds—hence American subscribers had provided the funds. The federal budget had to allow for interest payments on these bonds, and this was reflected in increased taxes. Reimbursement of the U.S. loans, it was clear, would lighten the burden on the American taxpayer. Congress did not fail to emphasize this fact when in 1932 it voted a resolution requiring the Federal Government to demand such reimbursement.

The debtor states could maintain, as France did, that while it was legally justified, this demand was not equitable. Had not the supplies provided by the United States to her allies contributed to a common war effort? At the least, there should be some correlation between the settlement of inter-Allied debts and the payment of German reparations. In 1923, Great Britain abandoned this argument and agreed to a settlement under which she undertook to repay the major part of her debt within fifty years, and obtained the cancellation of the remainder. Nevertheless, in July, 1932, when the Lausanne Agreement put an end to reparations payments, Great Britain joined France in advising the German Chancellor that its ratification was subject to a satisfactory agreement on the inter-Allied debts. And in December, 1932, the French Chamber of Deputies rejected any payment in respect of such debts, now that reparations had been canceled.

What was the significance of this long international controversy? The French public felt that an injustice had been committed and vigorously expressed its bitterness. The American public remained almost overwhelmingly convinced of the rightness of its cause and accused France of ingratitude. But this American resentment of her French ally did not have the serious repercussion in trade relations that the French commercial and diplomatic representatives in Washington had feared. It undoubtedly strengthened isolationist sentiment, however, and supplied a weighty argument, three years later, to the sponsors of the neutrality acts.

IV. CONCLUSION

In the history of international relations, is it possible to determine precisely the interrelation of business policy and diplomacy and to distinguish the roles played respectively by material and political interests?

The primary goal of the businessman is to make a profit. History shows that industrialists and financiers might have invoked the national interest, but they usually identified it with their private interests. In the eager search for "fruitful employment" of the capital they administered or hoped to attract, they sought first to expand their sphere of action at the expense of rivals, secondly to ensure the security of their investments. To do these two things, they needed the support of their governments. They might therefore be disposed to support or even precipitate imperialist policies, accepting the risk of international conflict—financial interests, in such cases, motivating political action. (It would be more accurate to say *some* financial interests, for they were far from unanimity; banking syndicates were only temporary alliances.)

Governments usually had other motives. They were not indifferent to material advantages and financial profit of course; the success of undertakings abroad and the profits from foreign investments were factors in national prosperity. Moreover, politicians, diplomats, and businessmen often belonged to the same social class; personal ties encouraged this convergence of aims.[39] But governments also took into account the advantages that the development of investments might procure for the *political* interests of the state—the extension of its influence, power, security, or prestige. Conse-

---

[39] See Bouvier, *op. cit.*, and "Les Intérêts financiers et la question d'Egypte, 1875–1876," *Revue historique* (Paris), July, 1960, pp. 75–105.

quently, they sought to use foreign investments to promote these interests, to channel them to regions where they wanted to intensify their political "presence," to take advantage of the opportunities afforded by the necessity of "protecting" them. Financial interests, far from *motivating* political action, were its instruments.

When the historian tries to explain these events, then, should he give pride of place to material and financial interests or political purposes? The observations we have made in this chapter show how useless this question of primacy is.[40] In some cases, the pressure exerted by private financial interests undoubtedly determined political action; in others, it is equally clear that financial interests served as instruments of a political plan. It is impossible to arrive at any explanation of permanent validity or even to determine some kind of hierarchy among possible explanations.

Is it possible, at least, to arrive at some value judgment about the policy of a particular state? Not really, for within that state, financial interests appear at times to have been a decisive influence, at others, to have played only a subordinate role. Moreover, the study of a particular issue—for instance, a specific example of dollar diplomacy in Central America, or France's political-financial intervention in Egypt in 1875–81—shows that in one and the same question financial interests have sometimes generated and sometimes been the tool of political action.

Is this to say that any attempt to establish a distinction between financial and political interests would be artificial[41] because they are simply "two aspects of the policy of the ruling classes"? This would be an evasion of the problem. Historical research can reach valid conclusions when it abandons the vain hope of arriving at a general explanation and confines itself to the study of particular cases. It is not a matter of indifference whether, in particular circumstances of time and place, financial considerations directed political action or the reverse. Much still remains to be done in this respect in a critical study of imperialism. Such research will promote the understanding of the behavior of human groups. The mistake would be to believe that research of this kind might lead to the establishment of "laws."

---

[40] See above, Chapter Four, pp. 85ff.
[41] Such is Jean Bouvier's argument; his analyses are in other respects masterly.

6

THE SENSE OF NATIONHOOD

I. THE CONCEPT OF NATION

The historian, like any observer of events, sees at every point in international relations the expressions of collective ideas or emotions. These ideas and feelings develop within a community whose members are aware of the interests or traditions uniting them, and who are prepared, in case of conflict with others, to sacrifice their individual interests to that of their community. This group solidarity, this consciousness of belonging to a distinct community, and this acceptance of sacrifice also exist in social groups organized along quite simple lines—for instance, in the tribe, but there they are based on the kinship among families or groups of families. When collective consciousness occurs in larger human groups, independent of any family ties, there we have the rudiments of *national* sentiment.

But any analysis of the concept of *nation* is beset with difficulties. In the first place, the terminology has changed during the past century and is still changing. Then there is the matter of boundaries, which change according to historical circumstance. And there are deep psychological differences. Complexity, obscurity, confusion—these are the terms found in the writings of those who have studied the *nation* and *national feeling*.

The real source of these difficulties lies in the multiplicity of factors involved in the genesis of a nation and in the development of a sense of nationhood. Historical interpretation has to make considerable allowances for conflicting accounts of the facts.

How about *territory?* Living together in the same area makes for similarities in modes of life, largely related to the climate, the terrain, watercourses, and vegetation. It may also lead to "cultural integration." But such similarities are not enough to create a nation. In many regions, homogeneous geographical conditions have led neither to union nor even to reconciliation among the communities inhabiting them; after centuries of cohabitation, they remain hostile to one another.[1] Nor is this homogeneity a necessary element to the sense of nation; the dispersed Jewish "nation" preserved its sense of solidarity for centuries even though, prior to the establishment of the Jewish National Home in Palestine in 1919, it had lost its territory.

---

[1] This is true in Transylvania, the coastal regions of Syria and Lebanon, and many other regions.

139

Race? Similarity of physical features—stature, shape of the skull, of the nose, and of the eyes, pigmentation—is certainly conducive to solidarity among men. Gobineau[2] thought that this justified the conclusion that peoples with common ethnographic characteristics must be of the same nationality. But ethnographic studies have shown that none of the great regions of the world have been racially homogeneous and that, indeed, only a few regions at all could be said to possess such homogeneity—Mongolia, the Iranian plateau, the Anatolian interior, the Arabian peninsula.

Language? The use of the same language—by reason of its structure, vocabulary, and, especially, literature—clearly leads to analogous thought patterns and makes for the creation of a patrimony of common concepts. Johann Fichte, the German philosopher, maintained—in his Fourth Address to the German Nation—that a group which speaks the same tongue in an entity that nature herself has united in advance by multiple and invisible bonds. In modern Europe, governments have been very conscious of the advantages of linguistic unity in the development of national solidarity; pioneers in the national movements of the nineteenth century shared this conviction. And governments of recently independent Asian states—India, Indonesia, the Philippines—taking the same view, are seeking to establish common languages in their lands. Yet, a sense of nationhood developed in Switzerland and in Belgium, for instance, among populations speaking different languages, and the use of a single tongue has not eliminated the divergencies among Serbs and Croats. Plebiscites held in 1920 and 1921 in the aftermath of World War I showed in a number of cases that no necessary connection existed between the expression of national sentiment and adherence to a linguistic group.[3]

A *common history?* This often is an important factor in the development of national sentiment. The names of the country's military heroes are cherished, and the struggles against foreigners and achievements that increased the country's influence are emphasized. Such historical memories are recalled with particular strength when a state and its people have experienced reversals of fortune. In Spain, for example, at the end of the nineteenth century and the beginning of the twentieth, references to the colonial achievements of the sixteenth and eighteenth centuries and to the war of independence against Napoleon were constant in the expression of national sentiment.

Tradition? Provided that national traditions are not confined to the diplomatic service or to a few political or academic circles, and that they

---

[2] In his *Essai sur l'inégalité des races humaines* (1853).

[3] For instance, at Sopron (Ödenburg), the Hungarian town transferred to Austria after World War I and returned to Hungary after the plebiscite of 1921; and among the Masurians, the indigenous Poles of East Prussia; and, especially, in the Balkans.

find an echo in the country as a whole,[4] they lend a particular color to national sentiment: Washington's and Jefferson's counsels to the American people; French insistence, from the sixteenth to the nineteenth centuries, on the fragmentation of the German territories; and British isolationism in the late nineteenth century. But such traditions are rarely spontaneous; they are created by statesmen or political writers and kept alive by publicists. They appear as a consequence, not as a cause, of national feeling.

Intellectual development? National consciousness presupposes the existence of a certain state of civilization: the emergence of intellectual trends; the development of a literature; the spread of ideas through education.[5] The quality and luster of this civilization are important to a sense of national pride—in Spain, for example. But a common civilization has never sufficed to make a nation: China and India, although they were matrices of great civilizations, did not show any sense of *nation*hood before the end of the nineteenth century.

Religion? The fact that a human group is animated by a common religious faith is conducive to solidarity, which is why governments often try to maintain or establish religious unity among peoples whose destinies they propose to direct. The creation of a religious community, in the case of the Anglican Church, for instance, was a means of asserting the special qualities and the power of the state. Religious sentiment then becomes an instrument of state policy. But what is more interesting is to what extent religious sentiment has been a source of national sentiment.

In Europe, the connection was frequently apparent. Religion was sometimes more important in the creation of a nation than linguistic unity or similarity: the experiences of Flemings and Dutch, Croats and Serbs, Slovaks and Czechs, Bulgarians and Serbs, are sufficient proof. But the reverse has also been true: it suffices to consider that German unity was eventually achieved despite religious differences; on the other hand, a common Lutheran faith did not suffice to prevent the divorce between Norwegians and Swedes.

In Asia, religious sentiment exerted an uneven influence. It seems to have played no part in the formation of national sentiment in China. In the countries conquered by Islam, it often helped in the birth and growth of a sense of nationality—such was the case, in 1919, in Indonesia—but in India, where Muslims were a minority, it obstructed the nationalist movement and ultimately forced partition. On the other hand, more recent history has shown the active role of Buddhist monks in national movements in Burma, Ceylon, and Vietnam. Japan provides an even better example of close asso-

---

[4] In this connection, see the remarks of James Joll in J.-B. Duroselle, ed., *La politique étrangère et ses fondements* (Paris, 1954), p. 164.

[5] See Friedrich O. Hertz, *Nationally in History and Politics* (New York and London, 1944), p. 24.

ciation between religious sentiment, in the form of Shintoism, and national sentiment; but manifestations of this national sentiment occurred prior to the resurgence of Shintoism, which merely served as a tool of nationalist propaganda.[6]

Economic conditions? Solidarity established between producers and businessmen has certainly fostered the development of national sentiment. In the nineteenth century, the Zollverein contributed to the success of the German nationalist movement since it prepared the ground for political union. But does this observation have any general validity? The history of the Zollverein, to take the same example again, shows that the solidarity established after 1850 among the south German states and Prussia, within the framework of the customs union, did not prevent them from taking up arms against each other in 1866. The Danes of northern Schleswig preserved their Danish national sentiment after 1865 despite the economic advantages they derived from membership in the North German Confederation and then in the German empire. In Alsace-Lorraine after 1871, participation in the prosperity of the German Reich certainly favored, for some twenty-odd years, the cause of those who wanted an autonomous province within the German Empire at the expense of the "protesters" who favored union with France; but it did not affect the ultimate survival of French national sentiment, which was vigorously expressed in the years before World War I. And what place should be ascribed to economic interests in Norway's nationalist claims, or in Flemish nationalism?

Social inequalities? In regions where the peasants, as a result of historical circumstance, were subject to the economic domination of great landowners from another region, belonging to another linguistic group, and in political power, the solidarity of interests among the peasants—tenant farmers or freeholders—vis-à-vis the landowners was doubtless conducive to the development of a sense of nationality. Complaints about heavy rents and about the exercise of the "rights" enjoyed by the landowners became more vigorous and found a sort of additional "justification" when they were directed against a "foreigner." On the other hand, conditions of this kind long remained unchanged—sometimes for centuries. Social discontent did not, therefore, give rise to national sentiment but was only fertile grounds for the seeds sown by other movements and prompted by other motives.

As for the *labor movement* and the development of *socialist doctrine*, they should, logically, have mitigated the expressions of national feeling and placed class solidarity uppermost in men's minds. In fact, however, in parts of Europe where the nationality question was most acute, especially Austria-Hungary, this rarely occurred. (The history of trade unions in Austria is instructive in this regard.) But the study of the relations between

---

[6] See below, Chapter 7, pp. 198–200.

socialism and nationalism has not yet received all the attention the problem deserves.[7]

None of these factors, then, is a matter of indifference, but none can provide a complete explanation. This uncertainty has governed the whole problem of relations between nation and state, a crucial problem for the historian of international relations.

II. NATION AND STATE IN MODERN EUROPEAN HISTORY

Political philosophers in Europe at the close of the eighteenth century— Herder, Burke, and Bentham—sought to determine the factors that differentiated human groups and the signs whereby a group might be recognized as belonging to a "nation." From the outset, these interpretations varied greatly, and the divergent views were reasserted throughout the nineteenth century, by Fichte and Schlegel, by Mazzini, by John Stuart Mill, Fustel de Coulanges, and Ernest Renan.

One theory, popular chiefly among German intellectuals, was that the nation was a living being that developed "through the unconscious action of a superior force"; this force was the "national genius," the *Volkgeist*. Its existence was to be recognized by a number of external marks—common language, loyalty to custom, the cult of ancient traditions. (Some theorists added racial kinship.) Such marks were easily discernible, and one needed to go no farther than to affirm that human groups belonged to the same "nationality" and thus formed a "nation." It mattered little if groups sharing these traits were unaware of their solidarity or showed no desire to live together; the external marks constituted an indisputable criterion.

For others, membership in a nation was a "matter of consciousness." A common language, historical memories, and tradition might be effective elements in the development of national sentiment, but they were not reliable indexes. The essential element was the desire to live together—regardless of the origin of that desire. "The mother country," Mazzini wrote, "is primarily consciousness of the mother country." The French historian Fustel de Coulanges added little to Mazzini's definition: "It is not race or language that constitutes nationality. . . . The mother country is the country one loves."[8] In 1882, Ernest Renan took up the same theme and expanded it: "What constitutes a nation is not the fact of speaking the same language or belonging to the same ethnic group; it is the fact of having done great things together in the past and wanting to do more in the future."[9] Among other

---

[7] Jacques Droz has prepared one study, however, originally presented to the International Congress of Historical Sciences in 1965 (not yet published).

[8] "Open Letter to Mommsen" (1870).

[9] "Qu'est-ce qu'une nation?" Lecture delivered at the University of Paris, reproduced in *Discours et conferences* (Paris, 1887).

supporters of this theory, Emile Boutroux gave the clearest definition of national sentiment: "the desire men have to live together, to cherish the same memories, to pursue the same ends." It is a concept that takes from eighteenth-century political philosophy the principle of "self-determination"— the right of each people to choose its political future.

These varying interpretations had one element in common: the wish to give the state a national basis, to make it coincide as far as possible with the nation, so that it would embrace all the peoples of a single nationality and only those. That was the intention expressed in the nineteenth-century "nationality principle."

But the difficulties in applying this principle were flagrant whenever historical arguments or linguistic factors contradicted the collective sentiments concerned. The theory of "unconscious nationality" permitted apostles of German unity to overlook expressions of particularist sentiment in Hanover, Bavaria, and Saxony, and also to claim Alsace-Lorraine as part of Germany. The theory of nationality as a "matter of consciousness" strengthened the moral position of the Italian patriots in regard to dynasties or sovereigns and bolstered French protests against the Treaty of Frankfurt ending the Franco-Prussian War, in which Alsace and part of Lorraine were ceded to Germany.

For the most part, theories were formulated at the precise moment they were needed to support a political position; they were thus tied to the hope of achieving practical results or to the wish to justify claims. This singularly diminishes their significance in the eyes of the jurist or political scientist. But the historian must recognize that national sentiment, despite these theoretical weaknesses, gives indisputable evidence of vitality and has been a particularly strong catalyst for action in international affairs.

The "nationality question" has taken two forms, often complementary: (1) the liberation of national groups presently under the authority of a government whose members belong to another nationality, thereby giving "national minorities" the opportunity to constitute an independent state; and (2) the union within a single state of peoples of similar nationality previously subject to different sovereignties, either as independent states or as "national minorities."

Between 1815 and 1848, the nationality movement assumed both these forms. We have only to consider the beginnings of Italian and German unity movements, or the protests of national groups against foreign domination— in Belgium in 1830, and in Russian-dominated Poland in 1831.

In 1848–49, attempts at national unification became particularly prominent in the German and Italian states and in the Rumanian principalities, but this was possible only because of the crisis in Austria's power, a crisis caused directly by the stirring of national minorities within the empire.

During the following two decades, forces of disintegration continued to operate in Austria, Poland, and Ireland; they were eclipsed by the success of the Italian and German national unity movements and by the beginnings of Rumania's national unification. In twenty years, the nationality principle had transformed the political map of Europe.

After 1871, and for the next half-century, the protest movements of national minorities made great strides: southern Slavs, Czechs, Slovaks, Poles, Ruthenians, Serbs, and Italians in the Austro-Hungarian Empire; Bulgarians, Greeks, Serbs, and Kutso-Vlachs in Macedonia, subject until 1912 to the Ottoman Empire; Poles, Finns, and Rumanians of Bessarabia in the Russian Empire; Poles again, Danes, and the peoples of Alsace-Lorraine in the new German Empire; Irish in the United Kingdom; Norwegians in the Swedish state before 1908; and Catalans and Basques in Spain—not to mention the Flemish movement in Belgium, which, according to the report of a commission of inquiry published in 1858, appealed to similar national principles, although it can be placed in the same category only by stretching the terms somewhat.

In the early twentieth century, some 60 million persons—one-fifth of the population of the European continent—were involved, or assumed to be involved, in these movements; they affected every European state except Switzerland, Portugal, and the Netherlands. Some nations feared the activities of the discontented minorities in their territories; others hoped that irredentism would operate in their favor. Austria-Hungary, where three-fifths of the population belonged to these minority groups, felt its very existence threatened.

World War I provided the protesters with a favorable opportunity, and the policy of each coalition in the war was to support national movements to the extent that they might weaken the other coalition. The states of the Entente Cordiale had an obvious advantage here, since the nationality movement endangered Austria-Hungary most of all. The armistice of 1918 paved the way to success for the national-minority claims, a success strongly aided by Woodrow Wilson's Fourteen Points.

The "experts" and statesmen who handled these matters at the Versailles Peace Conference came to realize that the strict application of the nationality principle was often impossible, given the inextricable intermingling of populations. It was possible to establish the existence of a language frontier between Germans and Italians in the Alto Adige, or between Germans and Danes in northern Schleswig, but it was far from easy to draw "clearly recognizable lines of nationality," as stipulated in the ninth of Wilson's Fourteen Points, between the different nationalities in the zones of contact between Poles and Lithuanians, or in the Sudetenland, or at the northern and southern edges of Silesia around Katowice or Teschen, in Transylvania, in Dalmatia.

Remarkably, the peace treaties of 1919–20 did a great deal to meet the demands of national minorities throughout central Europe—from Poland to Alsace-Lorraine, and from Schleswig to the Adriatic—but only to the extent that the victorious states and the national groups under their protection were likely to gain an advantage from the adjustments. Under the provisions of the peace settlement, 30 million persons who prior to 1914 had belonged to these "national minorities" acquired the right of self-determination.

But the solution could only be partial, since the peace treaties did not deal with the question of minorities in the United Kingdom, one of the victorious powers, or in Spain, which had not taken part in the conflict; and since the new frontiers, especially in the Danube region and the Balkans, had created new discontented minorities by attaching several national groups to states they regarded as alien.

Protesting minorities still numbered some 30 million, half the total of 1914.[10] But they now included certain groups—Magyars in Czechoslovakia, Germans in the southern Tyrol and Poznania—that had been in the political ascendant before 1914 and consequently found their new position harder to endure. In effect, in the years immediately after the conclusion of the peace treaties, the protests of these minorities and the disputes to which they gave rise kept a number of active foci of war alive in Europe; in Memel, Vilna, Teschen, or Fiume, as in Bessarabia, Macedonia, or Poznania, the right to national independence was always at the heart of the controversy.

The peace treaties of 1919–20 granted a certain protection to national minorities, at least in the states actually constituted by those treaties. The proponents of this special clause in the treaties had in mind to reduce the occasions for conflict arising over educational systems and "national tongues." They therefore secured "cultural" and sometimes administrative autonomy for minority groups, but not the political guarantees that might have jeopardized the sovereignty of the states in which this system prevailed. But how effective would this be? The governments of the "new" or "rejuvenated" states that thus undertook to protect their national minorities feared that cultural autonomy would pave the way for separatist political propaganda.

The nationalities question therefore remained until 1939 either the cause or occasion of dispute. And the right of national self-determination was applied only four times: in Ireland, in Iraq, in Saudi Arabia, and in Egypt after the elimination of the "reserved" points of the 1922 Declaration.

In studying the nature of these movements as they appear in the history of international relations during the past one hundred years, it is clearly necessary to distinguish between the formation of nations on the one hand and the action of national minorities within a given state on the other.

---

[10] Ervald Ammende, *Die Nationalitäten in den Staaten Europas* (Vienna, 1931), and W. Winkler, *Statistisches Handbuch der europaischen Nationalitäten* (Vienna, 1932).

A. MOVEMENTS OF NATIONAL UNITY

The development of national units was governed by a single, basic objective: to persuade peoples sharing a common or similar tongue and a common heritage from the historical past, but owing political allegiance to different states, to live together in a single state. It was thus a matter of fostering and propagating a particular attitude. The obstacles were: attachment to tradition; strength of personal ties forged within existing states; fear of changes in acquiring rights or economic interests; and, especially, the existing sovereigns, the loyalty of their subjects, and the desire of their administrators to preserve a state of affairs from which they benefited.

In order to overcome these particularist stresses, it was necessary to organize propaganda campaigns to give the people a sense of kinship and to show them the advantages of belonging to a great state. Such propaganda emphasized the political prospects far more than the economic; it sought in particular to show that unity would pave the way to *power*.

In Germany, arguments developed by political writers and philosophers were propagated in university lecture halls; students and, as a consequence, members of the liberal professions and civil servants were the best agents of this propaganda. Professional politicians did not take over until later, with the creation of that great powerhouse of propaganda, the Nationalverein. In Italy, where the universities did not enjoy the same kind of authority or power, the unity movement was at first led by secret societies, then by literary societies which spread the works of political writers. The foundation of the National Society in 1857 was the crowning achievement of activities pursued for more than thirty years. In Rumania, the national movement was spearheaded by sons of the great landowners who had been educated in west European universities.

Economic groups at first took no active part in these movements. Not until 1835, twenty years after the publication of the first great literary or philosophical works of "patriotic" inspiration and fifteen years after the organization of the *Burschenschaft* movement, did Rhenish businessmen begin to take an interest in German unification. And it was only around 1845, after thirty years of effort by the secret societies and manifestoes by political writers, that the first vestiges of an economic program appeared in the Italian unification platform.

Isolated thinkers and groups of activists were not alone in influencing the national unity movements. Everywhere the policies of kings and governments played an important part, either by encouraging such movements in the hope of benefiting from them, or by opposing actions that might endanger their own position. The offensive was much better organized than the defensive and displayed greater dynamism. Frederick William IV,

William I, and Bismarck, Charles Albert, Victor Emmanuel, and Cavour, and also Couza, dominated the history of the unification movements not only by their political decisions, but also, and especially, by the impetus they gave to transform the collective mentality.

B. MINORITY NATIONALITY MOVEMENTS

The protest movements of "national minorities" were everywhere characterized by much the same traits: the daily struggle between minority populations and the governmental administration over the language to be used in the schools, and over administrative and judicial incidents about the use of an "official language." But over and above these similarities, there were distinctive features to be discerned.

In the cases of Poland and Ireland at the beginning of the nineteenth century, the minority populations had been subject to direct foreign domination for too short a time to have been assimilated, and their sense of national cohesion remained intact. In a single generation, men had witnessed the third partition of Poland (1795) and the disappearance of the autonomous regime of Russian Poland (1831). Ireland had been independent between 1782 and 1800. So the wounds were still open, the protests against the new governments spontaneous. These minorities were from the outset prepared to listen to political slogans. (The same was true of the people of Alsace-Lorraine after 1871.)

The position of national minorities in the European part of the Ottoman Empire was an exceptional one. Greeks, Bulgarians, and Serbs, because they were Christians, were not entitled to the privileges the Ottoman administration granted to people converted to Islam—for example, the Albanians; in the midst of the Ottoman empire, they were thrust into a position of inferiority and suffered from this foreign domination. Each of these groups naturally then had national aspirations vis-à-vis the Turks, but their sense of nationality also worked within the context of the Christian communities themselves, arousing antagonism among Greek, Bulgarian, and Serb despite the solidarity that sometimes united them against the Turks.

Such national feeling was not always based on linguistic unity. The unique aspect of the nationality movement in this part of Europe was the active part played by religion—more specifically, by ecclesiastical institutions. The Greek and Serbian Orthodox churches, and the Bulgarian Orthodox Church after the creation of the exarchate in 1871, had become ardently "politicized," and then placed all their propaganda and proselytizing powers at the service of the cause of kindling or rekindling national feeling. Almost everywhere, the clergy were agents and leaders of protest movements. Their activities were not only directed against Ottoman domination; the three Orthodox churches contended as well for the religious allegiance of the faithful. Their rivalry grew in proportion as Turkish power declined, for they were intimately linked to the new Balkan states created at the expense of the Ottoman Empire. In the liberation and partition of Macedonia—which after 1880 became the political objective of Greece, Bulgaria, and Serbia—each of the three states relied on its church's propaganda to give it the advantage.

Foreign observers in the first years of the twentieth century[11] were disconcerted when they saw the forms that the cause of "nationality" had assumed in the Balkans. In many cases, membership in a church had been a more important factor in the development of national feeling than a common language; some groups who spoke Serb, for instance, regarded themselves as Bulgarians because they belonged to the exarchate.

At the beginning of the nineteenth century, the national minorities in most of central and western Europe were passive, and they were not aroused until the years between 1830 and 1870. What were the essential features of this awakening?

The decisive initial impetus came from the intellectuals: they revived the memories of a common national history and underlined the permanence of common traditions; they realized, and made others realize, the importance of linguistic unity; they were able to recognize and articulate sentiments that had previously lain dormant, and they gave these feelings authority. In every national movement—German, Czech, Italian, Croatian, Norwegian, and Flemish—the heroic names of the early struggles were always those of philosophers, writers, and historians of language, literature, and law, even more than political theorists. Their ideas were spread among the educated classes through the schools and universities and in their literary or historical works. They were disseminated in the public at large by newspapers and periodicals and by propaganda groups such as the Sacred Union in Flanders or the Society for the Advancement of Popular Education in Norway. Much of this propaganda was dedicated to the memories of great moments in the nation's past, the evocation of the nation's "glorious" accomplishments, and the cult of national traditions. The Czechs were reminded of the Defenestration of Prague of 1618; southern Slavs, of the empire of Dushan; the Italians, of the supremacy of ancient Rome; the Germans, of the role of German thought in the Reformation. Even among less sophisticated peoples—the Slovaks of northern Hungary, the Ruthenians of Austrian Galicia—the memory of the past was an active element in the national awakening. This sort of propaganda did not really reach the peasant masses, most of whom were illiterate, but it touched a chord among the semi-intellectuals and the middle class.

We may ask whether the spread of this propaganda was facilitated by financial and commercial concerns and whether social inequalities had any effect on it. The intellectual propagandists usually paid little attention to

---

[11] In particular, those who conducted the Carnegie inquiry in 1913.

these factors (some, like Mazzini, even declaring them negligible), but they did have some importance.

The industrial and commercial middle class in the Czech territories believed that the Austrian administration, would give greater consideration to Czech interests in the arrangement of the daily details of economic life if it were to be taken out of German hands. Another example of support from the business class can be found in Spain, where the Catalan movement was supported by economic interests in Barcelona whose position on tariff policies was at variance with the one prevailing in Madrid.

But the influence of economic and social forces sometimes operated in the opposite direction. Producers often realized the advantages of belonging to a large economic entity in which it was likely that they would have a wider market. Hungarians, for instance, even when they complained about the dualist regime of the Austro-Hungarian empire established in 1867, could not become separatists without losing the Austrian market, which was essential to their agricultural export trade. The Flemish nationalists could not overlook the economic ties that bound together the Belgian populations. And the success of the "autonomists" at the expense of the pro-French "protesters" in Alsace-Lorraine after 1890 was certainly connected with the opportunities offered by the rapid advance of the German economy.

The social struggle between a peasantry belonging to a "minority" group and alien landed proprietors certainly encouraged nationalist aspirations in many lands—Ireland, Transylvania, Istria, and the Balkans. But it did not spark the movement, it simply strengthened it after other issues had led the way.

Norway seems to have been the only country where the peasantry took an initiative in the national movement. Despite Norway's subjection to Sweden, she enjoyed considerable autonomy; Norwegians had no reason to complain of linguistic constraints; and economic interests were not endangered. The "upper classes"—civil servants and the commercial bourgeoisie—were not the architects of the national awakening. Its sponsors, especially Henrik Wergeland, were intellectuals who turned to the peasantry because it had been far less vulnerable to Danish or Swedish influences than the city dwellers, and because it was, as they said, the image of "national permanence."[12] This was the theme which the Nobel Prize winner Bjornstjerne Bjornson fostered widely in his "peasant tales." But the Norwegian peasants were independent owners of small holdings and very different, therefore, from the peasants of central Europe; their mentality, far more than material issues, separated them from the "upper classes."

Similarities notwithstanding, therefore, the awakening of national

---

[12] The groundwork was laid by John Neergard, who came of peasant stock; but Wergeland, in 1833–34, was the movement's spokesman. See Erica Simon, *Réveil national et culture populaire en Scandinavie* (Paris, 1960).

sentiments presented clearly different features from one group to another. But the study of these features has often been obscured by prejudice or sympathy: historians belonging to "minorities" have unconsciously tended to reconstruct the past in the light of subsequent triumphs; they have easily convinced themselves that the national movement concerned was deep and spontaneous even when there are grounds to doubt this. In order to give a really accurate account of the national feeling of a particular people at a particular time, it would be necessary to embark on new critical studies— a hazardous and difficult undertaking.

We may say, then, that in the evolution of international relations, the nationality movement has sometimes served as a force of association, when its object was to effect a union among national groups, and sometimes as a force of dissociation that undermined the structure of certain states.

1. The Nationality Movement as a Force of Association

We need only think of how the political map of Europe was transformed between 1850 and 1871, with the unification of Italy and Germany. Before that, the political fragmentation of the central part of the continent had been a permanent fact of international relations, even at the time of the Holy Roman Empire. The emergence of two great new states—one along the North Sea and the Baltic, the other in a central position on the Mediterranean— forced nearly all the other countries to modify the foundations of their foreign policy. The gains already made were significant of what might follow: Italian unification was incomplete as long as Austria-Hungary retained its sovereignty over the Alto Adige valley, Trieste, and Gorizia, and as long as Italians were established on the Dalmatian coast; the German Empire of 1871 did not fulfil the ideal of a "greater Germany" that had inspired some of the men of 1848. The Italian irredentist movement was almost constantly restrained by the policy of the government in Rome, but it was at the bottom of the wave of public opinion that eventually bore Italy into the European war in 1915. Again, between 1871 and 1914, the Anschluss between the Germans in Austria and the Reich was disavowed by Bismarck, and even in Austria only temporarily echoed in the line taken by the Christian Socialist Karl Lueger; but the idea reappeared immediately after the shock of 1914.

2. The Nationality Movement as a Force of Dissociation

Nationality movements resulted in the partitioning of certain states—the Netherlands in 1831, Sweden in 1905. It was the cause of the Ottoman Empire's abandonment of most of its European territories in 1912–13, the disintegration of Austria-Hungary in 1918, and, finally, the creation of the new Baltic states. These were major results that introduced essential or important changes in the political map.

But even when success was not secured, the threat that the protests of national minorities brought to bear on foreign-policy decisions in some of the Great Powers was a factor whose significance in international politics must not be underestimated.

Between 1871 and 1914, Germany may have had nothing immediate to fear from the opposition of the Danes in northern Schleswig, the Poles in west Prussia and Poznania, or even the people of Alsace-Lorraine; they constituted an insignificant part of the total Reich population. But in Great Britain, the Irish question weakened the international position of the government on several occasions; Salisbury recognized this in 1887, and Grey in the spring of 1914. In the Ottoman Empire, the hostility of the Christian peoples of the Balkans had been a source of unrest for thirty years before touching off the wars of 1912–13, playing into the hands of the Great Powers or setting them at odds in their defense of particular interests: insurrections in Bosnia-Herzegovina and Bulgaria in 1875 and 1876; a Rumelian independence movement in 1885; the uprising in Crete in 1897; and repeated armed attacks by the Macedonian revolutionary organization between 1899 and 1902. And the Polish question, notwithstanding the crushing of the Polish national movement in 1831 and again in 1863, threw a constant shadow over the foreign policy of Tsarist Russia up to World War I; it even affected the strategic plans of the Russian general staff, which, in the event of war with Germany, would have to conduct operations in regions inhabited by Poles and, since it could not trust locally recruited reserves to defend the territory, was obliged to transport these Poles to the interior and amalgamate them with Russians.

The nationalities problem weighed most heavily on Austria-Hungary— the multinational state par excellence; decision-making in the joint Ministry of Foreign Affairs of the Dual Monarchy was hindered often by the concern to avoid head-on clashes with the national minorities,[13] and always by the consequent sense of precariousness.

3. The Effect on International Politics

If we are to assess the practical significance of the national minorities protest in international politics, we have to remember the goals of these movements and the prospects before them.

Was the objective independence or merely autonomy? The answer depended largely on the policy pursued by the government to which the

---

[13] See Lord Acton's remarks in his chapter on nationality in *The History of Freedom and other Essays* (London, 1905).

minority was subject. Was it prepared, in order to give partial satisfaction to the nationality movements, to reform its structure, transform a unitary state into a federal one or even a confederation—in other words to abandon the safeguards offered by administrative cohesion? If the leaders of the minority group had no hope of achieving autonomy, they were all the more determined to demand independence.

The scope of the objective also depended on circumstances of human and political geography. One minority group attracted to an already existing national state, was likely to demand secession from its present authority and, therefore, independence; another, whose national feeling was no less strong, was satisfied to demand autonomy because it lacked an "external nucleus" it could eventually join and was took weak to constitute an independent state. The Serbs of southern Hungary wanted independence in 1910–12 in order to join Serbia, whereas the Czechs, who were no less imbued with a sense of nationality, were content to demand autonomy.

It was the existence of focuses of attraction that made the nationality problem so violent in the Danube area and the Balkans. The small nations formed in the Balkans during the nineteenth century achieved a political importance entirely out of proportion to their real power simply because they were able, by propaganda and by supporting clandestine groups, to maintain centers of agitation among the national minorities of the Ottoman Empire and Austria-Hungary. And, of course, the governments of these great multinational empires tried to check, or even to crush, these activities.

It is hardly necessary to remind ourselves that nationality movements were the direct cause of an increased number of international disputes. In view of the intermingling of national groups in most of central and south-eastern Europe, this was inevitable. How could nation and state coincide when in one and the same region peoples with different national sentiments were inextricably mingled?

Yet this problem was not immediately apparent to political observers prior to 1914, or in any event they gave it little thought, perhaps because they did not really believe that an experiment in the practical application of the nationality principle was possible. But it became inescapably clear in 1919, when the authors of the peace treaties had to take Wilson's Fourteen Points into account. Americans at the peace conference were surprised and disconcerted by the realities of this issue, of which they had not even been aware. The story of the disputes of 1919–20 over Vilna, Teschen, Fiume, and Macedonia is evidence of this embarrassment.

The methods finally adopted after 1919 to try to eradicate this permanent cause of unrest led to other difficulties. The treaty statute providing protection for the minorities, and entrusting the matter to the League of Nations, was intended to establish at least a theoretical guarantee of peace, even if it did not apply to all the states with varied populations. In practice, however, the protection system fell far short of ensuring peace. The minority groups, eager to have the system strictly enforced, voiced continuous complaints, relying on the publicity the Geneva platform gave to their grievances. The defeated states—especially Germany, after it joined the League—seized every opportunity to encourage these protests as a means of undermining the treaties. The political exploitation of the right to national self-determination became a characteristic feature of international relations between 1919 and 1939, far more than it had been before 1914, when governments had been more reluctant to intervene in the domestic affairs of other states.

In all its implications, then, the nationalities movement in Europe was a source of territorial change and, consequently, of serious disturbances in the political and economic relations of states.

III. NATION AND STATE OUTSIDE EUROPE

A. IN INDEPENDENT STATES

In the development of national sentiment and in the relation between nation and state, a comparison of non-European examples with the European experiences reveals more differences than similarities.

1. In the Western Hemisphere

In America, the revolt of European colonists against their mother countries was at the origin of most independent states. The English colonies that joined together to form the United States were not completely homogeneous; they included, in addition to the Indians and the English settlers (a majority among the Europeans), Dutch and French settlers as well. There was no religious unity: Anglicans, Puritans, Calvinists, and even Catholics lived side by side. Common attachment to the soil could not be a significant unifying factor, since the land was not their ancestors'.

So, prior to the Revolutionary War, the essential elements for the development of a nation did not exist. American historians have shown how a common sentiment asserted itself in the course of this war[14]; the Declaration of Independence was the first expression of it. But it was only after the creation of the Republic that the former colonists became aware of their national vocation and mission: to build a "new and better world" far from the foolish complications of European politics. What is most striking here is the novelty of this political and social experiment.

But a "unitary" spirit was not strongly in evidence until the War of 1812

---

[14] In particular, Hans Kohn, *American Nationalism: An Interpretative Essay* (New York, 1957).

against England. The westward territorial expansion of the United States between 1820 and 1850 helped to strengthen this national spirit, as the new territories were slowly populated by citizens from all parts of the Union who forgot their particularism and acquired a common "frontier" outlook. It is possible to see the first signs of a "cultural nationalism" stressing the differences between American and European cultures at this point. Yet, at the same time, this national sentiment was threatened by sectional antagonisms and by the rise of southern nationalism, the danger of which was already perceptible twenty years before the Civil War. It was only after the military defeat of the South that Charles Summer, in 1867, could declare that the United States constituted "one nation."[15]

The solidarity, unsure and shaky as it was, that the former English colonies of North America demonstrated after winning their independence never developed among the former colonies of Spain. Owing to geographical disparities, the circumstances of the military struggle, and the personal rivalries among the leaders of the revolution, the area once under Spanish domination was fragmented into eighteen states, each asserting its individuality against the rest despite the kinship among their ruling classes. It is no exaggeration to say that, in Latin America, the existence of independent states, rather than solidarity among them, "nourished" national sentiment.

During the second half of the nineteenth century, however, the volume of migrations from Europe threatened national cohesion in several states of the Western Hemisphere. The influx of migrants, who had nothing in common with the eighteenth-century settlers and often retained strong national sentiments of their own, threatened to touch off serious disturbances.

The United States was able to overcome the problem because the Anglo-Saxon majority remained vigorous and large and because the public authorities conducted a broad campaign of assimilation in the schools and were supported by the press and by various patriotic societies. Throughout the late nineteenth century, the immigrants appeared easily to adopt the modes of thought and life of the American people. In the early years of the twentieth century, however, the effectiveness of the "melting pot" began to show signs of failing, and assimilation became more difficult. This threat to the strength of national unity was realized by members of the government even before World War I,[16] and it was publicly expressed in President Wilson's Address to the American people of August 17, 1914. It was probably one of the reasons why U.S. immigration policy was radically altered in 1921.

In Brazil, on the other hand, where Spanish and Italian immigrants

---

[15] The studies by Merle E. Curti are interesting in this regard. See *The Making of an American Community* (Stanford, Calif., 1959) and *The Roots of American Loyalty* (New York, 1960).

[16] See *Reports of the Immigration Commission*, U.S. Senate, 61st Cong., 3d Sess., Document No. 7475 (2 vols.; Washington, 1911).

appeared alongside the Portuguese population, and in Argentina, where Italian immigration far exceeded Spanish immigration after 1880, there was an obvious danger that the original population would be outnumbered. How did this affect national feeling?

In practice, the development of strong national sentiments in Latin America seems to have been uneven.[17] In Honduras, Nicaragua, and Paraguay, it was found only among the social or intellectual elites. In Bolivia, Venezuela, and Brazil, national sentiment appeared strong also in the urban middle class. In Mexico, Chile, and Uruguay, the spread was wider. Argentina had exceptional difficulties (in 1914, foreign-born inhabitants constituted 30 per cent of the total population, 75 per cent of the population of Buenos Aires), yet in Argentina national integration was best achieved. Immigrants soon learned to shout "Long live our country!" and Argentinians displayed their faith in the "greatness" of their nation and in its future.

These differences can be traced to parallel disparities in economic and social development. In Argentina, 80 per cent of the men were employed in the secondary and tertiary sectors and in the higher categories of the primary sector of the economy; in Honduras, only 16 per cent. In countries where social groups remained strongly traditionalist, it was more difficult for national sentiments to take root. But the principal explanation for the differences lies in the quality of education. In all the Latin American states, military rallies and patriotic ceremonies doubtless awakened the sense of nationality; the press did much to foster it, too. But how history was taught in the schools was even more important. In Argentina, teachers emphasized the role of national heroes in the war of independence and the attempts to organize the government at the end of the war; they stressed the liberal principles on which the Constitution of 1835 was based; they sought to promote the idea that there existed an Argentine concept of political life different from that prevailing in other parts of Latin America, and to give the students a sense of pride in being Argentine.[18]

The debates in 1923–25 of the National Congress of Workers organized by the Argentine Patriotic League are instructive in this regard. In defining what the Argentine nation was, the League's president stressed the concepts of "culture" and "progress." Argentina's civilization, he said, was original in its moral and social aspects; the nation had created its own "type of political society." It was truly a nation, but a nation in process of development. National sentiment, said another, was based on territory, the solidarity of the citizens, and the consciousness of common traditions. But

---

[17] Judging by evidence shown in the latest monographs, particularly K. Silvert, "Nacionalismo y desarollo," *Rivista de la Universidad de Buenos Aires*, January, 1961, pp. 63–75.

[18] It is this spirit that informs the work of the Argentinian historian José P. Otero, for instance.

education also aided the development of that sentiment: the study of geography, citizenship, and, especially, history. For a young people "made up largely of immigrant, nonassimilated elements," such education was an "irreplaceable factor of unity," because history could and must define the significance of the "Argentine spirit," and point to the "spiritual conquests that have been achieved."[19] In a word, one could not assume that national sentiment would develop spontaneously; education, organized and given direction by the government, must be the instrument of that development.

Canada, which did not accede to independence but passed from the status of a colony to that of a dominion and thereby acquired most of the attributes of a state, was faced with even greater difficulties in maintaining national cohesion.

The survival of national sentiment among French Canadians (in 1940, 30.9 per cent of Canada's population) and the antagonism between them and the victorious English were at first the salient features of the situation. This antagonism was modified when the federal system enacted in 1867 provided the French Canadians with safeguards for their cultural and administrative autonomy. A French Canadian, Sir Wilfrid Laurier, was even elected Premier; he called for the moral unity of all Canadians and was supported by the majority of the inhabitants of the Province of Quebec.

French Canadian nationalists vigorously opposed the Federal Government during World War I, especially as regards the education laws and the requirement of compulsory military service. Why go off to defend French civilization in Europe, asked Henri Bourassa, when British Canadians sought in Canada's schools to "destroy French civilization in America"? A pastoral letter from Pope Benedict XV in October, 1919, counselling French Canadians not to resort to "illegitimate means" to state their case, diminished the furor for a time, but French Canadian sentiment between 1921 and 1925 reappeared—and in two forms.[20]

The traditional form was expressed most forcefully in the work of the historian priest Lionel Groulx: that French Canadians must defend the integrity of the "ethnic type" and of the "moral and social" powers of the French population; they must protect the originality of their culture and the vitality of Catholic religious sentiment. These themes, articulated in the periodical *Action Française*, were clearly related to those of nationality movements in Europe.

The other line, promoted by the economic historian Edouard Monpetit, appealed to material interests. The establishment in Montreal and Quebec of large companies controlled by British or American concerns, Monpetit

---

[19] M. Torrez Ibanez, "La educación nacionalista," *Report of Fourth Congress of the Argentine Patriotic League*, p. 220. See also G. Correa Luna's remarks in *Report of the Fifth Congress*, p. 343.

[20] See Mason Wade, ed., *Canadian Dualism* (Toronto, 1960).

argued, tended to relegate French Canadians to secondary and subordinate positions in industry and trade; the national movement should champion the "economic independence" of French Canada. And between 1929 and 1933, in the worst years of the depression, this argument fell upon receptive ears. The Prime Minister of Quebec refused to subscribe to this isolationist doctrine, however, and the Federal Government continued to include a number of French Canadians.

Since 1950, the French Canadian nationalist protest has asserted itself really vehemently. Some nationalists believe that the Canadian confederation will not long survive the centrifugal forces that threaten it, but they themselves will do nothing to hasten the disintegration; others openly advocate a separate French Canada, although they have been unable to show on what basis French Canada would exist were it to become independent.

At the turn of the century, immigrants directly threatened the Dominion's cohesiveness; the Canadian west was settled by Slavs and Scandinavians; and by 1910, newcomers amounted to nearly one-third the population of the country. Was there any national sentiment at all to bind together these many groups of diverse language, race, religion, and culture? Was there a Canadian *nation*? Did Canadians feel they formed a distinct people? Were they conscious of their individuality?

The terms in which Canadians formulate their reply are significant. A common life under a common government, says one,[21] has established a "political sympathy" among the varied populations; they feel an attachment to the governing institutions and a "territorial loyalty"—a desire to preserve the independence of Canada against other states. Political conditions, then, are the fundamental features. The national sentiment thus defined "varies with the individual, the local group, and with the occasion," and the nation's future depends "on the capacity of the people to tolerate marked dissimilarities and yet cultivate mutual interests and loyalties." The Canadian nation, then, is not indestructible, since it has no roots in the past. It is that basic trait which distinguishes it from the European concept of "nation."

2. In Asia

In Asia, national sentiment was first apparent in Japan in the nineteenth century. Conditions after 1637, when the shogunate government had decided to forbid all contact with foreigners (except in a few cases), undoubtedly led the Japanese people to consider themselves very different from all other peoples; the religious traditions of Shintoism convinced them of their special rights and gifts.[22] Yet, despite the temporal and religious authority of the

---

[21] Hugh MacDowall Clokie, *Canadian Government and Politics* (Toronto and New York, 1944).

[22] See below, Chapter Seven, pp. 198–200.

emperor, Japan's division into feudal estates operated against any developing sense of nationality. The notion of common interests existed among nobles and the intellectuals, but the peasants recognized the authority only of their feudal lord, the *daimyo*, the only object of their loyalty.

When feudal Japan was obliged to open her doors to foreign influence in 1854, there was a wave of xenophobia. Can one say that this movement had the features of a "nationality movement"? Not yet, for the *daimyos* and their clans were not yet unified in action against the external threat. National sentiment was apparent only when the *samurai*—members of the social elite—realized the need to transform Japan's institutions in order to enable them to resist foreign pressure. The reformers proposed to abolish the feudal system, and they hoped to gain the support of the imperial court to break down the resistance of the shogunate and those who benefited from it. They succeeded in rallying a majority of the *samurai* to their views and immediately instituted an educational program intended to inculcate "public spirit" in the peasant masses. When the Meiji period began in 1868, the Emperor and the reformers labored to achieve a systematic exaltation of Japanese national sentiment; they were completely successful.

Prior to 1884, Korea had been a virtually independent state, although in theory bound by ties of vassalage to the Chinese Empire. Her people enjoyed one language and a common heritage of tradition. Circumstances were thus conducive to the development of a sense of nationality, but no such feeling was expressed with any clarity when Japan first began to threaten Korea's independence in 1884 and then again in 1894. Only when confronted with *faits accomplis*—the establishment of a Japanese protectorate in 1905, the "deposition" of the king in July, 1907, the disbanding of the Korean Army, and, finally, the proclamation of annexation by Japan in 1910—did Korean national resistance movements appear. Even so, this national movement was not really strong until 1919, when Korean intellectuals hoped to appeal to the principles laid down by President Wilson in his Fourteen Points. The magnitude of the demonstrations on March 1, 1919, when the Korean National Committee proclaimed independence, and the violence of their repression, are evidence that the movement enjoyed widespread support. The Japanese Resident General reported that the "upper classes" had been prudent enough to avoid compromising themselves, but he did not dispute the extent of popular cooperation that the rebellion received.

The situation in China was altogether different, since the Chinese people had been subject since 1644 to the foreign domination of the Manchus. Despite the multiplicity of their dialects, the Chinese had one common written language, that of the mandarins; they were conscious of the great history and power of their civilization; and they felt as a group intellectually superior to the Manchus. (Other sectors of the population—the Muslims of Yunnan, the Hakkas of central China, the Tibetans and Mongols—were too inconsiderable[23] to shake these factors of cohesion.) These were surely circumstances conducive to the assertion of national sentiment, yet national sentiment emerged only slowly. The secret societies that had tried, especially since the end of the eighteenth century, to foster a spirit of resistance to the dynasty and prepare the ground for a Ming restoration, were limited in membership, and their propaganda found no response among the masses. Even the great T'ai P'ing rebellion, which gravely undermined the authority of the dynasty for two decades in the 1850's and 1860's did not generate a Chinese national movement; the imperial court called on the higher administrative echelons and the generals to help crush the revolt. And of course the Boxer Rebellion in 1900 was an anti-foreign, not a national, movement.

It was only after the defeats inflicted on China by Japan in 1894–95 and by Europeans in 1900–1901 that the anti-Manchu movement broadened. A sense of nationality now began to appear among the intellectuals, and they turned to the problem of how to preserve China and Chinese traditions from foreign influences. But, while Sun Yat-sen was preparing the revolution he was to initiate in 1911, notions of patriotism and duty to the state were in point of fact still alien to the masses; their horizon was narrow—local or at most provincial—and foreigners found their indifference to the common interests of the Chinese people striking.

Recent studies throw light on the process whereby this general outlook was gradually modified.[24] The process was initiated by Chinese scholars whose contact with Westerners and Japanese had given them the idea of a "national patriotism." K'ang Yu-wei, the great reformer of 1898, stressed the importance of patriotism in the unification and modernization of Japan after the fall of the shogunate. Liang Ch'i-ch'oa, his disciple, was convinced that, in order to "preserve the Chinese race," it was essential to awaken the "spirit of patriotism" and make the Chinese people aware of their unique characteristics. Both declared their conviction that the defense of China's civilization depended on solidarity in the face of foreign pressure.

It was to this conviction that Sun Yat-sen appealed in his revolutionary party's first publication: was not the sense of nationhood at the very foundation of Europe's progress? At this time, however, Sun Yat-sen's concern was to assert Chinese solidarity against the Manchus, and it was only later, in 1924, that he was to insist (in *The Three Principles of the People*) on the necessity of "promoting the national spirit."

The schools and the press, in China as everywhere else, were the most

---

[23] They did not number more than about 10 million out of a total population of well over 300 million (in 1910).

[24] See, in particular, Cyrus H. Peake, *Nationalism and Education in Modern China* (New York, 1932) ; J. de Francis, *Nationalism and Language Reform in China* (Princeton, N.J., 1950) ; Chow Tse-tsung, *The May Fourth Movement* (Cambridge, Mass., 1960).

effective instruments in the nationality campaign. Chinese newspapers came into existence only in the last years of the nineteenth century but from the outset struck a patriotic note. Nevertheless, they reached only a small minority: at the end of World War I, 90 per cent of the Chinese population was still illiterate; moreover, circulation was hampered by linguistic differences. (The situation was remedied in 1919 when a uniform written language was adopted for purposes of education.) The schools, for their part, were not encouraged to embark on a program stressing Chinese national pride until November, 1912, when the Ministry of Education ordered that elementary and secondary schools seek to instill in the students a "patriotic spirit" and the sense of belonging to a single *nation*.

The years of the civil war, from 1916 to 1928, showed how ineffective those instructions had been. But it was during this period—in 1919 with the May Fourth Movement, and in 1926–27—that the first great demonstrations of national feeling occurred, albeit with only a temporary effect and only in the urban population. Instructions issued to the schools in 1928, after the triumph of the Kuomintang had finally restored the unity of the state at least in theory, did little more than reiterate those of 1912. And when Chiang Kai-shek launched the New Life movement in 1934, he continued to underline the need to develop a "national consciousness." More than thirty years after the fall of the Manchu dynasty, this was still the chief problem of the Chinese Government.

3. In the Middle East

The Ottoman Empire of the nineteenth century, like Austria-Hungary, was a multinational state. In the Asian part of the Empire, the Turks (the great majority of the population of Anatolia) lived side by side with Armenians and Greeks; in the rest of the Empire, Arabs predominated over other groups such as the Kurds, Druses, Maronites, and the Jews in Palestine.

Here, then, was a situation that at first sight looks analogous to the position of national minorities in Europe. Certainly the Greeks and Armenians considered themselves as distinct groups—from the point of view of language, religion, and culture—and regarded the Turks as enemies. The Greeks in Asia Minor, especially after the Cretan uprising of 1866, were not indifferent to the proclamation of the Greek national program. And the Armenian national movement was active well before 1895. But what about the Arabs?

The Arab "national awakening," directed against Turkish domination, began to develop around the middle of the nineteenth century. Its sponsors were not Muslims, but Arabs who had been converted to Christianity. The literary work of Ibrahim el Yazidji, a Lebanese Christian, contains the first clear expression, in 1868, of the national idea, and it was at this date that secret societies were formed in Beirut and Damascus to promote that idea. The movement found support in the teachings of a political writer who was a Muslim but not an Arab—Jamal al-Din al-Afghani—who stressed the importance of the Arabs' role in the spread of Islam. Like the European nationalists, Jamal al-Din regarded community of language as the surest foundation of solidarity for a human group; he called on the Ottoman Empire to reform its structure and transform itself into a confederation of national states.

The principal propagandists in the 1870's were a Syrian, Butrus al Bustani, who published an encyclopedia, and a Lebanese, Takba, publisher of the Egyptian newspaper *Al-Ahram,* who developed the theme that membership in the same religion—Islam—did not necessarily mean a community of political fortunes. These innovators were in touch with the Lazarist missionaries in Syria and Lebanon as well as with the Protestant college at Beirut. Fifteen or twenty years later, another Syrian, Abd el Rhaman al Kawaliki, went so far as to say that the Ottoman sultan had usurped the caliphate, and to suggest the establishment of an Arab caliphate, so that the Arabs would no longer have an obligation of obedience to the Ottoman authority.

Finally, during the last years of the century, Mohammed Raskid Rida, a Syrian, asserted the superiority of the Arabs over the Turks. This line of thinking laid the groundwork for the establishment of the League of the Arab Motherland and the publication, in 1905, of a manifesto demanding independence.

Thus the linguistic factor, historical memories, and a sentiment of frustration, in addition to cultural kinship, played a predominant part in the emergence of the Arab nationalist movement, as they had in the European nationalist movements half a century earlier. Regardless of other differences, the meaning of this is clear: the promoters of "Arabism" were viewing the situation from a "Western" point of view. But the fundamental difficulty remained: that the Arabs also belonged to the Islamic community. Jamal al-Din, it is true, proclaimed that linguistic unity was a "stronger bond" than religious unity, but the ulemas remained hostile to the nationalist idea. Condemning the Arab movement, they invoked the *hadiths* of the Prophet, who had repudiated the "clan spirit"; reminded the people of their duty of obedience of the Ottoman caliphate; and stressed the danger of a split in the Islamic world. To overcome their opposition, promoters of the Arab movement took pains to present their program as one that could "regenerate" Islam, and they accused the Turks of having misunderstood the Koran—in a word, they adapted religion to their political designs. Nevertheless, until 1914, the religious factor continued to hinder the growth of Arab sentiment.

World War I was the Arab independence movement's great opportunity, destroying the Ottoman Empire and, only four years later, the caliphate. Now "Arabism"—with religious faith and national sentiment working hand in hand—turned against European influences, and economic interests too began to work to the advantage of national resistance. The commercial middle class in Beirut, Aleppo, and Damascus supported independence in order to be able to limit the importation of European goods and keep a hold on the domestic market.

In addition to the Greek, Armenian, and Arab national movements that had at first been directed against the Ottoman hegemony and grew steadily stronger after 1919, there now appeared a *Turkish* national movement, arising from the ruins of the Ottoman Empire. The doctrinal basis of this movement was set out by Ziya Gokalp, a political writer and member of the Society of Union and Progress, in a number of tracts and articles between 1908 and 1918.

According to Gokalp, the continued decadence of the Ottoman Empire since the end of the eighteenth century was the result of the exaggerated place held in the life of the state by Islamic civilization, the origins of which were Arab and Persian, not Turkish; this civilization had obstructed the adoption of European techniques, because the life of society had been regulated by the Koran and because the Ottoman sultan had been Caliph. The remedy? To modernize the Turkish regions of the empire; create a Turkish state which, without abandoning the spiritual values of Islam, would adopt a system of separation between religious and socio-political organizations and forms; and adopt the techniques and scientific methods of the "Westerners." The Turkish populations in this way would be shown that they must and could regain a controlling position. To instill this desire in them, it was necessary to appeal to the idea of "nation"; national sentiment must take pride of place over religious solidarity.

Here, then, was an ideology that appealed directly to the European "nationalities movement." But how effective would it have been had it not been taken over by Mustafa Kemal, who, without sharing all of Gokalp's ideas, retained his essential themes and used them as support for his political and patriotic plans—secularization, "Westernization," and "Turkism"? It is interesting to note that when the Turkish Republic finally achieved stability after ten years of struggle and effort, Mustafa Kemal attached great importance to the teaching of history and the study of the origins of "Turkism." The publication in May, 1932, of a bulky new textbook of general history, and the convening two months later of a historical congress, were intended to affirm the "personality of the Turkish nation"; the Ottoman Empire had not been the "true image" of that nation; it had been but a "passing phase"; if the Turkish people were to become "prouder," they must be shown that they were the heirs to a great and ancient civilization.

B. IN COLONIES

Resistance to the imperial expansion of European powers sometimes took forms analogous to national protests in Europe. What value should we place on this similarity?

The fact is that the colonial resistance movements did not begin to appeal to the nationality principle and the right of self-determination until the colonies had an intellectual leadership trained and formed by European example and education. But on the other hand, the circumstances varied enormously, and we must examine this diversity briefly here.

1. In Asia

Vietnam had an ancient civilization, but it was the civilization of China. There was no "national culture"; the scholastic written language was Chinese. But during the period when Vietnam (or Annam) was a vassal of China, the population regarded itself as distinct from its Chinese or Cambodian neighbors, and the mandarins showed a will to resist Chinese suzerainty when the latter was asserted by force of arms. Between 1863 and 1867, believing that it would give the state the means to preserve its independence, a reformer named Nguyen Truong To drew up a program for "modernization" of the administration, educational system, economy, and army but the occupation of Cochinchina by the French interrupted his plans. After 1884, the resistance of the mandarins was expressed against the French; teachers in the private nationalist schools founded by the young teacher Nguyen Hien in 1907 were often former scholars who felt a deep sense of humiliation at this latest turn in their country's history. They were supported in their views by revolutionary movements whose leaders came from the "people": De Tham, who for ten years led the struggle against the French, seems to have had an ideal of patriotic resistance. The deposition in 1917 of Emperor Duy-Tan deepened the humiliation. But was there any *national* sentiment? The highly organized nature of village life and its administrative autonomy continued to check its spread.

In 1919, the national movement found new leaders, trained not in the Chinese but in the western school. A typical case was that of Nguyen Ai Quoc, who is better known today as Ho Chi Minh. His father was a scholar who had refused to learn the language of the protectorate power and who had inculcated in his son an attitude of resistance to French domination. At the same time, he had judged it advisable to have his son attend classes at the Franco-Vietnamese *lycée* in Vinh. The study of the classics of French political literature inspired the young Vietnamese intellectuals there with the European ideal of the "nation"; Pham Quynh, the director of the periodical

Nam Phong, was a nationalist of the Maurice Barrès type.[25] And the many revolutionary movements of 1930 in Vietnam were undoubtedly inspired by the national idea. Active participants were recruited among minor officials, sales personnel, laborers, and teachers in direct contact with the French, much more than among the peasantry, which long remained indifferent to the struggle. Yet, despite these revolutionary trends, the French administration encouraged the teaching of national history in the primary schools. The objective was doubtless to show that Vietnam had often managed to checkmate China; this fostering of a sense of nationality among the peasantry naturally resulted in the further undermining of French domination.

The Philippines, with a far from homogeneous population, experienced three centuries of Spanish rule and in 1898 passed to United States control. The First Philippine Commission, under J. G. Schurman, noted the following spring that there was "no Philippine nation, no public spirit in the archipelago." There was, of course, an oligarchy of propertied and educated men who were in a position to express their opinions, but given their economic dependency, these men supported U.S. interests.

The Aguinaldo rebellion against the American administration almost immediately belied these optimistic views. The United States therefore deemed it advisable to permit the establishment of only a single political party, constituted under its aegis.

Soon after this order was rescinded, in 1907, the Partido Union Nacionalista came into being, demanding independence by law-abiding means. This was the party that triumphed in every election for fifteen years. It recruited its leaders from among the great landowners whose real objective was autonomy without breaking with the United States. But by 1925, American authorities were ready to admit that a large part of the Philippine population desired, not autonomy, but independence; and by 1926, the leaders of the Philippine national movement were sure enough of success to propose that a plebiscite be conducted—a proposal the American governor was careful not to accept. Eight years later, in 1934, after the economic depression had led American producers to wish to eliminate the competition of Philippine sugar, and after the demonstration of Japanese imperialism, politicians in Washington recognized this aspiration to independence by granting the Philippines transitional commonwealth status.

In India, the origins of the national movement go back to 1885. Its sponsors were Hindu intellectuals supported by some humanitarian "Westerners" who thought it right that the inhabitants enjoy self-determination and the benefit of politically liberal principles. From the start, the National Congress Party sought to foster a sense of solidarity among India's varied

---

[25] As Philippe Devillers has called him. See his "Vietnamese Nationalism and French Politics," in William L. Holland, ed., *Asian Nationalism and the West* (New York, 1953).

populations, despite the obstacles posed by the political fragmentation of "India of the Rajahs" and the caste system. But the national movement only really gained strength as English education created a native elite familiar with English thought. Economic circumstances favored the development of the movement once the native commercial middle class began to realize the divergence between its interests and those of the British traders—that is, when they felt the effects of the competition with European goods and realized how the customs policy imposed by the British favored the latter.

Should it be inferred that this national protest was in any way related to the national movements in Europe? The Indian national movement could appeal neither to linguistic unity nor to a common history, and it was not overly concerned with the attitude of the masses. Above all, it was undermined from the outset by religious differences. As soon as the nationalists demanded the participation of Indians in the administration and asked for elected Indian representatives, Muslims feared they would be swamped by Hindus—a fear clearly shown in 1906 and even more in 1926. National aspirations existed to the extent that Muslims and Hindus were both interested in conducting a common action against England, but the success of the national liberation movement in 1947 led immediately to the collapse of the Indian "nation."

2. In North Africa

In Egypt, the disposition to oppose British rule began to appear among intellectuals and rural leaders about 1905.[26] Among the factions into which this movement of ideas was divided, only one, led by Mustafa Kamel, a man of action as much as a publicist, clearly asked for independence—pointing to the examples of Japan and the Young Turks—without attempting to give any of these demands a doctrinal basis. The others wished to rely solely on persuasion to get the British to evacuate Egypt, but were concerned to act on principles.

They were not in agreement, however, on which principles. Muhammad 'Abduh and Ali Yusuf appealed to the interests of Islam; Ahmad Lutfi, on the other hand, considered that religion could no longer be a decisive element in politics in the twentieth century. He counted on education to open the way to "moral and social regeneration" and to restore to the Egyptian people a sense of their dignity. Only then, he said, would the existence of an Egyptian "nation" become a reality. (In that nation, the Copts would have their place, since Lutfi relegated religious sentiment to the background.) But none of these leaders, even when they based their theories on Islam, appeared to have considered joining forces with the Arab national movement, although

---

[26] On this early period, J. Mohammed Ahmed's study of *The Intellectual Origins of Egyptian Nationalism* (London, 1960) is particularly instructive.

some Arab nationalists had taken up residence in Cairo. The Egyptian regarded himself as having a distinct personality in the Arab world: was he not a descendant of the Pharaohs, of the Ptolemies? Did he not possess a "political education" superior to the Syrians'?

We may ask why these impulses came to a head between 1914 and 1918 and why in 1919 the National Party (Wafd) became a dominant mass movement. There were a number of reasons: the intellectual middle class objected to the suspension of the legislative assembly for the duration of the war; above all, it was aware, after January, 1918, of the possible implications of President Wilson's messages and addresses. The peasants, who before the war had been indifferent to the first demonstrations of national sentiment, were hard hit in 1917 and 1918 by the requisition of men and draft animals; they objected, moreover, to being treated as suspects by the British military authorities who conducted house searches and in May, 1917, demanded that all arms be turned in. Nevertheless, without the personal action of Zaghlul Pasha, without his ascendancy over the masses and his efforts to associate Copts and Muslims, the movement might never have developed as it did.

In Tunisia, Algeria, and even Morocco, where there existed a "strong political personality" despite the multiplicity of languages and ethnic groups, opposition to European domination prior to 1914 did not take the form of national movements. In all three territories, at the time of their conquest, the French found "loyal" tribes that helped them to quell the "rebel" tribes. It was not until after 1919, when Wilson's Fourteen Points awakened among Arab and Berber intellectuals and religious leaders a hope of escaping French domination, that a "national" protest began to emerge; the manifesto of the Algerian nationalists in 1918, and that of the Tunisian party, the Neo-Destour, in 1920, appealed to the right of national self-determination. But it does not necessarily follow that they were analogous to European national movements.

In Algeria, Kabyl and Mozabite particularism remained vigorous enough to jeopardize the existence of an Algerian nation. In 1919, the French Governor General Jonnart, who favored a policy of increasing the rights of the native inhabitants, underlined this heterogeneity: "We do not harbor the illusion that a common spirit will emerge in Algeria. But we have the duty and the will to enable diverse races to live and prosper side by side, through an association of interests." And indeed, the young Muslim intellectuals who had been active in the protest movement since 1900, especially since 1910, were by and large concerned only to achieve political rights. They would be satisfied for the time being, they said, to achieve equality with the French in Algeria—"assimilation," in fact. Their manifesto did not appeal to national principles at all.

In 1919 and 1920, the Young Algerians kept to much the same line. Only the emigrants from North Africa who had taken refuge in Geneva appealed to the Wilsonian principles of national self-determination and demanded independence. Finally in 1921 a *national* movement began to emerge; its sponsors were religious reformers who asserted that the Muslim populations of Algeria constituted a "nation" with linguistic, racial, and historical bases; they relied primarily on the awakening of Islam to bring about "salvation."[27]

In Tunisia, the Young Tunisians began to voice their opposition to the French Protectorate in 1910–12, but they invoked religious and economic grievances and made no attempt to evolve a "national" doctrine. In 1919, however, when Abd el Aziz Taalbi took over the leadership of the movement, the prospects were different. Abd el Aziz had spent the war years in India, where he had seen nationalism in action; he was in contact with the Egyptian national movement; and he had the Libyan uprising against Italian rule as an example before him. The Young Tunisians now denounced economic and social injustices and blamed them on the protectorate; it appealed to Wilson's principles and the basic principles of French law; still, it did not appeal to "national" sentiment any more than it did to Islam.

In Morocco, the first genuine expression of national sentiment appeared in 1930, when Allal al Fassi presented the Sultan with a reform program drawn up by the Moroccan Committee of Action—a group led by intellectuals who sought, in the name of Islam and Arab civilization (even in Berber territory), to resist any attempt at assimilation. In appealing to the right of national self-determination, they perforce turned to European ideology and cited Ernest Renan and Fustel de Coulanges. They also sought to propagate the national ideal among the population, but their progress here was very slow. Only after Morocco's proclamation of independence in 1955 was a consistent effort made to eliminate, or at least "neutralize," tribal particularism.[28]

3. In Sub-Saharan Africa

The emergence of national sentiment among the peoples of Africa south of the Sahara raises more complex questions. Resistance to European colonial penetration had been widespread. But does it follow that national movements existed? The idea of "nation" implies coordinated action, common sentiments, and a common program. But in most of southern and central Africa, the peoples were of diverse origin and spoke different languages; they had been grouped under the authority of different governments only as a result of historical "accidents," the latest of which was colonization; they possessed

---

[27] On the Young Algeria movement, see A. Ageron, "Le Mouvement jeune algérien de 1900 à 1923," *Bulletin de la Société d'histoire moderne*, No. 21 (January, 1962); and A. Nouschi, *La Naissance du nationalisme algérien, 1914–1954* (Paris, 1962).

[28] See J. M. Piguin, *Les Thèmes unitaires du nationalisme marocain à travers Al-Istiqlal* (Rabat, 1959).

neither common traditions nor common attitudes to their future. Tribal solidarity was very strong, but there was little solidarity beyond it. Consequently, if a national mentality was to be attained, the tribal mentality must first be transcended.

Colonial rule actually paved the way for this development. The policies of the colonial powers usually succeeded in destroying the authority of the tribal chiefs and notables. Moreover, through the demarcation of colonial frontiers, an artificial framework was established within which a common administrative authority created ties among tribes. The European plantations and commercial enterprises attracted young natives, who, leaving their tribes, became "uprooted"; a new society sprang up alongside the traditional one—a rural proletariat and the beginnings of a petit bourgeoisie. European Catholic and Protestant missions, for their part, attempted to undermine the tribal system by denouncing the errors of traditional African society and by propagating European social and ethical ideas through their schools.[29] Finally, in the sphere of agriculture, the advantages achieved by well equipped and mechanized European methods in contrast to mediocre indigenous husbandry, led native farmers to believe that only a national economic system could enable them to meet and overcome this competition.

These were the various causes that seem to have contributed to the development of independence movements within the colonies—led by persons belonging to different tribes wanting to inspire common aims among the people in order to combat European domination. But the effect of these influences and the pace of development were uneven, depending on varying circumstances of the native environment and varying European administrative methods. It is therefore no exaggeration to argue, as Rupert Emerson has done, that the nature of colonial policies influenced the development of national sentiments in sub-Saharan Africa.

But where, in fact, was national feeling expressed? Nowhere in France's African colonies, it seems, before 1914. In the German colonies, the great Herrero Insurrection in Southwest Africa in 1904–8 and the Manga Bell rebellion in the Cameroons in 1913 were both tribal revolts. But the situation changed after World War I. The Bantus of South Africa, for instance, felt that they constituted a homogeneous group, they possessed common historical memories, and they displayed a spirit of solidarity. Hence their demands showed the characteristics of a national movement. A similar solidarity existed among the inhabitants of the Gold Coast and Liberia; it began to evolve, also, in the Cameroons, where in 1938 a Cameroonian youth movement emerged that was to unify the populations of the territory. But in none

---

[29] Virtually all of the postwar African political leaders passed through Christian schools, writes Ndabaningi Sithole in *African Nationalism* (London and New York, 1959). The role of the native clergy was insignificant before 1914. In 1913, however, in the Cameroons, a native Baptist pastor decided to found a church independent of European ecclesiastical organizations; it was one of the leaders of this church who headed the resistance movement to white domination among the Douala people in 1921.

of these cases was the movement spontaneous. In Liberia, some 20,000 Negroes from the United States had spread "Western ideas." In the Gold Coast, the British administration had fostered such solidarity. And in the Cameroons, the youth movement had been initiated by the French Mandate officials, who hoped in this way to gain support among the people and frustrate German colonial ambitions. In the Belgian Congo, on the other hand, the liberation movement launched in 1921 by Simon Kimbangu, the "Messiah of the Negroes," was spontaneous, but it was not an expression of a Congolese national sentiment. In sum, then, the watchwords spread at the instigation of the four congresses of the Pan-African movement did not evoke much response.

Only after 1945 did a new spirit assert itself among Africans; collective demands were voiced to establish governments under African leaders. The organized movements supporting these claims appealed not only to the right of national self-determination, but to the right of the "nation" to constitute an independent state.

Yet the territorial frameworks in which these aspirations to nationhood were expressed were artificial, in most cases provided by the former European colonies, whose frontiers were drawn with no consideration for linguistic or religious factors. To what extent, then, has the aspiration to independence been an expression of "national sentiment"? Studies made on the subject are still too few and too inconclusive to permit final answers, but it would seem that the idea of "nation" was used by native intellectuals because it gave their claim to independence a moral basis and corresponded to a doctrine that Europeans could hardly disclaim.

The "national" movements found followers mainly among the *déracinés* who had left their tribes and joined labor unions organized on European models. After the success of the independence movements, the governments of new black African states then turned to the business of establishing solidarity among its peoples, no matter what their tribes. According to Léopold Sédar Senghor, President of Senegal, the way to "achieve nationhood" was to create a state that would draw the people together and make of them "a single people animated by a common faith and striving toward a common end." The bases of the national community, then, were laid *after* the activists who appealed to the national idea had entered the scene; the existence of the state became (much more than in Latin America) the principal catalyst of national feeling; the nation developed out of the state.

IV. CONCLUSION

The development of a sense of nationality and the ideology of national sentiment clearly take very different forms from one region of the world to another. These differences are linked to differences in the level of civilization and in social structure, to the uneven progress of "liberty" and "democracy," and also to circumstances external to each community concerned with the issue—that is, to threats or constraints imposed by alien forces. In order to try to account for and understand all these varied forms of national sentiment, a new terminology and methodology would be necessary to undertake broad critical studies. That is something that has scarcely begun.[30] But this general survey of the historical evolution of national sentiment may suggest a few remarks.

A. Can history prove the existence of a nation as a *fact?* When certain given external signs, or certain features of a community's collective psychology, appear, it is possible to say that this community constitutes a nation. At the same time, we must be clear about the validity and significance of these signs or criteria. The criteria most often cited by Europeans (on the strength of their own experience), such as linguistic or religious community, or common traditions, are applicable to Japan and China, partially applicable in the Americas, but hardly at all to Africa south of the Sahara. The only valid criterion remains the expression of a common will, of the "will to live in common."

Further questions arise. How is the genuineness of "national" sentiment to be recognized? And how does one gauge the level the sense of nationality has reached? Analysis is difficult enough with contemporary societies; it is clearly far more difficult when applied to the past.[31] Moreover, historical research is likely to be distorted by present preoccupations. New states all too often have sought to show that the national sentiments to which they appeal are of ancient origin. Vietnamese historiographers, for instance, endeavor to find antecedents to modern nationalism in fifteenth-century Annam. And Cameroonian intellectuals cite the insurrection of Manga Bell as an expression of national sentiment, although it was confined to a single tribe and was basically a protest against land expropriation. Leaders of the Moroccan independence movement sought to prove that "Morocco" had existed before the establishment of the French Protectorate and even attempted, at the cost of some quite considerable straining of the facts, to explain how tribal feeling had "engendered" Morocco's national spirit. There is no reason to believe that the proliferation of this type of historical writing will clarify this complex problem.

B. What are the relations between *nation* and *state?* Here again, European examples are seldom valid outside Europe. In Europe, the nation asserted itself in the nineteenth century as an autonomous force, either independent

---

[30] I am indebted, however, to a study group established by Raoul Girardet, which has done some important pioneering work in this field.

[31] I have limited myself here to the historical aspect of this problem, and have not discussed the rather debatable attempts made, by Karl Deutsch in particular, to determine tests that would permit one to foresee the evolution of national sentiment in a given region or regions.

of the state (in the case of national minorities) or antecedent to the state (in the case of unifying nationality movements). Outside Europe, on the other hand, the state in most cases preceded the nation and was the principal agent in the development of national sentiment—at least in Latin America, Canada, and Africa south of the Sahara. Arab national movements, however, bore greater analogies to their European counterparts.

Yet there were so many differences! The Chinese national movement in certain respects resembled Western ones; but again, it was the state that, after the elimination of the Manchu dynasty, succeeded in developing a national consciousness. The United States was a different case again; here national sentiment emerged spontaneously among the greater part of the population, but it would have been seriously threatened by the enormous influx of immigrants had not the government supported the idea of the "melting pot."

C. What political systems were most conducive to the development of national feelings?[32]

In Europe, favorable circumstances existed wherever the government was liberal or democratic and permitted the free expression of public opinion. The principle of national self-determination was essentially democratic. But a constant relation cannot be shown; national minority movements often emerged under quite unfavorable circumstances. And outside Europe, where the role of the state was important in fashioning national sentiment, it is difficult to attribute any influence to "democracy." In most cases, national sentiment was effectively promoted by authoritarian or oligarchic regimes.

Looking at the question with the issue that primarily concerns the historian of international relations in mind—that of war and peace—there is less uncertainty. The development of national feeling has seldom contributed to the maintenance of peace in any part of the world. Mazzini regarded the nationality movement as a means of establishing an "international fraternity" in Europe, but he first envisaged a complete realignment of the political map of Europe. And when Woodrow Wilson argued in 1918 that the application of this principle was the prerequisite to the formation of a League of Nations and a system of collective security, it was found that the principle was impossible to apply.

It must be repeated, therefore, that national sentiments, because they were directed against existing territorial arrangements, were almost everywhere a factor of serious disturbance in international relations.

---

[32] See Rupert Emerson, *From Empire to Nation* (Cambridge, Mass., 1960), p. 214. Emerson has interesting views on the subject, although they are obscured by a confusion between *national sentiment* and *nationalism*.

7

NATIONALISM

National sentiment, although it often manifests itself in opposition to national sentiments of other communities, is not by definition a dominating force; it is in theory prepared to respect the rights of others. Or so the sponsors of the national movements of the nineteenth century argued. To the extent that the aim was to give the state a national basis, mutual respect was possible at least in regions where distribution of "nationalities" made it possible to establish "clearly recognizable lines" between them.[1] But this condition was far from fulfilled everywhere. A nation-state was thus obliged to include a variety of groups within its frontiers. But this was a mere infraction of the principle, imposed, or apparently imposed, by circumstances.

In practice, however, as soon as a nation-state gathered strength and substance, it seldom respected the rights of other nations; the history of relations among European states since the sixteenth century is sufficient proof of this. The desire to assert the interests of a particular nation as against other human groups; the conviction that the nation had a "mission" to fulfill; the determination to increase its strength, power, and prosperity; pride in belonging to that state; the sense of material, moral, or intellectual superiority; the wish to make known or to impose this superiority—such have been the characteristics of that exaltation of the national sentiment which has been defined in the French language since the end of the nineteenth century by the term *nationalisme*. (In English and American usage, the word "nationalism" covers both national sentiment and the exaltation of that sentiment. In this chapter, "nationalism" is used in the French sense.)

I. FORMS OF NATIONALISM

Nationalism has for the most part been expansionist—both in "intercontinental" relations and in relations among states of one continent.

In the relations *between* continents, expansionist nationalism has taken the form of colonial imperialism; this, between 1880 and 1914, was a primary concern of most of the major European states. The arguments and rationales

---

[1] This was the expression President Wilson used in his Fourteen Points. But he allowed for exceptions—either for economic reasons (e.g., Poland's access to the sea) or in order to take historical factors into account (e.g., in the Balkans).

of statesmen who promoted colonial expansion in Great Britain, Germany, France, and Italy (the most active colonial powers) are strikingly similar.

There was the economic argument: to secure outlets for commercial products and supplies of raw materials. "Colonial policy is the daughter of industrial policy," Jules Ferry said. Bernhard Dernburg, German Minister of Colonies in 1907, agreed, and of course so did Joseph Chamberlain.

There was the strategic argument: to secure naval bases and ports for merchant shipping on the great international sea routes.

There was the moral argument (sometimes colored by religious considerations): to extend the sphere of Western civilization. Chancellor Hohenlohe, for instance, believed that the establishment of colonies would give "full freedom of action" to the religious missions.

There was the prestige argument: colonial expansion was a "natural law" that a great state could not avoid without resigning itself to decadence. In a speech of December 11, 1894, Hohenlohe referred to it as "a requirement of national honor," and Bethmann-Hollweg stated in January, 1914, that expansion was necessary to every growing being.

There was the power argument: rival states must not be allowed to gain an advantage in this division of the world. Such was Lord Rosebery's concern when he sought to show that the British Empire was not large enough and that Great Britain must continue to take part in the carving up of far-distant regions.[2]

The importance accorded to ·these arguments[3] differed, of course, in different countries. In Germany and Great Britain, the economic argument carried more weight than it did in France or Italy; in Great Britain, the conviction grew that "Englishmen" were a "governing race" of peerless quality—a claim that other colonial powers do not seem to have challenged. But the general lines remained the same. Everywhere, force was regarded as a legitimate means if the objective was to carry out a plan of colonial expansion; everywhere, too, the needs and interests of the natives themselves were said to justify the undertaking.

On the continental level, the principal manifestations and essential arguments of nationalism during the last century differed from one state to another. Nationalism asserted itself most forcefully in Europe—in Germany, Russia, France, and Italy. In the Americas, only United States nationalism showed aggressiveness. In Asia, Japanese nationalism held the center of the stage. The features of these various nationalisms should now be compared.

---

[2] Speech to the Royal Colonial Institute, March 1, 1893.

[3] Italian nationalists, beginning early in the twentieth century, added a demographic argument: that national emigration should be directed toward colonial territories.

A. In Germany

In the German Empire established in 1871, nationalism was based on the belief that Germany, by reason of her successes since 1850 in the military, economic, and even cultural spheres, had demonstrated indisputable superiority. The German people, it was said, had shown that they possessed special qualities, not only because they cheerfully accepted the sacrifice of individual interests to those of the state and were vigorously patriotic, but also because they had a "genius for organization."

This sense of superiority was encouraged by Germany's universities and schools. It was confirmed by the militaristic mentality of the middle class which, after showing hostility to the Prussian military system between 1848 and 1866, was "converted" by the brilliant successes of which a unified German empire was the final result. And finally, toward the end of the nineteenth century, it was further strengthened by racist ideas. In 1898, the French writer Gobineau's *Essay on the Inequality of Human Races* (1852) appeared in translation, and in 1899, Houston Stewart Chamberlain exalted the "historical and world mission" of the Germanic peoples.

German nationalism in its most radical form found expression in the Pan-German League, whose theories were advanced *ad nauseum* between 1891 and 1914.[4] The League's aim, according to its bylaws, was to "stimulate German thought," in particular to cultivate a sense of the racial and cultural community among all sectors of the German people, and everywhere to advocate "a vigorous policy in furtherance of German interests." The state's mission, the League declared, was to secure for Germany the most favorable possible conditions of existence and the means to play a great part in the world. It must, therefore, give the people an accessible ideal, central to which must be the need for expansion, which, said Secretary General Ernst Hasse, was a "necessary stage in the growth of a living and healthy organism." Economic expansion? —certainly: Germany needed the "world market"; but also territorial expansion: "land hunger stamps its imprint on our times; it demands and must receive satisfaction"; it appears among the German people as a "duty," wrote Hasse's successor, Heinrich Class, in 1913.

The League's program made the nationality principle basic to this desired expansion, interpreting nationality along lines indicated by the whole of nineteenth-century German thought on the subject[5]: the nation was the totality of men speaking the same language and conscious of their solidarity; if consciousness of solidarity did not occur along with language factors, the

[4] In the weekly *Alldeutschen Blätter*, in the League's *Flugschriften* (of which 35 issues appeared), and in a number of other works, the most important of which were by the Secretaries General of the League, Ernst Hasse and after him Heinrich Class.

[5] See above, Chapter Six, pp. 140, 143.

latter took precedence. But the right to expand, even the right to political existence, might not be exercised by every nation, but only those nations with a *Kultur* of indubitable value. This latter condition led theorists of Pan-Germanism to establish a distinction between "dominant" and "minor" nations. Germany at the time—although a "dominant" nation—was not yet a "national state," since it did not embrace all the peoples of "Germanic'' language—Germans of Austria, Bohemia, Hungary, or Switzerland, Dutch, Flemings, and Luxemburgers. It must therefore seek to expand in those directions.

The League agreed that this program was not feasible in its entirety; there was no question, for instance, of destroying Austria-Hungary in order to incorporate the Germans of that empire. On the other hand, it believed that the principle could be applied in the border zones, at expense of small groups "unfit and incapable of ever forming a state"—the Walloons, Lithuanians, Poles, Czechs, Magyars, and Slovenes. Germany should even consider expansion into Belgium and the Baltic countries, beyond the German-language sphere.

Judging only by statistics, the influence of the Pan-German League was slight. At its peak, in 1901, membership (despite modest dues) was no more than 22,400 persons, only half of whom subscribed to the weekly bulletin. Among members of the Reichstag at that date, there were thirty-eight registered members of the League; they belonged to the National Liberal or Free Conservative parties. The Left and Center parties were hostile to the League, and at no time, moreover, did the government adopt the League's program and only in a few instances did it give it any apparent encouragement.[6] But observers agreed that the League enjoyed an influence far greater than the strength of its membership indicated;[7] Pan-Germanism had many sympathizers in the higher echelons of the army and, especially, the navy, as well as in the teaching profession and in big business.

World War I led to closer ties between government policies and the League program. In the "bases of peace," which he drafter in 1914, Chancellor Bethmann-Hollweg adopted some of the essential themes of Pan-Germanism.[8] The League continued to serve as the moral spearhead of German nationalism, and it campaigned against the chancellor when he hesitated, in the winter of 1916–17, to wage all-out submarine warfare; it went even further than the war aims set by the General Staff, although this was simply a case of improving a bargained position, unrelated to any position of principle.[9]

---

[6] In 1907 and 1910–11 especially, when a *de facto* but short-term alliance was concluded between the League leaders and the government.

[7] Ludwig Dehio, "Gedanken über die deutschen Sendung, 1900–1918," in *H. Zeitschrift*, 1952 (T. 174), pp. 479–502.

[8] This is one of the most important points made by F. Fischer in *Griff nach der Weltmacht* (Dusseldorf, 1961).

[9] The League wanted a naval base at Toulon to be ceded to a victorious Germany.

The defeat of Germany in 1918 drove the League into obscurity. Nevertheless, in an Executive Committee declaration of February 16, 1919, the League called for a "national renaissance" and persisted in declaring that Germany must claim the German-speaking territories of Austria and around the Baltic. In 1925, Pan-Germanic themes gained a hearing in the National Party, which by the autumn of 1928 had fallen largely under the League's influence. That influence was even more marked, of course, in the early beginnings of the National Socialist movement; in 1920, Hitler declared himself the "faithful student" of Heinrich Class. But by 1924, notwithstanding the identity of foreign-policy aims, disagreement was apparent. The League did not approve of the Nazis' propaganda style or of the "adventurist" demeanor of its leader; the Nazis, for their part, regarded the League as an obsolete institution they had to bypass. By November, 1932, barely three months before Hitler's accession to power, the rupture was complete; and the Gestapo put an end to the League's existence in 1939.

The National Socialist program nevertheless retained the basic themes of Pan-Germanism: *Lebensraum*—the right of the state to territorial dimensions "proportionate to the size of its population" which would assure the "German race" of the necessary means of existence; the direction territorial expansion should take—namely, to the east, at the expense of the Polish, Lithuanian, and Baltic peoples. But Hitler did not hesitate to go beyond Pan-Germanism when he made war with Russia as an ultimate objective of German policy.

B. In Russia

The Pan-Slav movements had existed in embryo before 1850, when there were already Slavophiles who believed that Russia, as heir to the civilization of ancient Greece, was appointed to direct the future of all Slavs. But these Slavophiles, especially Alexis Khomiakov, identified Slavism and the Orthodox Church; the only "true" Slavs, they believed, were those who belonged to the Orthodox Church.

Nicholas Danilevsky, in his book *Russia and Europe,* which was published in 1871, went beyond that definition, and he gave impetus to a much broader Pan-Slav movement. The essential themes were clearly asserted: the Slavs had preserved a unique "type of civilization," for they had not been subject to Latin or Germanic influences; this Slav civilization was called on to take over the heritage of "Western" civilization, which had reached its apogee in the seventeenth century but was now in decline; all Slavs, Orthodox or Catholic—Russians, Czechs, Croats, Slovenes, Serbs, Slovaks, and Poles[10]—must be aware of this solidarity and consider forming a "union of Slav peoples" under Russian aegis.

---

[10] Danilevsky even added the Bulgarians.

Pan-Slavism, however, like Pan-Germanism, was not to be stopped by language barriers. In the Pan-Slav union, Danilevsky included Greeks, Romanians, and even Magyars, who might "benefit" from ties with Russia. And it became Dostoyevsky's theme: "Russia, at the head of Slavism, will be able to give European humanity and its civilization a new and healthy watchword, a watchword which the world has never heard before."

But Pan-Slav influence in official Russian circles was of short duration. Only between 1875 and 1878 did Tsarist policy and Pan-Slavist views appear to coincide; even then, Chancellor Gorchakov was reluctant to endorse or encourage Pan-Slav ideas. By 1881, the movement was on the wane; the Slav Committee was dissolved; General Fadayev, a disciple of Danilevsky, was dismissed from active service. During Alexander III's reign, some Russian nationalists, together with Katkov and Aksakov, repudiated Pan-Slav ideas; German and Austro-Hungarian diplomats noted this reaction in 1884 and again in 1891 and observed the apathy of Russian society as regards "everything Slavic."

Pan-Slavism was not revived until 1908, but a kind of "neo-Slavism" advocated "cultural and economic" collaboration among Slavs, ruling out any idea of altering frontiers or destroying states. After 1908, the movement had actually abandoned its political goals; the government, in a letter to the sponsors of the Pan-Slav congress of 1908, formally repudiated such Pan-Slav aims. At no time did Pan-Slavism try to become a mass movement. The organizers of the movement did not even act concertedly to influence public opinion—an essential difference from Pan-Germanism—and attracted only intellectuals, an occasional diplomat, and, after 1906, a few members of the Duma.

C. IN ITALY

Italian nationalism revealed its broadest ambitions in the mid-nineteenth century (before Italy was unified) in the political doctrine of the Risorgimento. More than a decade before the moderate republican nationalist Abbé Gioberti published his tract on *The Moral and Civil Primacy of the Italians,* Mazzini had proclaimed the "moral supremacy" of Italy and described the "great mission" he felt she should fulfill in the world.

After the establishment of the Kingdom of Italy in 1861, the appeal to Italian greatness, based on memories of ancient Rome, continued to inspire certain intellectuals, but the aims of the nationalist movement were better defined than this. Like Pan-Germanists or Pan-Slavists, the Italians appealed to the nationality principle, since their purpose was to unite to the young kingdom those territories settled by Italians which, after the peace of 1866 ending the war with Austria, had remained in foreign hands—Trentino, Trieste, and the western portion of Istria, sections of Veliki Kvarner and the Dalmatian coasts—areas that altogether held some 700,000 Italians. But the analogy with the German or Slav movements is only superficial. In the first place, the argument about a common or "related" language was used in Germany and Russia to promote annexationist programs; the real preferences of the populations concerned were not taken into account at all—or rather, they were assumed *a priori* to be favorable. But in the case of Italy, the people that the nationalist program sought to "liberate" did in fact (at least in Trentino and Venezia-Giulia) desire to be freed from Austro-Hungarian domination. Secondly, at no time did the Italian nationalist program include any plans for overstepping the "natural frontiers" of Italy. Its aims were thus limited and clear.

Although the irredentist movement occasionally met with some response among the public, it did not have a broad popular base. Originally and primarily, it was a movement of intellectuals, students, and a few politicians (usually republicans) who sought to embarrass the government by charging it with neglect to the "dignity of the mother country." They made no attempt to give their policies a doctrinal basis but confined themselves to invoking the interests of the "unredeemed" populations. The middle class was mostly indifferent and the peasant masses passive. Political apathy, a distinctive trait of the 1880's, persisted in the last years of the century.

Only in the early twentieth century did a new factor emerge in the Italian nationalist movement—the development of a doctrine on the rights and duties of the Italian people. Along lines hinted at earlier by Gabriele d'Annunzio, the extreme nationalist Enrico Corradini in 1903 launched his appeal: he protested against the "decrepitude" and "senility" of the Italian middle class; he wanted to restore to the Italians a sense of "greatness," to instill in them a sense of duty to the state and a spirit of sacrifice to the national interest. Expansion was central to his program, but he attached little importance to irredentism: "We cannot concede that all the external action of a great power should be confined to the reconquest of two provinces." His great concern was with *colonial* expansion, and he proposed that it be achieved by force of arms.

Such nationalism aroused no lasting response among the people, however, who continued to show only the faintest interest in military and naval matters. In 1912–13, however, thanks to the support it received among young intellectuals, the movement began to become a genuine political force.

What of the government's attitude? It could not lend support to irredentist claims, since they were contrary to the general trend of Italy's stated foreign policy. Italy had chosen in 1882 to enter into alliance with Germany and had resigned herself to political collaboration with Austria-Hungary; she could hardly encourage nationalist aspirations in directions that affected either ally. On the subject of colonial expansion, the government was reticent, but finally in 1911 gave in and undertook action in Libya which was expressly demanded by the nationalists' program. The episode, however, did not signify governmental support for the main ideas of the nationalist movement.

Italy's entry into the war in May, 1915, fulfilled the nationalists' dreams. It even opened up horizons that Corradini and his emulators had not even considered: the annexation of the upper Adige valley as far as the Brenner Pass, and the occupation of the strategic position of Vallona. The nationality principle was transcended. Nevertheless, the nationalists now in the government who conducted this policy, Sonnino at the head, did little more than to seize as many opportunities as they could; they did not attempt to act solely on nationalist principles.

After the war, the fascist movement incorporated the essential nationalist themes, especially after 1925. Contempt for the "flabbiness" of middle-class traditions; assertion of the "absolute and intangible" sovereignty of the state in international relations and, consequently, the repudiation of internationalism; belief that war must decide the fate of peoples and that it stamped a "mark of nobility upon the peoples who had the courage to face it"; belief in the primacy of political over economic objectives—all these themes Mussolini borrowed from Corradini, who was only too pleased to assume the role of "spiritual father" of fascism.[11]

But the Duce broadened the perspectives and added new themes: on the one hand, the primacy of the rights of the state over the rights of the individual, and the role of the "hero" who embodies the soul and destiny of a people; on the other, the idea of a necessary hierarchy among states, the exaltation of the virtues of the Italian people, and the determination to inaugurate a "great period of history" that would show "Caesar's Rome" as the arbiter of politics on the European continent.

D. IN FRANCE

French nationalism before World War I was of an entirely different kind. It was not "aggressive." It wanted France's frontiers revised, of course, since it gave pride of place to the question of Alsace-Lorraine, but in the minds of all Frenchmen this was merely a restitution that corresponded to the wishes of the annexed populations. At no point did the nationalists' program invoke the linguistic argument; it did not forget that German nationalism appealed to linguistic "kinship" in regard to Alsace, whereas the French argued from the basis of the peoples' expressed preference. Finally, it was careful to avoid launching a radical "revolutionary" program, such as the Pan-German and Pan-Slav programs. In a word, it was conservative.

---

[11]Dino Grandi, chief of staff for the *quadrumviri* of Mussolini's March on Rome in 1922, had been a militant nationalist of the Corradini stripe before World War I.

The main features of French nationalism (offering some analogies with the Italian experience in this respect) underwent a transformation between 1890 and 1895, moving from a "lef.-wing" position—or at least one sympathetic to the left, with vague ties to the Jacobin nationalism of 1792–99 but no basic theory—to a "right-wing" movement intent on establishing a doctrine.

Following France's defeat at the hands of Prussia in 1871, republican intellectuals, throwing the whole responsibility for the disaster on France's imperial regime, had attempted to offer France a new order—cultivating patriotism, establishing compulsory military service, and instilling in the youth of France a sense of national fraternity—that would unite democratic, republican convictions with the ardor of national sentiment. They hoped that a "democratic" educational system would foster this attitude, but they also considered the army as an instrument of reform. This was the period when popular writers extolled the "military virtues," when the Education League. a hotly anti-clerical organization, took on the job of "developing a taste for military institutions among the young," and when the new Ligue des Patriotes included on its Executive Committee the government's Director of Elementary Education and was supported by a leading association of teachers. All this was an instinctive reaction to the humiliation of defeat among a people who continued to fear the initiatives of Bismarck's Germany. This kind of nationalism felt no need to rely on any system of ideas defining France's role in the international community. After the Boulanger crisis, leftist circles began to depart from this position and soon adopted a very different one, a process completed by and defined in the Dreyfus case.

Just as the left was turning pacifist, the right became nationalist. This time, nationalism was given a doctrinal foundation, outlined by Maurice Barrès and Charles Maurras.

To be a nationalist, Barrès said, was to be fully aware of the close solidarity between the individual and "his entire past" and to seek "to turn that undivided heritage to good account"; to be firmly determined to preserve that heritage from foreign influences which might distort it and to assert the national tradition; to be prepared to "solve each question in relation to France" by repudiating internationalism. Maurras accused "Gambettist" nationalism[12] of being based solely on the "memory of our disasters" and "unconcerned with history." His thought was thus connected to that of Barrès' in that his principal emphasis was on tradition and the concern to preserve it against foreign influence (especially the influence of German philosophy), and in that he contrasted the permanence of national interests with the "fleeting destiny of individuals." Both wished to provide

---

[12] That is, derived from the views of Léon Gambetta (1838–82), whose earlier republican "Program of Belleville" envisaged a free press, freedom of association and meeting, universal suffrage, separation of Church and State, etc.

an "intellectual discipline," a "means of recovery" to combat the decadence of France. The democratic and parliamentary regime of the Third Republic, they maintained, was incapable of regenerating the country.

It was a pessimistic and anxious nationalism, defensive and conservative, and concerned above all with protecting a France threatened by Germanism. It thus had nothing in common with Pan-Germanism and Pan-Slavism. "When you come to think of it," wrote Maurras in 1912, "it is an odious and abominable expedient to have had to call a spirit of nationalism into being in order to be able to defend the nation."

E. IN GREAT BRITAIN

British nationalists never had expansionist designs on the Continent, but they did have vast imperialist ambitions which were asserted vigorously after a period of hesitation in the 1860's. When Benjamin Disraeli became Prime Minister for the second time in 1874, the nationalist trend showed new features. Its accent was on the idea of empire and on the "mission" of the British people in spreading European civilization. It appealed to the imagination, to a sort of romanticism, instead of invoking economic necessities (which were still indisputable).

In the work of British theorists of imperialism—Sir John Seeley, Sir Charles Dilke, Spencer Wilkinson—as in the writings of its great apostle Rudyard Kipling, and even in the declarations of certain statesmen like Cecil Rhodes and Joseph Chamberlain, there appeared themes not unlike some of the tenets of Pan-Germanism or Pan-Slavism: imperial expansion was a "law of historical development"; it expressed the designs of a "Providence whose wisdom transcended the art of statesmen"; the English people were destined to play a decisive part in the future of the world and were a "governing race." "Far from appealing to the self-interest of their audience," these champions of imperialism called upon them "to sacrifice their private interests, even their very lives, in pursuit of a lofty national ideal."[13]

Prior to 1894, the main concern was to maintain and organize the British Empire; it was a "defensive" nationalism. But between 1895 and 1902, this nationalism became "aggressive"; it sought to ensure the *growth* of the Empire; it affirmed, as Bernard Bosanquet put it in *The Philosophical Theory of the State* (1899) that the state, the depository of all the nation's "moral tradition," must exercise a dominant power over individuals; it sometimes went so far as to suggest that war was an "occasional tonic required by the social organism."[14]

---

[13] Elie Halévy, *A History of the English People in the Nineteenth Century* (2d rev. ed.; London and New York, 1949; trans. from the French by E. I. Watkin and D. A. Barker), V, 21.

[14] Sydney Low, "Should Europe Disarm?," *Nineteenth Century*, October, 1898.

Such injunctions, according to the most reliable testimony,[15] met with a broad response among the public. But the upsurge of belligerence was of short duration. After the harsh experience of the Boer War, the British public wearied of noisy jingoism; it sensed the exaggeration of the nationalist slogans and felt that Britain had committed an "error of judgment." That the liberal Sir Henry Campbell-Bannerman, who in 1899 had led the opposition to nationalist policies, should become Prime Minister in January, 1906, was symptomatic of this new state of mind.

F. IN THE UNITED STATES

From about 1840 on, American nationalism became expansionist and aggressive. This is well illustrated in the doctrine of America's "manifest destiny," as elaborated during this period. Let us look at the main themes of that doctrine.

There was the idea of "natural growth"; a young and healthy state must "have an appetite." (This was the self-same biological law to which Pan-Germanists were to appeal a half-century later.) There was the theory of "political gravitation," first propounded by John Quincy Adams and then by Robert Winthrop in 1846 and Charles Sumner in 1849: a great state exerts a "power of attraction" on neighboring territories. It was therefore logical to assume that the United States would ultimately control the whole of North America. There was the idea of a vocation to fulfill a "mission of regeneration" by spreading American political institutions, whose superiority, to the expansionists, was beyond dispute. The United States was entitled to expand the "domain of liberty" and to regenerate "unfortunate peoples" who did not yet enjoy the blessings of democracy.

These themes, widely propagated from the middle of the nineteenth century on in the press and in Congress, were revived in the last years of the century by John Burgess, John Fiske, and Albert J. Beveridge. Theodore Roosevelt gave them broader application when the "regenerative mission" of the United States was used as the basis of the doctrine that the United States had the right and the duty to exercise international police powers in Latin America in order to put an end to "chronic disorders."

G. IN JAPAN

For twenty-six centuries, the Japanese archipelago was spared invasion. The Japanese people concluded that this immunity was proof of the peculiar qualities of their race, and the feudal nobility adopted an honor code whose essential principle was the sacrifice of the individual to the superior interests

---

[15] See below, p. 190, letter of Sir Edward Grey to President Theodore Roosevelt.

of this collectivity. These convictions remained present in the minds of the creators of modern Japan. The desire for more land, first in the islands adjacent to the archipelago, then in Korea, was expressed as early as 1873, at a time when the modernization of Japanese state and society had hardly begun. The government then regarded expansion as premature; external action, they felt, would remain inopportune so long as the internal transformation of the country had not been achieved. But it was agreed, in 1887, that a program of expansion would have to be instituted as soon as improving economic and social conditions made new military and naval means possible: Japan was destined to become the "leading nation" of the Far East. She would be able to fulfill this destiny when a conflict among the European powers gave her the opportunity.

The original aims of the program were strictly practical: to establish a "protective barrier" by securing a foothold on the continental coasts nearest Japan, and to prevent the establishment of a European or American naval base threatening Japanese security; to find on the mainland the coal and ore she required for her industrial development; and to ensure the supply of rice. (After 1890, the Japanese population began to increase more rapidly than its food resources.)

But it was not long before a theory emerged to go with this program, and it soon took definite form. Pride in belonging to the Japanese nation, belief in the superiority of the "Japanese race," the conviction that a nation was doomed to decadence if it did not seek to extend its power, the determination to preserve the "national essence," the awareness of a "mission" to fulfill in the world—these, from the early 1880's, were the essential themes of Japanese education,[16] political propagandists, and the cult of the emperor's ancestors.

The Sino-Japanese War of 1894–95, primarily a struggle over Korea and the first designed to carry out Japan's expansionist program, aroused national enthusiasm. From the time of this first success (as a result of the war, Japan acquired Formosa and the Pescadores), Japanese nationalism transcended the goal of making the country "secure" and became openly aggressive. The "Japanist" movement that developed in 1897 among intellectuals had as its announced intention the "protection" of China against European influences and its "modernization."

From then on, a characteristic feature of Japanese nationalism was a proliferation of patriotic societies. In 1881, the *Genyōsha* society had been founded, advocating strengthened armed forces, the abolition of "unequal treaties," and expansion into Korea. It had not attempted to influence the general public, but it exerted vigorous pressure on the civil service and army officers. In November, 1898, the Cultural Society of East Asia broadened this program—spreading the idea of "modernizing" China by means of

---

[16] An imperial order of October 13, 1890, laid down the principles which must govern patriotic education.

Japanese economic penetration, prior to assuming the "protection" of that ancient empire; the Cultural Society appealed to businessmen as well as politicians.

The nationalist movement continued to make headway after 1901. New societies[17] advocated the acquisition of land on the Chinese mainland and labored to foster a military spirit. Their membership was fairly limited, but at the start of the Russo-Japanese War in 1904, their propaganda contributed considerably to a great wave of patriotic fervor among the people. These societies were in close contact with the General Staff and were subsidized by big businessmen. They naturally sought to influence political decisions in a way that often embarrassed the government; responsible statesmen, however (with the exception of Shigenobu Okuma in November, 1898), refused to adopt their program in its entirety.

After 1919, nationalist arguments took on a broader scope. The demographic argument was pressed—some remedy, it was said, must be found for the overpopulation of the Japanese islands; and economic considerations were adduced—Japanese industry must secure the outlets it needed. But the forms of nationalist activity remained unchanged: there was always the same fervent action by patriotic societies. New societies came to the fore: the Society of Military Virtues, for instance, and the Veterans' Society, which had been founded before the war but had not yet exercised any political power. These now sought to turn the nationalist cause into a mass movement and, thanks largely to the depression of 1930–33, succeeded in gaining a wide hearing among the peasants, from whom the lower officer ranks of the army were recruited. For success, they relied on threats against political leaders and threats of a popular uprising.

How successful were they? In 1919–21, the "super-patriots," despite intense propaganda efforts, were unable to affect government policy, which expressed agreement to abide by the forthcoming Washington Conference. This government attitude persisted until 1930. But in 1931, in connection with the question of a Japanese "presence" in Manchuria, the government was outmaneuvered by the nationalists in the Mukden incident, when Japanese forces seized strategic points in Manchuria and expelled the Chinese without prior authorization from Tokyo. Between 1934 and 1937, the right-wing patriotic societies firmly established their ascendancy, despite the failure of a *coup d'état* attempted in February, 1936, by young army officers hoping to establish a military dictatorship. In Japan's version of the Monroe Doctrine, in her preparation for war against China, in her definition of a plan to expand in the South Pacific, nationalism was triumphant.

Under this heading of "nationalism," then, we may associate movements whose scope, duration, and vitality varied markedly.

---

[17] The best known of these was the Society of the River Love, known to Westerners as the Black Dragon.

1. Where nationalism advocated both local and colonial expansion, were the two harmonized? They were completely so in the Germany of William II, where colonial and European Pan-Germanism were associated in theory and in practice. They were also harmonized to a degree in Italy. The nationalist congress held in Florence in 1910 (on the initiative of Enrico Corradini and his friends) named Scipio Sighele, a champion of irredentism, as chairman, and outlined a program for colonial expansion. But this collaboration had limits; most irredentists wanted their program to have priority over colonial ventures. In Russia, Pan-Slav nationalists showed little interest in Russian expansion in Turkestan or the Far East. In France, "Gambettist" nationalism was not averse to colonies, but "Barrèsian" nationalism was more restrained; in its view, colonial expansion was a kind of "turning away from more urgent European problems, a sort of cheap revenge."[18]

2. Nationalism in different countries showed unique and varying features. Prior to 1914, aggressive nationalist aims in Germany, Japan, Russia, and the United States had similar arguments: the need to expand, regarded as a natural law; the duty to fulfill a regenerative mission; the claim that a nation's or a state's sense of superiority over neighboring peoples conferred upon it a right to mastery over them. These themes, expressed earlier by Mazzini in Italy, were not revived there at the turn of the century by the irredentists; in France at the same period, nationalism was on the defensive, as we have seen.

These differences are not hard to explain. They were linked in the first place with general moods in each of the countries concerned: a mood of infectious optimism in Germany after the victories of 1866 and 1871; the excitement of full demographic and economic growth in the United States; Russia's conviction that despite her defeat in 1856 in the Crimean War she must, by reason of the size of her territories and the tenacity and "creative originality" of her people, assume leadership of the Slav peoples; France's anxiety after her defeat in 1871 in the face of German power.

They were also closely linked to these nations' material power—the primacy of German arms on the European continent between 1871 and 1914; the manpower resources that afforded Russia broad opportunities with the context of the military system of the period; the overwhelming demographic and economic preponderance of the United States in relation to Mexico and Canada; the organization of modern armed forces in Japan which enabled it in 1894 to impose her will on China, whose population was ten times larger. In a word, the will to power became apparent when a state began to acquire the means to pursue such a policy—a not surprising coincidence.

3. Lastly, the development of nationalism was not continuous. It is per-

---

[18] This was also the position of Paul Déroulède, President of the Ligue des Patriotes: "I have lost two children [Alsace and Lorraine], and you offer me twenty servants."

haps easy to observe such continuity in Germany, where Hitler's imperialism revived most of the Pan-Germanic themes; in Italy, where fascist nationalism was heir to Corradini's extremist nationalist doctrines and tendencies; and in Japan, where patriotic societies pursued the same endeavor for nearly half a century. But French nationalists, whose principal concern was to combat the "German peril," lost their principal justification between 1919 and 1933, and in England, the wave of national pride that gathered ·force between 1895 and 1899 had subsided by 1902.

To study various nationalisms as autonomous trends without constantly relating them to the circumstances of the period makes them meaningless phenomena.

II. CAUSES OF NATIONALISM

What were the principal motivations for these nationalist trends of thought and currents of opinion, and what effect should we attribute to them in the development of nationalism?

Material interests were certainly frequently involved: rivalries for export markets and sources of raw materials; activities and propaganda of the arms industries; the effect of economic recessions, which sometimes led to attempts to broaden a nation's field of expansion.[19] But in our search for explanations, we must also consider more tangible factors.

A. TEMPERAMENT

All peoples of the world display certain characteristics that contribute to the nature of public opinion in their land and that may in part explain their attitude toward neighbors. To study these characteristics is an immensely difficult task, for the methods are uncertain and the data of unequal value. Social psychologists and cultural anthropologists are not satisfied with empirical comments and intuitive conclusions provided by analysts, travellers, or moralists whose sole contribution is personal observation, for their conclusions are usually affected by prejudice or preconceived opinions. Within one country, there are constant differences of opinion as to the character of one's fellow citizens; the differences are naturally even greater when observations of foreign lands are concerned. All we intend to do here is to mention the least disputed "national" traits and characteristics—those, that is, on which both native and foreign observers tend to agree.[20]

The Frenchman, to begin with, is said to be characterized by intellectual

---

[19] See above, Chapter Three.

[20] I am attempting here to present briefly the conclusions reached in a number of individual studies, some of which are cited in the Bibliography to this chapter. (See below, pp. 395–98.)

vivacity, a desire to exchange ideas and opinions on the problems of the day, a taste for debate even if it leads to negative conclusions. Individualism and independence of spirit make him reluctant to submit to collective discipline, and attachment to his native land makes him reluctant to emigrate. Lastly, he has a basic tendency, appearances notwithstanding, to a static "conservatism," a tendency to conceive of the development of civilization in the context of a few basic ideas—those established by *reason*.

The Englishman is said to be characteristically slow in his intellectual responses, averse to abstractions and metaphysical speculations, disposed to adapt action to experience and consequently to avoid long-range plans, which he feels are vain and will probably have to be changed by circumstances. He is tenacious, self-controlled, and proud of belonging to a people sure of their superiority. Finally, he habitually injects moral into political considerations, a disposition that has helped to give British patriotism the serene firmness of religious conviction.

In the German, a sense of realism in practical affairs coexists with intellectual activity marked by abstract speculation, imaginative sensibility, and the aspiration to "vastness" (to use Keyserling's term). There is also a strong sense of duty, discipline, mass organization, hierarchy, loyalty to the leader, submission to established power; and, finally, a need for order that obscures the notion of political liberty.

The Russian's taste for metaphysical speculation is also highly developed. But the outstanding features of the pre-Revolutionary Russian temperament were patience, resignation, passive stoicism (these did not rule out a certain passion); the peasants' attachment to their land, which is probably at the root of the admirable capacity for resistance that the Russian people have shown in the face of invasion; and an attitude of warm hospitality toward foreigners, devoid of xenophobia.

Turning next to the American, we find that he is not given to elaborate theorizing and is quite willing to conform. His cult of energy and willingness to take risks are legacies of the "pioneer spirit." But history has shown him the need to incorporate individual effort in the community and to safeguard the community's interests. In the nineteenth and twentieth centuries, there was no question of his having to defend those interests by force of arms, since the risk of invasion was nonexistent. Hence the Americans' sense of superiority over Europeans was not related to the notion of "power" but was based on the conviction that Americans better understood the conditions of social life and that the solutions to social problems adopted in the United States were valid all over the world. Finally, the American tends to attribute his successes to energy and his failures to "providential fatality."

The Japanese, finally, is said to lack imagination and inventiveness, but he shows extensive intellectual curiosity and a desire to develop contacts with foreigners, since the imitation of their techniques and, sometimes, their institutions is a condition of power. He also has respect for authority, a sense of discipline, and the conviction that the individual must without the slightest hesitation accept every sacrifice—including that of his life—in the interests of the social group and the state.

There are clearly certain similarities between these "national character traits" and the conduct of peoples in international relations. The "pottering" mentality of the Frenchman explains why French overseas expansion, for example, even during the establishment of the "second" colonial empire between 1880 and 1914, never aroused much enthusiasm among the public, which preferred to let things simply go their way; the British character was brilliantly and fully revealed in all forms of colonial expansion; the German and Japanese temperaments were in many ways receptive to the development of nationalism.

But such observations are only *relatively* valid, since the temperament of each of these peoples has varied in the course of history. Scholars do not always draw as much attention to this point as they should.

The French people, at least the most activist among them, experienced a wave of expansionist nationalism between 1792 and 1815 which, despite the collapse of the Napoleonic empire, left traces in liberal or democratic circles until 1848; the prudence and caution of Louis Philippe's foreign policy was one of the principal targets for attacks on the July Monarchy. The French public subsequently made no effort to obstruct Napoleon III's foreign adventures, although rarely supporting them with any deep conviction. But, after the defeat of 1871 in the Franco-Prussian War, nationalism became defensive and conservative; the public showed little interest in colonial ventures or, indeed, in foreign-policy problems at all. After 1919, this interest awakened, but victory did not arouse a surge of active nationalism.

Similarly, changes can be seen in the national mood over the years in Germany. It was not until around 1840 that writers began to expound the idea of a conflict between "Romanism" and "Germanism"; at the same time, Germans became convinced that within the orbit of "Germanism" they were entitled to supremacy. Subsequently, Bismarck's victories confirmed the Germans in their sense of superiority and prompted them to desire to extend the sphere of action of the "Germanic genius."

In Great Britain, where for the last part of the nineteenth century bellicose sentiments were only rarely expressed, expansionist and aggressive nationalism became rampant at the turn of the century and young people avidly devoured tales of feats of arms.[21] This burst of enthusiasm coincided with the concern aroused by Germany's competition in the economic sphere, but it also coincided with new trends of thought that had first been expressed long before these anxieties arose. It quickly abated after the Boer

[21] On this period, see Esmé Wingfield-Stratford, *The Foundations of British Patriotism* (London, 1939).

War. In 1906 Sir Edward Grey wrote to President Theodore Roosevelt that, during the previous twenty years, any British government could have had a war by raising a finger; the people would have applauded it, they were hot-headed and in need of excitement. The present generation, however, had had enough of such excitement; it had lost some blood, it was healthy and normal, and its instincts seemed sound. Grey concluded that the British had had enough of war for a generation.

In the United States, the expansionist imperialism of 1898 showed some of the same ideas that had been current in the 1840's; but in the years between displays of nationalism had been infrequent. At the time of the Civil War and Reconstruction, Americans were understandably absorbed in domestic problems.

In Japan, before the "opening" of the country in the 1850's, most Japanese seem to have been indifferent to the samurai's honor code, but after the revolution of 1868, at the very time when the feudal nobility was losing its privileges, this feudal code of honor, with its spirit of sacrifice and its sense of discipline, became influential among a large segment of the population (thanks to the schools, the military, and the presence of many former samurai in the higher ranks of the civil service).

It is essential, therefore, to avoid hasty generalizations. Although certain tendencies do appear to have been virtually permanent among certain peoples, others have come and gone as a result of national or international political events.

What is more important is to assess the distance separating the image one people forms of the character of another people, and the reality. Obviously, stereotypes are often far from "fair," but they have influenced political opinion and have been a factor in the history of relations between the peoples concerned. How are such false images created? How are they spread?

B. Sense of National Destiny

It is easier to analyze a nation's concept of its interests, its honor, and its future than to analyze its people's temperament. But here again, circumstances are important, such as the memory of recent experiences, and the conscious or unconscious evaluation of available means of action.[22]

Some observers have diagnosed as a trait of "peasant civilization" the preoccupation with stability and security that was one of France's most

---

[22] The distinction Harold Laski tried to make between "national character" (permanent) and "national comportment" (related to drives and necessities born of historical circumstances) (*The New Statesman*, October 31, 1942) is not convincing, for historical circumstances can also influence character traits. On this point, see Denis W. Brogan, *The English People: Impressions and Observations* (London, 1943), p. 210.

marked features from 1871 to 1939 and the reason why nationalist movements found so little response among the mass of Frenchmen. Yet this preoccupation could also be interpreted as the response to a *de facto* situation. Following her defeat in 1871, France's dominant emotion was fear of German power; after her victory in 1918, there was a general feeling that she must expect a German revenge now that she was depleted and exhausted by the effort of the war, and left without the external support that had brought victory. Conversely, German belief in the superiority of the "Germanic genius" and the desire to extend the "Germanic" field of action had been expressed in political literature as early as 1840, but only after the military victories of 1866 and 1870 did they become widespread and distinctive features.

The Bolshevik Revolution considerably modified the Russian concept of national interest, since it destroyed the traditional social structures, favored the city-dwellers at the expense of the rural population, reduced contact with foreign countries to a minimum, and actively sought to give the people a new ideal. On the other hand, the Soviet Government has on a number of occasions shown precisely the same concern and preoccupation as the Tsarist government did in its day. And the fascist movement in Italy hoped to instill in the people a new attitude toward foreign relations and the idea that war was a valid moral "discipline" but, after twenty years, discovered it had not succeeded.

In the United States, isolationism had been a basic feature before 1914; it was set aside in 1917, when the people became convinced that the general interests of the country required them to take part in the world conflict, but reappeared after 1919 and influenced public opinion right up until the eve of World War II. The experience of 1939–45 was needed to eliminate it.

It is the historian's duty to insist on these fluctuations, but he must not confine himself to merely noting them. There are certain fundamental questions he must answer. How did the concept of the "national interest" develop? How did the images people made of others develop? How much was due to spontaneous response and how much to active indoctrination? To what extent did nationalist ideas and themes, as expressed by intellectuals and politicians, permeate the mass of the population beyond the "ruling classes"?

To answer these questions, we have to know more about propaganda methods and techniques. The development of elementary education, of the cheap daily newspaper and then radio, affected and marked different phases in the development of nationalism. How was the propaganda organized? How effective was it? The problem is of primary concern in the study of international relations and is also pertinent to the possible relation between nationalism and types of political systems. But the present state of research in this area is insufficient.

C. POLITICAL OR SOCIAL IDEOLOGIES

The next point to consider is whether political or social ideologies, and the prejudices and received opinions underlying them, have played an active part in the development (or decline) of nationalism.

At the end of the nineteenth and beginning of the twentieth century, democrats in most of the major states expressed reservations about nationalism. Yet under the July Monarchy, French liberals and democrats had been nationalists; they had revived the tradition of Jacobin nationalism, traces of which were to reappear in the "Gambettist" brand of nationalism of 1910. And German democrats of 1848 had had an annexationist program. The Mazzini democrats, who sought to rebuild Europe on the nationality principle, were at the same time Italian nationalists—a tradition represented in the early years of his career by Francesco Crispi, an apostle of colonial expansion but also a "liberal." In the United States, expansionist and nationalistic sentiments were written into the Democratic Party platform in 1844 and the Republican platform in 1898 and expressly endorsed in the presidential elections. It is therefore fair to conclude that liberal democracy and nationalism have often been associated. However, parliamentary control has in some cases made it possible to moderate nationalist excesses.

Usually, however, conservative political doctrines, based on the principle of authority, fostered the rise of nationalism. The individual, according to that principle, must submit to the dictates of authority, and in that authority is vested all responsibility for determining the national interest. Pan-Germanism may have disturbed traditional nineteenth-century Prussian conservatives, but it found supporters prior to 1914 in the Free Conservative and Liberal National parties and later took on the role of the declared foe of the Weimar Republic. And in France, the basic principle of the conservative nationalism preached by Barrès or Maurras was the inability of any parliamentary or democratic system to protect national traditions and interests. In Italy, Corradini's nationalism was at first related to these French nationalists, echoing their scorn of the "rights of man," their contempt for liberalism and democracy, their exaltation of the sacrifice of the individual to the nation, their belief that only the "ruling classes" could effect a national renaissance; it added to all this certain features borrowed from the Prussian concept of the state. Although at times it sought the support of young liberals and even of trade-unionists in 1910–11, it was always anti-parliamentary, and in December, 1912, Corradini broke off with those of his friends who favored an attempt to seek popular support. And Japanese nationalism was sponsored by conservative former samurai, eager to preserve "national characteristics" in the face of the invasion of Western ideas and also to regain some of the influence that the destruction of the feudal regime had caused them to lose. The first of the great nationalist associations, the *Genyōsha* (founded in 1881), immediately asserted its contempt for political parties and did not seek support from the public, but exerted pressures on politicians and civil servants and even engaged in terrorist acts. Similar societies created after 1919 adopted similar methods.

The common feature of all these conservative ideologies was the importance they attached to the military establishment and the role they assigned to the leaders of the armed forces (or allowed them to assume) in government operations.[23] These army and navy officers encouraged hero-worship and the idea of the sacrifice of the individual to the nation. When given the opportunity, they were the best possible promoters of nationalism.

We must not forget, however, that Danilevsky, the "father" of Pan-Slavism, had originally been a disciple of a French social philosopher famous for his utopian socialism, Charles Fourier, and that the neo-Slavists of 1908 belonged both to the Constitutional Democratic party and among rightist elements in the Duma. Nor should we forget the anxiety that Pan-Slavist propaganda aroused in the most conservative circles of Russia in the period around 1880; after all, it aimed to destroy the status quo in all of central and eastern Europe and was therefore revolutionary. And British nationalism at the end of the nineteenth century, which was combated by "orthodox" liberals of the Campbell-Bannerman school, found a champion in Joseph Chamberlain, a deserter from radicalism, and support in the imperialist wing of the Liberal Party.

D. RELIGIOUS SENTIMENT

The relation between nationalism and religious beliefs confronts the historian of international relations with particularly knotty problems. How is one to understand a given religious outlook without personally sharing in its convictions? The nonbeliever frequently tends to be contemptuous of attitudes that appear to him vain or even hypocritical. On the other hand, if one shares these beliefs, how is one to study the situation objectively and keep oneself from being unconsciously influenced by conventional viewpoints? This is an area where interpretation requires special restraint and prudence.

1. In the West

Roman Catholic doctrine is opposed, almost by definition, to aggressive nationalism. The internationalism of the Catholic Church necessarily obliges the Holy See to view with suspicion any tendencies that would dispose Catholic nations to divide among themselves or damage Catholic solidarity.

---

[23] Especially in Japan and Germany, where the military general staffs enjoyed a distinctive position that gave them direct contact with the emperor, bypassing the prime minister or chancellor.

The major Catholic political parties (those in Germany and Italy), while displaying vigorous national feeling, have avoided the pitfalls of excessive nationalism. The German Center Party was always opposed to Pan-Germanism, as it was to Hitler's nationalism; the Italian Catholic party, the Partito Popolare, founded in 1919, remained aloof from fascist nationalism. But it is also true that the clergy and the faithful did not always hold to these principles.

In France, between 1890 and 1914, most of the higher clergy were susceptible to nationalist influence. Catholic organizations and periodicals usually tried to link religious feeling and patriotic fervor. "Church and fatherland!" cried a leading Catholic educator, while *Le Correspondant* aligned the "enemies of the army" with "friends of Germany" and "destroyers of Catholicism." The beatification of Joan of Arc was the occasion for a flood of such pronouncements.[24]

In Italy, prior to 1867, Catholic clerical and lay circles were often fervently patriotic; but when the "Roman question" was resolved by force in 1870—when Italy deprived the Pope of his temporal power and rendered him "a prisoner of the Vatican"—they broke off all relations with the state. Catholics were virtually unrepresented in parliament until 1904, for the Holy See maintained the rule of *Non expedit.* (Pius IX had pronounced it inexpedient [*Non expedit*] for Catholics to participate in politics.) The Catholic viewpoint was expressed, of course, at Catholic Action congresses, but never on foreign-policy problems. Between 1904 and 1914, Catholics began again to play a role in the political life of the nation, allied, in fact, with the liberal middle classes and thus endorsing policies of colonial expansion. But they were not active in the nationalist movement; at the 1910 nationalist congress, when Corradini openly canvassed for Catholic support, the only response he got was from the "democratic" group of Father Murri, with whose political views he was at odds.

In Austria-Hungary during the decade before World War I, the clergy for the most part placed their moral influence at the service of the Hapsburg dynasty; nationalism was particularly strong in the Christian Socialist party between 1909 and 1914. Catholic intellectuals would have nothing to do with this trend, however. On the other hand, reports of Austro-Hungarian diplomats show that the Vatican Secretary of State encouraged Vienna in July, 1914, to embark on a war against Serbia in order to strengthen the Dual Monarchy for the future.

It would be arbitrary, therefore, to attribute to the papacy a consistently hostile attitude to certain kinds of nationalism during this period. After 1914, the attitude of the Holy See was entirely different.[25]

---

[24] Charles Juillard has gathered considerable material on this subject, as yet unpublished, with which he was kind enough to acquaint me.

[25] See below, Chapter Eight, pp. 211–13.

The Protestant churches, closely linked to national states as they often were by origin and constitution, had different reasons to fear the development of nationalism. But did they endorse it or lend it support?

In Germany, the Prussian Evangelical Church before 1914 certainly displayed consistent and unreserved loyalty to the national ideal and to the belief in German "greatness"—it regarded the exaltation of "national greatness" as a moral duty—but it does not seem to have encouraged extreme nationalism, even though the Pan-German League included a number of pastors among its active membership. On the whole, its attitude corresponded to the line of conduct adopted by the German Government itself. After 1919, and especially after 1933, German Protestants by and large accepted the slogans and commands of nationalism, although the Nazis were opposed, from 1934 on, by the Confessing Church under the leadership of Pastor Martin Niemöller. (The German Christian Church organized under the aegis of the Nazi Party was a minority; it secured only one-third of the seats in the ecclesiastical elections of November, 1932.)

In England, religious vitality was greater among Nonconformists than within the Church of England. At the time of the nationalistic upsurge at the end of the nineteenth century, Nonconformists, on several occasions, expressed dismay with this trend; as for the Anglicans, they taught that God had entrusted the English nation with a mission to perform in the world, and in 1898, the Bishop of Oxford went so far as to preach on the moral efficacy of war.

Neither in Great Britain nor in Germany do the apostles of nationalism appear to have sought direct support from religious bodies; they were satisfied with tacit consent or simply acquiescence.

In the United States, some of the Protestants—primarily Baptists and Presbyterians—actively supported the expansionist movement of 1898, for they considered it a duty to spread the Christian message among the Asian peoples.[26]

The Orthodox churches of eastern Europe, also closely linked to established governments, were in a somewhat different position.

In Russia, the Slavophile movement from the beginning sought support in religious sentiments. Ardent Slavophiles were profoundly attached to the Orthodox faith and believed it to be the strongest bond tying Slavs together and clear evidence of a fundamental opposition between Russian and Western civilization. Danilevsky played on the same themes in a minor key—Russia as the protector of Orthodoxy and Slavism; the Orthodox Church as the medium through which Greek and Byzantine civilization was to be trans-

[26] The views expressed on this subject in 1885 by Josiah Strong were reiterated in 1895 by the Rev. J. Barrows in his lectures at Union Theological Seminary in New York. See Albert K. Weinberg, *Manifest Destiny: A Study of Nationalist Expansionism in American History* (Baltimore, 1935), and Julius W. Pratt, *Expansionists of 1898* (Gloucester, Mass., 1959).

mitted—but they were not revived by the neo-Slav movement in 1908. At no time did the Russian Orthodox Church actively identify itself with such Pan-Slav ideas (this would have been contrary to the government's wishes), but it certainly supported, and perhaps helped to orient, Russian foreign policy in specific cases. In March and April, 1915, for instance, during negotiations with Italy on the subject of the Adriatic, the Russian Government zealously defended Serbian interests but was much more lenient over territories whose people were Catholic (Croats and Slovenes).

In the Balkans, the Orthodox churches, as they became emancipated from the Patriarchate of Constantinople, were eager and effective supporters of nationalism, in full accord with the governments of their respective countries.

When Serbia was under Turkish rule, the Serbian clergy had labored to keep national sentiment alive. When Serbia became an autonomous principality in 1830, the clergy was placed under the direct authority of the government. The Serbian Orthodox Church, now an established state institution, found itself in the vanguard of foreign policy-making; it propagated "the religion of the nation" and inculcated in the faithful passionate devotion to Serbia's past. During the last decades of the nineteenth century, it was the most ardent apostle of the struggle for "Serbianism"—for the liberation of Serbian populations still under foreign domination—even when this struggle was directed against other Orthodox powers (Bulgaria). Whenever church-state difficulties arose before 1914, the principal cause was foreign policy; ecclesiastical authorities would accuse the government of being too "soft" in its demands for the return of "unredeemed" Serbs.

The Bulgarian Church became autonomous in 1870 and in 1872 severed all connections with Constantinople. It immediately embarked on a propaganda campaign to extend the religious authority of the exarchate over the Slav populations of Macedonia, then subjects of the Ottoman Empire— asking these people whether they wished to remain under the religious authority of the Orthodox Patriarch of Constantinople or to pass under the control of the exarchate. This "exarchist" propaganda was really a political operation. The Bulgarian clergy was ardently "national"; they looked on religious autonomy as a prelude to political autonomy, then independence. Once the Bulgarian state was constituted and sought to expand into Macedonia, would it not be entitled to claim those Macedonians who had recognized the authority of the exarchate?

In point of fact, then, it was not religious faith that provided the impetus to nationalism in these cases. What happened was that the church identified itself with the national ideal and placed itself at the service of the state for the achievement of the state's purposes.

2. In the East

The close bond between political and religious forces in Islam, where the distinction between spiritual and temporal powers did not exist, did not suffice to prevent national movements which undermined Islamic solidarity. But these movements never wholly destroyed Islamic unity. Muslims, perforce divided in a number of separate states, often joined together when it came to combating "outsiders"—against Europe, that is. The question is whether this unity was used to further defensive or expansionist designs and whether it is still an important factor in the contemporary world.

In theory, Islam proposed to subjugate other peoples politically with a view to religious proselytizing, a policy by means of peaceful penetration or a "holy war," the *jihad*. The Muslim's duty was to sacrifice "his life and his goods" in order to take part in this "just war against the infidels." Nevertheless, by the ninth century, Muslim jurists were interpreting this doctrine in a restrictive sense:[27] the *jihad*, they said, could not continue indefinitely; in Islam's own interests, lengthy "pauses" must be allowed for during which peaceful relations with the infidel could be organized. After the fall of the Abbasid caliphate of Baghdad in 1528 and the subsequent carving up of the Islamic world, the doctrine lost all practical significance. The Ottoman Empire's expansion into Asia Minor and the Balkans in the sixteenth century and Selim I's assumption of the title "Commander of the Faithful" (1517) failed to restore the unity of Islam, and the decadence of the Ottoman Empire in the nineteenth century enabled the Europeans to extend their domination over Muslim populations in North Africa and along the Persian Gulf. The attempt by Sultan Abdul-Hamid II at the end of the nineteenth century to revive the authority of the Ottoman caliphate and restore Islamic solidarity among the Sunnites met with vigorous doctrinal resistance in the Arab regions and in Afghanistan.

Nevertheless, in November, 1914, when the Ottoman Empire entered the war, the Young Turk government, although it had repudiated the policy of Abdul-Hamid II in 1909, had the Sultan proclaim a "holy war" against France, Great Britain, and Russia. (His call remained ineffective among Muslims in Africa, India, and Indonesia, with the exception of the Senussi movement in Cyrenaica.)

With the end of World War I and the destruction of the Ottoman Empire, as provided in the terms of the armistice of Mudros of November, 1918; with the policies asserted by 1919 by the Turkish national movement, which was reconciled to abandoning hope of restoring Turkish rule over the non-Turkish populations of the former empire (whether Muslim or not) and which was determined to secularize the Turkish state; with the suppression,

---

[27] On this point, see Majid Khadduri, *War and Peace in the Law of Islam* (Baltimore, 1955).

finally, of the Ottoman caliphate, by a vote of the Turkish National Assembly on March 1, 1924—with these developments, the hopes for Pan-Islamic unity were severely shaken. In vain did the Islamic congress at Cairo in May, 1926, express the hope that the caliphate would be restored. The establishment of new nations in the lands freed from Turkish rule ended the hope for political collaboration in the Islamic world. On the eve of World War II, Islam was no longer in a position to pursue a coherent and united policy in international affairs, and the new Muslim states were not disposed to base their foreign policies on religious considerations. But this did not mean that the Islamic religion ceased to be a force to reckon with. Muslims preserved their sense of solidarity and asserted it on several occasions in relations with western Europe (barring French expansion in Syria and British expansion in Iraq). They also resisted, nearly everywhere, the penetration of Communist ideas, which threatened their religious beliefs, family stability, and property rights. Finally, although Islam lost some of its influence in the Near East and North Africa, it retained it in Africa south of the Sahara, where it made considerable gains thanks to the proselytizing efforts of religious brotherhoods, and also thanks to the attitude of the French and British colonial administrations, which encouraged the spread of these groups until at least 1930.[28]

Official doctrine, of course, continued to condemn compromise. When the theory that Muslim states were entitled to conduct foreign relations simply in accordance with the principles of international law, without taking the principles of Islam into account, was asserted in 1926 by a member of the university of Al Azhar, it was expressly condemned by the rest of the ulemas, the powerful religious authorities.[29]

Shintoism was an altogether different matter. It was really a form of ancestor worship, the apotheosis of the Japanese imperial family.[30] The Japanese defined it in various ways, but their definitions had at least one point in common—namely, that Shinto consisted of "the characteristic ritualistic arrangements, and their underlying beliefs, by which the Japanese people have celebrated, dramatized, interpreted, and supported the chief values of their national life."[31] By definition, this religion was not intended to spread outside Japan; there was no question of proselytism among foreign populations. Hence Shintoism could not have directly inspired expansionist policies, but it nevertheless played an essential part in international relations because it lent an original and singular force to Japanese nationalism. It

---

[28] The number of new Muslims in French West Africa between 1920 and 1939 (not counting increases in families already converted to Islam) was estimated at 600,000.

[29] Khadduri, *op. cit.*, p. 292.

[30] See Yamashita Yoshitaro, in *Transactions of the Japan Society of London* (London, 1900), IV, 257.

[31] Daniel C. Holtom, *The National Faith of Japan: A Study in Modern Shinto* (London, 1938), p. 6.

achieved this role, largely by *fiat* of the government, after the restoration of imperial power in 1868.

After the introduction of Buddhism in Japan at the end of the sixth century, a syncretism occurred between Buddhism and Shintoism, as a result of which the original tenet of Japanese religious faith—the doctrine of the divine ancestry of the emperor—no longer carried as much conviction. The "renaissance" of Shintoism thus appeared as a means of restoring the authority and unity of state power as vested in the emperor. Nevertheless, during the Meiji period, the government hesitated. First it considered abolishing Buddhism and making Shintoism a state religion, but recognized, after 1872, that this step would be too radical and considered recognizing both religions. Finally, in 1884, as a result of the difficulties involved in getting Buddhist and Shinto priests to collaborate, it decided to adopt the principle of the separation of church and state and ceased to intervene in the appointment of any priests, whether Shintoist or Buddhist.

However, the government proceeded by legislative action to establish a new religion, state Shintoism. This was to take the form of offerings to the Great Ancestor of the imperial family, prayers for the reigning emperor, and tributes to the memory of all citizens who had given their lives for their country since 1853 (that is, since the "opening" of Japan). School children were to attend these ceremonies in force under the supervision of their teachers.

Could this state Shintoism, its ritual established in 1875, revised in March, 1914, and again in November, 1927, by the Ministry of the Interior, be regarded as a *religion*? The government thought not, for it wished Japanese Buddhists and even Christians to take part in the "official" worship. It pointed out that state Shintoism did not teach any doctrine or dogma, and it is a fact that, in May, 1936, the Congregation for the Propagation of the Faith authorized Japanese Catholics to take part in the ceremonies, on the grounds that they had a civic and patriotic, not a religious, significance.[32] But we must recognize that a system of beliefs in the "sacred mission" of the Japanese race and in the divine origin and eternal glory of imperial power underlay this state Shintoism. The principal aims of the worship were clearly to ensure obedience to the government and prevent the spread of revolutionary ideas. In this system of beliefs, the relations between sovereign and people were intangible; it was an essential factor in developing national solidarity and in nurturing a nationalist ideology. Since the civic education of the Japanese people assumed the external form of a religious faith, and since it was based on the belief that the emperor was endowed with a power superior to that of all other chiefs of state, how could Japan have agreed even in principle to any kind of order or organization in international

---

[32] This was the not entirely convincing argument that Rev. Yasuda propounded in 1937 at the Oxford Ecumenical Conference.

relations? More than that, the veneration of militarism and national power could hardly fail to encourage the ideas that participation in war, even in a war of aggression, was the highest of duties. It was precisely in order to destroy this "ultra-nationalist and militarist" propaganda that the United States occupation authorities decided in December, 1945, to require the Japanese Government to abolish state Shintoism.[33]

III. CONCLUSION

This rapid survey of nationalism indicates all too clearly the need for further critical studies, not confined to an analysis of the theoretical foundations of nationalism and its manifestations in various countries, but attempting genuine explanations, trying to determine the effectiveness of given nationalist ideas or slogans.

What was the influence of the books in which nationalistic opinions and programs were set out, for instance? To what extent did newspapers and journals take up nationalistic themes? What traces can still be found in school books? It is often possible to find out the size and number of editions of a book and, from reviews, to get some idea of its influence. The second question needs long investigation; unless circulation figures and types of readers are carefully analyzed and studied, erroneous conclusions are likely to be reached. Answering the third question requires, not so much research, as very delicate interpretation of the evidence, not only assessing the influence and distribution of textbooks—how many copies printed, how many schools using them—but also trying to discover how much they differ from the material taught orally. Historical sources are obviously able to provide very little information on this subject.

And even if these questions are answered with any degree of accuracy, we still do not know whether the answers lead to valid conclusions. How is the influence of a newspaper article on its reader to be assessed, or that of a textbook on a student? There is good reason to believe that the acceptance of nationalistic ideas was often obstructed by skepticism and indifference. On the other hand, nationalistic notions probably helped to create a subconscious attitude that at critical moments gave support to given policies or propaganda. The problem is how to establish a satisfactory method for studying the relation between the available evidence and the real state of public opinion.

Not only collective tendencies must be taken into account in studying

---

[33] Memorandum to the Japanese Government, December 15, 1945, from Colonel W. Allen on behalf of the Commander in Chief of the Army of Occupation, cited in *Political Reorientation of Japan, September, 1945, to September, 1948: Report of Government Section, Supreme Commander for the Allied Powers* (Washington, Government Printing Office, 1949).

the development of nationalism, but also the role of the men in power who, by law or in fact, directed foreign policy. The role of these men—sovereigns, dictators, or ministers—has always been important, often decisive, as the history of the past one hundred years amply proves.

Actually, kings and princes rarely took the initiative in this area: the Tsars did not encourage Pan-Slavism; Kaiser Wilhelm was occasionally disturbed by Bismarck's nationalist policies, and Kaiser Wilhelm II did not endorse Pan-Germanism; Mutsuhito and his heirs sought in vain to calm down Japan's "super-patriots." But it is impossible, on the other hand, to ignore the impetus and the note of glorification Bismarck and Cavour gave to German and Italian nationalist ideologies in the great upheaval that transformed Europe between 1850 and 1870. The surge of nationalism in Great Britain between 1895 and 1902 is incomprehensible without Joseph Chamberlain; and Greek nationalism in 1919 must obviously be viewed in direct relation to the personal attitude of Venizelos. And what form would Italian nationalism have taken without Mussolini, or German nationalism without Hitler? (Conversely, the failure of the national movements in Germany and Italy in 1848–49 may be explained at least in part by the absence of men who could take the lead and exploit the existing currents of emotion.) It is when the underlying forces of a nation's collective mentality have coincided with the initiatives of its leaders[34] that nationalism becomes a major force on the international scene.

[34] See below, Part II, on the statesman's role.

8

THE DESIRE FOR PEACE

Peace is said to be "rationally the goal to which societies tend."[1]
But have people really believed this to be true? The past century has been marred by one major war after another. What means have men devised to preserve peace? What has been the practical significance of pacifist endeavors?

I. THE BASES FOR PACIFISM

The "cosmopolitanism" of the eighteenth century was the result of efforts made by a few groups of intellectuals to reach a somewhat larger world of the cultured, educated classes. The pacifist movement of the nineteenth and early twentieth centuries, on the other hand, had quite different ambitions: it sought to reach the masses.[2] Its appeal was primarily to humanitarianism and to conscience. War, the pacifists argued, inflicts physical and moral suffering on combatants and even noncombatants. It perverts the human spirit because it leads people to admire the effectiveness of force and to consider as "noble" the art of killing one's fellow man. Hence, all the values implicit in respect for the human person call for the condemnation of war. In addition, war is useless, since it can solve nothing; at best, the solutions it claims to provide are only apparent or transitory.

The humanitarian and common-sense arguments are joined, then, and provide the main themes of pacifist literature. Naturally, they were voiced most forcefully in the aftermath of the great European wars and at times when revolutionary movements seemed likely to produce international conflicts.

These pacifist sentiments were supported by the arguments of certain economists and social reformers, and on religious grounds.

A. PACIFISM IN ECONOMIC AND SOCIAL THOUGHT

The essential economic argument for pacifism was that there was a radical antinomy between war and prosperity, a utilitarian argument borrowed from

---

[1] Raymond Aron, *Peace and War: A Theory of International Relations* (trans., Richard Howard and Annette Baker Fox) (New York, 1966), p. 150.

[2] On this point, see Théodor Ruyssen's remarks in *Les Sources doctrinales de l'internationalisme*, Vol. III (Paris, 1961).

Bentham.[3] Between 1830 and 1850, this theme was frequently sounded in France, Germany, and England, where Richard Cobden popularized it widely. War, he said, resulted only in the impoverishment of peoples and the ruin of states, and preparations for war forced nations to mobilize and placed intolerable tax burdens on the people.[4] In France, Frédéric Bastiat argued along the same lines: the cost of armaments delayed economic progress; wars produced industrial crises and greatly increased taxation; they were "always contrary to the true interests of the masses."[5] In Germany, Arnold Ruge's principal argument was the financial burden imposed by an "armed peace."[6]

The same ideas frequently reappeared later in the century and at the beginning of the twentieth century, when they were extensively propagated by Sir Norman Angell, a British economist and writer. "War doesn't pay" came to be a basic tenet of the pacifist movement.

To this fundamental argument, some economists added a rider based on their observations of the industrial revolution. A major European war, they said, would destroy the ties between producers in different countries and would disorganize the trade relations upon which major industrial centers depended. If this happened, how could Europe compete with the United States? This conviction that economic solidarity between the European states was necessary, and this fear of American expansion, were forcefully expressed by Michel Chevalier as early as 1866.[7]

It was true that business circles were often unenthusiastic about the prospect of war. The British position at the beginning of the nineteenth century was characteristic, and so were the reactions of British bankers to the prospect of imminent European conflict in 1914: they were opposed to British armed intervention because they feared that the war would dislocate trade, halt capital investment, and destroy the international position of the British market.[8] The pacifism of American businessmen in 1912–14 (Andrew Carnegie was one) was doubtless based at least in part on the same considerations, although such positions taken on principle in this way were unusual among representatives of major economic interests. On the eve of World War II, however, the commercial middle class rather clearly expressed their apprehension about the possible consequences of a conflict that could open the door to revolution. And today, the international pacifism of the capitalist middle classes has been noted by many political observers.[9]

---

[3] See Jeremy Bentham, *A Plan for an Universal and Perpetual Peace*, written between 1786 and 1789 but published posthumously.

[4] See his pamphlet entitled *England, Ireland and Russia*.

[5] See *Les Harmonies économiques* (Paris, 1847).

[6] In a speech before the National Assembly at Frankfurt on July 23, 1848.

[7] They were even better put in a report by Anatole Leroy-Beaulieu to the Congrès des sciences politiques in 1900.

[8] See above, pp. 128–29.

[9] See Aron, *op. cit.*, p. 704.

Pacifism was also influenced by socialist theories. The French socialist Henri de Saint-Simon was pacifist because he believed that the absence of war was in the best interests of producers. (But we should note that his pacifism, like the economists', was strictly limited to Europe. Colonial expansion was one of the principal goals of his "European Federation," and his disciples, notably Barthélemy Enfantin, thought that once Europe was "pacified," she would undertake large-scale economic activities on other continents and would not hesitate to use force to achieve that end.) And followers of Fourier—the most active in this field being Victor Considérant—emphasized the commercial advantages of peaceful international relations: no more prohibitions, no more tariffs, no more customs barriers. In 1842, Constantin Pecqueur stressed the theme of "ruinous war" along the same lines as Cobden had earlier: "We need fifty years of peace to get over the effect of a few years of victories!"

Neither economists nor socialists pointed out the special interests that the working classes had in the maintenance of peace, but it was true that the worker, as a participant in industrial prosperity, wished to avoid international conflicts that jeopardized such prosperity. Later, militants began to insist on the interests of the workers and to seek means of safeguarding them, but their doctrine was worked out slowly, and with lengthy controversies.

In September, 1867, a congress of the International Working Men's Association held at Lausanne (the "First International," which Marx had founded in 1864), condemned war, "the brunt of which falls on the working class"; peace, the resolution said, was "the first condition of general well-being." But the question of how the workers should in fact *respond* to war did not arise. The congress noted merely that the "first and principal cause" of war was poverty and lack of economic stability; if armed conflicts were to be ended, the "social organization" must be transformed.

A year later, the Congress in Brussels tackled the problem directly. While César de Paepe, a leading Belgian socialist, maintained the arguments of the previous year and Tolain was prepared to rely simply on the pressure of public opinion to prevent war, the report by the Frenchman Charles Longuet, which the congress adopted, recommended that the working class "stop all work in case of the outbreak of war." Here, then, is the idea of a general strike, but its introduction did not lead to any real exchange of views. The idea was not re-examined at the 1869 congress, even though the international situation had not improved in the interval.

When the Franco-Prussian War broke out, the possibility of a general strike was not even considered. The manifesto of the General Council of the First International, dated July 23, 1870, denounced the "Bonapartist aggression" as a "revised and corrected edition of the *coup d'état* of December 2, 1851," and declared that the Germans' position was "defensive."

Confining itself to an expression of hope that "this dynastic war" would not degenerate into a war between peoples, it added the further vague hope that "the alliance of the working classes of all countries" would eventually put an end to war. The First International evaded all questions of principle.

After the dissolution of the First International in 1876, an International Committee of Workers for Peace was formed, but its appeal was not very widespread. At a peace congress held in London in September, 1878, the central theme was sounded in a speech by John Bright when he remarked that while there were men and classes for whom war was sometimes profitable, for workers it was always a disaster. But this observation remained in the realm of abstraction, as did Engels' remarks in 1887, when he depicted the horrors and devastation a great European war would inflict, while asserting that such destruction and suffering would create conditions favorable to the "ultimate victory of the working classes."

For fifteen years the Second International displayed no active concern with the prevention of war,[10] despite certain tendencies in that direction in 1900 and again in 1904. Only after 1905, when a great international crisis appeared to be on the horizon, did the issue arise at its international congresses. The debates at Stuttgart (1907), Copenhagen (1910), and Basel (1912) did not turn on, certainly discussed very little, the question of the legitimacy of war. Those who presented themselves as "pure" pacifists—condemning all war and viewing the notion of the "fatherland" as "irrelevant to the proletariat"—met with no response among the delegates, most of whom, like August Beber and Jean Jaurès, were willing to accept the hypothesis of a "defensive" war, although of course all of them hoped that it could be avoided.

But how? Could one depend on methods advocated by nonsocialist pacifists? Or was it necessary to resort to means of action available to the working class? The idea of a general strike reappeared—this time in an Anglo-French motion presented by Keir Hardie and Edouard Vaillant, and supported by Spanish, Russian, Serbian, and Swedish delegates. It was demolished by the German delegation with simple arguments on the facts. Bebel and Karl Legien remarked that the effectiveness of a general strike was "not even a matter for debate." How could one have one when men were being mobilized and food rationed? "At the first call, they'll laugh at us!" And trade-union weakness in the face of the power of the German state was clear: "We cannot allow methods of action to be foisted on us that might endanger the development of our party and perhaps also the existence of our organizations." A general strike, as Vaillant put it, would be "fatal to German socialism." Karl Renner developed the same argument on behalf

[10] On this point, see James Joll, *The Second International, 1889–1914* (London, 1955; New York, 1956).

of the Austro-Hungarian delegation, and at the congress in Copenhagen in 1910, the Vaillant–Keir Hardie motion was rejected by 131 votes to 51.

A resolution on the prevention of war presented to the congress in Stuttgart in 1907 had recommended merely an arms limitation, compulsory arbitration, and the abolition of secret diplomacy. None of this had been specifically socialist, although the congress had added that in each country the working class should use whatever means appeared most effective, according to the political and social situation in that country, but of course this was tantamount to abandoning coherent international action. Yet the Basel congress in 1912 asserted that the Second International was "strong enough to impose its views on those in power." In July, 1914, in point of fact, it was powerless.

B. Pacifism and Religion

Christianity was established most strongly in regions where expressions of national sentiment and nationalism were particularly vigorous in the nineteenth and early twentieth centuries—that is, in Europe and Latin America. The Christian is undoubtedly a good patriot; he is entitled to believe that his nation has a special vocation in the world. Nevertheless, Christ's message, since it condemns violence and preaches charity—and, therefore, good will in relations between states as between individuals—should cause the Christian to abandon the use of force to impose his own country's will on others; it should dispose him to a sense of fraternity. In what circumstances does Christianity countenance war? The question "What is a 'just war'?" is familiar to theologians. The Catholic and Protestant positions might appear to differ on this point, insofar as Catholicism has always been an international and even supranational force, whereas the Protestant churches did not attempt until quite recently to find grounds for common action in international relations.

1. Protestantism

An extensive pacifist movement developed in the nineteenth century among Protestants, but outside the major "established" Protestant churches.[11] The first "peace society" was formed in August, 1815, in the United States by the Quakers; the first pacifist periodical, *The Herald of Peace*, began publication in 1816, edited by another Quaker, William Allen. When William Ladd, yet another Quaker, assumed the leadership of the movement in 1823, he emphasized the religious motivation; pacifism, he said, was essential to

---

[11] On this point, see A. C. F. Beales, *The History of Peace* (New York, 1931).

the "perfect development of Christian character." Methodist and Congregational ministers were the principal propagandists of the movement.

American pacifist activities were soon emulated in Europe, mostly in Protestant countries: in Great Britain, in Germany (especially under the influence of the distinguished theologian Friedrich Schleiermacher), in the Netherlands, and in the Geneva canton in Switzerland.[12] But when the first international congress of peace societies met in London in 1843, only the English "religious press" reported its debates. Protestant influence dominated again at another international congress in Paris in 1849, but this time the congress had a wide appeal; an American Protestant, Elihu Burritt, director of *The Christian Citizen*, had made contact with French pacifists and initiated the venture. Some of the speakers at the congress were eminent Catholics, but the delegates were mainly British dissenters.

Forty years later, a nonconformist minister, Evans Darby, Secretary of the British Peace Society, tried to prevail on the churches to take part in the international pacifist movement and established a Committee of British Churches for Arbitration, with Methodist support. These efforts, sponsored by a few enthusiasts, were far from popular among the faithful; in 1899, at the time of the Boer War, *The Methodist Times* supported the war and the nationalist movement.

As for the most powerful Protestant churches—the Anglican Church and the Prussian Evangelical Church—they did not participate in these pacifist endeavors and even refused outright to do so. In its annual report of 1885, the British Peace Society noted their indifference to pacifist activity, even though it was "eminently Christian work." Pacifist ministers believed that this refusal was the consequence of a system that placed the churches in a position of dependence on the state and caused them to accept temporal necessities as "axioms" of the Christian faith.

But in the years immediately preceding World War I, an effort was made to involve these Protestant churches in the peace movement. In 1906, Allen Baker, a Quaker, established the World Alliance for Promoting International Friendship through the Churches, whose immediate goal was to establish contacts between British and German pastors in order to improve political relations—an endeavor backed in both countries by leading ecclesiastics.[13] When the first ecumenical conference met in Edinburgh in 1910, however, the only major item on the agenda was mission work; there was no discussion of the "organization of peace."

The following year, proposals were worked out for an Anglo-German conference, but they were swept away in the backwash of the Agadir crisis.

---

[12] In France, the Société des amis de la morale chrétienne, founded by the Duc de la Rochefoucauld-Liancourt, had both Catholic and Protestant members.

[13] In Germany, by the theologian Adolf Harnack and the court preacher Ernst Dryander; in Great Britain, by the Archbishop of Canterbury, Randall Davidson.

The idea had been taken up in the United States, however, by Andrew Carnegie, who set up an Endowment for International Peace in 1910 and on February 10, 1914, founded the Church Peace Union. This second organization proposed to examine how religion could ensure peace, Carnegie being convinced that religious organizations could and must be more effective than any other in the pacifist movement.[14] Catholics were not excluded; the American Cardinal Gibbons attended its constituent session. But Protestant ministers and missionaries predominated in the Executive Committee and were its most active members.

This committee immediately organized a World Conference of Churches to meet in Switzerland in 1914. The conference opened on August 1 in spite of the international situation (a "state of war emergency" had been proclaimed in Germany the previous evening), but the general mobilization in France and Germany forced them to dissolve the very next day after addressing an appeal for peace to the European governments. It was a curious episode, and the sole pacifist exercise of this kind in the tumult of war.

For a real confrontation of opinion within the Protestant World, we must look to the growing ecumenical movement between the wars, and the convening of ecumenical conferences at Stockholm (1925) and Oxford (1937).

The Stockholm Conference met just as the Locarno Treaties—guaranteeing the Franco-German and Belgo-German borders, arranging for arbitration clauses between Germany and her former enemies, etc.—were being negotiated. A resolution submitted by one committee on the "action of the Church for peace" condemned all wars "but especially wars of aggression," and recommended that the churches work to form a "Christian public opinion, capable of resolutely opposing war." The only declared opposition came from part of the German delegation; the orthodox Lutherans believed in restricting "Christian action to the interior life" and wanted to leave political contingencies "to their natural laws." "We will have nothing to do with pacifism," declared Superintendent Wolff. The conference did not adopt a Swiss proposal in favor of disarmament and only endorsed the terms of a declaration to the effect that the churches were in duty bound to express "horror of war" and to assert that war was "radically incapable of settling international disputes." That was a text, declared one of the French participants ironically, "that would have been acceptable to Scipio, Napoleon —and William Penn."

The Oxford Conference of 1937 met in very different circumstances. The German Protestants were absent; those who accepted (or were resigned to) Hitler's regime did not wish to send delegates, and the others—members of the Confessing Church—were not able to obtain passports.

---

[14] See Charles S. MacFarland, *Pioneers for Peace Through Religion* (New York and London, 1946), pp. 17–22.

The conference did not confine itself to repeating the themes adopted in 1925; prompted by several noted laymen—Lord Robert Cecil, Max Huber, John Foster Dulles—it added that the churches must not be "enslaved by national ideology" and that it was their duty to support a "progressive limitation on arms." But it noted that there were divergent Christian positions on war: some considered all war contrary to divine will; others believed that war was "just" when its purpose was to ensure respect for international law or to assist the victims of unprovoked aggression; still others asserted the unreserved duty of obedience to the state, the organism "divinely willed to prevent anarchy." The conference did not choose between these positions but only hoped that the differences would eventually be resolved.

The final message of the Oxford Conference made no attempt to define the "duty of the Christian citizen of a belligerent state" or to say whether it was legitimate to resort to war in order to avoid an "intolerable violation of the law." The failure to do so was inevitable, a French participant noted, for on these points major differences divided "Anglo-Saxon" and "Continental" thought—"a painful divorce for the ecumenical Church."

2. Catholicism

At the beginning of the nineteenth century, Catholic thinkers were much more reserved than Protestants on the subject of pacifism, perhaps because the Church hierarchy wanted to avoid taking any stand that might displease governmental authorities. In some ecclesiastical circles, Joseph de Maistre's radical political philosophy was influential—the idea that war was "divine in itself, since it was a law of the world" and since the results of armed conflicts "altogether eluded the speculations of human reason." The vague internationalism of the French Catholic writer Lamennais left traces among Catholic socialists in 1848, some of whom were militant pacifists, but apparently the mass of the faithful remained indifferent to these trends, and the Vatican did not seem to be considering any moves that might encounter the opposition of national Catholic groups.

The growth of nationalism was a dominant feature of Europe between 1871 and 1914. Is it possible to perceive attitudes common to Catholic circles during that time, or any guide lines established by Rome?

Germany's Catholic political party—the Center Party—was theoretically not a confessional group, but in fact it championed the cause of Catholicism and got most of the Catholic vote. In Bismarck's time, it was almost constantly in opposition; on pacifist issues, it at first opposed the proposal for a military septennate in 1887, despite the recommendations of Rome; in December, 1892, it opposed the new army bill presented by Chancellor Caprivi. But this did not mean that the Center Party was pacifist; as soon as it became an essential element in German parliamentary life, it gave up its opposition to the arms bills (in 1897), and in 1904 Chancellor von Bülow congratulated it on its "German national policy." Nevertheless, it took great pains to steer clear of the Pan-German movement, whose excesses it condemned, although at the same time it associated itself wholeheartedly with the government's foreign policy and maintained complete confidence in Germany's "cause."

The Catholic Church in Austria-Hungary held an "altogether exceptional" political position, since the bishops were *ex officio* members of the upper chamber of parliament.[15] In both parts of the monarchy, the ecclesiastical hierarchy generally accepted the decisions of the government. At no time was any pacifist sentiment apparent among ecclesiastical leaders.

In France, as in Germany, most of the episcopate actively endorsed all patriotic manifestations, and during the last years of the nineteenth century, at the time of the Dreyfus case, nationalistic sentiment asserted itself in most Catholic circles; spokesmen sometimes went so far as to revive de Maistre's arguments. Some years later, this tendency gained active support among members of the Sillon movement (one faction of which, led by du Roure, was won over by nationalistic argument), and in Joseph Lotte's *Bulletin des professeurs catholiques.*

Nevertheless, a Catholic pacifist movement existed in France. Its leader, Vanderpol, found backing in Belgium and in 1911 founded the International League of Catholic Pacifists. But the League of French Catholics for Peace numbered only 700 members, and the International League endeavored vainly to obtain some sign of approval from Rome. When Vanderpol, with the support of the Bishop of Liège, tried to organize an international ecclesiastical congress with a view to opening the way to a Franco-German *rapprochement,* only four French bishops agreed to send representatives.[16]

Thus, in nearly all the European Catholic churches, national sentiment triumphed over religious solidarity. And the Vatican made no serious attempt to correct this tendency, dangerous as it might have been. In 1870, Pius IX offered to mediate the Franco-Prussian conflict, but his offer did not come until war had actually been declared, and he did not persevere when the German Government refused the offer on the grounds that the war was a necessary action to preserve national honor.

Leo XIII, a "political pope" and a diplomat of vast experience, was only too ready to play an active part in international relations in order to restore the prestige of the Vatican, which had been shaken by the events of 1870, and therefore he agreed to act as mediator between Spain and Germany in the Caroline Islands affair in 1885. For the same reason, he wished to take

---

[15] The Austro-Hungarian Ambassador to the Vatican drew Pius X's attention to this point. See F. Engel-Janosi, *Oesterreich und der Vatikan* (Vienna, 1958), II, 47.

[16] A study by Charles Juillard, as yet unpublished, will provide further information on this movement. Here I am following the broad lines of his analysis.

part in the Hague Conference of 1899.[17] In his encyclicals,[18] Pope Leo declared that the system of an "armed peace" and the arms burden were "intolerable"; and he indicated his wish that an international court of arbitration be established. But these were only vague allusions, and he had no intention of taking the initiative.

Pius X, who had no wish to be a diplomat, was even more reserved. In 1911, it is true, he gave the Carnegie Endowment for International Peace an endorsement (he failed to do so for the International League). But in late July, 1914, the Vatican Secretary of State approved Austro-Hungary's ultimatum to Serbia and expressed the hope that Austria-Hungary would "stand firm"[19] and that the Dual Monarchy, a "Catholic state *par excellence*," would escape, if need be by force, the dangers that threatened it from Slav nationalist movements. Here, noted the Austro-Hungarian chargé d'affaires, the "apostolic viewpoint and the martial spirit" coincided.

Benedict XV gave a new orientation to the Vatican's approach to the pacifist movement. World War I was inflicting a "terrible ordeal" on the Catholic Church, and the Holy See obviously desired the end of hostilities, but the Pope did not confine himself to vague expressions of this hope—he took repeated action. On July 28, 1915, he appealed to the belligerent nations for a negotiated peace; on January 16, 1917, he suggested to Kaiser Wilhelm II the "general bases" of a peace offer; finally, on August 1, 1917, he offered personally to be a mediator. In each case, Benedict XV was doubtless moved by the desire to "fulfil a duty toward humanity," but he wished above all to remove the dangers threatening the Church, and he also wished to prevent the cause of international socialism from acquiring a monopoly in the area of action for peace. And when he considered (as early as the end of 1915) participating in the future peace conference, he probably thought, as Leo XIII had in 1899, that it would give him the opportunity to raise the "Roman question." These interventions were thus linked with the Vatican's political preoccupations. But Pope Benedict went beyond these preoccupations when he recommended, in a Papal Letter of September 28, 1917, the abolition of compulsory military service, and when, in the encyclical *Pacem* (May 23, 1920), he declared that mutual love and concord among peoples was a duty and expressed his hopes for the success of the League of Nations

[17] Statements of the Vatican Secretary of State to the French chargé d'affaires made it clear that the Holy See wished to raise the "Roman question" before the conference (*Documents diplomatiques français, 1871–1914*, first series, vol. XIV, No. 325). It was precisely this prospect that prompted the Italian and then the German governments to refuse the Vatican's request.

[18] *Nostris errorem*, February 11, 1889; and *Ad principes*, June 20, 1894.

[19] See the reports of the Bavarian Minister to the Vatican (*Bayerische Dokumente*, July 24, 1914, p. 266) and of the Austro-Hungarian chargé d'affaires (Oesterreich-Ungarische Akten, July 27, 1914, VIII, 893). See also the statements made by the Pope's private secretary to the Austro-Hungarian Ambassador in August, 1914 (Engel-Janosi, *op. cit.*, II, 151).

(as in November, 1921, he was to express his hopes for the success of the talks on naval disarmament).

The line traced by Benedict XV was followed by Pope Pius XI, albeit in hesitating fashion, when he contrasted patriotism, "the source of virtue and heroism," with "inordinate nationalism, the source of "injustice and iniquity." The remedies he proposed were "inviolability of the rights of man" and the "pacification of the spirit" through the action of the Catholic Church, the only body capable of infusing society with Christian principles.[20] In point of fact, however, the Vatican did not dare to censure Italy's aggression in 1935, or Germany's in 1938, apparently because it feared to create a conflict of conscience between national sentiment and the duty of obedience to the papal injunction.

Pius XII, who in 1917 had been the principal agent of Benedict XV's policy, was the first pope to take decisive action on the eve of a war. In 1939, he made repeated public appeals for peace and repeated diplomatic initiatives: an Easter sermon on April 9; a proposal to governments on May 4 to convene an international conference to seek a solution to the conflicts between Germany and Poland and between France and Italy; an address on June 2 before the Sacred College, where he represented "pacification" as the Church's specific duty; a proposal for a compromise on Danzig, submitted to the Polish Government on August 18; a broadcast message on August 24; an appeal addressed on August 31 by the Vatican Secretary of State to his diplomatic representatives. It was a continuous endeavor, in marked contrast to the attitude of Pius X in July, 1914.

The new line adopted by the Vatican during the twenty years between the two world wars encouraged the development of Catholic pacifist movements.[21] In 1921, twenty-one countries were represented at the first Catholic peace congress, held in Paris, and in 1931, at Fribourg, a "written consultation" on "peace and war" by eight theologians from Catholic countries met with a wide response. Here, again, the contrast with the difficulties encountered in a similar situation prior to 1914 was marked. Yet the results of these efforts were meager; none of the organizations ever numbered more than a few thousand members at best, and most of them (except Pax Romana), merely marked time after 1933. At no time and in no country did these Catholic groups succeed in defining a common attitude to the League of Nations and on the principles of collective security. Despite the appeals of the Holy See, nationalism maintained its strongholds in the Catholic world.

---

[20] The encyclical *Ubi arcano*, December 23, 1922. The idea was revived in the Pope's Christmas message in 1930 and in the encyclical *Caritate Christi*, May 3, 1932.

[21] We have made use here of an unpublished study by Janine Monier, *Le Mouvement paçifiste catholique internationale de 1919 à 1939*. The principal movements were the Catholic Council for International Relations, the Catholic Union for International Studies, the Catholic International League, and Pax Romana.

An inquiry on nationalism undertaken by Maurice Vaussard in 1924–25 among 160 leading Catholics is significant in this connection. The answers turned basically on the relations between Catholicism and nationalism on the one hand, and Catholicism and pacifism on the other.

Nationalism, wrote Father de la Brière, a leading French Catholic figure, was justified if it remained "in harmony with the fundamental obligations of natural and divine law" and, therefore, with the principles of justice, order, and "social morality" of which the Church was the guardian. When did it become excessive and dangerous? "Within the limits of the strictest orthodoxy," he admitted, "the zone of legitimate controversy remains considerable."

True enough, and the answers to the inquiry made that very clear. One respondent argued that Catholicism did not "exclude conflicts . . . among nations, when they are necessary for the triumph of a legitimate right or interest;" war is "just" when a state acts to achieve its natural frontiers or protect its rights to economic expansion. According to Jacques Chevalier, another respondent, religion could not counsel a nation "to forget an injustice." And yet another lamented:

In the face of all these ideas, all these trends appealing to our times, we active and thinking Catholics do not always know what our line of conduct should be, how far we should go either in resistance or conciliation. This uncertainty explains why there unfortunately does not exist a united Catholic front with regard, for instance, to the League of Nations.

The same writer expressed the hope that the Vatican would issue "positive instructions," but it was a vain hope. Vaussard was obliged to note that "most Catholics, under the guidance of their priests, in *practice* set the national interest above the interests of the Church."

On the eve of World War II, the French Catholic (and pacifist) philosopher Emmanuel Mounier attempted to define more exactly what should be the Christian attitude to the "problems of peace."[22] The Christian, he said, should not be an "absolute pacifist"; he does not condemn war when it is "just"; he recognizes "the legitimacy of violence in the service of justice." But how is this legitimacy to be determined? "International justice," Mounier said, "is not abstract; it changes with the times." In 1939, the essential issue was "between war and spiritual dishonor"; the Christian should not "buy peace at the price of an increase in moral turpitude, of another retreat of the Christian spirit before the forces of anti-Christ." He should, in such a case, accept the risk of war. Here, the argument in favor of resisting National Socialism was based no longer on national interest but on moral principle.

[22] *Pacifistes ou bellicistes?* (Paris, 1939), reprinted in *Oeuvres*, Vol. I (Paris, 1961).

Would the effectiveness of these religious movements in favor of peace have been enhanced had it been possible to establish common action among the churches? On the initiative of the Church Peace Union of America, an international congress of delegates from Catholic and Protestant pacifist organizations met in Geneva in 1928, but this was an isolated move. "As long as the Catholic church keeps to itself," declared the Archbishop of Canterbury in his opening address to the Oxford Conference in 1937, "it will not be possible fully to focus the forces of Christianity on the needs and problems of the contemporary world."

Religious sentiment, then, was not much more effective in promoting the pacifist movement than were materialist concerns. The solidarity that new industrial and commercial conditions had established among nations was less influential than economic rivalries, and the sentiment of Christian fraternity did not triumph over national feeling.

II. METHODS OF PACIFISM

Militant pacifists pursued their aims by three different methods: refusal to take part in acts of violence; attempts to remove the causes of war; and advocacy of a system of peace based on law, founded on the rules of jurisprudence, and supported by international institutions. These three general trends were not mutually exclusive. Those who practiced nonviolence were also prepared to use constitutional means; apostles of "peace through law" were not usually indifferent to efforts to "neutralize" the causes of conflict. But the distinctions are not artificial: each had its place in the development of the peace movement, and they do express the differences among spiritual families.

A. NONVIOLENCE

The principle of nonviolence had early been taken up by the Quakers, who remained for many years its most vigorous exponents.[23] The founders of the American peace societies opposed all forms of war, even defensive; they believed that no Christian should actively resist an act of violence. "I do not believe that a Christian has the right to fight in defense of life, liberty or religion, much less for property; but to leave vengeance to God, to whom it belongs," wrote William Ladd in 1838, and this was also Elihu Burritt's belief when he founded the League of Universal Brotherhood in 1846. But these apostles of peace did not generally attempt to require whole-hearted support for their doctrine, even from their friends. Ladd refrained from taking his position publicly because he realized that propaganda of

---

[23] On this point, see Beales, *op. cit.*

that nature would make it harder for pacifist groups to recruit members. Only a group founded by Henry Wright in September, 1838, openly proclaimed a program of nonviolence, but it collapsed at the time of the Mexican war because some of the members believed it to be a "just" war. And pacifist leaders who actively supported the abolitionist drive were reluctant to oppose a Union war against the southern secessionists; they went so far as to say that condemnation of war applied only to international conflicts. These differences of opinion hampered the development of the American pacifist movement.

The doctrine of nonviolence and the idea of refusing to serve in the armed forces found many supporters among members of the British Peace Society, but nonviolence made little headway on the Continent, where the Société des amis de la morale chrétienne, the first pacifist organization, refrained from taking a stand on the issue. European pacifists found it difficult to remove themselves from the realities of international politics.

In the late nineteenth century, the doctrine of nonviolence was no longer so vigorously proclaimed, even among British pacifists, who for the most part opposed neither the Crimean War nor the Boer War. Only the Society of Friends demanded of its members "to maintain Christian witness against all war, as being incompatible with the precepts and the spirit of God." (Even that doctrinal point was criticized, overtly or covertly, by some Quakers.[24]) "Radical" pacifism thus continued to lose ground.

B. ABOLITION OF THE CAUSES OF WAR

The second method—to work for peace by removing the causes of war— was far more popular than nonviolence within the pacifist movement.[25]

Let us take the *economic* reasons first, for mid-nineteenth-century pacifists most frequently criticized economic imperialism and restrictions imposed on free trade. Since "commercial jealousy" fanned international rivalries, they argued, the remedy was to establish a system that would facilitate the peaceful development of international trade. As early as 1828, the French economist J. B. Say asserted that this would persuade people of the "solidarity of their interests." The development of trade would weave a network of common interests, William Henry Channing, a prominent American Socialist, added in 1838. Peace would thus be ensured, since any conflict would disturb the order and industry of all the other states. Customs barriers that impeded trade development must therefore be broken down.

In the 1840's, Richard Cobden popularized this argument widely. Peace and free trade, he declared, were but a single cause. The elimination of

---

[24] See Margaret E. Hirst, *The Quakers in Peace and War* (London, 1923).
[25] On this point, see Aron, *op. cit.*, pp. 704–9.

customs barriers, in fact, was the only human means of achieving effective peace. It would permit the growth of voluntary cooperation, and this in turn would surmount the obstacles of nationality and race. Private interests operating in a framework of freely set contracts and free competition would be the true instrument of progress and social harmony.

The same note was sounded by Frédéric Bastiat. The spirit of free trade, he maintained, was inimical to the spirit of war, conquest, and domination; it tended to erase international friction and jealousy because it showed producers that real prosperity in industry was based, not, as he put it, on monopolies harmful to the masses, but on the prosperity of their customers— that is, of the entire world. Once the general public understood this, he declared, the death knell of violent aggression would sound.[26]

Joseph Garnier, permanent secretary of the Société d'économie politique, broadened this perspective in his book *Traité d'économie politique* (which went through seven editions between 1850 and 1875). Free trade, he thought, would not only establish common interests, but also permit a reciprocal penetration of ideas and awaken feelings of respect and fraternity among peoples.

As the nineteenth century drew to a close, pacifists gradually had to abandon this faith in free trade, and the United Kingdom alone remained faithful to its principles. Free trade made an appearance again in 1933 in the United States, however, at the start of the Roosevelt administration, when Secretary of State Cordell Hull tried to revive the argument that "economic disarmament" and freedom of trade were the two essential conditions of a durable peace.

The *social* arguments for "removing the causes of war" derived principally from Marxist teaching, which stressed the role of big business in conflicts of economic interests, pointing to the greed of businessmen who urged governments to press for commercial competitive advantages, by force if need be, in order to increase their own profits and to the munitions manufacturers believed to be responsible for the accelerated arms race. By abolishing these capitalist incitements to conflict and establishing a classless society, the Marxists argued, peace would be assured. The duty of the working class was to defeat the machinations of big business in case of threatened war by means of the revolutionary general strike.

This recourse to class warfare had been suggested in 1855 by the American pacifist Elihu Burritt, who had envisaged what he termed "an organized strike of all the workers of Christendom against war," but it was Marxism that popularized the notion.

The *political* argument for the movement to abolish the causes of war rested on the theory that differences in existing systems of government were

---

[26] From an address delivered in Lyons, August, 1847. See *Oeuvres complètes* (Paris, 1862), II, 270.

a cause of international conflict—a theory held by men as different as Mazzini, the French social theorist Victor Considérant, and Alexis de Tocqueville.

Between 1850 and 1870, and especially between 1867 and 1869, the idea took root in the pacifist movement that the establishment of republican and democratic governments was the necessary and sufficient condition for an enduring peace. The theme was suggested by Victor Hugo in a speech in 1855, and it dominated the debates of the Peace Congress at Geneva in 1867; only after "despotic regimes" were abolished would it be possible to "unite the peoples." The main objective of the International League of Peace and Liberty, which this congress decided to found, was to arouse public opinion to pave the way to the collapse of "old systems of government."

The Peace Congress of 1869 (Victor Hugo was its honorary president) hoped to establish a "federation of peoples of Europe," but proposed to include only those nations whose citizens enjoyed universal suffrage, the right to vote on taxes, and a system of government in which "individual and public liberties were assured." But this kind of argument was used mainly as a weapon against authoritarian regimes—those of Tsarist Russia, the German Empire and Bismarck, and Napoleon III—and peace was clearly a secondary concern.

The *moral* arguments supporting this second form of pacifism began with the tenet that excessive nationalism was the chief obstacle to peaceful international relations. This distortion of true love of nation was often encouraged in the press and in the schools, it was believed. How was it to be checked? —By a policy of enlightenment and education which was the responsibility, in all countries, of the intellectual elite.

This had long been a concern of all pacifist theorists. The first Universal Peace Congresses of the 1840's and 1850's, the new series of Universal Peace Congresses from 1889 to 1914, Andrew Carnegie's various endeavors between 1910 and 1914—all focused on this as a principal objective. But not until after 1919, under the aegis of International Federation of the League of Nations Societies was there any systematic and continuous action.

As far as "correcting" the wayward tendencies of the press and school system was concerned, all attempts were abortive. Surveys made in the 1920's and 1930's denounced the nationalist incitements found in many textbooks but could do nothing to remedy it. The only attempt to work out revisions—by agreement between French and German instructors in 1935—had no practical effects, as might have been expected, given the international situation at the time. (After World War II, the effort was revived by UNESCO.) As for the press, appeals were addressed to journalists—appeals to their conscience or their sense of responsibility—and the League of Nations attempted in the late 1920's to draft an international statute for journalists and to organize a campaign against inaccurate news reporting. But the League's efforts never became more than evidence of good intentions, which may also be said of further studies initiated by the United Nations General Assembly (but aimed at freedom of information rather than journalism's international responsibilities).

Lastly, for those who argued on *demographic* grounds for the abolition of causes of war, the question was, how significantly does overpopulation in fact act as a cause of international conflict? Or, how significant is the poverty it engenders, or the disparity in living standards for which it is partially responsible?[27] Before World War I, the pacifist movement paid little attention to these questions. Between the wars, sociologists and economists discussed them, but primarily in order to analyze the concept of *Lebensraum* and the arguments advanced in Germany and Italy in support of expansionist policies. Only after World War II, in the context of the international political and economic problems posed by the newly independent (and underdeveloped) nations, has a reversal of the population explosion appeared to many pacifists to be a prerequisite for peace.

It would seem that we can fairly infer that the peace movement's declared plan to eliminate causes of international conflict—a plan based on a critique of the "theory of war"—often served quite different ends. Free-trade economists of the mid-nineteenth century realized that pacifist ideas might reinforce theories they had originally advanced for purely utilitarian ends.[28] Revolutionary socialists before World War I desired a transformation of society far more than a strengthened peace. French republican democrats of 1867 were much more concerned to defeat Napoleon III or Bismarck than to eliminate war from international relations. These forms of pacifism were only "interested ideologies," to use Max Scheler's expression.

C. PEACE THROUGH LAW

Only the third tenet of the pacifist movement—organized "peace through law"—was ever translated into a genuine plan of action. Most theorists of this kind of pacifism felt from the start that the Quaker objective, the total abolition of war, was utopian. And they were careful to distinguish between their concern for peace for its own sake and the views of those who regarded pacifism as an aid to promote other political, social, or economic ideas. What they wanted was to establish a set of juridical rules or institutions that would ensure the peaceful settlement of international disputes. It may be useful to recall the themes and principal stages in the history of this endeavor.

---

[27] See above, Chapter Two.

[28] See Cobden's letter to Ashworth, April 12, 1842, cited by John Morley, *Life of Cobden* (London, 1903), I, 230.

In 1815, Europe was exhausted, depleted of energy after an international crisis that had continued for more than twenty years and had profoundly shaken the political and social found..tions of Europe. Men desired first and foremost to prevent a repetition of this experience. It is not surprising, then, that this was the era when essays on the reorganization of European society— by Saint-Simon and Karl Krause, among others—and, in the United States and England, pacifist societies first appeared. Between 1830 and 1848, when revolutions, diplomatic crises, and continuing "nationality" agitations raised fears of another general war, the evidence of this concern for peace mounted. Four distinct, if sometimes overlapping, trends may be distinguished: a religious trend, sponsored by American Quakers and English nonconformists; a socialist trend, chiefly French; a Mazzinian trend, strongly republican; and a trend inspired by free-trade theories. Slowly, the great themes emerged around which the pacifist movement was to develop: (1) the need to organize a system of international arbitration (the basic item on the agenda of the first world congress of peace societies in London in 1843); (2) disarmament (on which free-trade proponents placed most emphasis, since they believed it essential to free people from heavy tax burdens); and (3) the concept of a new organization of international relations—a limitation of national sovereignties in the context of a confederal system (advocated by socialists like Saint-Simon and Considérant, "humanitarian" pacifists like Philippe Marchand, "religious" pacifists like William Ladd and his European disciples, and the Mazzinians). Such an international organization might include all countries, but it should at least include all Europe. But each pacifist developed his ideas without knowing, or at least without discussing, those of others, and there was no confrontation of points of view until the great turning-point of 1848–49.

The first Universal Peace Congress, meeting in Brussels in 1848, heard a report from Elihu Burritt in which he outlined a plan for a society of European nations. He envisioned an elected international assembly that would establish a European constitution, which would then be submitted for ratification to the national legislatures, and a court of justice that would exercise *moral* jurisdiction in all controversial international questions. But Burritt's report did not provoke any real debate.

The idea of a United States of Europe later gained currency thanks to Victor Hugo but was never discussed substantively; pacifists simply repeated the slogan but did not commit themselves on the issue of what institutions should be established. On June 12, 1849, however, a debate was held in the House of Commons on a motion introduced by Richard Cobden and backed by a petition bearing 200,000 signatures, which invited the British Government to negotiate with foreign governments with a view to concluding a treaty under which contracting parties would undertake to submit to arbitration disputes that could not be settled through normal diplomatic channels.

Cobden believed that responsibility for rendering an arbitral award should be placed not in a "neutral" sovereign power, but in "individuals," in agents designated by each state. He rejected any idea of constraint by force of arms to execute the verdict, wanting to rely solely on moral pressure; the state that broke its promises would become an aggressor in the eyes of world public opinion. Cobden's proposal was rejected and never followed up.

During the next thirty years, the movement for peace through law declined, as nationalistic passions aroused in Italy and Germany made the prospect of unity among peoples (or states) less and less likely. While the "religious" pacifists continued to discuss questions of disarmament and arbitration, they seem to have abandoned the idea of a European federation. Socialists, with Proudhon, went so far as to hold that a United States of Europe was incompatible with the existence of large nation-states. The Mazzinians were silent, since it was becoming obvious that the application of the nationality principle was no guarantee of peace. Only some free-trade economists, in particular Michel Chevalier, continued to recall the "European idea." Newcomers to the pacifist movement—the promoters of the International League of Peace and Liberty—were really interested only in the struggle against authoritarian regimes.

But pacifism received a new lease on life in 1877 when, for the first time in the nineteenth century, studies of possible institutions of a European federation were undertaken by a number of noted jurists—the Scottish authority James Lorimer and the Swiss Johann Bluntschli, a professor at Munich and Heidelberg universities. Positions were now more carefully defined and complex alternatives clearly set out: equality among states vs. preponderance of great powers; respect of national sovereignty vs. a supernational organization; association among *governments* vs. representation of "popular will"; power directly exercised by an executive federal organ vs. delegation of power to certain states.[29] And, more important, pacifist societies made a real effort to secure a broader audience. After 1889, the regular sessions of Universal Peace Congresses and the Inter-Parliamentary Union popularized the movement.

The results of all this activity, however, despite the successes of the International Peace Conferences of 1899 and 1907 (the Hague Conferences), were not proportionate to the effort involved. The balance sheet for the twenty years preceding World War I was disappointing.

A United States of Europe, a central theme of the movement for so long, was now relegated to the background. Most of the members of the Congrès des sciences politiques (Paris, 1900) felt that it would be useless to examine the possible forms of such a federation. Moreover, the pacifists realized that European powers had such important interests outside Europe that they

---

[29] Subsequent studies, for instance, Novicov, *La Fédération de l'Europe* (1901), introduced nothing new into this doctrinal debate.

could not establish a federation that did not associate other continents in it. There was also the potential role of the United States to consider. A *global* solution would have to be found. The concept of a Congress of Nations, suggested in 1840 by William Ladd and since forgotten, now replaced that of a United States of Europe.

The disarmament issue, which had headed the agenda for some years (particularly between 1895 and 1899) was ignored after the partial failure of the First Hague Conference; arms limitation no longer seemed a feasible way to achieve peace, but only a consequence of such an achievement.

The possibilities of international arbitration remained central to pacifist ambitions, however. The work of the Hague Conferences endorsed the idea when they established the Permanent Court of Arbitration and prepared the ground for its procedures—the first conference by proposing an investigation procedure to determine the exact nature of the disputes, the second by laying down a conciliation procedure. But recourse to this form of settlement was still voluntary, and the execution of the arbitral award depended on the good faith of the states concerned. Compulsory arbitration, and compulsory agreement to the arbitral awards, were thus the objectives the pacifist movement most insistently pursued. The most noteworthy pacifist efforts, however—William Jennings Bryan's at the conference of the Inter-Parliamentary Union in 1906 and Andrew Carnegie's in the spring of 1914—remained abortive.

World War I threw new light on these problems. Since the war paralyzed all international cooperative activities, it seemed to threaten the very existence of a pacifist movement; the groups that survived were isolated and disorganized in the face of strong nationalistic currents.[30] But the length of the war, the extent of the suffering, and the spectacle of ruin aroused in much of the public and among statesmen the desire to prevent a repetition of the ordeal. In 1916, the problem of "organizing the peace" was beginning to be discussed; in 1919, it entered the realm of practical politics. But despite the establishment of the Permanent Court of International Justice and despite the League of Nations' General Act of Arbitration in 1928, progress was slight. Major pacifist efforts were concentrated on the organization of a confederal system. What, in fact, happened to pacifist theories when they confronted reality, first in the League system, then in the United Nations?

Preparatory studies for the League of Nations Covenant, and the debates in the committee of the Paris Peace Conference responsible for working it out, had won acceptance for the idea of an association of states, a "society of governments" that accepted a limitation of their sovereign rights, but no agreement to the establishment of an international government. The principle of equality among states was established in the League Assembly; but the

---

[30] In all the belligerent powers, even in the United States, pacifist organizations, with the exception of Quaker groups, approved of participation in the war.

preponderance of the Great Powers was officially recognized by their desig-
nation as permanent members of the Council. Appointment of members to
the Assembly, as to the Council, was the responsibility of governments.
Lastly, war was regarded as permissible not only in cases of legitimate self-
defense, but as a form of sanctions against a state that violated the League
Covenant.

Agreement on all these points was achieved without serious controversy
at the Paris Peace Conference. But the effectiveness of the system, gravely
jeopardized from the outset by the abstention of the United States and Russia,
was limited by the unanimity rule in the Council—a corollary of the state
sovereignty principle—which made it almost impossible to condemn an
aggressor; it was also limited by the inadequacy of the prescribed sanctions,
which the French Government vainly sought to remedy in 1924 by the Geneva
Protocol.

The pacifist movement now resorted to a return to "continentalism."
The "crisis" of the League of Nations, Georges Scelle observed, showed how
necessary it was to give the organization a regional basis.[31] The emergence
of the Pan-American idea (however timorous and inadequate) also provided
an argument in favor of continentalism, although the European problem was
not comparable to the Western Hemisphere situation, where the United
States enjoyed an undisputed hegemony. Still, the idea of the organization
of Europe, abandoned during World War I and at the Peace Conference,
when the United States became the arbiter of international relations, now
re-emerged. A Pan-European movement, championed by Count Richard
Coudenhove-Kalergi, began to take shape in 1926 and now aroused interest
among statesmen. Still, when, on May 17, 1930, Aristide Briand proposed
a European Union, he introduced no new theme into the study of the complex
questions involved, for he did not wish to alarm either the League of Nations,
within the framework of which a European Union would have to operate,
or national susceptibilities.[32] By insisting on respect for national sovereignty,
he appeared to endorse the League's unanimity rule and the optional character of its sanctions.

It was possible that this weakness could be remedied by other, less
ambitious, juridical means that did not require a system of international
institutions. In April, 1927, American pacifists suggested to Briand that
he propose an agreement under which France and the United States renounce
war as an instrument for settling disputes that might arise between them—
hoping that this might lead to a general agreement. But the Americans were
divided into two factions on this issue. The Carnegie Endowment for Inter-

---

[31] Georges Scelle, *Une crise de la S.D.N.* (Paris, 1927).

[32] See the important observations of Paul Bastid on this point, in "L'Idée d'Europe
et l'organisation de l'Europe," *L'Europe du xix et du xx siècles: Interprétations
historiques* (Paris, 1964), V, 415–16.

national Peace favored the principle of collective security, as conceived in the framework of the League of Nations; more "radical" pacifists, led by Salmon Oliver Levinson, advocated an international agreement completely outlawing war (all disputes would be referred to a court) but were deeply opposed to any system of military or even economic sanctions. If war were outlawed, would this mean that the use of armed force even to counter aggression was outlawed too? The question of sanctions re-emerged here— precisely the problem the League of Nations was unable to resolve.

"Radical" pacifists (including prominent senators like William Borah of Idaho) remained faithful to the American pacifist belief in the efficacy of moral sanctions. Levinson thought it best to rely on the good faith of nations and the influence of public opinion; war, he felt, must be proscribed even if this meant imposing a court's decisions; since people placed confidence in treaties of alliance which, as he said, "constrain nations to make war," why not have the same confidence in a treaty imposing the obligation *not* to go to war?

The supporters of peace "by juridical means," advocates of the League of Nations, could not accept what they considered to be a naïve argument, divorced from political realities, which favored a rule that would ruin the Genevan system. Briand therefore encouraged another formula as an alternative to outlawing war, according to which war would be renounced as an instrument of national policy, but recourse to armed force would remain licit when the Council of the League of Nations decided it to be "in the common interest." This was the formula adopted in the Kellogg-Briand Pact (the Pact of Paris, 1928), approved and implemented by the League members.[33] But the Pact contained no provisions for sanctions against the state that might violate it. It was impossible to harbor illusions about the Pact's future effectiveness.

The objective of the Charter of the United Nations, like that of the League Covenant, is to avert the "scourge of war" or, more accurately, to devise means to ensure that "armed force shall not be used, save in the common interest." The Charter proposes to achieve this peaceful international order by methods that do not substantially differ in principle from those of 1919, but simply try to improve the system. To what extent do the Charter articles defining collective security strengthen the right to act and the means of action?[34]

Under the Charter, the members of the Security Council are not bound by a unanimity rule, as they had been in the League, and may therefore theoretically make decisions more easily. But the unanimity rule does apply to

---

[33] For an analysis of the origins of this pact, see Duroselle, *From Wilson to Roosevelt: American Foreign Policy, 1913–45* (Cambridge, Mass., 1963). See also below, Chapter Eleven, pp. 303–5.

[34] See Aron, *op. cit.*, pp. 710–17.

the five *permanent* members of the Council—that is, each has the right of veto on any decision. This does not represent much progress; in the League, temporary Council members had rarely cast vetoes.

Secondly, the Security Council can act to use armed forces made available to it by U.N. member states; the controversy over sanctions that so disturbed the history of the League has thus in principle been resolved in favor of those who supported the idea of armed sanctions. But the U.N. in 1945, no more than the League in 1919, made no provision to establish a permanent international army. Implementation of Council decisions continues, therefore, to depend on the sovereign will of the individual states.

Lastly, the Security Council has no more competence than the League Council did to intervene in "matters which are essentially within the domestic jurisdiction of any state," but it is authorized to act when these matters threaten international peace; in attempting to keep the process of decolonization peaceful, the U.N. has appealed to and used this new clause.

In reality, these extensions of the powers and means of action available to the Security Council have been useless, since the rivalry between the Soviet Union and the United States has paralyzed the implementation of the Charter and virtually destroyed the very idea of a collective-security system. "Continentalism" has therefore once again reappeared to make up for the deficiency of the system. The U.N. Charter, recognizing the existence of the Organization of American States, expressly recognizes the legitimacy of "regional arrangements or agencies" and permits them to take autonomous action. But if such action includes recourse to force, the Charter requires the prior authorization of the U.N. Security Council. Clearly, neither NATO, nor the Council of Europe, nor the Soviet alliances can obey this stricture. Consequently, instead of developing within the collective-security framework, these regional arrangements have developed outside the framework—a return to coalitions, to the very situation the authors of the Charter desired to remedy—which makes clear the bankruptcy of the notion of "peace through law."

The "essential imperfection of international law" has thus become apparent. The very notion of collective security presupposes the existence of an international agency capable of imposing respect for decisions taken in common. But such decisions, under the U.N. Charter as under the League Covenant, require the agreement of all the great powers that are members of the organization. And, as Aron remarks, "when the major powers agree, with or without collective security, there is no major war."

III. THE INTERNATIONAL SIGNIFICANCE OF THE
PACIFIST MOVEMENT

Among the various difficulties that have thwarted the development of the pacifist movement, two stand out: the disagreements among pacifist thinkers; and the always cautious, sometimes antagonistic, attitudes of national governments toward pacifist ideas. Intra-pacifist disagreements occurred over both the basic principles and practical forms of an organized peace; naturally, they become more frequent as the questions raised become more complex.

The idea of international arbitration—involving agreement on conciliation procedures in case of a threat to peace, on the judges to settle the dispute, and on the undertaking to respect their decision—first emerged as an expedient way to resolve specific cases; there was no question of a permanent agency. Only in the last two decades of the nineteenth century did pacifists (from Leone Levi to Emile Decamps and Kamarovsky) examine the idea of an arbitral court, which the First Hague Conference eventually created. Was it possible to submit *all* international disputes to arbitration? Leading pacifists, Henry Richard at their head, had not even dared to suggest it. At the Universal Peace Congress of 1897, however, the pacifists began to think it a possibility; but in the same year, the Inter-Parliamentary Union (which included pacifists and men active in politics and familiar with political problems) concluded that limits must be set to the area in which arbitration should apply. In 1902, on the initiative of the French delegates, the Universal Peace Congress again supported a motion for compulsory arbitration of all disputes, but the British pacifists remained divided. Total agreement among the pacifist societies was finally achieved on this point at the peace congresses held after World War I, after more than thirty years of debate.

On the question of sanctions, on the other hand, agreement seemed impossible. What constraints should be exercised against a state that refused to arbitrate or respect the arbitral award? Moral sanctions? Economic boycotts? Armed sanctions? On a number of occasions, debates on this issue threatened to disrupt the British and American Peace Societies; they were a regular feature of the Universal Peace Congresses.

Advocates of moral sanctions believed that the censure of public opinion was enough to bring a state that had violated its obligations back to the straight and narrow path. Encouraged by British and American "religious" pacifists, but also with the support of Cobden and his disciples,[35] they declared that the use of force in sanctions would be tantamount to recourse to war. Advocates of armed sanctions invoked practical arguments: how could a state that remained unmoved by public indignation be brought to reason? Economic sanctions were envisaged as a compromise. In 1892, the

[35] See above, pp. 219–20, on Cobden's speech in the House of Commons in 1849.

Universal Peace Congress rejected armed sanctions but accepted economic sanctions; at its 1904 session, where advocates of armed sanctions were clearly in a minority, the debate developed on "peaceful"—that is, economic—sanctions. The chairman of the British Peace Society opposed economic sanctions, however, because, he said, they involved a threat of war. His argument prevailed by a small majority, and the matter was not taken up again until 1913, when it was referred to a special committee, which had not yet drafted a report when the war broke out.

This conflict between "idealists" and "realists" was a permanent theme of the pacifist movement even after 1919. In 1924, the British Conservative government refused to subscribe to the Geneva Protocol on the grounds that the enforcement of economic sanctions against an aggressor might oblige it to take a stand contrary to the interests of the United States. And in 1937, at the time of the Oxford ecumenical conference, Anglo-Saxon pacifists, coming as they did from states where the threat of foreign invasion was virtually nonexistent, voiced reservations over measures which Continental pacifists considered self-evident necessities.

When pacifists attempted to outline a plan for an international society— a Congress of Nations or a United States of Europe—the differences of opinion were no less great. Would the covenant concluded among the states provide for an association that would fully respect the rights of national sovereignty? Or would it be a confederation that would secure a closer and more durable union but would limit the exercise of national sovereignty? Or a form of federal state to which national governments would be subject? Almost every possible type of organization was suggested.

An extreme tendency was represented as early as 1814 by Saint-Simon, who conceived of a "general government" of Europe "altogether independent of national governments," with a parliament chosen by direct but hardly universal suffrage—only scholars, judges, administrators, and business men being permitted to vote; a chamber of hereditary peers; and a sovereign, the manner of whose appointment Saint-Simon never specified.

The idea of an international parliament reappeared in 1868; some writers proposed that the United States Constitution serve as the basis of an international organization—for instance, Charles Lemonnier, editor from 1867 to 1887 of the journal *Etats-Unis d'Europe*.

In his report to the Universal Peace Congress of 1848, Elihu Burritt proposed not an *elected* international assembly but one appointed by the legislatures of each state. James Lorimer also advocated this plan, in 1877, but, whereas Burritt envisaged limited powers for the assembly, whose decisions he believed should be submitted to national ratification, Lorimer envisaged the establishment of an executive power, consisting of a council elected by the assembly, with a chairman elected from among the council's members.

These proposals—aimed at achieving a fairly integrated form of inter-

national organization and providing for direct or indirect popular suffrage—
contrasted sharply with those for a confederation of states that would respect
national sovereignty. Philippe-René Marchand in 1842, and Emile de
Girardin in 1848, proposed a congress of ambassadors who would act under
instructions from their governments. Both cited the German Empire's Diet
as precedent and envisaged decisions by majority vote. Johann Bluntschli[36]
and Isambert (rapporteur in 1900 for the Congrès des sciences politiques in
Paris)[37] tried to arrive at a compromise: two assemblies, one appointed
by the national legislatures, the other consisting of representatives of
governments.[38] On the respective powers of these assemblies, their views
differed. Bluntschli favored wide powers for the assembly appointed by the
governments, which alone would be responsible for decisions on issues of
"major policy," questions implying a threat to national peace and independence. Isambert conceived of a more complex system, in which disputes
involving major issues would be referred to a congress in which representatives of governments and members appointed by national legislatures would
both participate. Bluntschli and Isambert also proposed different implemen-
tations of assembly decisions: the former entrusted this responsibility to
the states, the latter to a directorate. Two other theorists, Constantin Pecqueur
and Novicov,[39] envisaged a gradual progress from a confederation of states
to a federal state, with long intervals between each stage.

Thought on the subject of international organization was thus rich and
many-faceted, exploring every approach but never providing any systematic
analysis of the various theories. The only clear common trait was an awareness of the difficulties; bold concepts gradually gave way to more modest
ones. In the end, the system that commanded most attention was that of a
confederation of states.

Agreement was no easier on the responsibilities to be accorded these
international assemblies or councils. They would, of course, be responsible
for settling disputes between states; they would also have administrative
functions in the economic field, particularly as regards the organization
of transport and communications. Was it possible to go farther than this?
Pecqueur and de Girardin wanted them to be empowered to raise customs
and rule on the issue of paper currencies, in other words, to have some control over national economic and monetary policies. Girardin even favored
their control over social legislation, for no state, he believed could attempt
to regulate the length of the working day, for example, in isolation. But
what competence should these assemblies have in settling disputes arising

---

[36] "Le problème final du droit international," *Revue de droit international et de
legislation comparée*, 1878.

[37] "Die Organisation des europaischen Straatsverein," *Gegenwart*, 1900.

[38] Bluntschli called them "Senate" and "Federal Council"; Isambert, "High Court"
and "Legislative Council."

[39] Constantin Pecqueur, *De la paix* (1842), and Novicov, *op. cit.*

out of the claims of "national minorities"? Saint-Simon unhesitatingly proposed that the "European government" be responsible for settling conflicts between a government and a "population that wished to form a distinct nation"; Lorimer wanted the international congress to be empowered to decide matters of transfer of sovereignty. But there were very few who committed themselves to either of these extreme proposals, and no one took up the suggestion made by Marchand in 1840—that the federal congress establish uniform legislation on press offenses, in order to prevent newspapers from inflaming public opinion in international disputes. Here again, then, individual pacifists recognized the problems, but the pacifist movement as a whole did not attempt to resolve them.

If pacifist doctrine had been better defined, would it have been more effective? Governmental attitudes give reason to doubt it; at no time did any government seriously entertain pacifist ideas, whether on arbitration, disarmament, or a system of permanent international institutions.

Let us consider their attitude to arbitration. In June, 1849, in his reply to Cobden's motion in the House of Commons, Palmerston emphasized the difficulties: no government, he said, could agree to bind itself in advance to the decisions of a third party. Furthermore, who would be the arbitrators? Lawyers, chosen because of their ability and moral stature? They would have no power. Governments? If governments were "just," arbitration would be unnecessary, and if they were "unjust," they could not provide valid arbitration. In fact, an arbitration body would be ineffective unless there existed a tribunal of nations and a military force capable of ensuring compliance with it.

Still, governments have sometimes resorted to arbitrators. Between 1794 and 1900, 177 disputes were submitted to arbitral procedure, ninety of them between 1880 and 1900.[40] But few political issues were included in this number. Beyond such *ad hoc* procedures, other provisions have been made in anticipation of a future conflict. Recourse to arbitration was provided for in the Treaty of Paris of 1856 ending the Crimean War (in case of dispute, the Persian Shah was to make use of British good offices), but Protocol 23, which contained this provision, merely expressed the hope that, before resorting to arms, governments would appeal, "as far as circumstances permit," to the "good offices of a friendly power." On the occasions when this protocol was invoked—in 1869, at the time of the Greco-Turkish conflict, and in 1870, on the eve of the Franco-Prussian War, at the suggestion of the British Government—it was totally ineffective.

Bilateral treaties of arbitration were of two kinds. Some specified the cases where the contracting states undertook to resort to arbitration; others included a general undertaking, subject to reservations (the most common

---

[40] They are listed in H. la Fontaine, *Histoire sommaire des arbitrages internationaux* (Paris, 1902).

of which concerned disputes involving "national honor"); they did not attempt to define the scope of the exceptions, whose meaning remained very fluid.

Prior to 1899, no treaty on arbitration had been concluded between any of the Great Powers. (A proposal drawn up by the governments of London and Washington in 1896, on the initiative of the British Parliament, concerning their strained relations in the Venezuela boundary dispute,[41] had not been ratified by the United States Senate.) Arbitration procedures had been employed only in minor disputes which in any event did not seriously threaten the peace. But in 1899, the issue took on new importance. At that time, despite German hesitations, the nations represented at the First Hague Conference agreed to establish a Permanent Court of Arbitration. This organism was not really a court, nor was it permanent. At best, it was "an ephemeral tribunal in a permanent framework,"[42] which made its services available to states without "imposing itself on them." The principle of compulsory recourse to arbitration had been roundly rejected. "It is a serious matter," noted Louis Renault, "to commit oneself in advance to abide by an arbitral procedure without knowing what the nature of the disputes will be or what influence their settlement is likely to exert on the interests of the state."

The convention adopted at the Second Hague Conference, in 1907, noted merely that, in legal questions and above all in questions of interpretation or implementation of international conventions, arbitration was the most effective and equitable means to settle disputes that had not been settled through normal diplomatic channels. Even narrowly circumscribed in this way, the application of the principle was uncertain. (This time, however, the leader of the French delegation, Léon Bourgeois, spoke in favor of compulsory arbitration; the German delegation objected.)

The two Hague conferences gave their participants a strong impetus to conclude treaties of arbitration. The Great Powers did not oppose this trend, but those whose differences were more likely to lead to war (Germany and France, Austria-Hungary and Russia) concluded no arbitration treaties.

Not until September 26, 1928, in the General Act of Arbitration voted by the Ninth Assembly of the League of Nations, was the principle of compulsory arbitration for political conflicts established. It is scarcely necessary to point out how ineffective that principle remained.

Disarmament, the second major pacifist theme of the mid-nineteenth century, entered the field of diplomacy in 1869, when Lord Clarendon vainly

---

[41] Great Britain refused to submit to arbitration the disputed boundary between Venezuela and British Guiana, and took issue with Secretary of State Olney's assertion that the Monroe Doctrine would be violated by unilateral British action. In 1897, the dispute was arbitrated, the awards largely supporting the British position.

[42] Charles Rousseau, *Précis de droit international public approfondi* (Paris, 1960), p. 292.

attempted to act as mediator in the impending conflict between France and Prussia. But on that occasion, neither questions of principle nor practical problems were tackled. Two dates were crucial to any attempt to assess the position of various governments on disarmament: the First Hague Conference in 1899, and the Disarmament Conference of 1928–33.

In 1898, the Tsar took the initiative in proposing an international conference for the study of arms limitation. He had been prompted to do so by his perusal of pacifist works—by Baroness de Suttner and Jean de Bloch—and by reports of debates in the Inter-Parliamentary Union. But he was also thinking of his own country's interests. An international agreement to limit armaments would spare Russia the effort of reorganizing her military forces, a task that her present financial position rendered difficult.

The Tsar's proposal met with skepticism on the part of all the Great Powers, however. Lord Salisbury felt that one could not put faith in a government's mere promise to limit arms; Delcassé regretted that the study of these questions should be made under international auspices; Kaiser Wilhelm II wanted only to rely on his own "good sword"; the American delegate had instructions to make no commitments.

Germany's position was probably the clearest, and she led the way in turning down the disarmament idea; her delegates declared that arms control was unrealizable because the military systems of the various states were too disparate. But other governments were not unhappy when the disarmament idea failed; all the delegations were in fact determined to reject any measures that would reduce their countries' offensive or defensive forces, or even restrict the growth of those forces. At the Second Hague Conference, in 1907, all the participants agreed that a limitation on armaments could not be considered so long as the causes of war were not eliminated.

This approach, which made the limitation of armaments a consequence instead of a condition of peace, reappeared thirty years later in the Geneva Disarmament Conference debates. In 1927, the German Government demanded equality in armaments, which would have meant substantial reduction of France's armed forces; the French argued that such a reduction should be subject to a prior solution of security problems and therefore asked, not only for international policing of disarmament measures, but also that the inadequacies of the League of Nations system and its lack of sanctions be repaired. This disagreement sufficed to create a deadlock in the Disarmament Conference.

Permanent international institutions, envisaged for a century by pacifists in both Europe and America, finally came into being in 1919. The League of Nations was to secure the peace. But, in the minds of the authors of the Covenant, it was also to guarantee observance of the peace treaties—that is, of the territorial arrangements made in 1919–20; the victory was to be "transposed" into a "custodianship of the peace."[43] The Covenant provided for possible revision of those treaties, but Article 19 made revision subject to conditions that rendered the whole process unlikely. The territorial arrangements of 1919–20 thus received the stamp of permanency. This in turn weakened the League's moral authority, for the defeated nations naturally declared that an institution ostensibly designed to organize the peace was in fact perpetuating a situation achieved by victory, that is, by force.

As early as 1919, Foreign Office experts in London had regretted this rigid outlook, which, they felt, was irreconcilable with prevailing conditions. Quite apart from any desire for revenge, economic changes or migrations might well change the composition of certain populations so as to call into question the reasons for maintaining the old frontiers. It is arguable that the League of Nations could have better fulfilled its essential mission—to maintain the peace—had it been in a position to persuade both victors and vanquished to compromise, which would have required the broadening of Article 19 and the abandonment of the unanimity rule in the Council. But the League wished both to maintain the peace and to ensure the implementation of the peace treaties. In order to succeed in this double task, it would have had to have the power to impose sanctions on the states that refused to comply, i.e., the Covenant would have had to be changed. In the form in which it had been constituted by the Allied and Associated States, the League could not carry out the twofold task assigned to it.

Similarly, when Briand suggested strengthening the League of Nations with a European Union, his central concern was, apparently, to extend progressively to the entire European community the policy of international guarantees inaugurated at Locarno. He wished, therefore, to obtain assurances from Germany that she would respect the Czech and Polish frontiers. The security of the French system of alliances—and not some pacifist goal—was the first thing on his mind. And that is what provoked Germany's resistance and England's hesitation. No German Government, not even Chancellor Brüning's, whose desire for conciliation was beyond cavil, would be prepared to agree to a system under which it would have to abandon all hope of revising Germany's eastern frontiers. And the British Government, over and above the difficulties it foresaw in its imperial relations if it joined a European Union, was inclined to think that in giving France the moral advantage of initiating a plan for the organization of peace, Briand also hoped to consolidate a French "hegemony" on the Continent. It was not difficult to foresee the failure of Briand's scheme, long before the League Assembly, by a vote of September, 1931, rejected it in toto.

[43] Georges Scelle, "Le problème de la Société des Nations," *Année politique*, November, 1938, p. 383.

This somewhat hostile attitude on the part of governments toward pacifist proposals is largely to be explained by their responsiveness to their nations' collective psychology. If it is true that newspapers and parliamentary debates to a certain degree express popular ideas and sentiments, then we can fairly conclude that, prior to 1914, the pacifist movement apparently never enjoyed the active support of the public. This conclusion may best be judged in the light of the situation in Great Britain, where pacifist organizations were more numerous and more vigorous than elsewhere, and where their propaganda could be expected to gain a favorable hearing, given the general sense of security enjoyed by the English people. The pacifists' endeavors to prevent the Crimean War in 1854 provoked no response among the public; the British Peace Society noted in 1861 that the distinction between just and unjust wars was not so important to the public as the desire to maintain British supremacy and British military prestige. In 1873, it is true, the House of Commons defied the government and adopted a motion in favor of international arbitration; but Henry Richard, chairman of the Peace Society, vainly sought in 1882 to secure the adoption of a motion against the Egyptian expedition.[44] In 1899, when pacifist leaders condemned the Boer War, many people resigned from the peace societies, and the general elections of 1900 showed clearly that the efforts of these associations had enjoyed little sympathy among the public.

In France, at the time of the First Hague Conference, some newspapers and journals were suspicious of this gathering, wondering whether the purpose was not to bring about a repudiation of France's claim to Alsace-Lorraine. Most editorialists hoped that the deliberations on arms limitation would fail. The attempts of pacifist societies, socialists, and suffragette groups to "mobilize" opinion in favor of the conference received no support. And in 1917 in the United States, the leaders of the American Peace Society, the Carnegie Endowment for International Peace, and the organizers of the 1914 congress at Constance,[45] were all in favor of the United States taking part in the war, with only the Quakers objecting.

After 1919, the activities of pacifist societies in Europe were sometimes strengthened, and sometimes eclipsed, by the League of Nations societies. The pacifist movement became more broadly based, however, even though some organizations were sometimes critical of the League, whose organization they regarded as "undemocratic." It was strongest of all in England, but even there, the only time it became at all like a mass movement was in connection with the Peace Ballot in the autumn of 1935. And this crusade for peace happened then to coincide with Britain's political interests, since she wanted to prevent the formation of an Italian colonial empire along her imperial route through the Red Sea. In the United States, pacifists generally approved

---

[44] See Beales, *op. cit.*, pp. 162–79.
[45] See above, p. 221.

the Senate's rejection of the League Covenant, but they differed on the subject of whether to accede to the statute of the Permanent Court of International Justice. The movement disintegrated as the government's determination became more apparent to refuse to take on new responsibilities in international politics.

Théodor Ruyssen, the philosopher, sociologist, and great apostle of pacifism, was surely right when he said, "The sentiments aroused in men's souls by the pacifists' appeal never have the same depth or strength of the clarion calls of patriotism."

II
THE STATESMAN

by

JEAN-BAPTISTE DUROSELLE

9

THE PERSONALITY OF
THE STATESMAN[1]

No one should realize better than the historian the infinite variety of the human personality. Every man is different, every man complex and ambiguous. With a statesman who shoulders important responsibilities—even those who know him well will find elements in his attitude that are unpredictable or even inexplicable. No one can predict with any degree of certainty how he will act.

The historian therefore tends to concentrate on specific examples, specific moments. Having learned as much as he can about the forces that influence the statesman, it may seem possible to explain some aspects of his work in terms of his "temperament." The problem then is to find out all he can about that temperament—through the study of texts and eyewitness accounts, and through the study of his actual behavior.

Nevertheless, as the historian goes about this task—which requires a subtle, intuitive approach rather than a scientific, quantified one—he is bound to make comparisons. He compares the hero with his predecessors or his successors, with his friends or foes, and even with the hero himself at an earlier or later stage. Such comparisons—which do involve scientific precision—are not a mere exercise in rhetoric, in the manner of Plutarch's *Lives* or the classic comparisons between Aristides and Themistocles, Gladstone and Disraeli, or Briand and Poincaré. They are a means to understand better the part played by personality within the political framework.

I. PRINCIPAL TYPOLOGIES OF PERSONALITY

The human intelligence appears to be impelled to make classifications, even of so unfathomable a subject as a human being, endowed with consciousness and will. The historian, too, tends to refer, cautiously, to "typologies."[2]

---

[1] In the writing of this chapter, I have been greatly indebted to my colleague and friend Pierre Hassner.

[2] It is a striking fact that political scientists have by and large neglected this problem. Jean Meynaud, in his excellent *Introduction à la science politique* (Paris, 1959), notes that "most studies on the psychological factors of political phenomena have been made by social psychologists" (p. 110), and he mentions scholars such as Lasswell, but he largely confines himself to pointing to the difficulties of the subject

Our first concern will be to examine studies undertaken in the various human and social sciences in order to find out what classifications of personality have been suggested. But we shall not go into them very deeply, for obvious reasons. The historian is not competent to assess the intrinsic value of these theories; he is only a "user" of psychology in the same way that he "uses" political economy or international law, sociology or geography. It is sufficient to say simply that the historian should not disregard the studies made by other specialists.[3] It may be useful to provide here a summary of both the difficulties and the provisional results of personality studies that have led to the establishment of typologies.

All attempts to classify human personalities run up against two basic difficulties. The first is related to man's essential ambiguity. Man is a biological being, but he is also a thinking and reasoning one, and, finally, he lives in society. What are the elements in his personality which derive from his physical being, his psychological being, and his social being? Some theorists, like August Comte, simply deny the validity of psychological interpretations, regarding man as a biological being living in a collectivity—thus going directly from body to society. Gabriel Tarde writes that "man is a social being, grafted on a vital being." And Durkheim states that "in man there are two beings: an individual being, based on the organism, and a social being."

Such theories are clearly hard put to meet the challenge of the independent conclusions reached in psychology and, particularly, psychiatry and psychoanalysis:

> There exists in every human being a truly autistic domain, in the broadest sense of the word, which has been regarded as the "impregnable domain of the purely psychological. . . . The psycho-physiologist therefore must recognize that he is incapable of explaining a psychic type or function in terms of pure physiology. In each psychic event, he discovers the interaction of a physiological infrastructure and a psychological superstructure in which social factors play an essential, but most exclusive, part."[4]

The psychologist must thus "distinguish between what pertains to the physiological and the social, to the constitution and the institutions, and also to that unique something which cannot be reduced to any of them."[5] The task is not easy.

The second fundamental difficulty is in discerning the innate from the acquired. One writer has suggested that *character* be defined as "the complex

(pp. 111–15). Maurice Duverger, in his no less valuable study *An Introduction to the Social Sciences* (trans., Malcolm Anderson; New York and London, 1964), is briefer still.

[3] For more detailed information, see below, the works listed in the Bibliography for this chapter, pp. 402–3.

[4] Jean Delay, *La Psycho-physiologie humaine* (Paris, 1945), p. 94.

[5] *Ibid.*, p. 95.

of congenital dispositions that constitute the mental skeleton of a man," *personality* as the complex consisting first of character and then of "all the elements acquired during one's life, which have shaped the character in a way that might have been different,"[6] and finally, the *ego* as the "active center" that makes use of its freedom. Setting aside this last term, which is used as a transition between concrete observation and metaphysics, we shall follow this terminology; it has the advantage of being widely accepted.

The historian is obviously far more interested in the personality than in character alone. But the character too, the "nucleus," the "skeleton of the life of the psyche," the "solid and permanent" factor, must itself be discovered. Failing this, it is hard to determine how various circumstances— that is, what has been acquired—have contributed to the personality.

The acquired may come from the physical environment—climate, foods; from certain stimulants or drugs (alcohol, opium) that can basically transform the personality; from illness; and from social factors—environment, education, circumstances of life. The effects of illness in transforming the personality, for example, is familiar to the historian: Napoleon III's policies were modified after 1865 by his first attacks of stones, and Mussolini's after 1940 were seriously affected by the Duce's syphilis. Conversely, the attack of paralyzing poliomyelitis on the young Franklin D. Roosevelt helped to give this worldly, snobbish, and rather nonchalant young politician the fierce energy that was to lead him to the highest office in his land.[7]

A. PSYCHO-PHYSIOLOGICAL CLASSIFICATIONS

Psycho-physiological classifications attempt to establish a link between certain physiological and certain psychological features. Psycho-physiology is, in fact, the "objective study of relations between body and spirit."[8]

Some scholars, like J.-B. Charcot and the Swiss physiologist Walder Hess, made the nervous system the basis for their classification. Others based their classification on physical traits—a return, in subtler form, to the old notion that the face is the mirror of the soul. Ernst Kretschmer distinguishes between the *pyknic type* (from the Greek word for "stocky"), who is generally an extrovert—"overflowing with action," "glad to be alive," "bubbling with optimism"—and the *leptosomic* type (from the Greek word for "thin"), who is an introvert—"alienated from the world," a "sentimental idealist," "sarcastic ironist," or "coldly overbearing person."[9] Lastly, others return to the old Hippocratic distinctions between

[6] René le Senne, *Traité de caractérologie* (Paris, 1946), pp. 9, 11.
[7] Frank Friedel, *Franklin D. Roosevelt*, Vol. II: *The Ordeal* (Boston, 1954).
[8] Delay, *op. cit.*, p. 5.
[9] Kretschmer, *La Structure du corps et le caractère* (translated from the German; Paris, 1930).

sanguine, phlegmatic, choleric, and melancholic. The historian should use all such classifications with extreme caution.

B. Psychological Classifications

These classifications are made by and large by psychiatrists and psychoanalysts. The theories of the Swiss psychiatrist Carl Jung, for instance, are of particular interest to the historian, for in addition to clinical observation, he avails himself of what he calls the historical or folkways method, according to which individual psychological observation should be checked against the products left in humanity through the ages. We may note that Jung distinguishes two essential types, the introvert and the extrovert. (Another thinker has said that introverts lean to "classicism," while extroverts are "romantics."[10])

Still more interesting from our point of view are the studies of Harold Lasswell, who has made a vigorous attempt to synthesize political science and Freudian psychoanalysis with the aim of arriving at a typology of statesmen (not men in general, as in previous theories). He began by examining the more or less empirical classifications of philosophers, moralists, and sociologists from Aristotle to Machiavelli and Max Weber. But he concluded that these would be unsatisfactory unless they embodied the findings of psychology, in particular psychiatry and psychoanalysis.

Lasswell contends that politicians, like other men, act much less rationally than they think they do. The objectives they set themselves may be rational, but there is always a wide spectrum of apparently rational objectives, and the choice among them is inevitably determined by impulses of essentially nonrational origin.

In his *Psychopathology and Politics*, Lasswell classifies politicians as agitators, administrators, or theorists:

> [The essential mark of the agitator] is the high value which he places on the emotional response of the public. . . . He idealizes the magnitude of the desirable social changes which are capable of being produced by a specific line of social action. . . . The agitator easily infers that he who disagrees with him is in communion with the devil, and that opponents show bad faith or timidity. [The administrator] is a co-ordinator of effort in continuing activity.

The theorist, too, draws his convictions from unconscious private motives: "Political prejudices, preferences and creeds are often formulated in highly rational form, but they are grown in highly irrational ways."[11]

Clearly, all kinds of combinations are possible among these three terms.

---

[10] W. Ostwald, *Grosse Männer* (Leipzig, 1909).

[11] Harold D. Lasswell, *Psychopathology and Politics* (Chicago, 1930), pp. 78, 127, 153.

C. Classifications of Characterology

Characterology thus purports to be an objective science, but it analyzes the human spirit, and its techniques are consequently different from those of the natural sciences. Instead of selecting certain physiological or psychologial elements and treating them as the sole factors of differentiation among human types, characterology, by means of a long series of observations and inquiries, determines "constituent properties of the human being"; the different combinations of these properties are the criteria for establishing a certain number of types. Then, these types are further differentiated by the application of "supplementary properties" that make it "possible and legitimate to multiply characterological varieties indefinitely."[12]

Characterology appears to be a particularly French science. "The long and splendid sequence of French moralists from Montaigne through La Bruyère to Vauvenargues shows the inclination of the French mind for character analysis."[13] But the origin of scientific characterology is to be found early in the twentieth century in the works of two Dutch professors of Groningen University, the psychologist Gerard Heymans and the psychiatrist E. Wiersma. It was introduced and extensively\systematized in France in the 1930's and 1940's by René le Senne, and further explored by Le Senne's principal disciple, Gaston Berger. Finally, Roger Mucchielli introduced into it new psychological data. The study of characterology has made some headway in the Latin countries[14] but has been curiously ignored in the Anglo-Saxon countries.[15]

The "constituent properties of the human being," according to characterologists, are "emotivity," "activity," and "reverberation." Individuals are classified as emotive when their psychological and physiological life is more profoundly affected by events than most, and individuals will be classified as non-emotive who are less affected than most. Similarly, "an *active* man is one in whom the emergence of an obstacle intensifies the energy he expends in the direction the obstacle has just cut off; an *inactive* man is one whom the obstacle discourages."[16]

The notion of "reverberation" is more unusual. Any image that impresses itself on a man's attention has an immediate "reverberation" and also a subsequent, later one. "When the effects of a mental datum consciously perceived drive back the effects of earlier data, the *primary* function prevails

---

12 Le Senne, *op. cit.*, p. 59.
13 *Ibid.*, p. 47.
14 In France, there is even a journal devoted to *La Caractérologie* (published in Paris by Presses universitaires de France). See E. Forti, "La caractérologie en Italie," *La Caractérologie*, No. 4, 1961.
15 Neither Lasswell, in *The Analysis of Political Behaviour* (London, 1947), nor H. J. Eysenck, in *The Psychology of Politics* (London, 1954), make any mention of it.
16 Le Senne, *op. cit.*, p. 77.

over the *secondary* function; the man in whom this tendency is habitual is classified as belonging to the primary type. If, on the other hand, the persistent influence of past experiences prevails over the present—disguising it, repressing it, subordinating it—the man must be classified as belonging to the secondary type."[17] The primary type thus lives in the present; the secondary type lives in the past or future.

Given the basic categories, characterology permits infinite specification and diversification, not only by distinguishing all the possible degrees in each of the basic principles, but also by suggesting other combinations.

Knowledge of character, however, is not enough for the historian. As we said before, he is more interested in personality, including acquired factors. But here he comes up against a serious problem. Modern psychologists use the concept of the "situation," as do historians—"a certain concatenation of relationships between a subject (or group) on the one hand and on the other hand objects, events, external data, or other persons." A situation is, then, the "concatenation of forces" in which any individual at any time is involved.[18] Now the individual's personality is shaped by the successive situations he has confronted. His character, the structural innate nucleus, provides only a "predisposition" to meet situations in this or that manner. The essential question is: What can we predict about a person's reaction to a given situation? But it is an unanswerable question. For the response is determined by the situation and by the character. In certain extreme cases, the situation is decisive: a sickness that prostrates an energetic man may completely prevent him from reacting as he would normally have done. In other cases, the individual "restructures the situation."[19]

What, then, can the historian conclude from the theories we have mentioned? Certainly it is not enough to classify according to tentative "types." It is the historian's duty to enter more deeply into the study of man, for the complexity and contradictions which each of his heroes reveals cannot be reduced to formulas. Conversely, however, he would be unwise to disregard the explanations offered by the psychological sciences. Some of the distinctions mentioned enable the historian to understand certain decisions that might otherwise seem "out of character." (Lasswell's classification of statesmen as "agitators," "administrators," or "theorists" is very suggestive, and we shall return to it later in this chapter.)

---

17 *Ibid.*, p. 81.
18 Roger Mucchielli, *La Caractérologie à l'âge scientifique* (Neuchâtel, 1961), pp. 14–15.
19 *Ibid.*, p. 19.

II. THE STATESMAN'S PERSONALITY IN HISTORY

Since we want to find out to what extent the personality of statesmen explains their attitudes, we must ask what are the main traits we should focus on. The best way to distinguish the essential features is probably to try to discover—in sources such as diplomatic documents, memoirs, and speeches—the questions that statesmen and diplomats ask most frequently about the foreign statesmen they deal with. In this way, we can arrive at a simple empirical listing of contrasting types.

A. The Doctrinaire and the Opportunist

Doctrinaires—or "theorists," as Lasswell calls them—adopt a coherent system of thought and try, as far as possible, to harmonize their decisions with that system. Opportunists, or empiricists, do not cling to any one particular system; they regulate their conduct according to circumstances. Naturally, there are no wholly consistent doctrinaires, since circumstances sometimes impose decisions that are out of line with doctrine, and all opportunists have general ideas to which they are faithful.

History provides many instances of statesmen who were basically doctrinaire. The Bourbon pretender the Count of Chambord caused the failure of the attempted restoration of the monarchy in France in 1873 by unswerving determination to rule under the white flag of the Bourbons, and especially by his insistence that he was called to the leadership of the nation by divine right and not by the sovereign will of the French people.

One of the best examples of the doctrinaire is Hitler. We have only to consider the extraordinary coincidence between the plans set out in *Mein Kampf* and the effort to achieve them after 1933 for convincing proof.[20] The most tragic proof was the so-to-speak gratuitous extermination of several million Jews carried out in fidelity to a pseudo-scientific theory of racism. This fidelity may be explained as an hysterical, irrational passion, but it prompted Hitler to be "inhumanly cold and logical." In that respect, he was poles apart from Mussolini, "a man of indecision and skepticism . . . influenced . . . by personal motives, by vanity, or a desire for revenge."[21]

Before 1939, Western statesmen obviously did not realize Hitler's insane attachment to his doctrine. Had they done so, perusal of *Mein Kampf* would have made a greater impression. Hitler's admirable capacity for dissimulation was a tactical maneuver to disguise the systematic realization of his

---

[20] Certain authors, like Erich Kordt, in *Wahn und Wirklichkeit* (Stuttgart, 1948), see a contradiction between the plans set out in *Mein Kampf* and Hitler's actual performance. But this is noticeable only in regard to the war with Great Britain, which Hitler never wanted but which he could not avoid.

[21] Elizabeth Wiskemann, *The Rome-Berlin Axis* (London and New York, 1949), pp. 18, 19.

plans. But, as two American scholars have pointed out, few people in the Western democracies in 1939 took Hitler's book seriously.[22] There were exceptions: Newton, a British diplomat, realized that, unlike the Sudetenland, Bohemia would not be annexed to the Reich; those who had thoroughly studied *Mein Kampf* could affirm, he pointed out on May 16, 1938, that Hitler's plan was to establish vassal states with foreign populations.[23] And a number of French ambassadors—François-Poncet, Noël, and Coulondre— were considerably more perceptive on this score than the statesmen in Paris.

Another example of a doctrinaire, though a more flexible one with an extraordinary faculty for adaptation, was Lenin. Bertrand Russell said of him when he visited Moscow in May and June, 1920, that Lenin was "an embodied theory." "The materialist conception of history, one feels, is his life-blood. He resembles a professor in his desire to have his theory under- stood and in his fury with those who misunderstand or disagree."[24] Stalin followed the same doctrinaire line. It is easier to assess President Roosevelt's errors of judgment if one realizes how he minimized the doctrinaire spirit of the Soviet leader, believing that Stalin was more interested in good rela- tions with the United States than in the revolutionary expansion of Communism.

These essentially doctrinaire types may be contrasted with "opportunists." Men like Lloyd George, Aristide Briand, or Pierre Laval, however different they may have been in political stature and moral standards, were similar in that none of them were men of doctrine. Their ideal was a continuing series of successes, whatever the nature of the success.

In December, 1918, Lloyd George, the "crafty Welshman," favored the harshest possible penalties for Germany but in June, 1919, he sought to soften the terms of the draft peace treaty. The Italian statesman Orlando, observing him at the Versailles peace conference, wrote of the "excessive ease with which he passed from the defense of one position to that of a dif- ferent, if not contrary, one. I think that these changes in his thinking and judgment occurred under the pressure of responding to the necessities of the moment; they were not due to volubility or inconsistency, but to a real- istic sense that external circumstances had changed."[25] And Briand said in 1921, "There is no more difficult man to pin down than Lloyd George, and once one has pinned him down, it never lasts for more than twenty-four hours."[26] Lloyd George himself remarked, "I never believed in costly

---

[22] William L. Langer and S. Everett Gleason, *The Challenge to Isolation* (New York, 1952), p. 54.

[23] Great Britain, Foreign Office, *Documents on British Foreign Policy*, Series III, Vol. I (London, 1938).

[24] *Bolshevism: Practice and Theory* (London and New York, 1920), p. 36.

[25] Vittorio Emanuele Orlando, *Memorie, 1915–1919* (Milan, 1960), p. 357.

[26] Georges Suarez, *Briand: sa vie, son oeuvre, avec son journal et de nombreux documents inédits* (Paris, 1938–52), V, 163.

frontal attacks either in war or politics, if there were a way round. . . .
Whatever settlement is made will be suitable only to the circumstances
under which it is made, and, as those circumstances change, changes in the
settlement will be called for."[27]

Aristide Briand—the "man of the general strike" who became a moderate,
the man who early in 1921 advocated a tough policy with Germany and at
the end of the year a policy of accommodation, the foe of Poincaré who
became his Foreign Minister—is another good example of an opportunist.[28]
He confided his thoughts on this point to his biographer in 1923: "I have
known men so well, and so closely, that I have no prejudices. I look at events
and try to adapt myself to them. In politics, no human element should be
neglected. The good chess player uses the bishop as carefully as he does the
king."[29] Later, in connection with economic questions, he remarked, "Given
the circumstances we live in, most dogmas and doctrines explode every day
before our eyes. You must not count on me to stick the pieces together
again."[30] Joseph Caillaux, who was Briand's foe until their reconciliation
in 1925, gives a penetrating description of this opportunism:

> [Briand is] what Aristotle would have called a political animal, a man with
> a taste, a liking, a feeling for *immediate* politics, a man who excels in per-
> ceiving all the modulations and adapting to them, now by bending, now by
> straightening up. But these eminent gifts have their reverse. A man like this
> imprisons himself in the immediacy of politics. He only takes the "short view."[31]

As a final example, Pierre Laval, the Premier of France under German
occupation in World War II, whose flexibility was often akin to servility,
was an empiricist and an opportunist, "irresistibly drawn to facile solutions,"[32] "empirical rather than doctrinaire."[33]

Between these extreme cases of fanatical doctrinaires and determined
opportunists, we find many less clear-cut cases. Thus, over and above the
similarities, we may say that the principal difference between Wilson and
Roosevelt was that the former had worked out a doctrine—a "new diplomacy"—and the Treaty of Versailles was a means of ensuring the
triumph of that doctrine, whereas Roosevelt, for all that he was steeped

---

[27] David Lloyd George, address to the Trade Unions Conference, January 5, 1918,
in *War Memoirs* (London and Boston, 1933–37), IV, 2274. See also p. 2486.

[28] Briand once referred to the need for "long-range, tenacious plans," but this
does not imply that he advocated a doctrinal approach to politics. (*Journal officiel,
Débats parlementaires, Senat, 1929*, I, 3051.)

[29] Suarez, *op. cit.*, I, vi, vii; see also VI, 21.

[30] *Journal officiel, Débats parlementaires, Chambre des députés, 1926*, I, 431–32
(meeting of February 2, 1926).

[31] *Mes Mémoires* (Paris, 1943), II, 39–40.

[32] P. E. Flandin, *Politique française, 1919–1940* (Paris, 1947).

[33] J. Paul-Boncour, *Entre Deux Guerres* (Paris, 1946), III, 2.

in Wilson's ideas, was convinced that the important thing was to seize the opportunity.[34] Four years away from the Presidency and presumably referring to Al Smith, he gave this admirable definition of himself during the 1928 election campaign:

> If the vision of world peace, of the abolition of war, ever comes true, it will not be through the mere mathematical calculations of a reduction of armaments program, nor the platitudes of multilateral treaties piously deprecating armed conflict. It will be because this nation will select as its head a leader who understands the human side of life, who has the force of character and the keenness of brain to take, instinctively, the right course.[35]

In Bismarck, we have another good example of an opportunist. When in 1874 someone recalled to him remarks he had made in 1849, he replied that in politics it was absurd not to change: "The point is not what someone said twenty-five years back; the point is what is useful and necessary for the state."[36]

B. THE FIGHTER AND THE CONCILIATOR

Louis XIV made it clear that he preferred to conquer states than to acquire them without conquest. There are many statesmen like Louis XIV who are inclined more to combat than to conciliation; there are others who shrink from war. In French history, a good example of the former would be Georges Clemenceau, Premier in 1917–19; of the latter, Briand. It is no accident that in one and the same year (1917), Briand agreed to take part in preliminary feelers for negotiations, while Clemenceau expressed the essence of his policy with the statement "I am waging war." True, Clemenceau sometimes appeared as a conciliator—for instance, in March, 1871, or during his term of office in 1906–9—but he was essentially a fighter. He liked to make enemies (politicians were almost universally hostile to him), and he poured out contempt on his foes. This "wrecker of ministries," this "Tiger" justified his last fight, his posthumous fight with the dead Foch in these terms:

> When a man has placed the whole interest of his life in action, he is little likely to pause over unnecessary trifles. . . . I might perhaps have been capable of turning my back on my duty had not the breath of the great days magically fanned to new life the old, ever-burning flame of the emotions of the past."[37]

The policy of "conciliating" Germany, as practiced by Briand, was repugnant to Clemenceau. "Ten years after the signature of the treaty, what

---

[34] I have tried to analyze this point in my book *From Wilson to Roosevelt: Foreign Policy of the United States, 1913–45* (Cambridge, Mass., 1963).

[35] *The New York Times*, June 28, 1928.

[36] Cited in Paul Matter, *Bismarck et son temps* (Paris, 1905–8), III, 330.

[37] *The Grandeur and Misery of Victory* (New York, 1930), Foreword.

remains of it? Mr. Stresemann has been laying down the law. You'll tell me that faced with people like Millerand, Poincaré, and Herriot, the *Boches* cannot have found that very hard to do."[38] "What really makes a man," he wrote, "is not the momentary success which is the instinctive goal of the rabble. . . . It is a level of emotiveness boldly raised to that degree of disequilibrium required to launch the finest flights of energy." In the face of the crowd, "the solitary fighter for an idea will draw all his strength from his interior exaltation before the day of decision."[39]

Briand was not that type of man. If at first he appeared hot-headed, it was probably in the interests of his career to be so. But the same interests, and his temperament, inclined him to conciliation. The first great event in his political life was his report on the law of separation of church and state: here was a fighting issue par excellence, and he made of it a work of conciliation. At the Locarno Conference of 1925, Briand had the idea of setting up a *round* table: "It was an idea of our ingenious stage-manager designed to avoid rivalries as to precedence. . . . I knew an elderly ambassador who used to say to his young attachés, too quickly enamored of politics in the grand style, 'Learn first to set up a table.' Briand was certainly good at that."[40] In contrast, we have only to think of Bismarck lighting his cigar from the Austrian delegate at Frankfurt. The temperament was not the same.

Because a man is a conciliator, it does not mean that he is necessarily inclined to yield. It was possible to maintain harmony at the League of Nations—

> not because Briand always yielded, as his adversaries charged. . . . I wish the concessions of the Briand period could be compared with those made during the so-called tough period. But Briand was marvelously skilled in handling [the League]. He played it as he played the 'cello of his voice; those who never heard him, from his place in the Council, wind up a debate, yielding only on non-essentials and holding on to the essential, do not know Briand's greatest talent.[41]

Briand himself emphasized the relation between international conferences and the benefits of conciliation:

> These gatherings of peoples represented by the leaders of their governments are something new in world diplomacy. And even . . . if they do not produce all the results which might be expected, they are useful because they can dispel many misunderstandings, they can prompt many endeavors which will bring the peoples closer together, summoning them to make reciprocal concessions.[42]

---

[38] Cited in Jean Martet, *Le Tigre* (Paris, 1930), p. 71.
[39] *Au Soir de la pensée* (Paris, 1927), II, 490.
[40] Paul-Boncour, *op. cit.*, p. 161.
[41] *Ibid.*, p. 165.
[42] *Journal officiel, Débats parlementaires, Sénat, 1921*, II, 5244–45 (February 24, 1921).

But the figures of the fighters stand out more clearly. Beside Clemenceau, we may consider two other statesmen who in other respects were very different —Bismarck and Woodrow Wilson.

That Bismarck always preferred victory to compromise is obvious. We see it in the Seven Weeks' War of 1866, and again in the Franco-Prussian War of 1870. We see it in his *Kulturkampf* with the Catholic Church. We see it in his dispute with Harry von Arnim, and even in his major differences with Kaiser Wilhelm. If we consider their common taste for a fight, we can agree with Lord Keynes' comment that Clemenceau was the "French Bismarck."

In defense of altogether different principles, Wilson was also a "stubborn fighter." "I do love to feel in my blood," he said in 1913, "the splendid thrill of fighting for something, something that is bigger than myself."[43] As President of Princeton University from 1902 to 1910, he presented all his reforms as struggles either against reaction in general or individuals in particular, notably Andrew Fleming West. An episode which he himself describes throws considerable light on his own personality. The mother of a student whom he had decided to expel came to see him. After a ninety-minute session together, and despite the fact that the lady was about to undergo a serious operation, he remained adamant; his responsibility to the college, he insisted, was greater than his responsibility for anyone's health.[44]

As President of the United States, the man of "peace without victory" (January 22, 1917) reacted to the German policy of all-out submarine warfare by breaking off diplomatic relations, then by declaring war. The fears of the Allies that the man of "peace without victory" would wage only a token war were dispelled in the very first weeks: once involved in the war, Wilson wanted a victorious peace. And, similarly, German hopes of making him a man of compromise in October, 1918, foundered on the rock of his stubborn determination.

He demonstrated this will power in his relations with the Senate. At the risk of his life, for his health was poor, he wanted to campaign throughout the country against the amendments to the Versailles Treaty ratification proposed by Henry Cabot Lodge. He told Jusserand, the French Ambassador, in July, 1919, "I will agree to no concession; the Senate must take its medicine."[45] Colonel House relates another, still more characteristic, remark. A month earlier, after the Versailles Treaty had been signed, House begged Wilson to approach the Senate in a conciliatory spirit. " 'House,' he replied,

---

[43] R. S. Baker and W. E. Dodd, eds., *The Public Papers of Woodrow Wilson* (New York, 1926), II, 30.

[44] Charles Seymour, ed., *The Intimate Papers of Colonel House* (Boston, 1928), IV, 443. See also R. S. Baker, *Woodrow Wilson: His Life and Letters* (New York, 1927), II, 152.

[45] Quoted by Thomas A. Bailey, *Woodrow Wilson and the Great Betrayal* (New York, 1947), p. 14.

'I have found one can never get anything in this life that is worth while without fighting for it.' "[46] Although crippled by illness, he paid no heed to counsels of moderation and rejected any amendment; he preferred to break rather than to bend. "I break and do not bend" had been the motto of another great fighter, the French Catholic writer Lamennais.

C. The Idealist and the Cynic

Wilson and Bismarck were both fighters by temperament, but they were poles apart from another point of view—that of idealism, the idealism which is the contrary not of practical realism (one can be an idealist and at the same time an excellent tactician), but of cynicism. The idealist is the man who justifies his attitude by reference to universal values and who does so sincerely, as far as one can tell. The cynic invokes the authority of "sacred egoism" and *"raison d'état.* The idealist seeks to identify the true interests of his country with those of all humanity. The cynic asserts his disregard of the interests of humanity and loudly proclaims those of his country. Every variation is possible between these two terms. Clemenceau, for instance, was not merely the "French Bismarck," as Keynes described him—a cynic prepared to sacrifice international morality to French security—but also a man who believed in peace based on law, an old Radical enamored of freedom.[47] His place is somewhere between Wilson and Bismarck.

It is arguable that universalist idealism is principally the prerogative of the "satisfied" countries. The most satisfied of all, the United States, has supplied the world with the largest contingent of idealists, so much so that in 1951 a "great debate" began in America on this theme. George Kennan,[48] and especially Hans Morgenthau, asserted that American foreign policy was no more "moral" than that of other countries, and that if it sought to be so, it was dangerously deluding itself and leading the country to ruin. "The intoxication with moral abstractions," said Morgenthau, "which in our time has become the prevailing substitute for political thought, is indeed one of the great sources of weakness and failure in American foreign policy."[49] But the old tradition of American moralism has its defenders too, in Frank Tannenbaum, Dexter Perkins, and others.

Perhaps the most thoroughgoing example of universalist idealism is found in Cordell Hull. President Wilson combined idealism with a great tactical realism and remarkable skill in handling situations. But Hull felt he had achieved a real victory when he persuaded a realistic opponent—

---

[46] Seymour, *op. cit.,* p. 487.
[47] Clemenceau, *Grandeur and Misery of Victory,* Chap. XI: "A Europe Founded upon Right."
[48] *American Diplomacy, 1900–1950* (Chicago and London, 1951).
[49] *In Defense of the National Interest* (New York, 1951), p. 4.

Japan or Russia—to agree to abstract principles. For instance, he contrived in the spring of 1941 to get Japan to accept "four principles": respect for the territorial integrity of all countries, non-intervention in domestic affairs, commercial equality, and maintenance of the *status quo* in the Pacific. And in Moscow in October, 1943, he was little concerned to discuss with Molotov and Eden the concrete problems of Poland, Czechoslovakia, Greece, or Yugoslavia, producing instead a "Declaration of Principles," which was the more readily signed since it involved no specific commitments, and taking a naïve delight in the achievement—"an historic event," he called it.[50]

Hull's idealism was that of a generous and friendly man, not of a great statesman. Wilson's was much more imposing. Clemenceau, his future associate, was struck by this in Wilson's speech to the Senate of January 22, 1917, on "peace without victory." Clemenceau's comment on the idealism that prompted Wilson to disregard the Allied cause, a cause the Frenchman passionately identified with that of justice, was caustic and violent:

> Never before had a political assembly heard so fine a sermon on what human beings might do if they were not human. . . . As he is certainly sincere, he could not keep from dealing with the problem of Europe in flames, but, his gaze lost in the abyss of the ages, he projects himself, in one magnificent rush, into realms beyond time and space, there to hover in the void far above the things that are so inferior as to exist.[51]

Then came Wilson's stern reaction to all-out submarine warfare. Clemenceau hastened to voice his approval.[52] Wilson, he said, was "too deeply American for the excessive idealism that moves him to stand in the way of what he can learn from the facts of reality." Wilson had "suddenly felt himself growing to the dimensions of a spokesman for all mankind."[53]

Wilson's idealism consisted in the fact that he identified the interests of his country with those of mankind. "America," he asserted, "was born into the world to do mankind service."[54] The "new diplomacy" of which he was the apostle was based on the equality of peoples, a "world safe for democracy," and the League of Nations. This being the keystone of the system, Wilson demanded that the Covenant of the League be negotiated before territorial questions were taken up. When Japan threatened not to accede to it, Wilson resigned himself to turning over to Japan the former German rights to Shantung. The universalist principle took precedence over particular arrangements.

There are other examples of this attitude in Wilson's statements at his meetings with Clemenceau, Lloyd George, and Orlando. He argued, for

---

50 Cordell Hull, *Memoirs* (New York, 1948), II, 995, 1307.
51 *L'Homme enchaîné*, January 27, 1917.
52 *Ibid.*, February 5, 1917.
53 *Ibid.*, March 1, 1917.
54 Speech delivered in Pittsburgh, Pa., January 29, 1916.

instance, that U.S. policy was to secure an equitable territorial settlement and a lasting agreement among peoples—hence the United States' great desire to eliminate all sources of discord and antagonism. In other words, the ideal of a lasting peace could be promoted by the application of certain general principles, not by the furtherance of particular interests. This rejection of particular interests applied to the United States as well. What he sought, said Wilson, was not to deviate from the path of the world's great thrust toward justice. He wished to do nothing that would allow others to say of Americans that they professed fine principles but made exceptions wherever sentiment or national interest prompted them to depart from the rule.[55]

Such an attitude was completely foreign to Bismarck. Not that he did not have a passionate ideal—an historic Prussian monarchy, enlightened by Christian principles and a kind of liberalism, with hegemony over all Germany and an assured position of security in Europe—but his political ideal was never universalist. Heart and soul a monarchist, he was a republican in regard to France, since he thought that the monarchy would strengthen France, the hereditary enemy of his country. His "cynicism" was more than rough frankness, a verbal brutality which he used as a tried and true instrument of diplomacy. It was above all "sacred egoism," and an admission that the state was a supreme value. Yet Bismarck was not a totalitarian.[56] He recognized an international society based on certain rules—albeit rules he sometimes affected to despise.

The formulas in which he expressed this attitude are well-known: "The man with power proceeds on his own terms," he said once. And on April 17, 1863, replying to Twesten, who doubted his intention to act in response to Denmark's unilateral annexation of Schleswig-Holstein, he exclaimed: "When we judge it necessary to go to war, we shall go to war, with or without your blessing!"[57] Frederick William I had said that he was establishing his sovereignty like a rock of bronze. "That bronze rock," Bismarck told rebellious deputies, "is still standing. It forms the foundation of Prussian history. You will not succeed in budging it by either your *Nationalverein* or your motion of today."[58]

As for his brutal language, it was sometimes picturesque, sometimes malicious. Frederick of Augustenburg was "a blackguard"; Austria and Prussia meeting at Gastein in 1865 to divide up the spoils of the war over Schleswig-Holstein were like "hunters parceling out the game."[59] When

---

55 Paul Mantoux, *Les Délibérations du Conseil des Quatre (24 Mars–28 Juin 1919)* (Paris, 1955), I, 72 (March 28); II, 368 (June 10).

56 See Otto Pflanze, "Bismarck and German Nationalism," in *The American Historical Review*, April, 1955, pp. 548 ff. See also Friedrich Meinecke's *Machiavellism* (New Haven, Conn., 1957).

57 Erich Eyck, *Bismarck, Leben und Werk* (Erlenback-Zurich, 1941), II, 560.

58 See Matter, *op. cit.*, II, 235.

59 Eyck, *op. cit.*, II, 637.

Countess von Hohenthal asked him whether it was true that he wanted to expel the Austrians from Germany and conquer Saxony, he replied seriously: "Do not doubt it; I have never had any other idea, and I have never stopped preparing for it since I came into office."[60]

An equally cynical attitude is to be encountered in many statesmen, but with variations of style. Hitler's conversational tone, for instance, was usually pleasant but sometimes veered toward extreme violence. Mussolini, like Bismarck, liked trenchant expressions, but mainly for effect: "His Majesty the Cannon will have the last word!"

Generally speaking, the fascist and nationalist totalitarian regimes established in the years between the two world wars were governed by men who acted with the same amoral cynicism, displaying the same contempt for other people, the same selfishness—with infinitely more brutality than Bismarck.

D. THE INFLEXIBLE AND THE IMAGINATIVE

We should not confuse the inflexible man with the doctrinaire. The latter sets himself general goals but may carry them out in a variety of ways, as Hitler did. The inflexible man sticks closely to certain methods; he may be a good administrator, but the unexpected upsets him, and he is unable to devise new solutions. He is the man of precedent, not a creator. The imaginative man, on the other hand, can invent new solutions and is not disconcerted by any new development. We may, for instance, contrast Hoover with Franklin Roosevelt, or Poincaré with Briand.

Hoover, according to all his biographers, was a superb organizer and administrator. His administration of aid to Belgium left an indelible impression in that country; he ran the Department of Commerce skillfully during a period of prosperity. And as President of the United States, he might have made his mark as an administrator had not the great economic depression that began in October, 1929, completely disconcerted him. Respectful of precedents, he tried to behave as people had in previous recessions, which had always somehow resolved themselves. His policy was therefore to wait out the crisis, meanwhile proliferating optimistic statements on the subject. In 1931, with the Hoover Moratorium, he tried to suspend international payments for one year, but, despite the pleas of Secretary of State Stimson, he refused to extend it, as he did not wish to cancel the war debts. Moreover, although he expected that the crisis would be resolved in 1932 by an increase in international trade, he did not realize that this would require the lowering of the high Hawley-Smoot tariffs, passage of which in 1930 he had, as a good traditionalist Republican, approved.

[60] Cited by Matter, *op. cit.*, II, 387.

Temperamentally, Stimson and Mr. Hoover were wholly different. One was by nature and training an advocate and a fighter; the other was an organizer and planner. Mr. Hoover liked to calculate his moves as he would the building of a bridge, while Stimson preferred to choose his main objective and then charge ahead without worrying. confident that aggressive executive leadership would win followers.[61]

Franklin D. Roosevelt, on the other hand, confronted with the economic crisis, produced (with the help of his "brain trust") flexible and imaginative methods of governmental intervention. Halted in this endeavor by the Supreme Court, he hit on the expedient of reforming it; it was a *"Roosevelt revolution."*[62] Roosevelt, according to one writer, was "the supreme democratic leader of our time. . . . He moved with imagination and the skill of a 'creative artist' among the tangle of conflicting and confusing views and interests."[63]

The best evidence of Roosevelt's capacity for invention is probably to be found in the years 1940–41, when he personally conceived, and managed to have adopted, the great techniques that made the United States an "arsenal of democracy"—in particular, the profoundly new, not to say revolutionary, Lend Lease arrangement. The contrast with the moderate isolationist, faithful to tradition, was complete.

Another, less marked, contrast can be seen between Poincaré and Briand. Poincaré was remarkable for his extraordinary administrative talent, a talent that Briand possessed in the smallest possible quantities. Compared with Briand,

> Poincaré represented the severe, classical tradition of an unproductive soil, a scrupulous and narrow bourgeoisie, a hardworking and virtuous upbringing; he remained a man of one idea, one period, one system, one class. . . . Would this strict background explain the juridical marks with which he was indelibly stamped? And would this explain, too, his attempt to fit events, and life itself, into categories that were not always adequate for them?[64]

It is interesting to observe how Poincaré's legalism was put to the test. Poincaré was one of those who wanted to see the Treaty of Versailles carried out to the letter, simply because it had been signed. He gave up his Ruhr "victory" to return to a policy of reparations as it was expressed in the Treaty of Versailles—that is, with the agency of the Reparations Commission. Called upon to "save the franc," he employed the most conventional of all methods, and his love for precedent caused him for a time to attempt an impossible return to 1914 parity.

---

[61] Henry L. Stimson and McGeorge Bundy, *On Active Service in Peace and War* (New York, 1947), p. 196.
[62] Mario Einaudi, *The Roosevelt Revolution* (New York, 1959).
[63] *Ibid.*, pp. 59, 60.
[64] Georges Suarez, *De Poincaré à Poincaré* (Paris, 1928), pp. 104–5.

The extraordinary absence of any over-all view or synthesis in the ten volumes of his memoirs, *Au service de la France,* is proof of the administrative rather than imaginative quality of Poincaré's mind. According to whether one admires purely analytical intelligence or not, one can call him, as one friend did, a man of "brilliant intelligence" or one can simply call him stupid. It is said that Clemenceau once said of him: "One should never put a man whose heart is crammed with files in charge of a country. It's too dangerous."[65]

E. The Gambler and the Cautious Man

Some statesmen have a bent for danger, others abhor it. As a rule, the former make decisions quickly and the latter are slow, preferring to wait. Gamblers take risks more or less deliberately. We may include in this category two men as different as Jacques Lafitte, Premier of France in the first months of the July Monarchy of 1830, and Casimir Perier, who succeeded him.

Lafitte, a frivolous, presumptuous, and weak man, practiced what could be called a policy of letting events take their course, accepting risk out of vanity and without calculating the consequences. It was not so much a matter of having a taste for danger with him as it was recklessness. Whatever he might have said in private about wanting peace and good relations with foreign powers,[66] when pressed by Lafayette or the leftist groups to intervene in Poland and Italy, he became bombastic and bellicose: "In a very short time, we shall have, in addition to our fortresses, well supplied and defended, 500,000 well-armed men in the field. And the king, if need be, will place himself at the head of the nation. . . . If tempests break when the tricolor comes in view and aid our side, so much the worse for those who called upon them for aid!"[67]

Casimir Perier, by contrast, was a true gambler, daring, resolute, of prompt and bold decisions, never taking a risk without calculating the odds. "He was action personified, as vigorous in defense as he had once been in assault, giving it the same fire, the same fury, the same heroic fearlessness." It was necessary, he declared, for peace abroad as for peace at home, "that France be governed."[68] (Clemenceau said much the same thing in his policy declaration on taking office: "The country will know that it is being defended.") Perier strongly desired to maintain the peace, but he proposed to do so on the basis of a policy of force. The dispatch of a squadron to the Tagus estuary, of an army to Belgium against the King of the Nether-

---

[65] Martet, *op. cit.,* p. 192.
[66] Thureau-Dangin, *Historie de la Monarchie de juillet* (Paris, 1888–92), I, 223.
[67] *Ibid.,* p. 198.
[68] *Ibid.,* pp. 406, 410.

lands, of a French garrison to Ancona after the reoccupation of the northern portion of the Papal States by the Austrians—these were clear indications of that determination.

Vainglorious gamblers of the Lafitte variety are frequent in history, and dangerous to peace. The Duke of Gramont, in 1870, seems to have belonged to that category, and Mussolini also. It seems unquestionable that Mussolini made some of his most important decisions out of vanity of a kind, an emotional sense of honor. The Italian assaults on Albania in April, 1939, and Greece in October, 1940, were intended essentially to demonstrate that Mussolini would not play second fiddle to Hitler. The declaration of war of June 10, 1940, was perhaps related to the desire to share the future spoils, but certainly also to Mussolini's wish to give Hitler a certain impression. The reaction of the public, and Italy's real strength, were scarcely taken into account. On the subject of Albania, his son-in-law and Foreign Minister, Count Ciano, wrote: "I saw the Duce several times. He is calm, frightfully calm, and more than ever convinced that no one will want to interfere in our affair with Albania. However, he has decided to march, and he will march even though all the world may be pitted against him."[69]

The calculating gamblers of the Casimir Perier type are of another stature. Napoleon, Bismarck, and Hitler belong to that category. According to whether their general policy was defensive, semi-offensive, or offensive, we move along the spectrum from Casimir Perier to Bismarck, from Bismarck to Hitler. But in every case, the plan is coldly pushed to its logical conclusion. Only the intoxication of the successes achieved thanks to these calculations can prompt such a man to embark on a wild venture, as Hitler did on June 22, 1941, when he attacked the Soviet Union. The statesman par excellence, like Bismarck, knows when to stop, when to move from the offensive to the defensive, when he has achieved his purposes.

Vis-à-vis the gamblers, we have the cautious men—cautious because they are satisfied with what they are doing, and cautious by temperament. Despite the "shameful treaties of 1815," for example, Louis Philippe preferred a policy of prudence and moderation. This was very apparent in 1840. After dismissing the Thiers ministry, the King remarked, "I am conscious of keeping my royal oath when I do all I can to keep France from a war that would be, I feel, without cause or purpose and, consequently, without justification in the eyes of God or man."[70]

One finds this cautious attitude frequently in history. It presupposes a cool head, control over one's emotions, and also a total disinclination for danger. In its extreme form, it may take on the aspect of renunciation and

---

[69] Hugh Gibson, ed., *The Ciano Diaries, 1939–1943* (New York, 1946), p. 60 (entry for April 5, 1939).

[70] André Marie Jean Jacques Dupin, *Mémoires de M. Dupin* (Paris, 1855–61), IV, 99.

become appeasement, as it was known under Neville Chamberlain in the 1930's. In the face of an extremely daring gambler, extreme caution may be imprudent. Chamberlain, incidentally, practiced appeasement more out of conviction than by temperament.

Between the gamblers and the cautious men, we find many permutations. Napoleon III, for example, combined a certain taste for danger with extreme irresolution in executing his decisions. At Biarritz, he said several times to an astonished Bismarck: "We should not make circumstances; we should let them develop and then adapt our decisions to them"[71]—the "wait and see" attitude, often the policy of the irresolute. Marshal Pétain in 1940–44, whose advanced age doubtless had something to do with his indecision (witness his hesitations over whether to choose Baudouin or Laval as Foreign Minister on June 16, 1940, and again over what response he should take to the British attack on the French fleets at Mers-el-Kebir on June 3), was the very embodiment of the "wait and see" advocate. It was probably a deep-rooted personaliy trait: "I am waiting for the Americans and the tanks," he had said in 1917.

If we turn from politics to military strategy, we find the same opposition between gamblers and cautious men. Here too there are frivolous gamblers—like General Nivelle, who commanded the French in their counterattacks at Verdun in 1916—and the great gamblers like Napoleon or the German General Ludendorff. And there are also cautious militarists. They may well make good generals, but the greatest strategists are gamblers who calculate their risks. Ludendorff, for example, twice preferred to take a major risk than "wait and see": when he persuaded the Kaiser to wage all-out submarine warfare (the stake was victory by strangling the Allies, the risk was American entry into the war), and when he decided to launch the great spring offensives in 1918 in order to snatch victory instead of maintaining the German Army's capacity for resistance for years to come. The "crucial problem" in the fall of 1917, as he put it, was whether to "strike hard to the west" or simply "to maintain a systematic defensive." Among his arguments in favor of the first alternative, the following seemed typical of him—that the offensive is the most powerful form of combat, which alone can clinch the victory, a fact proven on every page of military history.[72]

One could go on and on with a list of types of statesmen, but these we have mentioned seem to be most frequently used by historians, and the easiest to distinguish. It would be much harder, for instance, to divide the intelligent from the unintelligent (one is likely to judge the evidence rather subjectively) or the emotional from the coldly calculating (a decision can

---

[71] Cited by Charles H. Pouthas, *La Politique étrangère de la France sous la Seconde République et le Second Empire* (mimeo., University of Paris), IV, 268.
[72] Erich Ludendorff, *Memoirs, 1914–1918* (London, 1936), pp. 234 ff.

be made under the influence of a deep passion, yet be skillfully and cynically executed). Or, again, it is hard to label some leaders ambitious and others not, since it is impossible to imagine a statesman, aside from those who inherit power, coming to power without ambition. "Politics is the art, the will, the passion to rule. Those who do not like to rule find it hard to get into the habit; those who like it find it even harder to give it up."[73] In any case, the line between personal ambition and an ambitious policy that purports to serve the national interest is often blurred. In historical analyses, it is preferable, therefore, to use clearer and better defined categories.

III. CONCLUSION

The importance of knowing as much as they can about the *personalities* of statesmen has never escaped governments or diplomats, as official government instructions and personal memoirs make clear.

In eighteenth-century instructions to ambassadors, for instance, we find many descriptions of the sovereigns and ministers whom the new envoy is to meet when he takes up his post, and often, too, the ambassador is requested for information on some public figure. When the French ambassador Blondel was about to depart for Vienna in 1749, Secretary of State Brulart de Silleri asked him for details concerning the future Austrian envoy to Paris: "[You are] to spare no effort to obtain as accurate information as [you] can on the character and personal qualities of the minister whom that court will send."[74] Or the ambassador may be requested to verify his predecessor's conclusions: "Baron de Breteuil, who has seen what is contained on the subject in reports of the Marquis de l'Hopital, is himself to ascertain whether the views expressed therein on the talents, character, and intentions of the Russian princes, ministers, or courtiers are based on sufficiently thorough and sufficiently impartial information."[75] Or again (a practice Vergennes usually followed), the minister requests an annual report on prominent personalities, with "an exact account of all the most important things [the ambassadors] have learned in the countries where they have resided, both on the character and tastes of the princes and their ministers and on any other matters which may be of concern to the department or of interest to the King."[76]

Works on the "art of diplomacy" are also significantly revealing of this need to have personal information of leading statesmen. Not only do they attach importance to such knowledge, but they sometimes adopt the "dichotomous" method, the same presentation by contrast, which we have

---

[73] Louis Barthou, *Le Politique* (Paris, 1923), p. 16.
[74] *Instructions données aux ambassadeurs*, I, Austria, March 25, 1749, p. 286.
[75] *Ibid.*, IX, Russia, March 16, 1760, p. 133.
[76] *Ibid.*, IX, Russia, May 6, 1780, p. 371.

discussed in earlier sections. Pierre Danès, writing in 1561, lists all the facts an ambassador should gather, and concludes: "Finally, the disposition and the genius of the prince, his ability, his occupations, his inclinations, his virtues, his vices, since the knowledge of all these details can throw considerable light on all matters to be negotiated with him."[77] Another Frenchman made the same point: "If it is a prince, get to know his disposition and inclination."[78] François de Callières, a negotiator of the Treaty of Ryswick (1697) and the author of one of the most remarkable of all treatises on diplomacy,[79] which was to be quoted throughout the eighteenth century, calls the ambassador "an honorable spy." Among the matters on which the ambassador must spy, he lists the "general interests of states," but he adds, "since the passions and whims of the men in power regulate the destinies of those subject to them, it is the duty of the skillful negotiator to instruct himself as accurately as he can concerning the inclinations, type of mind, and plans of the men in authority." Similarly, in a rather confused treatise of 1763, we read that the negotiator should know the "character of princes, generals, ministers" in order to make a "topography of politics."[80] And in the early nineteenth century, the Count d'Hauterive observed that it was necessary to have "an accurate idea of the persons in authority—their influence, their character, their talents, the qualities that might assist the progress of negotiations, of those which might hinder them."[81]

Surprisingly enough, Jules Cambon, in a book on diplomacy written in 1926, did not so much as mention this subject, although Louis Barthou, writing on "politics" in the same series, presented numerous picturesque and detailed portraits of statesmen ("Mosanus," or Poincaré; "Namnetus," or Briand; "Lugdunus," or Herriot). It is surprising, too, to find a similar omission in Léon Noel's *Conseils à un jeune Français entrant dans la carrière*,[82] and in the works of Sir Harold Nicolson and Lord Strang.[83]

Many "dichotomous" classifications of statesmen can be found in different treatises. The most celebrated dates from 1513 and is found in Machiavelli's *Prince*:

> I state that all men, and especially princes, who are placed at a greater height, are reputed for certain qualities which bring them either praise or blame. Thus one is considered liberal, another miserly . . .; one a free giver, another rapacious; one cruel, another merciful; one a breaker of his word, another

---

[77] "Conseils à un ambassadeur," edited by L. Delavaud, in *Revue d'Histoire diplomatique*, 1915.

[78] Jean Hotman, *De la Charge et dignité de l'ambassadeur* (Paris, 1604).

[79] *De la manière de négocier avec les souverains* (Paris, 1716).

[80] Charles-Armand L'Escalopier de Nourar, *Le Ministère du négociateur* (Amsterdam, 1763).

[81] A. M. d'Hauterive, "Conseils à un élève du Ministère des relations extérieures."

[82] Paris, 1948.

[83] Sir Harold Nicolson, *Diplomacy* (London and New York, 1963); and William, Lord Strang, *The Diplomatic Career* (London, 1962).

trustworthy; one effeminate and pusillanimous, another fierce and high-spirited; one humane, another haughty; one lascivious, another chaste; one frank, another astute; one hard, another easy; one serious, another frivolous; one religious, another an unbeliever, and so on.[84]

Callières established a briefer list: "He may and should find out what are the dominant passions and inclinations of the Prince to whom he is accredited, whether he is studious and hard-working, whether he loves war or whether he prefers rest and pleasure to business; whether he rules himself or is ruled, and to what extent."[85]

Antoine Pecquet, first commissioner of Torcy and a disciple of Callières, drew up a list of the alternatives that are presented in the choice of a diplomat:

> According to one's ideas, one will choose a man who is quick or temperate, a man more or less likely to inspire confidence or distrust; an easy or a difficult negotiator; a man who is flexible or firm; a man who is friendly or haughty; an industrious man or a man about town; a magistrate or a man who sticks to his desk; a man of high birth or merely one of respectable lineage.[86]

Finally, another French eighteenth-century writer even suggested that the diplomat study what today we would call psychology:

> It is necessary to learn the character of men, which vary nearly as much as their features; to know the mechanics of their behavior, the range and perspective of their minds and plans; to walk with them cautiously, to know how distrustful or trustful they are, how difficult or easy, how liberal or avaricious, how presumptuous or modest, how candid or devious, how quick or slow of wit, how intelligent or stupid, how prone to anger or restrained, how able or ignorant, how inclined or disinclined to particular pleasures, and above all how interested or disinterested in one's business with them.[87]

To sum up, I think we may say the following: We should never be done were we to try to make an exhaustive enumeration of men, especially if we wanted to define all the motives that bring their passions into play. Nevertheless, men who hold public office must have some smattering of the maxims by which they rule themselves, failing which they will be at a singular disadvantage in their negotiations.

---

[84] Chapter XV, "Of the things for which men, and especially princes, are praised or blamed."
[85] Callières, *op. cit.*, p. 153.
[86] *De l'Art de négocier avec les souverains* (The Hague, 1738).
[87] J. de la Sarraz Du Franquesnay, *Le Ministre public dans les cours étrangères, ses fonctions et ses prérogatives* (Paris, 1731).

10

THE STATESMAN AND THE "NATIONAL INTEREST"

The notion of a "national interest," as opposed to the "interest of the Prince," appeared with the development of national sentiment and came into its own with the emergence of democratic institutions. It would seem to correspond to a somewhat confused belief that, in a given situation, one can objectively determine the immediate and long-term goals the nation should set itself. A simplistic portrayal of its historical evolution would begin with the state in which the king pursued his own interests without regard for the goods or lives of his subjects; then would come the state governed by a small aristocracy or "upper middle class," again using the lives and resources of the mass of the people to promote its interests—its prestige, commerce, or accumulation of wealth—across the globe. And finally would come the state genuinely "of the people," whose leaders were obliged, whether they liked it or not, to act *only* in the general interests of the nation.

Woodrow Wilson was doubtless thinking along these lines—influenced by Louis Brandeis, probably, who in turn traced the doctrine back to Jefferson—when he promised during the 1912 campaign to devote his administration to the "national interest" rather than to the defense of "special interests." Thus did he reject on principle the "dollar diplomacy" of his predecessor, Taft, being unwilling as he was to place the powerful mechanism of the American Government at the service of big banks and industrial companies.

But the reality is unfortunately less simple. We see infinitely complex and diverse societies around us, divided not only into "classes" but also into "interest groups," and we constantly observe that the aspirations of these classes and groups conflict. What common denominator can be found between the demands of those Englishmen in 1846 who wanted the Corn Laws upheld, and those of consumers who were lured by Richard Cobden's propaganda in favor of cheap bread? Or between shareholders of a company that supported the conquest or retention of a colony, and the soldiers and their families, who were little disposed to risk death and bereavement for the sake of financial profit? Within one and the same state, contradictions among the interests of groups and individuals is such that one is hard put to admit that *objectively* a national interest exists. Are the much-vaunted "higher interests of the state" in fact a mere cover (except in special cases) for interests that are certainly less noble and in any case private?

Still, governmental authorities must make choices between various possible foreign-policy objectives. Consciously or unconsciously, they will say that the results of those choices is in the "national interest."

I. AMBIGUITIES IN THE CONCEPT OF THE NATIONAL INTEREST

Statesmen are subject to forces which they either endure or try to control. But their acts should not be viewed simply from the angle of *causality*. In order to explain international relations—or, for that matter, domestic politics—it is not enough to examine the causes—that is, the operative forces—and the consequences. One must also view the matter from the point of view of *finality*. Indeed, it is precisely the responsible authority who *must* define the nation's ultimate aims and act to achieve them, taking into account the risks and the available resources. Statesmen, like all men of action, live to a degree in the future.

Needless to say, this general truth has innumerable variations. We referred earlier to the doctrinaire leader who sets himself a goal and will not be swayed from it, and the opportunist who modifies his aims in the light of circumstances. There is similarly a wide disparity between the man who handles the nation's affairs on a day-to-day basis without any over-all plan, and the man who, like Hitler, seeks to forge the destiny of his country for the next thousand years, not to mention the man in between, who feels, like Bismarck, that he can anticipate the events of the next two years and does not look much further, this margin being sufficient for his plans and more distant forecast appearing impossible. Whichever they are, short-sighted politicians or visionaries, all responsible statesmen must, and in point of fact do, evolve a more or less stable, more or less definite, more or less well-thought-out image of the national interest. But some of them deny this and claim the interests of all humanity, not merely those of their own nation, as the primary objective. This is a typically Anglo-Saxon attitude and, especially, an American one. It seems to this writer to posit a false intellectual problem, but it has played a significant role in history and should be considered here.

Surrounded by weak or friendly countries, far away from Europe, possessing an immense extent of land and abundant resources, Americans very early came to believe that their exceptional position was the result of the special protection of Providence, itself due to the "moral" character of American foreign policy. This morality, superior to other peoples', consisted in the fact that Americans did not try—or so they thought—to augment their power. The expression "power politics" was used only in a pejorative sense. "Few French authors," writes Raymond Aron, "have glorified the *politique de puissance* as the German doctrinaires have extolled *Macht Politik,* and few French authors have condemned the *politique de puissance* in the way American moralists have condemned *power politics.*"[1] And this was true not only of moralists but also of statesmen. In 1913, Wilson said: "It is a very perilous thing to determine the foreign policy of a nation in terms of material interest. It not only is unfair to those with whom you are dealing, but it is degrading as regards your own actions."[2] The condemnation of power politics and pursuit of material gain extended to the idea of the balance of power, hence of alliances and political or economic regional groupings. Cordell Hull wrote: "I was not, and am not, a believer in the idea of balance of power or spheres of influence as a means of keeping the peace."[3]

The assertion of an American "national interest" that entailed conquest or diplomatic pressure at the expense of other nations was thus naturally unpopular. If one waged war, it was in defense of principles—a "crusade" in favor of the oppressed Cubans, or in favor of "freedom of the seas."[4] When Americans talked of the national interest, they meant, as Wilson did in 1912 and Charles Beard in his great work *The Idea of National Interest* (1934), the development of the economic well-being of the masses as opposed to the material interests of big business.

The circumstances following World War II caused a number of American historians to question whether this moralist tradition, with its aversion to the idea of interests, was not delusory—the United States, after all, like other nations, had sought to develop her resources and power, sometimes at the expense of other countries—and dangerous, moreover, since it was liable to blind American governments concerning imperative political necessities. The debate on this issue began, as we saw before, in 1951, with the appearance of Morgenthau's *In Defense of the National Interest* and Kennan's *American Diplomacy.* These partisans of a return to a certain form of "sacred egoism" of the state were immediately challenged by ardent, sometimes naïve, defenders of America's moral superiority. Professor Frank Tannenbaum, for instance, argued that the American tradition was still a moralist one and that Americans should at all costs avoid imitating the European admiration for Machiavelli, and for the European heroes like Napoleon, Bismarck, and Clemenceau.[5] Dexter Perkins, with somewhat greater moderation, expressed the view that American diplomacy, as compared with that of other countries, was indeed marked by a high level of morality, but he did not go so far as

---

[1] *Peace and War: A Theory of International Relations* (New York, 1966), p. 47.
[2] Speech at Mobile, Alabama, October 27, 1913. Cited in August Heckscher, *The Politics of Woodrow Wilson* (New York, 1936).
[3] Cordell Hull, *Memoirs* (New York, 1948), II, 1452.
[4] See Robert Osgood, *Ideals and Self-Interest in American Foreign Relations* (Chicago, 1953).
[5] "The American Tradition in Foreign Relations," *Foreign Affairs,* October, 1951.

to assert that morality was at the very foundation of American diplomacy; the promise of virtue, he remarked, was not the same thing as virtue. Yet when Americans conquered foreign lands, however unjustifiably, and when they pursued an imperialistic policy, they always did so, Perkins argued, with a bad conscience.[6] To which Morgenthau had already replied, citing Alexander Hamilton: "It may be affirmed as a general principle, that the predominant motive of good offices from one nation to another, is the interest or advantage of the nation which performs them."[7]

Many authors have tried to reconcile these two theories[8] by showing that statesmen have a moral duty to promote the national interest:

> Today, the alternative to a policy of the national interest to which people refer is of a different character. They fear policy-makers may be unduly concerned with the "interest of all mankind." . . . The issue, then, is not one of transcending narrow group selfishness, as it was at the time of Beard's discussion, but rather one of according more exclusive devotion to the narrower cause of the national self.[9]

This problem of idealism, or the illusion of idealism, *versus* selfish national interests, certainly appears to be a false problem. It apparently arises only in countries that feel themselves for the time being safe from external danger, like the United States before 1940. (There is a curious parallel here with the attitudes of Indian leaders when they felt themselves sheltered by the Himalayas.) It is certainly a very noble moralism, but it is sometimes irritating when it appears to others as a hypocritical justification of sordid interests.[10]

Basically, the question is whether private morality and the best conceived national interest can coincide with the interests of all humanity. Spiritual authorities constantly remind the people and their leaders of this possibility, and there is no doubt that they carry some weight with the public; there is also no doubt that statesmen stay far removed from such aspirations. Pope John XXIII was unanimously acclaimed when he wrote in his encyclical *Pacem in Terris*:

> The same moral law which governs relations between individual human beings serves also to regulate the relations of political communities with one another. We must remember that, of its very nature, civil authority exists, not to confine its people within the boundaries of their nation, but rather to protect, above

---

[6] *The American Approach to Foreign Policy* (Cambridge, Mass., 1952).

[7] *In Defense of the National Interest* (New York, 1951), p. 15.

[8] See Osgood, *op. cit.*, and Kenneth Thompson, *Christian Ethics and the Dilemmas of Foreign Policy* (Durham, N.C., 1959), and *Political Realism and the Crisis of World Politics* (Princeton, N.J., 1960).

[9] Arnold Wolfers, *Discord and Collaboration* (Baltimore, Md., 1962), p. 148.

[10] See the remarks on this subject in Arnold Wolfers and Laurence W. Martin, eds., *The Anglo-American Tradition in Foreign Affairs* (New Haven, Conn., 1956).

all else, the common good of that particular civil society, which certainly cannot be divorced from the common good of the entire human family.

But that does not mean that nation-states were in fact prepared to act along these lines.

The concept of the national interest in practice raises a much more serious difficulty: how to distinguish, in a statesman's words and writings, what is sincere and what is not—in other words, how to determine whether what he calls the "national interest" is not a disguised form of his own particular interests. In the *ancien regime,* the problem scarcely arose for the sovereign, since the interests of the state in theory coincided with his own. Louis XIV was aware of the role of kings "who have the public interest in their hands and whose decisions make for the weal or woe of the whole land." If the king is good, his interests coincide with those of his people. "For, after all, my son, we have to consider the good of our subjects much more than our own. . . . This power which we have over them should serve us only to labor more effectively to procure their welfare." And it is easy for him, being subject to constraint or limitation, to think that what benefits him is beneficial to his people. "My right," "my honor," are constantly recurring expressions. "I hope," Louis XIV said to his son, "that I shall leave you still more power and greatness than I have myself."[11]

In a parliamentary democracy, especially one where the executive authority is unstable, the prime minister's immediate concern is political survival. He may therefore be led to neglect to do certain things that would probably mean his downfall, yet that he knows are necessary. It is generally conceded, for instance, that it was vital for France to prevent Hitler from reoccupying the demilitarized zone of the Rhineland. The ministers responsible for the armed forces in Albert Sarraut's cabinet, particularly General Maurin, believed that any counter-measure would mean general mobilization (in addition to support from Great Britain), but the cabinet—appalled at the thought of an unpopular general mobilization two months before elections—decided to take no action. Or again, Paul Reynaud, in March, 1940, had to give the defense ministry to his predecessor, Daladier, in order to secure a one-vote majority in the Chamber of Deputies, although this meant the retention of General Gamelin as chief of staff and Reynaud judged Gamelin's presence in that post to be disastrous.

Another type of divergence between the announced intentions of a government and its real intentions is evident in many colonial histories, where the announced colonial activity was a *mission civilisitrice,* a war against slavery, the "white man's burden" to be borne on behalf of the rest of the world. In 1876, when Leopold II of Belgium founded the African International Association, its purposes were ostensibly scientific and humani-

---

[11] Jean Longnon, ed., *Louis XIV, Mémoires* (Paris, 1923).

tarian. Ferdinand de Lesseps called it "the most humanitarian creation of our century." But, as historians have pointed out, the king, who did not yet have political control in mind, was aiming at a single goal: "to create a great commercial enterprise endowed with as many economic monopolies as possible."[12] The cases of Tunisia or Morocco, let us say, are more problematical, since political considerations were also involved, but the idealistic dressing-up of policies actually intended to advance economic interests is a constant phenomenon in colonial history.

Should one go further and assert that *all* references to the national interest in capitalistic countries are in fact a delusion, and that the only interests involved are those of a single class, the bourgeoisie—in other words, that an over-all national interest cannot really exist? So Marx, Engels, and Lenin frequently argued. Yet, although Marx and Engels went too far in underestimating the coherence of the nation—Engels admitted it later— they regarded the Franco-Prussian war of 1870 as a defensive war as far as Germany was concerned. All Germans, of no matter what class, Engels wrote to Marx on August 15, 1870, had realized that the basic issue at stake was their nation's very existence.[13] Lenin went further, and World War I gave him an opportunity to pursue his attack on "bourgeois countries." His *Imperialism, the Highest Stage of Capitalism* and *Imperialism, the State and Revolution* are permeated with the notion that the foreign policies of existing states were *class* policies and by no means motivated by "national interest":

> In Russia chauvinism is hiding behind the phrases of *la belle France*, unfortunate Belgium, and enmity to the Kaiser and Kaiserdom. Therefore it is our absolute duty to fight against this sophistry, and, in order that this fight travel along a clear and straight path, a slogan is necessary to summarize the entire question. The slogan should show that, from the standpoint of the interests of the Russian working class, there is little doubt that the defeat of Tsarism is the lesser catastrophe, because Tsarism is a hundred times worse than Kaiserism.[14]

Discussion of the value of this theory is really more a philosophical than historical task, but the historian should observe two facts. First, in many cases, leaders of so-called bourgeois nations genuinely believe that the policies they pursue are furthering the over-all national interest. If they confuse the national interest with the interests of their class (which is open to question), they do so unconsciously. Secondly, it may happen that the policy of a

---

[12] See J. Stengers, "Léopold II et la fixation des frontières du Congo," *Le Flambeau* (Brussels), March–April, 1963, pp. 156–57.

[13] See Karl Marx, *The Civil War in France* (Chicago, 1934); and *Der Briefwechsel zwischen Friedrich Engels und Karl Marx, 1844 bis 1883* (Stuttgart, 1913), IV, 319, cited by Milorad Drachkovich, *Des Socialismes français et allemands et le problème de la guerre, 1870–1914* (Geneva, 1953), p. 226.

[14] Letter to Shliapnikov, October 17, 1914, cited by David Shub, *Lenin* (New York, 1948), p. 135.

"bourgeois state" is objectively advantageous to all its citizens, all its classes. This issue generated considerable heat in relation to colonial enterprises pursued in the years preceding World War I. A great debate took place in France, for instance, between the socialists Jean Jaurès and Charles Andler over the imperialism of German socialists.[15] Andler cited Gerhard Hildebrand, who advocated a "socialist distribution" of colonial territories, and Atlanticus, who argued (in a book to which Karl Kautsky wrote the preface) that "Germany's colonial possessions were a decisive factor in solving the social problem," and many others. Jaurès, on the other hand, optimistically continued to praise the "courageous and persevering effort of our comrades against the militarists beyond the Rhine, against the spirit of chauvinism, against all thoughts of imperialism and aggression."[16] Lenin, of course, did not accept the notion that colonization might benefit all classes. (Here he followed the English analyst Hobson.) He wrote, rather, that imperialism, by procuring valuable monopolies for a handful of very rich countries, created the economic possibility of corrupting the highest level of the proletariat.

The historian should analyze the advantages that each social class, or at least most of the people, may derive from a given national policy—colonization at one period, development of international trade at another, economic expansion, maintenance of peace, etc. It suffices that such advantages exist for the idea of the national interest to be preserved.

In any case, the historian's duty is not to determine an *objective* national interest, but to show what *subjective* notions of it statesmen have evolved.

Another difficulty in regard to the concept of the national interest is that domestic and foreign policies are inextricably bound together in it. An "active," "dynamic," perhaps even aggressive foreign policy inevitably has major repercussions on the daily lives of a nation's citizens. It requires, for example, a strong army and, consequently, a high defense budget and extended military service. Such burdens are sometimes accepted with enthusiasm, but this enthusiasm is usually ephemeral; more often, the reaction is weariness. When Poincaré pursued an "activist" policy in the Ruhr in 1923, he was remarkably successful; the Germans gave up their "passive resistance" and agreed to pay regular reparations. But by November, Poincaré had agreed to "internationalize" the reparations problem, which implied in the foreseeable future the evacuation of the Ruhr: why did he abandon the activist policy which had been so successful? There are several explanations, but one is of decisive significance: the French were exhausted by the war.

---

[15] See Andler's articles in *Action nationale*, November–December, 1912, and Jaurès' reply in *L'Humanité*, March 4, 1913.

[16] Address of June 17, 1913, cited by Alexandre Zevaes, *Le parti socialiste de 1904 à 1923* (Paris, 1923), p. 39.

General elections were to take place in May, 1924, and the French people would have the chance to express their hostility to a policy of "mounting a major offensive every time important foreign-policy issues arise," as Herriot had described it as early as 1921.[17] Poincaré was anxious not to lose the elections and believed (mistakenly) that he could appeal to the public as an arbiter of peace—hence his about-face.

In innumerable cases, then, a political leader is obliged to abandon his ambitious designs as a result of domestic pressures. Another phenomenon may also be observed: the use of foreign-policy issues to distract attention from specific domestic grievances.

The "Ultra of Ultras," the Prince of Polignac, for instance, undertook the conquest of Algiers in 1830 in order to get the country to accept the Five Ordinances he had secretly prepared against the liberals. His failure, in this case, was flagrant, but there are cases when such diversionary tactics achieve results. Although Bismarck certainly did not go to war against Austria in 1866 merely to have an issue with which to resolve his dispute with the Prussian Landtag, he undoubtedly intended to use his victory to allay domestic tensions. The indemnity bill approved by a large majority in the Landtag on August 5, 1866,[18] shows how closely linked the major foreign success and domestic policies were. And Lloyd George in December, 1918, and Clemenceau in November, 1919, won elections because they had won the war. But the rule is not infallible; two months after the elections, Clemenceau lost out in the presidency; and Churchill, notwithstanding his glory as a war leader, had the majority of the electorate turn against him in 1945.

What is very hard for the historian to determine is whether a specific foreign-policy decision was intended to achieve success abroad or at home. There are statesmen who care only about the high politics of foreign affairs. But even such "politics of greatness" will have an ultimate *domestic* purpose.

But is not the ultimate goal of this policy of "greatness" a domestic one? We may recall the celebrated opening phrases of General de Gaulle's memoirs: "Only vast enterprises are capable of counterbalancing the ferments of dispersal which are inherent in [the French] people." Thus, a grandiose foreign policy would be intended ultimately to preserve French unity.

This problem is linked to another one in the concept of the national interest: When a statesman pursues a given objective, does he think of the attainment of that objective as an end in itself or as a means to attain another end? (There are only a few cases that are clearly one or the other: France, for example, when she set herself the task of eventually recovering Alsace and Lorraine after her defeat in the Franco-Prussian war, undoubtedly considered this as an end in itself.) The problem arises chiefly in relation to

---

[17] Georges Suarez, *Briand* (Paris, 1938–52), V, 235.
[18] Erich Eyck, *Bismarck, Leben und Werk* (Erlenbach-Zurich, 1941), 278–79.

the question of power. Many authors believe that the acquisition and increase of power is of the very essence of the state—that power vies with power for survival and supremacy,[19] that power is sought as an end in itself,[20] and that foreign policy aims at the acquisition of optimum, and sometimes maximum power.[21]

This extreme position, which would reduce the concept of national interest to that of a constant effort to achieve power, does not withstand the test of historical analysis. It is possible, of course, that in case of doubt a statesman may adopt a certain course because he believes that it is likely to enhance the nation's power, and this, on the surface at least, can do no harm. But it is much more common for power to be regarded as a *means* to obtain other advantages—wealth, the satisfaction of a specific need related to the national sentiment (for instance, the annexation of a territory populated by compatriots). Raymond Aron and Arnold Wolfers have both demonstrated that nations set themselves many objectives.[22] While in some cases one of these objectives may be power, in others power is only a means to attain altogether different ends.

II. DIFFERENT CONCEPTS OF THE NATIONAL INTEREST

Whatever the magnitude of these difficulties and ambiguities, the historian must try to solve them in each instance as they arise. He will not always succeed, but the attempt will not be in vain. It may be facilitated, we believe, by understanding what the different elements are which alternately or simultaneously, make up the "national interest."

The first, and most general, concerns a nation's survival—in other words, its *security*. It is unthinkable for a statesman not to place security at the forefront of his concerns, especially if the state he heads is a nation-state. But even when it is an historical, multinational state, he will consider it his duty to preserve the state.

The concept of security contains a number of elements: preservation of sovereignty and independence; preservation of territorial integrity; preservation, as far as possible, of the lives of the inhabitants. It is understood that lives may have to be sacrificed to defend the country's independence or even its territory. But when all indications point to the hopelessness of defense, or if the loss in human lives will be excessive, then a country may be prepared to give up its land or its independence.

Compare the cases of Belgium in 1914, Czechoslovakia in September,

---

[19] Hans Morgenthau, *Scientific Man versus Power Politics* (Chicago, 1946), p. 71.

[20] Frederick Schuman, *International Politics* (New York, 1953), p. 262–63.

[21] Robert Strausz-Hupé and Stefan Possony, *International Relations in an Age of Conflict* (New York, 1954), p. 2.

[22] Aron, *op. cit.*, Chapter III, and Wolfers, *op. cit.*, Chapters I and VI.

1938, Czechoslovakia in March, 1939, and Denmark in 1940. In the first case, Belgium was faced with Germany's demand to permit invading German forces to cross Belgium in return for a promise to uphold the country's integrity. To accept meant, in effect, to lose both independence and honor. There remained two alternatives: token resistance, which would preserve national honor and spare human lives, but which would jeopardize the chances of recovering independence in the future; or fierce resistance, which would be very costly in human lives, but which, if Belgium were supported by strong allies, would allow the possibility of ultimately regaining independence. Minister Woeste proposed the first: "The situation is very grave. We are faced with a formidable power. Belgium is a small country. . . . We cannot simply submit, and we must sound our guns. But after this demonstration—essential but, in view of our weakness, vain—we shall have to withdraw to Antwerp and let things take their course." Paul Hymans replied with the second alternative:

> We must resist with all our might. That is our duty. We shall be supported by France and England. We may be defeated, but we shall have saved our honor, and we shall live. Otherwise, we are lost. The final outcome is uncertain, but, if Germany is victorious, the humiliation to which Belgium had resigned herself would deprive her of any title to the respect of the victor or to support from abroad.[23]

As we know, the second alternative prevailed.

For Czechoslovakia, in September, 1938, territorial integrity, not independence, was at stake. Her chances of military success against Germany's demand for Sudetenland were slight unless her allies, France and the Soviet Union, went to war against Germany. It was after France's threat of desertion that, in the night of September 20–21, the Czechoslovak Government resigned itself to the loss of Sudetenland. (A minority, centered around the Czech agrarian party, it is true, desired at all costs to avoid war.)

The situation in March, 1939, was different. By that time, Czechoslovakia's independence was at issue; resistance might therefore be considered. But resistance had no chance of success: the loss of Sudetenland had deprived Czechoslovakia of her fortifications, and she could count on no support from abroad. When President Hacha was summoned by Hitler to Berlin on March 13, he found himself faced with a tragic choice. Either he must sign a document placing "the fate of the Czech people . . . trustingly in the hands of the Führer," or Prague and other cities would be destroyed by bombing. In order to prevent the physical destruction of the country, he resigned himself to surrendering its independence. This was an extreme case, of course,

---

[23] Paul Hymans, *Mémoires* (Brussels, 1958), I, 86. It is Hymans who cites Woeste. Carton de Wiart maintains that Woeste actually supported the policy of resistance but voiced that support in "cold and realistic" tones. (*Souvenirs politiques* [Bruges, 1948], pp. 207–8.)

of a situation that normally occurs only after a country has suffered total defeat—Germany, for instance, in 1945—when the vanquished agrees to unconditional surrender.

Denmark's position in April, 1940, was rather similar. She had no means to resist the German invasion. The king decided to accept the German ultimatum, under protest but without a fight. Denmark lost her independence but had the hope of recovering it if the Allies were victorious. At least the capitulation saved human lives.

Thus, in the most dramatic cases, concern for physical survival may outweigh concern for the maintenance of independence and *a fortiori* of territorial integrity. Nevertheless, in the overwhelming majority of cases, security remains the cornerstone of the national interest.

But to desire security does not always mean to achieve it. The "Great Powers" are those which are capable of ensuring their own security against any other single power. There were eight such powers prior to 1914, six of them in Europe; the disappearance of Austria-Hungary reduced the number to seven. World War II reduced it to two: France and Italy had been regarded as Great Powers, but events proved they were no longer able to ensure their security; two others, Germany and Japan, showed that they were Great Powers but were defeated and thus deprived of means of action; as for Great Britain, while she was included among the victors, she could not continue to compete with the United States and the Soviet Union.

The great majority of states—now, all but two—have always had to look abroad for guarantees for their security. Such guarantees might include an alliance with a Great Power, or recognized international status as a neutral which, hopefully, would be respected, or some delicate balance calculated on the shifting rivalries among the Great Powers. This latter is how some "buffer states" managed to retain a certain independence—Persia and Afghanistan, for instance, thanks to Anglo-Russian rivalries, or Siam thanks to Anglo-French rivalries. But when powerful neighbors come to an "understanding," dismemberment and partition may soon follow for the powerless nation in between. Such was the case with Poland in 1795 and again in 1939.

The search for security may be active or passive. A country may seek to conquer an advanced line of defense, a strategic frontier—that was Italy's policy between 1915 and 1920, and Clemenceau's in the Rhineland during the Versailles Peace Conference—or it may seek to force an attitude favorable to it among its weaker neighbors. It may also try, in order to gain time to arm, to fend off the likelihood of war by making concessions to the potential aggressor. Such was Neville Chamberlain's so-called policy of appeasement.[24] Security may be sought by doing everything possible to avoid risks, or, to

---

[24] According to A. J. P. Taylor (*The Origins of the Second World War* [London and New York, 1961]), this was a deliberate policy based on a genuine theory. The same cannot be said of Georges Bonnet's parallel policy in France.

achieve a more complete security, by being prepared to take risks that jeopardize the very existence of the state. There is thus an absolute contradiction between the policy of immobility as practiced by Louis Philippe and Guizot, for instance, and the policy of conquest as practiced by Hitler. Between the two, many theorists argue, we find states that seek to acquire and hold an "optimum" strength. If a country is overly weak, it tempts an aggressor, if it is overly strong, it arouses anxieties and provokes the creation of hostile coalitions. Bismarck was particularly aware that, after Prussia's victory over France, she must cease her expansion—failing which, other powers, Russia in particular, would turn against her.[25] This is probably what he meant when he wrote to Henry von Reuss on February 28, 1874: "Prince Gorchakov is pursuing a policy of Russian power; we are pursuing not a policy of power but a policy of security."

Finally, in attempting to achieve security, a country may hesitate between what Wolfers calls "possession goals" and "milieu goals."[26] The first are goals a country sets itself in order to gain improved means of defense—human resources, territories, etc. In pursuing milieu goals, a country seeks to change the international environment so that aggression against it will be less easy and less profitable—endeavors to strengthen international law, or to create international organizations that, hopefully, will maintain the peace.

Here, the idea of collective security is relevant. Thus far, endeavors to achieve it have been largely unsuccessful. But is that because collective security itself is illusory? Or is it because, for precautionary reasons, nations "reassure" themselves against deficiencies in collective security by using the traditional old methods—arms buildup, alliances—that weaken collective security? The question was hotly debated in France between the two world wars and particularly when the foreign minister, Jean Louis Barthou, was trying to negotiate a Franco-Soviet mutual-assistance pact. "The Socialist Party," wrote Léon Blum, "must make it absolutely clear that in this matter as in all others it will fight the National Bloc [coalition] administration. It remains opposed to closed pacts that divide Europe into hostile groups."[27] The solution Blum advocated was a strengthened League of Nations and progressive disarmament.

We have emphasized security because it appears to us to be the most general and most essential form of national interest. But each country can choose among other objectives; the endlessly variable combinations of these objectives constitute formulations of the national interest. "Though all governments," wrote Montesquieu, "have the same general end, which is that of preservation, yet each has another particular object. Increase of dominion

---

[25] Eyck, *op. cit.*, III, 29.
[26] Wolfers, *op. cit.*, pp. 73–74.
[27] *Le Populaire* (Paris), July 13, 1934.

was the object of Rome; war, that of Sparta; religion, that of the Jewish laws; commerce, that of Marseilles."[28]

Raymond Aron has suggested that one can distinguish between abstract objectives and parallel concrete objectives. The abstract series concerns the desired prospective advantages; the concrete series concerns the desired objectives themselves—under which is subsumed the historical, empirical, *real* objectives such as a certain province, a certain source of wealth, etc. Taking Aron's idea as a starting point, we may list in a slightly different manner the following goals[29]:

> *Abstract series:* Power, Wealth, Values
> *Concrete series:* Land, Gold, Souls

A statesman, according to his preferences, may aim to procure power or wealth for his country. Power is the ability to impose one's will beyond the confines of the nation's sovereignty. It is of course a relative thing, and there have been instances where a weak country has imposed its will on a strong one (for example, Egypt on France and Britain in 1956). But on the whole, it is directly related to a country's forces and, in the long run, to its potential, its capacity to increase its strength. Directly after Pearl Harbor, Japan was stronger than the United States, but the latter's enormous potential enabled her within two years to achieve a crushing superiority.

Power and wealth are linked in many ways. A country may seek to increase its wealth in order to increase its power; for wealth will enable it to finance more powerful armies—this was the policy of King Frederick William II of Prussia and, to a great extent, of Louis XIV's controller general, Colbert. A country may also seek to increase its power in order to become wealthier; power, for example, will enable it to acquire territories rich in natural resources. Then there is the idea of acquiring wealth through booty rather than labor, as old as the world itself; Bonaparte proposed it to his tattered soldiers when they reached the rich plains of northern Italy. And power can also be sought for its own sake or for the "glory" it brings, or simply for the sake of security. Or a country may disdain power and choose rather to be "mercantile." In history, the alternatives are never so clear-cut. Nevertheless, a choice is necessary between power and wealth, and the choice is a definite one: what portion of the national revenue, what portion of the budget, should be devoted to the national defense, what part to economic and social investment? Goering put it neatly when he said that Nazi Germany preferred guns to butter. But it is always difficult to decide how much to allot to butter and how much to guns.

The idea that the national interest can be served by promoting certain

---

[28] *The Spirit of the Laws*, Book XI, Chapter V.

[29] See Duroselle, *"Paix et guerre entre les nations:* La théorie des relations internationales selon Raymond Aron," *Revue française des sciences politiques*, XII, No. 4 (December, 1962), 963–79.

"values"—a religion, an ideology—is found primarily among peoples who experience crises of revolutionary fanaticism. A "crusade" is meant to ensure the triumph of a faith. "Revolutionary expansion" rationalizes conquest by invoking a duty to free other peoples from tyranny, to "bring fraternity and aid to all peoples who wish to recover their freedom" (decree of the Convention, November 19, 1792). The conviction that one is moving "in the direction of history" is considered to justify one's imposition by force of arms of a certain type of government on foreign countries.

But nonrevolutionary peoples, accustomed to tolerance, may also come to believe that it is in their interest to promote certain values—liberty, democracy, respect for law—and, in extreme cases, to fight to defend them. General Eisenhower, significantly, entitled his memoirs *Crusade in Europe*. But nonrevolutionary democracies are more reluctant than revolutionary states to attempt the conversion of others. It is usually harder to persuade them that power may be considered an end in itself. One might even ask whether there is not some incompatibility between opting for wealth and opting for a crusade. "Satisfied" people usually make poor revolutionaries.

If we turn now to the objectives that the national interest prompts a country to pursue—the "concrete" series—we find parallel complex relationships.

We may immediately discard the self-serving theme advanced by German geopoliticians that territorial conquest is of the very essence of statehood. There are greedy states, but also satisfied peoples. Territorial conquest has certainly played a primordial role in human history. But the idea of "living space," of *Lebensraum*, is simply an abnormal extension of the attraction exerted by the conquest of land. During the *ancien régime*, the conquest of a province meant an increase in tax returns and, therefore, a chance to strengthen one's army. The conquest of colonial empires in the late nineteenth century meant an opportunity to do profitable business, to solve manpower problems (by incorporating native soldiers in the national army), or to hold key positions on a trade or strategic route. The notion of colonies as overseas bases, as vast territories for the deployment of armies, was an afterthought. In any case, even an unknown territory is probably a source of wealth: Leopold II's annexation of the mining province of Katanga was more or less accidental,[30] yet that province is the source of the Congo's wealth; similarly, the wastes of the Sahara have now revealed long-buried treasures.

It is quite another matter, again, when the land in question is peopled by compatriots. In that case, its conquest or reconquest—not of land in general but of a strictly delimited territory—becomes a national aspiration, a kind of "duty" that the country's leaders set themselves, usually with the public's strong backing. A new definition of the national territory may then

---

[30] J. Stengers, paper read to the Société d'Histoire moderne (Paris), May, 1963.

be coined: a territory "open to nationals." Statesmen have often been concerned to offer their country's citizens vast areas to colonize in order to
prevent them from emigrating to other nations. Mussolini's conquest of
Ethiopia was not solely motivated by a desire for prestige; he was also
conscious of the wastage of national energies, as he saw it, in Italian emigration to Argentina and Brazil. The high Abyssinian plateaus were healthy,
and they would provide Italy with a good field for colonization. In this case,
the attractiveness of the conquest obliterated the sense of commonly accepted
values—which included the right of the Ethiopian nation, member of the
League of Nations, to life and independence.

The pursuit of gold, that is, of all possible means of wealth, sometimes
coincides with the pursuit of land to conquer. But more often, it is at variance
with it. There are two types of trading nations: seafaring, colonizing nations,
like England or Venice; and nations content with their own territories
(because they are unable to enlarge them) which devote all their energy
to business, like Switzerland. *All* trading nations, however, tend to consider
a piece of land as a source of wealth. (Statesmen sometimes consider it
expedient to put the colonial problem in terms of the profits derived from
the territory.[31]) Once the land is no longer profitable, therefore, there is a
strong tendency to abandon it. Thus Great Britain, both in the mid-nineteenth
century and after World War II, experienced a "nadir of colonization."
The phenomenon had already been described long before: "If this nation
sends colonies abroad, it must rather be to extend its commerce than its
dominion."[32] There have been, of course, and there still are, many im-
perialists in England who think of the Empire in terms of power. But the
trend in favor of decolonizing, voiced by Cobden and others, was active for
a century in England and explains, perhaps, why it was easier for her to shed
her colonies than for France.

The conquest of a people, of "souls," may entail their acceptance of an
ideology or, more simply, their assimilation into the national community
that absorbed them. It too is one of the concrete forms sometimes assumed
by the national interest.

These general considerations have the merit of helping us to classify and
understand the historical phenomena which reveal the complexity of the
"national interest." At any given moment, a statesman has his own idea of
what is in the national interest, but his fellow citizens do not necessarily
agree, except in special cases of a "Sacred Union," a "National Union," or
a bipartisan policy. Frequently, his personal view is openly challenged.

---

[31] See Henri Brunschwig, *French Colonialism, 1871–1914: Myths and Realities*
(New York and London, 1966), and J. Stengers, *Combien le Congo a-t-il coûté à la
Belgique?* (Brussels, 1957).

[32] Montesquieu, *op. cit.*, Book XIX, chap. 27.

III. COLONIALISM AND CONTINENTALISM

The sudden acceleration of European colonial conquests after 1880 corresponded to a development in European concepts of national interest. Superficially, one can say that among European statesmen, there were two kinds: those who confined themselves to traditional diplomacy and regarded European problems alone as important; and those who discovered in colonial expansion a new and essential national objective. But the historical realities were obviously more complex than this. "Colonialists" like Jules Ferry were far from unconcerned with Europe; "Europeans" like Bismarck allowed themselves to be persuaded that colonies were of some importance. Still, there was a quite profound divergence between the two attitudes.

Jules Ferry is a good example of a "colonialist," having the advantage of being clear and well defined. Under the Empire, Ferry was a republican activist, totally unconcerned with the issue of colonies. For him, the essential problem was that of France's "natural frontiers." Unlike more starry-eyed republicans, he took a strong position as early as 1860 against acquiring the Rhine frontier:

> There are two ways of understanding France's destiny and seeking her greatness. Some believe the country will be stronger when she is more feared and when she increases the radius of her bellicose and triumphant nationhood. Others would prefer to see her grow only in moral action and industrial strength, in the power of her labor, in the power of her ideas, in the power of her example.[33]

As an adversary of Napoleon III, Ferry deliberately opted for the second position: "From neither a financial nor a military point of view would territorial expansion to the Rhine promote France's honor—that is obvious— or her real security, or her policies of progress." Moreover, he long remained hostile to permanent armies, "which nourish hatred and suspicion from one end of Europe to the other and which at home perpetuate swollen budgets."[34]

France's defeat in 1871, then the subsequent triumph of the opportunists, caused Ferry to revise his position. He admitted it frankly in the Senate, when he recalled Jules Simon's program for the abolition of standing armies:

> *A voice from the right*: "You too, you abandoned it!"
> *M. Jules Ferry*: "Yes, my dear colleague, I abandoned many of my youthful utopias, once I came in contact with realities and became involved in the conduct of business and the exercise of power [signs of considerable approval]."[35]

---

[33] *Courrier de Paris,* May 28, 1860. Reproduced in Paul Robiquet, ed., *Discours et Opinions de Jules Ferry* (Paris, 1893–98), I, 25–28.
[34] Ferry's circular as candidate in the sixth electoral district of Paris, 1869, in *ibid.,* I, 191.
[35] *Journal officiel, Débats parlementaires, Sénat, 1891,* November 24; and *ibid.,* I, 192.

We need not enter here into the complex history behind France's conquest of Tunisia; our purpose is merely to show how Jules Ferry, Prime Minister at the time, explained it. One thing is certain, that his "conversion" to imperialism came very late: "An affair in Tunis in an election year? You can't be serious," was his initial reaction.[36] Once Tunisia was conquered, however, the idea took shape in his mind that here lay the future for French greatness. In May, 1881, Gambetta wrote to Ferry to congratulate him "on this prompt and excellent result. The gripers will have to make the best of it: France is resuming her place as a Great Power."[37]

Ferry did not accept his opponents' argument that the conquest of Tunisia had been effected by "financial concessions and finagling"; it was not a "stock-market manipulation." "I say that it was a patriotic thing," he argued in 1891, "an honest and useful thing, and that it was a stroke of luck for France."

In the years after Tunisia, Ferry's ideas on empire developed more fully. How *did* he justify colonization? What were his reasons for choosing the territories he did for colonial conquest? What place did European politics occupy in his system?

"Colonial expansion," he said in a speech of July 28, 1885—his major declaration on colonial policy—"is a political and economic system . . . that [can] be linked with three realms of ideas: economic ideas, concepts of 'high' civilization, and political and patriotic ideas."[38] (This threefold justification had already appeared in an unsigned preface to a book entitled *Les Affaires de Tunisie,* published in 1882 by Ferry's private secretary Alfred Rambaud but which we know to have been written by Ferry.[39] Ferry spelled it out in more detail in later speeches.)

The economic motivations were essential, in Ferry's view. A colonial policy was incumbent in the first place on nations that depended on emigration to relieve the pressure on their poor or overcrowded population. It was no less incumbent on those with a surplus of either capital or goods. France, which had always had plenty of capital and had exported considerable amounts of it abroad—

> would be well advised to consider the colonial question from that aspect. . . . But there is another, far more important, aspect to this question. For countries like ours, foreordained by nature itself and by the industry of their people to a great export trade, the colonial question is essentially a question of outlets. Political predominance leads to the predominance of goods, that is, to economic predominance.[40]

---

[36] Cited in Maurice Reclus, *Ferry le Tonkinois* (Paris, 1964), p. 250.

[37] *Ibid.,* p. 255.

[38] Speech of July 28, 1885, *Journal officiel, Débats parlementaires, Chambre, 1885,* p. 1666.

[39] Robiquet, *op. cit.,* VI, 521.

[40] See Alfred Rambaud, *Les Affaires de Tunisie* (Paris, 1882), "Preface."

To Ferry, it was clear that the problems of outlets was related to pro-tective tariffs.[41] "Why? Because Germany is putting up barriers everywhere, because, beyond the seas, the United States of America has become protectionist, indeed extremely protectionist. . . . I do not say that these great markets are closing, but they are contracting."

"Colonial policy is the daughter of industrial policy."[42] "Do you not see that all the big industrial countries are becoming colonialists, one after the other? Can one say that this colonial policy is a luxury for modern nations? No, gentlemen, this policy is a necessity for all of them, in just the same way as outlets themselves."[43]

But the political reasons for having a colonial empire were equally important to Ferry. He was haunted by the need to restore French "greatness." "An irresistible force is impelling the European nations to conquer new lands. . . . This point-to-point race has been going on for barely five years, but from year to year it accelerates, as if gathering its own speed."[44] For France, this colonial race had two consequences. First, she must beware of timorous policies: "In the world as it is, a policy of meditation and abstention is simply the high road to decadence. . . . To try to be influential without doing anything, without involving oneself in world affairs . . . is to descend from the first rank to the third or fourth."[45] France "would not lightly resign herself to being a big Belgium."[46] Secondly, such self-effacement would result in "vacant" territories being occupied by others: that was exactly what had happened in Egypt in 1882, "the day the Chamber of Deputies, swayed by M. Clemenceau's passionate words, left England alone in Egypt."[47] "Should the French flag withdraw from Tonkin, for instance, as some advocate, Germany or Spain would replace us there forthwith. The competition among European nations is increasingly fierce."[48]

Political interests, Ferry felt, could not be measured in terms of "greatness" alone. France was, in fact, "the second maritime power in the world, and, when a country holds such a position, it has interests throughout the world."[49] This was the policy of naval bases.

Ideological motivations probably played a minor part in Jules Ferry's theories, except as rationalizations. There is no reason to doubt his sincerity; at most, one can say he was guilty of naïveté and a kind of robust optimism. Ferry was convinced of the inequality of races: "Gentlemen, we must speak

---

[41] See his speech of July 28, 1885.
[42] *Le Tonkin et la Mère Patrie*, "Preface," and Robiquet, *op. cit.*, V, 557.
[43] Speech of December 11, 1884, *Journal officiel, Débats parlementaires, Sénat, 1884*, p. 1892.
[44] Robiquet, *op. cit.*, V, 555–56.
[45] Speech of July 28, 1885.
[46] Robiquet, *op. cit.*, V, 524.
[47] *Le Tonkin et la Mère Patrie*, p. 36.
[48] Robiquet, *op. cit.*, V, 525.
[49] Address at Perigueux, April 15, 1884, *ibid.*, VI, 275.

more plainly and more truthfully! We must say openly that the superior races . . . I repeat, that the superior races have a right because they have a duty. Their duty is to civilize the inferior races."[50] He was replying to Clemenceau, who had said earlier:

> Superior races? Inferior races? That's easily said. Personally, I have had little use for the distinctions since I heard German scientists offer scientific proof that France should be defeated in the Franco-Prussian War because the French were inferior to the Germans. Since then, I confess, I take a long look before pointing to a man or a civilization and pronouncing them inferior.

The difference in race and, especially, in civilization, gave the superior country special rights, according to Ferry. "There are times when . . . the honor of France demands that we should no longer allow ourselves to be led around by the nose by a barbarous little people."[51]

How, in fact, did Ferry decide to intervene in Tunisia, in the Congo, in Tonkin, and even in Madagascar, and not in other parts of the world? He was opposed to what he called "a policy of hazardous and systematic expansion, a megalomaniac policy, as they say in Italy."[52] But if colonies were not to be sought at random, should not France have a colonial program? Ferry did not favor this. In his great speech of July 28, 1885, he said:

> It has been held against me that I have said that, in these distant undertakings, circumstances often guide policy rather than the reverse. . . . I say, gentlemen, that no colonial enterprise, no matter how great and how productive, no matter what its origin, was ever conceived in full or pursued from the outset in accordance with a set program, in fulfillment of a deliberate purpose.

But between the broad, preconceived plan, and living by circumstances, there are many intermediate positions. Ferry cleverly declared that he had "taken advantage of circumstances" but had not wished to "let himself be guided by chance."

Thus he gave his policy the somewhat curious name of "colonial conservation."[53] There was a continuity between the Third Republic and the preceding regimes that had bequeathed to it, "in trust," rights that must be made to bear fruit. The colonial effort was "based on national traditions."[54] "In a given spot in the world, it is essential to preserve the established structures; in another, to take a step forward; and in another, a decisive, all-embracing solution is required, because the opportunity is there, is passing, and may never recur."[55]

---

[50] Speech of July 28, 1885. Ferry borrowed this expression, which he used frequently, from Albert de Mun.

[51] *Ibid.* (On the other hand, on December 10, 1883, he had called China a "civilized Power.")

[52] *Le Tonkin et la Mère Patrie,* "Preface," and Robiquet, *op. cit.,* V, 555–56.

[53] Speech of December 10, 1883, *Journal officiel, Débats parlementaires, Chambre, 1883,* p. 272.

[54] Speech of October 31, 1883, *ibid.,* p. 2194.

[55] Speech of March 27, 1884, *ibid.,* p. 935.

Ferry's colonial policy, then, may be summed up as follows: (1) **France** should acquire a good part of the available lands, as long as they were being seized by force on every side; (2) she should not extend herself haphazardly, but only around positions she already held; (3) she should be careful in availing herself of opportunities, avoiding both preconceived plans and excessive reliance on luck.

In this global perspective, what was Europe's place? What part did Continental politics play in the French national interest? We know that Ferry sought an accommodation with Germany, particularly in 1884, in order to have his hands free for overseas enterprises. Only the hesitations of the French public and the passionate attacks of the "continentalists" prevented him from proceeding further along this road.

Yet Ferry often said that European politics came first. "The first of these sentiments is a concern and respect for our continental forces, a preoccupation with having the necessary concentration; we must be careful never to undermine it in the slightest degree."[56] Colonization, consequently, must not jeopardize security, but "it is wrong to say that the colonies have weakened the security of the motherland.[57] Moreover—this he did not say in public—"we live on a hand-to-mouth basis, since Bismarck wants peace at any price."[58] Ferry thought one should not overrate Bismarck: "Is one no longer a good Frenchman if one does not confess as an article of faith that in this world Bismarck holds the reins?"

Since Bismarck was fundamentally peace-loving, correct relations could be maintained with him. Ferry wrote, "Unless it is axiomatic that the ideal of French policy is to have difficult relations with Germany in peacetime, we must establish a relationship with Germany, and it is useful to enter into agreements in areas of common interest."[59] This presupposed that republican France would not immure herself "in a discouraged and threatening isolation,"[60] and that she took her place in the concert of Europe—to the extent that such a concert existed. "It is in our interest that there should continue to be a Europe, and that we should be present wherever it assembles"—whence French participation in the Congress of Berlin in 1878 and the Berlin Conference on African Affairs in 1884. We should note, however, that Ferry spoke little, and always as an exception, of possible alliances. It is here that his policy most radically differed from that of the "Europeans" or "continentalists," men hostile or unfavorable to overseas colonies, like Clemenceau, or who regarded them as of secondary importance, like Bismarck.

---

[56] Speech of October 31, 1883, *ibid.*, p. 2194.

[57] Speech of July 28, 1885.

[58] *Lettres de Jules Ferry* (Paris, 1914), letter to Joseph Reinach, September 8, 1886, p. 427.

[59] Letter of August 18, 1884, in *Documents diplomatiques français*, First Series, V, 274, No. 1.

[60] *Le Tonkin et la Mère Patrie*, pp. 34–35.

In contrast to Ferry's theories on France and empire, Bismarck's ideas on the German national interest have been amply studied. They are more or or less "classic," "traditional"; at the same time, Bismarck was original in that he was "satisfied" with the Germany he had created in 1871, rejected any idea of an Anschluss, and practiced a "conservationist" policy. To conserve what he had acquired and to forestall any inclination to revenge on France's part, the "hereditary enemy," he relied primarily on the army and on alliances. It was really he who re-introduced into Europe the system of permanent alliances that had disappeared after the collapse of the Quadruple Alliance in 1815. He felt thoroughly at ease in a system of European equilibrium in which Germany occupied a position of pre-eminence without exercising hegemony.

All this greatly resembles Ferry's European policy, for although Ferry in theory was "unsatisfied" with France's territorial status, he in fact spoke very little of Alsace-Lorraine; he was fundamentally opposed to any idea of "revenge," and for that reason he abhorred Boulanger, "that Minister Bluster who allows his general staff of journalists to set him up, in prose or verse, as General Revenge."

But there was a difference between Ferry and Bismarck. For Ferry, colonies came first. Bismarck, on the other hand, regarded colonial policy only as a means. He wanted to build up rivals to France and to prevent her from finding allies; he wanted to use France to further his domestic policies.[61] Germany entered the colonialist arena in 1884, before the general elections. De Courcel, the French Ambassador, wrote to Ferry: "The colonial issue has become so popular in Germany, and it provides the Chancellor with so useful a theme for the coming elections, that he probably wishes to emphasize before the public the importance he attaches to it himself."[62]

Bismarck very probably looked on colonial conquests—those of others especially—as a means of continuing and completing his European balance-of-power politics. As early as January 10, 1875, he wrote to Hohenlohe that France should be encouraged to conquer Tunisia: "It is no disadvantage to us, nor a tendency to be combatted, that French policy should seek a field of action in North Africa and the Far East. The forces that France uses and ties up there, and the difficulties she makes for herself, will serve as an outlet for her aggressive tendencies in regard to Germany."[63] In 1880, he put it even more plainly: "I believe," he said to Saint-Vallier, "that if you find in the Mediterranean the means of satisfying your natural and legitimate need for expansion, your people at home will feel less bitter about your lost provinces."[64] Bismarck's "conversion" to colonialism was linked, apparently not with any policy of national aggrandizement, but only with

[61] See Eyck, *op. cit.*, III, 396 ff.
[62] *Documents diplomatiques français*, First Series, V, No. 399, September 15, 1884.
[63] *Politique étrangère de l'Allemagne*, Vol. I.
[64] *Documents diplomatiques français*, First Series, V, No. 395, September 13, 1884.

economic considerations: "Our policy is not concerned with the dimensions of our colonial possessions; we seek only to secure access to Africa for German trade."[65]

Thus there was no clear-cut division between "colonialists" and "continentalists," the difference being rather one of emphasis and intensity. In France, "continentalists" like Clemenceau did not gain office at the end of the nineteenth century, and later, Clemenceau was "converted." In the last years of the century, there was a general trend to a policy of synthesis between colonialism and continentalism. Delcassé, who became Foreign Minister in June, 1898, sought both to extend French possessions and to strengthen France's position in Europe. At precisely the same time, Kaiser Wilhelm II launched his *Weltpolitik* in conjunction with a broad program of naval development. The expression itself is proof of the break with a purely European policy. And the British, colonialists by tradition, especially since Disraeli, also arrived at a synthesis—their policy of "splendid isolation" being succeeded by an active policy of European alliances and accommodation.

IV. TRADITIONAL SECURITY AND COLLECTIVE SECURITY

In analyzing how statesmen construed the national interest after World War I, one realizes that the war itself modified their attitudes. After untold suffering, after a slaughter the magnitude of which no one could have foreseen, the complete exhaustion of the people determined the policies of their leaders. Most politicians sincerely believed in peace but had not necessarily made it the first of their concerns; now it became a major objective in its own right. To keep the peace was the aspiration of both the "satisfied" and the "dissatisfied" states, at least during the early postwar years. The only essential difference was that the former desired peace *and* the *status quo*, whereas the latter wanted a peaceful revision of the *Diktats*. Only in the 1930's, with Hitler and Mussolini, did the idea of war as an instrument of policy re-emerge—and then there also arose the idea of a regenerative war, symbolizing the virtues of a strong people. During the 1920's, the German Stresemann no less than the French Briand was disinclined to foresee violence.

But the response of statesmen to these deep aspirations of the people was neither as clear nor as simple as the ordinary citizen would have wished. For no statesman could in fact permit himself to place peace at the absolute summit of his scale of values. A government must in the first place ensure security, and the ideal of security does not precisely coincide with the ideal of peace. Pacifist dreams of nonviolence, nonresistance, the outlawing of war, or unilateral disarmament[66] cannot be accepted *per se* by the men who

[65] *Ibid.*, III, No. 307, November 29, 1884.
[66] See above, Part I, Chapter Eight.

are responsible for ensuring the permanence and the integrity of their states. The apparent pacifist triumphs were never complete, for the governments which the pacifists succeeded in convincing always tempered their high principles with certain reservations. Thus, the Kellogg-Briand Pact provided only for the renunciation of war "as an instrument of national policy"; war remained possible if decided on by the League of Nations. The United States Neutrality Acts of 1935 and 1937, by obliging the President to proclaim an embargo on arms intended for active belligerents, certainly attempted to restrain his executive power and to render war less likely; and a constitutional amendment offered by Congressman Louis Ludlow in 1937 (narrowly defeated in the House of Representatives) would have made a declaration of war subject to popular referendum. But neither the Neutrality Acts nor even the Ludlow Amendment absolutely excluded the eventuality of war. War remained licit—particularly in case of a direct attack upon United States territory.

It is thus clear that a statesman cannot really be a pacifist, and that he must think of security first. But it is equally clear that the essential concern is to find a way of ensuring *both* security *and* peace. This was the theme around which new formulations of the national interest developed in the 1920's. But was it to be peace through collective security, or peace through traditional security? A few examples will show that neither could be applied consistently. Historical studies always reveal that the application of abstract formulas to concrete realities involves modification and adaptation.

One of the best contrasting set of examples of these two concepts is provided by Wilson and Clemenceau. At first sight, their opposition appears complete, and many historians have regarded it as such—John Maynard Keynes, in his celebrated book *The Economic Consequences of the Peace,* drew a misleading picture on that score.[67] On the one hand, Keynes saw Wilson as "this blind and deaf Don Quixote," more of a theologian than a political philosopher, poorly informed, slow to understand, stubborn, easily fooled by cleverer men than he. "Then began the weaving of that web of sophistry and Jesuitical exegesis that was finally to clothe with insincerity the language and substance of the whole treaty." Wilson allowed himself to be duped, according to this view, and concluded an unjust treaty in the name of justice. Facing this simple man—or rather, this man oversimplified by Keynes—was the infinitely subtler Clemenceau. But again, Keynes was guilty of oversimplification when he described Clemenceau's objectives: "He felt about France what Pericles felt of Athens—unique value in her, nothing else mattering; but his theory of politics was Bismarck's. He had one illusion—France; and one disillusion—mankind, including Frenchmen, and his colleagues not least."

[67] New York and London, 1920. See Chapter III, "The Conference."

The literary beauty of these passages, the apparent logic of the contrast, make it difficult for the historian to shake off Keynesian prejudices. Yet the documents show that the conflict between the two men was much less marked, much subtler. This becomes apparent if one compares them both with Lloyd George.

A. THE EXAMPLE OF WOODROW WILSON

Wilson's interpretation of the "national interest" has been often and abundantly studied. (The relevant documents are numberless, Wilson's private papers open to study; they in no way contradict the public documents. There is no need, therefore, to support the basic themes with direct citations, and our analysis will concentrate on the special nuances of his theories.) As far as "national security" was concerned, Wilson's conception was both novel—the "New Diplomacy" based on the League of Nations—and traditional. He was influenced by the moralist tradition of the United States and by the currents of liberalism originating in Britain and in France,[68] and he dreamed of a world in which international affairs would be transformed by a new type of security, a so-called collective security.

"What we seek is the reign of law, based upon the consent of the governed, and sustained by the organized opinion of mankind."[69] But public opinion was not enough. Law, as Pascal had said, must be backed by force—"Force, Force to the utmost, Force without stint or limit, the righteous and triumphant Force which shall make Right the law of the world, and cast every selfish dominion down in the dust."[70] This force, which the United States employed in the war, would belong to the League of Nations, not as an autonomous international force, but as a coalition of all peoples against aggressors.

Even before America's entry into the war, Wilson made it clear, in his great address in the Senate on January 22, 1917, that he conceived of this collective force as "so much greater than the force of any nation now engaged or any alliance hitherto formed or projected that no nation, no probable combination of nations, could face or withstand it."[71] He described it elsewhere as a "well-established concert of power."

Wilson definitely believed that the League would make possible the

---

[68] See Arno Mayer, *The Political Origins of the New Diplomacy, 1917–1918* (New Haven, 1959).

[69] Address at Mount Vernon, July 4, 1918, cited in R. S. Baker, *Woodrow Wilson and World Settlement* (New York, 1922), I, 12.

[70] Speech of April 6, 1918, in *Woodrow Wilson: Presidential Messages, Addresses and Public Papers, 1917–1924* (New York, 1927), Vol. III: *War and Peace*, p. 202.

[71] Woodrow Wilson, *Why We Are at War: Messages to Congress, January–April, 1917*, pp. 7–8.

creation of such a force and that this force would ensure security; disarmament, which he envisaged in the fourth of his Fourteen Points, would be carried out only insofar as this force existed.

But behind this universalism, Wilson's realism soon emerged. First, he was prepared to make concrete concessions in order to give the League a greater chance of success. Thus, he resigned himself to accepting German rights in Shantung being turned over to Japan (instead of China) so as to make sure that Japan would accede to the League of Nations. One scholar has interpreted Wilson's position on this point as follows: if Japan did not enter the League, "there was the danger of a Japanese-Russian-German alliance, and a return to the old 'balance of power' system in the world, on a greater scale than ever before. He knew . . . that he would be accused of violating his own principles, but nevertheless he *must* work for world order and organization against anarchy and a return to the old militarism."[72]

He did not intend, however, to reject this militarism for the United States, which, he believed, would be the principal power in the future League. After some hesitations, he authorized in 1916 a program to build up naval armaments, so that America would have, as he put it, "the strongest navy in the world." We should note the remarkable ease with which he identified the interests of the United States with those of humanity. The United States, he told Isaiah Bowman in late 1918, was "the only disinterested people at the Peace Conference."[73] America, he had said earlier, "was born into the world to do mankind service":

> My dream is that, as the years go by and the world knows more and more of America, it . . . . will turn to America for those moral inspirations which lie at the basis of all freedom; that the world will never fear America unless it feels that it is engaged in some enterprise which is inconsistent with the rights of humanity; and that America will come into the full light of the day when all shall know that she puts human rights above all other rights, and that her flag is the flag not only of America, but of humanity.[74]

With such a doctrine, one is sure of being always in the right, and those who see it as merely exaggerated idealism surely misjudge the power it gives to American positions. Wilson's universalism, then, never neglected the interests of the United States. In the name of the United States' special "mission," Wilson could successively proclaim neutrality, attempt to serve as a mediator, make peace proposals, proclaim the principle of peace without victory, break off diplomatic relations with Germany, enter the war, develop a program of peace based on victory, and intervene in the Peace Conference. And he could regard himself as the only real representative of world opinion,

---

[72] Baker, *op. cit.*, II, 266.

[73] Charles Seymour, ed., *The Intimate Papers of Colonel House* (Boston and New York, 1928), IV, Chap. 9, 280.

[74] From a speech of July 4, 1914, cited in Baker, *op. cit.*, I, 18.

of the weak nations, vis-à-vis Europe's ambitious leaders. The gigantic role he cast himself in was consequently out of all proportion. That he ultimately failed was the result not of the ineffectiveness of his methods, but of lack of understanding on the part of the American people. Americans felt their security so well assured in their traditional isolationism that they did not think· it wise to place their country's immense power at the service of a complex international agency. Wilson was defeated, not, as Keynes would have it, by the weakness of his own ideas, but by a narrow "nationalism."

B. THE EXAMPLE OF CLEMENCEAU

Was Clemenceau the antithesis of Wilson? On most points, the two men were in fact in agreement. The old Radical militant could. recall that he too had always backed the cause of justice against excessive national ambitions. The Europe that Clemenceau wanted was a Europe based on the rule of law. He put it succinctly in the political testament written at the very end of his life:

> A Europe founded on right, instead of a dismembered Europe, was a fine dramatic turn of events. Our victory did not allow us to hesitate. The nations had appeared on the battlefield in response to our appeal. The shedding of blood and the winning of rights went together. . . . Dying nations were about to revive. Throughout Europe the words "right," "liberty," and "justice" would mean something. Already deputies were coming to us from the tortured towns and provinces, raising their bow.ed heads and demanding reparations. We promised this, and we have kept our promise.[75]

It should not be imagined that Clemenceau was thus placing a belated halo of justice over a cynical achievement. The records of his meetings with the other members of the Council of Four furnish abundant proof that Clemenceau sought a just peace. For example, when Wilson, on May 26, 1919, proposed to the Italians that a plebiscite be held in Istria, Orlando refused but Clemenceau fully supported Wilson and condemned an Italian policy based on strategic considerations: "I beg you not to offer us a solution which would be nothing more than a continuation of the war. I do not repudiate the Treaty of London. But we have to recognize the truth in what President Wilson has said. At a given moment, we glimpsed this great ideal of the liberation of all peoples, and since then our policy has necessarily been modified."[76]

This relative similarity of ideals notwithstanding, Clemenceau differed profoundly from Wilson in his general philosophy of international relations and on the specific details of the Paris peace settlement.

---

[75] *Grandeur and Misery of Victory* (New York, 1930), p. 193.

[76] See Paul Mantoux, *Les Délibérations du Conseil des Quatre (24 Mars–28 Juin 1919)* (Paris, 1955), II, 227.

In the first place, he was infinitely more skeptical about the chances of achieving justice, a problem he discussed in some of the finest pages of his book *Au soir de la pensée*: "Justice," he writes, "is an abstraction on the absolute level; man, a complex of relativities." Whereas ideology "knows no obstacle" and firmly fixes itself in an utopian world, reality demands the recognition that a just peace is only just in relative terms and does not exclude the possibility of future war. "Justice and injustice in their turn will be gained by force. But force changes place constantly, just like the ideal of justice. How many irreparable miscalculations in our ideal solution!"[77] Wilson, he said, was the "inspired prophet of a noble ideological venture"—that was both his exceptional greatness, which Clemenceau emphasized, and his weakness, since he believed that the League of Nations would of itself assure the victory of an ideology. "There are probably few examples of such a misreading and disregarding of political experience in the maelstrom of abstract thought."[78]

For Clemenceau, as for Pascal, whom he cited with admiration, justice must be backed by force, and the force of the League of Nations was inadequate. At the same time, force must not violate justice, and that was a difficulty.

Against Wilson, Clemenceau fiercely defended the necessity of protecting French security—by permanently occupying the Rhineland and politically severing it from Germany. "We are offered the League of Nations as an instrument for affording us the security we need. I accept that instrument. But if the League of Nations were unable to enforce its decisions by military sanctions, we should have to find such sanctions elsewhere."[79] Against Foch or Poincaré, on the other hand, he rejected the idea that the occupation of the Rhineland should be a national ambition. Clemenceau's only territorial claim—to the southern Saar—was based on "rules of justice and common sense. . . . It is erroneous to believe that the world operates on abstract principles."[80] The annexation of this small territory, he maintained, was both just and necessary.[81] At the same time, it was preferable to maintain good relations with the Allies than to attempt to annex more land. "The drive to the Rhine was the tradition of our ancestors," he said during the French parliamentary debate on ratification of the Paris Peace Treaty, but, he added, "Is it my fault if, now, when I march toward the Rhine, I find German populations in my path?"[82]

---

[77] *Au Soir de la Pensée* (Paris, 1927), II, 405–8.
[78] *Grandeur and Misery of Victory*, pp. 167, 173.
[79] Mantoux, *op. cit.*, I, 45 (March 27).
[80] *Ibid.*, I, 70 (March 28).
[81] The Saarland, a rich coal-producing region north of Lorraine and southeast of Luxembourg, had become part of France in 1766 but was divided between Prussia and Bavaria in 1815. By the Treaty of Versailles in 1919, its coal mines were assigned to France and its territory placed under a League of Nations administration.
[82] Speech of September 25, 1919, *Journal officiel, Débats parlementaires, Chambre, 1919.*

Thus, to Clemenceau, the detachment of the Rhineland from Germany was not an element of the French national interest. It was a means of providing *security*. Security alone was the goal, whether it was assured by the detachment of the Rhineland, or by treaties of guarantee signed with the United States and Great Britain, or, failing these, by recourse to Article 429 of the peace treaty, which provided for extending the occupation. But on precisely this point lay the essential difference between Clemenceau and Wilson. Clemenceau did not believe in collective security; Wilson believed only in collective security. For Wilson, German disarmament, the demilitarization of the Rhineland, the temporary occupation—these were minor details compared with the great idea of the League. For Clemenceau, the League of Nations was at best a contributory force for security, which in the end could only be achieved by traditional methods. There was to be no more severe judge than he of the "so-called League of Nations."[83]

C. The Example of Lloyd George

We shall not attempt any detailed presentation of Lloyd George's successive views on what constituted the British national interest. The "crafty Welshman" was a man of great mobility, with a remarkable ability to change his viewpoint according to altering circumstances or because he sensed changes in public opinion. Orlando found him one of the most prodigiously intelligent men he had ever encountered, less profound than quick, but of really extraordinary quickness. His changing positions, Orlando thought, were due not to volubility or inconstancy but to a realistic sense of how external conditions were fluctuating.[84] All this shows how difficult it is to "nail him down."

Still, one can place him in relation to Wilson and Clemenceau. Although he nearly always supported the former, he resembled the latter more closely in his approach to the problem of security. For him, collective security was subordinate, and he envisaged the future in terms of traditional security. His terms of course were different from, even contradictory to Clemenceau's. An anecdote related by Jean Martet illustrates this well. One day, Clemenceau told Martet, he met Lloyd George in London, and Lloyd George asked him whether there was anything which he (Clemenceau) held against him. Clemenceau answered that there was—namely, that, within an hour of the armistice, he had had the impression that the British had again become the enemies of France, to which Lloyd George replied by asking whether that had not always been the traditional policy of his country.[85]

Indeed, Lloyd George does not seem to have departed appreciably from traditional British policies. He had a sincere horror of war, but, he pointed

---

[83] *Au Soir de la pensée*, II, 404.
[84] *Memorie, 1915–1919* (Milan, 1960), pp. 356, 357.
[85] Jean Martet, *Le Tigre* (Paris, 1930), p. 59.

out, national honor was a reality, and any nation that ignored it was lost. And Great Britain's honor had been involved because, he said, she had been pledged to defend the independence, the liberty, and the integrity of a small, peaceable, neighboring country. Victory, he told the war cabinet on March 20, 1917, would be one "in which the British Empire will lead. It will easily then be the first Power in the world. And I rejoice in that not merely for selfish reasons, but because, with all its faults, the British Empire is the truest representative of freedom—in the spirit even more than in the letter of its institutions."[86] On the same occasion, he enumerated British war aims: the evacuation of German forces from lands they occupied, and the restoration of independence on the basis of "national rights" (including Poland's) —goals that would ensure a more durable peace; secondary aims were the creation of a "peace league," the "democratization" of Europe, and the "destruction of the Turkish empire."

Faithful once more to his country's traditions, Lloyd George also desired the abolition of standing armies.[87] He wished to return, as far as it was possible, to the position of "nonintervention." On April 16, 1919, he told Parliament, "there is the fundamental principle of all foreign policy in this country—a very sound principle—that you should never interfere in the internal affairs of another country, however badly governed."[88] This would apply, for instance, to Bolshevik Russia, once the war was over, and soon, also, to Poland and the Balkan states. The trend was clearly back to Britain's policy of "splendid isolation."

On the subject of a European balance of power, Lloyd George said nothing, but he seems to have thought of it constantly. Before 1914, he had told Count Metternich "that the real ground for the growing antagonism in this country towards Germany was not jealousy of her rapidly developing commerce but fear of her growing navy."[89] Once the German navy was destroyed, it was hard not to imagine (as Clemenceau did) that France would be regarded as the potential adversary. In any case, Lloyd George made repeated references to the necessity of "not destroying Germany." "Our generals believe that a large French army on the Rhine will endanger the peace of Europe.[90]

All these tenets of Lloyd George's political creed combined with his faith in the future of a rejuvenated Commonwealth, present nothing new. He appears more of a traditionalist, even more of a nationalist, than Wilson—and also than Clemenceau. What particularly distinguishes him is the extreme importance he attached to Britain's economic interests. Wilson's New Diplomacy and Clemenceau's "security" took precedence over the idea of

---

[86] David Lloyd George, *War Memoirs* (London, 1934), IV, 1784.
[87] *Ibid.*, 1756.
[88] David Lloyd George, *Memoirs of the Peace Conference* (New Haven, 1939), I, 378.
[89] *War Memoirs*, I, 12.
[90] Mantoux, *op. cit.*, II, 272 (June 2).

accumulating wealth, of material expansion; in contrast, Lloyd George favored "economics first." In his program of March 20, 1917, he declared: "I shall be very disappointed if this war does not lead to a reconstruction of our own country in many respects, economic and industrial . . . the relation of capital and labor, the conditions of life amongst the people, and generally in an improvement, in a raising of the standard of life of the vast multitudes of this kingdom."[91]

Lloyd George's statements at the meetings of the Council of the Four show this concern for economic issues conclusively. On the first day of the meetings, it was Lloyd George who raised the question of war reparations. On the next day, he demanded 30 per cent for Britain—since he had introduced military pensions there. But he also considered the question of the various countries' capacity to pay, which he estimated far more realistically than did Loucheur. One could not "make extravagant promises without keeping them," he said. And, when the question of the Saar came up, his first question was, "What is the annual production of the Saar basin?"; one of his objections to the French policy position in favor of dividing the Saarland was that "the unity of this industrial region should be maintained." Again, he opposed the idea of military occupations to ensure payment of reparations and preferred the economic weapon of a blockade. And he favored the idea that Poland should pay reparations for Upper Silesia if she annexed that province! The few questions he raised concerning the city of Fiume[92] on April 3 were even more revealing of his "economist's" turn of mind: Had not Fiume once been a great port? When had the railroad been built? Had the Hungarian Government initiated these developments? What were Hungary's and Bohemia's outlets? Did Yugoslav banks have any branches in Croatia? What trades did the Italians in Fiume practice?[93] And in 1921, Lloyd George took the same line, for the vast British plan of December, 1921, for the economic restoration of Europe (combined with a treaty guaranteeing French security) had an "essentially economic" purpose.[94]

Despite all their contrasts, Wilson, Clemenceau, and Lloyd George all belonged to "satisfied" countries. (It is true that Britain and France, following colonial tradition, as it were, gained additional control through the mandate system over former German colonies and Ottoman provinces. But this was in the nature of a luxury. Lloyd George had told the war cabinet in

[91] *War Memoirs*, IV, 1775.

[92] Fiume, now called Rieka, was a city on the Adriatic coast that during its long history had been variously held by Austria, Croatia, France, and Hungary, but that was occupied by Italy in 1918. Its disposal became an issue that caused Italy to leave the Paris Peace Conference in 1919. Occupied by irregular troops under D'Annunzio during that year, it was set up as an independent free city in the Treaty of Rapallo between Italy and Yugoslavia in 1920.

[93] Mantoux, *op. cit.*, I, 28 (March 26), 65 and 68 (March 28), 90 (March 31), 127 and 133–37 (April 3).

[94] See Georges Suarez, *Briand* (Paris, 1938–52), V, 342.

1917 that he was not eager to add further millions of square miles to the British Empire. As for Wilson, he went further and refused a possible mandate over Armenia. [It would anyway have aggravated his difficulties with the Senate.]) In contrast to the "satisfied" countries, concerned with conservation and security, there were the "dissatisfied," revisionist nations. In order to have a more complete picture of the ways that statesmen may subjectively view their nations' interests, we now turn to one example of an aggressive imperialist. The wealth of sources illuminating his program, and the clarity of his plans, make him a good subject for study.

V. HITLER'S CONCEPT OF LEBENSRAUM

"The German Reich," Hitler wrote to Neville Chamberlain on August 23, 1939, "like every other state, possesses certain definite interests which it is impossible to renounce."[95] The expression of "definite interests" would indicate that Hitler had a well-planned program in the international sphere and that it was so to speak restrictive. But if the plan existed, its outline was unclear. Indeed, Hitler's originality consists in the fact that *three* plans were superimposed on one another in his mind: one was to wipe out the humiliation of the Versailles *Diktat* and force its revision; the second was to unite Germans within a greater Reich; the third was to conquer for this Reich a vast expanse of land to live in, a *Lebensraum,* beyond its own frontiers.

If one compares Hitler with most of the German statesmen of the Weimar Republic, one can see that they shared identity of views on the first point. Stresemann, just like Hitler, fought for the recognition of the principle of equal rights, *Gleichberechtigung.* He rejected the idea of "German culpability" and unworthiness to possess colonies. He was hostile, like all Germans, to the occupation, to reparations, to the internationalization of the Saar, to Germany's enforced unilateral disarmament. Stresemann also shared Hitler's views on the second point: the gathering together of Germans within a great empire. In a famous letter to the Crown Prince, he advocated the "readjustment of our eastern frontiers; the recovery of Danzig and the Polish corridor; and a correction of the frontier in Upper Silesia. In the background stands the union with German Austria."[96]

But Stresemann envisaged limits to this greater Germany. He freely ceded Alsace and Lorraine under the Treaty of Locarno, as well as Eupen and Malmédy. He was not concerned, apparently, with the Sudeten Germans, with the southern Tyrol under Italian sovereignty, or with the Baltic states. Hitler, on the other hand, coveted all these territories, whatever he may have

---

[95] *Documents on German Foreign Policy, 1918–1945,* from the archives of the German Foreign Ministry (Washington, 1956), Series D, Vol. VII, No. 201.
[96] Eric Sutton, ed., *Gustav Stresemann: His Diaries and Papers* (London, 1937), II, 503.

said for purely tactical reasons (for instance, his solemn declaration that he was "sacrificing" Alsace and Lorraine). And his racist views were curiously linked with his linguistic theories that all who spoke German should belong to the greater Reich; he regarded Croats and Slovenes as Germans who had forgotten their language—which would justify the annexation of Trieste. On October 15, 1943, after the Italian capitulation, he appointed a *Gauleiter und Reichstatthalter* for the "zone of operation of the Adriatic littoral" (Trieste, Ljubljana, Gorizia, Friuli, Istria)—territories he regarded as German.[97]

Hitler's real originality, then, lay in his concept of *Lebensraum*.

He set out the principle clearly in *Mein Kampf*. There were four ways, he said, of feeding a German population that was increasing by nearly 900,000 a year. One was birth control, as practiced in France; that, however, flouted the will of nature. The second was domestic colonization: but one cannot exploit a limited amount of natural resources indefinitely; the policy would lead in the end to famine, and then nature would make its selections and eliminate the weak. The third was to acquire new territories. The fourth was to increase German settlements abroad through commercial and colonial means.

Of these four solutions, Hitler of course chose the third—the conquest of new territories, of "living space." These territories he saw basically as those lying east of Europe. He was not very interested in colonies. He wanted to recover former German colonies, and he also talked of Morocco, but his objective here was simply to wipe out past humiliations. The German *Lebensraum* would be the great plains inhabited by the inferior Slav race: "We must calmly and coldly adopt the view that it cannot be in accordance with the divine will that one people should possess fifty times more territories than another." The "one people," of course, were the Slavs, whereas the territorially underprivileged nation was Germany. The "rights" of the superior race was clearly stated. The doctrine of Aryan superiority inherited from Gobineau, Vacher de Lapouge, Houston Stewart Chamberlain, and others was here combined with the pseudo-scientific theories of geopolitics championed by Karl Haushofer.[98] The superior race needed land because land was a source of power; *Lebensraum* was much more a source of power than an appetite for raw materials. Roosevelt, consequently, like Sumner Welles, was wrong when he thought, as early as 1937, that Hitler could be stopped if he were given free access to raw materials. Hitler wanted conquest, and the idea of justice never overly worried him: "We are not concerned with having justice on our side, but solely with victory," he told his generals on August 22, 1939. "Close your hearts to pity. Act brutally. . . . The stronger man is right. . . . On the one hand, we have highly civilized people in Europe who are reduced to stonebreaking. On the other hand, we

---

[97] Louis P. Lockner, ed., *The Goebbels Diaries, 1942–1943* (New York, 1948), p. 474.
[98] See above, Chapter One, p. 19.

have those stupid masses in the east. It is for those masses to do our menial chores."[99]

It is interesting to analyze the limits that Hitler set on German "living space." We cannot rely on his various concepts of "division into zones of influence" (for instance, as he described them to Molotov in Berlin in November, 1940), but in *Mein Kampf*, indistinctly, and more clearly in statements made after June 22, 1941, when Germany was winning major victories, we can find more accurate information.

> Many people thought, after World War I, that we should look toward the mineral wealth of the west, toward the raw materials in the colonies, toward gold. Personally, I have always considered the possession of land in the east as indispensable to us, and I have no reason to alter my opinion today.[100]

Why this ambition? Because "it is ridiculous to think of a world policy when we do not dominate the continent. . . . For a colonial policy to have any meaning we must first dominate Europe. In any case, it is only our Cameroons that I should like to possess again—nothing else!"[101]

It was thus Europe in the traditional sense—that is, extending to the Urals—that Hitler wished to conquer. As a measure of security, the frontier might be drawn some 150 miles east of that mountain range. Along a kind of Limes Germanicus, soldier-settlers would if necessary repel "barbarians" from Siberia. "It is our duty to place [this frontier] where we want it."[102] Within the "living space," there were to be apparently two types of colonization. There were to be German peasant colonies, possibly also Dutch, Norwegian, and Danish ones too "and even Swedes, on an individual basis,"[103] in the Baltic states, the Ukraine, and the Crimea; elsewhere, German cities would be connected by highways and each surrounded by a circle twenty miles deep of "beautiful villages. . . . whatever lies beyond is another world in which we intend to allow the Russians to live as they please. All that is necessary is that we control them. In case of a revolution, we can simply drop a few bombs on their towns, and the whole business will be settled."

This system would produce several results. First, Germans would no longer be permitted to emigrate to America. Secondly, they would get "the feel of great spaces." The immense Europe thus created would be able to live as an autarky. It would give up "the desire to export goods all over the world" and would become "an impregnable fortress protected from any threat of blockade."[104]

---

[99] *Documents on German Foreign Policy, 1918–1945*, Series D, Vol. VII, Appendix 1, p. 559, No. 193; and Adolf Hitler, *Libres propos sur la guerre et la paix* (ed., Martin Bormann) (Paris, 1952), Note 68, November 12, 1941.

[100] *Libres propos*, Note 12, July 27–28, 1941.

[101] *Ibid.*, Note 53, October 26–27, and Note 45, October 18.

[102] *Ibid.*, Note 23, September 23.

[103] *Ibid.*, Note 11, July 27.

[104] *Ibid.*, Note 20, September 17–18, and Note 25, September 25.

What role would other European peoples play in this system? As far as can be determined, Hitler envisaged a pyramid in which the relative positions would depend on the percentage of Aryan blood in a people's veins. At the top, lording it over all, would be Greater Germany. Then would come a group of peoples who could be progressively Germanized Scandinavians, Dutch, even English. (Hitler admired England and foresaw the day when Germany and England would march together against America. "I believe that this war will mark the beginning of a lasting friendship with England. But first we have to deal it a knock-out blow. The Englishman is capable of respecting only a man who has first put him out of action."[105] Norway would be "the central power station of northern Europe; Norwegians will thus at last have a European mission to fulfill."[106] The Swiss, on the other hand, would only just qualify as innkeepers. Below all these would come the satellites: the Latin countries—France, Italy, Spain, Portugal, Romania—and Hungary and Greece. Below even them would come the Slavs, born to be slaves, to whom access to higher education would be forbidden. As for the most inferior race of all, the Jews, it would be exterminated.

Beyond this Europe, with its African dependencies (Italy would extend its dominion from Tunisia to Suez and the Indian Ocean, and France would be compensated at the expense of the British Empire—at least, so Darlan was promised at Berchtesgaden in May, 1941), what would happen to the rest of the world? Except in the short foreword to *Mein Kampf*, Hitler does not seem to have thought in terms of global domination. Setting aside the Russian "barbarians" of Siberia, he seems to have envisaged two other great world powers, both of them autarkies: the United States in the Western Hemisphere, and Japan in the Far East. Hitler recalled that, at the time of the fall of Port Arthur, the Czechs in his class at school had wept, "whereas we were jubilant! That was the time my feeling for Japan was born."[107] But his racism would not permit him to accept Japan as a Great Power save to the degree that it came under Aryan influence:

If, as of now, Aryan influence should cease to operate in Japan . . . Japan's advances in the sciences and technology might continue for a while; but after a few years, the source would dry up, the specific Japanese characteristics would come to the fore again, and its present civilization would become petrified, returning to the slumber from which it was awakened, seventy years ago, by the wave of Aryan civilization.[108]

This, then, is how Hitler saw the world of the future at the time of his

---

[105] *Ibid.*, Note 6, July 22–23.
[106] *Ibid.*, Note 16, August 2.
[107] *Ibid.*, Note 21, September 21.
[108] Mein Kampf, Chapter XI, "Nation and Race," Sec. 6.

greatest triumphs, the world he hoped to create to last for a thousand years. Not that there weren't pathological features about his concept—but it was in any case a subjective concept concerning the national interests of his country, to be examined like those of any other political leader.

Having elaborated this concept, Hitler turned his ruthless energy to the task of putting it into effect. Some of his acts, if not all of them, may be explained in terms of these objectives he had set himself. For Hitler was not content either to endure or merely to use the underlying forces that help to shape his country and its foreign affairs. He constantly outstripped or disregarded them. When he wanted to recover Danzig and the Polish Corridor, he had the support of many Germans who thought that the Corridor violated their most sacred rights. But can it be said that the same ineluctable forces obliged him to attack the Soviet Union or exterminate the Jews? No, it was because the conquest of *Lebensraum* was a central part of his plans, that he took the tremendous risk, which was to prove fatal to him; it was because he firmly believed in the validity of his racist theory that, with no compelling force to urge him on, he ordered the Jewish massacres. The impression is of a series of "gratuitous" acts emanating from a single man—functions of his ideas, not of external forces.

This will to conquer obviously implied war. For pacifism, Hitler had nothing but contempt. But he was not so mad as to want war for war's sake. For him, it was simply an element of necessary risk. He made his position clear at a meeting reported in the "Hossbach Protocol" of November 5, 1937. "Only violence can effect a solution of the German problem, and violence is inseparable from risk." Without wanting war, Hitler knew that his politics made war inevitable. Unlike pacifists, or even reasonable statesmen, he did not abhor war; he saw in it the operation of the "law of selection," which "allows the best to survive." "War," he said, "has returned to its primitive form. War between one people and another is giving way to another war—aimed at the possession of vast territories. Originally, war was nothing but a struggle for the possession of pastureland. Today, it is a struggle for the possession of natural riches. These riches, by virtue of an immanent law, belong to him who conquers them."[109]

Between a statesman's views on the national interest and the results he ultimately achieves there is always a margin, sometimes an abyss—the distance that separates the dream from reality. Yet, whatever the compelling force of circumstances, the study of political leaders' conceptions of the national interest is not irrelevant. The will of the political leader can alter the course of history.

---

[109] *Libres propos*, Note 32, October 10, 1941.

11

THE INFLUENCE OF BASIC
FORCES ON THE STATESMAN

That there is a relation between the collective forces which constitute the "infrastructure" of international relations and that privileged individual, the statesman in office, is clear. But how do these forces exert their influence? How does the statesman attempt to resist or temper them? In this and the following chapter, we shall try to answer these two questions—at least partially.

We shall examine first the problem of how underlying historical forces influence the statesman. He, after all, is one of the people, which is the source of these economic and ideological forces. Like everyone else, he is subject, consciously or unconsciously, to many pressures: there is direct pressure, concretely applied by representatives of "pressure groups"; indirect pressure, by which various groups, or even the public as a whole, acts or moves so as to force him to take certain decisions; the general "atmosphere"—the economic state of the nation and the prevailing "state of mind," not necessarily as they exist objectively, but as the statesman assesses them; finally, social pressure, the complex of educational, environmental, and class prejudices which affect statesmen as they affect all men (even if they are not always aware of it).

I. DIRECT PRESSURE

The statesman devotes a great part of his time to receiving people. He sees his assistants and subordinates, but also persons or delegations who are not dependent on him. The tasks these persons take on is that of "asking" for things—for support in a job, for honors, for patronage, but also for changes in current policy. The demands carry greater weight in proportion as the person or delegation represents greater "forces" in the country, larger groups, wider interests. The nature of the conversation between the statesman and his guests may vary between exchange of information, arguments, appeals to the national interest, and also threats or blackmail. To gain satisfaction, "pressure groups" may announce that if their demands are not met, they will take reprisals: a bank may threaten to refuse to assist the government; a union may threaten to organize social disturbances or appeals to the public.

Of course, for such representations to reach the appropriate level of authority, they must not have been intercepted at a lower level. A filtering process usually takes place, whereby the closest associates of the man at the top decide whom he should see, whom they should see themselves and then report on (whence the importance of accurate reports), and who should not be received at all. Ministerial waiting rooms are haunted by the importunate, the deranged, and the visionary. The public records reveal hundreds of letters from bizarre individuals, utopians, "purveyors of advice." The problem of how to filter them out concerns all government departments; the agencies concerned in foreign affairs are certainly not the ones where such representations are most frequent. Most interests of groups are more closely related to the domestic departments and ministries—finance, economy, labor, commerce, etc. Nevertheless, foreign offices are not exempt from solicitations and pressure.

There are pressures, first, concerning material interests: certain foreign-policy measures may have economic implications; as a matter of fact, this is more and more frequent in contemporary international life. And in the realm of ideology, pressures may be brought to bear to have action taken or to prevent action that has been planned or undertaken by the government. In addition to representations on general themes ("anti-war," "pro-disarmament," "pro-decolonization"), there are innumerable ones on specific points: requests for intervention in favor of a man sentenced to death in another country, for an embargo on arms shipments to a particular power, for the severance of diplomatic relations as a form of protest, and sometimes (more seldom) for armed intervention.

The historian's problem is to discover exactly what representations were made and how successful they were. Very often, neither the politician nor his interlocutor wish anything to be known of their conversation. That is of course the case whenever the politician makes concessions in exchange for personal, financial, or other advantages. When this comes out in the open, there is a "scandal," especially since the public has become more conscious of its power in this respect. In the eighteenth century, certain ministers "sold themselves" almost openly. Talleyrand had no hesitation about it. But the advances of liberalism and democracy have sensitized the public, and where such practices now exist, they must be carefully concealed. But many perfectly honest representations remain unheard of, for different reasons.

When a government official and a banker, for instance, have a private conversation at a reception, they are observed, but who knows what they say to each other? There are times when statesmen deliberately escape the journalists; Briand and Stresemann went off alone for a tête-à-tête lunch at

Thoiry in 1926. Indeed, history reveals that extreme precautions have very often been taken to guard the secrets of a discussion. Painstaking statesmen—men like Cavour, Stresemann, or Barthou—took careful notes on their conversations, but the careless, like Napoleon III, were little concerned to do so. Papers in the files of banks, companies, and associations may perhaps be more instructive concerning some of these negotiations than the public records.

Valuable studies are available that show that such negotiations are at most times constantly in progress,[1] but we still have no clear notion about how this type of influence operates. Interpretations differ widely on their effect in this or that colonial conquest; some think it wholly economic—direct pressures exerted by the companies concerned; others prefer political explanations—the will to power, the desire for prestige, strategic interests.[2]

An example will give some idea of the nature of these direct pressures: we have ample information concerning representations made by Harvey Firestone, the tire-company tycoon, to the White House and State Department in early 1933 (particularly between January 17 and February 27) with a view to securing American intervention in Liberia.[3]

Great Britain, which controlled 80 per cent of the world's rubber production, had set strict limits on the cultivation and export of rubber under the Stevenson Rubber Restriction Act. The price had risen from $.15 per pound in 1922 to $1.23 in 1925. American companies using rubber, Firestone in particular, turned to the problem of developing rubber sources outside the British Empire—for instance, in Liberia—and Firestone invested $10 million in Liberia to that end. In this, he had been strongly encouraged by Herbert Hoover, at the time Secretary of Commerce. In December, 1932, however, Liberia, wishing to shake off the yoke that Firestone's dominance had placed on the country with no appreciable benefit to the national treasury, declared a moratorium on its debts and took various other measures hostile

---

[1] See, for example, Bertrand Gille on the politics of the Rothschilds, *Lettres adressées à la maison Rothschild de Paris par son répresentant à Bruxelles (Louis Richtenberger)*, Vol. I: *Crise politique et financière en Belgique (1838–1840)* (Louvain, 1961); Jean Bouvier on the role of the Union Générale, *Le Krach de l'Union Générale* (Paris, 1960); and Claude Fohlen on the activities of French textile concerns during the American Civil War, *L'Industrie textile au temps du Second Empire* (Paris, 1955).

[2] See Henri Brunschwig, *French Colonialism 1871–1914: Myths and Realities* (New York and London, 1966), which emphasizes the primacy of the political element; and reviews of the original French edition of this book by Lucien Genet, *Revue historique* (Paris), July–September, 1962, pp. 219–20 and Marcel Emerit, *Annales des sciences politiques* (Paris), November–December, 1962, pp. 1206.

[3] See especially Jay Pierrepont Moffat, *The Moffat Papers* (Cambridge, Mass., 1956); *Papers Relating to Foreign Relations of the United States, 1933*, II, 880 ff.; Alfred Lief, *Harvey Firestone* (New York, 1951); Nnamdi Azikiwe, *Liberia in World Politics* (London, 1934); and George W. Brown, *The Economic History of Liberia* (Washington, D.C., 1941).

to the American company's interests. An International Committee on **Liberia** had been set up at the League of Nations under the chairmanship of **an** Englishman, Viscount Cecil. Firestone was convinced that this committee was hostile to American interests, and he wanted the United States to intervene directly in Liberia—for instance, by dispatching a naval vessel there, the implication being a possible future use of force.

Without going into too great detail, let us look at the series of steps Harvey Firestone and his son now took. On January 17, 1933, they approached Under Secretary of State William R. Castle, who promised to back them.

Next, they went to see Henry Stimson, the Secretary of State, and "took up two hours of his valuable time."[4] They knew that President Hoover was well disposed toward them, both because he had formerly encouraged their investment and because Firestone was an influential member of the National Committee of the Republican Party. But Stimson was more restrained. He knew that, on the following March 4, a Democratic administration would take over, with Franklin D. Roosevelt and Cordell Hull. Moreover, he had undertaken to cooperate with the League of Nations in regard to Liberia and did not share the view that Lord Cecil was maneuvering against Firestone's interests. Then too, he disliked the idea of armed intervention against weaker countries, and knew what sort of repercussions this would mean in Latin America. To cap it all, the Firestones' tactics were "deplorable." "Knowing that he [Stimson] likes terse, clear-cut statements, and a logically built up case, they wandered all around the field for three-quarters of an hour before coming to the point, and even read aloud eight pages of what purported to be purloined minutes of the Liberian Cabinet impeaching Lord Cecil's integrity."[5] (This charge Stimson repudiated with indignation.) The upshot was that Stimson agreed to support them, but along his lines, not theirs.

On leaving Stimson, the two men went to see Jay Pierrepont Moffat, chief of the State Department's Bureau of Western European Affairs, and spent another hour with him. They explained that they wanted *immediate* action on the Liberian issue (which would then tie the hands of the future Democratic administration, with which their pressure tactics would be less effective.)

On January 24, further representations were made, after Liberia had rejected an American note. The Firestones had seen Hoover earlier and had requested him to send a warship to Africa, a suggestion that Stimson and his aides had violently opposed; and the Secretary of State had even threatened to resign. Hoover, put in a somewhat awkward position, had suggested to the Firestones that they try to convince Stimson—hence a

---

4 Moffat, *op. cit.*, p. 82.
5 *Ibid.*, p. 82.

meeting of January 24 between Everett Sanders, chairman of the Republican National Committee and the Firestone Company's attorney, another lawyer, and Moffat, who suggested the compromise that a mediator be dispatched to Liberia, rather than a warship.

Two days later, Sanders went to see Stimson, with Moffat present. He met with a very poor reception, for Lord Cecil had just written to Stimson saying that the Firestones had treated the League Committee "with grave discourtesy." "I am afraid," Cecil's note had continued, "that several members of the Committee have arrived at the conclusion that the object of the Firestone Corporation was . . . to drive the Liberian Government into such straits that they would be at the mercy of the corporation."[6] Stimson therefore insisted that the Firestones first make their peace with the League, and Sanders' efforts failed. "We are left wondering anew," wrote Moffat, "why the Firestones should employ the Chairman of the Republican National Committee five weeks before the Democrats come in."[7]

But the Firestones were obstinate. "The tenacity surpasses belief." On February 7, they returned to Stimson, who had just received a cable from Cecil announcing the Committee's dispatch of a strongly worded telegram to Liberia. "Mr. Firestone brushed it aside, however, as of no consequence. . . . He was here to ask for a warship. . . . Firestone concluded by stating that the only way in which Liberia would be convinced that America was prepared to stand up for its rights was to make a show of force." This would suffice to enable the Liberian opposition, who were pro-American, to oust the present president. Stimson, who disliked the Firestones' tactics of going over his head by appealing to the White House, was opposed to the plan and said so. Firestone thereupon accused him of sacrificing American interests to political considerations; "he grew more and more excited and got up, walking around the room waving his arms, etc." The interview, during which Stimson controlled himself as best he could, lasted forty minutes.[8]

On February 14, the two Firestones returned, but this time Stimson refused to see them. They saw Under Secretary Castle instead and then went on to Hoover, but it was too late. The Democrats were about to take over. Hull had been consulted and had announced his agreement to the dispatch of a mediator, and the Firestones were unable to persuade him otherwise.

The Firestones' failure is instructive. Their cause was not bad in itself, and they had some political leverage with the President. But they proceeded awkwardly, antagonizing Stimson, and the moment was against them.

Legislators are among those who exert more direct pressure than most on policy-makers. They have easy access to the Foreign Minister; and, in

---

[6] Cited in *ibid.*, p. 84, note.
[7] *Ibid.*, p. 85.
[8] *Ibid.*, pp. 85, 86.

a parliamentary system of ministerial responsibility, they have special leverage since the cabinet's survival depends on their votes. If they are members of the opposition, their favorable or unfavorable attitude to a given policy determines the tranquility of the executive branch and, consequently, its power of action. And if they head legislative committees on foreign affairs, they are especially important. In the United States, the President rarely makes a major foreign-policy decision without assuring himself of the support of the Chairman of the Senate Committee on Foreign Relations. Wilson failed to do so with Henry Cabot Lodge and was unable to obtain ratification of the Treaty of Versailles. Roosevelt was more careful, and always tried to associate in his decision not only the Chairman (Tom Connally in particular), but also the most influential minority member (Republican Arthur Vandenberg). When President Truman sought to embark on a policy of global alliances that ran contrary to the Republican isolationist tradition, he prevailed upon the Republican chairman of the committee to act, with the Vandenberg Declaration of 1948.

Memoirs of former foreign ministers (Austen Chamberlain or Anthony Eden), or heads of cabinet secretariats (like General Mordacq for Clemenceau), or heads of ministries (Paléologue, for instance, or Charles-Roux), indicate that most of the significant attempts to bring pressure on the government have been made by legislators. Sometimes, they group together unofficially in a "lobby" to advocate a particular policy. They also exert *indirect* pressures, which we shall discuss next.

II. INDIRECT PRESSURE

A statesman is influenced not only by direct approaches, by conversations with representatives of interest groups, but also by the activities and effects of these groups among the public, or among opinion-makers. Let us consider the case of the Hoare-Laval proposal to end Italian aggression in Ethiopia in 1935; rarely has any foreign-policy measure raised such a storm or had such concrete results.

It will be recalled that, after the Italians attacked Ethiopia on October 3, 1935, Great Britain and France officially protested and, in the League of Nations, called for economic sanctions against Italy—although these were in fact more symbolic than efficacious. Despite the existence, particularly in France, of pro-fascist right-wing and extreme left-wing minorities advocating more effective action, most Frenchmen and Englishmen appeared to favor this moderate policy. A kind of public-opinion poll—a peace ballot—had been conducted in England from late 1934 to June 1935, eliciting more than 11 million responses, and an immense majority had expressed itself in favor of the League of Nations and disarmament, yet only 6.8 million votes were in favor of military sanctions (2.4 million against).[9] But on December 7, 1935, the Foreign Secretary, Sir Samuel Hoare, secretly agreed to a proposal worked out by Pierre Laval that involved a complete reversal of this policy. Its purpose—a reasonable one—was to restore the "Stresa Front" of April, 1935, with Italy; this was regarded as the only effective obstacle to Hitler's growing ambitions. To win Mussolini over, he would be offered a considerable part of Ethiopia. Morally speaking, it was a plan to reward the aggressor.

To understand the reactions that followed, we must remember that Hoare had on several occasions expressed faith in the League of Nations; that British policy appeared to be moving in the direction of strengthening the economic sanctions by extending them to oil (which was indispensable to the Italian campaign); that, on December 5, Hoare explained to the House of Commons that he was pursuing a two-pronged policy of collective sanctions and conciliation endeavors.

When he arrived in Paris on the afternoon of Saturday, December 7, en route to Switzerland for a rest cure and vacation, Hoare proceeded directly to the Quai d'Orsay. There, Laval, who was personally opposed to any oil embargo, succeeded in outmaneuvering him, a success the real reason for which is probably that Hoare was ill.[10] Hoare himself admitted to accepting Laval's proposals out of physical exhaustion. "It may be that I was so pulled down by overwork that my judgment was out of gear."[11] Yet, to the astonishment of some members of the British Cabinet (particularly Eden), the cabinet as a whole, led by Prime Minister Stanley Baldwin, dared not repudiate the Foreign Secretary's signature to the agreement.

On December 9, when Hoare had left for Switzerland, the French papers, notably *L'Oeuvre* and *L'Echo de Paris,* published the substance of the Hoare-Laval plan—probably a deliberate attempt by Laval to force the British hand, but perhaps the result of negligence. A storm broke out over the news that England and France were going to propose a negotiated peace between Italy and Ethiopia (with Italy to receive a good portion of Ethiopia). It went on for nine days, and those nine days sufficed to force Sir Samuel Hoare's resignation. "The reaction of public opinion," Eden wrote in his memoirs, "was indignant and ashamed. It was said that we should have no part in rewarding aggressors."[12]

General elections had taken place a month before and had returned the Conservatives with a substantial majority. The new members of Parliament

[9] G. M. Gathorne-Hardy, *A Short History of International Affairs* (London, 1952), p. 409.

[10] The Earl of Avon, *The Eden Memoirs: Facing the Dictators* (London and New York, 1962), p. 295.

[11] Templewood, Sir Samuel Hoare, *Nine Troubled Years* (London, 1954), p. 178.

[12] Earl of Avon, *op. cit.,* p. 306.

were submerged in a flood of indignant letters from constituents, accusing them of having gained the election through deceit. British papers reproduced articles from the American and Commonwealth press condemning the Anglo-French plan. Eden, who had meanwhile proceeded to Geneva, noted on December 14 that opposition to the proposal was mounting dangerously. On December 11, the Laborite *Daily Herald* had demanded that Prime Minister Baldwin inform Laval that the British Government would accept no agreement that was not in accordance with the principles of the League of Nations. The trade unions, led by Ernest Bevin, were in the forefront of opposition to the plan, organizing protest meetings, but Conservatives were almost equally aroused. Members of Parliament found themselves under increasingly severe pressure from their constituents. Baldwin was obliged to recall Hoare from Switzerland (where he had had to stay on a few days longer because of an accident) ; he arrived in London on December 17 and was given to understand by Baldwin that the Prime Minister was backing him. "Later in the day, however, Chamberlain returned after another Cabinet meeting with a very different story. He had been asked to tell me that my proposed statement did not go far enough, and that it was necessary for me to say that my plan was bad, that I had been mistaken in accepting it, and that, in view of the general opposition, I withdrew my support of it."[13] Rather than retract, Hoare decided, on December 18, to resign.

Seldom has the public reacted to an event so vividly, so tersely, or so violently as it did to the publication of the Hoare-Laval proposal. Seldom, too, does it succeed in reversing national policy. For Hoare's resignation caused Baldwin to declare in the House of Commons on December 19 that an error had been made. "It is perfectly obvious now that the proposals are completely and absolutely dead. The Government is certainly going to make no attempt to resurrect them."[14] Usually, governments try to ride out such storms, for leaders who allow themselves to be buffeted about by waves of public opinion would be failing in one of their most essential duties.

Following this example of indirect pressure brought to bear by the public as a whole, let us examine the influence that individual opinion-making groups try indirectly to exert on governments. Press campaigns are one of the best-known forms of such action; lobbying is another—systematically laying siege not only to the men at the top, which leads us back to direct pressures, but also to all persons who might exert some influence on them. The practice has been best studied in the United States, probably because nowhere is the government more sensitive to lobbying, haunted as it always is by the problems of winning the next presidential elections.

Robert Ferrell has well described the type of activities conducted in the

---

[13] Templewood, *op. cit.*, p. 185.
[14] Cited by the Earl of Avon, *op. cit.*, p. 310.

1920's by the pacifist groups. The agencies he calls "conservative" and pro-League of Nations—the Carnegie Endowment for International Peace, the World Peace Foundation, the League of Nations Association—

operated through the influence of their highly placed members. These groups found it easier to obtain a private interview with a Secretary of State, or with an Under Secretary, or perhaps an Assistant Secretary, than to plan a public campaign to influence the American people and thereby the American government. The conservatives championed what could be known (depending on how one looked at it) as either a direct or an indirect approach. They knew, better than the radicals, that to enlist support for a course of action which a political leader or diplomat considered unwise was a most difficult task, subject to evasion, vague promises, and obfuscation of issues. The conservative peace men knew also that the world moved slowly.[15]

The so-called radical movements, on the other hand, "employed every device known to the new science of public relations, in an effort to make congressmen and diplomats sense the importance of American measures for world peace."[16] Their policy was to approach political leaders individually and try to convert them by repeated maneuvers of various kinds. One method was to inundate them with petitions. Another method was to have hundreds or thousands of letters or telegrams sent to them, so as to create—artificially—the impression that concern was widespread. (The method had been well known, particularly in Great Britain, for some time; witness the great Chartist movement of 1839.)

The interesting thing about the example I discuss below is that the "indirect pressure" was successful—leading to the signing of the Kellogg-Briand Pact. Let us see, now, how pressure was exerted on those two men in particular.

Pressure on Briand was both direct and indirect. A number of Americans, among them two eminent members of the Carnegie Endowment—Nicholas Murray Butler, President of Columbia University, and Professor James Shotwell—requested him to make a gesture that would satisfy the American public's desire for peace. The public, they maintained, was disturbed at France's delay in ratifying the treaty on the settlement of war debts, and newspapers were accusing France of militarism.

Shotwell, at the time an Associate Professor at the Hochschule für Politik in Berlin, came to Paris on March 15, 1927, after visiting Stresemann, the German Foreign Minister. During a short trip through the Saar, he had met the administrator of the French-controlled mines, Fontaine, a friend of Briand's private secretary, Alexis Léger, who undertook to transmit Shotwell's "peace plan" to him. However, Shotwell reports, "Briand had the

---

[15] In Alexander de Conde, ed., *Isolation and Security* (Durham, N.C., 1957), p. 102.
[16] *Ibid.*, p. 103.

reputation of not reading his own letters . . . and I decided that Léger was, to say the least, not helpful in getting the idea through to Briand."[17] Shotwell therefore asked his old friend Albert Thomas to arrange an interview for him with Briand. At this interview, which took place on March 22, Shotwell suggested that Briand would satisfy American public opinion by issuing a declaration that included a renunciation of not only the instruments of war but war itself. The declaration should be made public on April 6, the tenth anniversary of the United States' entry into the world war.[18] Briand was interested but had doubts, and he requested Shotwell to draft him a note. Shotwell did so and on March 24 gave the document to Léger, after which he left for London, then for the United States; on board ship, he learned of the success of his endeavor. For on April 6, Briand addressed a message to the American people through the Associated Press, proposing a renunciation of war as an instrument of national policy to be embodied in a pact between the United States and France.

What was Briand's intention? Certainly not the conclusion of a multi-national pact such as the Kellogg-Briand Pact of 1928. He feared being accused of Messianism, a malady which, he said, like fate, made men deaf and blind. The right-wing press was leveling just this charge at him, and he had repudiated it in a speech of February 6, 1927.[19] What he wanted was to satisfy certain aspirations of French and American opinion: for the French, the conclusion of a Franco-American pact, however vague, had about it a certain aroma of alliance, of "guarantee"; to the Americans—and Briand, we may note, addressed himself in the first place to the American *people,* over the head of the government—it was necessary to talk of peace.

Secretary of State Frank Kellogg's case was even more characteristic. He was a man of somewhat mediocre capacities, quick-tempered rather than energetic, abrupt rather than tenacious, with a profound contempt for pacifists and a horror of what he called their "private diplomacy." When he saw the sympathy with which the American press welcomed the Briand plan, he was stubbornly silent, but the extreme pacifists, Salmon O. Levinson in particular, had made a notable recruit in the person of Senator Borah, Chairman of the Senate Committee on Foreign Relations. Borah, who was an isolationist and hostile to the League, favored the idea of "outlawing war," but the principle of a bilateral Franco-American treaty was repugnant to him. It was Levinson who suggested that the French proposal might be transformed by extending the renunciation of war to all countries of the world.

On December 22, Kellogg had this new plan proposed to him at a meeting of the Foreign Relations Committee. He accepted it enthusiastically,

---

[17] *The Autobiography of James T. Shotwell* (New York, 1961), p. 207.
[18] *Ibid.,* p. 208.
[19] See Georges Suarez, *Briand* (Paris, 1938–52), VI, 248–49.

for it enabled him to reply to the pacifists' insistent demands and the impatient criticism in the press, and at the same time to regain the diplomatic initiative, which he had lost not only to Briand but also to private citizens.

Here, then, we have a curious example of effective indirect pressure, since the men in question adopted a policy for which they had no liking as a consequence of action by a well-organized sector of public opinion. "American diplomats were capable men, well intentioned, as full of good will as the peace leaders and workers who bothered them. But they had to cope with a public opinion whose only virtue often was that it was public and opinionated."[20]

III. THE CLIMATE OF OPINION

In addition to being subject to direct or indirect pressures, the statesman must also try to ascertain the general condition of the nation and its economy. Sometimes he trusts his intuitions, but more often he seeks "hard" information—from articles, from conversations, from reports by subordinates —from local officials for opinion throughout the country, from ambassadors for opinion abroad; nowadays, there are also public-opinion polls, sometimes initiated by the government. All this enables him to form some idea of the "atmosphere"—a vague term, but it shows that the reality involved is not easy to grasp. The statesman, incapable like everyone else of understanding the situation *objectively*, is constantly obliged to form a *subjective* idea about it. It is through the agency of this idea that the basic, underlying forces act upon him. That, indeed, is as far as he can go.

If his subjective view is seriously mistaken, a statesman's decision may lead to unexpected, sometimes violent or even catastrophic, relations. Polignac's "confidential report" to King Charles X, on April 14, 1830,[21] stated that the disturbances marking French political life were merely a surface matter, the fault of a few small groups, not affecting the masses. This view encouraged Polignac to prepare the Four Ordinances that led to the fall of the government. A similar example, concerning an economic rather than a political situation, was Hoover's mistake, as Secretary of Commerce, in believing that prosperity was permanent, and then, as President, in thinking that the depression precipitated in October, 1929, would simply solve itself. This assessment of the situation not only cost Hoover the election in 1932; it also helped to plunge the country into sufferings that a better analysis of the situation might certainly have mitigated.

A mistaken interpretation of the underlying forces at work often results in certain events being attributed to "plots"—to action organized by small

[20] Robert H. Ferrell, *Peace in Their Time: The Origins of the Kellogg-Briand Pact* (New Haven, Conn., 1952), p. 265.
[21] A. T. de Vaulabelle, *Histoire des deux Restaurations* (Paris, 1857), VIII, 102–3.

groups or minorities—whereas they are in fact the result of these basic forces. Thus, for instance, governments in conflict with native nationalist movements in rebellious colonies have often believed that the masses remained faithful to the mother country, that the independence movement was merely an artificial agitation sponsored from abroad, and that it would therefore suffice to arrest a few leaders to subdue it.

In any event, it is clear that politically responsible statesmen make constant attempts to take the "atmosphere" into account. The negotiators at the Paris Peace Conference in 1919 made constant references to public opinion —asking what it would or would not accept. And the memoirs and other papers of the members of the Council of Four do much to illuminate their respective attitudes to the "atmosphere." (We do not always know, of course, whether their references to this matter of public opinion were sincere or whether their purpose was simply to strengthen an argument.)

Lloyd George was probably most sensitive of all of them to fluctuations of public opinion. He realized that the English desire to "punish" Germany was progressively being overcome by concern *not* to destroy the German economy, if only in order to benefit from the vast market it normally offered. In assessing the situation in his country, therefore, he made the following observations, *inter alia:* the British worker did not wish to overwhelm the Germans with excessive demands; unrestrained hostility to the Germans was, rather, an upper-class phenomenon; if the Allies' conditions seemed too moderate, he (Lloyd George) would have great difficulties in Parliament, but those difficulties would not come from the masses.[22]

As for possible intervention on behalf of the Poles, Lloyd George expressed the view that in neither America nor England would public opinion support intervention under existing conditions. And concerning Russia, he believed that, in England, the feeling against action by British forces in Russia was growing increasingly strong.[23]

Lloyd George's attitude was most strikingly expressed during the dramatic meeting of June 2, 1919. He was eager to sign the treaty as quickly as possible, fearing insoluble complications if the Germans rejected it, and he therefore declared himself in favor of major concessions, proposing them in the name of the public; British public opinion, he said, was primarily concerned with peace and did not attach much importance to the conditions of that peace. It would not support a government liable to provoke war without the most compelling reasons. He reminded the other negotiators that the British people did not have the same military tradition as France. They wanted to stay at home and would not lend themselves to renewed hostilities if the treaty contained anything they might consider unjustifiable.

Clemenceau's reply to Lloyd George was based on the same principle.

[22] Paul Mantoux, *Les Délibérations du Conseil des Quatre* (Paris, 1955), I, 46 (March 27).
[23] *Ibid.*, I, 47, and II, 202 (May 24).

I am informed of the trend of public opinion in my country, and I have to take it into account. I think that everyone is in a hurry to reach a settlement. In England, the view is that the way to reach it is to make concessions. In France, we believe it necessary to be tough. Unfortunately, we know the Germans better than anyone. . . . British opinion is not sorry that Germany must give up her colonies, her navy. That is natural; everyone sees things from their own point of view. It is no less natural that in France one should feel that British criticism concentrates on Continental questions.[24]

Clemenceau's evaluation too was based on a certain subjective concept of what the French people thought; he believed he could lead and educate the public, but only up to a point. "Our parliaments," he said, "all believe that we will not be given enough. Some newspapers, sometimes with very influential backing, tell me every day that I am not doing enough for my country. I am doing my duty, and that is enough for me."[25] As for Germany, Clemenceau's outlook was pessimistic. Lloyd George, on the other hand, remarked that while France thought Germany to be the greatest danger, he believed the danger had been averted for the next century; "I am much more afraid of the Slavs."

Wilson, as we know, had a very different notion of the "atmosphere." He believed that the American public—disinterested, favorable to peaceful solutions—could be identified with a "world public" of which he believed himself to be the spokesman. This concept emerged in particular in his discussions with Clemenceau and Orlando. The feeling that had drawn together men from every point of the globe, he said, had been the feeling that they were fighting together for justice. "That is I have on occasion been able to say that we in Paris represent not so much the nations as the opinion of the world."[26] "I did not write the Fourteen Points in my own name, nor to express my personal opinion. I tried to voice the feeling of the people of the United States—and it coincides with that of all the great peoples of the world. My only wish has been to articulate, as it were, what has been sensed by the masses." His idea of public opinion in the United States is well summed up in one statement: "If I may be permitted to continue to speak on behalf of my fellow countrymen, to be, so to speak, their spiritual representative, it is impossible for me to agree to a population being handed over to foreign domination without its consent."[27]

Of the Big Four, Wilson was probably the one whose subjective concepts were furthest removed from objective reality. Events were cruelly to give

---

[24] *Ibid.*, II, 265 ff. (June 2).

[25] *Ibid.*, I, 419 (April 29).

[26] *Ibid.*, I, 71–72, (March 28).

[27] *Ibid.*, I, 293 (April 20) and II, 223 (May 26). We might note a comment in *Le Figaro* of January 26, 1919: "In spite of himself, he is a citizen of the United States before being a citizen of the world, since he wants the world to resemble the United States."

him the lie. On the matter of Fiume, he thought he could appeal to Italian public opinion over Orlando's head. (Orlando, too, was constantly talking about this, but he arbitrarily associated "Italian public opinion" with the views of the *arditi* groups—the ultra-nationalists.) At first, he believed the Fiume problem was soluble. Orlando's difficulty, he said, was "similar to that which concerns Lloyd George in England and Clemenceau in France. It is how to satisfy a badly informed and anxious public. I am not unfamiliar with the problem."[28] When Orlando persisted in claiming Fiume, Wilson felt he could appeal to the Italians in his own right. He was confident, he said, that "when the man in the street in Italy hears what I have to say, he will think it over; there may be a reversal in Italian opinion."[29]

But Italians reacted in a manner quite contrary to Wilson's expectations. On April 24, Orlando announced to his fellow negotiators that he was leaving for Rome; "I must," he declared, "return to the sources of my authority."[30] In Rome, he obtained a unanimous vote in parliament for his claims to Fiume, and Italian political circles were swept by a vast movement of passionate hostility to Wilson and the United States, causing Wilson to remark wryly that the American public took great interest in the dispute and could not understand why they were apparently alone in this. "It seems to me that the support of American opinion is more important than that of Italian opinion." He was forced to the same conclusion regarding his two principal Allies: "the present impression in America is that the United States does not enjoy the sympathy of France and Britain." Lloyd George replied that Clemenceau had told him that the (hostile) Paris press was not truly representative of French opinion. "And I am glad to hear it. All I know is that in England there is a certain feeling [against America], it is there and it is growing."[31]

Wilson thus realized quite early that his assessment of European opinion was mistaken and that the European nations, ravaged by war, were now thirsting for more or less justified "compensation" for the immense sufferings they had endured. On the other hand, he nourished more durable and more dangerous illusions concerning the nature of opinion in his own country.

He was right, of course, when he told the others in the Council of Four on June 17 that he must leave for home and face the Senate as soon as the treaty was signed: "the Senate has taken the bit between its teeth, but fortunately the same is not true of the American people."[32] Many American

---

28 *Ibid.*, I, 242 (April 13).

29 *Ibid.*, I, 329 (April 22).

30 *Ibid.*, I, 354.

31 *Ibid.*, I, 454 (May 2), and 471 (May 3). See also George Bernard Noble, *Policies and Opinions at Paris, 1919: Wilsonian Diplomacy, the Versailles Peace and French Public Opinion* (New York, 1935). The author seems to have somewhat exaggerated the hostility of the French press to Wilson.

32 Mantoux, *op. cit.*, II, 446.

historians, however, have made it clear why even a current of opinion favorable to the treaty and Covenant could not have helped.[33] European problems were far away in comparison with domestic ones; interest in the treaty was mild and courteous but unenthusiastic; Senators cared little about the public response anyway since elections were a long way off; and finally, there was a deep longing to return to "normalcy"—the slogan on which the Republican Warren Harding was to base his victorious campaign in 1920.

The examples of the Big Four and their interpretation of public opinion are similar, in that they all represented and were responsive to democratic countries. Consider, however, the example of a dictator, Mussolini.

Public opinion, which in any case is not easily expressed, is sometimes thought to be a negligible factor in a dictatorship. In fact, however, a dictator usually tries to have some idea of what the public thinks of certain basic issues. The press, which he controls, can be of no help to him here, and he must rely instead on reports from his aides. Yet the latter, who need to be in his good graces, describe the situation not as they see it, but as he would like it to be. The discrepancies between the objective reality and a dictator's assessment of it may be considerable.

Thanks to the diaries of Count Nobile Galeazzo Ciano, Mussolini's son-in-law and his Foreign Minister until 1943, we possess almost a complete daily record of evaluations of Italian opinion on the war in 1939 and 1940.[34] On August 16, 1939, for example, he wrote that war "would be a mad venture, carried out against the unanimous will of the Italian people, who as yet do not know how things stand, but who, having had a sniff of the truth, have had a sudden fit of rage against the Germans." Starace, Secretary of the Fascist Party, Ciano continued, "who is in good faith in this matter, says that when Germany attacks Poland we must keep our eyes open to prevent public demonstrations against the Germans. A policy of neutrality will, on the other hand, be more popular, and, if it were necessary later, war with Germany would be every bit as popular."[35]

Did Mussolini subscribe to Ciano's interpretation of the Italians' "readiness for war"? Hardly. On August 27, Ciano wrote:

I have been completely abandoned by the large group of men who are concerned with telling the Duce only those things that please him. To tell the truth is the least of their cares. Starace, with his intellectual and moral short-sightedness, has the cheek to tell Mussolini that the Italian women are happy about the war because they are going to receive six lire a day and will not have the encumbrance of their husbands.[36]

[33] See in particular Thomas A. Bailey, *Woodrow Wilson and the Lost Peace* (New York, 1944), and *Woodrow Wilson and the Great Betrayal* (New York, 1945).
[34] Hugh Gibson, ed., *The Ciano Diaries, 1939–1943* (New York, 1946).
[35] *Ibid.*, p. 122.
[36] *Ibid.*, p. 131.

Not all advisers were so servile. In the entry for August 30, we read: "Bocchini [chief of police], whom I have urged to send to our Chief *true* reports on the situation, is very pessimistic. He went so far as to tell me that in case of uprisings in connection with the preservation of neutrality, the carabinieri and police would make common cause with the people." Again, on September 13: "Bocchini reports on the state of mind of the country, which is gradually getting better with the spreading of news of the certainty of our neutrality. Nevertheless, the country is and remains fundamentally anti-German."[37]

Did Mussolini know all this? It seems clear that he continued to delude himself on the state of public opinion, on the army, and on the air force. "He has figures given him by Valle, which are absurdly optimistic" (September 18). In early October, Ciano wrote, "In the country rumors are being spread against everything and everybody, himself included. But he has always acted in good faith. He was betrayed by four or five individuals whom he inadvisedly put into high positions and whom he still has not punished severely."[38] Starace, who was dismissed at this time, was evidently one of the individuals who had been misleading Mussolini.

The problem of Italy's attitude to entering the war came up again in the spring of 1940. How was it assessed in high quarters? By now, Mussolini realized that intervention, to which he was increasingly attracted, was unpopular. "When the instincts in a people are stationary and without ideas, only the use of force can save them," he told Ciano. "The Italian race is a race of sheep" (January 29). "Beat them and beat them and beat them" (February 7).[39]

Italians, meanwhile, feared the worst and were restless. Ciano's entry for February 15: "Bocchini's report on the internal situation was very pessimistic. The poverty of the nation is growing and all kinds of difficulties increase. The prestige of the regime is not what it used to be. But is Bocchini telling these things to Mussolini? He swears to me that he is." Again, "the people of all social levels want nothing to do with war" (March 23). "The population, among whom rebellion is still alive, would revolt as soon as they got any inkling of our difficulties. I talked about this to the Duce, and, for whatever it was worth, repeated that Italy unanimously detests the Germans" (April 6).[40]

Slowly, however, German successes in the war had some effect on Italian attitudes. "News of the German action in the north has had a favorable echo among the Italian people" (April 10). Mussolini inferred that opinion had really changed.

---

[37] *Ibid.*, pp. 133–34, 143.
[38] *Ibid.*, pp. 147, 157.
[39] *Ibid.*, pp. 202, 205.
[40] *Ibid.*, pp. 208, 225, 232.

The Duce . . . starts from this premise: "The feeling of the Italian people is unanimously against the Allies." Where does he get this information? Is he really sure of what he writes, or is it not true that, conscious of his personal influence, he is thinking of the opportune moment for modifying the national mood at his whim? [May 2]

On May 15, Ciano wrote, "Great excitement over the news of the piercing of the Maginot Line at Sedan. . . . Public opinion has now improved because of German victories, but the real feelings of the people have not changed." And on May 25, "The people want to know what will be done, and I hear many voices calling for war. This never happened up to a few days ago." A week later, Ciano had an audience with the king, who, he said, "feels that the country is going to war without enthusiasm. There is interventionist propaganda, but there is not in the least that enthusiasm we had in 1915."[41]

Finally, the fateful day of June 10, 1940: "Mussolini speaks from the balcony of the Palazzo Venezia. The news of the war does not surprise anyone and does not arouse very much enthusiasm. I am sad, very sad. The adventure begins. May God help Italy!" Mussolini, with habitual inconsistency, has proceeded once more to inveigh against the Italians: "His reflections on the Italian people . . . are extremely bitter this evening" (June 17). "[He] is taking it out on the Italian people: 'It is the material that I lack. . . . A people who for sixteen centuries have been an anvil cannot become a hammer within a few years' " (June 21).[42]

IV. SOCIAL ORIGINS

The underlying forces that shape history and men exert an influence even when they go unnoticed. It is not irrelevant, for example, to investigate from what classes, groups, or regions statesmen are recruited. It is true, for instance, that "those whose heritage has included graciousness, manners, and what is known as worldly wisdom in addition to substantial possessions are most beset by that failing—common, indeed, to all diplomats—of basing their estimation of opinion in the country where they are posted on views advanced in the worldly circles in which they normally move."[43]

That there exist class outlooks and even outlooks peculiar to social groups is a self-evident truth which not only Marxists have observed. This kind of class mentality can become "class consciousness," marked by the determination to favor those of the same birth or rank. But very often one protects and gives privileges to one's peers almost as a matter of course, because it seems the natural thing to do.

[41] *Ibid.*, pp. 234, 242, 250, 254, 258.
[42] *Ibid.*, pp. 264, 265, 267.
[43] François Mauriac, "Preface" to Jacques Dumaine, *Le Quai d'Orsay* (1945–1951) (Paris, 1955), p. 9.

It would be fascinating to explore more fully the question of what social "circles" and types of men govern foreign policy. It would be interesting, for example, to analyze the recruitment of European diplomats among wealthy and noble families in the nineteenth century, to see whether this directly affected the creation of a kind of international solidarity and common diplomatic language.

In our century, many diplomats of the traditionalist school expressed consternation at the brash new Bolshevik diplomatic service, in which, along with a few men of the old regime like Chicherin, "ill-mannered" revolutionaries were to be found. The American diplomatic corps, during the same period, was staffed principally by businessmen, some of them millionaires, and by writers and lawyers. And a spoils system of making political appointments to ambassadorships resulted in what were often wholesale changes of personnel with every new administration. The Americans were usually more forthright than their European colleagues, whom they frequently shocked by their methods.

The present-day Yugoslav foreign service includes many veterans of the International Brigade of the Spanish Civil War, and nearly all its members took part in the struggle of the Partisans during World War II.

The make-up of the diplomatic corps often changes within a single country. It would be interesting, for example, with regard to France, to study what effect the institution of a "major competitive examination" (ordered in 1868, decreed in 1877) and the establishment of the Ecole Nationale d'Administration (1945) has had on French diplomacy. For a long time, the men of the career service were stamped by their training at the Ecole Libre des Sciences Politiques. At present, the absorption of former supervisory personnel (civilian controllers from Tunisia and Morocco, overseas administrators) into the French Foreign Service is effecting new changes. The "unity of style and training, which was clearly justified at a time when diplomacy was still largely a career centered around a Europe with monarchical and aristocratic traditions, began to be criticized between the two wars as indications of the Quai d'Orsay's outdated attachment to a bygone era."[44]

Similar developments have taken place in England, where the great reform dates from 1943.

> The British diplomatist of past times was commonly said to have several grave defects. On the assumption that he had been recruited from a rigorously restricted social class—an assumption which was no longer justified from the end of the first world war onwards—he was accused of being incapable for this reason of representing fairly the interests of the nation as a whole; of having led too sheltered a life in his own class to be able to understand

[44] Jean Baillou and Pierre Pelletier, *Les Affaires étrangères* (Paris, 1962), p. 200.

economic and social questions; and of consorting through social prejudice with too narrow a section of the population in the countries where he served. These criticisms were not entirely without substance.[45]

The conduct of foreign affairs in most countries was long "the preserve of social oligarchies with an acute sense of class." We may also note this mournful comment: "Almost all diplomatists . . . deplore the tyranny of the cocktail party as a diplomatic institution, yet almost all of them feel obliged both to give and to attend such parties. The fact is that, though tiring and bad for the digestion, they have their uses. They are a form of clearing house or exchange and mart for political rumors."[46] Yet anyone who has attended such functions is well aware that they are far from representative of all classes of a population.

In addition to class, there is the problem of the language barrier. It is interesting to compare the attitudes of statesmen who knew only their own language and were circumscribed by it, and those who knew several. Bismarck, for example, spoke fluent French and English; Hitler knew only German. "Beware," said Bismarck, "of an Englishman who speaks French without an accent." Palmerston knew French, Spanish, and Portuguese well enough to check the texts of the Quadruple Alliance agreements of 1834. At the 1919 Peace Conference, Lloyd George knew French; Clemenceau was perfectly at home in English; Orlando was fairly fluent in French; only Wilson knew no other language but his own. At Munich, in 1938, Mussolini was the only one familiar—although not so familiar as he imagined—with the four languages of the countries represented. And in the 1939 negotiations in Moscow between Britain, France, and the Soviet Union—when Molotov spoke Russian, the British Ambassador English, and the French Ambassador French—the two latter understood one another; Potemkin, Deputy People's Commissar for Foreign Affairs, translated their statements into Russian; and Molotov translated the Russian ones into French. The two Soviet representatives thus had a distinct advantage over their fellow negotiators.[47]

Of all statesmen, Americans seem least able to escape from the confines of their mother tongue. Perhaps this explains certain characteristic tendencies of American diplomacy—isolationism or, as Morgenthau calls it, neo-isolationism, which consists of minding other people's business without taking account of their views. According to the American diplomat E. Wilder Spaulding, Americans—

> are at the mercy of the bilingual "local" who summarizes what he sees fit to summarize and translates conversations in phrases intended to flatter the American participants. Marion Folsom's indictment that "the United States

---

[45] William, Lord Strang, *The Foreign Office* (New York, 1955), p. 70.

[46] *Ibid.*, pp. 72, 101.

[47] On this subject, see the memoirs of Paul Schmidt, Hitler's interpreter, *Statist auf diplomatischer Bühne* (Bonn, 1949).

is probably weaker in foreign language abilities than any other major country in the world" underscores the sorry situation. The recent [1960] estimate that 10 million Russians are studying English while only 5,000 students in 180 American colleges are studying Russian seems to lead to the conclusion that the Russians can outsmart our diplomats on any and every occasion.[48]

We obviously cannot establish general laws regarding the influence of education and native environment on any nation's statesmen. Each case must be studied separately (whence the evident need for good biographies). But there are certain salient traits that reveal the sometimes decisive importance of this unconscious or semi-conscious "social pressure."

It is not irrelevant that Bismarck came from a Junker family in which the French were looked on as the hereditary foe. On the other hand, the few "liberal" ideas he derived from his mother and her family vanished after 1840. He had by then become a landowner, immersed in Brandenburg's society of country gentry, and here he absorbed the more "reactionary" notions that marked him in the years 1848–50. Although he stood out head and shoulders above the narrow and mediocre environment of his family's world, Bismarck was deeply influenced by it, and it was to mark his behavior. "As a class, the Junkers were always politically of one mind."[49] Bismarck himself told a liberal in 1848, "I am a Junker and want to profit from it,"[50] and on the first page of his memoirs he wrote, "My historical sympathies remained on the side of authority." Whatever influences were brought to bear on him at school, he added, "were not strong enough to extirpate my innate Prussian monarchical sentiments."[51] "Innate" is not the right word; this was a case of characteristics acquired through environment and education. "My views, as regards the War of Liberation, were taken from the standpoint of a Prussian officer. On looking at the map, the possession of Strasbourg by France exasperated me."[52]

Similarly, we find certain features in Napoleon III's upbringing that influenced subsequent political attitudes. From his mother, Queen Hortense, he derived the "Napoleonic cult" and the notion of his "star of destiny." He lacked fatherly, male direction,[53] but his tutor, Philippe Lebas, a republican and an admirer of Robespierre, exerted some influence. There was a "leftist" side to Napoleon III that was to be revealed in 1830–31, when he fell under the influence of the Carbonari, a secret society in Italy with various Christian, Masonic, humanitarian, and republican elements in its ideology. In fact, there is an entire aspect of his Italian policy which stems from these ideas imbibed in his youth. Perhaps those sources should

---

[48] *Ambassadors Ordinary and Extraordinary* (Washington, 1961), p. 4.
[49] Erich Eyck, *Bismarck and the German Empire* (New York, 1964), p. 12.
[50] Cited in *ibid.*, p. 13.
[51] *Bismarck, the Man and the Statesman* (New York, 1899), I, 1.
[52] *Ibid.*, p. 3.
[53] Albert Guerard, *Napoleon III* (Cambridge, Mass., 1943), p. 17.

also be credited with his sympathies with the theories of the socialist theorist Saint-Simon, which led him to take a keen interest in economic expansion and even, in the commercial treaty signed by France in 1860, made of him an exponent of free trade.

The oft-cited contrast between Briand and Poincaré[54] may also be pursued in terms of their social and educational environments:

[Briand] cannot be classified among the usual products of the universities or great schools. In the long series of statesmen who have made their mark on history, Clemenceau and he are the only men who did not belong by birth to the so-called ruling class. They were not among those who, by temperament, training, or tradition, considered power as the legitimate and almost inevitable culmination of a well-ordered career, meticulously punctuated by diplomas and titles.[55]

Everything disposed the young Briand to become the flexible, imaginative intellectually, if not actively, opportunistic statesman who was to play so great a role in the 1920's: the unassuming family life, his father, eccentric, optimistic, and somewhat excitable, who ran a small cafe at Saint-Nazaire; and the influence of Genty, one of the teachers in the local *lycée*, who "played an important part in his intellectual orientation." "He had contempt for the arbitrary and for received opinions. He loved reality too well to distort it."[56] It was also apparent in the adult Briand that he was a "poor man's son." "Without his exceptional gifts, he would never have traversed the distance that separated him from a world in which Poincaré had only to be born to be admitted."[57]

With Woodrow Wilson also, we can see clearly that certain factors in his youth and education strongly marked his future action: "The great environmental influences which built permanent habits of thought in Wilson as a youth were home, religion and 'the South.' "[58] Although later he acquired a kind of detachment in regard to the Civil War, he felt himself essentially a Virginian by temperament. He loved and admired his "incomparable father" and his mother. "You know," he wrote to Joseph Tumulty, his private secretary, "there are two natures combined in me that every day fight for supremacy and control. On the one hand, there is the Irish in me, quick, generous, impulsive, passionate, anxious always to help and to sympathize with those in distress. . . . Then, on the other side, there is the Scotch—canny, tenacious, cold and perhaps a little exclusive."[59] The Pres-

---

[54] See above, Chapter Nine, pp. 253–54.

[55] Suarez, *op. cit.*, I, 16.

[56] *Ibid.*, pp. 14, 15.

[57] *Ibid.*, p. 18.

[58] Harley Notter, *The Origins of the Foreign Policy of Woodrow Wilson* (Baltimore, 1937), pp. 4–5.

[59] Alexander L. and Juliette L. George, *Woodrow Wilson and Colonel House* (New York, 1956), p. xvi.

byterian influence was probably the stronger of the two; he learned from his family "that the world was governed by a righteous God; that every man was responsible to God for his actions; that the true perspective on life was spiritual and moral; . . . that one's conscience was a higher court than the opinion of one's fellows; and that the future rather than the immediate present was vital."[60] It is not hard to see here some of the sources of the "New Diplomacy" and the explanation of a number of Wilsonian attitudes.

Examples of this kind abound: in Disraeli, the influence of the Jewish environment—and of wealth—which prompted him, consciously or unconsciously, to defend himself against social exclusiveness by grandiloquence and startling achievements; in Mussolini, the distinctive mark of the journalistic profession. In her excellent portrait of the dictator,[61] Elizabeth Wiskemann shows that his taste for the sensational and his desire to astonish others must be ascribed to this as much as to his temperament. Thus, he was "indignant" at the German occupation of Romania in October, 1940. "Hitler," he said, "always faces me with a *fait accompli*. This time I am going to pay him back in his own coin. He will find out from the papers that I have occupied Greece."[62]

It is always hard for the historian to estimate the exact influence of a man's wife and close relatives. But marriage sometimes produces a decisive change by transferring a man from one social milieu to another. At opposite extremes are Wilson, who was strongly influenced by his second wife, and Lloyd George, who was virtually separated from his. The influence of other women is still harder to assess. There is no doubt that they sometimes play a considerable historical role by the mere fact that they are connected with an important political personality, see him constantly, and are in a position to sway his opinions. Some take deliberate advantage of that position.

It may be said that a political figure normally chooses his immediate collaborators among his friends, among those he trusts, because he knows them or because they are recommended to him. And these aides are tremendously important not only as advisers but also as "filterers." They can be virtually all-powerful as regards news or contacts. They can hide unpleasant truths, they can shield the man in question from influences they consider dangerous, or, to the contrary, they can encourage other influences. To the extent that they belong to the same social, political, and intellectual environment, they are formidable agents of social pressure.

The most extreme case known in a democracy of a man's "entourage" sheltering him from the outside world is probably that which occurred in connection with Wilson's illness in 1919. Mrs. Wilson and Wilson's personal physician were the only persons to see the President. Not only did they censor his visitors, but all the news that reached him passed through them.

---

[60] Notter, *op. cit.*, p. 9.
[61] *The Rome-Berlin Axis* (New York and London, 1949), p. 6.
[62] Gibson, *op. cit.*, p. 300 (October 12, 1940).

To calm the poor patient Mrs. Wilson persuaded him that the Senate would yield and ratify the Treaty of Versailles, and she consequently bears considerable responsibility for the President's rejection of amendments that might have saved the day.

It is interesting, therefore, to examine the role of ministerial staffs, private secretaries, and presidential aides—Colonel House for Wilson, Harry Hopkins for Franklin D. Roosevelt, Berthelot for Briand (although he held the job of secretary-general). Even more interesting would be the study of small groups.

Consider, for example, Gambetta's cabinet in the period when he combined the posts of French Prime Minister and Foreign Minister, from November, 1881, to January, 1882. His principal private secretary was Joseph Reinach. At the Ministry of Foreign Affairs, where Eugène Spuller was Under Secretary of State, a young diplomat, Auguste Gérard, was principal private secretary; his deputy was Gabriel Hanotaux, then draftsman of the Ministry's official records and contributor to *La République française*. Gambetta's personal secretary was Joseph Arnaud, whose mother presided over one of the great republican and Gambettist *salons* in Paris.[63]

The choice of Gérard as private secretary at the Quai d'Orsay may be explained by friendship. In the winter of 1869–70, Gérard, then a student, had gone to the Palais Bourbon and boldly asked to see Gambetta. Gambetta invited him to his home, and a lasting friendship was established. Gambetta took a lively interest in Gérard, trusted him, initiated him into politics, an encouraged him to apply for entrance to the prestigious Ecole Normale. When he called on him in 1881 he knew that he could count on him completely.

As for Hanotaux, Gambetta summoned him on June 19, 1881, to join the editorial board of *La République française*. "I was conquered right away," said Hanotaux.

Thanks to Gérard's memoirs, we possess some valuable particulars:

[Gambetta] worked a great deal, received many visitors, accepted outside invitations, and himself kept the most hospitable table at the Quai d'Orsay. . . . Every day he would go to the Chambers. . . . I had to wait for him every evening until he came home, sometimes quite late, to give him not only the latest telegrams but also the dispatches and letters that had come in the day's mail. I summarized most of the documents for him but read out the essential ones in full, noting in the margin his comments and instructions.[64]

We know also how Gambetta received visitors and whom he received. We may infer that Gambetta depended very closely on his immediate aides.

---

[63] See *Mémoires d'August Gérard* (Paris, 1928), pp. 64–80; and Gabriel Hanotaux, *Mon Temps*, Vol. II: *La Troisième République, Gambetta et Jules Ferry* (Paris, 1938), pp. 127, 139–238.

[64] Gérard, *op. cit.*, pp. 69, 70.

Hanotaux gives even more particulars. "As leader, [Gambetta's] first concern was to have a group, a battalion, an army." The group developed around *La République française:* Challemel-Lacour, Spuller, Weiss, Galiffet, Miribel, Reverseaux, Roux, Antonin Proust, etc.:

> It has rightly been said that Gambetta's entourage was a motley crowd. . . . Gambetta, the Prime Minister, Minister for Foreign Affairs, had long since dropped his Bohemian ways. . . . His contact with society, including luncheons with the Prince of Wales, the "arbiter of taste," had completed the solid middle-class education he had received from his mother and his good Aunt Massabie.[65]

V. CONCLUSION

We have briefly examined the channels through which the statesman receives the influences and marks of his nation's basic forces. Whether he is strongly aware of them or hardly at all, they are there, and it is not always easy to resist them. *Should* they sometimes be resisted? The problem really has two aspects, one normative (and beyond the scope of this study), one realist.

Democracy, however it is defined, is based on the idea of the "will of the people." But the will of the people is not the same thing as public opinion.[66] The will of the people proceeds from a general tendency that the elected representatives (or party in power) try to adapt to the procedures of government. Public opinion fluctuates, and has a constant ebb and flow of change.

In the Western democracies, the will of the people is expressed through periodic elections. Now these throw light on the state of public opinion, but only on a fleeting moment of it. New techniques for taking public-opinion polls, however, enable us to follow more closely the fluctuations of popular opinion.

George Gallup, the principal inventor of these polls, completely identifies "will of the people" and "public opinion." In a controversial article, he looks to a future in which periodic elections will be replaced by continuous public-opinion polls.[67] The statesman would then have his decisions dictated from day to day by the public's view of the issues. But this suggestion disregards the fact that the public is usually ill informed, whereas governments possess a great mass of information that sometimes enables them to

---

[65] Hanotaux, *op. cit.*, pp. 142, 145, 187.

[66] See on this subject the interesting analysis by G. Burdeau, "L'évolution des techniques d'expression de l'opinion publique dans la démocratie," in Gaston Berger, ed., *L'Opinion publique* (Paris, 1957), pp. 137–68.

[67] "The Next Twenty Years," *International Social Science Bulletin* (Paris, UNESCO), V, No. 3 (1953), 467–73.

look far ahead and to make decisions on a long-term basis. Conversely, it is precisely this complex and long-range character of foreign-policy problems that results in the public's general indifference to them. For the most part, the public is concerned with foreign policy only insofar as it produces visible domestic consequences (customs policy and price levels, length of military draft, etc.).[68]

When Mussolini declared war on June 10, 1940, he was probably acting against the wishes of most Italians. But he had a chance to win them to his side—by gaining an immediate success. He probably exaggerated the possibility of such a success, and, as the disasters multiplied, public opinion hardened in its initial position, and the Mussolini regime collapsed by successive stages in the midst of almost universal hostility.

Roosevelt, in 1939–40, started from a similar position: the extreme hostility of the country to war. Being better informed than the public, he came to the conclusion that war was inevitable and that the very existence of the United States was at issue. Nevertheless, he knew it was impossible to make decisions right away that were likely to lead to immediate war. His enormously skillful policy was to work *ahead* of the public, but to do things that the public would quickly understand were necessary. His victory in the presidential election of 1940 showed that it was possible to go far along the road from "neutrality" to "nonbelligerence." In general, the public "followed" Roosevelt.

But public opinion and economic forces are not only forces that impel the statesman to act. They are also relatively malleable entities, and the statesman can try to change them. In the next chapter, we shall examine the nature and limits of what he does in this respect.

[68] On this point, see the useful information published in *Sondages* (Paris), 1958, No. 1–2 (special issue on French foreign policy and public opinion, 1954–57). See also below, pp. 335–36.

12

THE STATESMAN'S INFLUENCE
ON BASIC FORCES

The statesman's power to influence a given event is undeniable—that is his function and his responsibility, whether in reacting to another nation's move, or in initiating policy. He probably can also modify circumstances by a series of deliberate acts—circumstances in this sense being the whole complex of events taking place at a particular time. The political leader is sometimes able to unravel this skein and determine the points where action is required or, sometimes, where action would merely aggravate the situation.

In an inflationary crisis, for example, there are certain policies one can and certain policies one should not follow. Poincaré, between July and October, 1926, "saved the franc" and succeeded in balancing the budget; Wilhelm Cuno, in the spring of 1923, managed to accelerate the runaway inflation that was sweeping Germany. In a major economic crisis, there is a deliberate choice to be made among possible remedies. In their different ways, Roosevelt through the New Deal, Hitler through rearmament, Ramsey MacDonald through the devaluation of the pound, the restoration of protective tariffs, and the establishment of imperial preference, mitigated the global depression of the early 1930's. The unstable French governments of the same period, with their policies of deflation by decree, probably helped to aggravate France's economic paralysis.

That, however, is not the real issue. The real issue is whether a statesman can, in sustained action, decisively transform the basic structures of the nation, or whether these are subject to unchangeable laws. (Perhaps we should speak rather of the underlying infrastructures and of superstructures. According to one theory, only the latter are not immune to the influence of political action; the former, the very substance of a nation's history, continue to evolve according to their own implacable laws.) If we could answer this question, we would solve one of the most crucial problems confronting the historian. Some writers, Marxists in particular, believe that the doctrine of historical materialism provides the answer—an answer, incidentally, considerably more subtle and complex than ill-informed or ill-intentioned commentators imagine.[1] Others contend that historical materialism is based on hypotheses that only history is capable of validating or invalidating, that the

---

[1] See below, pp. 323–24.

case is not proven, and that considerable objective research is required before any interpretation can be seriously asserted.

This is really an essential problem in the philosophy of history. Philosophy posits theories. Only the study of history can assess their validity. And, given the present state of historical research, it does not seem possible to provide clear and convincing assessments.

Our task here is far less assuming. It is to show what practical problems arise and to delimit those problems. We shall analyze a few cases, but we must resign ourselves to admitting that the data are often apparently contradictory.

To begin with, looking at the situation in historical perspective, we may say that neither the Battle of Waterloo, for example, nor even the whole series of wars arising from the French Revolution and the Napoleonic era affected the substantial similarity in standard of living and level of power of defeated France and victorious England. Moreover, however different their political systems were in practice, they were based on the same fundamental principles. This means that whatever the vicissitudes in the political histories of the two countries were, the basic structure of national life in each followed a parallel development. Or consider the question of decolonization. Almost twenty years after the conclusion of World War II, victors and vanquished alike have lost their colonial empires. Defeated Japan and Italy had to give them up immediately. Victorious England—and France, which had been a modest partner in the camp of victory—have given them up piecemeal. The only difference between vanquished and victors is that with the former the process was rapid and with the latter it spread out over several years. But in a century's time, it will all appear as a single, basic phenomenon.

Another example: all the nations that we now call medium-range powers which before the war already had a large industrial capacity have at least doubled their production since the war, whether they had colonies or not and whether they were well or badly governed. Japan, whose population has increased by 25 million and whose territory has shrunk back to the Japanese archipelago alone, now enjoys a standard of living twice as high as it was at the time when she maintained that she was "suffocating" and needed to conquer "living space." France, with more than thirty governments since the war, and Germany with a single chancellor in fourteen years, developed into the 1960's at an almost equal pace, if not along parallel lines.

Inversely, the recent horrifying developments in arms technology open up a clear possibility that a single decision by a political leader is capable of transforming not only an event, not only circumstances, but the very structure of societies. The decision to initiate thermonuclear warfare, or the irrational act that might turn a conflict into a war of mutual destruction, could send any surviving humanity back to a kind of dark ages. The virtually inevitable destruction of cities, of industry, of administrative personnel, and of intellectual and technical capabilities would in a few days transform sophisticated societies into heaps of rubble in which, in all likelihood, the rare survivors, banded together and armed like their ancestors of prehistory, would fiercely dispute for possession of the few inhabitable zones and scanty resources. And all this could depend on a single political act. Incredible as it may seem, one must regard such an act as a possibility.

The two world wars, terrible as they were, may be more modestly regarded as the result of political actions that also widely transformed structural conditions. It is true that in Europe both victors and vanquished—England, France, Germany, Italy—which in 1914 were powers equal in "rank" are today on roughly the same level in the hierarchy of power. But the "decline of Europe" and the absorption of the substance of power by the Soviet Union and the United States may surely be ascribed to the decisive weakening of Europe in consequence of wars that today appear to have been fratricidal. Believers in the autonomous development and endurance of national infrastructures, on the other hand, might reply that the wars were not in fact brought about by ephemeral political decisions but by the historical necessity of inescapable forces.

Even if we are unable to solve the problem of the actual influence of men on these basic structures of history, there remain the cases where political leaders *wanted* and *tried* to transform the underlying forces.

I. ATTEMPTS TO INFLUENCE ECONOMIC AND SOCIAL FORCES

We can take as a first example what is perhaps the most elementary social phenomenon, population trends and demographic movements. History would appear to indicate that in societies which become industrialized and where illiteracy disappears, the birth rate declines—a complex structural phenomenon as yet incompletely accounted for. Occasionally one finds a spontaneous reversal of this tendency—as was the case in the United States, where demographic forecasts in 1930 that the country would have 120 million people by 1960 were proved wrong, since the United States had a population of 190 million in 1963.

Political leaders in any case have means of action with which they can encourage or reverse the trend. We do not know whether the increase in the birth rate in France after 1946 had something to do with the 1938 law on family allowances, or with the "family code," or with some sort of structural revival of confidence, but it is reasonable to assume that the legislation played an albeit small, but not negligible, part.

Or again, since 1950, the Japanese Government has systematically pursued a policy favoring birth control. The results are staggering: from a 22 per cent increase, the birth rate has dropped in fifteen years to 16.2 per cent, considerably lower than France's. But again, one can argue that the decline is related to the rise in Japan's standard of living.

Is a government able to effect a decisive transformation of a country's social structure? Marxist-Leninists would be the first to say yes. After the proletarian revolution, in their view, a country will pass successively through the stage of "popular democracy," in which the class struggle continues but under the direction of the proletariat (which they draw into the revolution's vanguard, the Communist party); the stage of "socialism," in which the classes still exist but in which the class struggle is over; and finally the stage of "Communism," that is, of a classless society. But we have no historical example of such a society and cannot, therefore, know whether their prophecies can be fulfilled.

But in any case, this voluntary transformation will not really take place, according to them, until after the "revolution." On the one hand, the revolution is the inevitable result of active economic and social forces; on the other hand, the action of the proletarian government *after* the revolution consists basically in "moving with the current of history," encouraging the forces that shape the nation's infrastructure, and removing the obstacles in their way. For Marx, the superstructure is subordinate and grows from the infrastructure, from the forces of production and their interaction, which together constitute the real base upon which the legal and political superstructure is founded, and to which there correspond specific forms of social consciousness.[2] For Stalin, who viewed the situation as one where the proletarian revolution had already taken place and in the context of "socialism in a single country," the superstructure is more independent, with its own role:

> The superstructure is a product of the base; but this does not mean that it is passive, neutral, indifferent to the fate of the classes, to the character of the system. On the contrary, no sooner does it arise than it becomes an exceedingly active force, actively assisting its base to take shape and consolidate itself, and doing everything it can to help the new system finish off and eliminate the old base and the old classes.[3]

Thus we arrive at the idea that "the state is the most important component of the superstructure"[4]—making it possible to justify the strengthening of the Soviet state.

On the other hand, historical circumstances led the Bolsheviks to do things that seem little in accord with the laws Marx had enunciated—launching the Russian Revolution in 1917, although there existed no socialist economic

---

[2] Karl Marx, *A Contribution to the Critique of Political Economy* (Chicago, 1904).
[3] Josef Stalin, *Marxism and Linguistics* (New York, 1951), p. 10.
[4] A. I. Denisov and M. G. Karicento, cited by Henri Chambre, *Le Marxisme en Union Soviétique* (Paris, 1955). See the chapter entitled "Staline et la superstructure," pp. 457–83.

base in Russia, and "collectivizing agriculture in the 1930's by a revolution from 'on top,' in order to be in a position to develop the production forces of the agricultural economy by socializing them, instead of the reverse."[5]

Indeed, one can say that Marxism in its Soviet form abandoned the "mechanistic" theories which explained all development solely in terms of the infrastructure and minimized the role of the state. This had been central to Marx's position (Engels, however, showed that Marx exaggerated this aspect of his thought for polemical reasons), and it was also Georg Plekhanov's position, in *The Materialistic Conception of History* (1897), and Nikolai Bukharin's in *Historical Materialism* (1925). Most Marxist theorists now say that, at least in the socialist state, the superstructure (thus, ultimately, the decision of the men in power) can modify the infrastructure, provided, of course, that it does not infringe the general laws of dialectical materialism.

A mechanistic explanation is nonetheless possible. Even if the state has its own autonomous function and is able to modify the infrastructure, it may itself still be no more than a mere product of the infrastructure, so that the accession of certain men to power is in a sense predetermined, or so that any man placed in authority would act in the same way. But many Marxist thinkers vigorously reject this strict determinism. "As long as Stalin was in power," writes André Gorz,[6] Marxists presented his reign as the manifestation of a historical necessity: Stalin, it was claimed, had been produced by the material necessity of Stalinism; and Stalinism was the sole objective solution for the Soviet Union." Later, however, people began to wonder "whether acts hitherto explained by objective necessity were not in fact to be imputed to the individual and suddenly manifested will of the man Stalin." Gorz prefers an explanation somewhere in the middle. He maintains that "the brutality of Stalin's policy was not an accident, but a necessity." Nevertheless, even though,

> by his qualities, Stalin was the man of the situation . . . it is conceivable that, in the place of the "historical" Stalin, a contingent individual, another man might have been found with the same qualities in even greater measure, and with others that Stalin lacked. This ideal Stalin would probably have done basically the same things as the real Stalin did, but he would have done them in a different *way* and *at less cost*.

Most Marxist thinkers, then, now hold that in a system where the proletariat has assumed power, the state (the superstructure *par excellence*) exerts a controlling influence on the infrastructure (the underlying economic and social forces). They probably are also willing to concede the possibility of the government's being able, in a capitalistic system, to "apply the brakes."

---

[5] Chambre, *op. cit.*, p. 466.
[6] André Gorz, *La Morale de l'histoire* (Paris, 1959), pp. 24–29.

In simpler fashion, Tito has expressed a view on the function of the statesman that seems acceptable to both Marxist and non-Marxist thinkers:

> I admit that the role of man in history may be very important; it would be
> absurd, and a denial of the facts, to maintain the contrary. But the role of a
> man is the more considerable to the extent that it represents the will and
> the conscience of a people at a particular time. The people is the motor
> power of history.[7]

From this brief analysis of a particular theory of history, let us move on
to a more detailed presentation of actual examples of governments attempting
to fashion new infrastructures. The case of France and Mexico have been well
and clearly studied[8] and are also interesting because they are so dissimilar.

In France, the legislation passed in the revolutionary assemblies of the
1790's profoundly changed the country's social structures. The suppression
of feudal rights, the nationalization of church property, the abolition of
internal tariffs, and the Le Chapelier act of 1791 prohibiting coalitions did
much to promote the *economic* interests of the middle class, while the Declaration of the Rights of Man, effectively benefiting only one sector of the nation,
secured the foundations of middle-class *political* power. These developments
may certainly be explained as part of the interplay of basic socio-economic
forces; nevertheless, in combination with thousands of other decrees, they
gave a new structure to France. What is more interesting from our point of
view is that, by deliberate actions in the foreign-policy sphere—namely,
wars—these structural reforms were imposed on foreign countries where the
underlying forces were not really working in the same direction. Once these
transformations were achieved, it was virtually impossible to turn the clock
back.

It is striking that French theories on foreign economic policy, even at the
time of the Continental Blockade, remained broadly protectionist. While liberal economists were securing the triumph of domestic liberal policies from
the days of the Constituent Assembly on, all the European states maintained
strict customs barriers, prohibitions, and quota systems up to the time of the
British reforms of 1846–50 and the Cobden-Chevalier Treaty of 1860. "It is
difficult to exaggerate the effect of this commercial policy in retarding the
development of French industry and France's relations with other nations."[9]

It is certainly true that powerful forces were at work to retain protection-

---

[7] Vladimir Dedijer, *Tito parle* (Paris, 1953), p. 445.

[8] See in particular Rondo E. Cameron, *France and the Economic Development of
Europe, 1800–1914* (Princeton, 1961); and Charles Kindelberger, "The Post-War
Resurgence of the French Economy," in Stanley Hoffmann, *et al., In Search of France*
(Cambridge, Mass., 1963), pp. 118–58; also Raymond Vernon, *The Dilemma of Mexico's
Development* (Cambridge, Mass., 1963).

[9] Cameron, *op. cit.*, p. 36.

ism. There were many protection-minded businessmen in the legislature during the restoration monarchy and then during the July Monarchy, and the powerful journal *Moniteur Industriel* was much more influential than its opponent, the *Journal des économistes,* which reached only a few intellectuals. Similarly, the advent of free trade in England may be attributed to underlying forces, such as were represented by Cobden's Anti-Corn Law League. But there is a point where structural modification by deliberate will of the government is patently clear, as in the introduction of a form of free trade in France in 1860.

Napoleon III was in favor of free trade, but the legislature of the Empire, like the two chambers in the July Monarchy, was overwhelmingly protectionist, and there is every reason to believe that lobbyists favoring free trade were insignificant compared to the immense forces supporting a policy of protection. Twice, in 1856 and 1859, the legislature rejected bills voiding prohibitions. But we know that Napoleon III, on the advice of Michel Chevalier, decided to take advantage of a provision of the 1852 Constitution that authorized him to sign and ratify commercial treaties without legislative interference—thereby disrupting protectionism at one blow, despite the fury of the industrialists. Now it is difficult to regard this as the manifestation of some sort of historical necessity, and we are tempted to attribute the substantive basic reform to the specific decision of one man. Generalizing, we might regard the immense economic growth of France under the Second Empire—which was due principally to favorable circumstances such as the continued rise in prices combined with the new flow of gold from California—as due to the Emperor's deliberate and consistent policy, as shaped by his Saint-Simonian advisers.

One of the consequences of France's rapid economic development in the Second Empire was, of course, capital accumulation—clearly an essentially structural phenomenon. But political acts were to be decisive with regard to the employment of surplus capital, as was most apparent in the methods used to export capital. We might consider in this light, for instance, the government's role under the Second Empire in the politics of building railroads abroad with the assistance of French capital. An even more useful example would be the politics involved in making loans to foreign governments as we see it under the Third Republic. French loan policy at that time was motivated primarily by political considerations; its long-term economic consequences were disastrous. "Very little of the capital contributed in any significant way to economic development or material welfare,"[10] as the example of the Russian loans perhaps best shows. The "official solicitude on the part of republican France for the finances of Tsarist Russia may be attributed to France's persistent search for an ally against Germany." Even before the alliance, that policy was apparent. And after 1890, "abandoning their few remaining scru-

---

[10] *Ibid.,* p. 405.

ples regarding interference in the capital market, French ministers sought by every means at their disposal to encourage French investments in both government and private securities in Russia."[11]

Mexico provides us with a series of examples of governmental acts affecting what were first traditional structures, then structures in process of economic development.

When Benito Juárez became President of Mexico in 1858, his government undertook to transform a traditional and strongly structured society that had developed in the course of three centuries of Spanish domination. The economy was based on a complex system of monopolies, privileges, and controls governing both production and trade. Economically, Mexico was divided into watertight compartments of local markets; communication routes were virtually nonexistent. Since any undertaking required government authorization, bribery of the appropriate official was common practice. In the rural areas, the only protection the Indians enjoyed was that provided by the great landowner or the Catholic Church.

The policy of Juárez and the liberals was "to make a single nation of Mexico by reserving for the national government such powers as the maintenance of armies, the issuance of currency, and the regulation of foreign trade."[12] Monopolies, special privileges for industry, slavery, and forced labor were abolished, as were internal trade barriers.

Despite strong resistance, Juárez and his Finance Minister, Matias Romero, vigorously applied these new policies. Ecclesiastical property was confiscated and put up for sale, but as a rule it was purchased at low cost by well-to-do members of the bourgeoisie who were willing to brave excommunication (another feature in common with revolutionary France). And the railroad between Mexico City and Vera Cruz was completed. For the first time, a government was systematically attempting to alter Mexico's basic economic and social structures. Owing to the resistance it encountered, its success was only partial. Being liberals, Juárez and Romero would have wished to move in the direction of free trade also, but half of Mexico's federal revenues came from customs duties, and there were powerful groups favoring protection.

The dictatorial regime of Porfirio Díaz, who ruled Mexico from 1876 to 1911, substituted for this socially oriented policy one of systematic economic development which, it was believed, could be left in the hands of private enterprise. A decisive choice was made: to do everything possible to encourage the investment of foreign capital in Mexico. This meant that domestic order and tranquillity must be maintained—the justification for the dictatorship.

---

[11] *Ibid.*, pp. 423–24, 434. See also Herbert Feis, *Europe, the World's Banker* (New Haven, 1930). For a more complete discussion of how France carried out this loan policy, see above, Chapter Five, pp. 113–14.

[12] Vernon, *op. cit.*, p. 33.

The principal investments were made in railroads. From some 400 miles of track in 1876, total rail mileage had risen to 15,000 by 1900. Other investments made possible the development of mines, export crops, and some processing industries.

Although Díaz' policy had a considerable beneficial influence on Mexico's economic growth, it for the most part disregarded the interests of the peasantry and permitted the wealthy to accumulate enormous estates. In 1910, 80 per cent of the rural families of Mexico were landless, and one-seventh of Mexico's arable land was owned by a few foreigners. The situation was bound to provoke violent reactions. Díaz was indubitably transforming the economic structure of the country, but he was also encouraging profound discontent by doing so in a way that treated the Indians as inferior beings, on the principle of some sort of racist Darwinism. Discontent also developed among the workers and the rapidly growing urban middle class. Mexico needed only a more than momentary decline in prices on the world market (such as took place between 1907 and 1910) for her raw materials to be ripe for revolution. And revolution broke out, in fact, in 1910.

Between 1910 and 1940, revolutionary Mexico had first to endure a period of unrest; the authority of the federal state was only gradually restored. The uprisings were mainly agrarian rebellions: lands seized, *haciendas* burned, merchants attacked. Local autonomy was reasserted. But despite the confusion, the goal of the new Mexican politics was still clearly to take away the power of those who had supported Díaz: the Church, the great landowners, foreigners. The nationalization of the mines and mineral resources (which led to violent conflict with United States oil companies), confiscation of lands, expulsion of foreigners, restoration of collective village property, protection of labor, government arbitration in labor disputes—all these clearly showed Mexico's new determination to transform structures by giving social affairs priority over economic affairs.

Vigorous presidents like Venustiano Carranza, Alvaro Obregón, and Plutarco Elias Calles were gradually able to restore a strong central power, based on the dominant Institutional Revolutionary Party (PRI), comprising government officials, trade unions, and many other leading groups and individuals. When Lazaro Cárdenas became President in 1934, the government was once more in a position to make major decisions for the reform of the Mexican economy. Cárdenas was able, for instance, to put into effect the agricultural reforms enacted in 1917. By 1940, the number of Mexicans on the great *haciendas* had dropped to 800,000 from 3 million in 1910. Yet, despite his Marxist leanings and his links with the unions, Cárdenas decided to protect industrial and commercial enterprises, at the same time controlling them by forcing them to belong to the enormous government-controlled Confederacion de Camaras Industriales and the Confederacion de Camaras Nacionales de Comercio. Altogether, the transition period of 1910–40 was characterized

principally by the introduction of state management and by a growing awareness of the role of the public sector in economic development. The economy
began to move ahead after 1920, especially in industry, and proceeded much
more rapidly after 1935.

From 1940 on, government action on economic structures became more
defined, more conscious, and more obvious. "It was the year in which there
appeared the first of a succession of presidents devoted to the proposition that
industrial growth on the modern pattern was indispensable for Mexico."[13]
And the war, by increasing demand for Mexican products abroad, gave the
economy a considerable boost. By 1960, the gross national product had sur-
passed 82 billion pesos (taking the 1950 value as the base rate), as compared
with 23 billion in 1939.

Estimates naturally differ as to who benefited from this growth. Although
huge fortunes were amassed, the standard of living of part of the masses also
improved. This does not mean that Mexico has become a fully developed
country—far from it. But, to use W. W. Rostow's term, we may say that
Mexico has certainly reached the stage of economic "take-off."

The important feature of the Mexican example is that government action
on economic structures was conducted with a single goal over a long period.
The work of Díaz and the accomplishments since 1940 are most characteristic,
the latter especially; taking advantage of certain more or less socialist reforms
instituted in the revolutionary period, the government has had vast means of
action at its disposal. A flexible planning system developed after 1952 under
the immediate control of the president. "The administrative style of the Mexican government began to acquire certain new accents."[14]

Once again, it is hard to determine the exact relative roles of the government and the nation's basic forces in developing and transforming the social
structure. But the many political vicissitudes we have briefly described here
are clear evidence of the contribution made by the conscious will of a series
of political leaders. The examples of France and Mexico do not answer the
questions for us, but they enable us to state them more adequately.

In the first place, they both show that many statesmen have indeed set
about to reform the economic and social structures of their countries. They
also demonstrate that statesmen have sometimes succeeded in going against
the tide—in overcoming resolute opposition from entrenched forces. Such
was the case of Juárez' attempt at reform and still more with Napoleon III's
successful effort to establish a kind of free-trade policy. These cases were
exceptions, however. More usually, the men in power used existing forces to
defeat other, newer powers. Thus Díaz encouraged various forms of Mexican
and foreign capitalism to establish order and unity; and the French governments after 1887 allowed Russian propaganda to be disseminated freely, with

[13] *Ibid.*, p. 88.
[14] *Ibid.*, p. 115.

the result that large and small investors were encouraged to put their money in Russian bonds.

But however consistent and persevering the reforming efforts may be, and however long the period over which they extend, do they in fact effect deep structural changes? Here we shall have to admit ignorance more often than affirm definite conclusions. Napoleon III turned France to free trade, but do we really know whether he effected any profound transformation of the country's basic structure? Is it possible to assert (as some historians have done) that the government's encouragement of foreign bond issues discouraged investors from investing in French companies and thereby slowed down French economic development? The answer is certainly not clear. It is true that France suffered heavy losses of capital in Russia and other countries. But would that capital necessarily have been invested in France had it not been attracted abroad? Was France's slower economic growth after 1880 due to this or to other causes—business attitudes, the structure of the capital market, tax laws?

The problem remains, finally, to what extent political leaders may or may not be simply the expression of a country's underlying forces. "Bourgeois dynasties" have certainly existed that monopolized politics and business on behalf of their members, with the result that state policy was often inspired by the exigencies of high finance and big capital. Yet to claim that this connection is an absolute and more or less continuous one,[15] seems to sacrifice an extremely varied phenomenon, capable of different interpretations, to an occasionally seductive theory. It is true that generous social reforms have often been blocked by the "money wall"—this was apparent in France in 1924–25 and in 1936–37. But the state has often acted in the light of far broader considerations than those of business: the "national interest," as Wilson called it, has often opposed "special interests," and the state has often been able not only to resist pressures, but also to take action against them.

There is one last aspect of the effect of political action on economic forces to consider: the policy of seeking to induce certain economic phenomena in order to achieve concrete results in the area of foreign policy—economic reprisals, tariff wars, the initiation of free trade as a step toward peace, the granting of economic advantages in exchange for political ones, and, more recently, the attempt to achieve political federation through economic "integration." It will be enough to refer briefly to some of these points.[16]

The notion of strengthening peace through free trade, dear to liberal economists of the nineteenth century and enshrined in the third of President Wilson's Fourteen Points, also one of Cordell Hull's themes, finally received a form of abstract international sanction in the establishment of the General Agreement on Tariffs and Trade (GATT) after World War II.

---

[15] See Beau de Loménie, *Les Responsabilités des dynasties bourgeoises* (Paris, 1943–63).

[16] Government actions of this kind are treated in detail above, pp. 75–82.

Whereas thinkers like Friedrich List (in his *National System of Political Economy*, written in 1841) assert that the nation is the natural framework for economic development, others, the liberals, try to eliminate the barriers that separate human groups. One of their oft-cited arguments is that free trade—the product of a political decision—removes a basic cause of wars, economic rivalry. Cordell Hull returned to this theme constantly, entitling one chapter of his memoirs "War and Trade." Here he recalled that in the House of Representatives on June 8, 1916, he had suggested that a "permanent international trade congress" be established after the end of the war "to promote fair and friendly trade relations among all the nations of the world."[17] As Secretary of State, Hull became increasingly attached to this theory. Roosevelt, however, was less enthusiastic, and by and large Hull was unable to secure the adoption of his policy. "According to the mercantilists, *commerce is war*, according to the liberals, *commerce is peace*, on the sole condition that it be free. According to the national economists, *commerce will be peace* when all nations are developed; according to the Marxists, *commerce is war* under capitalism, *commerce will be peace* with socialism."[18]

Giving economic aid is perhaps a means of acting on a nation's infrastructure, as the Marshall Plan showed. And the extension of economic aid to the so-called underdeveloped countries reveals even vaster ambitions. Since undiluted altruism plays only the very smallest role in international relations, the underlying intentions must necessarily be mainly political, but they are based on economic hypotheses that have thus far not been proven. With their aid programs, industrialized nations of the West hope to encourage the beginnings of economic development; this will reduce the likelihood of unrest and revolution by raising the standards of living. The Soviet Union, on the other hand, whose aid often consists in financing the development of industry, is perhaps trying to encourage the creation and development of an industrial proletariat.

Here we are coming to the real heart of the matter. If it is demonstrated in the coming years that economic aid contributes appreciably to a rise in standards of living, then it will have been proved that states can effectively act upon national infrastructures. The fact that economic aid succeeded in Europe proved nothing, for the development structures already existed and the assistance simply revived once strong economies that had been exhausted by the war.

With international economic integration, we are confronted with an even more significant experiment. History shows us various examples of customs unions (to which reference was made earlier in this volume[19]), but the concept

---

[17] Cordell Hull, *Memoirs* (New York, 1948), I, 82. See also L. Robbins, *The Economic Causes of War* (London, 1939), and W. R. Allen, "Cordell Hull and the Defense of the Trade Agreements Program, 1934–40," in Alexander de Conde, *Isolation and Security* (Durham, N.C., 1957), pp. 107–32.

[18] Raymond Aron, *Peace and War* (Garden City, N.Y., 1966), p. 253.

[19] See above, Chapter Four, pp. 85–89.

of economic integration goes much further, beyond the simple issue of common customs and free-trade areas, to the idea of effecting a complete fusion of economies, implying complete mobility of goods, capital, and tariffs, a single banking system, equal levels of social security, and a single currency.

What is interesting for us about the politics of economic integration—inaugurated in Europe in our era in May, 1950, with the Schuman Plan and extended by the 1957 Treaty of Rome establishing the Common Market—is that its proponents actively sought to effect a complex stimulus to economic forces and political institutions. By the decision of six governments (informally approved by the public, but subject to strong opposition), machinery was established to transform the basic structures of the EEC member countries in twelve or fourteen years and to incorporate them in a single system. But the real purpose was to make Europe's political unification possible. (Even if some supporters of economic integration do not favor future political integration—General de Gaulle, for example—the process may not be reversible.) We thus have the following theoretical sequence: governmental action (superstructure) aimed at transforming the economic reality (infrastructure), in turn to lead to a transformation of institutions (superstructure). But the experiment is not yet finished and we cannot yet tell whether history will conform to this pattern.

II. ATTEMPTS TO INFLUENCE NATIONAL PUBLIC OPINION

Governmental efforts to transform or modify current public opinions are legion. In a parliamentary or presidential democracy, a kind of balancing movement occurs between the government, which tries to win the support of the public, and the popular will, which in the end, after all, chooses who will represent the public. It is a complex balance, for the government must both satisfy the public and persuade it. It is its attempts to do the latter that we shall examine here. We must also ask to what extent a government can act on deep, broad, and lasting tendencies, such as certain great ideologies. Finally, every government tries to influence the collective attitudes taken in foreign countries, both in time of peace and, especially, in time of war.

The vocabulary used in describing such governmental activity is not very precise. When a government wishes to give a correct version of the facts, it terms this version "information." But it seldom gives out "information" without ulterior motives, and the "facts" are therefore liable to be colored; it is a case no longer of information but of propaganda. Hitler did not hesitate to call the government department entrusted to Goebbels the "Ministry of Propaganda."[20] Totalitarian regimes, of course—with their control

[20] Derrick Sington and Arthur Weidenfeld, *The Goebbels Experiment: A Study of the Nazi Propaganda Machine* (London, 1942).

of press, radio, television, publishing, public meetings and associations—
have far more powerful propaganda means available than democratic nations
do, but some democracies have a "Ministry of Information" or the like
the real purpose of which is to spread propaganda.

The borderline between propaganda and psychological warfare is not
always clear. In Nazi Germany, a book by a Colonel Blau, *Propaganda als
Waffe* (1935), written for the Nazi high command, was based on psychology,
psychoanalysis, and sociology; during the war, Blau was put in charge of
the psychological-warfare operations of the Wehrmacht, with a large staff
and considerable financial means at his disposal. How does one, in fact,
distinguish between "propaganda" and "psychological warfare"? Both
techniques may be used in peacetime as in war; both, in theory, pursue the
same ends—namely, to strengthen the nation's morale, to project a favorable
image of it abroad, to demonstrate that it is resolute and that its cause is
good, and to discourage the enemy. The difference lies in the intention.
Propaganda seeks simply to give the nation a good reputation, a good moral
position, and even, in the case of internal propaganda, greater cohesion (by
improving the relations between the public and the government). Psychological warfare, on the other hand, is an aspect of war—indeed, of total
war; it is used, whether in the context of hostilities or not, when the intention
is to destroy a country, a system, or an ideology. It is first a "substitute for
violence"; since victory in this instance consists in achieving the submission
of the will of the foe, it is most economical if this aim can be achieved without using armed force. "War is psychological in the sense that the advance
of armies is simply a means toward negotiation. Warring kings, in pursuing
their objectives, appealed to the public and conformed to the rules of
psychology." Psychological warfare also serves to "heighten violence" where
the intention is to develop a warlike spirit and total mobilization of the
nation's energies. Finally, it may take the form of an endemic condition, a
"generalized conflict of minds."[21] The cold war that began after the end
of World War II expresses this on an unprecedented scale.

At the imperceptible point at which psychological warfare takes the place
of propaganda, a sort of perversion of methods sets in which only *raison
d'état*, or totalitarianism, can claim to justify. For total psychological warfare, there must be unqualified adherence to the principle that the end
justifies the means. Would that this entailed nothing worse than even the
most infamous lies! But it entails much more. Psychological warfare seeks
to instill terror by means of criminal assaults, massacre of the guilty and
even of the innocent (bombing civilian populations, destroying villages,
assassinations, or torture). It goes so far as to violate the human consciousness by "brain-washing"—euphemistically described as the "re-education"
of the vanquished. In a word, total psychological warfare is a continual and

---

[21] Maurice Megret, *La Guerre psychologique* (Paris, 1956), pp. 8 ff.

systematic violation of human dignity. It is hardly surprising, therefore, that the public should respond unfavorably and reject the terms "psychological warfare" and even "propaganda," independent of their technical connotation.

Still, political leaders must try to affect the basic forces of the collective psychology. We have chosen examples of such attempts from a period when the mass media were not yet fully developed;[22] and we have tried to distinguish between peace and war situations and between government action on its own country and on foreign peoples, whether friends or enemies.

In peacetime, governments have always tried to influence public opinion, on a short-term or long-term basis. Its principal tools, prior to the period of widespread radio broadcasting, were press campaigns. Less frequently— during election campaigns, for instance—these were supplemented by meetings. Of course, in a dictatorship, the government completely controls the press, but most of the public knows it and is skeptical, and it is also attracted to foreign information sources the government does not control. Frenchmen preferred the B.B.C. to the German and Vichy radio during the occupation in World War II and eagerly read clandestine underground papers. In countries where the press is free, the government tries either to win over the editors or, by means of secret payments, to subsidize them.

The French scholar Bernard Voyenne distinguished three uses of the press in this regard.[23] The first is "prolonged repetition of stimuli moving in identical directions," the second, "prestige effects," in which the press appeals to diverse authorities in an effort to persuade uncommitted readers at a critical moment. For instance, when Woodrow Wilson arrived in Paris in 1918, the Communist Party paper *L'Humanité* published a special issue on December 14 designed especially to increase its popularity in leftist circles; in addition to Party leaders, the contributors included well-known writers such as Anatole France, scholars like the historian Maxime Leroy, the sociologist Lévy-Bruhl, the economist Charles Gide, and public figures such as Ferdinand Buisson, chairman of the Ligue des Droits de l'Homme. Third and lastly, the press acts through the "orientation of news content," that is, the varying degrees of prominence given to different news items.

The government can employ the method of prolonged repetition if it controls the newspapers. And it is well placed to manipulate "prestige effects," since important statements by political leaders are usually highlighted in the press. But in a free country, such means are limited, since the government will not control all the paper. Of course, on major issues, the government may try to appeal directly to the public through a campaign of meetings, forums, and speeches.

---

[22] See Bernard Voyenne, *La Presse dans la société contemporaine* (Paris, 1962), particularly "Chronologie des techniques de diffusion," pp. 275–79, and the UNESCO statistics Voyenne cites on the distribution of newspapers, radios, and television sets.

[23] Voyenne, *op. cit.*, pp. 187 ff.

Take, for example, the tour that Wilson made through the United States between September 3 and September 29, 1919, to obtain popular support for the Treaty of Versailles and the League of Nations. Certain points about this trip are particularly interesting. First, Wilson chose to visit "decisive" zones: he left out New England, which was stoutly opposed to his views, and the South, where the senators all supported him, and went instead to the Middle and Far West, where opinion was divided. But after scoring a remarkable triumph in California, one of whose senators, Hiram Johnson, was strongly opposed to his views, he decided to go to Massachusetts after all, the home state of Senator Henry Cabot Lodge, the Republican chairman of the Committee on Foreign Relations and the principal foe of the Treaty. Illness alone prevented Wilson from carrying out this project.

The inherent difficulty in Wilson's procedure was that he could reach only part of the population. (In Columbus, Ohio, a city of 300,000, Wilson spoke before 4,000 persons.) He could not really affect the grass roots. (With radio and television, Wilson could have reached twenty times more listeners without strain or danger.) But direct contact with the people is not ruled out even in our own time. In contrast to the method used by Pierre Mendès-France when he was Premier—a weekly radio talk—think of General de Gaulle's practice of traveling through the French provinces.

For Wilson, as for others, the practice of traveling presented another disadvantage: it provoked immediate reactions from the opposing side. In every city through which he passed, the irreconcilable foes of the treaty— McCormick, Borah, Johnson—followed in their turn, hoping to destroy any gains Wilson might have made.

It must therefore be recognized that a government's attempts to create public attitudes, particularly on foreign-policy issues, are often unavailing and at any rate limited. Scholars have shown, incidentally, that in peacetime, the public is usually indifferent to foreign-policy issues and therefore not very receptive to propaganda:

> When the public is consulted on urgent problems, on the duties incumbent on the government, it points first to domestic affairs and, among the possible issues, to whatever concerns *material* conditions of existence—wages, prices, general standard of living, housing, or employment. [Only events] in which individuals are somehow directly involved [the Algerian war, for instance] can divert attention for a while from immediate personal or family preoccupations. Concern with peace, general worries about the relative positions of the powers, international politics, systems of alliances—all these take a secondary place in the public mind, as though in the background of consciousness.[24]

This analysis seems to hold true in a number of countries, certainly those

---

[24] *Sondages* (Paris), 1958, No. 1-2 (special issue on French foreign policy and public opinion, 1954–57), p. 10.

with a high standard of living. In the United States, 53 per cent of those questioned in a poll gave priority to domestic questions, and only 16 per cent to international problems.[25] If a government finds it difficult to act rapidly, it profits by this indifference, since it gives it great freedom of action. As Guizot remarked:

> You may take it as a fact that foreign policy does not preoccupy France at all and will not produce any great reaction there. Governments may do as they please; if they do foolhardy things, they will not be supported; if they simply do silly things, they will be jeered at, but not angrily; and they will not be overthrown provided they are at all adequate as regards domestic affairs, which is the only thing the public takes seriously.[26]

It is enough, in most cases, for the government simply to counterbalance the hostility of opposition groups.

Its "educational" task would appear more important. Can it, in the long run, mold outlooks, kindle patriotism, in some cases exacerbate it? Totalitarian governments can, for they can design textbooks, organize youth groups and thus reduce the influence of the family, control the press and publications. Democratic governments also act on school programs and textbooks, but are the results proportionate to the effort? Over a period of twenty years, Mussolini certainly did not succeed in convincing the Italians that war was a noble and magnificent enterprise. Even Hitler, although he took advantage of German grievances after the Treaty of Versailles, roused only a fraction of the country to bellicosity. All the evidence agrees that in September, 1939, German soldiers were resigned but not enthusiastic. The patriotic fervor of Paris or Berlin in 1914 could not be revived by mere propaganda.

The impression is rather that the great evolutions of national sentiment— its growth, its explosions into violent nationalism, its decline in favor of internationalism or supranationalism—are profound structural phenomena over which governments have only limited influence. The most a government can do during a period of ardent nationalism is to divert abroad the passions of a people eager for social reform. Thus Nasser's Egypt used the desire for revenge against Israel, the victorious nation of 1948, as a powerful lever for domestic political action. But in peacetime, the "politics of greatness" does not obliterate concrete demands. Polignac was not able to eliminate domestic French unrest by the conquest of Algiers. Venizelos' ambitious foreign policy in 1919–20 did not prevent his defeat in the Greek elections of November, 1920.

The action of statesmen on foreign populations is even harder to de-

---

[25] Jerome S. Bruner, *Ce que pense l'Amérique* (Paris, 1945), p. 22. See also Lester Markel, ed., *Public Opinion and Foreign Policy* (New York, 1949).

[26] Letter to Lord Aberdeen, September 16, 1849, in *Lettres de M. Guizot à sa famille et à ses amis* (Paris, 1884), pp. 270–72.

termine. Foreign governments often pay journalists or subsidize newspapers to present their point of view, but great precautions are taken to conceal these practices, and they come to light only accidentally.

For example, the Bolsheviks, after the October Revolution, published in *L'Humanité* a series of letters written principally by Arthur Raffalovich,[27] a private counsellor to the Russian Ministry of Finance in Paris between 1897 and 1917, that related to payments made for propaganda purposes by the Tsarist embassy in Paris to a large number of newspapers: "Since it is impossible to buy everyone, we must make a selection and take *Le Temps*, *L'Echo de Paris*, *Le Journal*, *Le Petit Parisien*, and four or five provincial papers." For 50,000 francs, "we have been promised real collaboration for six months in the financial sections of *Le Petit Journal*, *Le Figaro*, *Le Matin*, *Le Français*, etc. It is not a case of their being neutral, but of their rendering real assistance, of stimulating interest, and of educating the public."[28] The object was to "enlighten the public" by lauding the merits of Russian bonds. But, as Kokovtzev wrote to Poincaré in October, 1912: "I refer to the Paris papers, whose inclinations are of great importance, from the point of view not so much of our two countries' financial interests as of their political interests."[29]

A systematic study—the only one of its kind, to our knowledge, based on an extensive examination of the records—has been made concerning Greek propaganda in 1919–20.[30] By studying the documents of the Greek Embassy in London, the author was able to reconstruct the vigorous representations made by the Greeks—to the major allies, in Switzerland, to the British powers in Asia, and among specific Christian and Jewish, academic, and socialist groups—to gain support for Greek claims to northern Epirus, Thrace, the western coast of Turkey, Pontus, Rhodes, the Dodecanese, Cyprus, Imbros, and Tenedos. This propaganda was the more necessary since Greece had come late to the side of the Entente, and her former king, Constantine, had been emphatically pro-German and had therefore cast doubt in the minds of the Allies about Greek sentiments.

One of the ministers, Andreas Michalacopoulos, was instructed to set up a Greek propaganda organization in London, and a former journalist, Dimitri Caclamanos, was put in charge. Innumerable pamphlets and books, maps and statistics were published and distributed, and systematic "siege" was laid to the press. England's major papers—*The Times*, *The Manchester Guardian*, *The Morning Post*, etc.—were approached individually and persuaded to publish incidental articles in favor of the Greek position. Other,

---

[27] These were published in book form under the title *L'abominable vénalité de la presse* (Paris, 1931).

[28] *Ibid.*, pp. 5, 7 (October 13 and 26, 1901).

[29] *Ibid.*, p. 332.

[30] Dimitri Kitzikis, *Propagande et pressions en politique internationale: La Grèce et ses revendications à la Conférence de la Paix, 1919–1920* (Paris, 1963).

less important papers received money. The Greek Government also issued its own periodical, the *Balkan Review* (and in France the *Etudes franco-grècques*). Journalists were personally won over by means of subsidies.

On all these points we have a wealth of detail that reveals the scale of Greek action and its high degree of organization. Influential figures, in particular Sir Basil Zaharoff, a fabulously wealthy munitions manufacturer of Greek ancestry, actively engaged in putting constant pressure on politicians whom their position permitted them to meet and influence. "Venizelos and his men, who were very sensitive to all developments in techniques of international action, fully realized the importance of propaganda." There was some wastage, "for it was a new technique, which had never before been attempted on so great a scale." The Greek endeavor was too brief to be wholly effective, but Venizelos, "who received great awards from the Peace Conference, could only congratulate himself on having spent so much money and effort in this area."[31]

When wartime propaganda turns into "psychological warfare," of necessity it becomes greater in scope; funds are provided with greater liberality, and the stakes are higher. The aims are systematically to buoy up the nation's morale by extolling victories, minimizing defeats, and offering reasons for optimism, and at the same time to destroy the morale of enemy soldiers and civilians. (Thus the Japanese, during World War II, tried to make American soldiers in the Pacific homesick.) Action on civilian morale is another essential preoccupation. We know that, according to General Douhet of the Italian Air Force, the bombing of cities was considered an essential means of undermining the determination of the enemy. But on the other hand, neither the Battle of Britain nor the Allied bombing of Germany would appear to bear out this theory, since in both cases the morale of the civilian population remained firm.

We as yet know little about the organization of wartime propaganda. Let us take an example, however, for which some information exists—namely, British propaganda at the end of World War I.[32] Prior to 1916, British propaganda was administered by a hush-hush agency, the Office of War Propaganda (Wellington House), directed by Charles Masterman. Then, after various other experiments, a Ministry of Information was established in February, 1918; Lord Northcliffe, editor of *The Times* and *Daily Mail* and an extraordinarily talented journalist, was appointed director of propaganda for enemy countries. Propaganda at home and in the Allied countries was the responsibility of the National War Aims Committee. We have special information on one aspect of this propaganda—the part conducted in the

31 *Ibid.*, pp. 483–84.

32 Megret, *op. cit.*; J. Driencourt, *La Propagande, nouvelle force politique* (Paris, 1950); Harold D. Lasswell, *Propaganda Technique in the World War* (London and New York, 1927); E. H. Carr, *Propaganda in International Politics* (Oxford, 1939).

United States—for we have an account by the man in charge of the service, Sir Arthur Willert.[33]

Willert had long been chief of the press service at the Foreign Office. During the war, he became Washington correspondent for *The Times*, then secretary of the British War Mission and representative of the Ministry of Information in the United States, while remaining *The Times'* correspondent. Willert shows, first of all, how necessary British propaganda was in the United States. Despite the bond of a common language and other powerful factors, there was a great deal of anti-British feeling in the United States (particularly among isolationists), many prejudices, and many points of disagreement during 1914–17 and even in the summer of 1918.[34]

An even more essential figure than Willert was Sir William Wiseman, who arrived in the United States at the close of 1915 (he was then thirty years old) as liaison officer between Wilson and Colonel House and the British War Cabinet. Basically, Wiseman was concerned with counter-espionage, with Willert serving rather as his deputy in the propaganda field. Willert is highly critical, however, of the British Ambassador, Sir Cecil Spring-Rice, who was not adept at concealing his constant irritation with Americans.

It was after the Balfour mission to the United States in the spring of 1917 that an official British public-information agency was set up in New York. Previously, the American activities of Wellington House (where a Canadian novelist, Sir Gilbert Parker, directed the American section) had been limited: arrangement of lecture tours, supply of films, books, and pamphlets. The organization of an active center was thus long overdue, and Wiseman and Willert drew up plans. A young Cambridge don, Geoffrey Butler, was placed in charge of the New York bureau, his first job being to coordinate existing activities and to give precise information and aid to British journalists and lecturers who for one reason or another came to the United States. One of his major aims was to penetrate Catholic circles, often of Irish origin and in general violently hostile to the British.

Then in June, 1917, Northcliffe was appointed chief of the British war mission. This marked an immense step forward. Willert had no difficulty in getting along with him. Northcliffe, unlike Spring-Rice (who detested him), "understood Americans; they liked and trusted him."[35] William Randolph Hearst, who was regarded as pro-German, even agreed to give Northcliffe the run of the editorial page of *The New York Journal American* for one issue, where Northcliffe successfully took pains to inform the public of the extent

[33] *The Road to Safety: A Study in Anglo-American Relations* (London, 1952).

[34] However, Suzanne Tassier's *La Belgique et l'entrée en guerre des Etats-Unis* (Brussels, 1951) contains a useful study of the anti-German feeling aroused in the United States by Germany's violation of Belgian neutrality.

[35] Willert, *op. cit.*, p. 100. Spring-Rice was replaced by Reading in February, 1918.

of British participation in the European war—a participation that Tardieu's French mission preferred to minimize.[36] Northcliffe's mission, indeed, went far beyond propaganda, and his training and temperament caused him to attach exceptional importance to it.

III. CONCLUSION

The efforts of statesmen to affect the underlying forces is constant, whether in modifying, or attempting to modify, economic trends, or transforming, temporarily or permanently, the psychological tendencies of the people. But the essential question is still unanswered. How effective are they? The scarcity of historical studies dealing with this issue forces us once again to confess uncertainty.

One point seems clear, however: political leaders have become more and more aware of the importance of these basic collective forces. Whereas the leaders of the old absolute monarchies could disregard or disdain public opinion and were little concerned with what today we call economic "structures," political leaders in our day, even those at the head of dictatorial regimes, are constantly concerned with them. The growing "self-awareness" of the people, concurrent with the progress of democracy (whether of the "Western" or "socialist" type), the inexorable accumulation of economic responsibilities by the state, advances in economics and sociology—all these force governments to pay more and more attention to "structures" and, consequently, to understand them better. As a result, there are an increasing number of public, private, and academic agencies in the service of governments whose job is to analyze the existing condition of these underlying forces and to forecast future developments on the basis of that analysis. Techniques are improving and sometimes produce valuable results, at least in economics and demography. This new attitude among statesmen also results in an increasing number and variety of agents—"operators"—whose job it is to act on basic national forces. As the number of traditional diplomats has grown too, one sees at the same time the emergence of new professionals: psychological-warfare experts, statisticians, technicians, etc.[37]

Not only, then, do these basic underlying forces continue to affect the evolution of history, but political leaders now know they exist and seek to use them, however hesitantly or clumsily. This intellectual transformation has repercussions in research studies and government administration, but does it reduce the function of the statesman to a purely nominal one? On the contrary, we may say that because political leaders now possess certain means of action by which they can attempt to work with these hitherto untamed forces, they have in certain cases increased their effective power.

---

[36] *Ibid.*, p. 112.

[37] On the contrast between these new operators and traditional diplomats, see the interesting article by Hans Speier, "Elite vs. Masses," *World Politics*, 1950.

13

DECISION-MAKING

The highest of the many activities of a political leader in office, the one that justifies all the rest, the one that fulfills the statesman's ambition, is decision-making. Much of his time may be spent in receiving visitors, weighing the advice and reports of his subordinates, studying documents, making speeches, and taking part in official functions. But all this is secondary to his essential task, which is to make the decisions affecting the nation. The historian must, first, establish the facts—examine what decisions were made, who made them, and in what circumstances—and, next, *explain* the decision or sequence of decisions the existence of which he has established, a far more complex and revealing affair.

Decision implies choice. At a higher, so to speak metaphysical, level, the problem is whether man is free to choose at all, whether everything is not determined, whether the belief in his own freedom inherent in each individual is not a delusion, whether conscience is not an "epiphenomenon." But that is a *transcendent* consideration, and history belongs essentially to the realm of *immanence*. For the historian, it is enough to note that man believes himself to be free, believes that he is confronted with choices and acts in virtue of that irresistible conviction. For the historian, the problem of liberty is not metaphysical; it arises on the level of phenomena; when a man wants to choose, he knows that his choice is limited to certain practical alternatives.

The president of Finland cannot choose to recover Carelia, nor the president of Mexico to recover Texas. But in the complex of relations between Finland and the Soviet Union, or Mexico and the United States, the leaders of the two lesser countries retain a few alternatives. *A fortiori,* leaders of the powerful countries feel themselves still freer, the range of possibilities confronting them being vaster. But they, too, realize that the freedom of choice is limited and, within the limits, feel responsible for choices that, in some circumstances, can be dramatic.

Foreign-policy decisions, while they are closely similar and closely related to domestic policies, nevertheless have unique aspects. In theory, a government that decides to levy an income tax has the means to enforce its decision: a whole arsenal of administrative, police, and judicial weapons is available; it controls the nation's domestic affairs; and only in extreme and exceptional cases will such a domestic decision lead to revolution. On the other hand, if a government decides to levy a customs duty, it has no control over the response of foreign countries and does not know how they will react. In matters of foreign policy, we find ourselves in the realm of what Raymond Aron calls "competitive conduct," in which as a rule there exists no superior authority able to coordinate relations. If, before making a decision, in foreign affairs, one must always weigh all the consequences, one enters the realm of "incalculable consequences."

Our aim in the present chapter is first to list, define, and classify the questions that confront us when we study the decisions made by statesmen in office. We shall then consider the question of the rationality of decisions. Finally, we shall illustrate these considerations by reference to some major historical decisions.

I. THE GENERAL PROBLEM OF DECISION

The question of fact: "Who made a given decision?" is less easy to resolve than it appears at first sight. A study of the legal situation would of course indicate who is in authority. Under a parliamentary system, authority is vested in the Cabinet.[1] Under a presidential system, as in the United States, the Cabinet is simply a gathering of appointed secretaries without any independent power of its own, and authority resides wholly in the President. In a personal dictatorship like Hitler's or Mussolini's, the issue is of course clearer. The most complex case is that of a collective dictatorship of party leaders—as, for instance, in the Soviet Union, with its Politburo and Presidium of the Supreme Soviet. With the abolition of the Stalinist "personality cult," there is little way of knowing, even after the event, who among the Soviet leaders was ultimately responsible for any given decision.

Whatever the circumstances, the focus of decision-making is often obscure. The man in authority may delegate most of his foreign-policy powers to a subordinate—for instance, President Harding to Secretary of State Charles Evans Hughes, or President Eisenhower to Secretary of State John Foster Dulles. Or, especially in a weak government, a subordinate may actively take the initiative, a line of action that may be legitimized by the legal authority—as happened, for instance, after General Savov, chief of staff of the Bulgarian Army, opened military operations against Serbia on June 26, 1913, against the Prime Minister's wishes; or again, when the Laniel-Bidault ministers in the French cabinet assumed responsibility in August, 1953, for the deposition of the Sultan of Morocco. Or a government may repudiate the enterprising subordinate. A curious example is that of Admiral Persano, a Piedmontese, who was dispatched in pursuit of Garibaldi's "Thousand" in May, 1860, but who openly hinted to Cavour that he would make it his

---

[1] In our day especially. But Delcassé, for instance, did not submit all his decisions to the Cabinet, and Hoare concluded his pact with Laval without assurance of Cabinet agreement.

business not to catch up with them. "I think I understand you, Count," he said. "If necessary, send me to the fortress of Fenestrella."

The importance of determining this focus of decision-making does not escape the politicians of other countries. When the German gunboat *Panther* entered the port of Agadir on July 1, 1911, threatening the French position in North Africa, the new Prime Minister of France, Joseph Caillaux, felt that negotiations should be undertaken, but to ensure that they would bear fruit, he first tried to find out who had been personally responsible for the German decision. He was convinced that it was Kaiser Wilhelm II himself.[2] In order to enter into direct communication with the Kaiser without the knowledge of the Foreign Office, he undertook to negotiate secretly, through a French businessman called Fondère, with the Counsellor of the German Embassy in Paris, Baron von Lancken. But the interesting thing is that Caillaux was mistaken.[3] The impulsive, irresolute Kaiser had in fact been appalled at Germany's "Big Stick" policy, and its author was Kiderlen-Wächter, the Foreign Minister, who had had a hard time trying to secure his sovereign's approval. This mistake led to needless complications in the negotiations and, early in 1912, by a reverse swing of the pendulum, to the fall of Caillaux's cabinet, which was accused by one of its members, de Selves, of having practiced "personal politics."

Let us suppose that one knows to whom to attribute a given decision. The problem then arises to *explain* it. As an act of will, any decision must be explained by reference not only to causes, but also to ends.

Causes may sometimes dominate, and a man may be forced to make a certain decision because otherwise he would face personal risks he dare not take. For instance, President McKinley proposed a declaration of war on Spain on April 11, 1898, because, despite his own desire for peace, he could no longer resist the pressure of Congress, which in its turn was being pressured by the Hearst and Pulitzer newspapers:

> McKinley was an able politician, and by no means blind to political considerations. He could not have failed to see that if he tried to thwart the popular will, he would undoubtedly jeopardize, perhaps ruin, his chances of re-election in 1900. . . . A belligerent senator shouted to the Assistant Secretary of State, "Day, by ———, don't your President know where the war-declaring power is lodged? Tell him, by ———, that if he doesn't do something, Congress will exercise the power."[4]

Under the Constitution, the power to declare war does in fact reside in

---

[2] See Caillaux, *Agadir* (written in 1912–13) (Paris, 1919).

[3] As he admits in his *Mémoires*, Vol. II (Paris, 1942), written after he had seen the German documents.

[4] Thomas Bailey, *A Diplomatic History of the American People* (New York, 1940), pp. 506–8. See also Robert H. Ferrell, *American Diplomacy* (New York, 1959), p. 199: "It is doubtful if McKinley or anyone could have checked the course of events."

Congress, and it is possible to conceive of a situation where Congress would decide to act over the head of the President.

At the other extreme, a decision may be governed almost exclusively by *ends*. The decision governed by causes is a "forced decision"; the decision motivated by ends is a "gratuitous decision," and there are plenty of examples of the latter.

Nothing, for instance, *obliged* Hitler to attack the Soviet Union in June, 1941. A trial of strength was doubtless foreseeable in the long run between the Nazis and the Soviets—that, in any case, was Stalin's view—but neither economic considerations (the Soviet Union was scrupulously delivering the goods provided for in the commercial treaty of August 26, 1939) nor strategic considerations (a Soviet defeat would not have contributed directly to the destruction of Great Britain) justified a decision of such magnitude. The explanation must be sought in those grandiose dreams which Hitler had never abandoned of the conquest of *Lebensraum* in eastern Europe.

Another striking example is the Schuman Plan of May 9, 1950. The authors of the plan, Jean Monnet and Robert Schuman, were motivated by the desire to create something new; nothing forced them to it.[5] It was necessary, of course, to try to improve relations between France and the new German Federal Republic, which were aggravated by French policies on the Saar, but normal diplomatic relations would have sufficed to achieve that end. Schuman and Monnet had more ambitious plans: the reconciliation of France and Germany, and advancement along the road to European unity. In that sense the decision was "creative," and consciously so, as evidenced by Paragraph I of the Preamble to the treaty of April 18, 1951, establishing the European Coal and Steel Community: "Considering that world peace may be safeguarded only by creative efforts equal to the dangers which menace it. . . ."

Most decisions, of course, are situated somewhere between these two extremes and are the effect of causes *and* aspirations toward particular goals. In Chapter Eleven, we studied the processes by which the "underlying forces" exert their influence on statesmen, and we shall not, therefore, dwell here on the causality of decisions, but we shall consider their ultimate end.

This may be presented schematically as follows: given the objective which the author of the decision sets himself, what relation is there between the value of what is at stake and the degree of risk involved? What is the relation between the goals pursued and the available means? The first is a matter of diplomatic strategy, the second, of diplomatic tactics.[6]

---

[5] See Pierre Gerbet, "La genèse du Plan Schuman," *Revue française de science politique* (Paris), July–September, 1956, pp. 525–53; and William Diebold, *The Schuman Plan* (New York, 1959).

[6] I have tried to present these problems theoretically in Duroselle, "La stratégie des conflits internationaux," *Revue française de science politique* (Paris), June, 1960, pp. 287–308; and, especially, in Duroselle, *Le Conflit de Trieste, 1943–1954* (Brussels, 1966).

A. The Value of the Stakes and the Degree of Risk: Diplomatic Strategy

It may be assumed that any political leader holding national office seeks to achieve certain general goals—permanent goals if he is doctrinaire, short-term objectives if he is an opportunist. These goals as a whole constitute what he believes to be the "national interest."[7] But since, in the international arena, a decision by one state involves reactions that it cannot control on the part of other states, the author of the decision is obliged to consider all other possible national reactions. Any important decision implies some risks. But what risks?

There is first the domestic risk of weakening or destroying the government in power. Under the parliamentary system, countless cabinets have resigned or fallen in consequence of a foreign-policy decision—Freycinet's on July 29, 1882, when he wanted to intervene in Egypt; Briand's in January, 1922, in the face of the opposition to his policy of conciliation with Germany. In any regime, a given foreign-policy decision may lead to a *coup d'état*—for instance, that of Young King Peter II of Yugoslavia on March 27, 1941, against the regent, Paul, who two days earlier had aligned Yugoslavia on the side of the Axis by acceding to the Three-Power Pact. More simply, it can mean that the leader concerned will not be re-elected or that a candidate from the opposition party will be installed—as, for instance, when Woodrow Wilson's candidate, Cox, was defeated in 1920 by the Republican Warren G. Harding because he had based his campaign on the theme of acceding to the League of Nations.

But the *external* risks are even greater. There is the risk of retaliatory measures and reprisals; of ignominy (being branded as an aggressor, as a country which lets down its ally or violates treaties); of war, with the consequent loss in human lives, destruction, and financial disasters; of defeat, involving the loss of independence or territorial integrity. Finally, the atomic age has introduced the most terrifying risk of all—that of the total physical destruction of the population.

In calculating risks, statesmen may make mistakes. A political leader who thought he was risking no more than the loss of a few soldiers may find himself facing certain defeat. For a political leader to take risks means necessarily that he must have the temperament of a gambler, but also that he must attach great importance to what is at stake. Even if his goal is an exalted one, he will not pursue it if the risk is too great. It is remarkable, for instance, that none of the French governments between 1871 and 1914 seriously considered undertaking a "war of revenge" to recover Alsace and Lorraine. When General Boulanger was retained as War Minister—a sign appearing to mean that France would indeed pursue early revenge—the principal political leaders (President Grévy, Jules Ferry, Freycinet) joined forces to remove him from

---

[7] See above, Chapter Ten.

office, Bismarck meanwhile having skillfully used the crisis of the "Schnaebelé affair" to put pressure on France and call her to order. Very often, the two parties to a dispute announce that they do not wish to use force to resolve it and perhaps in doing so each sacrifice a chance of success; as Bismarck put it, "my opponent does not need to know if I do not intend to use force."

Nevertheless, the popular saying "Nothing wager, nothing win" can be applied to foreign policy. In general, we may say that a satisfied nation— "saturated," as Bismarck put it in regard to Germany—is less inclined to take risks than a dissatisfied one. But "satisfaction" in this context is in any case a difficult concept to define. A country dissatisfied politically and territorially is one that has not achieved its national unity (for instance, Serbia before 1918) or that has lost provinces (for instance, Germany thinking about the Polish Corridor between the two world wars). Expression of this dissatisfaction may be reduced to the two concepts of "irredentism" and "revenge." Such dissatisfaction is in any case a very relative thing, for opinions always differ as to the achievement of national unity.

We may recall the famous debate in revolutionary France of 1796–97 between the prudent Carnot, who advocated a return to the "frontiers of 1792," Reubell, who wanted France to achieve her "natural frontiers," and La Revellière-Lépeaux, who called for "revolutionary expansion" and the establishment of "sister republics" or satellite states around France.[8] Although the Carnot thesis in general prevailed after 1815, the champions of "natural frontiers" sometimes came to power (for instance, Napoleon III), and even after World War I there were groups that argued along those lines—for instance, the Action Française, at certain points.

In German history, we find not only the well-known conflict between champions of a "small Germany" and advocates of a "greater Germany," but also the Pan-Germanists who dreamed of Germany absorbing "Germanic" countries such as the Netherlands, Denmark, and German Switzerland. These ideas crystallized (with the addition of a racist doctrine) in Adolf Hitler's idea for his "Great Reich."

In 1919, Orlando sought Italian control over part of the east coast of the Adriatic, a program that Mussolini was to adopt in 1941, and in 1945, the aged Orlando, now a senator in the Italian Republic, was to thunder against the *renunciatorii* who went as far as to abandon the greater part of Istria.

Even the United States had its quota of expansionist theories with the doctrine of "Manifest Destiny" in the mid-nineteenth century.

The influence of the statesmen here is of course critical, for ultimately he must personally play a part in choosing between ambitious territorial aspirations, with their attendant risks, and being "satisfied," even if this entails conflict with the most chauvinist, ultranationalist sectors of public opinion.

---

[8] See in particular Jacques Godechot, *La Grande Nation: l'expansion révolutionnaire de la France dans le monde de 1789 à 1799* (Paris, 1956).

The concept of a nation's "economic satisfaction" is more complex still, taking into account not only the average standard of living, but also the percentage of the population enjoying a tolerable standard of living. In the past twenty years, American and European economists and political scientists— men like W. W. Rostow, John Kenneth Galbraith, François Perroux, Alfred Sauvy—have done much to increase our still meager knowledge in this field. Rostow, for instance, distinguishes five successive stages in a nation's economic development: the stage of "traditional society"; the "pre-take-off" point, before a nation can sustain its own economic growth; the "take-off" into self-sustained economic growth; "maturity"; and "high mass consumption."[9] Only the traditional societies and, at the other extreme, the "mature" and "high mass consumption" nations enjoy a degree of stability. We may note here Karl Deutsch's remark that a revolution (an "endogenous" revolution, in Ernest Labrousse's terminology[10]) has never taken place where the average annual per-capita income exceeded $900.[11]

As far as the statesman's position in regard to economic dissatisfaction is concerned, the only conclusions—and they are still tentative—that history permits us to draw are the following: first, economically dissatisfied nations, more often than satisfied nations, select leaders who are ambitious and eager to take risks; second, economic dissatisfaction is a general cause of unrest and revolution, but a political leader can sometimes *divert* revolutionary passions toward an international objective. In the second case, the revolutionary spirit turns into chauvinist nationalism, and the spirit of adventure (consequently the acceptance of risk) urges much of the country toward ambitious and aggressive goals. Without there being any perfect correlation between willingness to run risks and economic dissatisfaction, or between fear of adventure and economic satisfaction, history nonetheless reveals that there have been political leaders who were "rapacious," while others were "satisfied," "immobile," "sated."

A statesman's assessment of the importance of the stakes involved in a foreign-policy decision is a very personal matter.[12] There can be no *objective* determination of their value. One man will prefer to sacrifice prosperity to prestige (Thiers in 1840), another, prestige to prosperity (Guizot). One will place all his energies into territorial claims, another will decide that existing frontiers are after all sufficient. One will take the view that no acquisition is worth a war, another will accept the prospect of war. The "indetermination of

---

[9] *The Stages of Economic Growth* (New York and Cambridge, 1960).

[10] "Comment naissent les revolutions," *Actes du Congrès historique du Centenaire de la Révolution de 1848* (Paris, 1949), pp. 1–20.

[11] As of this writing, the present comparative figures on average annual per-capita income is less than $50 in Paraguay, Haiti, and Pakistan; $65 in India; $300 in Mexico; around $1,200 in France, Great Britain and West Germany; $1,600 in Switzerland; $2,400 in the United States.

[12] See above, Chapter Ten, pp. 260 ff.

foreign-policy attitudes," as Aron puts it, is thus considerable in the context of a decision's ultimate effect. Knowing that the conduct of his opposite numbers will be governed by many, varied motives, a statesman will usually be in the dark as to the possible consequences of his acts.

B. THE RELATION BETWEEN ENDS AND MEANS: DIPLOMATIC TACTICS

The given "stakes" to be risked in a foreign-policy decision and the immediate aim may coincide. But it is our view that, as a rule, what is at stake —the "national interest"—comprises the whole complex of national objectives, the ideal; whereas the immediate aims are pursued day by day and constitute what might be described as the successive elements of the stake.

In the case of Hitler, for instance, what he believed to be at stake was Germany's eventual domination of Europe and the possession of a vast *Lebensraum*. But if we consider each of his acts chronologically, we see that he was careful not to reveal his vast plans and after each success sought to reassure everyone. Take, for instance, a speech Hitler delivered on May 21, 1935, in the Reichstag. On the previous March 16, he had unilaterally voided a clause of the Treaty of Versailles and announced that Germany would rearm—thus achieving one specific goal he had in view. But he had to continue to disguise his successive future goals, so he therefore proclaimed an objection to territorial annexation:

> As there is no longer any unoccupied space in Europe, every victory—without making any difference to the fundamental distress in Europe—can at best result in a quantitative increase in the number of inhabitants of a country. But if the nations attach so much value to that, they can achieve it without tears in a simpler and more natural way. A sound social policy, by increasing the readiness of a nation to have children, can give its people more children in a few years than the number of aliens that could be conquered and made subject to that nation by war.[13]

He added that "no further territorial demands would be made on France" (a statement belied in 1940), and that "we recognize Poland as the home of a great and nationally conscious people" (although in 1939 he was to destroy Poland and annex part of it, extending far beyond the disputed zones inhabited by Germans).[14]

This is a clear example of the necessary coordination between ends and means. By rearming Germany, Hitler not only ensured "equality of rights" for the "master race," but he was also forging the instrument that would enable him to seize German territories one by one, to put France out of com-

---

[13] Norman H. Baynes, ed., *The Speeches of Adolf Hitler, August 1922–August 1939* (New York and London, 1942), II, 1219–20.
[14] *Ibid.*, pp. 1221, 1232.

mission, and finally to embark on the conquest of *Lebensraum.* The sequence was closely aligned to the development of German military power, and also the growing isolation of the Western democracies, which lost hope in the support of Italy and then of the Soviet Union. Conversely, however, Hitler was well aware that German rearmament and German acts of aggression encouraged his potential foes to rearm, and that the imbalance of forces he was systematically creating would inevitably be rectified and even operate against Germany.

In the celebrated "Hossbach Protocol"[15] (there exist many other convergent sources), Hitler set 1943 as the critical date. The power of potential enemies must be broken before then—whence the extreme importance of the time factor in Hitler's decision-making. His sense of urgency was further heightened by a conviction that he was the only man who, by virtue of the decrees of a mysterious providence of the race, was capable of achieving his great designs, of winning the stakes. He stated this belief at a meeting on November 5, 1937, and repeated it to his generals on August 22, 1939:

> Essentially all depends on me, on my existence, because of my political talents. Furthermore, the fact is that probably no one will ever again have the confidence of the whole German people as I have. There will probably never again in the future be a man with more authority than I have. My existence is therefore a factor of great value. But I can be eliminated at any time by a criminal or a lunatic.[16]

If diplomatic strategy consists in determining the risks to be taken in order to win the stakes, the tactics are the adaptation of ends and means. But this adaptation may proceed in either direction: the ends may be toned down for lack of means; or the means may be augmented in order to achieve the ends. Many episodes in international relations can be explained by this twofold operation—for instance, arms races. Bismarck, for example, was greatly disturbed at the French military laws of 1872 and 1875 (the "fourth battalion") and throughout his career, even in 1887, sought to obtain supplementary appropriations from the Reichstag for each military septennate. We know that this policy was motivated by purely defensive considerations. The French, however, never believed that he had renounced further territorial ambitions and tried on their part, too, to strengthen the military establishment in order to be capable of responding to any "preventive war." The cycle of the arms race was thus initiated, although the immediate national aims (if not the ultimate aim, Alsace-Lorraine) were wholly defensive.

The question of Alsace-Lorraine itself shows clearly that France constantly distinguished between the ultimate aim, the recovery of the lost prov-

---

[15] See *Documents on German Foreign Policy, 1918–1945,* from the archives of the German Foreign Ministry (Washington, D.C., 1956).

[16] *Ibid.,* Series D, Vol. VII, note 192; see also note 193.

inces, and immediate objectives. "Let us think of them always" (the ultimate stake), and "speak of them never" (the recovery of Alsace-Lorraine was not a reasonable immediate objective). The same type of distinction is clearly observable in a famous letter from the German Foreign Minister, Gustav Stresemann, to the Crown Prince in 1925. Since the letter was intended to placate German ultranationalists, it may have exaggerated the magnitude of what, for Stresemann, were the ultimate aims—settlement of the Rhineland question, protection of the "10 or 12 millions of our kindred who now live under a foreign yoke," rectification of the eastern frontiers (Danzig, the Polish Corridor, Upper Silesia), and, eventually, the union of Austria with Germany. "The most important thing . . . is the liberation of German soil from any occupying force. We must get the stranglehold off our neck." In other words, given Germany's meager means, the only attainable goals were of a much more modest order. And, Stresemann added, "on that account, German policy, like Metternich's for Austria after 1809, will be one of *finesse* and the avoidance of great decisions."[17] This goal, then, attainable in itself, would have to be presented circumspectly, skillfully, and only gradually.

Another good example of the adaptation of means to ends is provided by Woodrow Wilson's conversion in 1916 to the idea of creating a great naval force for the United States. For Wilson, the stakes seem to have been the accomplishment of a "mission" unique to the United States: to be the defender of moral principles and international law. But this ultimate stake presupposed a much more precise first aim: to defend the rights of United States nationals whose lives were endangered by German submarines when they traveled on vessels flying the flags of the Entente Powers, and whose property was endangered by both sides, particularly by the Entente's blockade. The theoretical formulation was the "defense of freedom of the seas"; the practical expression was a continuous stream of protest notes on particular incidents.

But Wilson gradually discovered that the *means* available to him—basically, diplomacy and "moral force"—were wholly inadequate, whence his rather sudden conversion to the idea of "military preparedness." "Fortunately, President Wilson, in the autumn of 1915, had revised his earlier ideas and was now ready to go before the country with a demand for vigorous preparation. In his speech before the Manhattan Club he confessed his change of mind, and he soon undertook an active campaign for preparedness in the pacifist centres of the Middle West."[18] On February 3, 1916, at St. Louis, Wilson went even further than the champions of a great American Navy could have hoped. From Admiral Mahan's dream of an American Navy second

---

[17] Eric Sutton, ed., *Gustav Stresemann, His Diaries, Letters, and Papers* (London, 1937), letter of September 7, 1925, pp. 503–5.
[18] Charles Seymour, ed., *The Intimate Papers of Colonel House* (Boston and New York, 1926), II, 84.

only to the British, Wilson proceeded to this: the "American Navy ought in my judgment to be incomparably the greatest navy in the world."[19]

Needless to say, the means to achieve a given end need not be military. They may be provided by the diplomatic situation, by alliances, by the support of other powers, by increased wealth, etc. The historian, therefore, is usually faced with this difficulty: he cannot determine whether a given decision was taken in order to achieve a particular goal, or to procure the means whereby a wholly different goal might eventually be achieved. For instance, it is difficult to tell whether, by encouraging the Hohenzollern candidacy to the Spanish throne in 1870, Bismarck sought simply to establish a friendly kingdom to the south of France, or whether he was looking for a pretext to start a war that he considered necessary for the realization of German unity; or again, when he encouraged France to conquer Tunisia, whether he intended this as a sop in order to induce her to give up any idea of "revenge" against Germany, or whether he regarded the undertaking as a means for fomenting trouble between Italy and France.

Just as, in chess, the capture of an important piece is both an end in itself and a means of increasing one's chances of winning the game, any limited goal is no more than a stage in the journey toward larger aims, and may be regarded in turn as a means. But if the historian finds it hard to distinguish between ends and means, that is perhaps because the statesman himself is often in the dark too. Sometimes, as Bismarck phrased it, he puts two irons in the fire.

II. THE PROBLEM OF THE "RATIONAL" DECISION

In the foreign-policy sphere, uncertainty regarding the possible reactions of the other side introduces extreme difficulty into the calculations of policy-makers. Theoretically, a decision may be defined as rational if it has every prospect of achieving the desired result. But this requires first and foremost that the statesman thoroughly understand the situation, and correctly appraise it. The need for *information* is thus of primary importance.

Disastrous decisions made on the basis of wrong information are legion. In general, an overly optimistic estimate of one's own strength and an underestimate of the foe's leads to catastrophe. Napoleon III in 1870 and Hitler in June, 1941, made errors of this kind. But one must also know what the opponent intends to *do* with its forces, its *will*. In September, 1935, the British massed the Home Fleet in the Mediterranean, but Mussolini (who had an excellent intelligence service) knew that they were determined not to use it. He could therefore ignore the fleet and launch a war against Ethiopia. Shortly before March 7, 1936, Hitler's military advisers told him that it would be

---

[19] Josephus Daniels, *The Wilson Era* (Chapel Hill, N.C., 1946), p. 378.

madness to reoccupy the Rhineland; they knew that the French Army was still much stronger than the German. Hitler nevertheless decided to act since he believed that the French leaders would not dare use force and that consequently, French military superiority need not be taken into account. In Mussolini's case, there appears to have been an attempt to procure and act on precise information; Hitler's decision, on the other hand, seems to have been based purely on intuition.

In practice, a perfectly rational decision, taken in full knowledge of the facts, is virtually impossible—for two reasons which the historian more or less constantly observes in the course of his investigations. First, even if the information available to the decision-maker is accurate, and accuracy is hard to obtain, it is never complete. Second, except in the case of "creative" decisions to embark on a wholly new and unprecedented course, which can be long and carefully prepared, there is usually not enough time to collect the necessary information, and the decision will be made on the basis of insufficient data.

The fact that information is incomplete almost of necessity is due to the extraordinary complexity of the factors involved in any foreign-policy decision. Even presupposing the absolute denial of a sensitive and subtle approach to international affairs in favor of a mathematical approach, the idea that it is possible to know all the facts and feed them to some electronic brain that would calculate the optimum result is absurd. The omission of a single factor can completely distort the results. In the pre-electronic age, we know of such catastrophic omissions. In 1914, for instance, the Germans believed that, with the Schlieffen Plan, they had loaded the dice in their own favor. But there was at least one element that no one could know before the actual experience of war: the force of *character* among the commanders. One of them, Von Moltke, was hesitant, worried, fearful; the other, Joffre, faced with the total failure of his earlier plans, displayed extraordinary strength of character and was able, in the very midst of defeat, to reverse the French position completely. What is true on the military level is also true on the diplomatic level. The human factor remains uncertain, and knowledge of the other party is never exhaustive.

The time factor is even more important. There are cases where decisions must be made almost immediately—as, for instance, when there has been an ultimatum or an act of aggression. A small power, faced with an ultimatum from a great one, sometimes must make a tragic choice within moments.

We may judge of the virtually total irrationality of the decision that the responsible authority in one of the two great nuclear powers would have to take in the face of flagrant aggression by the other: a few minutes in which to decide between sacrificing an ally or annihilating 100 million citizens— that would be the terrifying alternative. However much the specialists try to forecast all possible eventualities and determine in advance the decisions necessary in each one of them, it is highly probable that the event would constitute an unforeseen case, which would raise the necessity of a virtually instantaneous decision, in which the imponderable—and, therefore, the irrational—element would predominate.

But history provides many examples of another complication resulting from the time factor. It sometimes happens that a choice is available between a carefully deliberate rejoinder to an opponent's move and a lightning counterstroke. The first would appear to be the more reasonable, since it allows for information to be gathered. But the second is in certain cases the only satisfactory one, although it leaves no time for investigation. There are occasions on which it is imperative to act on impulse, almost spontaneously—incurring great risks—because any delay, any hesitation, would strengthen the opponent's position. Or it may be that gaining time is the best solution.

Attempts have been made in the last few years, particularly in the United States, to rationalize decisions that, for lack of time or information, are essentially irrational. The method consists of adapting "game theory," derived from mathematics, to international relations. The object is to discover, among all the possible alternatives, which would be likely to produce the most satisfactory results with a minimum of chances of failure.[20]

A resemblance does in fact exist between games and diplomacy, an analogy that is reflected in our everyday speech. We speak of the "diplomatic chess board"; we say of some bold action that it was "calling the other party's bluff"; we say that a given statesman is "a gambler," that he is "moving his pieces forward," that he is "finessing," that he is "using all his trumps." And since games, which comprise an effort of intelligence as well as chance, give rise to what are often calculable combinations, the temptation arises to embark on comparable calculations in foreign affairs.

Yet the differences are no less striking. The number of pieces on a chess board, or of cards in a bridge game, is limited. In foreign policy, the number of elements involved is unlimited. A game, moreover, may be interrupted. The player knows when he is playing and when he is not, but the statesman must remember that every waking decision involves consequences and sets off mechanisms that he cannot stop. Qualitative factors—evaluation of the opponent's intelligence and audacity—are certainly not lacking in a game, but they do not constitute its essence. There are rules of a game, but no one has been able to establish objective rules of diplomacy. Finally, a player may normally take his time and may either ponder his move (chess) or know that at each trick (cards) he has a certain amount of time left. In diplomacy,

---

[20] See in particular, Morton Kaplan, *System and Process in International Politics* (New York, 1957); and Thomas Schelling, *The Strategy of Conflict* (Cambridge, Mass., 1960). Some American universities go so far as to organize "diplomacy games" along the lines of the military *Kriegspiel*. See also the interesting, if not convincing, book by Harold Guetzkow *et al.*, *Simulation in International Relations* (New York, 1963).

time and time limits do not usually depend upon the actors but are imposed from without. One cannot compare a "diplomatic game," in which one or two persons represent each country, with real diplomacy, in which there are certainly responsible authorities, but in which those authorities know that they have behind them the enormous apparatus of a state and that they must take into account a multitude of domestic forces that are often contradictory and sometimes coercive. (On the other hand, one can be a great statesman and a poor chess player. Napoleon, at Saint Helena, was regularly beaten by Las Cases.)

Game theory, therefore, adds little to the rationality of decisions and is liable to seriously deceive those who, struck by the apparent analogy, might expect mathematical calculations and answers which, although mathematically exact, would generate catastrophe in the infinite complexity of the real world.

We must therefore re-introduce the most irrational and least quantitative possible notions: intuition, "sizing up," common sense. There is an art as well as a science of diplomacy, involving experience, skill, a feel for people, clarity, imagination, perseverence, and force of character. Suppleness of mind is not an archaic form of the intelligence slowly superseded through the march of science, but one of the constituent elements of human life.

On the other hand, we must not forget that a series of correct intuitions may cause a political leader to become excessively self-confident. Belief in his "guiding star" may cause him increasingly to disregard information or advice. Prior to 1941, Hitler had had a series of intuitions bordering on "genius," and this led him to conclude that he was infallible. Yet his "intuition" of a speedy victory in Russia was the origin of an historical catastrophe of the first order.

Apart from game theory, the application of mathematical methods is often very useful. "Operational research," "scientific methods to supply public authorities with calculated bases for their decisions,"[21] have in many cases become indispensable. It has thus been possible to determine that ships sailing in convoys would suffer fewer losses than those in isolation, and to define the ideal dimensions of convoys and most effective arrangements for escort vessels. When the quantitative factor far outweighs the qualitative, operational research must precede decision and even govern it. But one should not attempt to measure the immeasurable, and it must be conceded that the statesman cannot always elude the inexorable circumstances that force him to make a decision without all the data that would make it rational.

One student of the relations between operational research and decision considers that there are two kinds of decisions: those that express a compromise and those expressed in a choice. Compromise is a "weighing of several contrary or optimum conditions." "The search for this compromise, termed

[21] See the interesting study by Colonel Gonard, of the Swiss Army, *La Recherche opérationnelle et la décision* (Geneva, 1958), p. 39.

decision, is indisputably in the area of operational research" in all cases where the factors involved are of a quantitative type (volume of the order, number of workers and machines, prime cost). Choice, on the other hand, is the alternative between two contrary possibilities. It "thus eludes, by definition, the influence of any operational research." The leader is not "caught in the dilemma of the logical decision and the empirical formula. . . . Hence the *best* decision is not necessarily and always rational. . . . There exists . . . a qualitative hierarchy of decisions, whether rational or not."[22]

We may experimentally conclude, then, that in foreign-policy decisions, qualitative factors prevail over quantitative ones, and the notion of a decision's rationality is completely relative. The best decision is not necessarily one where the decision-maker sought to act rationally. The main thing is success, and one can succeed by luck, by chance, by virtue of the intervention of an unforeseen element (for instance, an error by the opponent). The rational attitude is, as far as possible, to play all one's cards, but ultimately, at the moment of decision, it is sometimes necessary to be able to dare, to risk, to take a chance.

III. EXAMPLES OF DECISIONS

Historians, particularly American historians, are increasingly concerned with the study of decision-making, as is apparent from a number of well-known works.[23] Some have in fact suggested that the study of decision-making should be central to any research in international relations.[24]

We shall confine ourselves here to a study of a few cases on which we have adequate information.

A. Caillaux' Decision to Offer Germany Part of the Congo in Exchange for Morocco

We select this case because it is a relatively simple one on which we have plentiful material.[25] When the French, called in on the request of the Sultan of Morocco, occupied Fez on May 21, 1911, it was likely that Germany would react. We know, indeed, from German diplomatic papers, that by May 2, when the French expedition was in preparation, the German Foreign Minister, Kiderlen-Wächter, had suggested a plan of action to the Kaiser and to Chancellor Bethmann-Hollweg. The plan was to send a German warship to a Moroccan port as "surety," which would make it possible not to annex or

---

[22] *Ibid.*, pp. 81–83.

[23] Among many, see in particular the books cited in the Bibliography, p. 411–12.

[24] Richard Snyder, *et al.*, eds., *Foreign Policy Decision-Making: An Approach to the Study of International Politics* (New York, 1962).

[25] See in particular, *Documents diplomatiques français*; Joseph Caillaux, *Agadir* (Paris, 1919) and *Mes Mémoires* (Paris, 1942–47), Vol. II; Paul Cambon, *Correspondance, 1870–1924* (Paris, 1940), Vol. II: *1898–1911*; and Ernest Jäckh, ed., *Kiderlen-Wächter, der Staatsmann und Mensch* (Stuttgart, 1924).

partition Morocco, as the Pan-Germanists would have liked (they would also like, wrote Kiderlen-Wächter on April 19, to annex the Department of the Rhone), but to obtain a fat compensation—for instance, the whole of the French Congo in exchange for a small African territory belonging to Germany. During his talks at Kissingen with the French Ambassador, Jules Cambon, on June 20 and 21, Kiderlen remarked, "You are organizing a real protectorate in Morocco." And he suggested a plan for compensation. That, replied Cambon, could not be found in Morocco but might be possible elsewhere, and he returned to Paris to discuss the matter with the government.

At this point, Caillaux, the Minister of Finance in Monis' cabinet, succeeded Monis as Premier. On June 30, he read his official policy statement from the rostrum of the Chamber. On July 1, the German gunboat *Panther* entered the port of Agadir. The crisis was on.

Caillaux had had little experience in the Foreign Ministry, and he knew nothing about the Kissingen talks before July. He wanted, therefore, a first-rate Foreign Minister at the Quai d'Orsay, and approached Léon Bourgeois, then Raymond Poincaré, but neither would accept the office. "The only choice left me was to go to the Quai d'Orsay myself or to appoint a second-rate man . . . de Selves. . . . I had no illusions about M. de Selves' ability. I knew it to be indifferent. . . . But I knew, also, that he had tact and shrewdness."[26] It is not certain that de Selves (a nephew of Freycinet) was in fact of such indifferent ability. But because Caillaux held that opinion of him he assumed the burden of the operation himself and de Selves exerted little influence on him.

De Selves' first thought was to send a French vessel to Mogador.[27] This plan was mentioned during the talks between Paul Cambon, French Ambassador in London, and the Foreign Secretary, Edward Grey, who counseled prudence.[28] But de Selves wanted to stand firm, and it was finally Caillaux who prevented him from so doing, perhaps on the advice of Delcassé, Minister of the Navy. "I put a stop to the intrigue I was lucky enough to uncover. But it showed me the attitude prevailing in certain circles of the Quai d'Orsay."[29] Taking advantage of the fact that he was taking de Selves' place for a few days (the latter was accompanying the President of the Republic to Holland), Caillaux instructed Jules Cambon to request fuller information from the German Foreign Minister.

26 *Mes Mémoires*, II, 77, 79, 48.
27 *Documents diplomatiques français*, Second series, Vol. XIV, No. 1 (July 1, 1911).
28 *British Documents on the Origins of the War, 1898–1914*, VII (London, 1932), 330–35 (letters from Grey to Sir Francis Bertie [British Ambassador in London], July 3 and 4, 1911); VII, 323–24 (letter from Cambon to Grey, July 1, 1911). See also *Documents diplomatiques français*, Second Series, Vol. XIV, No. 19, July 4, 1911 (letter from Cambon to Caillaux).
29 Caillaux, *Agadir*, p. 108; Cambon, *op. cit.*, Vol. II, letters of July 3 to Henri Cambon and July 18 to de Fleuriau; Caillaux, *Mes Mémoires*, II, 120.

The interview took place on July 9. Cambon was the one to broach the matter of "compensation," and he suggested that such compensation should be in the east. "I replied coldly," wrote Kiderlen-Wächter, "that in the east our desires were satisfied." Cambon rejoined that France would not agree to Germany's taking part of Morocco. "I replied to Cambon that so far nothing indicated any intention on Germany's part to proceed to a take-over." (In point of fact, Kiderlen-Wächter was waiting for France to make an offer.) The negotiations drew out on this point until July 16, when Kiderlen-Wächter finally told Cambon "that what we wanted was the French Congo—in fact, the whole of it. The ambassador was virtually stunned."[30]

How was Caillaux going to come to a decision? His principles were that war must be avoided and that, in order to avoid it, it was necessary to do something more than offer Germany a few "left-overs,". to use Cambon's expression. But at the Quai d'Orsay, de Selves, his principal private secretary, Maurice Herbette, and the Deputy Director of Foreign Affairs, Conti (the "Herbette-Conti set," as Caillaux called them), wanted to "insist on Morocco while refusing any compensation."[31] On the one hand there were the German demands, on the other, the Quai d'Orsay's refusal to concede. Since Caillaux did not want war, some compromise solution had to be found.

This Caillaux seems to have obtained from Paul Cambon (in complete agreement with his brother Jules). Paul Cambon came to Paris on July 15 and conferred with de Selves and the British Ambassador, Sir Francis Bertie. On July 18, Caillaux joined in the discussions. De Selves favored an international conference on the Moroccan issue; Cambon opposed it on the grounds that France might not have the support of a majority, and that a conference might jeopardize the advantages France had reaped in Morocco since the Act of Algeciras in 1906.

Caillaux evidently did not arrive at a clear idea of a solution to this particular point. He had rejected the plan for dispatching a French vessel and did not want war. Paul Cambon quotes him as putting his quandary in these terms: "What, then, do you suggest? There are only three possibilities: to hold a conference, to give up the Congo, or to give up Agadir." At that point Cambon made the suggestion, apparently quickly accepted, that *certain territories* of the Congo be offered, but not all, and certainly not coastal enclaves. Two possible developments could then be envisaged: Kiderlen-Wächter might tone down his demands, or he might announce that the Germans would stay at Agadir. If the latter, France could require him to obtain the authorization of the other powers, and she would thereby strengthen her own position in Agadir. " 'In that case,' [Cambon] told

[30] Jäckh, *op. cit.*, Bethmann-Hollweg to the Kaiser, July 15, 1911; Cambon's account is in *Documents diplomatiques français*, Second series, Vol. XIV, No. 71, July 16, 1911.

[31] Caillaux, *Mes Mémoires*, II, 149.

Caillaux, 'send handbills and hucksters to Agadir right away to set up booths on the beaches.' Caillaux thought this a splendid idea and rushed to the telephone!"[32]

Everything seems to point to July 18 as the date when Caillaux settled on this policy. From then on, the negotiations turned on the idea of offering Germany a "slice" of the Congo, the size of which would depend on the counterpart Germany was prepared to give. Caillaux tells us that as early as July 10, Jules Cambon had asked him "to have a hand in the negotiations" and that from July 16 he sought to "follow the negotiations."[33] It was probably between July 16 and 18 that he decided on the necessity of avoiding war and on the considerable advantages of a French protectorate in Morocco. He already had definite opinions on the Congo, as a result of having taken part in the discussions on the Ngoko-Sangh company, and now sought further information. And it was during this period that he read a report by the colonial Inspector General Frézouls, which revealed the virtual non-existence of French colonies in French Equatorial Africa, although Gabon, said Frézouls, "might well become a rich and prosperous agricultural colony." But most of the territories had little potential and boasted only forty French settlers and 150 administrators, officers, or N.C.O.'s.[34] It would be no great sacrifice to give them up. It was essential, on the other hand, to keep Gabon. That seems to be the position the Premier held from then on.

Caillaux had thus decided on a line of action by July 18. He left less and less initiative to the Quai d'Orsay and by the middle of August had taken over altogether.[35] The confusion in French policy seems to have originated in the fact that the nucleus of decision had not been clearly defined from the start. The Quai d'Orsay under de Selves functioned badly: "No firm principle, no program; stray impulses, intentions, alternate confidence and panic; a short-sighted attitude, fed by a weak will—this period of our history is certainly not one in which future diplomats should look for models."[36] General Messimy, Minister of War, shared this view. He regarded Caillaux as "a clear-headed man, who desired peace but did not bleat for it, who knew where he was going and succeeded in eluding the traps the Quai d'Orsay laid for him."[37] Caillaux alone, evidently, was able to make the basic decision, a decision founded on the moderate views of the experienced Cambon brothers.[38]

---

[32] Cambon, *op. cit.*, letter of July 18 to de Fleuriau. See also *British Documents*, VII, 370–75.

[33] Caillaux, *Agadir*, pp. 158–59.

[34] *Ibid.*, pp. 148–52.

[35] Caillaux, *Agadir*, p. 159.

[36] André Tardieu, *Le Mystère d'Agadir* (Paris, 1912), p. 447.

[37] A. Messimy, *Mes Souvenirs* (Paris, 1937), p. 58.

[38] Messimy mentions the "place of eminence that must be assigned, in the final triumph, to our illustrious representatives in Berlin, Jules Cambon, also the Premier's most admirable collaborator" (*ibid.*, p. 59). See Keith Eubank, *Paul Cambon, Master Diplomatist* (Norman, Okla., 1960), pp. 136–42.

B. Wilson's Decision to Break Off Diplomatic Relations with Germany

President Wilson's decision to break off diplomatic relations with Germany, announced in Congress on February 3, 1917, at 2:30 P.M., followed directly from the German decision to initiate all-out submarine warfare against the Allies, a decision communicated by Ambassador Bernstorff to Secretary of State Lansing at 4:30 P.M., January 31. The final decision, then, must have been made between the afternoons of January 31 and February 3.

Immediately on Bernstorff's departure, Lansing telephoned the White House. Wilson was not there. Upon his return, Joseph Tumulty, his secretary, "brought in a news bulletin announcing the German threat. Wilson read and re-read it. He was amazed at first, then incredulous. Color left his face as he took in the full meaning. His lips tightened and his jaw locked. Then he said with quiet grimness: 'The break that we have tried so hard to prevent now seems inevitable.' "[39]

At 8 P.M., he received the official documents from Lansing, accompanied by a short note,[40] and Wilson called Lansing to come to the White House. His other principal adviser, Colonel House, was in New York. (The day before, House had received a message from Bernstorff announcing an imminent "very important letter."[41]) Summoned now by the President, House took the night train for Washington and arrived in the morning of February 1.

Was the German move a complete surprise? Probably not for the State Department. The United States Ambassador to Berlin, Gerard, had sent a cable almost a year earlier pointing out that the National Liberals advocated "relentless submarine warfare," and Joseph Grew, chargé d'affaires in Berlin, communicated on December 12 the view of the Spanish Ambassador, who had just seen Chancellor Bethmann-Hollweg, that, if the German peace proposals were not accepted, there would be "a resumption of indiscriminate submarine warfare." The same theme was sounded the next day, after a meeting with the Danish minister.[42] In short, "that decision was not altogether unexpected."[43] Colonel House had seen Bernstorff on January 26 and been told that "the military have complete control in Germany"; Lansing, for his part, continued to write letter after letter to Wilson warning him of imminent danger.[44]

But, for Wilson, the imminence of the threat was hidden behind a smoke-

---

[39] Arthur Walworth, *Woodrow Wilson* (Boston, 1965), Book II, p. 82.
[40] Robert Lansing, *War Memoirs* (Indianapolis and New York, 1935), p. 212.
[41] Charles Seymour, *op. cit.*, II, 430.
[42] United States Department of State, *Papers Relating to the Foreign Relations of the United States, 1916, Supplement* (Washington, D. C., 1929), Nos. 3941, 4724, 4733, pp. 33, 86, 89. See also No. 4749 (December 19, 1916), p. 103.
[43] Seymour, *op. cit.*, II, 437.
[44] *Ibid.*, p. 429. Lansing, *op. cit.*, pp. 203–8.

screen. Bernstorff skillfully continued to negotiate with House on the basis of peace proposals Wilson had made in December. On January 31, the very day he communicated the German decision to the State Department, he sent House a letter on German conditions of peace. Wilson was deluding himself.

Wilson conferred with Lansing in his office during the evening of January 31. The Secretary of State advocated immediate severance of diplomatic relations with Germany, as Wilson had elaborated, after the sinking of the *Sussex,* in an American note of April 18, 1916. But the "President, though deeply incensed at Germany's insolent notice, said that he was not yet sure what course we must pursue, and must think it over; that he had been more and more impressed with the idea that 'white civilization' and its domination over the world rested largely on our ability to keep this country intact." Lansing replied that by not breaking off relations, the United States would be humiliated, that a break was in any case inevitable, and that it was important not to "lose our character as a great power and the esteem of all the nations." Wilson remained unconvinced for some time but eventually instructed Lansing to prepare a note announcing the break. It was to be a "tentative draft," however, "and a basis for further consideration of the subject." Lansing drafted his note and revised it the next morning, February 1. Before returning to Wilson, he refused to make any public declaration and discussed the matter only with Senator Gilbert M. Hitchcock, a Democrat and member of the Senate Committee on Foreign Relations, who thought it good to gain time.[45]

Meanwhile, on the morning of February 1, House arrived at the White House, where he breakfasted. The President told him of his instructions to Lansing, citing the exchange of notes between the United States and Germany on submarine warfare, and describing the new move as being "for the purpose of giving Bernstorff his passports if it was thought advisable."[46]

In other words, Wilson was still hesitating. The idea of breaking off relations had struck him as soon as Tumulty had brought him the news release on the previous day, but he had not wanted to take such action unless the case was crystal clear. But was it? "The President was sad and depressed. . . . He was deeply disappointed in the sudden and unwarranted action of the German Government. . . . The President said he felt as if the world had suddenly reversed itself."[47]

There were three possible solutions: to declare war on Germany; to sever diplomatic relations with her at once; or to wait for an overt act before breaking them off—that is, for the actual sinking of an American vessel. Wilson never for a moment considered the first. His debate with House turned on the choice between the second and third. "The President was

---

[45] Lansing, *op. cit.,* pp. 212–14.
[46] Seymour, *op. cit.,* II, 438.
[47] *Ibid.,* p. 439.

insistent," wrote House, "that he would not allow it to lead to war if it could possibly be avoided."[48] House, on the other hand, believed that war was unavoidable and pressed for an immediate rupture. The discussion drifted to a halt. Mrs. Wilson suggested a round of golf, but House thought that would make a bad impression on the public. Wilson nervously arranged his books and finally suggested a game of pool. "In great governmental crises of this sort," observed House, "the public have no conception what is happening on the stage behind the curtain."[49]

Lansing joined them late in the morning, bringing the documents he had prepared. He had long been convinced that war was inevitable.[50] House, who had once believed in at least the possibility of American mediation, was now more firmly on Lansing's side. The two men succeeded in winning Wilson over to the view that diplomatic relations must be broken off immediately (subject to one condition, as we shall see). "Lansing was so nearly of our mind that there was little discussion," writes House. "He read what he had written and we accepted it."[51]

Wilson's one condition was to call a cabinet meeting for the following day to consult his secretaries. He had promised William J. Stone, Chairman of the Senate Committee on Foreign Relations, not to proceed to a break without first talking to him. Stone was in St. Louis, and Wilson telegraphed to him to return to Washington. But, Lansing wrote, the President had practically made up his mind.[52]

House left Wilson at 2 P.M., still somewhat uncertain as to the solution. So was Lansing, who wrote a memorandum for Wilson the next day in which he stated that the rupture of diplomatic relations with Germany should be the "first course," and suggesting two possibilities for a "second course": either a declaration to the effect that the United States Government regarded Germany as an "international outlaw," or a declaration to Congress that there remained no other solution but "to employ every resource which [the country] possesses to punish the guilty nation"—that is, to resort to war. Lansing was clearly in favor of the latter. In the morning of February 2, Wilson and Lansing conferred three times by telephone.[53]

At 2:30 that afternoon, the cabinet met and remained in session until 4:45. After speaking of the "astounding surprise" of the German decision, Wilson asked his secretaries, "Shall I break off diplomatic relations with

---

[48] *Ibid.*, p. 440.

[49] *Ibid.*, p. 441.

[50] Daniel M. Smith, *Robert Lansing and American Neutrality, 1914–1917* (Berkeley, 1958). Smith made use of Lansing's unpublished papers, which bear out the *War Memoirs*.

[51] Seymour, *op. cit.*, p. 44. The text is in *Papers Relating to the Foreign Relations of the United States, 1917, Supplement*, No. I, pp. 106–16.

[52] Lansing, *op. cit.*, p. 214.

[53] *Ibid.*, p. 219.

Germany?" All but two, Secretary of Labor William B. Wilson and Postmaster General Albert S. Burleson, replied unreservedly in the affirmative. This, it seems, was the point at which Wilson definitely made up his mind. He proceeded next to Capitol Hill for discussion with members of Congress, in particular Senator Stone. When one of the legislators suggested a note of protest, Wilson replied, "Let us be done with diplomatic notes. The hour to act has come."[54] Whereupon he returned home and saw only members of his family for the rest of the day, with the exception of Lansing. Wilson worked until midnight drafting the message he intended to deliver in Congress the following day.

We see clearly, then, that Wilson hesitated for quite a long time. The two men whom he trusted most, House and Lansing, were virtually the only ones with whom he had prolonged discussions. Both were convinced that war was inevitable, especially Lansing. Josephus Daniels, Secretary of the Navy, who was inclined against this, believed that Wilson, in his noble aspiration toward peace, had no support from Lansing and House, who, along with Walter H. Page, United States Ambassador in London, desired war.[55] The argument defended in 1934 by Senator Gerald P. Nye to the effect that Wilson made this decision under the pressure of banks interested in the victory of the Entente powers is absolutely without foundation, at least as far as the rupture of diplomatic relations is concerned. Wilson does not seem to have been subject to any "direct" influence except Lansing's and House's during the two decisive days.

Wilson's decision can be explained, therefore, not by a system of causality based on the influence of the underlying forces of American life, but only in reference to the ultimate goal he had in mind. In the latter case, the relationship between stakes and risks may be fairly clearly perceived.

The risk Wilson took into account was American entry into the war, and this risk he wished to remove if he could. Rather than address an ultimatum to Germany to respect the maintenance of the freedom of the seas, he chose to break off relations without an ultimatum, precisely because he thought this would be less dangerous. But the danger of war remained. Naturally, he hoped that the Germans would in fact refrain from sinking American vessels so that there would be no "overt act" that would necessitate a declaration of war. But this was an error of judgment, for the whole purpose of all-out submarine warfare was to reduce the vulnerability of German submarines, which, in a given area, would no longer check whether the vessel they sighted was enemy or neutral—a technique designed to increase their security by going sooner on the attack. The process of checking to see whether a vessel was American or not would have reduced the advantage of the new policy to nil.

---

[54] Walworth, *op. cit.*, II, 83–84.
[55] Josephus Daniels, *op. cit.*, p. 584.

But although there was danger of war, Wilson never seriously entertained the notion that American territory would be threatened. The efforts to build up the Navy taken in 1916, which could be increased, seemed to assure protection of the "Fortress America" even in case of a German victory. Wilson did not think, therefore, that there was any major risk here.

This was not Lansing's view. He feared a German victory and had never believed in Wilson's attempts at mediation or in his peace proposals. On January 28, 1917, he wrote:

> Looking at the situation without bias and without undue weight to our selfish interests, we can no more avoid entering this war against Germany than we can avoid the progress of time. It is as certain as fate. I wish that we might be spared, because it will mean the waste of millions of lives and billions of treasure. While I claim no prophetic vision, I believe that I can declare that, by this time next year, Americans will be killing those German barbarians or at least getting ready to do their part in this war against the Kaiser and his military gang who rule over Germany. I hate the horrors of war, but I hate worse the horrors of German mastery.[56]

Lansing believed, then, that there was a direct, if not an immediate risk. For him, the stakes were the maintenance of the balance of power, and he believed that American intervention alone could ensure this. Similarly, he was haunted by the idea that right was on the side of the Entente—notwithstanding what he believed to be the implicit threat constituted by Tsarist Russia. "The present military oligarchy," he wrote to Wilson, "must be eliminated for the sake of civilization and the future peace of the world."[57]

Walter Lippmann, writing a decade later, gave as his view that the American decisions had been made to restore the balance of power and not, as Wilson had declared in his address of February 3, 1917, in order to defend the "undoubted rights of our people" or "the sacred and indisputable rules of international law" or "freedom of the seas."[58] But Lippmann, as it has been pointed out,[59] confused Lansing's views with Wilson's. Wilson thought in terms of justice, Lansing in terms of political balance. Lansing joined Wilson on the terrain of moral principles, but he was concerned with the national interest, whereas Wilson employed the formula, "We wish to serve no selfish ends."

What is remarkable is that Lansing and House should have prevailed upon Wilson. Perhaps—this is merely a hypothesis—Lansing touched on a sensitive nerve when he asserted (on a number of occasions, apparently, but certainly in his letter of February 2) that an active attitude on the part of the United States would "give this country a prominent place in the

---

[56] Lansing, *op. cit.*, pp. 208–9.
[57] *Ibid.*, p. 220.
[58] Walter Lippmann, *Men of Destiny*.
[59] Robert H. Ferrell, *op. cit.*

peace negotiations, which will prevent unjust treatment of the Central Powers." For it was already Wilson's ambition to play an essential part in the conclusion of a just peace and to bring to the world his program for a "new diplomacy."

C. Mussolini's Decision to Enter the War in 1940

Mussolini's decision to declare war on June 10, 1940, may be a good example of individual action taken in defiance of the realities of the situation; we have reliable sources to clarify this point.[60]

The origins of the decision go back to the offensive-defensive alliance (the Pact of Steel) of May, 1939, between Nazi Germany and Fascist Italy. When Count Ciano, Mussolini's foreign minister, met Hitler on August 12–13, 1939, he was stunned to learn that Hitler had definitely decided to attack Poland, "I realized immediately that there is no longer anything that can be done. He has decided to strike, and strike he will." Yet two days earlier, Mussolini had told Ciano that he was "more than ever convinced of the necessity of delaying the conflict." On Ciano's return, therefore, Mussolini found himself on the horns of a dilemma: "The Duce's reactions are varied. At first he agrees with me. Then he says that honor compels him to march with Germany. Finally, he states that he wants his part of the booty in Croatia and Dalmatia."[61] On the one hand, there were the arguments against intervention (Ciano asserted that the Italian people "will boil over with horror when they know about the aggression against Poland, and most probably will wish to fight the Germans,"[62] and that the Italian army was totally unprepared), and, on the other, the arguments in its favor: "honor," as Mussolini conceived it, and the lure of spoils.

By the end of August, Mussolini had settled on the idea of presenting requirements to Germany for raw materials and armaments as preconditions for entering the war, demands that were beyond the German ability to supply. Since Hitler was unable to satisfy them, Italy remained neutral. In this phase, however, Mussolini remained "worried," "nervous," "anxious." He passed alternately through neutralist and interventionist phases. "The Duce . . . is convinced that we must not march blindly with Germany" (August 15). "For a moment the fires of the old scruples of loyalty return to the Duce" (August 17). The Duce was in the grip of "his usual shifting feelings" (August 18). On August 21, Ciano went to Mussolini: "When I entered the room Mussolini confirmed his decision to go along with the

---

[60] Hugh Gibson, ed., *The Ciano Diaries, 1939–1943* (New York, 1946); Malcolm Muggeridge, ed., *Ciano's Diplomatic Papers* (London, 1948); and *Documenti Diplomatici Italiani*, Series IX, 1939–43, Vols. I–IV.

[61] Gibson, *op. cit.*, pp. 118–20 (August 10, 12, and 13, 1939).

[62] *Ibid.*, p. 120 (August 13).

Germans." Ciano protested and "cast aside every scruple." Mussolini, "much impressed" with this tirade, backtracked. At last, the note of August 26, following on the signature of the German-Soviet Nonaggression Pact, constituted a triumph for Ciano: "I have had to struggle hard to persuade the Duce to act as he has [but he] is now quite calm, as he always is after he has made a decision."[63]

The decision to remain neutral conformed with the wishes of most of the Italian people, of the King, and of his principal ministers; it was also economically profitable. What caused Mussolini to modify the decision later?

At the end of 1939, he seems to have been far from any thought of war, despite "the usual recurrent waves of pro-Germanism." Occasionally he referred to "intervention at the side of Germany during the second half of 1941," but these were mere phrases, and for the time being he remained "somewhat hostile to the Germans. . . . He repeats that we cannot indefinitely remain neutral. To preserve neutrality until the end of the war would make us play second fiddle among the European powers."[64]

The first sign of a change appeared on February 8, 1940, when the Duce turned down every request for war matériel from the Allied democracies; simultaneously, Hitler proposed a meeting on the frontier. "I fear this meeting," said Ciano. "When the Duce is with the Germans, he becomes excited."[65]

The prospect of this interview with Hitler was to have a profound effect on Mussolini, but for the moment he was content with the notion of a "parallel war"—an independent operation he believed himself capable of opening against Yugoslavia. On March 10, Ribbentrop arrived in Rome with a long and clever letter from Hitler.[66] Hitler praised the Duce's clearsightedness and, meeting possible Italian objections to Germany's course of action, justified the German attitude. He began with

> what for me, in its *people*, in its system, and above all in its leader, is the *first* friend, and will always remain the first, *Italy!* The outcome of the war will also be decisive for the future of Italy! If that future is considered in the light of security for the existence of the Italian people from an historical, geopolitical, and moral point of view . . . then the same enemies who today combat Germany will be your adversaries too. I know, Duce, that you yourself do not think otherwise.

It was an ingenious move; Hitler was flattering his emulator's ambitions and his sense of honor. Speaking with Ribbentrop, Mussolini declared that he intended to "intervene in the conflict and to fight a war parallel to that of Germany." He accepted the proposal for a meeting at the Brenner Pass,

[63] *Ibid.*, pp. 121–32 *passim.*
[64] *Ibid.*, pp. 186–200 *passim* (December 31, 1939; January 11, 17, 23, 1940).
[65] *Ibid.*, p. 205.
[66] *Documenti Diplomatici Italiani*, Series IX, Vol. III, No. 492, pp. 415–23.

in order, he maintained, to dissuade Germany from a great Western offensive, since "Italian inaction, which already weighs heavily on [Mussolini], would be unbearable if the German forces really entered the struggle." Ciano, who knew well that the Germans would not allow themselves to be overruled on this issue, felt that the Brenner meeting would commit Mussolini. "Neither can it be denied that the Duce is fascinated by Hitler, a fascination that involves something deeply rooted in his make-up."[67]

The meeting at the Brenner Pass took place on March 18. Again, Hitler's psychological tactics were superb: first a presentation of a magnificent picture of the German arms situation; then, a declaration that he hoped to conclude the struggle with France and England sooner than those countries expected;[68] finally, avoidance of any demand on Italy. "The Führer told the Duce that he had not come to ask anything of him, but that he intended simply to give a picture of the situation. . . . The Duce could then, basing himself solely on the facts, make his decisions. Of one thing, however, the Führer is firmly convinced, and that is that the fates of Germany and Italy are indissolubly connected."[69] As Ciano had feared, Mussolini committed himself: "As soon as Germany has by her military operations created what the Führer describes as a favorable situation, he would lose no time in intervening."[70]

Everything thus depended on the effectiveness of German action. But Mussolini was already "growing every day more definitely pro-German. He now speaks openly of entering the war at the side of Germany" (March 23), and on April 2, came a "violent turn of the wheel in the direction of war" in consequence of Allied threats to tighten the blockade. On April 9, Ciano wrote that Mussolini was delighted with the German invasion of Denmark and Norway. But "it is humiliating," Mussolini told Ciano, "to remain with our hands folded while others write history" (April 11). On April 22, Mussolini again considered postponing Italy's entry into the war until the spring of 1941. Three days later, Mussolini repeated "his faithfulness to the pacts, but as regards war he says that 'he will enter it only when he has a quasi-mathematical certainty of winning it.' " On May 3, "the news from Norway literally exalts the Duce."[71]

The German attack of May 10, 1940, was the turning point. Upon Ambassador von Mackensen's bringing him the news at 5 A.M. that morning, Mussolini told Ciano of his decision to intervene. The next day, however, Mussolini was "more disposed to wait." On May 13, he told Ciano, "Any delay is inconceivable. We have no time to lose. Within a month I shall

---

[67] Gibson, *op. cit.*, pp. 219–20 (March 11 and 12).
[68] Muggeridge, *op. cit.*, p. 362.
[69] *Ibid.*, p. 363.
[70] *Ibid.*, p. 365.
[71] Gibson, *op. cit.*, pp. 225–43 *passim*.

declare war. I shall attack France and England in the air and on the sea. I am no longer thinking of taking up arms against Yugoslavia." "Unfortunately," added Ciano, "I can do nothing now to hold the Duce back. He has decided to act, and act he will."[72]

This conversation preceded the German thrust through the Ardennes. When the news of that operation was confirmed, Mussolini had a few days' hesitation. "He plans to write a letter to Hitler announcing our intervention for the latter part of June." On May 28, Mussolini spoke of June 10; on May 29, of June 5. "Rarely have I seen Mussolini so happy. He has realized his dream: that of becoming the military leader of the country at war."[73] On the same day, he summoned his chiefs of staff—Badoglio, Graziani, Cavagnari, and Pricolo—and explained that, after deciding that Italy must enter the war in the spring of 1941, he had been persuaded by the German victories to advance the date to some time after June 5, 1940.[74]

The final decision was taken on May 30: "The die is cast. Today Mussolini gave me his communication sent to Hitler about our entry into the war. The date chosen is June 5, unless Hitler himself considers it convenient to postpone it for some days."[75] (Hitler requested the Duce to postpone the opening of hostilities to June 10.[76]) Mackensen was informed on the same day. There was no turning back now.

Mussolini's decision was made by himself alone. In contrast to Wilson, who had to be urged on by Lansing and House, Mussolini now chose to act in a way that corresponded to his dearest wish, which he had been impatient to fulfill for almost a year but from which he had been restrained by his entourage. He had public opinion against him. Prior to May 10, he had reasoned that he was not ready and that he must wait, but the prodigious successes of his friend and model, Adolf Hitler, intoxicated him and led him to believe that the time had come. He misjudged Britain's capacity for resistance even more than Hitler did and believed he was entering the war at the point where total victory was assured, where he need give only the final blow to acquire, at minimum cost, the right to share the spoils.

Today [he told the chiefs of staff on May 29] two sentiments excite the Italian people: first, the fear of arriving too late into a situation that would diminish the value of our intervention and, secondly, a certain emulation that stimulates and incites them to parachute-jumping, firing against tanks, etc. This is something that pleases us, because it shows that the Italian people are made of good material.[77]

---

[72] *Ibid.*, pp. 246, 248, 249.
[73] *Ibid.*, pp. 255, 256.
[74] *Documenti Diplomatici Italiani*, Series IX, Vol. IV, No. 642, pp. 495–97.
[75] Gibson, *op. cit.*, p. 257.
[76] *Ibid.*, No. 646, p. 500.
[77] *Ibid.*, No. 642, p. 496.

Mussolini's judgment was no doubt a subjective and mistaken one as to the basic tendencies of a peace-loving nation. But it was a judgment developed by auto-persuasion and encouraged, in his dictatorial regime, by flattery from his entourage. We may say, then, that Mussolini acted on a faulty analysis of the situation, but he arrived at that analysis because he *wanted* to make the decision; in order to justify it, he constructed an artificial representation of reality.

CONCLUSION

The preceding analyses prompt us to reflect on the respective importance of the various factors whose influence we have noted in international relations. Historians are usually divided on this question. Some think that economic, financial, and demographic conditions exert a compelling influence on the conduct of a country's foreign policy and on the development of international relations. Others believe that the fundamental explanation should be sought in people's sentiments, their psychology, and the "new directions taken by the human spirit." Still others attach primary importance to the specific value of decisions and acts of the men responsible for the conduct of foreign policy. It is not our intention to assess the value of any of these general interpretations from a theoretical point of view, which is the level on which the discussion is frequently conducted, but simply to offer a few observations based on historical fact.

In this area, we have to proceed very cautiously, for critical studies are still very inadequate. The development of major international markets, for example, "one of the major phenomena of contemporary economic history," is very poorly documented.[1] The part played by high finance or big business in international politics is often hard to trace. The development of national sentiment in Asia, Africa, and Latin America is still largely unexplored territory. Analyses of the movement of ideas have often failed to establish the extent to which ideas penetrate beyond intellectual circles to the mass of the people. And the study of the statesman's methods and means of action, if it is to be really valuable, should be undertaken in the light of as many specific examples as possible, which cannot usefully be done without consulting private papers.

As a first approach, however, within the terms of reference we have defined, it may not be superfluous to make some observations suggested by two basic aspects of the modern history of international relations: the rise, and then the decline, of colonial expansion during the past hundred years; and the causes of the great wars.

THE RISE AND FALL OF EMPIRES

The colonial or semi-colonial expansion of a number of European states, the United States, and Japan was a major aspect of international relations

---

[1] See the remarks of Bertrand Gille in "La Finance internationale et les Trusts," *Revue historique* (Paris), April, 1962, pp. 291–327.

in the nineteenth century. This imperialism was the immediate reason for major clashes of political interests between the Great Powers, but the significance of those clashes should not be overrated, since they were settled without recourse to war, even when they had reached that critical stage at which the opponents had evidently said the "last word." Colonial expansion also established new contacts between civilizations, partially destroyed many local social structures, and opened the way for the penetration of Western ideas and techniques into Asia, Africa, and the Middle East. It also created new centers of production.

Among the motives for this expansion, economic and financial interests claim first attention. Large-scale modern industry could not maintain the tempo of production without new outlets and privileged markets—at a time (around 1879–80) when most states except Great Britain were adopting increasingly stringent protectionist policies—and without new sources of raw materials. Furthermore, the great industrial states possessed considerable capital funds that could not always be used profitably enough at home and for which investments were sought abroad. In some cases, the influence of big financial and industrial concerns is clearly apparent in the opening of new markets and the protection of capital investments. This influence may have been constant, but what facts we do have do not warrant asserting this as a fact.

In some cases, too, demographic motives should be taken into account, either when a state tried to direct its emigrants toward a territory under its own sovereignty, or when the establishment of a "colony without a flag" opened the way to economic or political expansion.

But the urge to expansion did not proceed solely from the lure of material interests. It was also related to the psychology of various social groups: the desire of Christian missions to develop their apostolate among the faithful of other religions; the desire of certain officers of the army and navy not only to hoist the national flag on new territories, but also to fulfil their personal ambitions and to satisfy temperaments which the humdrum monotony of professional life at home was unable to satisfy. Finally, it was prompted by the conviction of serving the national interest—raising the prestige of the state, giving a great people a "mission" to accomplish in the world, assuring the nation of military bases to protect its communications.

The question is whether the respective importance and effects of these motives can be properly determined. The facts, from one case to another, appear to differ considerably.

In the famous Fashoda Incident of 1898, for instance, economic and financial considerations seem to have been quite subordinate in the French policy behind the dispatch of French soldiers to occupy the Egyptian town of Fashoda. The main concerns were prestige and the desire to force Great Britain to reopen negotiations on the future of Egypt.

At about the same time, to take another example, the Spanish-American War was supported in the United States by economic and financial groups with interests in Cuban plantations, but the "big interests" opposed it until, after the first victories, it looked as though it would be a short operation. American Protestant missions favored the idea of extending their operations in the Pacific, and they looked to China. Nevertheless, the determining motives of Theodore Roosevelt's decision were altogether different. He desired to inculcate in the citizens of the United States a conviction that they had a "mission" to fulfill in the world; he wanted, he wrote, to give the American people something other than material gain to think about.

The role of certain business circles in Germany's Moroccan policy between 1904 and 1907 is indisputable, for the mineral wealth of the Rif Mountains was of great interest to them. But the promoter of this policy in the government, Baron von Holstein, was primarily pursuing prestige and diplomatic advantage; as he admitted himself in a note written in April, 1904, he hoped to break up the Anglo-French Entente Cordiale.

In the origins of the Boer War, economic and financial interests of the Europeans working the gold and diamond deposits in the Boer republics seem to have been decisive. Yet among the Uitlanders, as the British High Commissioner noted in May, 1899, there were many who did not want Great Britain to intervene militarily, since that would interfere with business. But the motives which ultimately inspired Cecil Rhodes and Joseph Chamberlain were determination to destroy the Boer republics so as to secure "the future of British South Africa," and a belief that any postponement of a solution would be an "admission of weakness" that would adversely affect Britain's world position.

In China, at the end of the nineteenth century, it was certainly economic and financial interests that determined the European powers' railway policies and the "spheres of influence." But the European Powers' governments also knew that economic and financial influence could lead to political influence. The same was true in the Ottoman Empire between 1911 and 1914.

Often, too, motivations varied in the course of one and the same undertaking. At the beginning of French expansion in Indochina, between 1860 and 1867, we meet primarily missionaries and navy men concerned to acquire naval bases; economic or financial interests were altogether secondary. Twenty years later, however, these interests had a certain influence, whether in regard to the coal deposits coveted by certain industrialists, or the much more important question of access to the Chinese market. But, in the mind of Jules Ferry, advocate of French colonial policy in 1883–84, the essential consideration was to restore French prestige after the defeat of 1871.

British policy in Egypt was governed at first by strategic considerations—control of the Suez Canal. Financial interests were probably also at hand, but not decisive. Economic interests came into the picture only after the *fait accompli* of the occupation.

Japanese plans for expansion on the Asian mainland were connected in the first place with strategic considerations, since the establishment of a European power in Korea would threaten Japan's security. It was only at the beginning of the twentieth century, when Japan wanted to develop her metallurgical industry, that the coal and iron-ore deposits of Manchuria became an incitement to conquest. As for the demographic argument, it did not arise until twenty years later. The only *constant* factor at all stages of Japanese expansion was the "will to power" and the fervor of national sentiment which Japanese leaders sought to inculcate in the population.

Can we say that economic and financial considerations, in cases where they were obviously paramount, served as stimulants to action? Undoubtedly, in a number of cases. But often, too, business interests were put at the service of plans relating to security, prestige, or political power.[2] In 1911, American banks received advice from the State Department to invest in China, and they yielded to this pressure. In Persia and the Ottoman Empire, at the beginning of the twentieth century, the British Government clearly subordinated the interests of its banks to strategic interests, which required that the security of India be ensured. In France, the policy of foreign loans to Egypt, Tunisia, Morocco, or the Balkans was governed by political considerations. In a single instance, these diverse interests were mingled: economic and financial considerations were now the motive, now the instrument of political action.

To come to a valid conclusion on the motivations of colonial or semi-colonial expansion, we should have to turn to a great number of critical studies based primarily on private records. This type of investigation has barely begun.

THE CAUSES OF WAR

The great war crises—of 1870, far more of 1914 and 1939—were essential agents of change during the past one hundred years. Not only did they profoundly modify or completely disrupt the power relations among states, but they also had major consequences in the fields of demography, political economy, and social structure. They also led to the development of new intellectual and political movements.

Economic interests evidently played a negligible part in the origins of the Franco-Prussian War. The economic and financial expansion of France in Europe was not markedly affected by competition from Prussia, and Prussian industrial development did not encounter obstacles for which French

---

[2] On this point, see above, Chapter Three, **pp. 53 ff.**

economic policies might be held responsible; moreover, a trade treaty of 1862 had expanded the area of free trade between the two countries. True, Prussia's economic interests prompted her to advocate the establishment of German unity, but such unity was already achieved within the Zollverein, which was strengthened in July, 1867, by the formation of a customs parliament (the object being to accustom southern Germans to permanent collaboration with the "North German Confederation").

The desire to achieve a "national mission," the will to power, however, played the principal part in Prussian policy. In French policy, the objective was similar: France's *de facto* pre-eminence on the Continent would be seriously jeopardized by German unification.

Would these impulses alone have been decisive on either side? No, what was decisive was the individual action of statesmen. Bismarck wanted to achieve German unity not by mere diplomatic pressure exercised on the south German states, but by an act of force; in his view, victory over France would be the necessary completion of the unity movement. Napoleon III, by refusing to be satisfied with the Hohenzollerns' renunciation of any claim to the Spanish throne, and by attempting to extract from Kaiser Wilhelm a commitment for the future, sought to preserve his personal prestige and secure the future of his dynasty.

The origins of the 1914 war raise far more complex questions. Demographic pressures played no part at all at this period, when migration could occur freely and when the United States was prepared to welcome all those from Europe who were dissatisfied with their conditions. But conflicts among national economic interests undoubtedly were far more important than they had been in 1870—the consequence of the "second industrial revolution" and colonialist expansion.

These conflicts were particularly apparent between Great Britain and Germany, rivals in nearly all the export markets of Europe and elsewhere. German commercial successes had aroused a sense of frustration in the British public, particularly between 1895 and 1897. And the need for a constant expansion of export markets was a *leitmotiv* for German businessmen.

On a lesser scale, commercial conflicts were also apparent between France and Germany. The Germans complained about French customs policies, which placed the French colonies under a "game preserve" system; moreover, they would have liked freer access to French iron-ore reserves and to the Paris financial market. French political leaders, on the other hand, were concerned at the position which German capital was beginning to occupy in France in certain mining ventures. More generally, the rivalry between colonial or semi-colonial imperialisms kept local antagonisms alive.

Nevertheless, it does not appear that the action of economic or financial interests operated in favor of war in July, 1914. In Great Britain, industrialists were less worried about German competition than they had been in 1908 or 1909; the financial interests in the City quite obviously displayed keen apprehension concerning possible British intervention in a continental war. The government, for its part, in the spring of 1914 had given proof of its willingness to encourage German economic expansion in Central Africa and Asia Minor. In Germany itself, there was no immediate threat to prosperity; there was no evidence of potential economic crisis that might prompt industrialists to gain new markets by force. In order to formulate any valid judgment on the place of economic questions in the origins of World War I, therefore, we would have to undertake lengthy critical studies of the economics of the day, the relations between business circles and governments, and the state of public opinion.

The influence of emotional forces, on the other hand, was clear. It took two forms: the "national minorities" movement and the growth of nationalism.

The movement of national minorities fostered unrest, especially in the Balkans and Danubian Europe. In the Balkans, it provided opportunities for intervention by the Great Powers and thus aggravated antagonism between Austria-Hungary and Russia. In Danubian Europe, it was serious enough for the political leaders in Vienna and Budapest, to conclude in July, 1914, that an Austro-Serbian war was necessary to assure the existence of the Dual Monarchy.

Nationalism, particularly between 1890 and 1914, made considerable strides in all the great European states, strengthening the desire for prestige and the will to power. The repeated clashes and threats of conflict accustomed Europeans to the idea of a war, and some political leaders thought it would be inevitable. In that context, the maintenance of the alliance system took on particular importance. This explains why there was virtually universal public agreement about the possibility of war in 1914, although the public does not actually appear to have given any impetus to governmental decisions. The churches did little to restrain the advances of nationalism, and international socialism proved powerless to oppose the principle of war.

The part played by individuals, although less considerable than it had been in 1870, was not negligible. Twice, in the Moroccan affair, German political leaders resorted to measures of intimidation, although most of them did not want to go as far as war. These diplomatic pressures aggravated the state of tension. During the crisis of July, 1914, all statesmen put fidelity to their alliances at the forefront, since the alliances seemed to them essential either for the preservation of their security or for the maintenance of their prestige. This was the motive that inspired the German Government to give Austria-Hungary full support and the French Government to accept the *fait accompli* of the Russian general mobilization. But in Vienna, the government decided to reject any compromise solution because they believed that the Dual Monarchy would, in three or four years' time, find itself facing a similar crisis under less favorable circumstances. Yet this decision might have been different, even given the economic and emotional context of the period.

In the origins of World War II, the German claim to "living space" takes pride of place. The argument Hitler developed in *Mein Kampf* was the inadequacy of German resources to feed a population that must continue to grow, and the consequent need to expand German territory; the reasons were demographic and economic. Yet these reasons are far from convincing: German population growth was declining in 1933, and as for insufficiency of foodstuffs, it was easily compensated in an industrial state whose exports enabled it to cover the deficit in national resources by imports. But it was just this need to resort to foreign imports that Hitler wanted to lessen. The economic difficulties he emphasized existed only to the extent that the German state sought to achieve autarky. But autarky was advocated because it would make it easier to assure the subsistence of the population in case of war, and to counteract a blockade. In point of fact, the economic argument was dominated by a political design and became the instrument of that design.

The same was true in 1938, when the Hitler government "settled" the Sudetenland question. The annexation of that part of Czechoslovak territory gave Germany the means to augment its arms potential by enabling it to control the Skoda works. There again, economic interests served political interests.

Finally, between 1934 and 1939, the German Government sought to ensure access to the mineral and agricultural resources of southeastern Europe, and its attempts at penetration there met with considerable success. These successes, it is true, may have been precarious, since they were achieved in the context of short-term agreements; nevertheless, in the summer of 1939, British political leaders were disposed to concede that the Reich possessed a preferential zone of economic influence in southeastern Europe, provided that Germany undertook to refrain from further recourse to force. The fact that the Nazi government disregarded such offers proves that it assigned a minor role to economic questions.

It is nevertheless possible that this German policy was influenced (perhaps not even consciously) by the pressure of economic and financial necessities. The "machinery of the German economy," as organized by the Nazi regime, was showing signs of weakness. In order to prevent economic and social collapse at home, the government had developed the system of placing orders itself and had therefore rapidly increased the public debt. It was thus faced with a possible monetary crisis. To escape these difficulties, it had to secure broader foreign outlets, and it might have envisaged acquiring them by force. But did the Nazis really reason in this way? We have to concede that this is pure hypothesis. Moreover, according to the Chairman of the Reichsbank,

Germany's financial difficulties were caused by an overrapid enactment of the rearmament program. It would therefore have been simple to reduce those difficulties by slowing down the program; but that the government did not want. There, again, political considerations were a stronger factor than economic necessity.

German national sentiment and nationalism served as props for this policy, but they did not initiate it. The successes achieved by the German Government in the foreign-policy field over a period of six years, together with the restoration of German military traditions, certainly gave the German public the satisfaction it had been yearning for since 1919. That is why so much of the population accepted the Nazi regime or gave it at least passive support. But the government took pains to strengthen this nationalism by education and propaganda, since it regarded a favorable "collective psychology" as a prerequisite to the success of its foreign policy. The thrust of mass feeling merely buttressed political action.

In the final analysis, therefore, the essential factor is the will of an individual or of a group of individuals.

The motives for the behavior of human groups are never simple. What happens, in fact, is that the diverse influences which govern the power of international relations—economic, financial, demographic, psychological, or emotional factors on the one hand, and the impetus given by the will of the men in power on the other—contradict one another or combine in accordance with constantly varying circumstances of time and space. Consequently, when the historian tries to explain certain events, he must examine the play of each of these influences as they affect each individual case. Sometimes, he finds that economic or demographic forces were dominant; that is often the case with changes that occurred over a long period of time. Sometimes, he will emphasize emotional or ideological forces. Sometimes, he sees individual initiative as having played the decisive part. Any attempt to single out one of these explanations as *a priori* and permanently preponderant would falsify the purpose of historical research. The same may be said of any attempt to study a particular aspect of the behavior of human groups in isolation without considering the interaction of the various motives influencing behavior. To establish some kind of hierarchy among these explanations would be as useless as to establish laws. The historian can avoid major errors in his study of international relations only by keeping an open mind.

SELECTED BIBLIOGRAPHY

In a book on the history of international relations a full bibliography could cover virtually the same ground as that for world history in general. We have tried to provide a somewhat more helpful selective bibliography, the selection being determined not only by the intrinsic value of the books listed, but also, and particularly, by their contribution to the positions we have adopted in the present study.

Many of the books listed for the chapters in Part I touch on the issues discussed in Part II, The Statesman. In the bibliography for Part II (Chapters Nine through Thirteen), no books have been listed that are concerned exclusively with the personalities used as examples in the text (such references will be found in the footnotes to each chapter); we have listed only works of a more general theoretical or methodological nature. One must bear in mind that many areas of this vast subject remain unexplored.

GENERAL

There are two important general works by French authors:

ARON, RAYMOND. *Peace and War: A Theory of International Relations*. Translated by RICHARD HOWARD and ANNETTE BAKER FOX. New York: Doubleday, 1966. Aron's work is a remarkable synthesis of reflections on the theory, forces, value systems, and recent developments of the "international system."

La Politique étrangère et ses fondements: rapports préparés sous la direction de J.-B. Duroselle. Paris: Armand Colin, for the Association Française de Science Politique, 1954. This series of studies does not claim to cover the whole field.

American works are more numerous. Among the best known are:

FOX, WILLIAM T. R. (ed). *Theoretical Aspects of International Relations*. Notre Dame, Ind.: University of Notre Dame Press, 1959.

MORGENTHAU, HANS J. *Politics Among Nations: The Struggle for Power and Peace*. 3d rev. ed. New York: Alfred A. Knopf, 1960. The author adheres to the theory that the quest for power constitutes the basis of international relations.

PULESTON, W. D. *The Influence of Force in Foreign Relations*. Princeton, N. J.: D. Van Nostrand, 1955.

STRAUSZ-HUPÉ, ROBERT, and POSSONY, STEFAN. *International Relations in an Age of Conflict*. New York: McGraw-Hill, 1954. The authors deal with factors of power, techniques of foreign policy, and, more briefly, the role of ideologies and economic interests in the conduct of foreign policy.

WOLFERS, ARNOLD. *Discord and Collaboration: Essays on International Politics*.

Baltimore, Md.: The Johns Hopkins Press, 1962. A collection and revision of previously published articles; one of the most intelligent evaluations of international relations to be found.

WRIGHT, QUINCY. *The Study of International Relations.* New York: Appleton-Century-Crofts, 1955.

Other recent works to which we should draw attention are:

BALL, MARGARET M., and KILLOUGH, HUGH B. *International Relations.* New York: The Ronald Press, 1956.

DUCHACEK, IVO D., and THOMPSON, KENNETH W. *Conflict and Cooperation Among Nations.* New York: Holt, Rinehart & Winston, 1960.

FRANKEL, JOSEPH. *The Making of Foreign Policy: An Analysis of Decision-Making.* London and New York: Oxford University Press, 1963. A study of the influence of environment on the statesman.

HOFFMANN, STANLEY (ed.). *Contemporary Theory in International Relations.* Englewood Cliffs, N. J.: Prentice-Hall, 1960. A collection of acute commentaries showing how far removed we still are from any absolute theory of international relations.

PADELFORD, NORMAN J., and LINCOLN, GEORGE A. *The Dynamics of International Politics.* New York: Macmillan, 1962.

PALMER, NORMAN D., and PERKINS, HOWARD C. *International Relations: The World Community in Transition.* 2d ed. Boston: Houghton Mifflin, 1954. In this now somewhat outdated work, the authors stress the elements of state power, the instruments available for the protection of the national interest, and the legal and diplomatic means through which international relations can be controlled.

SPROUT, HAROLD and MARGARET. *Foundations of International Politics.* Princeton, N. J.: D. Van Nostrand, 1962.

Elsewhere in the bibliography,* we shall mention some works concerned with the issues of realism in foreign affairs, in particular those of Hans Morgenthau, Reinhold Niebuhr, and Kenneth Thompson. Here, it may suffice to mention the following:

FOX, WILLIAM T. R. "Inter-War International Relations Research: The American Experience," *World Politics,* I (October, 1948), 67–79. A study of the evolution of methodology.

SCHWARZENBERGER, GEORG. *Power Politics: A Study of World Society.* 3d ed. New York: Frederick A. Praeger, 1964.

On the nature and history of imperialism, see:

BUKHARIN, NIKOLAI I. *Imperialism and World Economy.* New York: International Publishers, 1929.

HALLGARTEN, WOLFGANG. *Imperialismus vor 1914.* 2 vols. Munich: C. H. Beck, 1951.

* See below, bibliography for Part II, Chapter Ten.

LANGER, WILLIAM L. "A Critique of Imperialism," *Foreign Affairs*, XIV (October, 1935), 102–19.

———. *The Diplomacy of Imperialism*. New York: Alfred A. Knopf, 1935.

———. "Farewell to Empire," *Foreign Affairs*, XLI (October, 1962), 115–30.

MOON, PARKER T. *Imperialism and World Politics*. New York: Macmillan, 1926.

SCHUMPETER, JOSEPH A. *Imperialism and Social Classes*. Translated by HEINZ NORDEN. Edited by PAUL M. SWEEZY. New York: Augustus M. Kelley, 1951. Originally published in 1919. (Paperback ed.: Meridian.)

SEILLIÈRE, ERNEST. *Introduction à la philosophie de l'impérialisme*. 2d ed. Paris: F. Alcan, 1911.

STRACHEY, JOHN. *The End of Empire*. New York: Random House, 1960. (Paperback ed.: Frederick A. Praeger.)

WINSLOW, E. M. "Marxist, Liberal, and Sociological Theories of Imperialism," *Journal of Political Economy*, XXXIX (December, 1931), 713–58.

———. *The Pattern of Imperialism*. New York: Columbia University Press, 1948.

CHAPTER ONE. GEOGRAPHY

FRIEDRICH RATZEL's pioneering work *Politische Geographie*, Leipzig: 1897, remains essential. Professor of Geography at the University of Leipzig, Ratzel established a considerable reputation with his studies on bio-geography. Later, he attempted to establish the relation between geography on the one hand, and history and political science on the other. This relation between geography and politics remained central to the thought of other writers who attempted to widen the scope of Ratzel's theories.

The two leaders of the school of thought that maintained that national power depended on geographical factors were Sir Halford J. MacKinder and Karl Haushofer.

SIR HALFORD J. MACKINDER, in an address before the Royal Geographical Society in 1904 (republished in 1951 by the Royal Geographical Society, London, under the title *The Scope and Methods of Geography and The Geographical Pivot of History*), and later, in his book *Democratic Ideals and Reality*, New York: Henry Holt; London: Constable, 1919 (Paperback ed.: Norton), avoided taking a doctrinaire position and called his views only "an approach" to the truth. Haushofer, by contrast, claimed to propound a doctrine and at the same time thought himself to be establishing a number of "palpable facts" and "proven laws" that, he felt, could guide political leaders. The essence of his argument is contained in KARL HAUSHOFER, *et al.*, *Bausteine für Geopolitik*, Berlin-Grunewald: K. Vowinckel, 1928; Haushofer wrote the first part. Among his collaborators, Professor OTTO MAULL of the University of Graz, author of *Politische Geographie*, Berlin: Gebruder Borntraeger, 1925, and Richard Henning, a professor at the Dusseldorf Hochschule, were noteworthy. See also:

KJELLÉN, RUDOLF. *Staten som Lifsform*. Stockholm, 1916. German translation: *Der Staat als Lebensform*. Berlin-Grunewald: K. Vowinckel, 1917. Kjellén was the first to use the term "geopolitics."

SEMPLE, ELLEN CHURCHILL. *Influence of Geographic Environments*. New York: Henry Holt, 1911.

VOGEL, WALTHER. *Das neue Europa und seine historisch-geographischen Grundlagen*. Bonn: K. Schroeder, 1925.

The actual influence of this school of geographers has been much debated. According to HANS W. WEIGERT, *Generals and Geographers: The Twilight of Geopolitics*, London and New York: Oxford University Press, 1942, Haushofer's ideas exerted considerable influence on Hitler. Weigert points out that the conclusion of the Soviet-German nonaggression pact of August, 1939, was the fulfillment of an oft-repeated aspiration of the "geopoliticians." CARL TROLL, however, in an interesting study published in *Erdkunde* (Bonn), Vol. I (1947), disputed the extent of that influence: Haushofer, he pointed out, did not succeed in having geopolitics included in university curricula; after 1938, he ceased to be *persona grata* among the Nazi leadership (possibly because his son, who was also a geographer but who was opposed to his father's views, had been arrested by the Gestapo).

ADMIRAL ALFRED T. MAHAN's *The Influence of Sea Power upon History: 1660–1783*, Boston: Little, Brown, 1890 (paperback ed.: Hill & Wang), occupies a special position. It appeared earlier than Ratzel's work and concentrated on the history of naval wars. Mahan's essential concern was not to establish a relation between geography, history, and politics, but to analyze the foundations of naval strategy and to show how sea power explains the greater part of history. The only approach to a general theory is contained in scattered reflections throughout the volume. Mahan's work may usefully be compared with that of RAYMOND DE BELOT and ANDRÉ REUSNER, *La Puissance navale dans l'histoire*, Vol. III: *De 1914 à 1919*, Paris: Editions Maritimes et coloniales, 1960.

The main critique of the theory of geographical determinism was provided by French geographers and historians. VIDAL DE LA BLACHE made his response to Ratzel's book clear in "La Géographie politique: à propos des écrits de M. Frédéric Ratzel," *Annals de Géographie*, 1898, pp. 98–111. His views are set out with especial authority in the preface to *Tableau de la Géographie de la France* (Vol. I of Ernest Lavisse, ed., *Histoire de France*), Paris: Hachette, 1911, CAMILLE VALLAUX, in *Géographie sociale: Le Sol et l'Etat*, Paris: O. Doir, 1911, objected to Ratzel's idea of political geography and particularly to his "space" theory, on the grounds that it was not sufficiently detached from "concern with the immediate" and that it sought to legitimize German imperialism. CAMILLE VALLAUX and JEAN BRUNHES, in *La Géographie de l'histoire*, 2 vols., Paris: F. Alcan, 1921, contribute some interesting points to the discussion without actually attacking Ratzel. ALBERT DEMANGEON directed his critique against "geopoliticians" in general but not Ratzel specifically: "La Géographie politique," *Annales de Géographie*, 1932, pp. 22–31; see also PIERRE GEORGE, "Sur une nouvelle présentation du déterminisme en géographie humaine," *ibid.*, 1952, pp. 250–54. JEAN GOTTMANN, in *La Politique extérieure des états et leur géographie*, Paris: Armand Colin, 1952, seeks to explain what he considers to be the fundamental fact of political geography—namely, the "compartmentalization" of the world into individualized communities. The causes of this compartmentalization, he believes, are psychological and sociological and do not correspond to geographical characteristics.

Among historians, LUCIEN FEBVRE, in *A Geographical Introduction to History*, New York: Alfred A. Knopf, 1925, most vigorously attacks Ratzel's "ambitious generalizations" and "geographical fatalism." JACQUES ANCEL, in *Manuel géographique de politique européenne*, Paris: Delagrave, 1936, mistakenly identified Ratzel with the "geopoliticians" and attacks a political geography determined by geographical, spatial factors. He attempts to show that varying modes of living on the one hand, and "spiritual factors" on the other, are more valid explanatory elements, but he does not clearly define his own concepts. On the general aspects of this question, see also ROBERT STRAUSZ-HUPÉ, *Geopolitics: The Struggle for Space and Power*, New York: G. P. Putnam's Sons, 1942.

It is obviously impossible to mention all the works that might usefully be consulted here. But certain studies reveal particularly interesting points of view on various aspects of this vast subject:

HUNTINGTON, ELLSWORTH. *Civilization and Climate*. New Haven, Conn.: Yale University Press, 1915.

LE ROY-LADURIE, E. "Histoire et climat," *Annales de Géographie*, January, 1959, pp. 3–34.

SORRE, MAXIMILIEN. *Les Fondements de la géographie humaine*. Vol. I: *Les Fondements biologiques: Essai d'une écologie de l'homme*. Paris: Armand Colin, 1943.

SPYKMAN, NICHOLAS J. *The Geography of the Peace*. New York: Harcourt, Brace, 1944.

UTTERSTROM, GUSTAF. "Climatic Fluctuations and Population Problems in Early Modern History," *The Scandinavian Economic History Review*, XXX, No. 1 (1955), 3–47.

CHAPTER TWO. POPULATION

General

BEAUJEU-GARNIER, JACQUELINE. *Géographie de la population*. 2 vols. Paris: M. T. Génin, 1956–58.

BOUTHOUL, GASTON. *La Population dans le monde: les grands évènements historiques*. Paris: Payot, 1935.

CHEVALIER, LOUIS. *Démographie générale*. Paris: Dalloz, 1951.

LANDRY, ADOLPHE, et al. *Traité de démographie*. Paris: Payot, 1945.

MARSHALL, THOMAS H., et al. *The Population Problem: The Experts and the Public*. London: George Allen & Unwin, 1938.

REINHARD, MARCEL R. *Histoire de la population mondiale de 1700 à 1948*. Paris: Domat-Montchrestien, 1949–50. The best general study available.

SAUVY, ALFRED. *Théorie générale de la population.* 2 vols. Paris: Presses universitaires de France, 1952–54.

UNGARN-STERNBERG, R. VON, and SCHNUBNELL, H. *Grundriss der Bevölkerungswissenschaft.* Stuttgart: Piscator, 1950.

The Population Increase

FROMONT, P. *Démographie économique: les rapports de l'économie et de la population dans le monde.* Paris: Payot, 1947.

MOMBERT, P., "L'adaptation internationale de la population à l'économie," *Revue économique internationale* (Brussels), December, 1936, pp. 493–520.

MYRDAL, GUNNAR. "Industrialization and Population," in *Economic Essays in Honour of Gustav Cassel*, pp. 439–58. London: Allen, 1933.

THOMPSON, WARREN S. *Danger Spots in World Population.* New York: Alfred A. Knopf, 1929. Brief and often controversial.

———. *Population and Peace in the Pacific.* Chicago: The University of Chicago Press, 1946.

See also the records of the Congress for the Science of Population (Congrès international de la population) that met in Paris in 1937 (Vols. I–VIII, Paris: Hermann, 1938), and of the World Population Conference that met in Rome in 1954 (6 vols., New York: United Nations, 1956–57); and the reports presented in 1937 to the International Studies Conference.

Comparative study of demographic policies between 1929 and 1939 have been made by F. SECRETAIN, *Le problème de la population: Etude des solutions données aux problèmes démographiques en Allemagne, en Italie et au Japon,* Paris: Presses universitaires de France, 1942.

The concepts of optimum population and overpopulation are examined in a number of studies. The following, in particular, should be consulted:

BOUTHOUL, GASTON. *La Surpopulation dans le monde.* Paris: Payot, 1958.

BUQUET, LÉON. *L'Optimum de population.* Paris: Presses universitaires de France, 1956.

EFFERTZ, OTTO. "Théorie ponophysiocratique de la population," *Revue d'économie politique*, XXVIII (1914), 129–52.

FERENCZI, IMRE. *The Synthetic Optimum of Population: An Outline of an International Demographic Policy.* Paris: International Institute of Intellectual Co-operation, League of Nations, 1938.

Migrations

CITROEN, H. A. *Les Migrations internationales.* Paris: Librairie de Médicis, 1948.

GREGORY, JOHN W. *Human Migrations & the Future: A Study of the Causes, Effects & Control of Emigration.* London: Seeley Service, 1928.

HERSCH, L. "Les Migrations internationales comme facteurs de guerre et de paix," *Revue internationale de sociologie*, September-October, 1929, pp. 367–82.

Numelin, Ragnar. *The Wandering Spirit: A Study of Human Migration*. London: Macmillan, 1937.

Sorre, Maximilien. *Les Migrations des peuples*. Paris: Ernest Flammarion, 1955.

Varlez, Louis. *Les migrations internationales et leur réglementation*. The Hague: Academy of International Law, *Recueil des cours*, 1927, XX, 167–348.

Willcox, A. *International Migration*. 2 vols. ("Publications of the National Bureau of Economic Research," Ser. No. 14, 18.) New York, 1930–31.

The League of Nations publications should also be consulted. See in particular: *Migration Movements, 1920–1924* ("Publications of the International Labour Office," Special Report Series), Geneva: ILO, 1926; and *Methods of Compiling Emigration and Immigration Statistics* ("Publications of the International Labour Office," Special Report Series), Geneva: ILO, 1922. See also *International Migration Statistics*, New York: United Nations, 1953. One can also consult Winifred Gregory (ed.), *International Congresses and Conferences, 1840–1937*, New York: H. W. Wilson, 1938. The two reports of the International Conference on Emigration and Immigration—Rome, 1924, and Havana, 1928—are also important.

Questions bearing on the years since World War II are studied in C. Martí-Bufill, *Nuevas soluciones al problema migratorio*, Madrid: Ediciones Cultura Hispanica, 1955; and Jacques Vernant, *The Refugee in the Post-War World*, London: George Allen & Unwin, 1953.

On national policies and problems with regard to migrations, see:

BRAZIL

Cornelius, Carl G. *Die Deutschen im brasilianischen Wirtschaftsleben*. Stuttgart: Ausland und Heimat, 1929.

Oberacker, Karlheinrich. *Die volkspolitische Lage des Deutschtums im Rio Grande do Sul*. Jena: G. Fischer, 1936.

Roche, Jean. *La colonisation allemande et le Rio Grande do Sul*. Paris: Institut des hautes études de l'Amérique latine, 1959.

Wagemann, Ernst F. *Die deutschen Kolonisten im brasilianischen Staate Espirito Santo*. Munich and Leipzig: Dunker & Humblot, 1915.

CANADA

Clokie, Hugh McDowall. *Canadian Government and Politics*. Rev. ed. Toronto and New York: Longmans Green, 1950.

Corbett, David C. *Canada's Immigration Policy: A Critique*. Toronto: University of Toronto Press, 1957.

Massey, Vincent. *On Being Canadian*. Don Mills, Ont.: J. M. Dent & Sons, 1948.

CHINA

Ch'en, Ta. *Emigrant Communities in South China*. New York: Institute of Pacific Relations, 1940.

Mosolff, Hans. *Die Chinesische Auswanderung*. Rostock: C. Hinstorff, 1932.

ITALY

BOYER-MONTÉGUT, R. DE. *L'Immigration italienne dans le Sud-Ouest de la France.* Paris: Editions Spes, 1928.

FOERSTER, ROBERT F. *The Italian Emigration of our Times.* Cambridge, Mass.: Harvard University Press, 1919.

VIRGILII, FILIPPO. *Emigrazione.* Vol. II: *Le leggi Fasciste.* Rome: Libreria del Littorio, 1928.

————. *Il problema della popolazione.* Milan: F. Vallarde, 1924.

WOOG, CLAUDE. *La Politique d'émigration de l'Italie.* Paris: Presses universitaires de France, 1930.

JAPAN

BAILEY, THOMAS A. *Theodore Roosevelt and the Japanese Crisis.* Stanford, Calif.: Stanford University Press; London: Oxford University Press, 1934.

IYENAGA, TOYOKICHI, and SATO, KENOSKE. *Japan and the Californian Problem.* New York and London: G. P. Putnam's Sons, 1921.

OGISHIMA, TORU. "Japanese Emigration," *International Labour Review,* November, 1936, pp. 618–51.

YOSHITOMI, MACAOMI. *Le Conflit nippo-américains et le problème du Pacifique.* Paris: A. Pedone, 1926.

The proceedings of the 2d Conference of the Institute of Pacific Relations, held in Honolulu in 1927, have been reprinted with slight variations in: JOHN B. CONDLIFFE (ed.), *Problems of the Pacific,* Chicago, 1927.

PALESTINE

HUREWITZ, JACOB C. *The Struggle for Palestine, 1920–1950.* New York: W. W. Norton, 1950.

KULISHER, YEVGENII M. *Jewish Migrations: Past Experience and Post-War Prospects.* New York: The American Jewish Committee, 1943.

UNITED STATES

BERNARD, WILLIAM S. (ed.). *American Immigration Policy: A Reappraisal.* New York: Harper & Bros., 1950.

Reports of the Immigration Commission, U.S. Senate, 61st Cong., 3d sess., Document No. 7475. 2 vols. Washington: Government Printing Office, 1911.

CHAPTER THREE. INTERNATIONAL ECONOMIC RIVALRY AND CONFLICT

General

BROCARD, LUCIEN. *Principes d'économie nationale et internationale.* Paris: Recueil Sirey, 1929–31.

CONDLIFFE, JOHN B. *The Reconstruction of World Trade: A Survey of International Economic Relations.* New York: W. W. Norton, 1940.

CULBERTSON, WILLIAM S. *International Economic Policies: A Survey of the Economics of Diplomacy.* New York and London: Appleton, 1925.

ENKEN, W. *Die Grundlagen der Nationalökonomie.* Jena: G. Fischer, 1941. See the chapter entitled "Die wirtschaftliche Macht."

HEILPERIN, MICHAEL A. *Economic Nationalism.* Geneva: Droz, 1960.

PANTALEONI, M. "Tentative di analysi del concetto di forte e debole in economia," *Erotemi de Economia,* I, 229–55.

PERROUX, FRANÇOIS. "Esquisse d'une théorie de l'économie dominante," *Economie appliquée,* I (1948), 243–300.

———. "Note sur le dynamisme de la domination," *ibid.,* III (1950), 245–58.

TRUCHY, HENRI, and BYÉ, MAURICE. *Les Relations économiques internationales.* Paris: Recueil Sirey, 1948.

National Economic Policies and International Relations

ABELARDE, PEDRO E. *American Tariff Policy Toward the Philippines, 1898–1946.* New York: King's Crown Press, 1947.

BACHI, R. "Politique douanière entre la métropole et les colonies," *Mélanges dédiés à M. le Professeur Henri Truchy.* Paris: Recueil Sirey, 1938, pp. 32–51.

BONN, JULIUS-MORITZ. "La Paix économique: Dans quelle mesure les régimes autarciques sont-ils conciliables avec le maintien de la paix?" *Esprit International* (Paris: Hachette), XII (1938), 238–55.

DUMONT, CHARLES. *Les Conditions internationales de la paix douanière.* Paris: Report to the International Chamber of Commerce, 1928.

GRIZIOTTI-KRETSCHMANN, JENNY. *Autarchia economica e finanziaria ed economia mondiale.* Padua: Cedam, 1937.

GUILLAIN, ROBERT. *Les Problèmes douaniers internationaux et la Société des Nations.* Paris: Recueil Sirey, 1930.

HELANDER, SVEN. *Das Autarkieproblem in der Weltwirtschaft.* Berlin: Dunker & Humblot, 1955.

HÉRISSON, CHARLES D. *Autarcie, économie complexe: politique, commerciale, rationelle.* Paris: Librairie technique et économique, 1937.

ISAACS, ASHER. *International Trade, Tariff and Commercial Policies.* Chicago: Richard D. Irwin, 1948.

LANDRY, ADOPHE. Report to the Congress of French-speaking Economists in Paris, 1930, and discussion of that report. Unpublished.

LAUFENBURGER, HENRY. *L'Intervention de l'Intervention de l'Etat en matière économique.* Paris: Librairie générale de droit et de jurisprudence, 1939.

PERROUX, FRANÇOIS. *Autarcie et expansion; Empire ou empires.* Paris: Librairie de Médicis, 1940.

Economic Expansion

Of the economic rivalries that existed during the period of expansion in export trade, 1871–1914, the Anglo-German has received most attention. See Ross J. HOFFMAN, *Great Britain and the German Trade Rivalry, 1875–1914,* Philadelphia: University of Pennsylvania Press, 1935. For European rivalries for export markets in the Near and Far East, see:

HOU, HON-LUN. *Histoire douanière de la Chine.* Paris: Presses Modernes, 1929.

NEBIOGLU, OSMAN. *Die Auswirkungen der Kapitulationen auf die türkische Wirtschaft.* Jena: G. Fischer, 1941.

SOULIÉ, CHARLES G. *Exterritorialité et intérêts étrangers en Chine.* Paris: P. Geuthner, 1925.

WILLOUGHBY, WESTEL W. *Foreign Rights and Interests in China.* Rev. ed. Baltimore, Md.: The Johns Hopkins Press, 1927.

On the German economic penetration of Southeast Europe, see:

BASCH, ANTONÍN. *The Danube Basin and the German Economic Sphere.* New York: Columbia University Press, 1943.

EINZIG, PAUL. *Bloodless Invasion: German Economic Penetration in the Danubian States and the Balkans.* London: Gerald Duckworth, 1938.

RUHM VON OPPEN, BEATE (ed.). *Documents on German Foreign Policy, 1918–1945.* ("Publications of the Royal Institute of International Affairs," Series D.) London and New York: Oxford University Press, 1953. The documents included here are particularly important.

The quest for raw materials and sources of energy was the subject of an interesting study begun at the outbreak of World War II as part of a long report presented by ETIENNE DENNERY to the International Studies Conference: *Peaceful Change,* Vol. IV: *Le problème des matières premières,* Paris: International Institute of Intellectual Co-operation, League of Nations, 1939.

On the relation between economic and political issues in the matter of oil, see the following books (some of which go to extremes of interpretation):

BÉRENGER, HENRY. *Le pétrole et la France.* Paris: Ernest Flammarion, 1920.

BROOKS, BENJAMIN T. *Peace, Plenty and Petroleum.* Lancaster, Pa.: The Jacques Catell Press, 1944.

FAURE, EDGAR. *Le Pétrole dans la paix et dans la guerre.* Paris: Nouvelle Revue Critique, 1939.

FISCHER, LOUIS. *Oil Imperialism: The International Struggle for Petroleum.* New York: International Publishers, 1926.

JOESTEN, JOACHIM. *Öl regiert die Welt: Geschäft und Politik.* Düsseldorf: K. Rauch, 1958.

ROBERT-PIMÍENTA. "Une Politique du pétrole," *Colonies et marine,* IV (1920), 224–43. A review of Bérenger's book.

ZISCHKA, ANTON. *La Guerre secrète pour le pétrole.* Paris: Payot, 1933.

On oil in particular regions, see:

ELWELL-SUTTON, LAURENCE. *Persian Oil: A Study in Power Politics.* London: Lawrence and Wishart, 1955.

FATEMI, NASROLLAH S. *Oil Diplomacy: Powderkeg in Iran.* New York: Whittier Books, 1954.

LENCZOWSKI, GEORGE. *Oil and State in the Middle East.* Ithaca, N.Y.: Cornell University Press, 1960.

LONGRIGG, STEPHEN H. *Oil in the Middle East: Its Discovery and Development.* 2d ed. London and New York: Oxford University Press, 1961.

SHWADRAN, BENJAMIN. *The Middle East, Oil, and the Great Powers.* 2d ed. New York: Council for Middle Eastern Affairs Press, 1959.

VAGTS, ALFRED. *Mexico, Europa und Amerika, unter besonderer Berücksichtigung der Petroleumpolitik.* Berlin-Grunewald: Dr. W. Rothschild, 1928.

The international issues posed by railroad construction are studied in:

BODE, F. *Der Kampf um die Bagdadbahn, 1903–1914.* Breslau, 1941.

EARLE, EDWARD M. *Turkey, the Great Powers and the Bagdad Railway: A Study in Imperialism.* New York: Macmillan, 1923.

HALSEY, FREDERIC M. *Investments in Latin America and the British West Indies.* ("Publications of the U. S. Foreign and Domestic Commerce Bureau," Special Agents Series, No. 169.) Washington, D. C.: Government Printing Office, 1918.

IBBEKEN, RUDOLPH. *Das aussenpolitische Problem Staat und Wirtschaft in der deutschen Reichspolitik, 1880–1914.* Berlin, 1924.

MACMURRAY, JOHN VAN A. *Treaties and Agreements With and Concerning China, 1894–1919.* Washington, D.C.: Carnegie Endowment for International Peace, 1929.

NGAN, CHIANG-KIA. *China's Struggle for Railroad Development.* New York: John Day, 1943.

WOLF, JOHN B. *The Diplomatic History of the Bagdad Railway.* Columbia, Mo.: University of Missouri Press, 1936.

ZEN SUN, E-TU. *Chinese Railways and British Interests, 1898–1911.* New York: King's Crown Press, 1954. The author has utilized the papers of the Director of Railroads.

The diplomatic history of the Suez and Panama canals is well known. Among the many available works, see:

ANCHIERI, ETTORE. *Il canale di Suez.* Milan: Libreria lombarda, 1937.

BONNET, GEORGE EDGAR. *Ferdinand de Lesseps: le diplomate, le créateur de Suez.* Paris: Plon, 1951.

HALLBERG, CHARLES W. *The Suez Canal: Its History and Diplomatic Importance.* New York: Columbia University Press; London: P. S. King, 1931.

McCAIN, WILLIAM D. *The United States and the Republic of Panama.* Durham, N.C.: Duke University Press, 1937.

REINHARD, E. *Kampf um Suez.* Dresden: Kadon, 1930.

SIEGFRIED, ANDRÉ. *Suez and Panama.* Translated by H. H. and DORIS HEMMING. New York: Harcourt, Brace, 1940.

SMITH, DARRELL HEVENOR. *The Panama Canal: Its History, Activities and Organizations.* Baltimore, Md.: The Johns Hopkins Press, 1927.

WILSON, LT.-COL. SIR ARNOLD T. *The Suez Canal: Its Past, Present and Future.* London: Oxford University Press, 1933.

Coercive Measures

TARIFF WARS

BILLOT, ALBERT. *La France et l'Italie: Histoire des années troubles, 1881–1899.* 2 vols. Paris: Plon et Nourrit, 1905.

LIENS, H. G. Untitled memoirs on the origins of the tariff wars in 1887–88. Unpublished.

SCHULTZ, MAURICE, "La Politique économique d'Aehrenthal envers la Serbie," *Revue d'histoire de la guerre mondiale*, October, 1935, pp. 325–47; January, 1936, pp. 23–42.

EMBARGOES AND BOYCOTTS

CHAMBERLAIN, JOSEPH. *The Embargo Resolutions and Neutrality.* ("International Conciliation," No. 251.) Worcester, Mass., and New York: Carnegie Endowment for International Peace, 1929.

LAMBERT, EDOUARD. *Les Embargos sur l'importation et l'exportation des marchandises.* Paris: Librairie générale de droit et de jurisprudence, 1936.

MICHELS, ROBERTO. *Il Boicotaggio, saggio su un aspetto delle crisi.* Turin: Einaudi, 1934. There is a French edition, translated by G. BOUTHOUL, *Le Boycottage international*, Paris: Payot, 1936.

ROUSSEAU, CHARLES. "Le boycottage dans les rapports internationaux," *Revue générale de droit international public*, 1958, pp. 5–25.

SÉFÉRIADÈS, STELIO P. *Réflexions sur le boycottage en droit international.* Paris: Rousseau, 1912.

WALZ, GUSTAV. *Nationalboycott und Völkerrecht.* Berlin: Dunker, 1939.

The boycotts directed by China against Japan between 1925 and 1931 were studied in the *Report* of the Commission of Inquiry of the League of Nations (Lytton Commission), Geneva, 1932, pp. 124–30, and in S. MATSUMOTO, *The Historical Developments of Chinese Boycotts*, Tokyo: Council of International Relations, 1933. See also DOROTHY ORCHARD, "China's Use of the Boycott as a Political Weapon," *Annals of the American Academy of Political Science*, CLLII (1930), 252–61; and CHARLES F. REMER, *A Study of Chinese Boycotts, with Special Reference to Their Economic Effectiveness*, Baltimore, Md.: The Johns Hopkins Press, 1933.

CHAPTER FOUR. INTERNATIONAL ECONOMIC AGREEMENTS

This subject has been taken up in general, and in full, in only one study:

JACQUES A. L'HUILLIER, *Théorie et pratique de la coopération économique internationale.* Paris: M. T. Génin, 1957.

Customs Unions

THE ZOLLVEREIN

BENAERTS, PIERRE. *Les Origines de la grande industrie allemande.* Paris: F. H. Turot, 1933.

EISENARTH-ROTHE, W. VON. *Vorgeschichte und Begründung des deutschen Zollverein, 1815–1834.* 3 vols. Berlin: Hobbing, 1934.

HENDERSON, WILLIAM O. *The Zollverein.* Cambridge: Cambridge University Press, 1939.

PRICE, ARNOLD HEREWARD. *The Evolution of the Zollverein.* Ann Arbor, Mich.: University of Michigan Press, 1949.

THE FRANCO-BELGIAN CUSTOMS UNION

DESCHAMPS, HENRY T. *La Belgique devant la France de Juillet: l'opinion et l'attitude françaises de 1839 à 1849.* Paris: Les Belles lettres, 1956.

RIDDER, ALFRED DE. *Les Projets d'union douanière franco-belge et les puissances européennes, 1836–1843.* Brussels: M. Lamertin, 1932.

THE PROJECT OF 1931

KRULIS-RANDA, JAN. *Das Deutsch-österreichische Zollunionsprojekt von 1931.* Zurich: Europa [ca. 1955].

Condominiums and Spheres of Influence

HOWARD, HARRY N. *The Partition of Turkey: A Diplomatic History, 1913–1923.* Norman, Okla.: University of Oklahoma Press, 1931.

JOSEPH, PHILIP. *Foreign Diplomacy in China, 1884–1900.* London: George Allen & Unwin, 1928.

PIGLI, MARIO. *L'Etopia moderna nelle sue relazioni internazionali, 1859–1931.* Padua: Cedam, 1933.

RENOUVIN, PIERRE. *La Question d'Extrême-Orient, 1840–1940.* 3d. ed. Paris: Hachette, 1958.

SIASSI, ALI AKBAR. *La Perse au contact de l'Occident: Etude historique et sociale.* Paris: E. Leroux, 1931.

Of the books concerning the 1884 Berlin Conference on the Congo, see in particular SYBIL E. CROWE, *The Berlin West African Conference, 1884–1885,* London and New York: Longmans Green, 1942; and G. KÖNIGH, *Die Berliner Kongo-Konferenz,* Essen, 1938. JACQUES WILLEQUET's important work *Le Congo belge et la Weltpolitik, 1894–1914,* Brussels: Université Libre de Bruxelles, 1962, should also be consulted. On the Moroccan crisis, ANDRÉ TADIEU's *Le Mystère d'Agadir,* Paris: Calmann-Lévy, 1912, is still useful; the negotiations of February, 1909, are discussed in Part I. But one may best consult the diplomatic documents available in *Documents diplomatiques français, 1871–1914,* 2d. ed., Vol. XI, and in *Die Grosse Politik der europäischen Kabinette.* Critical analyses are provided in a thesis by M. FREMICACCI, the manuscript of which was placed at this author's disposal.

International Cartels

Studies on this subject are numerous, even when one leaves aside the many books dealing with purely juridical aspects. See in particular:

BALLANDE, LAURENCE. *Les Ententes économiques internationales: Etude monographique et statistique.* Paris: Librairie technique et économique, 1937.

BENNI, A., *et al. Etude sur les aspects économiques de différentes ententes industrielles internationales.* Geneva: League of Nations, 1930.

EDWARDS, CORWIN D. *Economic and Political Aspects of International Cartels.* (Prepared for the Subcommittee on War Mobilization, U.S. Senate Committee on Military Affairs, 78th Cong., 2d sess. Senate Committee Print, Monograph No. 1.) Washington, D.C.: Government Printing Office, 1944.

ELLIOTT, WILLIAM Y., *et al. International Control in the Non-Ferrous Metals.* New York: Macmillan, 1937. This includes a study of international cartels in general.

HEXNER, E. *International Cartels.* Chapel Hill, N.C.: University of North Carolina, 1946.

———. *The International Steel Cartel.* Chapel Hill, N.C.: University of North Carolina, 1943.

LEBÉE, EDMOND. *Trusts et cartels internationaux.* The Hague: Academy of International Law, *Recueil des cours,* 1927, IV, 143–246.

LEWINSOHN, RICHARD. *Trusts et Cartels dans l'économie mondiale.* Paris: Librairie de Médicis, 1950.

OUALID, WILLIAM, with the assistance of LAURENCE BALLANDE. *International Raw Materials Cartels: Causes—Effects—Regulations.* Paris: International Institute of Intellectual Co-operation, League of Nations, 1938. One of a series of monographs prepared as supplements to the 10th International Studies Conference.

PICARD, ROGER. *Les ententes de producteurs.* The Hague: Academy of International Law, *Recueil des cours,* 1939, LXVII, 539–624.

RESPONDEK, ERWIN, *Wirtschaftliche Zusammenarbeit zwischen Deutschland und Frankreich.* Berlin: C. Heymann, 1929.

WAGENFUHR, HORST (ed.). *Deutsche ausländische und internationale Kartellvertrage im Wortlaut.* Nuremberg: Kirsche, 1931.

WHITTLESEY, CHARLES R. *Governmental Control of Crude Rubber: The Stevenson Plan.* Princeton, N.J.: Princeton University Press, 1931.

———. *National Interest and International Cartels.* New York: Macmillan, 1946.

The reports of the International Chamber of Commerce, in 1927 and 1929, supply interesting information and points of view; see also the United Nations memorandum *International Cartels,* New York: United Nations, 1947.

CHAPTER FIVE. INTERNATIONAL FINANCE

The International Flow of Capital Investments

The history and development of international capital investment are covered in:

CAMERON, R. E. *France and the Economic Development of Europe, 1800–1914.* Princeton, N.J.: Princeton University Press, 1961.

JENKS, LELAND. *The Migration of British Capital to 1875.* London, 1927; Camden, N.J.: Thomas Nelson, 1963.

PHILIP, ANDRÉ. "L'évolution des investissements internationaux du XIXe siècle à nos jours." (Roneo.) University of Paris, 1958.

RIPPY, J. FRED. "British Investments in Latin America and India: An Inspection of Comparative Returns," *Inter-American Economic Affairs,* VII (1953), 3–18.

The economic consequences of the international flow of capital are discussed in:

LEWIS, CLEONA. *The United States and Foreign Investment Problems.* Washington, D.C.: Brookings Institution, 1948.

TACKE, GERD. *Kapitalausfuhr und Warenausfuhr: Eine Darstellung ihrer unmittelbaren Verbindung.* Jena: G. Fischer, 1933.

The Role of the State

HERBERT FEIS, *Europe, the World's Banker, 1870–1914: An Account of European Foreign Investment and the Connection of World Finance with Diplomacy before the War,* New York: Augustus M. Kelley, 1930, is an essential study, both on the methods and on the distribution of English, French, and German investments. See also PAUL EINZIG, *Finance and Politics,* London: Macmillan, 1932, and, on problems of documentation, BERTRAND GILLE, "Finance internationale et trusts," *Revue Historique,* CCXXVII (April-June, 1962), 291–326.

On investment policies of the major powers, information is widely dispersed and critical studies are rare. Satisfactory introductory material is provided in:

BOUVIER, JEAN. "L'installation des groupes financiers au Moyen-Orient: emprunts gouvernmentaux, investissements bancaires, et rapports internationaux, 1862–82," *Bulletin de la Société d'Histoire moderne,* May 3, 1959, Series 12, pp. 10–13.

CAIRNCROSS, A. K. *Home and Foreign Investments, 1870–1913: Studies in Capital Accumulation.* Cambridge and New York: Cambridge University Press, 1953.

CALCHSI, E. "Les Relations financières de la France et de la Russie de 1886 à 1892." Unpublished thesis, University of Paris, 1963.

FIELD, FREDERICK V. *American Participation in the China Consortiums.* Chicago: The University of Chicago Press, for the Institute of Pacific Relations, 1931.

HALSEY, FREDERIC M. *Investments in Latin America and the British West Indies.* ("Publications of U.S. Foreign and Domestic Commerce Bureau," Special Agents Series, No. 169.) Washington, D.C.: Government Printing Office, 1918.

HENDERSON, W. *L'exportation des capitaux anglais avant et après la guerre.* Paris: Editions de la vie universitaire, 1924.

LABICHE, GEORGES-PIERRE. *Textes réglementant l'exportation des capitaux et l'importation des valeurs mobilières.* Paris: Librairie générale de droit et de jurisprudence, 1924.

RENOUVIN, PIERRE. "La politique des emprunts étrangers aux Etats-Unis de 1914 à 1917," *Annales,* July, 1951, pp. 289–305.

RICHARDSON, J. HENRY. *British Economic Foreign Policy.* London: George Allen & Unwin, 1936.

ZABRISKIE, EDWARD H. *American-Russian Rivalry in the Far East: A Study in Diplomacy and Power Politics, 1895–1914.* Philadelphia, Pa.: University of Pennsylvania Press, 1946.

Financial Imperialism and Political Conflict

CHINA

REID, JOHN GILBERT. *The Manchu Abdication and the Powers, 1908–1912: A Study of the Role of Foreign Diplomacy During the Reign of Hsiian-T'ung.* Berkeley, Calif.: University of California Press, 1935.

REMER, CHARLES F. *Foreign Investments in China.* New York: Macmillan, 1933.

EGYPT

BOUVIER, JEAN. "Les Intérêts financiers et la question d'Egypte, 1875–1876," *Revue historique* (Paris), LXXIV (July, 1900), 75–105.

MARLOWE, JOHN. *A History of Egypt and Anglo-Egyptian Relations, 1800–1953.* London: Cresset Press; New York: Frederick A. Praeger, 1954.

MEXICO

DÍAZ DUFOO, CARLOS. *México y los capitales extranjeros.* Paris: Bouret, 1918.

VAGTS, ALFRED. *Mexico, Europa und Amerika, unter besonderer Berücksichtigung der Petroleumpolitik.* Berlin-Grunewald: Dr. W. Rothschild, 1928.

MOROCCO

GUILLEN, PIERRE. "Les Milieux d'affaires français et le Maroc à l'aube du XXe siècle: La fondation de la Compagnie Marocaine," *Revue Historique*, CCXXIX (April-June, 1963), 397–442.

MIÈGE, JEAN-LOUIS. *Le Maroc et l'Europe, 1850–1889.* Paris: Presses universitaires de France, 1961.

SOUTH AFRICA

LOVELL, REGINALD IVAN. *The Struggle for South Africa, 1875–1899: A Study in Economic Imperialism.* New York: Macmillan, 1934.

POEL, JEAN VAN DER. *Railway and Customs Policies in South Africa, 1885–1910.* London: Longmans Green, for the Royal Empire Society, 1933.

On financial capitalism in the development of imperialism, the essential interpretations (in addition to those listed on pp. 378–79 in the General Bibliography) are:

HILFERDING, RUDOLF. *Das Finanzkapital: Eine Studie über die jüngste Entwicklung des Kapitalismus.* Berlin: Dietz, 1955. Originally published in 1910.

HOBSON, JOHN A. *Imperialism.* 5th ed. New York: Macmillan, 1949. Originally published in 1902.

LENIN, V. I. *Imperialism: The Highest Stage of Capitalism.* New York: International Publishers, 1939. Originally published in 1917. (Paperback ed.: International Publishers.)

Critics of the theses advanced in these books include:

ROBINSON, RONALD, et al. *Africa and the Victorians: The Official Mind of Imperialism.* New York: St. Martin's Press, 1961.
SCHUMPETER, JOSEPH A. *Imperialism and Social Classes.* Translated by HEINZ NORDEN. Edited by PAUL M. SWEEZY. New York: Augustus M. Kelley, 1951. Originally published in 1919. (Paperback ed.: Meridian.)
STRACHEY, JOHN. *The End of Empire.* New York: Random House, 1960. (Paperback ed.: Frederick A. Praeger.)

Other interesting points of view are represented in:

HALLGARTEN, WOLFGANG. *Imperialismus vor 1914.* 2 vols. Munich: C. H. Beck, 1951.
KOEBNER, RICHARD. "The Concept of Economic Imperialism," *The Economic History Review,* Second Series, II (1949), 1–29.
MYRDAL, GUNNAR. *An International Economy: Problems and Prospects.* New York: Harper & Bros., 1956.
SEMMEL, BERNARD. *Imperialism and Social Reform.* Cambridge, Mass.: Harvard University Press, 1960.
WINSLOW, E. M. *The Pattern of Imperialism: A Study in the Theories of Power.* New York: Columbia University Press, 1948.

The workings of "dollar diplomacy" have been thoroughly studied. See in particular:

BEMIS, SAMUEL FLAGG. *The Latin American Policy of the United States: An Historical Interpretation.* New York: Harcourt, Brace, 1944.
DIAMOND, W. *The Economic Thought of Woodrow Wilson.* Baltimore, Md.: The Johns Hopkins Press, 1943.
FEIS, HERBERT. *The Diplomacy of the Dollar: First Era, 1919–1932.* Baltimore, Md.: The Johns Hopkins Press, 1950.
NEARING, SCOTT, and FREEMAN, JOSEPH. *Dollar Diplomacy: A Study in American Imperialism.* New York: B. W. Huebsch and the Viking Press, 1925.
WILLIAMS, BENJAMIN H. *Economic Foreign Policy of the United States.* New York: McGraw-Hill, 1929.

CHAPTER SIX. THE SENSE OF NATIONHOOD

I have not listed here many of the works on forms of national sentiment from which most of the documentary information in this chapter was drawn. The reader will not find any bibliographical information on nationality movements in Ireland, Poland, Alsace-Lorraine, China, or the Middle East. I have limited the bibliography to general works; special studies are referred to in the notes throughout Chapter Six.

The Concept of Nation

HERTZ, FRIEDRICH OTTO. *Nationality in History and Politics: A Study of the Psychology and Sociology of National Sentiment and Character.* London: K. Paul, Trench, Trubner; New York: Humanities Press, 1944. An important study, particularly on forms of, and elements in, national sentiment, and on the historical development of ideology.

CHABOD, FEDERICO. *L'Idea di nazione.* Edited by ARMANDO SAITTA and ERNESTO SESTAN. 2d ed. Bari: Giuseppe Laterza e Figli, 1962.

GENNEP, ARNOLD VAN. *Traité comparatif des nationalités.* I.: *Les éléments extérieurs de la nationalité.* Paris: Payot, 1922.

HAYES, CARLTON J. H. *The Historical Evolution of Modern Nationalism.* Peterborough, N.H.: Richard R. Smith, 1931.

KEDOURIE, ELIE. *Nationalism.* New York: Humanities Press, 1960. (Paperback rev. ed.: Frederick A. Praeger.)

KOHN, HANS. *The Idea of Nationalism: A Study in its Origins and Background.* New York: Macmillan, 1944. (Paperback ed.: Macmillan.)

SNYDER, LOUIS L. *The Meaning of Nationalism,* New Brunswick, N.J.: Rutgers University Press, 1954.

STANNARD, HAROLD M. *What is a Nation?* ("Looking Forward" Pamphlets, No. 3.) London: Royal Institute of International Affairs, 1945.

KOPPEL S. PINSON's *A Bibliographical Introduction to Nationalism,* New York: Columbia University Press, 1935, is useful, despite its age; see also KARL DEUTSCH, *Interdisciplinary Bibliography on Nationalism, 1935–53,* Cambridge, Mass.: Technology Press, 1953.

National Sentiment

BARKER, SIR ERNEST. *National Character and the Factors in Its Formation.* London: Methuen, 1927.

BUCK, CARL DARLING. "Language and the Sentiment of Nationality," *American Political Science Review,* X (February, 1916), 44–69.

FELS, JOSEF. *Begriff und Wesen der Nation: Eine Sociologische Untersuchung und Kritik.* Münster in Westfalen: Aschendorffsche, 1927.

LE FUR, LOUIS. *Races, Nationalités, Etats.* Paris: F. Alcan, 1922.

LENZ, MAX. "Nationalität und Religion," *Preussische Jahrbücher,* Berlin, 1907.

SIMAR, THÉOPHILE. *Etude critique sur la formation de la doctrine des races au XVIIIe siècle et son expansion au XIXe siècle.* Brussels: M. Lamertin, 1922.

VOSSLER, KARL. *The Spirit of Language in Civilization.* Translated by OSCAR OESER. New York: Harcourt, Brace, 1932. See Chapter VII in particular.

Nation and State

A major formative work on relations between nation and state is JOHN STUART MILL's *Considerations on Representative Government,* first published in 1861. See also JOHANN KASPAR BLUNTSCHLI, *The Theory of the State,* authorized

English translation, Oxford and New York, 1885; IGNAZ SEIPEL, *Nation und Staat*, Vienna: W. Braumüller, 1916; and PIERRE VERGNAUD, *L'Idée de la nationalité et de la libre disposition des peuples dans ses rapports avec l'idée de l'Etat (étude des doctrines politiques contemporaines) 1870–1950*, Geneva: Droz, 1955.

On the history of nationality movements, see, in addition to Carlton Hayes' book listed above:

HENRY, PAUL. *Le Problème des nationalités.* Paris: Armand Colin, 1937.

WEILL, GEORGES. *L'Europe du XIXᵉ siècle et l'idée de nationalité.* Paris: Albin Michel, 1938.

And on national minorities in Europe, see:

BAUER, OTTO. *Die Nationalitätenfrage und die Sozialdemokratie.* Vienna: Wiener Volksbuchhandlung, 1924.

ERLER, GEORG H. J. *Das Recht der nationalen Minderheiten.* Münster in Westfalen: Aschendorffsche, 1931.

MACARTNEY, CARLILE A. *National States and National Minorities.* London: Oxford University Press, 1934.

MAIR, ERICH. *Die Psychologie der nationalen Minderheit.* Münster in Westfalen: Aschendorffsche, 1933.

RENNER, KARL (pseudonym, R. SPRINGER). *Das Selbstbestimmungsrecht der Nationen in besonderer Anwendung auf Oesterreich.* Vol. I: *Nation und Staat.* Leipzig: F. Deuticke, 1918.

Lastly, on the problem of nationhood in Africa, see:

DIA, MAMADOU. *The African Nations and World Solidarity.* New York: Frederick A. Praeger, 1961. (Paperback ed.: Praeger.)

EMERSON, RUPERT. *From Empire to Nation.* Cambridge, Mass.: Harvard University Press, 1960. (Paperback ed.: Beacon Press.)

HODGKIN, THOMAS. *Nationalism in Colonial Africa.* New York: New York University Press, 1957. (Paperback ed.: New York University Press.)

SITHOLE, NDABANINGI. *African Nationalism.* London and New York: Oxford University Press, 1959.

CHAPTER SEVEN. NATIONALISM

National Character and Temperament

American sociologists and cultural anthropologists (Karl Deutsch, Harold Sprout, and Margaret Mead) since World War II have sought to establish new methods for studying national character. The psycho-sociological approach has been used well in the important German work by WILLY HUGO HELLPACH, *Einführung in die Völkerspsychologie*, Stuttgart: F. Enke, 1954.

Perhaps the most interesting line of approach for the historian of international relations is the study of stereotypes that citizens of one nation have of citizens of another nation—an approach that focuses on the deformations of reality revealed in these stereotypes and on how they happened. The study of HADLEY CANTRIL and WILLIAM BUCHANAN, *How Nations See Each Other: A Study in Public Opinion*, Urbana, Ill.: University of Illinois Press, under the patronage of UNESCO, 1953, provides, in this regard, interesting information applying to new countries. See also HEINZ SIEBURG, *Frankreich und Deutschland in der Geschichtsschreibung, 1915–1948*, Sarrebruck, 1955. In the 1957 *Bulletin international des sciences sociales* (p. 128), there is a summary of a symposium on plans to further this area of studies.

Comparative Studies

KEYSERLING, COUNT HERMANN. *Europe.* Translated by MAURICE SAMUEL. New
   York: Harcourt, Brace, 1928.
MADARIAGA, SALVADOR DE. *Englishmen, Frenchmen, Spaniards: An Essay in
   Comparative Psychology.* With a Prefatory Note by ALFRED ZLMMERN. London:
   Oxford University Press, 1928.
SIEGFRIED, ANDRÉ. *Nations Have Souls.* Translated by EDWARD FITZGERALD. New
   York: G. P. Putnam's Sons, 1952.

I have also used the notes by R. GIRARDET delivered to a meeting of the "working group on comparative nationalism," May 2, 1960, and published in the *Bulletin de liaison de la Fondation des sciences politiques.* See also the now outdated synthesis provided by GEORGES HARDY in *La Géographie psychologique*, Paris: Nouvelle Revue Française, 1939. The *Revue de psychologie des peuples*, published by the Institut Havrais (A. MIROGLIO, Director), includes a large number of studies on ethnic psychology.

Country by Country

On nationality movements in Europe during the late nineteenth and early twentieth centuries, the essential book is FRIEDRICH OTTO HERTZ, *Nationality in History and Politics: A Study of the Psychology and Sociology of National Sentiment and Character*, London: K. Paul, Trench, Trubner; New York: Humanities Press, 1944. But see also EUGEN LEMBERG, *Geschichte des Nationalismus in Europa*, Stuttgart: C. E. Schwab, 1950.

FRANCE

The basic sources are MAURICE BARRÈS, *Scènes et doctrines du nationalisme*, 2 vols., Paris: Plon et Nourrit, 1925; and CHARLES MAURRAS, *Enquête sur la monarchie*, Versailles: Bibliothèque des oeuvres politiques, 1928. See also:

CURTIUS, ERNST ROBERT. *Maurice Barrès und die geistigen Grundlagen des
   französischen Nationalismus.* Bonn: F. Cohen, 1921. (2d ed., 1962.)
DIGEON, C. *La Crise allemande de la pensée française, 1871–1914.* Paris: Presses
   universitaires de France, 1949.
FRANK, W. *Nationalismus und Demokratie im Leben der dritten Republik.* Hamburg: Hanseatische Verlagsanstalt, 1933.

MADAULE, JACQUES. *Le Nationalisme de Maurice Barrès.* Marseille: Sagittaire, 1943.

WEBER, EUGEN. *The Nationalist Revival in France, 1905–1914.* Berkeley: University of California Press, 1959.

GERMANY

ANDLER, CHARLES P. T. *Pan-Germanism: Its Plans for German Expansion in the World.* Translated by J. S. Paris: Armand Colin, 1915.

DROZ, J. *Le nationalisme allemand de 1871 à 1939.* (Roneo.) University of Paris, 1963.

KRUCK, ALFRED. *Geschichte des alldeutschen Verbandes, 1890–1939.* Wiesbaden: F. Steiner, 1954.

MOLISCH, PAUL. *Geschichte der deutschnationalen Bewegung in Oesterreich.* Jena: G. Fischer, 1926.

WERNER, LOTHAR. *Der alldeutsche Verband, 1890–1918.* Berlin: Emil Eberling, 1935.

GREAT BRITAIN

BARDOUX, JACQUES. *Essai d'une psychologie de l'Angleterre contemporaine. Les crises politiques: protectionnisme et radicalisme.* Paris: F. Alcan, 1907.

WINGFIELD-STRATFORD, ESMÉ. *The Foundations of British Patriotism.* London: Routledge & Sons, 1939.

ITALY

ARCARI, PAOLA MARIA. *La Elaborazione della dottrina politica nazionale fra l'Unita e l'intervento (1870–1914).* 3 vols. Florence: Marzocco, 1934–39. The standard work on the subject.

CHABOD, FEDERICO. *Storia della politica estera italiana del 1870 al 1896.* Vol. I: *Le premesse.* Bari: Giuseppi Laterza e Figli, 1951. Very good on the characteristics of the Italian "collective psychology."

CORRADINI, ENRICO. *Discorsi politici (1902–1923).* Florence: Vallecchi, 1923.

VAUSSARD, MAURICE. *De Pétrarque à Mussolini: Evolution du sentiment nationaliste italien.* Paris: Armand Colin, 1961. Excellent on the 1930's.

JAPAN

BROWN, DELMER M. *Nationalism in Japan: An Introductory Historical Analysis.* Berkeley, Calif.: University of California Press, 1955.

HIBINO, YUTAKA. *Nippon Shindo Ron, or, The National Ideas of the Japanese People.* Translated with an Introduction by A. P. McKENZIE. Cambridge, England: Cambridge University Press, 1928.

HOLTOM, DANIEL C. *The National Faith of Japan: A Study in Modern Shinto.* London: K. Paul, Trench, Trubner, 1938.

KUNO, J. *Japanese Expansion on the Asiatic Continent.* Berkeley, Calif.: University of California Press, 1937.

STORRY, RICHARD. *The Double Patriots: A Study of Japanese Nationalism.* New York: Houghton Mifflin, 1958.

RUSSIAN NATIONALISM AND PAN-SLAVISM

FISCHEL, A. *Der Panslavismus bis zum Weltkriege.* Berlin, 1929.

KOHN, HANS. *Pan Slavism: Its History and Ideology.* Notre Dame, Ind.: University of Notre Dame Press, 1953. (Paperback ed.: Vintage.)

STRÉMOOUKHOFF, D. *Vladimir Soloviev et son oeuvre messianique.* Paris: Les Belles lettres, 1935.

UNITED STATES

BEARD, CHARLES A., with the collaboration of G. H. E. SMITH. *The Idea of National Interest: An Analytical Study in American Foreign Policy.* New York: Macmillan, 1934.

COMMAGER, HENRY STEELE. *The American Mind.* New Haven, Conn.: Yale University Press, 1950.

KOHN, HANS. *American Nationalism: An Interpretative Essay.* New York: Collier Books, 1957.

PRATT, JULIUS WILLIAM. *Expansionists of 1898: The Acquisition of Hawaii and the Spanish Islands.* Gloucester, Mass.: Peter Smith, 1959. Originally published in 1936. Good on this special topic.

WEINBERG, ALBERT K. *Manifest Destiny: A Study of Nationalist Expansionism in American History.* Baltimore, Md.: The Johns Hopkins Press, 1935. A basic and essential study.

Religion and Nationalism

ALIX, CHRISTINE. *Le Saint-Siège et la nationalisme en Europe, 1870–1960.* Paris: Editions Sirey, 1962.

BOBTCHEV, S. *La Lutte du peuple bulgare pour une Eglise nationale indépendante.* Sofia: Société slave en Bulgarie, 1938.

CHARLES, RAYMOND. *Le Droit musulman.* Paris: Presses universitaires de France, 1956.

FERNAU, FRIEDRICH WILHELM. *Moslems on the March: People and Politics in the World of Islam.* Translated by E. W. DICKES. New York: Alfred A. Knopf, 1954.

HOLTOM, DANIEL C. *The National Faith of Japan: A Study in Modern Shinto.* London: K. Paul, Trench, Trubner, 1938.

KHADDURI, MAJID. *War and Peace in the Law of Islam.* Baltimore, Md.: The Johns Hopkins Press, 1955.

MOUSSET, JEAN. *La Serbie et son Eglise (1830–1914).* Paris: Droz, 1939.

RONDOT, PIERRE. *Les Forces religieuses et la vie politique: l'Islam.* (Roneo.) University of Paris, 1957.

VAUSSARD, MAURICE. *Enquête sur le nationalisme.* Paris: Editions Spes, 1921.

CHAPTER EIGHT. THE LONGING FOR PEACE

The basic study is A. C. F. BEALES, *The History of Peace: A Short Account of the Organized Movements for International Peace,* New York: The Dial Press, 1931. See also:

CURTI, MERLE EUGENE. *The American Peace Crusade: 1815–1860.* Durham, N.C. Duke University Press, 1929.

LANGE, CHRISTIAN L. *Histoire de la doctrine pacifique et de son influence sur le développement du droit international.* The Hague: Academy of International Law, *Recueil des Cours,* 1926, III, 175–246.

SCHELER, MAX. *L'idée de paix et le pacifisme.* Translated from the German by R. TANDONNET. Paris: Editions Montaigne, 1953.

The Arguments for Pacifism

IN ECONOMICS

BASTIAT, FRÉDÉRIC. *Bastiat and the ABC of Free Trade.* Translated and edited by LORENZA GARREAU. London: T. F. Unwin, 1926.

———. *Le Libre échange.* Paris, 1882.

GARNIER, CLÉMENT JOSEPH. *Abrégé des éléments de l'économie politique.* Paris: Guillaumin, 1858.

MORLEY, JOHN. *The Life of Richard Cobden.* London: Chapman & Hall; Boston: Roberts, 1881.

SILBERNER, EDMUND. *La Guerre et la paix dans l'histoire des doctrines économiques.* Paris: Editions Sirey, 1957.

THE ROLE OF SOCIALIST THOUGHT

The basic material is found in the documents collected in *La Première Internationale,* 2 vols., Geneva, 1962, and the reports of Congresses of the Second International, especially the 1907 Congress in Stuttgart and the 1910 Congress in Copenhagen. See also:

DRACHKOVITCH, MILORAD. *Les Socialismes français et allemands et le problème de la guerre, 1870–1914.* Geneva: Droz, 1953.

JOLL, JAMES. *The Second International, 1889–1914.* London: Weidenfeld and Nicolson, 1955; New York: Frederick A. Praeger, 1956.

KAUTSKY, KARL. *Sozialisten und Krieg.* Prague: Orbis, 1937.

THE ROLE OF RELIGION

A good general study is JOSEPH MÜLLER, *L'oeuvre de toutes les confessions Chrétiennes (Eglises) pour la paix internationale,* The Hague: Academy of International Law, *Recueil des cours,* 1930, I, 297–392.

Catholicism

BOSC, R. *La Société internationale et l'Eglise: Sociologie et morale des relations internationales.* Paris: Editions Spes, 1961.

EPPSTEIN, JOHN. *The Catholic Tradition of the Law of Nations.* London: Burns, Oates & Washbourne, for the Carnegie Endowment for International Peace, 1955.

FESSARD, GASTON, S. J. *Pax nostra: Examen de conscience international.* Paris: B. Grasset, 1936.

GOYAU, GEORGES. *L'Eglise catholique et le droit des gens.* The Hague: Academy of International Law, *Recueil des cours,* 1925, I, 127–329.

LA BRIÈRE, YVES DE. *L'Organisation internationale du monde contemporain et la Papauté souveraine.* 3 vols. Paris: Editions Spes, 1924–30.

———. *Le droit de juste guerre. Tradition théologique. Adaptations contemporaines.* Paris: A. Pedone, 1938.

MOUNIER, EMMANUEL. *Pacifistes ou bellicistes?* Paris: Editions du Cerf, 1939. Reprinted under the title *Les chrétiens devant le problème de la paix,* in *Oeuvres,* vol. I. Paris: Editions du Seuil, 1961.

VANDERPOL, A. "Le catholicisme au Congrès de la paix," *Le Sillon,* October, 1906, pp. 251–55.

———. *La Guerre devant le christianisme.* Paris: A. Tralin, 1912.

Protestantism

HIRST, MARGARET E. *The Quakers in Peace and War: An Account of Their Peace Principles and Practice.* London: Swarthmore Press, 1923.

LYNCH, FREDERICK H. *Through Europe on the Eve of War: A Record of Personal Experiences Including an Account of the First World Conference of the Churches for International Peace.* New York: Church Peace Union, 1914.

MACFARLAND, CHARLES S. *Pioneers for Peace Through Religion, Based on the Records of the Church Peace Union, 1914–1945.* New York and London: Fleming H. Revell, 1946.

SCHIAN, MARTIN. *Die evangelische Kirche in der Heimat, 1914–1918.* Berlin: Mittler, 1925.

The Ecumenical Movement

GRUTZMACHER, RICHARD HENRICH. "Le Protestantisme, puissance de politique intérieure et extérieure," *Esprit International,* VI (1932) (Paris: Hachette), 262–72.

ROUSE, RUTH, and NEILL, STEPHEN CHARLES. *A History of the Ecumenical Movement: 1517–1948.* Philadelphia, Pa.: Westminster Press, for the Ecumenical Institute, Château de Boissey, 1954.

Methods of Pacifist Action

ARBITRATION

EFREMOFF, JEAN. *La Conciliation internationale.* The Hague: Academy of International Law, *Recueil des cours,* 1927, III, 5–145.

HUDSON, MANLEY O. *The Permanent Court of International Justice: A Treatise.* New York: Macmillan, 1934.

POLITIS, V.-N. "Les Commissions internationales d'enquête," *Revue générale de droit international public,* 1912, pp. 149–88.

SCELLE, GEORGES. "Critique du soi-disant domaine de compétence exclusive," *Revue de droit international et de législation comparée,* 1933, pp. 365–95.

DISARMAMENT

CHAPUT, ROLLAND A. *Disarmament in British Foreign Policy.* London: George Allen & Unwin, 1935.

D'ESTOURNELLES DE CONSTANT, BARON PAUL. *Report on the Limitation of Armaments.* London: The Peace Society, 1906.

————. *Limitation of Naval and Military Expenditure: Report Drawn Up in the Name of the Commission Entrusted with the Discussion of the Problem at the Conference of the Union of Rome . . . October, 1911.* Brussels: Misch & Thron, 1912.

LYON, JACQUES. *Les Problèmes du désarmement.* Paris: Boivin, 1931.

NOEL-BAKER, PHILIP J. *Disarmament.* London: The Hogarth Press, 1926.

TATE, MERZE. *The Disarmament Illusion: The Movement for a Limitation of Armaments to 1907.* New York: Macmillan, 1942.

WHEELER-BENNETT, JOHN W. *The Disarmament Deadlock.* London: Routledge & Sons, 1934.

THE LEAGUE OF NATIONS AND A UNITED STATES OF EUROPE

CHABOD, FEDERICO. *Storia dell'idea d'Europa.* Edited by ERNESTO SESTAN and ARMANDO SAITTA. Bari: Giuseppi Laterza e Figli, 1961.

COUDENHOVE-KALERGI, COUNT RICHARD N. *Kampf um Europa: Aus meinen Leben.* Zurich: Atlantis, 1949.

CURCIO, CARLO. *Europa: Storia di un'idea.* 2 vols. Florence: Vallecchi, 1958.

CURTI, MERLE EUGENE. *Bryan and World Peace.* ("Smith College Studies in History," Vol. XVI.) Northampton, Mass.: The Department of History, Smith College, 1931.

FERRELL, ROBERT H. *Peace in Their Time: The Origins of the Kellogg-Briand Pact.* New Haven, Conn.: Yale University Press, 1952.

FIELDING-RATHMANN, R. "La Mission de la France et le Fédéralisme européen selon Victor Hugo." Unpublished thesis, University of Paris, 1951.

KNAUSS, A. *La Guerre hors la loi.* Paris: Editions Spes, 1927.

MEULEN, JACOB TER. *Der Gedanke der internationalen Organisation in seiner Entwicklung.* 3 vols. The Hague: M. Nijhoff, 1917–40.

PLAYNE, CAROLINE. *Bertha von Suttner and the Struggle to Avert the World War.* London: George Allen & Unwin, 1936.

RAPPARD, WILLIAM E. *The Quest for Peace since the World War.* ("Lowell Institute Lectures.") Cambridge, Mass.: Harvard University Press, 1940.

ROUSSEAU, CHARLES. *La Compétence de la S.D.N. dans le règlement des conflits internationaux.* Paris: Imprimerie administrative centrale, 1927.

RUYSSEN, THÉODORE. "Pour et contre la S.D.N.," *Cahiers des droits de l'homme,* October 1, 1927.

SCELLE, GEORGES. *Une Crise de la Société des Nations: La Réforme du Conseil et l'entrée de l'Allemagne à Genève, mars-séptembre 1926.* Paris: Presses universitaires de France, 1927.

SHOTWELL, JAMES T. *War as an Instrument of National Policy and its Renunciation in the Pact of Paris.* New York: Harcourt, Brace, 1929.

STONER, JOHN E. *S. O. Levinson and the Pact of Paris.* Chicago: The University of Chicago Press, 1943.

CHAPTER NINE. THE PERSONALITY OF THE STATESMAN

Typologies of Personality

ADORNO, THEODOR W., *et al. The Authoritarian Personality.* New York: Harper & Bros., 1950. (Paperback ed.: Science Editions; 2 vols.)

BERGER, GASTON. *Caractère et personnalité.* Paris: Presses universitaires de France, 1954.

———. *Traité pratique d'analyse du caractère.* Paris: Presses universitaires de France, 1950.

DELAY, JEAN. *La Psycho-physiologie humaine.* (Collection "Que sais-je?") Paris: Presses universitaires de France, 1945.

JUNG, CARL G. *Psychological Types.* Translated by H. GOODWIN BAYNES. New York: Pantheon Books, 1959.

KLINEBERG, OTTO. *Social Psychology.* Rev. ed. New York: Henry Holt, 1954. See Chap. 20, "Psychology and International Relations," in particular.

LASSWELL, HAROLD D. *The Analysis of Political Behaviour: An Empirical Approach.* London: K. Paul, Trench, Trubner, 1947; Hamden, Conn.: Shoe String Press, 1966.

———. *Power and Personality.* New York: W. W. Norton, 1948. (Paperback rev. ed.: Compass.)

———. *Psychopathology and Politics.* Chicago: University of Chicago Press, 1930. (Paperback rev. ed.: Compass.)

LE SENNE, RENÉ. *Le Mensonge et le Caractère.* Paris: F. Alcan, 1930.

MUCCHIELLI, ROGER. *La Caractérologie à l'âge scientifique: Essai sur les méthodes et les limites de la caractérologie.* Neuchâtel: Editions du Griffon [1961].

The empirical classifications proposed in the text do not derive from any other published work. While there is no "scientific" study on the personality of the statesman, the reader will find useful discussions in some of the following works. On diplomats, who after all play a major role in the making of foreign policy, the literature is, in contrast, abundant.

BARTHOU, LOUIS. *Le Politique.* Paris: Hachette, 1923.

BLOCH-MORHANGE, JACQUES. *Les Politiciens.* Paris: A. Fayard, 1961.

BOURRICAUD, FRANÇOIS. "La Sociologie du 'Leadership' et son application à la théorie politique," *Revue française de science politique,* III (July–September, 1953), 445–70.

CALLIÈRES, FRANÇOIS DE. *De la manière de négocier avec les souverains, du choix des ambassadeurs et des envoyez, et des qualitez nécessaires pour réussir dans ces employs.* Paris, 1716.

CAMBON, JULES M. *The Diplomatist.* Translated by CHRISTOPHER R. TURNER. London: P. Allan, 1931.

FREYMOND, JACQUES. *The Saar Conflict, 1945–1955.* London: Stevens & Sons; New York: Frederick A. Praeger, 1960. See Part Two, Chap. 10, "The Men and Their Actions," pp. 208–22.

HAUTERIVE, A.-M. BLANC DE LA NOUTTE, COMTE D'. "Conseils à un élève du Ministère des relations extérieures." Paris [1813].

Hotman, Jean, sieur de Villiers. *De la Charge et dignité de l'ambassadeur.* 2d ed. Paris, 1604.

La Sarraz Du Franquesnay, J. de. *Le Ministre public dans les cours étrangères, ses fonctions et ses prérogatives.* Paris, 1731.

L'Escalopier de Nourar, Charles-Armand. *Le Ministère du négociateur.* Amsterdam, 1763.

Machiavelli, Niccolò. *The Prince.* Firenze [1513]. (Paperback ed.: Mentor.)

Nicolson, Sir Harold. *Diplomacy.* 3d ed. London and New York: Oxford University Press, 1963. (Paperback ed.: Galaxy Books.)

Noel, Léon. *Conseils à un jeune Français entrant dans la carrière.* Paris: La Jeune Parque, 1947.

Pecquet, Antoine. *De l'Art de négocier avec les souverains.* The Hague, 1738.

Spaulding, E. Wilder. *Ambassadors Ordinary and Extraordinary.* Washington, D.C.: Public Affairs Press, 1960.

Strang, William, Lord. *The Diplomatic Career.* London: André Deutsch, 1962.

Wicquefort. *Mémoires touchant les ambassadeurs et les ministres publics.* 2 vols. Cologne, 1676–79.

Wolfers, Arnold. "The Actors in International Politics," in William T. R. Fox (ed.), *Theoretical Aspects of International Relations,* pp. 83–106. Notre Dame, Ind.: University of Notre Dame, 1959.

CHAPTER TEN. THE STATESMAN AND THE "NATIONAL INTEREST"

Concepts of the National Interest

The best theoretical studies are:

Aron, Raymond. *Peace and War: A Theory of International Relations.* Translated by Richard Howard and Annette Baker Fox. Garden City, N.Y.: Doubleday, 1966. (Paperback ed.: Frederick A. Praeger.)

Morgenthau, Hans J. *In Defense of the National Interest: A Critical Examination of American Foreign Policy.* New York: Alfred A. Knopf, 1951.

Wolfers, Arnold. *Discord and Collaboration: Essays on International Politics.* Baltimore, Md.: The Johns Hopkins Press, 1962.

On the opposition between the national interest and universal concerns, and between realism and idealism—issues discussed most frequently in the United States and Great Britain—see:

Cook, Thomas I., and Moos, Malcolm. "Foreign Policy: The Realism of Idealism," *The American Political Science Review,* XLVI (June, 1952), 343–56.

Herz, John H. *Political Realism and Political Idealism.* Chicago: The University of Chicago Press, 1951.

Kennan, George F. *American Diplomacy, 1900–1950.* Chicago: The University of Chicago Press, 1951. (Paperback ed.: Mentor.)

Morgenthau, Hans J. *Politics Among Nations: The Struggle for Power and*

Peace. 3d rev. ed. New York: Alfred A. Knopf, 1960. See also above, Morgenthau's *In Defense of the National Interest*.

OSGOOD, ROBERT E. *Ideals and Self-Interest in American Foreign Relations*. Chicago: The University of Chicago Press, 1953. (Paperback ed.: Phoenix.)

PERKINS, DEXTER. *The American Approach to Foreign Policy*. Cambridge, Mass.: Harvard University Press, 1952.

TANNENBAUM, FRANK. "The American Tradition in Foreign Relations," *Foreign Affairs*, XXX (October, 1951), 31–50.

――――. *The American Tradition in Foreign Relations*. Norman, Okla.: University of Oklahoma Press, 1955.

THOMPSON, KENNETH W. *Political Realism and the Crisis of World Politics*. Princeton, N.J.: Princeton University Press, 1960.

WOLFERS, ARNOLD, and MARTIN, LAURENCE W. (eds.). *The Anglo-American Tradition in Foreign Affairs: Readings from Thomas More to Woodrow Wilson*. New Haven, Conn.: Yale University Press, 1956.

On religious aspects of this problem, see above, the bibliography for Chapter Eight, pp. 398–401, and also:

BUTTERFIELD, HERBERT. *Christianity, Diplomacy, and War*. New York: Abingdon Press, 1954.

NIEBUHR, REINHOLD. *Christian Realism and Political Problems*. New York: Charles Scribner's Sons, 1953.

THOMPSON, KENNETH W. *Christian Ethics and the Dilemmas of Foreign Policy*. Durham, N.C.: Duke University Press, 1959.

On the national interest as the search for power, see, in addition to Morgenthau:

ADLER, MORTIMER J. *How to Think About War and Peace*. New York: Simon & Schuster, 1944.

MEINECKE, FRIEDRICH. *Machiavellism: The Doctrine of "Raison d'Etat" and Its Place in Modern History*. Translated by DOUGLAS SCOTT. New Haven, Conn.: Yale University Press, 1957. (Paperback ed.: Frederick A. Praeger.)

PARSONS, ELSIE CLEWS. *Social Rule: A Study of the Will to Power*. New York: G. P. Putnam's Sons, 1916.

RITTER, GERHARD. *Die Dämonie der Macht: Betrachtungen über Geschichte und Wesen des Machtproblems im politischen Denken der Neuzeit*. Munich: Leibniz, 1948.

RUSSELL, BERTRAND. *Power: A New Social Analysis*. New York: W. W. Norton, 1938. (Paperback ed.: Barnes & Noble.)

SPYKMAN, NICHOLAS J. *America's Strategy in World Politics*. New York: Harcourt, Brace, 1942.

Traditional Security and Collective Security

On the search for power and the search for security, see Herz, above, and:

BURNHAM, JAMES. *The Struggle for the World*. New York: John Day, 1947.

FOX, WILLIAM T. R. *The Super Powers: The United States, Britain, and the*

Soviet Union—Their Responsibility for Peace. New York: Harcourt, Brace, 1944.

LASSWELL, HAROLD D., and KAPLAN, ABRAHAM. *Power and Society.* New Haven, Conn.: Yale University Press, 1950. (Paperback ed.: Yale.)

LIPPMANN, WALTER. *U.S. Foreign Policy: Shield of the Republic.* Boston: Little, Brown, 1943.

ROGGE, HEINRICH. *Kollektiusicherheit, Bündnispolitik, Völkerbund. Theorie der nationalen und internationalen Sicherheit.* Berlin: Junker und Dünnhaupt, 1937.

SCHUBERT, GLENDON A. *The Public Interest: A Critique of the Theory of a Political Concept.* Chicago: The Free Press of Glencoe, 1960.

SCHUMAN, FREDERICK L. *International Politics: An Introduction to the Western State System.* 6th ed. New York: McGraw-Hill, 1958.

SPROUT, HAROLD and MARGARET. *Foundations of National Power.* 2d ed. Princeton, N.J.: D. Van Nostrand, 1951.

STRAUSZ-HUPÉ, ROBERT, and POSSONY, STEFAN. *International Relations in an Age of Conflict.* New York: McGraw-Hill, 1954.

On the concept of collective security, see:

HAAS, ERNEST B. "Types of Collective Security: An Examination of Operational Concepts," *The American Political Science Review,* XLIX (March, 1955), 40–62.

JOHNSON, HOWARD C., and NIEMEYER, GERHART. "Collective Security: The Validity of an Ideal," *International Organization,* VIII (February, 1954), 19–35.

LISKA, GEORGE. *International Equilibrium: A Theoretical Essay on the Politics and Organization of Security.* Cambridge, Mass.: Harvard University Press, 1957.

THOMPSON, KENNETH W. "Collective Security Re-examined," *The American Political Science Review,* XLVII (September, 1953), 753–72.

Examples of the National Interest

Studies of the national interest, country by country, have only occasionally been attempted. There is one great classic, on the United States:

BEARD, CHARLES A., with SMITH, G. H. E. *The Idea of National Interest: An Analytical Study in American Foreign Policy.* New York: Macmillan, 1934.

HARRINGTON, FRED HARVEY. "Beard's Idea of National Interest and New Interpretations," *American Perspective,* Summer, 1950, pp. 335–45.

Interesting discussions can also be found in:

BLACK, JOSEPH E., and THOMPSON, KENNETH W. (eds.). *Foreign Policies in a World of Change.* New York: Harper & Row, 1963.

CRAIG, GORDON A., and GILBERT, FELIX (eds.). *The Diplomats, 1919–1939.* Princeton, N.J.: Princeton University Press, 1953. (Paperback ed.: Atheneum; 2 vols.)

KERTESZ, STEPHEN D., and FITZSIMONS, M. A. (eds.). *Diplomacy in a Changing World*. Notre Dame, Ind.: University of Notre Dame Press, 1959.
MACRIDIS, ROY C. (ed.). *Foreign Policy in World Politics*. 2d ed. Englewood Cliffs, N.J.: Prentice-Hall, 1962. (Original paperback.)

FRANCE

DUROSELLE, J.-B. "Changes in French Foreign Policy Since 1945," in Hoffmann, Stanley, *et al.*, *In Search of France*, pp. 305–58. Cambridge, Mass.: Harvard University Press, 1963.

GERMANY

BRACHER, KARL D. *Die Auflosung der Weimarer Republik: Eine Studie zum Problem des Machtverfalls in der Demokratie*. Stuttgart: Ring-Verlag, 1955. (2d ed., 1957.)
DEUTSCH, KARL W., and EDINGER, LEWIS J. *Germany Rejoins the Powers: Mass Opinion, Interest Groups, and Elites in Contemporary German Foreign Policy*. Stanford, Calif.: Stanford University Press, 1959.
GROSSER, ALFRED (ed.). *Les Relations internationales de l'Allemagne occidentale*. Paris: Armand Colin, 1956.

GREAT BRITAIN

Royal Institute of International Affairs. *Political and strategic interests of the United Kingdom: an outline*. London: Oxford University Press, 1939.
STRANG, WILLIAM, LORD. *Britain in World Affairs: The Fluctuation in Power and Influence from Henry VIII to Elizabeth II*. New York: Frederick A. Praeger, 1961. (Paperback ed.: Praeger.)

ITALY

TOSCANO, MARIO. "The Foreign Policy of Italy," in BLACK and THOMPSON, *op. cit.*, pp. 171–98.

JAPAN

REISCHAUER, EDWIN O. *Japan, Past and Present*. New York: Alfred A. Knopf, 1946. (3d ed., 1964.)

RUSSIA

FISCHER, LOUIS. *The Soviets in World Affairs: A History of Relations Between the Soviet Union and the Rest of the World*. London: Jonathan Cape, 1930. (Abridged paperback ed.: Vintage.)
KENNAN, GEORGE F. *Russia and the West Under Lenin and Stalin*. Boston: Little, Brown, 1961. (Paperback ed.: Mentor.)
MOSELY, PHILIP E. *The Kremlin and World Politics: Studies in Soviet Policy and Action*. New York: Vintage Books, 1960. (Original paperback.)

SPAIN

FERNÁNDEZ ALMAGRO, MELCHOR. *Historia Política de la España contemporanes*. 2 vols. Madrid: Ediciones Pegaso [1956–59].

SWITZERLAND

BONJOUR, EDGAR. *Swiss Neutrality: Its History and Meaning.* Translated by MARY HOTTINGER. London: George Allen & Unwin, 1946.

LLOYD, WILLIAM B., JR. *Waging Peace: The Swiss Experience.* Washington, D.C.: Public Affairs Press, 1958.

YUGOSLAVIA

DEDIJER, VLADIMIR. *Tito.* New York: Simon and Schuster, 1953.

CHAPTER ELEVEN. THE INFLUENCE OF BASIC NATIONAL FORCES ON THE STATESMAN

Most of these works deal with the recent past:

EHRMANN, HENRY W. *Interest Groups on Four Continents.* Pittsburgh, Pa.: University of Pittsburgh Press, 1958. (Paperback ed.: Pittsburgh.)

MEYNAUD, JEAN. *Les Groupes de pression en France.* (Cahiers de la Fondation nationale des sciences politiques.) Paris: Armand Colin, 1958.

———. *Les Groupes de pression internationaux.* ("Etudes de science politique.") [Lausanne], 1961.

———. *Nouvelles Etudes sur les groupes de pression en France.* Paris: Armand Colin, 1962.

MEYNAUD, JEAN, and MEYRIAT, JEAN. "Les 'Groupes de Pression' en Europe Occidentale," *Revue française de science politique,* IX (March, 1959), 229–46. Includes 149-title bibliography.

———. "Les 'Groupes de Pression' en Europe Occidentale," *ibid.,* XII (June, 1962), 433–55. Includes 268-title bibliography for works published in 1959–61.

SARTORI, GIOVANNI. "Gruppi di pressione o gruppi di interesse," *Il Mulino,* VIII (January, 1959), 7–42.

The books listed below are useful for their relevance to international relations:

FRANCE

EHRMANN, HENRY W. *Organized Business in France.* Princeton, N.J.: Princeton University Press, 1957.

GERMANY

NIPPERDEY, THOMAS. "Interessenverbände und das Parteien in Deutschland vor dem Ersten Weltkrieg," *Politische Vierteljahresschrift,* III (September, 1961), 262–80.

PRITZKOLEIT, KURT. *Die neuen Herren: Die Mächtigen in Staat und Wirtschaft.* Vienna: K. Desch [1955].

GREAT BRITAIN

BUTLER, ARTHUR. "The History and Practice of Lobby Journalism," *Parliamentary Affairs,* XIII (Winter, 1959–60), 54–60.

FINER, SAMUEL E. *Anonymous Empire: A Study of the Lobby in Great Britain.* London: Pall Mall Press, 1958.
POTTER, ALLEN. *Organized Groups in British National Politics.* New York: Hillary House, 1961.

MEXICO

KLING, MERLE. *A Mexican Interest Group in Action.* Englewood Cliffs, N.J.: Prentice Hall, 1961.

UNITED STATES

BAKER, ROSCOE. *The American Legion and American Foreign Policy.* New York: Twayne, 1954.
COLE, WAYNE S. *America First: The Battle Against Intervention, 1940–1941.* Madison, Wis.: University of Wisconsin Press, 1953.
———. *Senator Gerald P. Nye and American Foreign Relations.* Minneapolis, Minn.: University of Minnesota Press, 1962.
ENGLER, ROBERT. *The Politics of Oil: A Study of Private Power and Democratic Directions.* New York: Macmillan, 1961.
JOHNSON, WALTER. *The Battle Against Isolation.* Chicago: The University of Chicago Press, 1944.

On legislative parties and pressure groups, see:

BLAISDELL, DONALD C. *American Democracy Under Pressure.* New York: Ronald Press, 1957.
——— (ed.). *Unofficial Government: Pressure Groups and Lobbies.* Philadelphia, Pa., 1957.
KEY, V. O. *Politics, Parties, and Pressure Groups.* 5th ed. New York: Crowell, 1964.
STEWART, J. D. *British Pressure Groups: Their Role in Relation to the House of Commons.* London and New York: Oxford University Press, 1958.
TRUMAN, DAVID B. *The Governmental Process: Political Interests and Public Opinion.* New York: Alfred A. Knopf, 1951.

CHAPTER TWELVE. THE STATESMAN'S INFLUENCE ON BASIC NATIONAL FORCES

On the statesman's role in economic, financial, and tariff decisions, see the bibliographies for Chapters Three, Four, and Five.

The Statesman and the Schools

ISAAC, JULES. "L'Histoire des origines de la guerre, dans les manuels allemands," *Revue Historique, CCXXVIII* (July–September, 1962), 73–106.
Revue d'Histoire de la guerre mondiale, January, 1932, pp. 25–52.
NORA, PIERRE. "Ernest Lavisse: Son rôle dans la formation du sentiment national,"

————. *Le Nationalisme français d'après les manuels scolaires.* (Multigraph.) Paris: Roundtable conference of the Association Française de Science Politique, May, 1962.

PAGÈS, GEORGES, *et al.* "L'Histoire contemporaine dans les manuels allemands," *Revue d'Histoire de la guerre mondiale,* April, 1938, pp. 113–214.

PIERCE, BESSIE LOUISE. *Civic Attitudes in American School Textbooks.* Chicago: The University of Chicago Press, 1930.

PUBLIC OPINION AND OPINION POLLS

ALBIG, WILLIAM. *Public Opinion.* London and New York: McGraw-Hill, 1939.

DUROSELLE, J.-B. *De l'Utilisation des sondages d'opinion en histoire et en science politique.* Brussels, 1957.

FRAENKEL, ERNST. *Offentliche Meinung und internationale Politik.* Tübingen: Hugo Sinzheimer, 1962.

POWELL, NORMAN J. *Anatomy of Public Opinion.* Englewood Cliffs, N.J.: Prentice-Hall, 1951.

RASSAK, JULES. *Psychologie de l'opinion et de la propagande politique.* Paris: M. Rivière, 1927.

STOETZEL, JEAN. *Théorie des opinions.* Paris: Presses universitaires de France, 1943.

PROPAGANDA AND POLITICS

CARR, E. H. *Propaganda in International Politics.* Oxford: Clarendon Press, 1939.

CHILDS, HARWOOD LAWRENCE (ed.). *Propaganda and Dictatorship: A Collection of Papers.* Princeton, N.J.: Princeton University Press, 1936.

DOMENACH, JEAN-MARIE. *La Propagande politique.* Paris: Presses universitaires de France, 1950. (4th ed., 1962.)

DOOB, LEONARD W. *Public Opinion and Propaganda.* New York: Henry Holt, 1948.

DOVRING, KARIN. *Road of Propaganda: The Semantics of Biased Communications.* Introduction by HAROLD D. LASSWELL. New York: Philosophical Library, 1959.

DRIENCOURT, JACQUES. *La Propagande, nouvelle force politique.* Paris: Armand Colin, 1950.

FRASER, LINDLEY. *Propaganda.* London and New York: Oxford University Press, 1957.

HUMMEL, WILLIAM, and HUNTRESS, KEITH G. *The Analysis of Propaganda.* New York: Henry Holt, 1949.

IRION, FREDERICK C. *Public Opinion and Propaganda.* New York: Crowell, 1950.

LASSWELL, HAROLD D., and BLUMENSTOCK, DOROTHY. *World Revolutionary Propaganda: A Chicago Study.* New York: Alfred A. Knopf, 1939.

MARTIN, LESLIE JOHN. *International Propaganda: Its Legal and Diplomatic Control.* Minneapolis, Minn.: University of Minnesota, 1958.

OGLE, MARBURY B. *Public Opinion and Political Dynamics.* Boston: Houghton Mifflin, 1950.

Propaganda in World Politics. (*Journal of International Affairs,* Vol. V, No. 2.) New York: School of International Affairs, Columbia University, Spring, 1951.

TCHAKHOTINE, SERGE. *Le Viol des foules dans la propaganda politique.* ("Collection Problèmes et documents.") Paris: Nouvelle Revue français, 1939.

WHITAKER, URBAN G., JR. *Propaganda and International Relations.* San Francisco: H. Chandler, 1960. (Paperback rev. ed.: Chandler.)

PROPAGANDA, WAR, AND INTERNATIONAL RELATIONS

DAUGHERTY, WILLIAM E., and JANOWITZ, MORRIS. *A Psychological Warfare Casebook.* Baltimore, Md.: The Johns Hopkins Press, 1958.

DYER, MURRAY. *The Weapon on the Wall: Rethinking Psychological Warfare.* Baltimore, Md.: The Johns Hopkins Press, 1959.

HOLT, ROBERT T., and VAN DE VELDE, ROBERT W. *Strategic Psychological Operations and American Foreign Policy.* Chicago: The University of Chicago Press, 1960.

LIFTON, ROBERT JAY. *Thought Reform and the Psychology of Totalism: A Study of "Brainwashing" in China.* New York: W. W. Norton, 1961. (Paperback ed.: Norton.)

LINEBARGER, PAUL M. A. *Psychological Warfare.* Washington, D.C.: Infantry Journal Press, 1948. (2d ed., 1954.)

MEGRET, MAURICE. *La Guerre psychologique.* (Collection "Que-sais je?" No. 713.) Paris: Presses universitaires de France, 1956.

POSSONY, STEFAN T. *A Century of Conflict: Communist Technique of World Revolution.* Chicago: Henry Regnery, 1953.

TRINQUIER, ROGER. *Modern Warfare: A French View of Counterinsurgency.* Translated by DANIEL LEE. With an Introduction by BERNARD B. FALL. New York: Frederick A. Praeger, 1964.

Propaganda in World War I and II and on the Peace Conference

A Catalogue of Paris Peace Conference Delegation Propaganda in the Hoover War Library. Stanford, Calif.: Stanford University Press, 1926.

BRUNTZ, GEORGE G. *Allied Propaganda and the Collapse of the German Empire in 1918.* London: H. Milford, for the Oxford University Press; Stanford, Calif.: Stanford University Press, 1938.

HOVLAND, CARL I., LUMSDAINE, ARTHUR A., and SHEFFIELD, FRED D. *Experiments in Mass Communication.* Princeton, N.J.: Princeton University Press, 1949. (Paperback ed.: Science Editions.)

LASSWELL, HAROLD D. *Propaganda Technique in the World War.* London: K. Paul, Trench, Trubner; New York: Alfred A. Knopf, 1927.

MENDELSSOHN, PETER DE. *Japan's Political Warfare.* London: George Allen & Unwin, 1944.

NOBÉCOURT, RENÉ GUSTAVE. *Les Secrets de la propagande en France occupée.* Paris: Fayard, 1962.

PETERSON, HORACE C. *Propaganda for War: The Campaign Against American Neutrality, 1914–1917.* Norman, Okla.: University of Oklahoma, 1939.

WILLIS, IRENE COOPER. *England's Holy War: A Study of English Liberal Idealism During the Great War.* New York: Alfred A. Knopf, 1928.

Germany

HAGEMANN, WALTER. *Publizistik im Dritten Reich; ein Beitrag zur Methodik der Massenführung.* Hamburg: Hansischer Gildenverlag, 1948.

HEIBER, HELMUT. *Joseph Goebbels.* Berlin: Colloquium [1962].

MÜLLER, GEORG WILHELM. *Das Reichsministerium für Volksaufklärg und Propaganda.* Berlin: Junker und Dünnhaupt, 1940.

SEMMLER, RUDOLF. *Goebbels, the Man Next to Hitler.* With an Introduction by D. McLACHLAN and Notes by G. S. WAGNER. London: Westhouse, 1947.

Soviet Union

BARGHOORN, FREDERICK C. *Soviet Foreign Propaganda.* Princeton, N.J.: Princeton University Press, 1964.

EVANS, FRANK BOWEN (ed.). *Worldwide Communist Propaganda Activities.* New York: Macmillan, 1955.

INKELES, ALEX. *Public Opinion in Soviet Russia: A Study in Mass Persuasion.* Cambridge, Mass.: Harvard University Press, 1950.

United States

LERNER, DANIEL (ed.). *Propaganda in War and Crisis: Materials for American Policy.* New York, 1951.

CHAPTER THIRTEEN. DECISION-MAKING

General

BEAUFRE, ANDRÉ. *An Introduction to Strategy: With Particular Reference to Problems of Defense, Politics, Economics, and Diplomacy in the Nuclear Age.* Translated by E. H. BARRY. With a Preface by B. H. LIDDELL HART. New York: Frederick A. Praeger, 1965.

DEUTSCH, KARL W. "Mass Communications and the Loss of Freedom in National Decision-Making: A Possible Research Approach to Interstate Conflicts," *The Journal of Conflict Resolution,* I, No. 2 (June, 1957), 200–211.

FINETTI, B. DE, *et al.* "Les Recherches sur la décision," *Bulletin S.E.D.E.I.S., Futuribles,* No. 813, March 1, 1962.

FURNISS, EDGAR STEPHENSON. *Weaknesses in French Foreign Policy-Making.* (Policy Memorandum No. 5.) Princeton, N.J.: Center of International Studies, Princeton University, 1954.

GONARD, SAMUEL. *La Recherche opérationnelle et la décision.* Geneva: Droz, 1958.

GORE, WILLIAM J., and SILANDER, FRED S. "A Bibliographical Essay on Decision-Making," *Administrative Science Quarterly,* IV (June, 1959).

GREENFIELD, K. F. (ed.). *Command Decisions.* New York: U.S. Department of the Army, 1959.

HOFFMANN, STANLEY. "Théorie et relations internationales," *Revue française de science politique,* XI (June, 1961), 413–33. Translated and revised version in STANLEY HOFFMANN, *The State of War: Essays in the Theory and Practice of International Politics,* Chap. 1: "Theory and International Relations." New York: Frederick A. Praeger, 1965.

JOUVENEL, BERTRAND DE. "Les Recherches sur la décision," *Bulletin S.E.D.E.I.S., Futuribles,* No. 809, January 20, 1962.

KAPLAN, MORTON A. *System and Process in International Politics.* New York: John Wiley, 1957. (Paperback ed.: Science Editions.)

LANDHEER, BARTHOLOMEUS, *et al. Ethical Values in International Decision-Making.* (Conference on Ethical Values in International Decision-Making, Institute of Social Studies, The Hague, 1958.) The Hague: M. Nijhoff, 1960.

MARVICK, DWAINE. (ed.). *Political Decision-Makers: Recruitment and Performance.* Chicago: The Free Press of Glencoe, 1961.

MERLE, MARCEL. *Les Problèmes du pouvoir exécutif dans la Société internationale.* (Multigraph.) Paris, 1959.

SCHELLING, THOMAS C. *The Strategy of Conflict.* Cambridge, Mass.: Harvard University Press, 1960. (Paperback ed.: Galaxy.)

SHACKLE, GEORGE L. S. *Decision, Order and Time in Human Affairs.* Cambridge and New York: Cambridge University Press, 1961.

SIMON, HERBERT A. "Theories of Decision-Making in Economics and Behavioral Science," *The American Economic Review,* XLIX (June, 1959), 253–83. Includes a 71-title bibliography.

SNYDER, RICHARD C., BRUCK, H. W., and SAPIN, BURTON (eds.). *Foreign Policy Decision-Making: An Approach to the Study of International Politics.* New York: The Free Press of Glencoe, 1962.

THRALL, ROBERT M., COOMBS, C. H., and DAVIS, R. L. (eds.). *Decision Processes.* New York: John Wiley, 1954.

VON NEUMANN, JOHN, and MORGENSTERN, OSKAR. *Theory of Games and Economic Behavior.* Rev. ed. Princeton, N.J.: Princeton University Press, 1955. (Paperback ed.: Science Editions.)

Special Historical Studies

AMRINE, MICHAEL. *The Great Decision: The Secret History of the Atomic Bomb.* New York: G. P. Putnam's Sons, 1959.

GROSSER, ALFRED. *La IVe République et sa politique extérieure.* Paris: Armand Colin, 1961.

HARTMANN, FREDERICK H. (ed.). *World in Crisis: Readings in International Relations.* Paperback 2d ed. New York: Macmillan, 1962.

KENNAN, GEORGE F. *Soviet-American Relations, 1917–1920.* Vol. II: *The Decision to Intervene.* Princeton, N.J.: Princeton University Press, 1958.

SNYDER, RICHARD C., and PAIGE, GLENN D. "The United States Decision to Resist Aggression in Korea: The Application of an Analytical Scheme," *Administrative Science Quarterly,* Vol. III (December, 1958).

WOHLSTETTER, ROBERTA. *Pearl Harbor: Warning and Decision.* Stanford, Calif.: Stanford University Press, 1962. (Paperback: Stanford.)

INDEX

Bosnia-Herzegovina, 78, 81, 152
Bosporus, 14, 92
Boulanger, Georges, 181, 280, 345–46
boundaries: linguistic, 6, 145; political, 7, 22, 139, 146
Bourassa, Henri, 157
Bourbon dynasty, 243
Bourgeois, Léon, 229, 356
bourgeoisie, 43, 150, 169, 253, 265, 327, 330; *see also* middle classes
Boutroux, Emile, 144
Bowman, Isaiah, 284
Boxer Rebellion, 96, 160
boycotts, 53, 75, 80–82, 225
Brandeis, Louis, 260
Brandenburg, 9, 11, 314
Brazil, 13, 26, 40, 70; immigration to, 43, 50, 155–56; U.S. and, 122, 123
Brenner Pass, 6, 180, 365–66
Breteuil, Baron de, 257
Briand, Aristide, 88, 89, 222, 237, 281, 296, 303–5, 345; personality of, 244–45, 246–47, 252, 253, 258, 315
Brière, Father de la, 213
Bright, John, 205
British Empire, 15, 125, 170, 174, 182, 274, 288, 290
Brüning, Heinrich, 89, 231
Bryan, William Jennings, 119, 221
Buddhism, 141, 199
Buenos Aires, 42, 156
Buisson, Ferdinand, 334
Bukharin, Nikolai, 324
Bulgaria, 11, 13, 62–63, 115, 118, 177, 196; nationalism in, 141, 145, 148, 149, 152; Serbia and, 78, 86, 87, 196, 342
Bülow, Bernhard von, 96, 210
Burgess, John, 183
Burke, Edmund, 143
Burleson, Albert S., 362
Burma, 141
Burritt, Elihu, 207, 214, 216, 219, 226
business interests: foreign policy and, 262, 312, 326, 369; pacifism and, 129, 203, 216
Bustani, Butrus al, 162
Butler, Geoffrey, 339
Butler, Nicholas Murray, 303

C

Caclamanos, Dimitri, 337
Caillaux, Joseph, 245, 343, 355–58
California, 49, 50, 74, 326, 335
Calles, Plutarco Elias, 328
Callières, François de, 258, 259
Cambodia, 164
Cambon, Jules, 93, 258, 356–57

Cambon, Paul, 357–58
Cameroons, 91, 169–70, 171, 292
Campbell-Bannerman, Henry, 183, 193
Canada, 22, 56, 104, 111, 118, 157–58; emigrants from, 34, 42; immigrants to, 40, 41, 42, 50, 158
Canal Zone, 56, 74
canals, interoceanic, 14–15, 73–74
Canterbury, Archbishop of, 207, 214
Canton, 60, 72
Cape of Good Hope, 15
capital, export of, 109, 110, 112, 113, 116, 118, 120, 128, 130, 276; *see also* finance, international
capital investment, 27, 40, 102–8, 118, 127, 326–27, 329–30; imperialism and, 125–26, 130–31, 370; political influence and, 122–25, 132, 135, 137–38; war and, 203; *see also* finance, international; foreign investment; railroads
capitalism: critics of, 99, 265, 331; imperialism and, 125–27; U.S. aid and, 122–23
Caprivi, Leo, 118, 209
Carbonari, 314
Cárdenas, Lazaro, 328
Carnegie, Andrew, 203, 208, 221
Carnegie Endowment for International Peace, 208, 211, 222–23, 232, 303
Carnot, Lazare, 346
Caroline Islands, 210
Carranza, Venustiano, 328
cartels, international, 97–101
Carthage, 12
Castle, William R., 298, 299
Catalan minority, 145, 150
Catholic Action, 194
Catholic Church, 154, 157, 193–94, 206; Bismarck and, 248; in Mexico, 327, 328; pacifism and, 209–14
caution, statesmanship and, 255–56, 346
Cavagnari, 367
Cavour, Camillo, 148, 201, 297, 342–43
Cecil, Robert, 209, 298, 299
Central America, 21, 79, 104, 118, 130, 131–32, 138; *see also* Honduras; Nicaragua; Panama
Ceylon, 141
Chaco War, 11–12
Chamber of Deputies, French, 76, 91, 137, 264, 277
Chamberlain, Austen, 300
Chamberlain, Houston Stewart, 175, 291
Chamberlain, Joseph, 56, 174, 182, 193, 201, 371
Chamberlain, Neville, 58, 64, 256, 270, **290, 302**

I

Iceland, 14, 15
idealism, statesmanship and, 249–51, 263, 284
ideology: government policy and, 332; nationalism and, 170–71, 192–93, 199, 201, 273; pacifism and, 218; pressures and, 296; Wilsonian, 286
Ilg, Alfred, 71
illiteracy, 149, 161, 322
imagination, statesmanship and, 252–54
immigration, 39–52, 155, 172; international conference on, 48; restrictions on, 43–44, 47–51, 81; *see also* emigration
imperialism, 59, 265–66, 369–70, 373; British, 15, 45, 79, 182–83, 193, 274; colonial, 173; financial, 125, 130–33, 215; French, 276; German, 187; Italian, 32, 232; Japanese, 15, 28, 46, 165, 321; U.S., 126, 190, 263; *see also* colonialism
import duties; *see* tariff regulations
Import-Export Bank, 107, 123
income, per capita, 347
indebtedness, international, 135–37
independence, movements for, 152, 153, 154, 156, 163, 164, 165, 166, 168, 169, 170, 306
India, 9, 12, 15, 19, 28, 55, 70, 140, 141, 197, 263, 347; boycott, 81; Britain and, 81, 93, 95, 111, 372; and capital investment, 127–28; nationalist movement in, 165–66, 168; population of, 30
Indian Ocean, 14, 55, 90, 293
Indians, North American, 12, 154, 328
Indochina, 6, 14, 26, 34, 55, 56, 80, 371; *see also* Vietnam
Indonesia, 15, 140, 141, 197
industrial development, 26, 53, 58, 59, 65, 102, 104, 110, 321, 331; British, 10, 110, 289; cartels and, 98; colonial policy and, 277, 379; French, 325; immigrants and, 40, 41, 43; Italian, 9; Japanese, 61–62, 184; Mexican, 327–29; military strength and, 24; Russian, 113
Industrial Revolution, 126, 203, 373
industrial securities, 112, 116
industry, nationalization of, 136
inflation, monetary, 320; *see also* devaluation
inflexibility, statesmanship and, 252–53
Institute of Pacific Relations, 51
insurrections; *see* uprisings
intellectual development, nationhood and, 141
intellectuals: Catholic, 194; Chinese, 160; colonial, 164; Egyptian, 131, 167; émigré, 36; French, 181; German, 143;

in national movements, 149, 150, 156, 164, 165, 167, 170, 171, 179; in pacifist movement, 202; Korean, 159; Russian, 178
intelligence services, 351–52
interest groups, 260, 296; *see also* lobbying
interest rates, 106, 113
International Chamber of Commerce, 101
International Emigration Commission, 48
International Justice, Permanent Court of, 221, 233
International Labor Office, 35, 48
international law, 78, 198; peacekeeping and, 218–24
International League of Peace and Liberty, 217, 220
international organization, proposals for, 220–24, 226–27
International Working Men's Association, 204, 205
Inter-Parliamentary Union, 220, 221, 225, 230
Iran, 13, 67, 140; *see also* Persia
Iraq, 79, 146, 198
Ireland, 23, 27, 145, 146, 148, 150, 152; emigrants from, 42, 339
iron and steel industry, 10, 88, 98, 99, 112, 113
iron ore, 10, 65, 372, 373
irredentism, 145, 151, 179, 186, 346
irrigation, 21
Isambert, 227
Islam, 6, 12, 141, 148, 161, 163, 166, 168, 197–98
islands, 15–16, 22, 93
Ismail, Khedive of Egypt, 131
isolationism: British, 141, 288; French Canadian, 158; Japanese, 15–16, 158–59; U.S., 137, 191, 285, 300, 304, 313, 339
Israel, 336
Istanbul, 61; *see also* Constantinople
isthmus regions, 13
Istria, 150, 178, 285, 291, 346
Italy, 6, 7, 24, 69, 196, 270, 285, 289, 290, 322; Catholic Church in, 212; emigration from, 35, 37–42, 45, 48, 155, 274; France and, 45–46, 76–77, 112, 114, 117, 131, 254, 272, 314; Germany and, 76, 179, 293, 309, 364–65; industrial development of, 9, 10; nationalism in, 145, 149, 174, 178–80, 186, 187, 192, 194, 201, 220; population of, 23, 24, 32; public opinion in, 308–11, 319; unification of, 144, 145, 147, 151; U.S. and, 105, 121; *see also* colonialism; Ethiopia; expansionism; fascism; irredentism; Mussolini
Izmir (Smyrna), 92, 93

World Court; *see* Permanent Court of International Justice
World Economic Conference, 57
World War I, 7, 11, 24, 57, 73, 104, 126, 145, 151, 157, 163, 211, 221, 265, 281; British in, 287-88, 338; causes of, 373-75; financers and, 128-29, 203; oil concessions and, 67-68; U.S. in, 43, 80, 105, 136, 203, 248, 359-63; *see also* Germany
World War II, 15, 24, 106, 268-70, 272, 334; causes of, 375-76; U.S. and, 129, 200, 203; *see also* Germany; Lend Lease Act
Wright, Henry, 215

X

xenophobia; *see* isolationism

Y

Yangtze River, 96
Yap, island of, 15
Yazidji, Ibrahim el, 161
Yellow River, 96
Yüan Shih-k'ai, 133-34
Yugoslavia, 62-63, 116, 250, 289, 312, 345, 365, 367; *see also* Trieste
Yunnan, 71, 96, 159
Yusuf, Ali, 166

Z

Zaghlul Pasha, 167
Zaharoff, Basil, 338
Zanzibar, 16
Zionism, 47
Zollverein, 85, 86, 88, 142, 373